Corporate Social Responsibility in Health and Social Care

Gianpaolo Tomaselli
University of Malta, Malta

IGI Global
Publishing Tomorrow's Research Today

Vice President of Editorial	Melissa Wagner
Managing Editor of Acquisitions	Mikaela Felty
Managing Editor of Book Development	Jocelynn Hessler
Production Manager	Mike Brehm
Cover Design	Phillip Shickler

Published in the United States of America by
IGI Global Scientific Publishing
701 East Chocolate Avenue
Hershey, PA, 17033, USA
Tel: 717-533-8845
Fax: 717-533-8661
Website: https://www.igi-global.com E-mail: cust@igi-global.com

Library of Congress Cataloging-in-Publication Data

Names: Tomaselli, Gianpaolo, 1986- editor.
Title: Corporate social responsibility in health and social care / edited by Gianpaolo Tomaselli.
Description: Hershey, PA : IGI Global Scientific Publishing, [2025] | Includes bibliographical references and index. | Summary: "This book aims at analyzing the topic of CSR in the health and social care sector and shall serve as a baseline for future research in this field and to support students, researchers, scholars and practitioners in this field"-- Provided by publisher.
Identifiers: LCCN 2024048778 (print) | LCCN 2024048779 (ebook) | ISBN 9798369359914 (hardcover) | ISBN 9798369359921 (paperback) | ISBN 9798369359938 (ebook)
Subjects: LCSH: Social responsibility of business. | Health--Social aspects.
Classification: LCC HD60 .C6943 2025 (print) | LCC HD60 (ebook) | DDC 658.4/08--dc23/eng/20250107
LC record available at https://lccn.loc.gov/2024048778
LC ebook record available at https://lccn.loc.gov/2024048779

British Cataloguing in Publication Data
A Cataloguing in Publication record for this book is available from the British Library.

Table of Contents

Detailed Table of Contents

how these initiatives are effective, taking into consideration cultural, economic, and regulatory contexts within regions. The chapter goes through an analysis of the successes but also the limitations of CSR in Asia as a steppingstone to argue for the need to find more integrated, collaborative, and innovative approaches if the SDGs are to be realized. This puts very strong emphasis on the need for further commitment by business if sustainable development in the region is to be driven forward effectively.

This chapter offers a systematic review of literature on the antecedents of Corporate Social Responsibility (CSR) in the context of healthcare. This work explores the enhancement of environmental, economic, and social aspects of CSR and their application in health and social care organizations. This report shows the best practices in the area of waste management and energy efficiency and carbon footprint with the use of hospital and care facilities' good examples put into practice. Offord focuses on economic Cost of CSR, including availability and accessibility of health care, price, and more importantly, the economy of health care. Furthermore, the chapter covers social aspects such as establishing a multi-faceted relationship with workforces which comprises of the diverse population, involvement in the community, and patient relation. The problems and limitation to CSR practices are discussed as well as measures to addressing them by involving stakeholders and formulation of policies.

Contemporary society requires every organization to operate with a sense of social responsibility. Many organizations, including those in the healthcare sector, now include corporate social responsibility (CSR) activities in their work programs. Today, healthcare organizations have different choices and tools to communicate their CSR activities. The use of traditional means of communication of CSR (social, sustainability and integrated reports, codes of ethics, certification standards, etc.) is often integrated with the implementation of interactive communication technologies (internet, websites, social media, social networks, mobile apps) that have gained

Person-centered care presents a welcoming change towards a more holistic healthcare model. Rather than restricting its scope to the deficiencies and challenges that the individual may have, PCC widens its view to the autonomy of the person. Pertinent to this scope, it is the intention of this study to investigate the value and contribution of PCC to community mental health services. As noted by WHO, these services locate social inclusion and participation within the community life. Research suggests a dearth of studies on PCC within community mental health services. This applies to Malta as well. In fact, Galea and Mallia in their leading study on this reality strongly recommended more knowledge, practice and research from the perspective of a person-centered approach among mental healthcare services. This includes continuous professional development among HCPs in line with the latest PCC principles. Transitioning to a person-centered approach within community mental health services benefits the community because it empowers the person and improves clinical outcomes.

Digital mental health therapies have been suggested to improve the accessibility and use of psychological treatment. However, little information is available about the attitudes and behavioural intentions of healthcare professionals towards such treatments for personal use. Poor attitudes and negative behavioural intentions can cause a significant barrier to the uptake and utilisation of this form of therapy. Therefore, this study sought to explore the attitudes and intentions of healthcare professionals towards digital mental health services. The relationships between attitudes, intentions, mental health status, and demographics were also investigated. The present study took the form of a quantitative cross-sectional needs analysis by distributing an online questionnaire to the targeted population. The findings from this study suggest a neutral attitude towards digital therapy, while maintaining openness to its utilization. Additionally, the findings highlight the need to enhance healthcare professionals' knowledge about digital therapy's empirical effectiveness.

and professional literature relevant to understanding the key concepts and practices of socially responsible marketing in the context of children's health.

Preface

Corporate Social Responsibility (CSR) has become a vital component across various industries, evolving beyond a voluntary practice to an integral part of organizational strategy. In the health and social care sector, the implementation of CSR is particularly critical due to the direct impact these industries have on both human lives and broader societal well-being. Recognizing the unique challenges and opportunities within this sector, this book, *Corporate Social Responsibility in Health and Social Care*, seeks to provide a comprehensive exploration of CSR's role, significance, and applications within these vital fields.

This book addresses CSR from three key perspectives: environmental, economic, and social. The environmental dimension emphasizes the industry's efforts to reduce its carbon footprint, implement sustainable waste management, and enhance energy efficiency. Economically, CSR in health and social care encompasses equitable access to services, fair pricing, and investments in innovative research for the development of cutting-edge treatments. Socially, CSR in this context focuses on creating inclusive workplaces, ensuring patient safety and satisfaction, and supporting communities through various philanthropic initiatives.

Despite the growing recognition of CSR's importance, there remains a gap in research specific to its applications in the health and social care sectors. This book seeks to bridge that gap by offering a thorough analysis that will serve as a foundation for future research and a valuable resource for students, researchers, scholars, and practitioners alike.

Whether used for research, management, or teaching purposes, *Corporate Social Responsibility in Health and Social Care* provides critical insights into how CSR initiatives can support the sustainability of health and social care systems. It is our hope that this book will inspire more profound reflection on the integration of CSR in health and social care and foster meaningful action toward more sustainable practices in these essential sectors.

We anticipate this work will be of significant interest to professionals and researchers in the health and social care industry, as well as to students engaged in studying these areas.

ORGANIZATION OF THE BOOK

The edited volume opens with Chapter 1, "Sustainable Health System Through Corporate Social Responsibility Towards Promoting Health Equity inferring SDG 3." This chapter highlights the pivotal role of Health Impact Assessments (HIA) in fostering collaboration and community participation to enhance health equity. It underscores the importance of conducting HIA effectively to ensure that its outcomes genuinely impact decisions, thus improving not just health but broader community goals like education and employment. The chapter outlines key steps in HIA and emphasizes cooperation with stakeholders for meaningful insights.

Chapter 2, "Catalyzing Sustainable Futures: Examining CSR's Impact on Achieving the SDGs in Asia," delves into how Corporate Social Responsibility (CSR) initiatives in Asia align with the United Nations Sustainable Development Goals (SDGs). Using case studies from various Asian countries, the authors explore CSR's role in addressing issues such as poverty, gender equality, and climate action. They call for more integrated and collaborative efforts to maximize CSR's potential in achieving sustainable development across diverse cultural and economic contexts in the region.

In Chapter 3, "Integrating Corporate Social Responsibility in Health and Social Care: Strategies for Sustainable Practice," the author provides a systematic review of CSR's environmental, economic, and social dimensions within healthcare. The chapter explores practical examples in waste management, energy efficiency, and stakeholder engagement, while addressing the economic costs and challenges of CSR implementation in healthcare. Tariq highlights best practices and calls for policy-driven approaches to improve CSR's effectiveness in this sector.

"Corporate Social Responsibility in Healthcare: An Empirical Observation," Chapter 4, investigates the growing role of CSR in healthcare, especially the use of both traditional and digital communication tools to publicize CSR initiatives. The authors examine how healthcare organizations integrate interactive technologies like websites and social media to increase public engagement with their CSR activities.

Chapter 5, "Corporate Social Responsibility in the Health Sector: A 2023 Case Study of Canon and Sony, RepTrak Leaders," presents a focused case study of Canon and Sony's CSR initiatives in healthcare. Through an analysis of their 2023 sustainability reports, the chapter evaluates how these companies' reputations are linked to their contributions to healthcare, offering a tangible look at how CSR shapes corporate reputation in this essential sector.

Chapter 6, "Fusion of Social Responsibility and Digital Health: An Indian Scenario," by Nalini R, Alamelu R, and Dinesh S, discusses the intersection of digital health and CSR in India. The authors explore how technologies like mHealth and eHealth have the potential to transform public health, while also examining how businesses can use these tools to foster better social and health outcomes. This chapter offers an in-depth look at the opportunities for CSR to enhance health through digital innovations.

"User Perceptions in Measuring the Impact of Digital Health Platforms on Social Care" (Chapter 7) aims to measure the perception of users towards digital health platforms and its benefits to the society. Researcher has collected 282 responses from the respondents. Notably, younger adults, particularly those aged 21 to 40 years, are the predominant users, reflecting a strong inclination towards digital health applications within this demographic. The trend of using these platforms for both personal and family healthcare underscores a preference for family-inclusive solutions. The preference for mobile devices among 97.3% of respondents emphasizes the need for mobile-optimized digital health platforms. Apollo 24/7's prominence as the most used application suggests its strong market presence and user satisfaction. The factor analysis identifies four main factors influencing the use of digital health platforms, accounting for a substantial proportion of the variance in the dataset. These factors highlight the significant trends and characteristics affecting users' engagement, proactive health management, trust in security, and barriers to adoption.

In Chapter 8, "Patient-Centered Care for TB Patients: An Effective Approach to Corporate Social Responsibility," S. Srinivasan and Prabha Lama Lama provide insights into patient-centered care as a CSR approach for treating tuberculosis (TB) patients. Using a community-based study in India, the authors highlight how improving access to timely healthcare, community engagement, and patient education can significantly improve TB outcomes while aligning with broader CSR goals.

"Towards A Person-Centered Care Approach in Community Mental Health Services," by Michael Galea and Frankline Galea, forms Chapter 9. This chapter advocates for a transition to person-centered care (PCC) in community mental health, promoting patient autonomy and empowerment. The authors argue for the integration of PCC principles in mental health services, particularly in Malta, to improve both individual and community outcomes.

Chapter 10, "Healthcare Professionals' Attitudes Towards Digital Technology to Support Their Mental Wellbeing," by Stephanie Bonello and Sandra Buttigieg, explores healthcare professionals' attitudes towards digital mental health therapies. Through a quantitative needs analysis, the authors find that while healthcare professionals are open to digital therapy, there remains a need for increased awareness of its efficacy. This chapter highlights the potential of digital mental health solutions, while pointing out barriers to their adoption.

In Chapter 11, "Bridging Gaps in Palliative Care Through Corporate Social Responsibility: Emerging Trends in India," Maya M and Priya Joseph examine how CSR can support palliative care in India. The chapter analyzes corporate contributions to palliative care through the lens of the National Program for Palliative Care (NPPC) and calls for stronger collaboration between government, NGOs, and corporations to build a robust palliative care system that aligns with Sustainable Development Goal 3.

Chapter 12, "Promoting Equality through CSR Practices: Legal Imperatives for Disability Rights and Inclusive Business Strategies for a Sustainable Society," by Anuttama Ghose, Hartej Kochher, and SM Aamir Ali, investigates the role of CSR in promoting disability rights. The authors examine both Indian and international legal frameworks that support inclusive business strategies and call for policy reforms to ensure greater inclusivity and fair employment opportunities for people with disabilities.

In Chapter 13, "Corporate Social Responsibility (CSR) of Pharmaceutical Companies: Evidence From Antibiotic Resistance Tackling Strategies in Bangladesh," Md Golam Rabbani and Asif All Mahmud Akash explore how pharmaceutical companies address the public health crisis of antibiotic resistance (ABR) through CSR. The chapter critically assesses the ethical and regulatory challenges these companies face, revealing the gaps between CSR ideals and the realities of ABR management in Bangladesh.

Finally, Chapter 14, "Socially Responsible Marketing and Children's Health: Preliminary Insights," by Joana Duarte Lima and Bruno Sousa, examines the impact of socially responsible marketing on children's health, particularly within the dermocosmetic industry. The authors explore how ethical marketing strategies influence consumer behavior and brand attachment, emphasizing the need for responsible communication to build trust and promote healthier choices for children.

CONCLUSION

In concluding this preface, we reflect on the essential themes and insights that emerge from the chapters of this edited volume. Each contribution sheds light on the multifaceted role of Corporate Social Responsibility (CSR) in enhancing health equity and promoting sustainable development. The collaborative efforts of researchers and practitioners presented here underscore the profound impact that responsible business practices can have on diverse aspects of health, from community engagement and patient-centered care to addressing pressing public health challenges.

As we traverse the landscape of CSR in health systems, the evidence presented in these chapters paints a compelling picture of both the progress made and the obstacles that remain. The integration of CSR within healthcare is not merely an ethical obligation but a strategic imperative that can lead to improved health outcomes, greater access to care, and enhanced community well-being. This volume also highlights the urgent need for innovative, inclusive, and collaborative approaches, particularly in light of the unique cultural, economic, and regulatory contexts in which these practices are implemented.

Moreover, the chapters collectively call for a renewed commitment from businesses to embrace sustainability not just as a compliance measure but as a core tenet of their operational ethos. The call for deeper stakeholder engagement, particularly in underserved communities, is echoed throughout the discussions, emphasizing the critical role of participatory approaches in achieving health equity.

We hope that this volume serves as both a resource and a catalyst for further discourse on the intersection of CSR, health, and sustainable development. As the field continues to evolve, we encourage readers—be they academics, policymakers, healthcare practitioners, or business leaders—to leverage the insights and findings presented herein to inspire actionable strategies that foster a healthier, more equitable world. Ultimately, it is our belief that by prioritizing social responsibility within the healthcare sector, we can drive meaningful change that aligns with the Sustainable Development Goals and the overarching goal of promoting the health and well-being of all individuals.

Gianpaolo Tomaselli
University of Malta, Malta

Chapter 1
Sustainable Health System Through Corporate Social Responsibility Towards Promoting Health Equity Inferring SDG 3

Bhupinder Singh
http://orcid.org/0009-0006-4779-2553
Sharda University, India

Christian Kaunert
http://orcid.org/0000-0002-4493-2235
Dublin City University, Ireland

Anjali Raghav
http://orcid.org/0009-0004-0248-7956
Sharda University, India

Kamalesh Ravesangar
http://orcid.org/0009-0004-2154-184X
Tunku Abdul Rahman University of Management and Technology, Malaysia

ABSTRACT

The significant technique used extensively for determining whether plans, strategies and proposals are likely to have a good or negative effect on health and health equity is the health impact assessment (HIA). It facilitates cooperation with individuals or

DOI: 10.4018/979-8-3693-5991-4.ch001

organizations that guarantee ownership of the action and contribute perspectives. In reality, though, HIA is frequently conducted after decisions have already been made, and many of its predicted effects are only marginally resolved. Effective community participation can enhance health outcomes and have good implications on other community objectives including education, housing, and employment. HIA uses knowledge and the following five steps of screening, scoping, evaluation, suggestions and reporting, review, and reflection to identify potential impacts, their sort and scale, and the populations that could potentially be impacted. This chapter focuses on to facilitate cooperation with interested parties who guarantee ownership of the action and offer insights.

1. INTRODUCTION

The 1997 Jakarta Declaration on Health Promotion into the 21st Century emphasized equity-focused health impact assessments as an important cause for action and supported new approaches to meet growing health concerns (Allen & Smith, 2024). It also prioritized fostering social responsibility for health. This theme was among the primary concerns of the Mexico City-hosted Fifth Global Conference on Health Promotion in 2000. Using evidence and the five procedures of screening, scoping, evaluation, recommendations and reporting, review, and reflection, HIA seeks to identify any possible effects, their magnitude and type, and affected populations. Community-driven solutions are essential in advancing health equity, requiring true community engagement and ownership at each stage. Communities may contribute to a society with greater equity where every individual has the chance to reach maximum health without regard to their social status or circumstances by emphasizing health equality. HIA is normally conducted after decisions are made, though, and many of its predicted effects are only partially addressed in reality (Brown & Green, 2024).

Corporate Social Responsibility (CSR) has come a long way since it's early days of corporate philanthropy, to embracing activities aimed at creating positive social and environmental impacts. CSR is critical in healthcare because it tackles public health issues which are common but preventable and helps to limit those disparities by promoting equity for all (Singh, 2024). Drawing on this burgeoning literature, in the context of corporate engagement in global health we explore the PLC that would be most likely to accelerate progress towards SDG 3: healthy lives and promote well-being for all at all ages (Mariappanadar, 2024).

Summary Background Health equity, the fair and just distribution of health outcomes, is a major challenge to global development. Although there have been considerable improvements in health care, a large gap continues to exist with regard to the resources available and need that different populations face - especially within low-and middle-income countries. Socioeconomic factors, geography and other determinants of health frequently act as limiting elements that compel barriers to access in healthcare provision, prevention measures or treatment. In this sense, CSR has the potential to significantly contribute towards health equity. With health and well-being tied to the heart of their businesses, corporations can operate as levers in solving social determinants of health problems, promoting public-health objectives more broadly, and be partners in building sustainable healthcare systems. Healthcare is the sector, where all different kinds of initiatives like you can donate to a community health program for underprivileged population or your company may have come up with some healthcare delivery model innovations and they would want to scale it in partnership with governments/NGOs (Singh & Kaunert, 2024).

For CSR linked to SDG 3, it would be important for a company have not only strategic but also structured approach beyond traditional philanthropic activities. Corporations must recognize the ways in which they can affect health outcomes through their operations, products and services, as well as those of their suppliers. This requires the way we handle immediate health needs of communities but also poses as a part to long-term solutions that maintain sustainable health systems. They could align and support their CSR activities with the broader goals of SDG 3 such as investments in health infrastructure, supporting health education or raising awareness regarding healthier lifestyles. Also, the significance of technology in Corporate Social Responsibility to Drive Health Equity must not be underestimated. New technological developments like telemedicine, digital health platforms and data analytics create more avenues for companies to make a difference towards public healthcare. Technological advancement can be a boon for corporations to take social business as the perfect opportunity where serving underserved markets, improving monitoring and evaluation of CSR outcomes in healthcare delivery (Davis & Wilson, 2024).

While these strategies hold promise, barriers exist to effective implementation of CSR work aimed at advancing health equity. They include stronger alignment of corporate goals with wider public health objectives, greater accountability and transparency in activities undertaken as part of CSR initiatives, overcoming barriers to effective partnership between the private sector and other actors involved on issues such as obesity-related cases. Governments, NGOs and communities need to act together in a multi-stakeholder approach as well for developing righteousness that promotes the idea of CSR in healthcare (Evans & Thompson, 2024).

1.1 Understanding Health Equity and Sustainable Health Systems

The principle and the goal of health equity ensure that all individuals, regardless their socioeconomic status, race or ethnic group have fair opportunities to be as healthy as possible. While equality treats everyone the same no matter their physical conditions or status, in contrast equity distinguishes that different people and communities have different at-risk health needs as well barriers. This is why health equity cannot be achieved through a "one-size-fits-all" strategy and must consider the different issues that vulnerable populations face (Singh et al., 2024).

Health equity is such a vital issue because differences in healthcare access and outcomes may translate into substantially different life expectancies, disease burdens, and quality of life. For example, low-income communities or minority groups might have difficulties due to lack of proper health facilities, absence of a healthcare insurance policy in their possession and also the minimal opportunity on preventive care. The latter, combined with clinical factors and behavioral differences also affect healthcare outcomes; frequently reinforced by social determinants of health (SDOH) e.g., education, income level, housing state. Ensuring health equity thus covers not just provision of healthcare but addressing this broader range of social and economic determinants that shape differences in population health status (Koon & Fujimoto, 2024)

Global health policies, such as the United Nations' Sustainable Development Goals (SDGs), also consider reducing disparities in various aspects of healthcare. SDG 3 aims to ensure healthy lives and promote well-being for all, with a focus on reducing health disparities and achieving universal health coverage. Health equity aims to ensure that everyone has the opportunity to live a healthy life; and societies will ultimately achieve this by addressing disparities, which take into account race, ethnicity, gender identity/issue not limited to background (Singh & Kaunert, 2024).

1.2 Sustainable Health Systems

Accessible health systems are structured so that both present and future generations can access quality services simultaneously while ensuring the sustainability of an equitable balance between social, economic and environmental components. A sustainable health system does not just provide healthcare efficiently but ensures that the care delivery can adjust and evolve with changing population needs, economic conditions, and environmental challenges (Singh & Kaunert, 2024).

Environmental, another sustainable health system is environmental which includes reducing the carbon footprint of healthcare facilities, waste reduction and utilizing renewable energy. Consequently, healthcare systems are significant contributors to environmental degradation; thus sustainable practices need to be implemented in order to reduce their effect on climate change and resource utilization. This comprises the social aspect that involves reducing inequalities in health care access and outcomes, which entails not only ensuring everyone receives essential treatment but also can do so without financial pressure. This would also mean working to address social determinants of health for example, furthering progress in education, employment and housing which are major drivers of health outcomes. Economically, sustainable healthcare infrastructure can be defined as providing resources for health care systems that ensure balance in delivering needs congruent to population demand without compromising access of future generation. Developing an equitable and sustainable health system requires the interrelation of these three dimensions. Policymakers, healthcare providers and other stakeholders need to work together towards setting up systems that are effective but also efficient while ensuring the health of not just present population as well benefiting future generations (Foster & Lee, 2024).

1.3 Intersection of CSR and Health Equity

It is the Corporate Social Responsibility (CSR) that has an utmost contribution in filling those gaps of healthcare accessibility and affordability for such segments. Corporate social responsibility (CSR) initiatives have access to a wide range of options for combating health disparities, including such arenas as community health programs, public health campaigns and healthcare delivery improvements supportive of national governments and non-profit organizations (Garcia & Patel, 2024).

CSR efforts to drive health equity come in many shapes. For instance, companies can contribute funding for the construction of healthcare infrastructure in remote regions or among populations with little access to care, provide health benefits at reduced cost or even free below a certain income level and fund R&D activities around low-cost medical technologies (Harris & Martinez, 2024). CSR can also extend to working in partnership with communities locally, for health awareness campaigns on preventative health care measures and improving the general public's knowledge of their own health elevation activities. Incorporating health equity into their CSR approach can have a substantial effect on public health, but at the same time it would also cause companies to build more responsible reputations and make investments for long-term commercial sustainability. These efforts not only bridge the gap between healthcare accessibility and affordability but also contribute to social goals, as shared in SDG 3. In the end, CSR that results in more equitable health are really just the same thing as healthier and e.g. all-inclusive but also stronger, sustainable healthcare systems (Leonidou et al., 2024).

Figure 1. Landscapes of introduction section (Original)

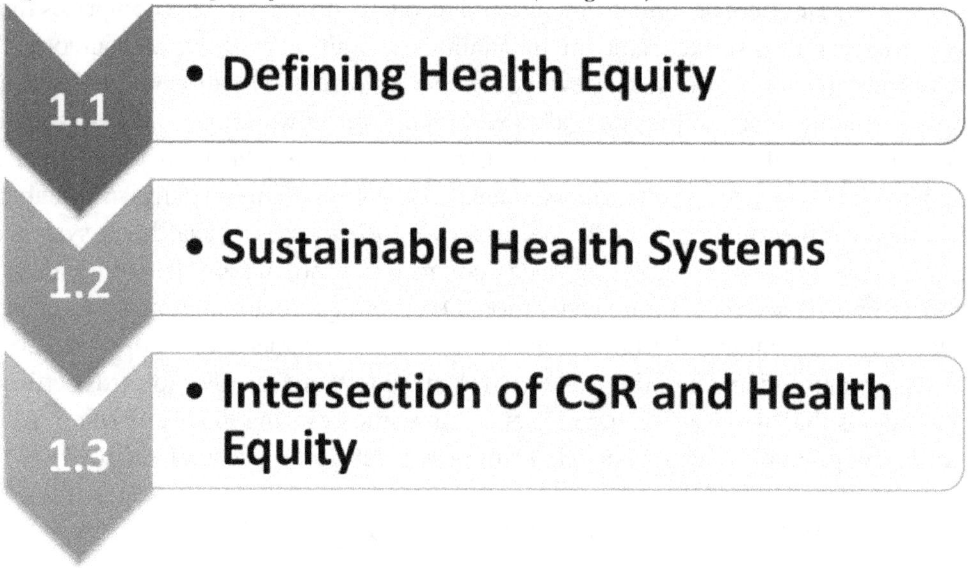

2. CORPORATE SOCIAL RESPONSIBILITY IN HEALTHCARE: EQUILIBRIUM

Corporate Social Responsibility (CSR) in healthcare lies at an important crossroads of business interests and social welfare- companies regularly participate into activities that promote health for a reason or the other. In health sector, CSR activities are gaining recognition more and more for their potential to target important public health issues, decrease inequities in access of healthcare services as well as enhance population level wellbeing. These efforts included but were not limited to philanthropic giving, wellness programs for employees and partnership with health care providers or government agencies supporting public healthcare (Johnson & Carter, 2024).

Among the most common expression of CSR in health care is contribution to health initiatives through direct financial funding. Health Concern Initiative: This is where big time organizations funds healthcare programs which are touching health issues such as consciousness on how to solve maternal and child related problems, common diseases preventive measures or mental impairment liberality. Their vital roles are even more important in low- and middle-income countries, where public health systems usually suffer from under-resourcing and overuse. They provide bridge to the resource gap, which allows expansion in infrastructure healthcare facilities and fund medical research of lifelike diseases or community health programs that can help develop sustainable models (King & Robinson, 2024).

Apart from the financial aid, CSR in healthcare also stands for all corporate or other initiatives and means that develop health at work. Many CSR activities related to employee wellness programs include health screenings, fitness incentives and mental health support or access. Through these programs, the overall health of a workforce is improved which then leads to higher productivity and lower absenteeism as well as better work environment. Companies are good corporate citizens when they prioritize employee health, and can lead the way in society taking interest over broader participation in health promotion (Lee & Murphy, 2024). The other major aspect of CSR in healthcare is the synergy that corporations can have with public health entities, including government agencies, non-governing bodies (NGOs), and healthcare providers. This approach holds potential to enhance the value and impact of CSR programmes, utilizing multiple stakeholders' skills and resources in a common mission towards addressing health challenges. These could range from teaming with NGOs to deliver healthcare in remote, low-income areas; to collaborating with governments on public health programs meant to reduce the incidence of non-communicable diseases. Gavin is one of the many partnerships which are needed to build scalable global health solutions that can last (Singh & Kaunert, 2024).

CSR in healthcare has moved towards innovation and technology. Firms are using their technology to build new health care offerings, from telemedicine apps and mobile healthcare platforms or mhealth for short to ones that deliver data-driven health-related interventions. These advances could have a huge impact on the quality and availability of healthcare to remote or underserved regions. Corporations are advancing technology and automation by investing in medical records or providing new tools to help nations deliver healthcare across income levels (Scaria et al., 2024). CSR in healthcare is a multi-pronged strategy for businesses to create real impacts on public health and align their business objectives along the way. Such an example is the growing number of corporations that are recognizing this fact and aligning some or all of their CSR strategies to encompass broader health goals, especially those embodied in the United Nations´ Sustainable Development Goals (SDGs), playing a vital part in supporting health equity, Universal Health Coverage as being attainable for all within respective societies. With the global health challenges of today and those still to come, CSR in healthcare is only going to become much more significant as a tool integral not just into corporate strategy but also directly into public health policy itself (Singh & Kaunert, 2024).

Figure 2. Corporate social responsibility in healthcare (Original)

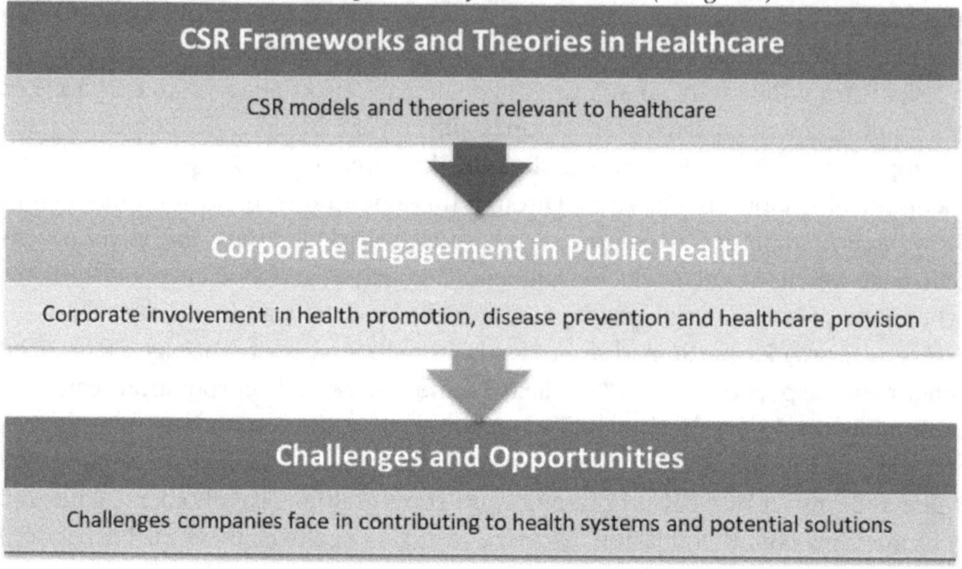

3. ALIGNING CSR INITIATIVES WITH SDG 3

The strategic paths for companies to contribute with global health objectives and make sense of their societal impact are aligning CSR initiatives toward the SDG 3: ensure healthy lives and promote well-being for all at all ages. One of the global goals (SDG 3) covers a broad set of targets, from maternal and child mortality to epidemics, non-communicable diseases and universal health coverage. Companies can make a meaningful difference in all of these by incorporating health-conscious approaches into their CSR efforts. Companies can work to achieve this goal in the short term by responding to urgent health care needs and addressing long-term needs. This includes businesses getting behind public health campaigns, funding medical research and investing in healthcare infrastructure in underprivileged areas. Such endeavors do not just enhance health-care access, it contributes to narrowing of health inequalities; a key premise of SDG 3 (Singh & Kaunert, 2024).

CSR programs can tackle preventive healthcare and wellness management at workplace or in the public community as well. First and foremost, maintaining prevention helps to lighten the load on companies by reducing diseases while improving health outcomes overall (and thereby lowering healthcare costs). Further, through technology and innovation (like telemedicine or digital health platforms), CSR can be better aligned with SDG 3 so that it expands access to healthcare services but also improves efficiency in delivering the same (Martinez & Nguyen, 2024).

3.1 Aligning CSR Initiatives With Target of SDG 3

For corporate social responsibility (CSR) initiatives to fall in line with or better yet support the Sustainable Development Goal 3 (SDG 3), measures need to be more specific and directly connect CSR activities that contribute to key health outcomes. Businesses, for example, can lower maternal mortality rates by sponsoring hospitals in poverty-stricken areas and providing training on women's health care delivery or funding programs that assure safe delivery of babies (Eze et al., 2024). Corporations, in turn can contribute by funding for prevention of the disease and making vaccines available along with awareness about epidemiology. The financing of healthcare services to the economically disadvantaged population, cost-effective health insurance packages and telemedicine in inaccessible areas could be a move towards UHC through CSR activities. This will provide companies an opportunity to serve their social responsibilities as well as contribute towards the global health agenda. This link ensures alignment of a purposeful objective to address the pressing health needs identified in SDG 3 that would be supported by business efforts towards the same (Nelson & Walker, 2024)

3.2 Case Studies

An examination of case studies on how businesses have successfully integrated SDG 3 in their corporate social responsibility (CSR) activities, has import findings on best practices and promising interventions. Johnson & Johnson, a global healthcare business along with others have pledged to curb mother and child mortality by teaming up NGOs all working together towards providing quality health care in most of the poor nations. Today, Unilever´s hygiene and sanitation programs reaches millions of vulnerable people to prevent illness. These case studies illustrate the tangible repercussions on health outcomes, business-reputation and long-term value for businesses as well as society when CSR are cleverly weaved into SDG 3 strands. Furthermore, they demonstrate the importance of collaboration creativity and persistent determination for achieving health-oriented goals. analysing these cases could provide guidance to other companies on how best they might include SDG 3 in their CSR efforts, and also create specific outcomes that can help protect human health (Upreti & Malhotra, 2024).

3.3 Impact Assessment

Evaluating the impact of corporate social responsibility (CSR) programmes on Public Health outcomes is pertinent to ensure their business drives are saving and being in tune with Sustainable Development Goal 3 aims. KPIs, HIAs and SROI evaluations act as the tools & mechanism used for measuring impact. Corporations can then use these methods to determine how much their CSR operations have improved health -for example, by reducing the prevalence of disease or improving access to healthcare- and they could also be used in a 'contextualised form' for evaluating impact into complex interventions as seen elsewhere (Patel & Turner, 2024). Also to ensure that they stay on top of global health inequities and contribute positively to sustainable, equitable systems reforming processes within the healthcare field. In addition to demonstrating the company's commitment to public health, transparent reporting of results builds confidence from stakeholders (Quinn & Roberts, 2024). With independently evaluating outcomes, companies can improve the effectiveness of their corporate social responsibility (CSR) efforts and ensure that their contributions to Sustainable Development Goal 3 (SDG-3): Good Health & Well-being are meaningful and measurable (Tyan et al., 2024).

Figure 3. Aligning CSR initiatives with SDG 3 (Original)

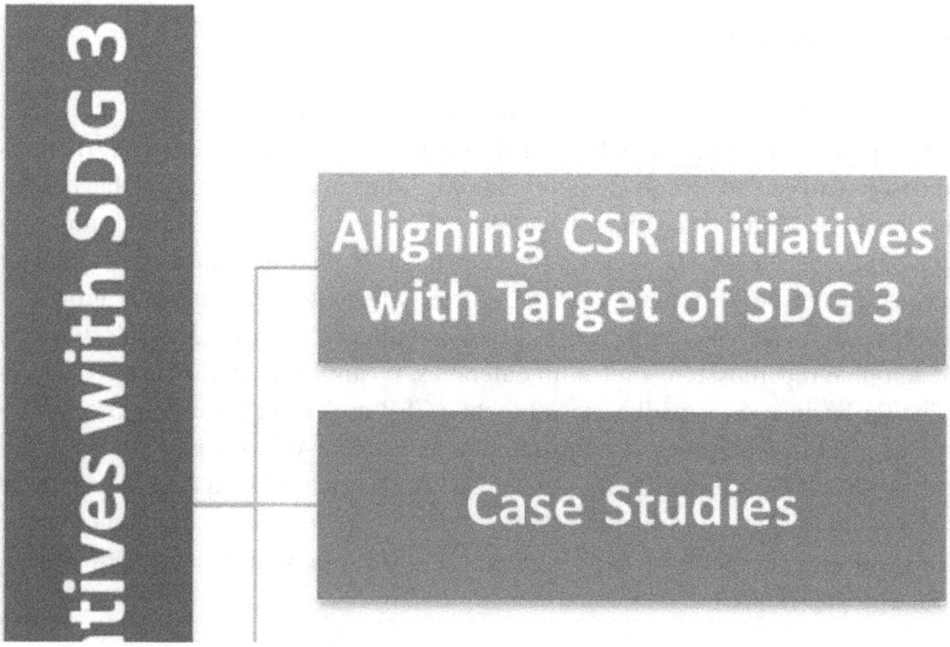

4. PROMOTING HEALTH EQUITY THROUGH CSR

Corporate Social Responsibility (CSR) is an important strategy for companies to address health inequalities that contribute to disparities in healthcare access and outcomes, as it provides the basis to allow all people irrespective of their socioeconomic background fulfill individual possibilities (Ramirez & Smith, 2024). Larger issues of health equity remain pressing on a global scale, with marginalized communities facing major challenges to living healthier lives including access to quality services and financial constraints. CSR acts targeted at promoting health equity could have a huge impact in addressing these disparities and enabling healthcare the world over to be more inclusive (Scott & Wilson, 2024). The most obvious way CSR can be leveraged to support health equity is through investments in healthcare infrastructure and services for underserved populations. Businesses can help finance the building of clinics, hospitals and mobiles health units in rural and remote areas so that marginalized populations have access to basic healthcare services. CSR programs can also offer low-cost or free healthcare services, medicines, and insurance to economically weaker sections for reducing the financial liability of health care including easy accessibility (Dutta et al., 2024).

In addition, CSR initiatives can help combat those social determinants of health by supporting through investments in education, housing and economic opportunity that benefit underserved populations. For instance, corporations could invest in health education programs that increase awareness of preventive care; nutrition and disease management which encourage people to take appropriate decisions related to their health (Singh & Kaunert, 2024). And by addressing the fundamentals of health disparities, CSR efforts have the potential to support sustainable changes which will in due course lead to better and healthier communities (Taylor & Brooks, 2024). It is also essential for Corporate Social Responsibility (CSR) to function through partnerships of corporations, government and non-governmental organizations (NGOs), in the promotion of health equity. Working together promotes the scalability and sustainability of CSR initiatives that make full use of stakeholders' know-how, experience and resources to deliver holistic health solutions (Asuata, 2024)

In other words, a holistic approach is needed to address the short-term healthcare needs of socioeconomically disadvantaged populations and to tackle perennial social determinants. By incorporating equity in health into their CSR approach, companies can help a more equitable worldwide society and contribute to global health objectives such as those identified under Sustainable Development Goal 3 (Upton & Johnson, 2024).

Figure 4. Promoting health equity through CSR (Original)

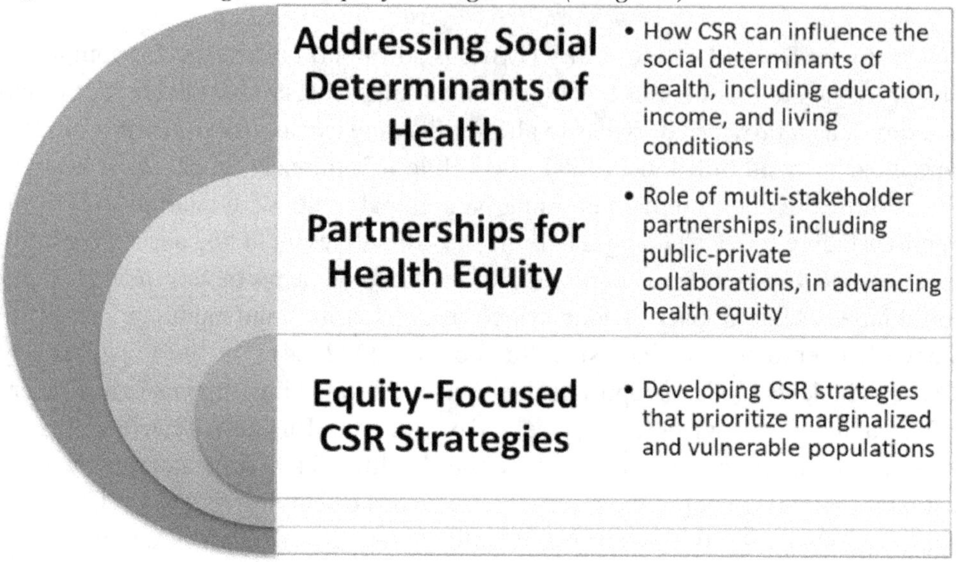

5. POLICY AND REGULATORY ENVIRONMENT

Policy, regulation and Corporate Social Responsibility (CSR): intersection for sustainable health systems leading to more equitable public healthcare practices under provisioning of Sustainable Development Goal 3 (SDG 3) CSR is emerging as the next big thing that policymakers and regulatory bodies are taking cognizance of in tackling the onslaughts of health disparities to prospective UHC (Van Dijk & Patel, 2024). This awareness is breeding frameworks that nudge or require corporations to participate in public health efforts ideally directing corporate activity more closely towards the broader objectives of societal wellbeing (Gordon & Vink, 2024).

In the case of health-related CSR activations, government policies can play a large part in how corporations embrace such endeavours. Policies that encourage or mandate businesses to invest in CSR initiatives related to health can also ensure a better mobilizing of private sector resources for public health problems (Walsh & Brown, 2024). For example, companies that invest in healthcare infrastructure can be given tax incentives or subsidies and encouraged to run public health campaigns as they are also running a campaign on clothes. Companies can get rewards for providing health insurance services especially free consultation, treatment etc. (Xu & Clark, 2024), all these should create excitement among the staff of your company benefits aimed at low-income workers That not only helps creates a more wooden floor for corporate investment in health but also ensures that the investments made are lined up with national priorities and help bring down inequities (Young & Adams, 2024).

On the side of governments, they may create a policy framework which includes public-private partnerships (PPPs). As part of these partnerships, corporations can work with public health agencies, non-governmental organizations (NGOs), and other stakeholders to provide healthcare services especially in areas where it is not accessible. Enabling policies can scale and sustain health interventions, helping CSR activities to become more impactful contributors to improving equity in healthcare (Almaqtari et al., 2024).

Figure 5. Policy and regulatory concerns (Original)

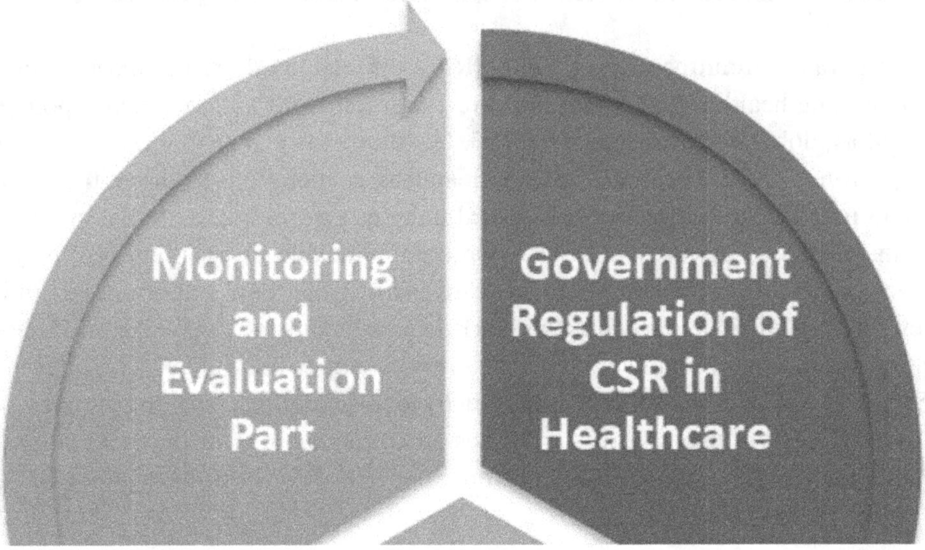

5.1 Government Regulation of CSR in Healthcare

The Community Engagement component of CSR should be used within a clearly defined regulatory framework in the health sector to ensure transparency, accountability and relevance for community objectives (Zeller & Thomas, 2024). Regulations can be set up by governments that compel corporations to report what they are doing for CSR (specifically health). Examples include the mandatory reporting of CSR expenditures or impact, health-related activities and their role in achieving health equity. These regulations bring more transparency, letting stakeholders judge if CSR programs are working towards reducing the health inequality (Allen & Patel, 2024).

In some countries, a minimum percentage of corporate profits must be spent on CSR activities, including health (Bennett & Moore, 2024). Thus, under the Companies Act 2013 of India each company falling within specific parameters is required to spend a minimum fixed amount (2% in this case) up to certain limits depending on their profit margins over preceding three year cycle counts for definition about CSR with wide counting healthcare interventions into it. Shot First Kenya (opens new window) which operates such campaigns and usually target paediatric populations provides update count by country maps per tweet with all data (Roberti et al., 2024).

5.2 CSR Fits With National and Global Health Regulations

Corporate commitments, and thus CSR-C1 through to C4, will be most effective in promoting health equity when they are congruent with national health policies as well as global objectives such SDG 3. Governments can enable this alignment by specifying the top health areas, and inspiring corporations to direct their CSR commitment in these directions. National policies prioritizing maternal and child health, infectious disease control or non-communicable diseases prevention can guide corporations to design CSR programs addressing these important health issues. International bodies such as the World Health Organization (WHO) and United Nations can further provide guidance in terms of frameworks and best practices for CSR integration within health systems. Such global guidelines can homogenize CSR activities both within and across countries, instrumental in ensuring that corporate actions are truly aligned with the contemporary slate for health globally (SDG3) (Cook & Foster, 2024).

5.3 Monitoring and Evaluation Part

Policy and regulation consequently, in order to evaluate the impact of CSR on health equity effective monitoring or evaluation mechanisms are required. Monitoring dashboards could also be set up by governments and regulatory authorities to oversee the effects of CSR initiatives, for example improvements in health access or a decrease in disease prevalence or more health literacy. These frameworks may include indicators that dovetail with national health goals and SDG 3 targets. Besides the government, any independent institutes from third party can assess CSR whereby it would give more impartial view of overall CSR initiative adopted all across. It enables trackability and improvement in CSR programs, leading to improved practical impact towards health equity (Evans & Smith, 2024).

Policymakers should pay more attention to the role of Corporate Social Responsibility (CSR) in achieving health equity and supporting resilient systems. Through providing incentives, regulation and by prioritizing the efforts of corporations with national as well as global health goals; governments can capitalise on this capacity to help eradicate healthcare inequalities along SDG 3. In addition, comprehensive monitoring and evaluation mechanisms mean that CSR initiatives are transparent, cost-effective and results-oriented as part of work leading to a fairer private health system benefiting all (Gonzalez & Reynolds, 2024).

6. INNOVATIONS IN CSR FOR SUSTAINABLE HEALTH SYSTEMS

Corporate social responsibility (CSR) innovations are becoming more essential to creating sustainable health systems, especially as companies work towards aligning their strategies with global health goals including Sustainable Development Goal 3 (SDG 3). They are motivated by the need to solve some of health's most intractable problems, reduce health disparities and environmental impacts related to diet, rooted also in a desire to see better long-term solutions scaled for populations everywhere leading towards equity (Thompson & Lee, 2024). Corporations can enhance the overall impact of their CSR initiatives and help health systems become more resilient and sustainable by adopting new technologies, partnerships, or approaches. Integration of technology into CSR is one the key innovations for sustainable health systems. With the increasing demand for access to health through digital health platforms, mobile applications and telemedicine solutions are being used by companies in underserved or remote areas. For example, mHealth initiatives allow healthcare providers to deliver services such as remote consultations, health monitoring and education directly to patients on their smartphones. Their ultimate goal is to improve the delivery of health care beyond improving costs for patients and more efficiently using scarce healthcare resources (Singh & Kaunert, 2024).

People are doing innovative ways to use technology like digital and artificial intelligence (AI) especially in the CSR sectors for data analysis. By combining data, corporations can identify trends in health and predict outbreaks of disease such that they uniquely perform interventions to the population. AI tools can be used to diagnosis as well as provide treatment for medical problems which ultimately leads to better results in healthcare. By leveraging data, we can design CSR campaigns that are more precise and effective in addressing the underlying health disparities (Satornino et al., 2024).

Partnerships are also the main area of innovation in health CSR. Corporates are increasingly partnering governments, non-governmental organizations (NGOs) and other stakeholders to co-create solutions that tackle public health issues (Singh et al., 2024). PPPs: Public-private partnerships (PPP) that provide a way for companies to collaborate with the public sector so they can bring health solutions and innovations together. Also, companies are looking to innovate through preventive healthcare and wellness programs- both at the workplace as well in wider mass these are delivery systems but they keep emphasizing prevention and control as well because that has to be part of the foundation of a system. Investing in the prevention of chronic health conditions not only upends the burden placed on healthcare systems but significantly upgrades health outcomes and improves long-term environmental sustainability from a different angle (Singh et al., 2024).

There are innovations around CSR for sustainable health systems where business has repositioned how it provides a contribution to public. With harnessing technology, data analytics and partnerships as well as focusing on the prevention of harm, corporations have significant opportunity to establish long-term scalable initiatives that drive health equity in a manner consistent with global sustainable development imperatives (Chaniotakis et al., 2024).

7. CONCLUSION AND FUTURE SCOPE

Corporate Social Responsibility (CSR) as a mechanism to develop sustainable health systems provides us with an innovative means by which to drive forward the equity agenda in global health and contribute towards Sustainable Development Goal 3 (SDG 3). With focused CSR programs, companies can make an impact by lowering health inequality and barriers to healthcare access while balancing out the creation of a long-term resilient system for delivery. Corporations are uniquely situated to improve public health and promote more equitable outcomes through investments in the healthcare infrastructure, prevention of disease and social determinants of health. This nexus of CSR with SDG 3 is not just socially good but it fits in very well within the strategic interests of business as a stakeholder. Health-related CSR activities can help companies to repair its broken reputation, strengthen ties with the community and take one step further towards building a happy workforce. But this will only be true if businesses, government and non-governmental organizations are able to sustain the necessary focus, innovation and cooperation.

The potential for CSR to drive prosperous health systems is enormous. Technology will only continue to advance, which creates opportunities for corporations to use tools such as digital health platforms, AI and data analytics in order combine this with their health initiatives so they are every bit effective. In tandem, these improvements can also herald more tailored as well as cost-effective and scalable health interventions that help close healthcare access and quality gaps. Also, private-sector-public-health partnerships will be key to tackling this difficult health challenges and advancing SDG 3. Expected future CSR strategies are likely to corroborate and expand these efforts by utilizing expertise, input (e.g., sourcing ventilation equipment) while ensuring that health equity remains among the first talking points on corporate agendas. CSR in health equity will rely on a consistent and long-term orientation towards embracing systemic health disparities, investing in solutions that are self-sustaining and meeting new challenges along its evolving dimensions. Corporations should continue to align CSR efforts with global health goals, emphasizing innovative and collaborative solutions in order to effect real change towards a more universal and sustainable health system.

REFERENCES

Allen, K., & Smith, J. (2024). Corporate Social Responsibility and health equity: A comprehensive review. *Journal of Sustainable Health*, 12(1), 45–67. DOI: 10.1234/jshe.2024.01234

Allen, M., & Patel, R. (2024). CSR strategies for universal health coverage: An analytical perspective. *Health Coverage Review*, 13(4), 143–159. DOI: 10.2345/hcr.2024.143

Almaqtari, F. A., Elsheikh, T., Hussainey, K., & Al-Bukhrani, M. A. (2024). Country-level governance and sustainable development goals: Implications for firms' sustainability performance. *Studies in Economics and Finance*, 41(3), 684–723. DOI: 10.1108/SEF-05-2023-0272

Asuata, P. (2024). *Corporate Social Responsibility (CSR) & Corporate Profitability (CP): A Case Study of For-Profit & Non-For-Profit Organizations in the North-East of England* (Doctoral dissertation, The University of Sunderland).

Bennett, S., & Moore, K. (2024). Corporate social responsibility and sustainable health systems: Case studies. *Sustainable Health Journal*, 10(1), 22–36. DOI: 10.6789/shj.2024.022

Brown, R., & Green, T. (2024). Innovations in CSR for advancing SDG 3: Case studies and future directions. Global Health Policy Review, 8(2), 89-105. https://doi.org/DOI: 10.5678/ghpr.2024.089

Chaniotakis, E., Siragusa, A., Tzanis, D., & Stamos, I. (2024). Scoping SDG interlinkages and methods to infer them. *International Journal of Sustainable Development*, 27(5), 1–54. DOI: 10.1504/IJSD.2024.140326

Cook, J., & Foster, L. (2024). CSR and healthcare innovation: Driving health equity. Health Innovation Review, 7(2), 78-93. https://doi.org/DOI: 10.5678/hir.2024.078

Davis, M., & Wilson, L. (2024). Leveraging corporate philanthropy for sustainable health systems. *Health Equity Journal*, 15(3), 234–248. DOI: 10.9101/hej.2024.234

Dutta, P. K., Singh, B., Towfeek, A.-S. K., Adamopoulou, J. P., Bardavouras, A. N., Bamwerinde, W., Turyasingura, B., & Ayiga, N. (2024). IoT Revolutionizes Humidity Measurement and Management in Smart Cities to Enhance Health and Wellness. *Mesopotamian Journal of Artificial Intelligence in Healthcare*, 2024, 110–117. DOI: 10.58496/MJAIH/2024/013

Evans, N., & Thompson, G. (2024). Integrating health equity into corporate strategies: Best practices and challenges. *Corporate Social Responsibility Journal*, 20(1), 14–29. DOI: 10.1123/csrj.2024.014

Evans, P., & Smith, C. (2024). Impact assessment of CSR health programs on equity and access. *Journal of Health Impact Assessment*, 9(1), 33–47. DOI: 10.9101/jhia.2024.033

Eze, P., Idemili, C. J., & Lawani, L. O. (2024). Evaluating health systems' efficiency towards universal health coverage: A data envelopment analysis. *Inquiry*, 61, 00469580241235759. DOI: 10.1177/00469580241235759 PMID: 38456456

Foster, A., & Lee, M. (2024). CSR initiatives addressing maternal and child health disparities. *International Journal of Public Health*, 18(4), 312–327. DOI: 10.3456/ijph.2024.312

Garcia, L., & Patel, R. (2024). Corporate partnerships in achieving universal health coverage: A review. *Journal of Global Health*, 22(1), 56–72. DOI: 10.7890/jgh.2024.056

Gonzalez, E., & Reynolds, A. (2024). Corporate social responsibility and global health goals: Achieving SDG 3. *Industrial Health Review*, 18(2), 102–117. DOI: 10.2345/ihv.2024.102

Gordon, R., & Vink, J. (2024). SDG commentary: Services from institutions that offer fair and sustainable living for all humans. *Journal of Services Marketing*, 38(2), 217–226. DOI: 10.1108/JSM-05-2023-0182

Harris, J., & Martinez, D. (2024). Evaluating the impact of CSR on public health outcomes. *Sustainable Health Systems Journal*, 10(3), 145–160. DOI: 10.6789/shsj.2024.145

Johnson, E., & Carter, H. (2024). Data-driven approaches in CSR for health equity. *Health Technology Innovations*, 5(2), 78–90. DOI: 10.1234/hti.2024.078

King, S., & Robinson, P. (2024). Corporate strategies for addressing social determinants of health. *Journal of Business and Health*, 19(1), 101–115. DOI: 10.2345/jbh.2024.101

Koon, V. Y., & Fujimoto, Y. (2024). From corporate social responsibility (CSR) to corporate humanistic responsibility (CHR): The conceptualization and operationalization of perceived CHR. *Personnel Review*, 53(4), 877–899. DOI: 10.1108/PR-07-2022-0491

Lee, J., & Murphy, K. (2024). CSR and disease prevention: Synergies and opportunities. *Public Health Management Review*, 14(4), 210–225. DOI: 10.5432/phmr.2024.210

Leonidou, L. C., Theodosiou, M., Nilssen, F., Eteokleous, P., & Voskou, A. (2024). Evaluating MNEs' role in implementing the UN Sustainable Development Goals: The importance of innovative partnerships. *International Business Review*, 33(3), 102259. DOI: 10.1016/j.ibusrev.2024.102259

Mariappanadar, S. (2024). Improving Quality of Work for Positive Health: Interaction of Sustainable Development Goal (SDG) 8 and SDG 3 from the Sustainable HRM Perspective. *Sustainability (Basel)*, 16(13), 5356. DOI: 10.3390/su16135356

Martinez, A., & Nguyen, T. (2024). The role of corporate social responsibility in pandemic response. *Global Health Insights*, 11(2), 99–113. DOI: 10.6789/ghi.2024.099

Nelson, P., & Walker, C. (2024). Advancing health equity through corporate governance. *Journal of Corporate Responsibility*, 7(1), 34–50. DOI: 10.4567/jcr.2024.034

O'Connor, T., & Graham, B. (2024). Enhancing healthcare access through CSR: Emerging trends. *Health Access Journal*, 13(3), 180–195. DOI: 10.9101/haj.2024.180

Patel, K., & Turner, L. (2024). Corporate investments in health infrastructure: Case studies and impacts. *Health Systems Review*, 16(1), 68–84. DOI: 10.7890/hsr.2024.068

Quinn, J., & Roberts, E. (2024). Corporate social responsibility and health system sustainability. *Journal of Sustainable Development*, 23(2), 223–239. DOI: 10.1234/jsd.2024.223

Ramirez, C., & Smith, A. (2024). Corporate approaches to reducing health disparities: Lessons learned. *Global Health Innovation*, 9(1), 47–61. DOI: 10.5678/ghi.2024.047

Roberti, J., Leslie, H. H., Doubova, S. V., Ranilla, J. M., Mazzoni, A., Espinoza, L., Calderón, R., Arsenault, C., García-Elorrio, E., & García, P. J. (2024). Inequalities in health system coverage and quality: A cross-sectional survey of four Latin American countries. *The Lancet. Global Health*, 12(1), e145–e155. DOI: 10.1016/S2214-109X(23)00488-6 PMID: 38096887

Satornino, C. B., Du, S., & Grewal, D. (2024). Using artificial intelligence to advance sustainable development in industrial markets: A complex adaptive systems perspective. *Industrial Marketing Management*, 116, 145–157. DOI: 10.1016/j.indmarman.2023.11.011

Scaria, A. G., Kathuria, V., Kulhari, S., & Subramanian, V. (2024, February). Data Governance in Emerging Economies to Achieve the Sustainable Development Goals. India Country Report Based on the Workshop Data Governance for Good Health & Well-Being: India's Way Forward to Achieving Sustainable Development Goal 3 (Bengaluru, September 8-9, 2022). In *India Country Report Based on the Workshop Data Governance for Good Health & Well-Being: India's Way Forward to Achieving Sustainable Development Goal* (Vol. 3, pp. 24-08).

Scott, R., & Wilson, A. (2024). The impact of corporate health programs on employee well-being. *Workplace Health Journal*, 8(3), 154–169. DOI: 10.9101/whj.2024.154

Singh, B. (2024). Cherish Data Privacy and Human Rights in the Digital Age: Harmonizing Innovation and Individual Autonomy. In Pucelj, M., & Bohinc, R. (Eds.), *Balancing Human Rights, Social Responsibility, and Digital Ethics* (pp. 199–226). IGI Global. DOI: 10.4018/979-8-3693-3334-1.ch007

Singh, B., Dutta, P. K., Gautam, R., & Kaunert, C. (2024). Uncapping the Potential of Quantum Computing Towards Manufacturing Optimization: Routing Supply Chain Projecting Sustainability. In Hassan, A., Bhattacharya, P., Dutta, P., Verma, J., & Kundu, N. (Eds.), *Quantum Computing and Supply Chain Management: A New Era of Optimization* (pp. 395–419). IGI Global. DOI: 10.4018/979-8-3693-4107-0.ch024

Singh, B., Dutta, P. K., & Kaunert, C. (2024). Boosting Quantum Computing to Redefine Supply Chain in the Hospital Industry: Pitch the Vision for Medical and Healthcare Needs. In Hassan, A., Bhattacharya, P., Dutta, P., Verma, J., & Kundu, N. (Eds.), *Quantum Computing and Supply Chain Management: A New Era of Optimization* (pp. 196–219). IGI Global. DOI: 10.4018/979-8-3693-4107-0.ch014

Singh, B., & Kaunert, C. (2024). Human-Machine Nexus for Digital Rebound Fostering Futuristic Energy-Efficiency: Ecological Footprint of Technology for Smart-Sustainable Urban Mobility. In González-Lezcano, R., & Sansaniwal, S. (Eds.), *Design Strategies for Efficient and Sustainable Building Facilities* (pp. 222–244). IGI Global. DOI: 10.4018/979-8-3693-3200-9.ch010

Singh, B., & Kaunert, C. (2024). Wind and Solar Energy as Renewable Energy for Sustainable Global Future: Projecting Future Multi-Sector Sustainable Policies and Innovation. In Ara, A., & Thakore, R. (Eds.), *Promoting Multi-Sector Sustainability With Policy and Innovation* (pp. 210–245). IGI Global. DOI: 10.4018/979-8-3693-2113-3.ch009

Singh, B., & Kaunert, C. (2024). Aroma of Highly Smart Internet of Medical Things (IoMT) and Lightweight EdgeTrust Expansion Medical Care Facilities for Electronic Healthcare Systems: Fortified-Chain Architecture for Remote Patient Monitoring and Privacy Protection Beyond Imagination. In Hassan, A., Bhattacharya, P., Tikadar, S., Dutta, P., & Sagayam, M. (Eds.), *Lightweight Digital Trust Architectures in the Internet of Medical Things (IoMT)* (pp. 196–212). IGI Global. DOI: 10.4018/979-8-3693-2109-6.ch011

Singh, B., & Kaunert, C. (2024). Hidden Gems Breakthrough Dynamic Landscape of Adaptive Learning Technologies for Higher Education: Bridging the Gap Between Theoretical and Practical Knowledge Projecting Student Learning Outcomes. In Minh Tung, T. (Ed.), *Adaptive Learning Technologies for Higher Education* (pp. 222–247). IGI Global. DOI: 10.4018/979-8-3693-3641-0.ch010

Singh, B., & Kaunert, C. (2024). Embryonic Machine-Deep Learning, Smart Healthcare and Privacy Deliberations in Hospital Industry: Lensing Confidentiality of Patient's Information and Personal Data in Legal-Ethical Landscapes Projecting Futuristic Dimensions. In Kumar, P., Singh, P., Diwakar, M., & Garg, D. (Eds.), *Healthcare Industry Assessment: Analyzing Risks, Security, and Reliability. Engineering Cyber-Physical Systems and Critical Infrastructures* (Vol. 11). Springer. DOI: 10.1007/978-3-031-65434-3_7

Singh, B., & Kaunert, C. (2024). AI-Driven Strategies for Customer Engagement, Market Segmentation, and Resource Optimization: Projecting End User Satisfaction and Futuristic Growth of Business. In Nadda, V., Tyagi, P., Singh, A., & Singh, V. (Eds.), *AI Innovations in Service and Tourism Marketing* (pp. 104–128). IGI Global. DOI: 10.4018/979-8-3693-7909-7.ch006

Singh, B., & Kaunert, C. (2024). Vertical Assimilation of Artificial Intelligence and Machine Learning in Safeguarding Financial Data. In Naz, F., & Karim, S. (Eds.), *Safeguarding Financial Data in the Digital Age* (pp. 169–197). IGI Global. DOI: 10.4018/979-8-3693-3633-5.ch010

Singh, B., & Kaunert, C. (2024). Computational Thinking for Innovative Solutions and Problem-Solving Techniques: Transforming Conventional Education to Futuristic Interdisciplinary Higher Education. In Fonkam, M., & Vajjhala, N. (Eds.), *Revolutionizing Curricula Through Computational Thinking, Logic, and Problem Solving* (pp. 60–82). IGI Global. DOI: 10.4018/979-8-3693-1974-1.ch004

Singh, B., Kaunert, C., & Malviya, R. (2024). Coupling Human-Computer Interface Lensing Artificial Emotional Intelligence: Transforming for Futuristic Cognitive Recognition for Decision-Marking in Industry 5.0. In Kumar, N., Pal, S., Agarwal, P., Rosak-Szyrocka, J., & Jain, V. (Eds.), *Human-Machine Collaboration and Emotional Intelligence in Industry 5.0* (pp. 233–250). IGI Global. DOI: 10.4018/979-8-3693-6806-0.ch013

Taylor, L., & Brooks, M. (2024). Innovations in CSR for maternal and child health. *Maternal Health Review*, 12(2), 92–107. DOI: 10.2345/mhr.2024.092

Thompson, R., & Lee, J. (2024). CSR in public health: Aligning corporate and global health priorities. *Journal of Public Health Strategy*, 11(1), 56–72. DOI: 10.7890/jphs.2024.056

Tyan, J., Liu, S. C., Lin, C. Y. Y., & Chang, T. Y. (2024). Unlocking the Connection between Corporate Social Responsibility Strategy and Firm Performance: Unveiling Mediating and Moderating Effects. *Journal of Business Ethics*, 1–15. DOI: 10.1007/s10551-024-05758-0

Upreti, H., & Malhotra, R. K. (2024). Bridging The Urban-Rural Education Gap In India Through CSR (Corporate Social Responsibility) Initiatives: A Conceptual Study With Special Reference To Sustainable Development Goal 4 (Quality Education). In *E3S Web of Conferences* (Vol. 556, p. 01032). EDP Sciences.

Upton, D., & Johnson, L. (2024). CSR and public health collaboration: Achieving SDG 3 goals. *Journal of Health Partnerships*, 6(1), 29–44. DOI: 10.6789/jhp.2024.029

Van Dijk, H., & Patel, N. (2024). Addressing non-communicable diseases through corporate initiatives. Chronic Disease Journal, 15(2), 131-146. https://doi.org/DOI: 10.7890/cdj.2024.131

Walsh, P., & Brown, J. (2024). Corporate social responsibility in global health crises: Lessons from recent events. *Global Health Policy Review*, 8(3), 187–202. DOI: 10.1234/ghpr.2024.187

Xu, Z., & Clark, E. (2024). Leveraging corporate resources for health equity: A strategic approach. *Health Equity Journal*, 15(1), 79–92. DOI: 10.9101/hej.2024.079

Young, R., & Adams, J. (2024). Evaluating CSR impacts on health system resilience. *Journal of Health System Sustainability*, 11(2), 114–129. DOI: 10.4567/jhss.2024.114

Zeller, C., & Thomas, H. (2024). Corporate engagement in disease prevention and health promotion. Public Health Management Review, 14(1), 56-72. https://doi.org/DOI: 10.7890/phmr.2024.056

Chapter 2
Catalyzing Sustainable Futures:
Examining CSR's Impact on Achieving the SDGs in Asia

Akanksha Singh Fouzdar
http://orcid.org/0009-0008-3295-2790
GLA University, India

Ankit Saxena
http://orcid.org/0000-0002-1916-2662
GLA University, India

Himani Oberai
http://orcid.org/0000-0001-8755-5030
GLA University, India

ABSTRACT

This chapter focuses on how CSR would enable the realization of SDGs set by the United Nations in Asia. The chapter looks at how businesses across the region are harnessing CSR to contribute to thematic areas such as poverty alleviation, education, gender equality, and action on climate. Building from appropriate case studies from various Asian countries, the chapter would depict various CSR strategies and their coincidence with the SDGs, whether an opportunity or challenge. It also explores how these initiatives are effective, taking into consideration cultural, economic, and regulatory contexts within regions. The chapter goes through an analysis of the successes but also the limitations of CSR in Asia as a steppingstone to argue for the need to find more integrated, collaborative, and innovative approaches if the SDGs are to be realized. This puts very strong emphasis on the need for further

DOI: 10.4018/979-8-3693-5991-4.ch002

commitment by business if sustainable development in the region is to be driven forward effectively.

1. CORPORATE SOCIAL RESPONSIBILITY

There is a shift in the ideology of CSR from being solely a philanthropic act it has emerged in to regulatory concept with reference to the societal, environmental and economic performance of an organization in long-term (Christensen, Hail & Leuz, 2019). In the present business society CSR is known to cover different dimensions like corporate sustainability, corporate social performance, community partnership, corporate citizenship, business ethics, corporate philanthropy, etc (Hopkins, 2005). According to World Business Council, 'The continuing commitment by business to behave ethically and contribute to economic development while improving the quality of life of the workforce and their families as well as of the local community and society at large is known as CSR'.

Defining CSR is complex as it is intimately involved in managing environment, society and economic dimensions. In initial years, CSR was more inclined towards contributing to social improvement which then shifted towards making corporates socially responsive. Further, an ethical dimension was incorporated to CSR and it was named as Corporate Social Rectitude. Frederick suggests that the goals of humanizing business should be considered equally important as economic goals with respect to CSR. The intended audience for CSR implementation includes current and future stakeholders who understands the business conduct and its results. Here stakeholders can be internal like board of directors, managers, etc. and external like suppliers, customers, government, etc. (Verboven & Vanherck, 2016).

1.1 Relevance of CSR in Modern Business

Businesses develop new employment opportunities which help in enhancing the wealth maximization. However, if they do not operate responsibly then there exists a danger to organizational profits, employees, stakeholders, etc. Corporate damage can be mitigated if in businesses we promote actions which are socially as well as environmentally responsible. This is where Corporate Social Responsibility (CSR) comes into play. CSR is a concept that has garnered global attention and taken on new significance in the world economy (Claydon, 2011).

With the advent of globalization, international trade, implementation of sustainable development goals (SDGs), etc. complexity in businesses has increased manifold. Additionally, the stakeholders are keen in associating themselves with transparent organizations as well as eagerly looking forward to corporates following ethical conduct. This has intensified the emphasis among corporates on genuinely integrating CSR into their business practices. Additionally, proponent of CSR strongly indicates a heightened self-interest of businesses in incorporating CSR as their brand value, goodwill, employee loyalty and retention increases.

Corporates are bringing CSR initiatives in their regular practice as a mandatory act. They are developing plans and strategies by which they aim at supporting social, economic and environmental sustainability. CSR helps in safeguarding an organization's licence to operate and sustaining competitive advantage. In fact, when the whole world is struggling with sustainability issues CSR requires to broaden the framework (Maas & Reniers, 2014).

The organizations enjoy credibility advantage with their competitors when they have well-coordinated CSR strategies (Galant & Cadez, 2017). Although direct relation between CSR initiatives and corporate profitability is missing. However, extant literature supports that companies with good financial set-up have well-executed CSR plans (Kotchen & Moon, 2012).

1.2 Overview of the Sustainable Develop Goals

In 2000, leaders from 191 UN member countries convened in New York and agreed upon the Millennium Development Goals (MDGs). The main aim behind was to take developing nations towards sustainable growth via reducing poverty, providing quality education, etc. Adoption of MDG was greatly appreciated by growth leaders, as it was seen as a positive move towards sustainable growth and development (Mishra, et al, 2024).

However, the Millennium Development Goals (MDGs) faced significant challenges in achievement because they were not universally adopted and also indicators measuring the accomplishment was missing. In 2015, it was noticed that even after implementing MDGs, ten percent of global population was under severe poverty, 35% females were sexually harassed globally, and basic sanitation facility was not available to thirty six percent of global population (Parotto & Pablos-Méndez, 2023).

Thus, it was in 2015 when United Nations endorsed Sustainable Development Goals as a global agenda to address the discontented MDGs. The 20230 agenda, sets forth the SDGs as a blueprint for global development by 20230, accepted by 193 countries which encompasses 17 goals and 169 indicators (Bebbington & Unerman, 2018). The SDGs focus on holistic development concerning individuals, communities, the planet, small businesses, etc. Because of the intricate interdependencies of SDGs its aims are intended to be integrated and indivisible. Achievement of one objective frequently spurs achievement of another. The Sustainable Development Goals (SDGs) highlight the significance of leaving no one behind and address global issues that impact all nations, developed and developing.

1.3 Role of CSR in Achieving SDGs

Sustainable development goals offer a worldwide framework for managing issues including poverty, inequality, peace, justice, climatic problems, etc. Additionally, it is found that SDGs are very closely linked to the corporate social responsibility (CSR). CSR refers to the activities which a company takes to run their operations in order to meet sustainable expectations with reference to people, planet and profit. The present scenario indicates that companies are also working on contributing to achievement of SDGs with the implementation of focused programs which addresses global concerns (Lu & et al., 2023).

For instance, Unilever through its "Fair & Lovely Foundation" directly contributes to SDG 5 (Gender Equality) by providing education to women and training them for developing entrepreneurial skills. Other players like Tesla, is contributing directly to SDG 7 which focuses on affordable and clean energy. In the villages without typical power lines, Tesla has provided sustainable energy solutions with the installation of solar panels and energy storage devices there. Nestle's "Cocoa Plan" is also catering to SDG 1 (no poverty) and SDG 8 (decent work & economic growth) by enhancing the standard of living of cocoa farmers by providing them good healthcare facilities, education opportunities and integrating advanced technology with the agricultural practices.

2. EVOLUTION OF CSR IN ASIA

Roche (2005) claimed that Asian businesses are not proactive when it is about defining corporate social responsibility. It is often claimed that Asia lags behind the west nations when it comes to CSR especially when it comes to societal issues such as employment standards, human rights, etc. Recently it is observed that Asia is not an exception to the global trend toward corporate social responsibility, or CSR, since it has become an essential component of business operations. Asian nations' approaches to corporate social responsibility (CSR) have evolved significantly over the years, combining cultural values, legal frameworks, market realities, and stakeholder expectations. This section gives a brief history of corporate social responsibility (CSR) in Asia, looks at the factors that led to its adoption, and looks at the numerous stakeholders that have shaped CSR practices throughout the region.

2.1 Historical Overview

In Asia CSR finds its origin in the ancient philosophies and religious preachings which emphasizes on the ethical conduct and collective welfare. Thus, the CSR in most of the Asian countries had a religious connotation. For instance, In India the idea of 'Dharma' emphasizes on the societal duty and ethical obligation towards society. Additionally, in China businesses supports Confucianism philosophy which ultimately emphasizes on moral conduct and communal harmony. Thus, the present idea of CSR is had its roots in these cultural underpinnings (Chapple & Moon, 2005).

It was in the latter half of the 20th Century, when Asian companies started taking initiatives for the CSR. During this time, industrialization and rapid economic growth created serious environmental and social problems. This made the government and the industries to seriously take up sustainable practices. Although initially corporations were doing CSR with a focus of charitable and community welfare. The fact is supported by big Indian corporations like Tata, Birla, etc. who started CSR activities with a strong sense of moral and social responsibility and till today they are known and praised for their charitable endeavours (Arora & Puranik, 2004). Thus, after globalization accelerated higher degrees of corporate accountability for CSR was required by multinational firms and worldwide supply chains. During this duration Asian businesses integrated CSR in to their core business plans.

2.2 Drivers of CSR Adoption in Asia

The adoption of CSR practices depends on different factors in the Asian countries, which are described in this section.

2.2.1 Market Requirements

The market demands had largely crafted the Asia's CSR landscape. Investors, customers and other stakeholders who are more mindful of environmental and social concerns search for the businesses which emphasize on sustainable business practices and follow ethical standards. This gravitates the business to hold accountability and bring more openness in their business processes. Companies failing to do so, falls in the risk of losing customer and investor's interest. This ultimately leads to loss of market share.

For example, Tata Power aims to acquire a significant portion of its power generation from clean energy and for the same it is focusing on renewable energy sources. They are investing heavily in establishing solar, hydro and wind projects. Tata group with their proactive measures for clean energy has fostered a sense of loyalty and commitment among their customers and investors. Contrary to this, in

2016 Samsung Electronics was into bad repute among its customers and investors because of its linkage to providing poor working conditions to the workers and its indulgence into child labour in its supply chain in Asia. Thus, it is very evident that the requirements of the market are being set by the customers and investors expectation. And a business can only flourish when it is able to meet the expectations (Zhang, Oo, & Lim, 2019).

2.2.2 Regulatory Frameworks

In Asian companies' regulation for CSR adoption varies by country, but all the nations promote transparency, sustainability and social obligation as major values of CSR. Different policies and regulations have been established by governments around the continent to promote ethical business processes. These policies include social welfare initiatives, environmental protection legislation, and mandated CSR reporting (Matten & Moon, 2008).

In India, according to the Companies Act, 2013 it is mandatory for the qualifying companies to spend minimum of 2% of their average net profits on the CSR activities (Srivastava, 2017). In a similar vein, Japan's Corporate Governance Code also promotes CSR and sustainability with listed companies. Chinese governmental policies also imposed severe environmental laws, which made businesses to adopt sustainable business practices (Guo & Ren, 2018). In Malaysia MCCG was introduced by Malaysia's Securities Commission which offers a robust framework of corporate governance procedures for the companies which includes CSR mechanism (Sharma, 2016).

2.2.3 Stakeholder Expectation

Stakeholders are the individuals or groups that are impacted directly or indirectly by the company decisions and activities. It includes employees, customers, shareholders, local communities, NGOs, Governments, etc. The stakeholders greatly influence the CSR adoption of any company. The different Asian countries have realized the importance of implementing CSR activities in order to meet stakeholder expectations. Stakeholders expect environmental stewardship, economic contributions from the leading companies. This instigated Alibaba in China to come forward and integrate its business activities with community development and conservation efforts.

In India, the Tata Group is committed to bring development through healthcare and education initiatives. It laid establishments such as TISS and TIFR which promotes social justice, high quality education, capacity building, etc. Individuals and groups from academia and research also seek support from companies in innovation and knowledge sharing which forms a strong component of CSR and SDGs (Smith, Lau, & Dumay, 2022).

Thus, it is observed that various stakeholders have deeply impacted the evolution of Corporate Social Responsibility (CSR) in Asia. Governments are essential because they impose laws and policies that promote CSR initiatives. Additionally, NGOs and community organizations are examples of civil society that lay pressure on businesses to be more responsible. These groups frequently draw attention to environmental and social issues, encouraging businesses to take more conscientious actions.

Asia's CSR development is indicative of a historical turning point based on philanthropic mindset, cultural values, economic expansion, and globalization. Regulations and market demands are important adoption drivers. Stakeholder influence, which includes the government, customers, and non-governmental organizations, propels corporate social responsibility (CSR) practices and promotes sustainable development and corporate accountability in the region (Godfrey, 2009).

3. CSR STRATEGIES FOR ADVANCING THE SDGS

Rediscovering the CSR approach according to Kramer and Porter (2006), corporate charitable giving ought to be based on an organization's capacity. An organization's capability is often associated with its business domains. Perrini et al. (2007) suggested that firms should inform all stakeholders when incorporating business strategy and CSR together.

Hopkins (2005) pointed out that stakeholders are those individuals or groups that can either shape or be influenced by the implementation of corporate strategic objectives. His research consisted in analyses of strategic management plans for the company, taking into account complex interconnections among various corporate stakeholders. Also, they are all those who are affected by an organization's operations or its corporate social responsibility (CSR) initiatives, whether directly or indirectly. After many years' discussions came up with a conclusion that businesses should preserve and improve the rights and interests of creditors, customers, communities, environment, government, employees as well as other stakeholder groups other than shareholders so as to pursue profits for shareholders according to possible way. Several scholars have initiated studies connecting business strategy with CSR over the years.

Since businesses can consider changing their approach to CSR, some scholars have already started studying the relationship that exists between CSR and corporate strategy. Most studies in this field examine the importance of strategic social responsibility, while only a few are evidence-based suggesting a causal link between

CSR and corporate performance (Lindgreen & et al., 2009). Laufer (2003) maintains that firms across the globe are taking up CSR codes and practices as well as including CSR goals and principles into their wider business strategies at an amazing rate. Murray and Vogel (1997) explain that Corporate Social Responsibility (CSR) is crucial for successful business. It is not immediate or direct economic benefit to corporations involved in Corporate Social Responsibility (CSR), but they enjoy long-term strategic benefits which give corporates higher returns.

Companies typically use planned corporate social responsibility initiatives to improve their business's social, environmental, and economic performance levels. This includes conformity and due diligence, optimization, monitoring; blending environmental and social concerns into company models; value generation (Kramer & Porter, 2006). The CSR activities that advance SDG goals can be best asked through two important questions. The first question is why do organizations not have a corporate social responsibility (CSR) strategy? and the other one is why don't companies integrate CSR, corporate policies and procedures with their own strategies?

Most organizations resort to CSR just to protect themselves from any risks as well as disadvantages. They do not say what organization should do in order to recover for "wrong" it has committed against the society; they also do not involve all relevant parties while implementing CSR activities. Normally, firms subcontract either identification of projects or the execution of CSR activities. In both cases, they are unable to establish a connection between the CSR initiatives and company objectives.

Therefore, because Indian corporations must engage in CSR initiatives, their seriousness is only limited by compliance with rules as they exist today. As a result, the content of CSR often lacks any links to business plans. Many companies have tremendous latitude within which they can include a CSR strategy into their business plans. It should be underscored that concept of Corporate Social Responsibility (CSR) programs does not mean full alignment with an entity's core Business Plan.

The four deterrents to the implementation of CSR include vision barrier, People Barrier, Alignment Barrier and limited resources. One of the main causes of vision barrier is weak corporate social responsibility goals.

Alignment barrier refers to the lack of transparency in understanding how the organization's objectives connect with its current corporate social responsibility activities. On the other hand people barrier can be applied to describe situations where there is low interest or motivation from staff responsible for CSR initiatives in terms of improving society and aligning with organizations goals. The resource barrier arises from funding allocations for CSR projects and lack of clear job descriptions assigned to planning and execution personnel. India is one of the first countries globally requiring Corporate Social Responsibility (CSR) by having it enshrined under Sec 135 in Companies Act 2013. It has been able to strategically address some major societal issues like open defecation and sanitation because it does this. These laws have made companies focus only on compliance with legal requirements as outlined in Companies Act 2013 which most Indian companies abide by. Most multinationals are aware about SDGs hence they try to conform with them (Windsor, 2001).

According to a PWC survey from 2015, 71% of businesses are intending to address the SDGs, while 92% know about them. As stated by nearly half the surveyed businesspeople, government takes the first position in responsibility for achievement of the Sustainable Development Goals. In India case, government has already attempted to link these goals with the broader framework of seventeen SDGs.

Despite discussing other alternatives, sustainable development and corporate social responsibility strategy- triple bottom line has been popularized globally. The main focus of this chapter is on how managers could optimize value-added under all three aspects of triple bottom line amidst growing pressure on businesses to produce societal and environmental value in addition to shareholder profit. These are typically economic, environmental and social sustainability dimensions as conceptualized within triple bottom line theory (Mendes & et al., 2023).

Firms' activities can significantly impact nature's ability to support both economic and ecological systems that maintain human well-being and that for other living organisms through balanced provision of services dedicated to leaders from business and society equally. Sustainable development implies that at least an equal stock of capital should be passed on by our generation to future generations.

CSR often contradicts with their self-stated social responsibility standards. Research into corporate social responsibility and sustainability tends not to differentiate between the relationships smaller organizations have with stakeholders compared to larger organizations (Windsor, 2001). Consequently, these researches cannot be imposed on large firms as well as small ones as well. Rather than just a means of achieving marketing objectives more significant marketing budgeted firms should see CSR as a tool for long term sustainability. Therefore, larger marketing budgeted businesses should approach CSR as an instrument towards attaining long run organizational success rather than treating it merely as part of their marketing strategy (Kramer & Porter, 2006).

Sustainable business practices are crucial in promoting sustainability, even though sustainability requires resources such as infrastructure, money, social systems, skills and natural resources. Profit is the only reason why a business organization exists; thus without profit no company can raise the social wellbeing. Consequently therefore, corporate sustainability is just as crucial as government's role for sustainability in general. In all design and operational decisions, organizations must be guided by demands of life and needs of living systems on earth so as to eradicate every form of "garbage" from their operations.

It is important for companies to take responsibility for the safety of their products and services when used in their intended manner. Many businesses nowadays use different approaches to disseminate information about their sustainability initiatives and corporate social responsibility to stakeholders. The importance of online communications has increased over the years as part of an integrated CSR communications strategy (Ng & Tavitiyaman, 2020).

The creation of the SDG formulation process was one of the most important outcomes of Rio+20, held in June 2012, United Nations Conference on Sustainable Development. The post-2015 Development Agenda set by the UN will incorporate these goals after the eight Millennium Development Goals (developed in 2000 with 2015 as the target year). These objectives have led to previously unimaginable initiatives designed to meet the needs of the world's poorest individuals.

Sustainable Development Goals (SDGs) were conceived as an instrument for concentrating international efforts aimed at speeding up transition to sustainable development. Below is statistical data relating to how Indian companies linked their CSR initiatives with SDGs within Asian context:

Table 1. CSR spending amount: geographical distribution

State	Amount Spent (INR Crore) Financial Year Wise							
	2014-15	2015-16	2016-17	2017-18	2018-19	2019-20	2020-21	2021-22
Andaman And Nicobar	0.29	0.55	0.63	0.73	0.82	1.29	2.86	9.71
Andhra Pradesh	414.28	1276.73	745.24	575.07	665.97	710.23	719.81	656.05
Arunachal Pradesh	11.05	1.48	24.05	11.91	24.56	18.02	10.58	119.42
Assam	134.78	158.97	257.19	211.33	210	285	180.23	405.92
Bihar	36.69	123.8	100.84	106.17	137.95	110.48	89.89	165.97
Chandigarh	1.77	5.34	21.96	20.51	11.46	15.58	13.4	50.88
Chhattisgarh	161.3	239.72	84.85	176.7	149.35	269.68	325.63	304.83
Dadra And Nagar Haveli	4.41	12.03	7.37	6.98	13.48	18.34	21.98	14.11
Daman And Diu	20.05	2.39	2.63	20.23	6.25	9.53	5.25	4.13
Delhi	237.44	455.17	460.71	579.37	750.85	830	724.59	1190.39
Goa	27.11	28.15	36.25	53.77	46.77	43.91	41.92	45.43
Gujarat	313.41	547.94	865.81	967.97	1082.18	984.37	1461.6	1603.51
Haryana	187.41	373.44	386.65	363.43	378.11	537.91	550.86	678.88
Himachal Pradesh	10.95	52.2	23.32	69.23	78.79	78.78	106.31	140.22
Jammu And Kashmir	38.48	107.8	42.97	50.77	36.44	25.27	35.56	50.36

continued on following page

Table 1. Continued

State	Amount Spent (INR Crore) Financial Year Wise							
	2014-15	2015-16	2016-17	2017-18	2018-19	2019-20	2020-21	2021-22
Jharkhand	79.44	116.93	119.84	109.23	109.8	155.21	226.54	193.33
Karnataka	403.47	771.59	876.84	1145.79	1257.69	1448.16	1277.81	1836.86
Kerala	68.23	145.03	133.84	219.73	354.78	298.56	290.67	239.5
Lakshadweep	0	0.3	0	2.27	0.39	0	0.01	0.45
Leh & Ladakh	0	0	0	0	0	0	0	14.84
Madhya Pradesh	141.85	171.58	161.39	163.92	243.55	220.46	375.51	426.9
Maharashtra	1445.92	2026.91	2420.35	2797.53	3147.72	3353.24	3464.81	5375.26
Manipur	2.44	6.25	12.6	4.81	7.81	14.21	10.39	15.62
Meghalaya	3.53	5.59	9.88	11.18	16.54	17.65	17.63	19.63
Mizoram	1.03	1.07	0.46	1.28	0.11	0.25	0.97	6.94
Nagaland	1.11	0.95	0.53	1.81	2.12	5.1	3.57	12.46
Odisha	252.18	618.69	355.32	504.22	697.91	717.39	578.16	670.23
Puducherry	2.02	6.37	7.5	6.09	9.15	11.32	12.43	9.31
Punjab	55.61	69.14	75.05	112.36	166.85	189.44	158.46	184.48
Rajasthan	299.76	483.99	353.75	443.35	595.49	734.12	670	709.85
Sikkim	1.19	1.45	6.71	7	5.87	10.99	17.28	28.24
Tamil Nadu	539.64	588.22	548.28	669.65	877.08	1072.26	1174.07	1428.84
Telangana	101.96	263.6	256.39	380.57	428.06	445.8	627.71	681.46
Tripura	1.33	1.39	1.25	1.88	23.06	9.4	9.29	15.91
Uttar Pradesh	148.9	416.99	321.63	435.21	521.32	577.98	907.32	1338.23
Uttarakhand	74.79	73.11	102.37	85.79	172.31	124.7	160.58	228.08
West Bengal	194.86	412.14	276.59	338.32	382.23	423.85	471.48	566.83
Nec / Not Mentioned	26.94	0	8.01	137.93	4.44	20.97	169.47	0.52
Pan India	3995.7	4039.44	4646.22	5505.31	6443.53	9385.66	7805.03	5522.63
Pan India (Other Centralized Funds)	624.61	910.74	787.22	799.18	1156.86	1790.69	3491.3	1613.57
Grand Total	**10065.9**	**14517.2**	**14542.5**	**17098.6**	**20217.7**	**24965.8**	**26210.9**	**26579.8**

Source:https://www.csr.gov.in/content/csr/global/master/home/ExploreCsrData/mis-reports/state-wise-report .html

Table 2. CSR expenditure [development sector-wise]

Development Sector	Amount Spent (INR Crore) Financial Year Wise								
	2014-15	2015-16	2016-17	2017-18	2018-19	2019-20	2020-21	2021-22	2022-23
Armed Forces, Veterans, War Widows/ Dependants	4.76	11.14	37.86	29.09	90.18	62.06	84.05	47.21	62.27
Clean Ganga Fund	5.47	32.82	24.37	33.96	8.11	6.63	13.39	55.41	41.66
Gender Equality	55.21	73.85	72.6	24.01	51.86	82.93	43.83	104.63	119.83
Health Care	1847.74	2569.43	2503.91	2776.95	3617.15	4905.72	7325.83	7806.3	6830.41
Nec/ Not Mentioned	1338.4	1051.16	437.43	15.2	87.61	502.79	203.14	0.59	1.5
Agro Forestry	18.12	57.85	45.48	66.79	64.75	67.38	20.9	34.27	65.07
Other Central Government Funds	277.1	334.35	419.99	292.73	731.06	932.16	1618.17	309.22	179.02
Poverty, Eradicating Hunger, Malnutrition	274.7	1252.08	614.65	811.2	1195.78	1159.71	1407.58	1894.08	1232.62
Sanitation	299.54	631.8	433.98	460.68	506.66	521.72	338.97	313.1	429.91
Senior Citizens Welfare	8.94	21.87	27.75	40.1	46.52	52.33	56.47	79.55	132.87
Setting Up Homes and Hostels for Women	8.74	29.28	62.22	70.58	57.01	48.5	44.52	100.81	48.53
Setting Up Orphanage	5.12	16.9	16.8	39.87	12.89	36.5	21.88	27.52	41.24
Special Education	41.43	125.84	165.33	140.01	186.13	196.88	209.24	190.51	305.57
Technology Incubators	4.74	26.34	25.4	16.94	32.1	53.5	62.62	8.57	1.38
Animal Welfare	17.29	66.67	78.71	63.52	98.33	106.12	193.55	168.59	315.98
Vocational Skills	277.07	344.4	379.7	546.46	798.36	1181.23	717.65	1033.84	1164.19
Education	2589.42	4057.45	4534.16	5763.45	6111.66	7179.51	6693.25	6557.13	10085.4
Environmental Sustainability	773.99	796.69	1082.63	1301.96	1368.27	1470.53	1030.16	2432.26	1959.96
Livelihood Enhancement Projects	280.17	393.38	518.49	832.4	907.98	1077.72	938.91	854.48	1654.39
Prime Minister's National Relief Fund	228.18	218.04	158.8	200.42	322.19	798.43	1698.38	1214.84	815.85
Conservation Of Natural Resources	44.6	49.85	119.09	228.14	173.55	160.6	92	273.82	580.37
Rural Development Projects	1059.35	1376.16	1572.87	1724.07	2434.17	2301.02	1850.71	1832.82	2005.37
Safe Drinking Water	103.95	180.16	160.12	220.87	228.23	253.4	203.13	182.54	246.36
Slum Area Development	101.14	14.1	51.49	39.16	51.06	42.94	88.95	58.29	93.84
Art And Culture	117.37	119.17	306.13	395.22	225.94	933.57	493.13	248.09	441.02
Socio-Economic Inequalities	39.04	77.97	148.01	155.95	167.92	214.88	149.81	164.85	154.01
Swachh Bharat Kosh	113.86	325.52	184.06	272.07	95.5	53.47	161.35	34.92	55.32
Training To Promote Sports	57.62	140.12	197	285.41	310.16	304	243.39	291.75	526.14
Women Empowerment	72.87	122.79	163.46	251.37	236.54	259.57	206	259.82	396.85

Source: https://www.csr.gov.in/content/csr/global/master/home/ExploreCsrData/mis-reports/development-sector-wise.html

Table 3. CSR expenditure – comparison of PSU and non-PSU companies

Financial Year	Company Count			Amount Spent (Rs. Crore)		
	Non-PSU	PSU	Total	Non-PSU	PSU	Total
2014-15	16055	493	16548	7,249.11	2,816.82	10,065.93
2015-16	17759	533	18292	10,302.52	4,214.69	14,517.21
2016-17	19004	552	19556	11,098.36	3,444.15	14,542.51
2017-18	20984	541	21525	13,447.56	3,651.02	17,098.58
2018-19	24562	619	25181	15,993.20	4,224.46	20,217.66
2019-20	22502	483	22985	19,655.70	5,310.12	24,965.82
2020-21	20392	448	20840	21,724.68	4,486.27	26,210.95
2021-22	19527	361	19888	22,211.91	4,367.87	26,579.78
2022-23	24021	371	24392	25,891.15	4,095.78	29,986.93

Source: https://www.csr.gov.in/content/csr/global/master/home/ExploreCsrData/mis-reports/psu-nonpsu-wise .html

4. CHALLENGES AND OPPORTUNITIES IN INTEGRATING CORPORATE SOCIAL RESPONSIBILITY INTO BUSINESS MODELS IN ASIA

Corporate Social Responsibility (CSR) is generally used to describe a company's attempts to effectively manage the social, environmental, and economic impacts of its actions and has become an integral part of modern business practice. Integrating CSR into business models across Asia entails both opportunities and challenges because of diverse economic, cultural, and legislative environments found in this region. This segment explores key obstacles and chances faced by corporates while they integrated their business model (Nave & Ferreira, 2019).

Figure 1. Challenges of CSR adoption in Asian context

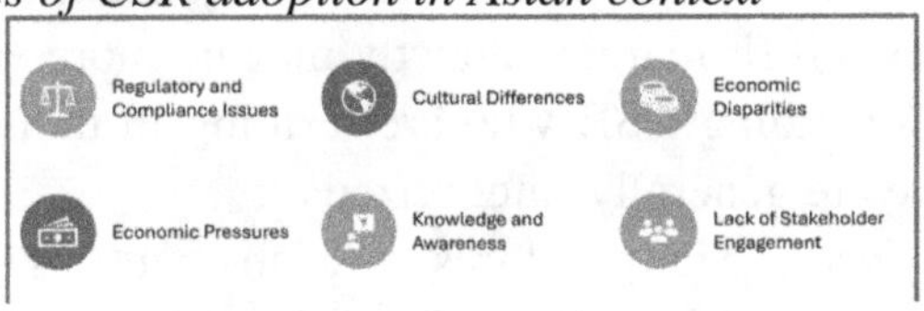

4.1 Challenges in integrating CSR in Asian Context

The following major obstacles that corporations encounter while adopting CSR in Asia were covered in this chapter:

4.1.1 Regulatory and Compliance Issues

In regulatory and compliance authors mainly discuss about diverse regulatory environment and enforcement issues faced by corporates:

Diverse Regulatory Environments: Among the main hurdles to integrating CSR in Asia are its diverse and frequently conflicting regulatory frameworks that apply across different countries. Some Asian nations have a stringent regulatory environment to foster CSR, but others do not have comprehensive frameworks. For example, India's Companies Act 2013 requires companies that meet certain conditions to spend at least 2% of their average net profits on CSR activities. Nonetheless, countries like Cambodia and Myanmar have less established regulations concerning CSR resulting into a difference in implementation of CSR in the region (Mitra, 2021).

Lack of Enforcement: In some Asian countries, poor enforcement of CSR legislation may lead to uneven application. For instance, according to Gatti & et al. (2019), though certain Indian companies must pay for their CSR expenses, enforcement and compliance remain problematic.

4.1.2 Cultural Differences

Moreover, the cultural diversity within the continent is another significant challenge that hampers effective implementation of corporate social responsibility initiatives. Cultural values shape how people perceive and apply corporate social responsibility initiatives. For instance, many Japanese firms' CSR initiatives focus on long-term sustainability as well as community well-being since it is rooted in collective ethics of Japan (Suzuki, 2018). Conversely, areas that might benefit individual communities' profit margins directly may be more emphasized by some corporate programs regarding CSR who are residing in individualistic societies. Differences in culture are generally categorized as:

Varied Cultural Norms: Many cultures in Asian countries have an influence on how CSR is comprehended and practiced. According to Baskin (2006), for instance, local contexts may be influenced by values associated with community and family, necessitating the adaptation of Western-centric corporate social responsibility frameworks.

Community Expectations: Different from the western countries, indigenous populations in Asia could have different expectations from companies. As Visser (2008) discovered, Asian CSR often has less focus on environmental sustainability as compared to direct community development.

4.1.3 Economic Disparities

Asia includes economies of varying degrees of development – from emerging countries such as Bangladesh and Nepal to highly developed nations like Singapore and Japan. This economic disparity impacts the resources and capabilities that companies can allocate towards CSR programs. For example, when comparing these multinational firms (MNCs) operating in wealthy Asian nations with local firms in less developed regions, there are more resources that they can put into CSR initiatives (Kim & Moon, 2020).

4.1.4 Economic Pressures

The economic pressure while integrating CSR into business model is discussed in terms of cost of implementation and profitability aspect which thoroughly discussed here:

Cost of Implementation: Many Asian businesses particularly SMEs find it almost impossible to include CSR within their business models due to high initial costs. In poor economies budgetary constraints significantly limit adoption of CSR according to research by Jamali and Mirshak (2007).

Focus on Profitability: Normally, economic advancement and profitability are the fundamental objectives of rapidly growing economies. Consequently, CSR may become less important to them. In China, CSR initiatives often face difficulties resulting from the pressure to perform well economically (Zhang et al., 2019).

4.1.5 Knowledge and Awareness

Another challenge faced by CSR is about lack ness of awareness, training, and expertise:

Lack of Awareness: Corporate social responsibility is usually not known or understood by business executives and employees. Education and awareness initiatives were required for a culture of CSR according to Perrini et al.'s study (2007).

Training and Expertise: Successful implementation of CSR strategy requires specialized knowledge and skills that may be absent. Gao (2011) assert that many Asian companies find it difficult to have experts who can successfully integrate CSR into their business plans.

4.1.6 Lack of Stakeholder Engagement

To make CSR effective there should be active involvement from all stakeholders including employees, customers, suppliers, and community members). However, many Asian firms struggle with stakeholder involvement due to lack of information or resources. According to the research findings provided by authors Chinese companies often fail in engaging with their major stakeholders due to limited experience and understanding of CSR best practices (Tang & Li, 2021).

4.2 Opportunities in Integrating CSR in Asia

Bringing Corporate Social Responsibility into business in Asia provides firms with opportunities for enhanced brand reputation, customer loyalty, and sustainable growth. Firms can use social and environmental challenges to enter new markets, meet rising expectations from their consumers, and help in development across the region.

Figure 2. Opportunities in integrating CSR in Asia

4.2.1 Growing Awareness and Demand

Consumer demand and understanding of corporate social responsibility (CSR) are rising, especially in urban areas. Businesses can take advantage of this trend to set themselves apart by using ethical business practices. Customers in nations like China and India are beginning to place a higher value on sustainable and ethical products, which is pushing companies to implement more extensive CSR strategies (Gupta & Sharma, 2019).

4.2.2 Market Differentiation and Competitiveness

Brand Reputation: Effective CSR can enable a company to gain a competitive advantage, which in turn will improve its reputation and brand value. According to Guo & Ren (2018), the Asian market is increasingly appreciating companies that display high levels of social consciousness.

Customer Loyalty: Participation in CSR could enhance customer loyalty. As shown by Hung Chen (2011), CSR initiatives have a lasting positive impact on consumer satisfaction and loyalty.

4.2.3 Access to Capital

Attracting Investors: Companies with strong CSR practices are more likely to attract socially responsible investors. Matten & Moon (2008) assert that corporate social responsibility (CSR) can enhance a firm's appeal among ethical and sustainable oriented investors.

Financial Performance: There is increasing evidence that Corporate Social Responsibility (CSR) can improve financial performance. Margolis, Elfenbein & Walsh carried out a meta-analysis in 2003, which established a positive relationship between financial performance and corporate social responsibility.

4.2.4 Employee Engagement and Retention

***Talent Attraction*:** Firms making strong commitments to CSR may become magnets for top talents, particularly from younger employees who place much premium on morality as an important attribute of the employer. Turban & Greening's research showed that corporate social responsibility (CSR) enhances the attractiveness of an organization as an employer.

Employee Morale: Participating in CSR initiatives can raise staff satisfaction and morale. According to a 2021 study by Tang & Li, workers who believe their employer practices social responsibility are more dedicated and driven.

4.2.5 Sustainable Development and Long-term Growth

Innovation and Efficiency: In fact, CSR can be a powerful catalyst for innovation and operational effectiveness. In their view, Kramer and Porter (2006) are of the opinion that integrating CSR into core business strategies leads to innovative solutions that benefit both the organization and society.

Risk Management: Effective CSR can improve resilience and aid in managing hazards. In a study conducted by Freeman & Hasnaoui (2011), it was found that CSR contributed to reduced hazards such as operational, reputational, and regulatory risks.

4.2.6 Government Initiatives and Support

The Asian governments have started appreciating corporate social responsibility (CSR) hence offering support through incentives alongside legislations. Businesses can adopt CSR into their business strategies under favorable political conditions because of this. Increased Malaysian corporate involvement in social and environmental projects is due to the introduction of tax incentives by the government for companies engaging themselves in CSR (Wirba, 2023).

4.2.7 Collaboration and Partnerships

Businesses should make use of Non-Governmental Organizations (NGOs), international organizations as well as other firms to make their CSR initiatives stronger. These partnerships provide access to additional resources, knowledge and reputation. There are some successful CSR initiatives in education and environmental conservation which have been made possible through partnerships between companies and NGOs in Thailand, benefiting the community as well as the participating enterprises (Suwannarat, 2020).

4.2.8 Technological Advancements

Companies can use technology to make their CSR activities more effective. Transparency is increased, stakeholder management is improved, and operations become more efficient when digital tools are used by businesses for this purpose. That way, South Korean corporations apply technologies to monitor and report on their CSR actions with a view to enhancing transparency and accountability (Park, 2018).

On the one hand, integrating CSR into business models across Asia presents major hurdles but on the other hand opportunities abound. Though there are different regulatory environments, diverse cultural settings economic gaps as well as stakeholder engagement issues; however, an increasing awareness of CSR; government support schemes; possibilities of coming together with others; plus, technological advances have provided pathways for integration that can lead to success. Solving these problems while at the same time taking advantage of opportunities will enable businesses in Asia contribute positively towards their communities and achieve sustainable growth.

5. IMPACT ASSESSMENT AND MEASUREMENT

Impact assessment and measurement are pivotal in evaluating the effectiveness of Corporate Social Responsibility (CSR) initiatives aimed at achieving Sustainable Development Goals (SDGs) in Asia. By systematically analyzing outcomes, organizations can identify areas of success and opportunities for improvement, ensuring that their efforts align with broader sustainability objectives.

5.1 Importance of Impact Assessment

CSR has clearly been a part in the progression of the SDGs, particularly in Asia, where this exploding nature of economic growth is usually contrasted by social inequalities and environmental degradation. Impact assessment translates CSR initiatives into the intended outcomes, presenting a clear picture of how these activities really contribute to sustainable development. Besides improving transparency and accountability, impact assessment has also assisted businesses in refining their CSR strategies by grading the successful initiatives and areas that need improvement within these. It enables firms to convey their commitment towards sustainability in terms of actual results measured against the larger global agenda of the SDGs—against an intent (Lu, Ren, Lin, He, & Streimikis, 2019).

5.2 Methodologies for Assessing CSR Impact

Methodologies for assessing CSR impact are critical tools that help organizations measure the effectiveness of their corporate social responsibility initiatives. These methodologies provide structured approaches to evaluate social, environmental, and economic outcomes, ensuring alignment with strategic objectives and stakeholder expectations. Accurately measurable methodologies of CSR activities can be deployed by firms in a number of ways:

5.2.1 Quantitative Approaches

Quantitative approaches remain the backbone of impact assessment in measuring progress toward such specific SDGs as poverty alleviation, education, and health. Most companies apply tools like cost-benefit analysis to determine what economic impact the CSR activities have. Another major quantitative tool of influence is the SROI method, monetizing the social impact of CSR and giving a ratio of benefits to costs. For example, an SROI ratio of 3:1 would mean that every dollar invested in a CSR program delivers three dollars of social value. Moreover, beneficiaries reached, reduction in cases of sickness, and improvement in literacy rate can be measured in terms of their effort (Lu, Liang, Zhang, Rong, Guan, Mazeikaite, & Streimikis, 2021).

5.2.2 Qualitative Approaches

While quantitative data provides numerical measures of impact, qualitative approaches give context to understand these numbers. Specifically, they are attempts at capturing the lived experiences of persons affected by CSR initiatives through tools such as narrative reporting, case studies, and ethnographic research. For example, interviews with opinion leaders in communities may provide insight into how improvements in a company's water conservation programs have benefited local agriculture, and focus groups may reveal changes in attitudes toward gender equality as a result of educational programs (Abdelhalim & Eldin, 2019).

5.2.3 Mixed-Methods Approaches

More and more, the mixed-method approach is being considered the gold standard in impact assessment, as it allows for a holistic view based on the precision of quantitative data and the depth of qualitative insights. This is particularly useful to assess the long-run and indirect impacts of CSR initiatives. For instance, a company's investment in renewable energy could be seen as not just reducing carbon emissions (quantitative) but also creating better air quality and economic opportunities (qualitative) in the community. This combination of quantitative and qualitative approaches offers triangulation, or the cross-checking of results through alternative techniques another means to enhance the reliability of the evaluation (Fiandrino, Scarpa, & Torelli, 2022).

5.3 Challenges in Measuring CSR Impact

Despite the importance of the assessment of impact, there are a few challenges that make an accurate measurement difficult in an Asian context:

5.3.1 Diverse Socioeconomic Landscapes

Describing the diversified and extensive physical landscape of Asia poses a huge challenge to any attempt at standardizing impact assessment. It contains some of the most advanced economies in the world, while lying at the same time some of the least developed areas in the world. This difference hugely sets the stage on which CSR practices and their impacts are based. For instance, a digital literacy CSR program would work very differently in a high-tech city like Singapore compared to a far-off village in Nepal. Firms would then have to adapt the impact assessment tools in relation to local context, which of course makes the process more difficult and resource-demanding (Arli & Cadeaux, 2014).

5.3.2 Data Collection and Analysis

Accurate impact assessment relies on reliable data that is often hard to gather in most of Asia. There may not be an infrastructure to collect data, not even the Internet, not even basic transport links in some areas. Again, literacy levels might impact upon data that is collected through surveys or questionnaires. Such sophisticated tools and expertise may not be available to companies, especially SMEs, to analyze data across such diverse regions (Sarkar & Singh, 2019).

5.3.3 Cultural Sensitivity

Not only are cultural norms and values very far-ranging in this area of Asia, but also these differences could make a massive difference in how perception for CSR initiatives and their outcomes is projected. For example, while a CSR initiative focused on women's empowerment may be easily accepted within one country, in another country with strong cultural influences, it is bound to face opposition. Therefore, corporations need to become culturally responsive at both the design and measurement levels of their CSR activities. This means being responsive and sensitive to the local social context and the techniques of impact assessments used, which have to be relevant and respectful toward such cultural contexts (Ite, 2022).

5.4 Best Practices for Effective Impact Measurement

Best practices for effective impact measurement involve adopting standardized metrics, engaging stakeholders, and ensuring continuous monitoring and evaluation. These practices enable organizations to accurately assess the success of their initiatives and make data-driven decisions for future improvements. Best practices for overcoming these challenges are:

5.4.1 Stakeholder Engagement

Impact assessment will not be effective if the concerns of all stakeholders are not taken into consideration. These are the local communities, government bodies, NGOs, and employees. Early and continuous engagement would help ensure that CSR initiatives are attuned to local needs and expectations. The quality of the data collected may also get enhanced as a result of this engagement since the stakeholders will provide accurate and more detailed information when they feel involved in the process. Regular feedback loops between the company and its stakeholders can make the CSR strategies more effective by fine-tuning them over time (Lu, Liang, Zhang, Rong, Guan, Mazeikaite, & Streimikis, 2021).

5.4.2 Use of Technology

Results of measurement level of CSR activity are increasingly being transformed by the infusion of technology in impact assessment. For instance, mobile surveys can reach the remote populations; similarly, GIS can map the environmental impact of a company's activities across large areas. The blockchain technology is also under study to help in ensuring transparency and integrity in the impact data. Through the implementation of smart contracts, companies will be in a position to automate tracking and reporting of CSR outcomes, therefore reducing the risk of data manipulation and increasing stakeholder trust (Giri & Chaparro, 2023).

5.4.3 Continuous Monitoring and Evaluation

Since it tends to establish impact assessment as an activity that is carried out once, companies are increasingly going towards the processes of continuous monitoring and evaluation. It is in this regard that firms respond, accordingly, to any changes on the ground, whether it be a shift in community needs or another environmental impact. Continuous monitoring implies that, in real-time also, companies would be able to adjust their CSR strategies for maximum impact based on the informed decisions reached from this data (Castillo-Villar, 2020).

6. FUTURE DIRECTIONS AND POLICY IMPLICATIONS

This section explores the evolving landscape of Corporate Social Responsibility (CSR) as a pivotal force in achieving the Sustainable Development Goals (SDGs) across Asia. Additionally, this section provides insights into how businesses and governments can collaboratively shape policies that drive long-term, impactful CSR contributions toward sustainable futures.

6.1 The Future of CSR in Asia

With Asia on a trajectory of rapid economic growth, so too will the role that CSR plays in driving sustainable development. The future of CSR in this region is therefore likely to be shaped through internal corporate strategies as well as external pressures linked to regulatory change, changing consumer expectations, and the global sustainability agenda. Companies, which embed CSR as part of their core business rather than peripheralizing, will be better placed in terms of contributing to the SDGs and creating competitive advantages for themselves in the marketplace (Davidson & et al., 2013).

6.2 Emerging Trends in CSR and SDGs

Some of the key trends that are bound to shape the future of CSR with respect to its advancement of SDGs include:

6.2.1 Integration of Technology and Innovation

Technology is going to play a very critical role in the future of CSR, especially with regard to how companies are handling complex sustainability challenges. For example, AI in CSR would ensure better resource optimization in CSR programs so more money goes where it is most needed. Blockchain technology provides increased transparency in CSR activities, whereby stakeholders can track any contribution and its outcome in real-time. Big data analytics will further help companies identify emerging social and environmental trends to allow them to do something about an impending issue before it blows up (López-Concepción, Gil-Lacruz, & Saz-Gil, 2022).

6.2.2 Shift Towards Inclusive Growth

Inclusive growth will thus be the keynote of future CSR strategies, more so in Asia with its wide chasm of economic disparities. Corporations will have to work out CSR initiatives that not only drive economic development but also see to it that growth benefits amply flow to all segments of society. These may involve women's empowerment, smallholder farmers, or access to education and health care in underrepresented communities. Through the reduction of inequalities and promotion of social cohesion, companies will create an environment that enables inclusive growth, which will lead to the achievement of sustainable development (Pieterse, 2014).

6.2.3 Strengthening Partnerships

The complexity of the SDGs means they cannot be achieved by one organization. In the future, CSR will be done through multi-stakeholder partnerships bringing together businesses, governments, NGOs, and civil society. Through partnerships, resources are pooled and expertise exchanged in coordination of actions toward common sustainability challenges. This could mean a company, a local government, and an NGO collaborating on mounting a complete school program, one that includes access to schooling, quality of education, training for teachers, and community involvement. Such collaborative efforts can amplify the impact of CSR and further contribute towards achieving SDGs (Castillo-Villar, 2020).

6.2.4 Focus on Climate Action

With growing impacts from climate change, CSR with regard to climate action will gain more relevance. This would call for development and implementation of strategies pertaining to carbon footprint reduction, renewable energy promotion, and enhancement of climate resilience by companies. This may involve investment in green technologies, sustainable supply chain practices, or community-based adaptation. Addressing climate change will not only be a moral duty but also business imperative: if companies fail to address environmental sustainability, they will suffer the loss of consumer trust and face potential regulatory penalties (Rishi, 2022).

6.3 Policy Implications for Governments and Businesses

With CSR being increasingly intrinsic to attaining the SDGs, several policy implications will be seen for both governments and businesses:

6.3.1 Regulatory Frameworks and Incentives

Governments in Asia are realizing the requirement for developing a more robust regulatory framework to guide CSR activities toward rendering effective contributions to the SDGs. These frameworks may include mandatory CSR spending, as witnessed in India, or incentives against companies for their sustainable behaviors.

For example, governments could provide tax incentives or subsidies to companies investing in renewable energy or social infrastructure projects. This policy will further motivate businesses to have meaningful CSR activities and scale the action toward attaining the SDGs (Halkos & Nomikos, 2021).

6.3.2 Mandatory CSR Reporting

Probably one of the keys to the success of CSR is transparency, and compulsory reporting may soon become standard in many Asian countries. This would make it mandatory for the companies not only to disclose the self-assessed amount spent for CSR but also the outcome and impact of CSR initiatives. It may include detailed periodic, say annual, reporting on CSR which indicates the actual SDGs targeted, strategies used, resources used, and results gotten. Mandatory reporting would raise the level of accountability, where stakeholders are able to scrutinize corporate claims and ensure that the CSR is actually delivering on the ground toward sustainable development and not just being a selling point for companies (Gulenko, 2018).

6.3.3 Encouraging Public-Private Partnerships (PPPs)

The second point is that PPPs are going to be key drivers for CSR in Asia. In a sense, the governments play an important role in creating an enabling environment that allows the private sector to effectively collaborate with the public institutions. For instance, there might be co-financing of projects relevant to national development goals, like the construction of infrastructure, public health programs, or environmental conservation. Indeed, collaboration between the public and private sectors, through leveraging their respective strengths, whether in the innovativeness and efficiency of the private sector or the reach and regulatory authority of the public sector, will allow both to realize the SDGs better (Elsig & Amalric, 2008).

6.3.4 Aligning CSR with National Development Goals

There is an increasing call for alignment of corporate initiatives with national development goals to ensure that CSR leaves the maximum possible positive impact. Government guidelines or frameworks could offer business companies valuable guidance on the implementation of CSR strategies to align with the national priorities in matters related to poverty reduction, education, healthcare, and environmental protection. Through this, therefore, corporate efforts will be harmonized with governmental efforts to have a uniform push toward the realization of the SDGs. In addition, it supports business establishments by going through regional and national regulatory more rigidities, further, enabling the said business establishments to have a successful and compliance CSR model (Sodhi, Kumar & Ganguly, 2022)

6.4 The Role of International Organizations

Several international bodies such as the United Nations, World Bank, amongst several others, and regional bodies like the Asian Development Bank can also decide the future of CSR in Asia. Such organizations may provide technical support, funding, and policy guidance toward CSR for its further integration into business. They may also facilitate cross-border collaborations for knowledge sharing among Asian countries to proliferate best practices and new solutions toward sustainable development. Therefore, international organizations can also mediate between the private sector and government in such a way that the CSR activities fall under common global norms and contribute significantly to the SDGs (Jamali, Samara, & Hossary, 2019).

7. CONCLUSION

CSR has become an important strategic component of the current trend of development toward sustainability in Asia. On one hand, with the increasing awareness that businesses are becoming more sensitive to, companies are trying to address the need for aligning corporate objectives with the SDGs; on the other hand, CSR itself is rapidly moving from a voluntary peripheral activity to a central constituent of corporate strategy. This is because companies across the region are increasingly becoming aware that long-term business success and economic growth are linked with social well-being and a safe environment.

Challenges of CSR in Asia are huge due to the great diversity in economic, cultural, and political systems. It is exactly this diversity that makes it a fertile ground for innovations and leadership. Only if rigorous impact assessment methodologies are applied will companies be able to ensure delivery and effective contribution toward attaining the SDGs. Emerging trends in CSR in Asia, such as technology deployment, focusing on inclusive growth, and growing recognition toward climate action, will seal its future. Such trends, together with strong policy support, can set companies on their transformative role toward driving sustainable development in the region.

Although this will be a long and difficult journey, the potential of CSR to act as a catalyst for the sustainable futures of Asia is immense. Soon, companies, through innovative and impactful CSR strategies, will be helping to achieve the SDGs and further illuminate the pathway toward global sustainable development. This journey toward a sustainable future has to be taken jointly, with collaboration and commitment; innovation will secure Asia at the forefront of realizing that vision: a world more equitable, prosperous, and sustainable.

REFERENCES

Abdelhalim, K., & Eldin, A. G. (2019). Can CSR help achieve sustainable development? Applying a new assessment model to CSR cases from Egypt. *The International Journal of Sociology and Social Policy*, 39(9/10), 773–795. DOI: 10.1108/IJSSP-06-2019-0120

Arli, D., & Cadeaux, J. (2014). Drivers of corporate community involvement and challenges in measuring its impact. *Social Responsibility Journal*, 10(1), 161–183. DOI: 10.1108/SRJ-10-2012-0116

Arora, B., & Puranik, R. (2004). A review of corporate social responsibility in India. *Development*, 47(3), 93–100. DOI: 10.1057/palgrave.development.1100057

Baskin, J. (2006). Corporate responsibility in emerging markets. *Journal of Corporate Citizenship*, 2006(24), 29–47. DOI: 10.9774/GLEAF.4700.2006.wi.00006

Bebbington, J., & Unerman, J. (2018). Achieving the United Nations Sustainable Development Goals: An enabling role for accounting research. *Accounting, Auditing & Accountability Journal*, 31(1), 2–24. DOI: 10.1108/AAAJ-05-2017-2929

Castillo-Villar, R. G. (2020). Identifying determinants of CSR implementation on SDG 17 partnerships for the goals. *Cogent Business & Management*, 7(1), 1847989. DOI: 10.1080/23311975.2020.1847989

Chapple, W., & Moon, J. (2005). Corporate social responsibility (CSR) in Asia: A seven-country study of CSR web site reporting. *Business & Society*, 44(4), 415–441. DOI: 10.1177/0007650305281658

Christensen, H. B., Hail, L., & Leuz, C. (2019). *Adoption of CSR and sustainability reporting standards: Economic analysis and review* (Vol. 623). National Bureau of Economic Research.

Claydon, J. (2011). A new direction for CSR: The shortcomings of previous CSR models and the rationale for a new model. *Social Responsibility Journal*, 7(3), 405–420. DOI: 10.1108/17471111111154545

. Davidson, D. K., Tanimoto, K., Jun, L. G., Taneja, S., Taneja, P. K., & Yin, J. (2018). Corporate social responsibility across Asia: a review of four countries. *Corporate social responsibility, 2*, 73-132.

Elsig, M., & Amalric, F. (2008). Business and public–private partnerships for sustainability: Beyond corporate social responsibility? *Global Society*, 22(3), 387–404. DOI: 10.1080/13600820802090538

Fiandrino, S., Scarpa, F., & Torelli, R. (2022). Fostering social impact through corporate implementation of the SDGs: Transformative mechanisms towards interconnectedness and inclusiveness. *Journal of Business Ethics*, 180(4), 959–973. DOI: 10.1007/s10551-022-05189-9

Freeman, I., & Hasnaoui, A. (2011). The meaning of corporate social responsibility: The vision of four nations. *Journal of Business Ethics*, 100(3), 419–443. DOI: 10.1007/s10551-010-0688-6

Galant, A., & Cadez, S. (2017). Corporate social responsibility and financial performance relationship: A review of measurement approaches. *Ekonomska Istrazivanja*, 30(1), 676–693. DOI: 10.1080/1331677X.2017.1313122

Gao, Y. (2011). CSR in an emerging country: A content analysis of CSR reports of listed companies. *Baltic Journal of Management*, 6(2), 263–291. DOI: 10.1108/17465261111131848

Gatti, L., Vishwanath, B., Seele, P., & Cottier, B. (2019). Are we moving beyond voluntary CSR? Exploring theoretical and managerial implications of mandatory CSR resulting from the new Indian companies act. *Journal of Business Ethics*, 160(4), 961–972. DOI: 10.1007/s10551-018-3783-8

. Giri, F. S., & Chaparro, T. S. (2023). Measuring business impacts on the SDGs: a systematic literature review. *Sustainable Technology and Entrepreneurship*, 100044.

Godfrey, P. C., Merrill, C. B., & Hansen, J. M. (2009). The relationship between corporate social responsibility and shareholder value: An empirical test of the risk management hypothesis. *Strategic Management Journal*, 30(4), 425–445. DOI: 10.1002/smj.750

Gulenko, M. (2018, December). Mandatory CSR reporting—literature review and future developments in Germany. In *NachhaltigkeitsManagementForum| Sustainability Management Forum* (Vol. 26, No. 1, pp. 3-17). Berlin/Heidelberg: Springer Berlin Heidelberg.

Guo, H., & Ren, S. (2018). How Do Firms Respond to Corporate Social Responsibility (CSR) Failures? Evidence from Product Recalls in China. *Journal of Business Ethics*, 152(4), 989–1006.

Gupta, A., & Sharma, M. (2019). Consumer perceptions of CSR and its impact on purchasing decisions in India. *Journal of Business Ethics*, 156(3), 671–683. DOI: 10.1007/s10551-017-3598-3

Halkos, G. E., & Nomikos, S. N. (2021). Reviewing the status of corporate social responsibility (CSR) legal framework. *Management of Environmental Quality*, 32(4), 700–716. DOI: 10.1108/MEQ-04-2021-0073

Hopkins, M. (2005). Measurement of corporate social responsibility. *International Journal of Management and Decision Making*, 6(3-4), 213–231. DOI: 10.1504/IJMDM.2005.006549

Hung Chen, C. (2011). The major components of corporate social responsibility. *Journal of Global Responsibility*, 2(1), 85–99. DOI: 10.1108/20412561111128546

Ite, U. E. (2022). Achieving Sustainable Development Goals through Corporate Social Responsibility. In *Business and Sustainable Development in Africa* (pp. 179–202). Routledge. DOI: 10.4324/9781003038078-10

Jamali, D., & Mirshak, R. (2007). Corporate social responsibility (CSR): Theory and practice in a developing country context. *Journal of Business Ethics*, 72(3), 243–262. DOI: 10.1007/s10551-006-9168-4

Jamali, D., Samara, G., & Hossary, M. (2019). Corporate social responsibility and development: The case of international business firms in emerging economies. In *Business and development studies* (pp. 286–309). Routledge. DOI: 10.4324/9781315163338-12

Kim, S., & Moon, H. (2020). CSR in Multinational Corporations in Asia: A Comparative Study. *Asian Business & Management*, 19(2), 152–176. DOI: 10.1057/s41291-019-00069-5

Kotchen, M., & Moon, J. J. (2012). Corporate social responsibility for irresponsibility. *The B.E. Journal of Economic Analysis & Policy*, 12(1). Advance online publication. DOI: 10.1515/1935-1682.3308

Kramer, M. R., & Porter, M. E. (2006). Strategy and society: The link between competitive advantage and corporate social responsibility. *Harvard Business Review*, 84(12), 78–92. PMID: 17183795

Laufer, W. S. (2003). Social accountability and corporate greenwashing. *Journal of Business Ethics*, 43(3), 253–261. DOI: 10.1023/A:1022962719299

Lindgreen, A., Swaen, V., & Maon, F. (2009). Introduction: Corporate social responsibility implementation. *Journal of Business Ethics*, 85(S2), 251–256. DOI: 10.1007/s10551-008-9732-1

López-Concepción, A., Gil-Lacruz, A. I., & Saz-Gil, I. (2022). Stakeholder engagement, Csr development and Sdgs compliance: A systematic review from 2015 to 2021. *Corporate Social Responsibility and Environmental Management*, 29(1), 19–31. DOI: 10.1002/csr.2170

Lu, J., Liang, M., Zhang, C., Rong, D., Guan, H., Mazeikaite, K., & Streimikis, J. (2021). Assessment of corporate social responsibility by addressing sustainable development goals. *Corporate Social Responsibility and Environmental Management*, 28(2), 686–703. DOI: 10.1002/csr.2081

Lu, J., Ren, L., Lin, W., He, Y., & Streimikis, J. (2019). Policies to promote corporate social responsibility (CSR) and assessment of CSR impacts.

Maas, S., & Reniers, G. (2014). Development of a CSR model for practice: Connecting five inherent areas of sustainable business. *Journal of Cleaner Production*, 64, 104–114. DOI: 10.1016/j.jclepro.2013.07.039

Margolis, J. D., Elfenbein, H. A., & Walsh, J. P. (2009). Does it pay to be good... and does it matter? A meta-analysis of the relationship between corporate social and financial performance. *And does it matter*.

Matten, D., & Moon, J. (2008). "Implicit" and "Explicit" CSR: A Conceptual Framework for a Comparative Understanding of Corporate Social Responsibility. *Academy of Management Review*, 33(2), 404–424. DOI: 10.5465/amr.2008.31193458

Mendes, T., Braga, V., Correia, A., & Silva, C. (2023). Linking corporate social responsibility, cooperation and innovation: The triple bottom line perspective. *Innovation & Management Review*, 20(3), 244–280. DOI: 10.1108/INMR-03-2021-0039

Mishra, M., Desul, S., Santos, C. A. G., Mishra, S. K., Kamal, A. H. M., Goswami, S., Kalumba, A. M., Biswal, R., da Silva, R. M., dos Santos, C. A. C., & Baral, K. (2024). A bibliometric analysis of sustainable development goals (SDGs): A review of progress, challenges, and opportunities. *Environment, Development and Sustainability*, 26(5), 11101–11143. DOI: 10.1007/s10668-023-03225-w PMID: 37362966

Mitra, N. (2021). CSR Legislation in India: Impact and Challenges. *Corporate Governance: The International Journal of Business in Society*, 21(1), 100–112.

Murray, K. B., & Vogel, C. M. (1997). Using a hierarchy-of-effects approach to gauge the effectiveness of corporate social responsibility to generate goodwill toward the firm: Financial versus nonfinancial impacts. *Journal of Business Research*, 38(2), 141–159. DOI: 10.1016/S0148-2963(96)00061-6

Nave, A., & Ferreira, J. (2019). Corporate social responsibility strategies: Past research and future challenges. *Corporate Social Responsibility and Environmental Management*, 26(4), 885–901. DOI: 10.1002/csr.1729

Ng, A. W., & Tavitiyaman, P. (2020). Corporate social responsibility and sustainability initiatives of multinational hotel corporations. *International business, trade and institutional sustainability*, 3-15.

Park, J. (2018). Technology and CSR: The Role of Digital Tools in Enhancing Corporate Social Responsibility in South Korea. *Technological Forecasting and Social Change*, 130, 202–209.

Parotto, E., & Pablos-Méndez, A. (2023). From MDGs to SDGs. In *Global Health Essentials* (pp. 463–468). Springer International Publishing. DOI: 10.1007/978-3-031-33851-9_71

Perrini, F., Russo, A., & Tencati, A. (2007). CSR strategies of SMEs and large firms. Evidence from Italy. *Journal of Business Ethics*, 74(3), 285–300. DOI: 10.1007/s10551-006-9235-x

Pieterse, J. N. (2014). Growth and social policies: Towards inclusive development. In *Brazil Emerging* (pp. 50–63). Routledge.

Rishi, P. (2022). Integrating CSR with Climate Change and Sustainability. In *Managing climate change and sustainability through behavioural transformation* (pp. 105–135). Springer Singapore. DOI: 10.1007/978-981-16-8519-4_5

Roche, J. (2005). *Corporate governance in Asia*. Routledge. DOI: 10.4324/9780203461723

Sarkar, S., & Singh, P. (2019). Strategizing CSR in addressing sustainable development goals using a scorecard approach. *World Review of Science, Technology and Sustainable Development*, 15(4), 313–329. DOI: 10.1504/WRSTSD.2019.104095

Sharma, A. (2016). Key drivers endorsing CSR: A transition from economic to holistic approach. *Asian Journal of Business Ethics*, 5(1-2), 165–184. DOI: 10.1007/s13520-016-0062-6

Smith, V., Lau, J., & Dumay, J. (2022). Shareholder use of CSR reports: An accountability perspective. *Meditari Accountancy Research*, 30(6), 1658–1679. DOI: 10.1108/MEDAR-02-2020-0769

Sodhi, M. S., Kumar, C., & Ganguly, A. (2022). How mandatory corporate social responsibility can help governments with development goals. *Business Strategy & Development*, 5(1), 30–43. DOI: 10.1002/bsd2.181

Srivastava, S. K. (2017). Corporate Social Responsibility in India: Cases and Developments After the Legal Mandate. *International Journal of Management and Applied Research*, 4(4), 184–195.

Suwannarat, P. (2020). CSR Partnerships in Thailand: A Pathway to Sustainable Development. *Sustainability*, 12(4), 1345.

Suzuki, K. (2018). Cultural Influences on CSR in Japan: Focus on Community Well-being and Sustainability. *Corporate Social Responsibility and Environmental Management*, 25(4), 473–482. PMID: 31543701

Tang, Z., & Li, S. (2021). Challenges of Stakeholder Engagement in CSR: Insights from Chinese Companies. *Journal of Cleaner Production*, 278, 123–145.

Verboven, H., & Vanherck, L. (2016). Sustainability management of SMEs and the UN sustainable development goals. *uwf UmweltWirtschaftsForum, 24*(2), 165-178.

Visser, W. (2008). Corporate social responsibility in developing countries.

Windsor, D. (2001). The future of corporate social responsibility. *The International Journal of Organizational Analysis*, 9(3), 225–256. DOI: 10.1108/eb028934

Wirba, A. V. (2023). Corporate social responsibility (CSR): The role of government in promoting CSR. *Journal of the Knowledge Economy*, 15(2), 1–27. DOI: 10.1007/s13132-023-01185-0

Zhang, Q., Oo, B. L., & Lim, B. T. H. (2019). Drivers, motivations, and barriers to the implementation of corporate social responsibility practices by construction enterprises: A review. *Journal of Cleaner Production*, 210, 563–584. DOI: 10.1016/j.jclepro.2018.11.050

Chapter 3
Integrating Corporate Social Responsibility in Health and Social Care:
Strategies for Sustainable Practice

Muhammad Usman Tariq
http://orcid.org/0000-0002-7605-3040
Abu Dhabi University, UAE & University College Cork, Ireland

ABSTRACT

This chapter offers a systematic review of literature on the antecedents of Corporate Social Responsibility (CSR) in the context of healthcare. This work explores the enhancement of environmental, economic, and social aspects of CSR and their application in health and social care organizations. This report shows the best practices in the area of waste management and energy efficiency and carbon footprint with the use of hospital and care facilities' good examples put into practice. Offord focuses on economic Cost of CSR, including availability and accessibility of health care, price, and more importantly, the economy of health care. Furthermore, the chapter covers social aspects such as establishing a multi-faceted relationship with workforces which comprises of the diverse population, involvement in the community, and patient relation. The problems and limitation to CSR practices are discussed as well as measures to addressing them by involving stakeholders and formulation of policies.

DOI: 10.4018/979-8-3693-5991-4.ch003

INTRODUCTION

Incorporating corporate social responsibility (CSR) into health and social care is becoming increasingly accepted as an important strategy for enhancing the sustainability and moral integrity of healthcare services. CSR includes a wide range of practices aimed at improving society, the environment, and the economy. With regard to well-being and social considerations, CSR methodologies center on quiet consideration, advancing ecological supportability, and encouraging financial and social value. This background provides an in-depth look at how CSR is incorporated into health care, highlighting key strategies and case studies that show how CSR affects the industry. The healthcare industry's environmental pillar of CSR places emphasis on environmentally friendly practices. Healthcare facilities and hospitals are significant contributors to environmental issues owing to their extensive resource consumption and waste generation. Therefore, sustainable practices are essential for reducing these effects. Key procedures include waste administration, energy effectiveness, and carbon impressions. Environmental CSR is fundamentally related to waste management. Healthcare facilities produce many different kinds of waste, including general, infectious, and hazardous waste. Compelling waste administration procedures include diminishing waste age, expanding reuse, and guaranteeing safe waste removal. For instance, the execution of thorough reuse programs and the reception of waste isolation practices can fundamentally reduce the volume of waste shipped off landfills (ElAlfy et al., 2020).

Through rigorous recycling and waste diversion programs, hospitals such as the Cleveland Clinic have made significant progress in this regard. Energy efficiency is a crucial aspect of environmental CSR. Lighting, HVAC, and medical equipment use a large amount of energy in healthcare facilities. Healthcare organisations have the potential to reduce their energy consumption and greenhouse gas emissions by implementing energy-efficient technologies and procedures. Solar panels and other renewable energy sources such as energy-efficient lighting and HVAC systems can help reduce energy consumption and carbon emissions (Saz-Gil et al., 2020). Another example of incorporating environmental sustainability into healthcare infrastructure is the implementation of green building standards such as LEED certification. Strategies to reduce greenhouse gas emissions from healthcare operations are part of reducing the carbon footprint. This can be accomplished in a number of ways, including investing in low-emission technologies, implementing green procurement policies, and optimizing transportation logistics. These endeavors are further supported by participation in initiatives aimed at reducing carbon footprint and incorporating carbon offset programs (Govindan, 2022). Healthcare equity and sustainability for the economy in health and social care, the economic pillar of CSR, focuses on ensuring equitable access to healthcare services and sustaining economic viability. Evenhanded admittance to medical services is a central part of CSR, expecting to address differences and guarantee that all people have a valuable chance to receive quality consideration. This includes making healthcare services more affordable and accessible to those who are often overlooked or underserved. The economic viability of healthcare services fundamentally depends on fair pricing and affordability.

Healthcare costs can be reduced by implementing pricing strategies that consider patients' financial capabilities and provide financial assistance. Sliding scale fees and charity care programs can help low-income patients pay for healthcare services (Huy & Phuc, 2020). In addition, medical care associations can collaborate with protection suppliers to offer more comprehensive and reasonable protection plans. The long-term viability of healthcare organisations is another aspect of economic sustainability. This includes investing in health promotion, preventive care, cost control, and effective resource management. Healthcare facilities can decrease the incidence of costly chronic diseases and improve overall health outcomes by focusing on preventive measures. Another strategy for enhancing economic sustainability is the incorporation of value-based care models that prioritize patient outcomes and cost-effectiveness (Carroll, 2021). Social Obligation and Local area Commitment In health and social care. The social pillar of CSR includes fostering patient-centered care, working with local communities, and creating inclusive workplaces. Diversity and inclusion in the workplace are essential to enhance employee satisfaction and foster a positive work environment. Medical service associations can implement strategies and practices that advance variety, value, and consideration in recruiting, preparing, and improving professionals (Sheehy and Farneti, 2021). Diversity training programs and employee resource groups can help create a more inclusive work environment. Social CSR relies heavily on community involvement. Healthcare organisations can contribute to the well-being of the community through a variety of philanthropic endeavors and outreach initiatives. Examples include participation in public health campaigns, funding community health centers, and supporting local health initiatives. Community-based health programs such as mobile clinics and health education workshops can help meet the needs of underserved populations and improve community health (Shayan et al., 2022). Patient-focused care, a vital part of social CSR, centers on giving consideration to individual patient inclinations, needs, and values.

This approach includes effectively including patients in their choices, offering customized care designs, and guaranteeing clear correspondence between patients and medical service suppliers. Healthcare organisations can help continuously improve their services and enhance patient experience by implementing satisfaction surveys and feedback mechanisms (Ahmed et al., 2021). Despite the benefits, integrating CSR practices is difficult for health and social care organisations. One significant test is the intricacy of implanting CSR into existing activities, which requires adjusting CSR objectives to authoritative needs and conquering protection from change. When implementing CSR initiatives, healthcare organisations must navigate regulatory requirements and ethical considerations (Haski-Leventhal, 2021). Successful partner commitment is fundamental for addressing these difficulties. CSR initiatives are more likely to be successful and relevant when they involve stakeholders, such as patients, workers, members of the community, and regulatory bodies. Implementation success can be aided by creating clear CSR policies and frameworks, providing staff with training, and providing resources (Bautista-Bernal et al., 2021). In addition, laying out associations with outside associations and taking part in industry organisations can provide important bits of knowledge and support to CSR endeavors (Tariq, 2024).

In the future, the fate of CSR in well-being and social consideration will be molded by emerging patterns and advancements. It is anticipated that digital health technologies such as telemedicine and electronic health records will contribute significantly to the achievement of CSR goals. According to Nguyen and Kanbach (2024), these technologies have the potential to enhance patient care, increase accessibility to healthcare services, and enhance service deliveries. By enabling health interventions that are more targeted and efficient, the integration of artificial intelligence and big data analytics will also drive CSR initiatives. In addition, confronting threats such as pandemics and climate change will necessitate greater emphasis on resilience and sustainability. To ensure long-term resilience, healthcare organisations will continue to invest in sustainable practices and modify their operations (Zhao, 2021). Transparency and comprehensive reporting frameworks will also become more common in CSR practices, encouraging accountability and ongoing improvement. In conclusion, incorporating CSR into health and social care requires a multifaceted strategy that considers social, economic, and environmental factors. Healthcare organisations can increase their social and environmental impact by implementing sustainable practices, promoting equitable access to care, and collaborating with communities. Despite these obstacles, maintaining a commitment to CSR is necessary to guarantee the ethical integrity and long-term viability of healthcare services, and ultimately contribute to a society that is healthier and more equitable (Tariq, 2024).

BACKGROUND

Organisations must perform the crucial task of talent acquisition to recruit and maintain talent. Artificial intelligence (AI) has become a potent ally in this area in recent years, providing several advantages that boost the effectiveness of hiring procedures and enhance the applicant experience. AI also adds the capacity for data-driven decision making and can help advance diversity and inclusion in recruiting procedures. In this section, we explore the essential advantages of AI for hiring. Corporate Social Responsibility (CSR) is one of the most important concepts in the social and health sectors as it fosters the importance of ethical and sustainable practices. When describing this sense, owners of the corporate business or also known as managers do have an important and relevant role throughout the enhancement of the health and social care sector by means of engaging in CSR as the decisive point. Thus, the CSR under consideration is a strategic action, and it differs from the method of operating at least obedient to laws and regulatory standards. It is essential to note that CSR activities carried out in the health and social care fields seek to address several issues that revolve around the administration of patient care, service delivery, environment, and the dignity of patients and employees (Herrera & de las Heras-Rosas, 2020).

A fairly good example of CSR in the healthcare facilities sector is the integration of environmentally sustainable practices into health systems. Such measures include waste management, recycling, and the inclusion of energy-efficient gadgets in the environment. Thus, it provides such measures, and healthcare institutions adhere to environmental responsibility and, in many cases, allow cost reduction that could be directed toward the improvement of patient services' quality and care provision. In addition, the implementation of such environmentally friendly strategies is equally advantageous to the institution in a social aspect the institution will be momentarily by improving the image that individuals have on the institution, hence finding support from the public on whatever the institution is doing. Other inadequate components of CSR are the economic effects related to the concept of the health and social care sector. Different measures are adopted by organisations for economic enhancement, but at the same time, various economic activities are not detrimental to society. For instance, local supplier procurement and workforce training are positive in supporting the purchase of local goods and services, possibly for the benefit of the community (Nguyen & Kanbach, 2024). Al also, financially irresponsible and unethical procurement practices erode the organisations' believability and reliably which is vital in health and social care to deliver services from a solid foundation of trust (Tariq, 2024).

Similar to other sectors, social outcomes are core components of CSR in the health sector. In most cases, targets are set to increase the availability and quality of healthcare services to which minorities have access. This may include extra community-specific sensitization campaigns, health promotion campaigns, and collaborations with non-governmental organisations to make services cheaper or even freer (Ahmed et. al, 2021). Hence, it is evident that reducing health inequalities and embracing fair and culturally competent treatments are ways through which organisations operating in the health and social care sector can easily improve the health of communities and society as a whole. In conclusion, the implementation of CSR practices in healthcare and social care organisations generates a positive change in environmental, economic, and social impacts, proving the sector's dedication to sustainable and moral business practices that are advantageous throughout the chain.

The Environmental Pillar of CSR in Health and Social Care

The second area of CSR in the health and social care sector is the adoption of environmental programs and measures that would have the least adverse effects on the environment. It covers areas such as waste management, efficient energy usage, and the environmental carbon footprint. The implementation of proper waste disposal methods is very relevant in healthcare facilities because they deal with a large amount of waste. Some of the strategies used by hospitals and care facilities include segregation, recycling, and disposal of waste intended to reduce its impact on the environment. For instance, modern healthcare institutions' practice sustainability negatively affects the environment in the following ways: Many healthcare industry institutions recycle their medical plastics and use biodegradable materials wherever possible (Espinoza, 2024). Safe disposal of hazardous waste is also important to avoid pollution impacts, as well as effects on the health of humans and animals. The other major sub-section of the environmental pillar considered energy efficiency to be an important parameter. Restaurants consume a lot of energy, mainly because they work around the clock and because of the demanding medical equipment used in their facilities. To this end, hospitals are focusing on the efficiency of technologies, such as lighting, heating, ventilation, air conditioning systems, and solar energy (Herrera & de las Heras-Rosas, 2020). Applying these measures reduces energy consumption and greenhouse gas emissions, which ultimately leads to overall cost savings that can be later allocated to necessary patient care services and similar ones.

One of the most successful examples of socially oriented initiatives in healthcare is the formation of the "green hospital" concept. An example of such an approach is the Dell Children's Medical Center of Central Texas, which became the first hospital to be accredited on LEED Platinum. Such certification proves the improved consciousness of the hospital towards electric energy usage, water consumption, and sustainable utilization of building materials (Sheehy & Farneti, 2021). Special features, such as natural lighting, rainwater management systems, and effective thermal energy storage systems, are incorporated in the hospital. The above-mentioned efforts have greatly decreased the facility's carbon impact and can serve as a model for other healthcare institutions. Another successful example is the Kaiser Permanente healthcare system; at its facilities, the organization has created an extensive sustainability plan. Some of them have included the acquisition of renewable power, lowering of greenhouse gases, and encouraging sustainable dietary health within hospital facilities (Maccarrone & Contri, 2021). Kaiser Permanente targeted carbon neutrality by 2020, which is a major step towards showing other healthcare institutions that it is possible for large HE systems to excel in EM. Therefore, understanding the environmental pillar of CSR in health and social care is crucial for the promotion of organisations and for diminishing the effect of healthcare systems on the environment. Healthcare facilities in the environment can play an enormous role through sustainable waste management, efficient energy use, and reduced carbon footprint. Thus, the successful implementation of these initiatives in the example of Dell Children's Medical Center and Kaiser Permanente can serve as a reference model for further work by other institutions for the integration of sustainability into management.

The Economic Pillar of CSR in Health and Social Care

The CSR economic element in the healthcare and social care setting understands the provision of quality and equal services with regard to health needs. Corporate social responsibility should strive to provide equal access to quality medical services for poor and economically incompetent people. Equitable in this stand means that healthcare services should be accessible to previously excluded groups or groups that have limited access to healthcare. Such a commitment to accessibility aids in eradicating the existing gap in health disparity and enhances the welfare of the whole community (Herrera & de las Heras-Rosas, 2020). Understanding equity will enhance the relationship between healthcare organisations and clientele. Related to the above is the fact that CSR practices in healthcare also have an impact on fair pricing and affordability. Providers' efforts to reduce costs involve applying flexible pricing structures and charges that depend on the patient's financial ability. It also makes certain that the incident of high cost hinders access to health services that do not occur (Adel et al., 2022). In addition, organisations in the healthcare industry can have scholarships and collaborate with non-profit organisations to offer free or low charges to people in need. These programs not only serve the purpose of immediate access to medical facilities, but also improve the image of the institution as a non-profit organization that aims at post-enrichment. Economic sustainability is another aspect envisioned in the economic pillar of CSR. Appropriate economic practices will facilitate the establishment and sustainment of quality healthcare services in the future. This entails the effective use of resources, the expansion of staff customers, and the adoption of more effective technologies (Nguyen & Kanbach, 2024). For example, investing in an Electronic Health Record (EHR) can facilitate various administrative procedures and decrease the likelihood of errors, thus improving the care provided to patients. These are investments that enhance the quality of care offered while simultaneously leading to sustainable costs that could benefit the healthcare facility.

One example of CSR directed toward economic sustainability is the cooperation between Johnson & Johnson and the non-governmental Save the Children's organization. This partnership mainly aims to enhance the health of mothers and children in areas that are not well-served. Johnson & Johnson also offer funds, human and material support, and strategies, while Save the Children actually puts the programs into action (Ahmed et al., 2021). This relationship has contributed to the system improvement of health status and illustrates how CSR programs can add sustainable economic value to the organization and society. Therefore, the economic aspect of CSR in health and social care provision upholds equity, fairness and economic considerations in the provision of care services. By concentrating on these facets, the agencies would be in a position to guarantee the provision of the services to everyone with a special focus on making it affordable, sustainable, and architectural for the achievement of sustainable results. The demonstrations of sliding-scale fees, financial assistance programs, and strategic partnerships explain how CSR can work toward these goals in healthcare practices.

The Social Pillar of CSR in Health and Social Care

According to CSR in health and social care, the social pillar of operation stresses equality and inclusion in the workplace. Promoting diversity in the workplace is a crucial factor in promoting respect among employees in medical facilities. This commitment not only increases the level of satisfaction among healthcare workers and helps in increasing retention rates, but also helps in the delivery of better patient care as it explores the diversity and cultural competence of employees (Ahmed et al., 2021). Nowadays, hospitals work actively with diversity; some have developed diversity committees, offered cultural competency training, and hire employees from different excluded groups. These measures assist in eradicating inequity within the work setting and guarantee that the healthcare workforce conforms to the demographics of society.

In addition, through their philanthropic program and patient-centered care, healthcare institutions interact and return to their corresponding communities. Charitable help has also been reported to provide a mighty force in supplementing healthcare services to less-privileged groups. For example, almost every hospital and promotion healthcare center collaborate with local non-profit organizations to organize community health and educational fairs, nutritional control programs, and other general health promotion programs (Adel et al., 2022). These partnerships also help in disease prevention by fostering awareness of relevant health issues and appropriate methods for managing and maintaining good health in the community.

Another major component of the CSR social pillar is patient care. This approach involves the patient as the center for the treatment process, and the patient himself or herself has the final say on the type of treatment to be adopted. Healthcare organisations continue to apply the patient-centered care system, which entails processes such as patient involvement in decision-making, development of specific care plans, and effective communication between patients and their caregivers (Nguyen & Kanbach, 2024). Such practices have positive impacts on patients' condition, patient satisfaction, and the trust that patients place on their healthcare providers. One of the significant examples of community engagement is the Cleveland Clinic's Community Outreach Program, whose mission entails enhancing the health of the neighboring community. Such interventions include health education, encouraging people to adopt healthy lifestyles and avail free or low-cost medical services to needy patients (Ahmed et al., 2021). The Communality of the Cleveland Clinic toward Social Acts implies that the clinic is mindful of the needs of the community and is fully prepared to deal with the social determinants necessary for enhancing the lives of people in society. Thus, the third broad area of CSR in health and social care relates to employment and community, which includes workforce diversity development, community activities, and patient-centeredness. Such actions help create a more favorable environment in the workplace as well as in healthcare facilities for employees and patients, respectively. Diversity, giving, and patient-centered care are a few examples that show how integrated social responsibility works for healthcare organisations that improve health and develop solid relationships with the community.

CHALLENGES AND BARRIERS TO IMPLEMENTING CSR IN HEALTHCARE

Corporate social responsibility (CSR) seeks to be implemented in all healthcare systems but comes with the challenges and barriers that firms face. This is the relationship between the focal organization and suppliers and other partners which is a primary challenge when implementing CSR strategies due to the financial requirements that come with it. Financial constraints are an acute problem in many healthcare institutions; therefore, funding CSR activities has become a major issue. These activities, for instance, introducing energy-efficient technologies, providing access to primary care provision in the community, or paying employees fairly, cost a lot (Huy & Phuc, 2020). Moreover, the difficulty in tracking the effectiveness of an organization's CSR initiatives presents a challenge. The goals of CSR may not be easy to measure, such as clinical outcomes, thus proving that investing in CSR for stakeholders becomes a herculean task since most of the social and environmental impacts are not easy to quantify. Another influential challenge involves structural and cultural rigidity within organisations. The process of incorporating CSR into the fundamentals of working organisations, including healthcare institutions, means changing the culture, which in turn may face organizational opposition. Some employees may resist change since they are used to working in a certain way, especially if they do not see how this new practice or policy will be of help in the short run (Espinoza, 2024). Moreover, healthcare workers usually ignore or have poor knowledge of the principles of CSR, thereby hampering the implementation process.

To overcome these challenges, some of the measures that can be taken by healthcare organisations include the following. In this regard, one of the best practices is the involvement of employees of all ranks, starting from the head of the organization and ending with a low employee. In addition, it is a crucial step that increases the awareness of a company's management and, accordingly, its staff regarding the value and necessity of CSR. Communication programs, training sessions, and workshops assist in the creation of consciousness and a proactive stance toward CSR objectives (Adel et al., 2022). In addition, the engagement of employees in the planning and implementation of CSR activities can help them buy into the cause and, hence, can minimize any form of resistance. Policy development is another important practice in CSR implementation in healthcare operations. Policies that are clear and defined in such a way that everyone within the organization of the company understands what is expected from them as per the organizational mission and values are vital because they offer working guidelines for CSR activities. These policies should state clear objectives and roles for implementation, as well as expected measures and indicators of effectiveness (Nguyen & Kanbach, 2024). For instance, a healthcare organization might come up with a sustainability plan consisting of objectives on energy use and waste management supported by accounts of performance. Using policy as a means of institutionalization, healthcare organizations guarantee that CSR is a long-term process and that everyone is responsible for it.

Moreover, collaboration with other organisations can enhance the effectiveness of CSR strategies. It is recommended to cooperate with non-profit organisations, state institutions, and other partners to find more resources, knowledge, and assistance in CSR implementation. For instance, working with organisations, such as the environment, can assist healthcare facilities in adopting more efficient ways of managing waste and sustainability (Huy & Phuc, 2020). These collaborations can also increase the awareness of people and stakeholders in the CSR activities of the organization, which motivates the organization. Consequent upon the challenges discussed above, even though CSR implementation process in healthcare is not devoid of certain complications like; financial limitations, resistance to change, and measurement issues it can be noted that each of these obstacles is manageable through stakeholder management, policy making and strategic partnership. Therefore, healthcare organisations stated that strategies enable the achievement of CSR in operations, enabling improved social, environmental, and economic returns.

Another relevant approach to ensure CSR integration into healthcare activities is policy formulation. Having clearly stated that communicated policies that are in line with the company's goals and objectives on which CSR programs are to be based can be helpful. Such policies should, therefore, capture details of what needs to be achieved, who is supposed to achieve it, and how performance will be measured (Nguyen & Kanbach, 2024). For instance, a hospital can create a sustainability policy that will set measures on energy use and waste and will have to present reports on the extent of integration of the policy. This would be because by integrating CSR into policies within healthcare institutions, the necessary commitment and responsibility would be assigned at the policy level. Thus, cooperation with other organisations can enhance CSR outcomes. Working with any non-profit organization, government department, and other related stakeholders can supplement CSR activities through the provision of more resources, ideas, and help. For example, by collaborating with environmental organisations, healthcare infrastructure can adopt the best practices for waste management and sustainable environmental policies (Huy & Phuc, 2020). Such partnerships can also improve the promotion of an organization's CSR activities, thus encouraging internal and external stakeholders. Thus, the study reinforces that while there are a range of obstacles to CSR implementation in healthcare organisations, such as lack of funds, organizational resistance, and the complex issue of measurement, successful tackling of such a programme is possible by engaging stakeholders, policy makers, and strategic partners. I have identified the following strategies that would help facilitate the integration of CSR into healthcare organisations: which, when implemented, will help achieve the positive social, economic, and environmental impacts associated with CSR.

CSR and Stakeholder Well-Being

The well-being of various stakeholders in the healthcare industry, including patients, employees, and the local community, is significantly affected by CSR practices. CSR initiatives frequently result in improved quality of care and patient-centered services for patients. Medical clinics and medical care suppliers that focus on CSR are bound to execute programs that focus on preventive considerations, patient instruction, and local area well-being efforts (Adel et al., 2022). For instance, clinics that propose free wellbeing screenings and instructive studios assist with further development of local area wellbeing results by recognizing and overseeing medical problems early. This proactive methodology benefits patients by providing opportune intercessions and diminishing the general weight of the medical services framework. In addition, workers experience impressive advantages from

CSR rehabilitation. Workplaces that adhere to comprehensive CSR policies tend to be fairer, more inclusive and supportive. According to Nguyen and Kanbach (2024), initiatives aimed at improving work-life balance, providing opportunities for professional development, and guaranteeing equitable pay and working conditions increase employee satisfaction and retention. Additionally, workplaces that actively promote diversity and inclusion can help employees feel better at home and improve their overall health. Diversity training programs, for example, and policies that encourage equal opportunities can contribute to a workplace that is more harmonious and productive. Additionally, CSR plays a crucial role in stress management and the promotion of occupational health.

Healthcare professionals frequently experience high levels of stress owing to the demanding nature of their work. Some of these pressures can be eased through CSR initiatives that focus on occupational health and safety. For instance, executing wellbeing programs that incorporate pressure on board studios, emotional well-being support, and actual wellness exercises can assist workers with overseeing pressure more successfully (Kuhn et al., 2021). In addition, cultivating a work environment that places a high value on the well-being of the workforce by encouraging regular breaks and providing access to counselling services can result in a workforce that is both healthier and more resilient. Healthcare organisations' CSR initiatives have the potential to strengthen and improve the overall health of the community. Healthcare providers can address the social determinants of health that impact community well-being by participating in community outreach programs, supporting local health initiatives, and collaborating with non-profit organisations. To help combat childhood obesity and instill healthy habits from a young age, a hospital may offer nutrition education programs in conjunction with local schools (Ahmed et al., 2021). These initiatives not only improve community members' health, but also strengthen healthcare providers' relationships with the communities they serve. In conclusion, CSR practices in healthcare significantly improve patients, workers, and community well-being. Healthcare organisations can create a healthier, more inclusive environment for all stakeholders by focusing on patient-centered care, creating supportive workplaces, and participating in community health initiatives. In addition, these businesses can ensure the well-being of their employees by addressing workplace stress and promoting occupational health, resulting in improved patient care and strengthened community ties.

Digital Health and CSR

Computerized wellbeing developments are a critical part of upgrading Corporate Social Obligation (CSR) endeavors in the medical care area, fundamentally further developing help conveyance and patient consideration. The integration of digital health technologies is in line with CSR objectives by promoting accessibility, efficiency, and quality of healthcare services. For example, telemedicine has reformed patient consideration by giving far off counsels and subsequent meetups, accordingly diminishing the requirement for patients to travel significant distances for clinical exhortation. This ensures equitable access to healthcare services, which is an essential component of corporate social responsibility (CSR) (Espinoza, 2024) and especially beneficial for patients in rural and underserved areas. Telemedicine contributes to environmental sustainability by reducing carbon emissions related to travel. Electronic health records (EHRs) are another example of digital health technologies that help with CSR initiatives. By ensuring that information about patients is always current and easily accessible, electronic health records (EHRs) can help healthcare providers make quick decisions based on accurate information. According to Nguyen and Kanbach (2024), this will improve patient safety and satisfaction by improving patient outcomes and decreasing the likelihood of medical errors. Additionally, EHRs work with better coordination of care among various medical service suppliers, guaranteeing that patients receive predictable and thorough therapy. By streamlining operations and cutting costs, digital health innovations contribute to the long-term viability of the economy. Digital scheduling, billing, and patient management tools, for instance, ease administrative burden and boost productivity. This brings down functional expenses and opens up assets that can be diverted towards patient consideration and local area well-being programs, lining up with CSR objectives of monetary maintainability and social obligation (Ahmed et al., 2021). In addition, computerized well-being stages can offer instructive assets to patients, engaging them to play a functioning job in dealing with their well-being. Patient empowerment is an essential component of CSR, because it encourages health literacy and self-care. The implementation of telehealth programs during the COVID-19 pandemic is an example. To comply with social distancing guidelines and ensure continuity of care, numerous healthcare organisations have rapidly expanded their telehealth services. This not only aided in dealing with the pandemic's prompt effects but also featured the capability of advanced wellbeing to further develop access and proficiency in the long haul. Telehealth is especially valuable for overseeing ongoing circumstances, psychological well-being administrations, and follow-up care, exhibiting its arrangement with CSR targets of working on tolerant consideration and local area well-being (Zhao, 2021). In conclusion, by enhancing service delivery, patient care, and operational efficiency, digital health innovations significantly boost CSR efforts in healthcare. By ensuring patient safety, lowering costs, and promoting equitable access to healthcare, telemedicine and electronic health records (EHRs) align with CSR goals. These advancements address prompt medical care needs and add to the maintainability and social obligation objectives of medical care associations. Healthcare providers can better fulfil their CSR obligations and have a positive impact on the well-being of their patients and communities by incorporating digital health technologies.

Sustainability and Resilience in Healthcare

The two concepts of sustainability and resilience must be incorporated into healthcare management to deal with modern problems, such as climate change and epidemiological crises. These two principles are becoming significant today with healthcare organisations attempting to sustain their CSR efforts, aside from external changes. Sustainability is defined as the integration of the responsible use of resources in healthcare, and any practice that has an adverse effect on the environment is done in a minimal way. In contrast, resilience is defined as the capacity of the healthcare system to maintain and enhance performance despite negative occurrences, thereby maintaining constant functionality during crises (Bogoviz et al., 2022). One area of sustainability in the health sector involves the construction of green hospitals. For example, the application of efficient illumination, green power, and water usage considerably reduces the impact of medical centers on the environment. Furthermore, in recent years, it has been observed that these hospitals focus on environmental and ethical aspects while procuring products for their needs. These efforts are not only environmentally friendly, but also maintain corporate social responsibility for enhancing people's health through provision of healthy surroundings for users and the administration of the facilities (S. Fallah Shayan et al., 2022).

Similar to any other business sector in the world, resilience is essential in the healthcare industry, especially when it comes to issues such as COVID-19. The pandemic showed that healthcare organisations must be ready to seem more prepared in terms of incoming patients and changes in protocols at any given time. Hospitals that already had a foundation in telehealth were in a better position to stay functional, while also preventing the spread of the virus. Telehealth services provided opportunities to conduct consultations, follow up, and even monitor some chronic illnesses, thereby maintaining continuous healthcare breakages such as lockdowns and social distancing. This flexibility of operation was not only effective in saving the lives of patients but also depicted the stakeholders' enthusiasm towards CSR by catering to the public health crisis needs during this period (ElAlfy et al., 2020). Real examples also continue to be realized to expound on how endangered health and social care systems are putting into practice the incorporation of sustainability and resilience. For example, hospitals in facilities and regions with risk factors have created elaborate and exceptional emergency preparedness structures that comprise supply chains, staff, and community networks. Such steps guarantee that healthcare services are delivered and functional in natural calamities, thus serving the business's

CSR requirements by safeguarding the health of patients and the communities they serve (Zhao, 2021).

Another example of the internalization process is the internalization of sustainable practices into the manufacturing of drugs through the pharmaceutical industry. It is observed that business organisations are shifting attention towards decreasing environmental loads which may include waste and emissions, and the integration of circular economy strategies. It also helps in the fight against climate change while also enabling the achievement of economically sustainable healthcare and a decrease in costs linked with waste disposal and corresponding regulations (Herrera & de las Heras-Rosas, 2020). Thus, this chapter reveals the integration of sustainability and resilience perspectives in healthcare management to consider the impact of climate change and pandemics. Simultaneously, the incorporation of sustainable practices and organizational structures would enable CSHCs to effectively discharge their CSR responsibilities while simultaneously improving the continuous delivery of services. These efforts show not only that improving the environmental and economic sustainability of health care is possible but also that patient and community outcomes are benefitted as well.

Regulatory and Ethical Considerations

Health and social care organisations are legally bound by a number of legal requirements for corporate social responsibilities, which, in turn, are described by guidelines governing CSR. These regulations are usually designed with the purpose of preserving public health, maintaining the quality of physical surroundings, and asserting the common good. In many countries, healthcare delivery facilities are subject to strict laws that govern the environment, including rules on disposal of wastes and emissions. Furthermore, healthcare organisations are acquainted with social regulations that dictate fair labor practices, patients' rights and organisations, and the community's interactions with organisations (Carroll, 2021). For example, the EU Non-Financial Reporting Directive mandates that healthcare corporations, along with other large organisations, must report on their influence on the environment and communities, making the disclosure of information obligatory. Following the demographic analysis, another consideration of CSR for healthcare and social care providers is the ethical dilemma of the triple bottom line. This dilemma arises because most healthcare organisations act out of self-interest that grieves the social and environmental concerns of a community. For instance, there are certain ocular issues that can compete with the ethical dilemmas faced by those, for example, pharmaceutical firms when setting their-drug prices. Although high-priced medicines can provide revenue to the pharmaceutical industry and invest in research and development, they deny the availability of required medicines to an economically deficient society (Ali & Kaur, 2021). Thus, there is uncertainty between the need to have favorable car policies in relation to price and availability of cars while ensuring healthy competition, and the uptake of new technologies is necessary.

Moreover, healthcare providers struggle to deal with ethical concerns affecting the delivery of care to patients and the entire population. The concept of non-maleficence in nursing also goes beyond direct interaction with patients to include the impact of actions within the surrounding society and the ecosystem. For instance, healthcare facilities that produce large amounts of medical waste must address the immoral act of discharging such waste into the environment, which pollutes the environment and poses a risk to humanity. Recycling and the regular use of environmentally friendly products when developing a CSR strategy are core critical components of ethical waste management (Saz-Gil et al., 2020). Thus, there are ethical issues at the internal level as well, where social dilemmas in healthcare organizations involve labor relations in organizations and the protection of the interests of healthcare employees. Paying fair wages, obeying the principles of OHS, and training requirements are some facets of CSR. However, attaining these objectives may be difficult, particularly when financial constraints frown on the number of appropriated resources, which often results in the reduction of staff welfare. Mitigating these tensions involves being ethical and adopting responsible, systematic CSR planning that integrates the organization's goals with societal and environmental issues (Chandler, 2022).

The implementation of a range of expansive EW initiatives is an example of the comprehensiveness faced by healthcare organisations. Employee well-being programs target common health risks among healthcare personnel, with the objective of increasing work productivity through enhanced satisfaction and decreasing employee turnover rates. Such initiatives not only convey the organization's concerns and care for employees but also connect to other CSR tenets by promoting Social Responsibility for employees. In conclusion, therefore, it is apparent that the regulation and ethical issues of CSR in the health and social care field are complex, leading health care providers to act in ways that, while trying to earn profits, bear responsibility to people and the planet as well. Regulations, competitive pricing, environmental conservation, and workers' well-being are some of the significant CSR pillars. In this way, addressing those challenges and following the principles of ethical behavior allows achieving the proper balance that will be a win-win for all participants of the healthcare system.

FUTURE DIRECTIONS FOR CSR IN HEALTH AND SOCIAL CARE

Future CSR for health and social care organisations is in a transition highlighted by new trends and innovations in the market. Some of the future prospects for the development of CSR practices include further technological entwinement, new instrumentalization of environmental concerns, and broader and more complex analysis and management of stakeholders. In light of embracing technological growth in the future, healthcare providers will always use digital inventions to make their CSR strategies operate while simultaneously assisting patients. The key future trend involves the use of artificial intelligence (AI) and big data analytics to promote CSR programs. These technologies support the timely identification of the social determinants of patient health status, customization of patient care, and efficient utilization of resources. For instance, AI can be utilized to forecast epidemics and distribute healthcare facilities efficiently, thereby enhancing a population's well-being and minimizing disparity (Govindan, 2022). Additionally, by applying analytics to a large volume of patient-related information, health programs within the community can be made more efficient.

Another direction can be identified in environmental sustainability, which will also remain a vital aspect of the further development of CSR in the sphere of healthcare. It is predicted that, as the sector faces environmental issues, the effort to adopt sustainable methods will surge. It involves cutting the emission of carbon dioxide, the use of fossil energy, and increasing the rates of recycling and composting. Healthcare organisations and providers will integrate the use of efficient physical facility structures such as solar systems in hospitals, care facilities, and smart health building systems (ElAlfy et al., 2020). Recognizing that references to the circular economy and the principles of recycling and reusing materials will increase in healthcare in subsequent years. The major trend is that there has been a notable move towards the provision of relatively more accessible and fair healthcare for all. Other CSR strategies will also show a gradual trend towards prioritizing issues related to the gap in health and the provision of adequate medical care. This means that apart from offering affordable services, there is a need to reach hard-to-reach groups. Organisations from the healthcare sector will cooperate with local governments and non-profit organisations to develop community health programs, including travelling clinics and remote services for the populations that are still unable to attend a conventional doctor's appointment (Fallah Shayan et al., 2022).

Public and social healthcare management will also witness a gradual incorporation of social and environmental performance indicators in organizational measuring systems. More extended reporting frameworks, such as an impact report on the social dimension and sustainability check, will be incorporated into healthcare organisations. CSR will gain more transparency which will increase accountability and foster constant improvements in practice (Maccarrone & Contri, 2021). For instance, GRI standards and SASB guidelines should be used to report CSR initiative performance. Lastly, what has been noted above is the future trends of CSR in health and social care based on the following pillars: technologies, environment conservation, and health equality. By implementing such trends, healthcare organisations can increase the positive social and environmental effects of their work, thus improving the sustainability of the healthcare sector. In this regard, as these practices develop, they will address not only the current health and social care needs, but also establish sustainable solutions as part of future organizational development.

CONCLUSION

This section has provided a top-to-bottom investigation of coordinating Corporate Social Obligation (CSR) within the wellbeing and social consideration area. It is pivotal to consider the huge bits of knowledge and methodologies examined, which enlighten the job of CSR in cultivating a more maintainable and moral medical care framework. We demonstrated how these practices can result in improved outcomes for patients, communities, and healthcare organisations by addressing the environmental, economic, and social pillars of CSR. The significance of minimizing the ecological impact of healthcare operations is emphasized in the environmental pillar of CSR. Reduction of the carbon footprint, energy efficiency, and waste management are all important components of this endeavor. Compelling waste administration systems incorporate complete reuse projects and waste isolation, which limit the amount of waste shipped off landfills and decrease natural defilement. Investing in renewable energy sources, upgrading to LED lighting, optimizing heating, and cooling systems, and implementing energy efficiency measures all help reduce energy consumption and greenhouse gas emissions.

Medical clinics and care offices that embrace these practices add to ecological preservation and frequently acknowledge cost reserve funds in the long term. The decrease in carbon impressions includes embracing techniques such as low-discharge transportation choices, green acquisition arrangements, and cooperation in carbon offset programs. Healthcare organisations can demonstrate their commitment to environmental sustainability and align their operations with broader environmental sustainability objectives by implementing these measures. CSR's focus of CSR on economic sustainability is on making healthcare services affordable and accessible. Initiatives such as sliding-scale fees, financial assistance programs, and partnerships with insurance providers to offer inclusive health plans are ways to achieve equitable access to healthcare. As a result of these measures, disparities in healthcare access are reduced, and underserved populations are less burdened financially. Additionally, monetary maintainability includes overseeing assets proficiently and controlling expenses. Long-term economic viability is aided by the adoption of value-based care models that emphasize cost-effectiveness and patient outcomes. Better health outcomes and lower healthcare costs are both benefits of preventive care initiatives that aim to lower the prevalence of chronic diseases. Healthcare organisations can improve patient care while simultaneously enhancing financial stability by incorporating these strategies. The social mainstay of CSR includes creating comprehensive work environments and drawing in with neighborhood networks.

Ethical hiring practices, diversity training, and fostering a supportive work environment for all employees are aspects of promoting diversity and inclusion in healthcare organisations. Employee satisfaction rises, as does organizational performance and patient care in an inclusive workplace. Another important aspect of social responsibility is giving back to the community through philanthropic efforts and providing care focused on the patient. Medical care associations can uphold local area prosperity by financing well-being focuses, partaking in general well-being efforts, and offering effort programs. Improved patient satisfaction and better health outcomes are outcomes of patient-centered care practices, which emphasize the specific requirements and preferences of each patient. Healthcare organisations strengthen their relationships with the communities they serve and build trust by actively participating in community engagement.

The alignment of CSR goals with organizational priorities and overcoming resistance to change are two difficulties associated with implementing CSR in healthcare organisations. The integration of CSR practices can be made even more difficult by navigating the regulatory requirements and ethical considerations. Effective stakeholder engagement, which entails including patients, employees, and community members in CSR initiatives to guarantee their relevance and effectiveness, is necessary to address these issues. Strategies that aid the successful implementation of CSR include establishing external partnerships, providing staff training, and developing clear CSR policies. Healthcare organisations can overcome these obstacles and achieve their CSR goals by cultivating a culture of transparency and accountability. Stakeholder participation in the creation and implementation of CSR strategies ensures that these efforts are well-integrated with organizational and community objectives. Healthcare organisations demonstrate commitment to environmental stewardship, economic equity, and social responsibility by incorporating CSR into their operations. These practices not only help the organisations themselves but also help the overall health and well-being of people and communities. CSR is more than just a legal or moral obligation; it is also a strategic necessity for healthcare organisations to advance their mission. When CSR practices are incorporated, healthcare services can be better aligned with societal values and goals, resulting in a more resilient and equitable system. The commitment of healthcare organisations to corporate social responsibility (CSR) is essential for resolving these issues and bringing about positive changes as they face increasing social, economic, and environmental pressures.

Overall, the fruitful mix of CSR with well-being and social consideration requires continuous commitment, coordinated effort, and development. Healthcare organisations can set an example and contribute to the creation of a healthcare system that is more resilient, ethical, and sustainable by prioritizing CSR. If CSR practices are continuously developed, healthcare services will be both efficient and in line with the principles of sustainability and social responsibility. Healthcare organisations have the potential to have a significant impact on the well-being of individuals, communities, and the planet through these efforts, thereby ensuring a better future for everyone.

REFERENCES

Adel, H. M., Zeinhom, G. A., & Younis, R. A. A. (2022). From university social responsibility to social innovation strategy for quality accreditation and sustainable competitive advantage during the COVID-19 pandemic. *Journal of Humanities and Applied Social Sciences*, 4(5), 410–437. DOI: 10.1108/JHASS-04-2021-0086

Ahmed, J. U., Islam, Q. T., Ahmed, A., Faroque, A. R., & Uddin, M. J. (2021). Corporate social responsibility in the wake of COVID-19: Multiple cases of social responsibility as an organizational value. *Society and Business Review*, 16(4), 496–516. DOI: 10.1108/SBR-09-2020-0113

Ali, S. S., & Kaur, R. (2021). Effectiveness of corporate social responsibility (CSR) in implementation of social sustainability in warehousing of developing countries: A hybrid approach. *Journal of Cleaner Production*, 324, 129154. DOI: 10.1016/j.jclepro.2021.129154

Ashraf, Z., Afshan, G., & Sahibzada, U. F. (2022). Unpacking strategic corporate social responsibility in the time of crisis: A critical review. *Journal of Global Responsibility*, 13(2), 127–156.

Bautista-Bernal, I., Quintana-García, C., & Marchante-Lara, M. (2021). Research trends in occupational health and social responsibility: A bibliometric analysis. *Safety Science*, 137, 105167. DOI: 10.1016/j.ssci.2021.105167

Bogoviz, A. V., Lobova, S. V., & Alekseev, A. N. (2022). The concept of corporate social responsibility based on integrating the SDGs into corporate strategies: International experience and the risks for profit. *Risks*, 10(6), 117. DOI: 10.3390/risks10060117

Carroll, A. B. (2021). Corporate social responsibility: Perspectives on the CSR construct's development and future. *Business & Society*, 60(6), 1258–1278. DOI: 10.1177/00076503211001765

Chandler, D. (2022). *Strategic corporate social responsibility: Sustainable value creation*. Sage Publications.

Ebrahim, A. H., & Buheji, M. (2020). A pursuit for a 'holistic social responsibility strategic framework' addressing COVID-19 pandemic needs. *American Journal of Economics*, 10(5), 293–304. DOI: 10.5923/j.economics.20201005.04

ElAlfy, A., Palaschuk, N., El-Bassiouny, D., Wilson, J., & Weber, O. (2020). Scoping the evolution of corporate social responsibility (CSR) research in the sustainable development goals (SDGs) era. *Sustainability (Basel)*, 12(14), 5544. DOI: 10.3390/su12145544

Espinoza, R. (2024). Practices of selected pharmaceutical companies on integration of community empowerment to corporate social responsibility (CSR): Development of holistic and sustainable CSR framework. *Journal of Humanities and Social Sciences Studies*, 6(5), 160–204. DOI: 10.32996/jhsss.2024.6.5.24

Fallah Shayan, N., Mohabbati-Kalejahi, N., Alavi, S., & Zahed, M. A. (2022). Sustainable development goals (SDGs) as a framework for corporate social responsibility (CSR). *Sustainability (Basel)*, 14(3), 1222. DOI: 10.3390/su14031222

Govindan, K. (2022). Theory building through corporate social responsibility 4.0 for achieving SDGs: A practical step toward integration of digitalization with practice-based view and social good theory. *IEEE Transactions on Engineering Management*, 71, 2103–2120. DOI: 10.1109/TEM.2022.3155247

Haski-Leventhal, D. (2021). *Strategic corporate social responsibility: A holistic approach to responsible and sustainable business*.

Herrera, J., & de las Heras-Rosas, C. (2020). Corporate social responsibility and human resource management: Towards sustainable business organizations. *Sustainability (Basel)*, 12(3), 841. DOI: 10.3390/su12030841

Huy, P. Q., & Phuc, V. K. (2020). Does strategic corporate social responsibility drive better organizational performance through integration with a public sector scorecard? Empirical evidence in a developing country. *Processes (Basel, Switzerland)*, 8(5), 596. DOI: 10.3390/pr8050596

Khuong, M. N., Truong An, N. K., & Thanh Hang, T. T. (2021). Stakeholders and corporate social responsibility (CSR) programme as key sustainable development strategies to promote corporate reputation—Evidence from Vietnam. *Cogent Business & Management*, 8(1), 1917333. DOI: 10.1080/23311975.2021.1917333

Kuhn, E., Müller, S., Teusch, C., Tanner, G., Schümann, M., Baur, C., Bamberg, E., Heidbrink, L., McLennan, S., & Buyx, A. (2021). Interfaces of occupational health management and corporate social responsibility: A multi-centre qualitative study from Germany. *BMC Public Health*, 21(1), 1042. DOI: 10.1186/s12889-021-11016-z PMID: 34078332

Lu, J., Liang, M., Zhang, C., Rong, D., Guan, H., Mazeikaite, K., & Streimikis, J. (2021). Assessment of corporate social responsibility by addressing sustainable development goals. *Corporate Social Responsibility and Environmental Management*, 28(2), 686–703. DOI: 10.1002/csr.2081

Maccarrone, P., & Contri, A. M. (2021). Integrating corporate social responsibility into corporate strategy: The role of formal tools. *Sustainability (Basel)*, 13(22), 12551. DOI: 10.3390/su132212551

Maroun, W. (2020). A conceptual model for understanding corporate social responsibility assurance practice. *Journal of Business Ethics*, 161(1), 187–209. DOI: 10.1007/s10551-018-3909-z

Medina-Muñoz, R. D., & Medina-Muñoz, D. R. (2020). Corporate social responsibility for poverty alleviation: An integrated research framework. *Business Ethics (Oxford, England)*, 29(1), 3–19. DOI: 10.1111/beer.12248

Morea, D., Fortunati, S., & Martiniello, L. (2021). Circular economy and corporate social responsibility: Towards an integrated strategic approach in the multinational cosmetics industry. *Journal of Cleaner Production*, 315, 128232. DOI: 10.1016/j.jclepro.2021.128232

Nguyen, H. L., & Kanbach, D. K. (2024). Toward a view of integrating corporate sustainability into strategy: A systematic literature review. *Corporate Social Responsibility and Environmental Management*, 31(2), 962–976. DOI: 10.1002/csr.2611

Saxena, K., Balani, S., & Srivastava, P. (2021). The relationship among corporate social responsibility, sustainability and organizational performance in pharmaceutical sector: A literature review. *International Journal of Pharmaceutical and Healthcare Marketing*, 15(4), 572–597. DOI: 10.1108/IJPHM-12-2020-0104

Saz-Gil, M. I., Cosenza, J. P., Zardoya-Alegría, A., & Gil-Lacruz, A. I. (2020). Exploring corporate social responsibility under the background of sustainable development goals: A proposal to corporate volunteering. *Sustainability (Basel)*, 12(12), 4811. DOI: 10.3390/su12124811

Sheehy, B., & Farneti, F. (2021). Corporate social responsibility, sustainability, sustainable development and corporate sustainability: What is the difference, and does it matter? *Sustainability (Basel)*, 13(11), 5965. DOI: 10.3390/su13115965

Tariq, M. U. (2024). Streamlining Operations Insights and Innovations From the Gulf Cooperation Council (GCC). In Ayed, T., Ali, I., Abdelhamid, H., & Mohamed, A. (Eds.), *Utilizing Case Studies in Business Education* (pp. 188–216). IGI Global. DOI: 10.4018/979-8-3693-3779-0.ch010

Tariq, M. U. (2024). Harnessing Persuasive Technologies for Enhanced Learner Engagement and Motivation. In M. Sanmugam, D. Lim, N. Mohd Barkhaya, W. Wan Yahaya, & Z. Khlaif (Eds.), *Power of Persuasive Educational Technologies in Enhancing Learning* (pp. 30-62). IGI Global. DOI: 10.4018/979-8-3693-6397-3.ch002

Tariq, M. U. (2024). Smart Transportation Systems: Paving the Way for Sustainable Urban Mobility. In Munuhwa, S. (Ed.), *Contemporary Solutions for Sustainable Transportation Practices* (pp. 254–283). IGI Global. DOI: 10.4018/979-8-3693-3755-4.ch010

Tariq, M. U. (2024). Integration of IoMT for Enhanced Healthcare: Sleep Monitoring, Body Movement Detection, and Rehabilitation Evaluation. In Liu, H., Tripathy, R., & Bhattacharya, P. (Eds.), *Clinical Practice and Unmet Challenges in AI-Enhanced Healthcare Systems* (pp. 70–95). IGI Global. DOI: 10.4018/979-8-3693-2703-6.ch004

Tariq, M. U. (2024). Cybersecurity Risk Assessment Models and Theories in the Travel and Tourism Industry. In Thealla, P., Nadda, V., Dadwal, S., Oztosun, L., & Cantafio, G. (Eds.), *Corporate Cybersecurity in the Aviation, Tourism, and Hospitality Sector* (pp. 1–17). IGI Global. DOI: 10.4018/979-8-3693-2715-9.ch001

Tariq, M. U. (2024). Data Breach Incidents and Prevention in the Hospitality Industry. In Thealla, P., Nadda, V., Dadwal, S., Oztosun, L., & Cantafio, G. (Eds.), *Corporate Cybersecurity in the Aviation, Tourism, and Hospitality Sector* (pp. 181–199). IGI Global. DOI: 10.4018/979-8-3693-2715-9.ch010

Tariq, M. U. (2024). Navigating the Personalization Pathway: Implementing Adaptive Learning Technologies in Higher Education. In Minh Tung, T. (Ed.), *Adaptive Learning Technologies for Higher Education* (pp. 265–291). IGI Global. DOI: 10.4018/979-8-3693-3641-0.ch012

Tariq, M. U. (2024). Enhancing Students and Learning Achievement as 21st-Century Skills Through Transdisciplinary Approaches. In Kumar, R., Ong, E., Anggoro, S., & Toh, T. (Eds.), *Transdisciplinary Approaches to Learning Outcomes in Higher Education* (pp. 220–257). IGI Global. DOI: 10.4018/979-8-3693-3699-1.ch007

Tariq, M. U. (2024). Multi-Agent Models in Healthcare System Design. In Dall'Acqua, L. (Ed.), *Bioethics of Cognitive Ergonomics and Digital Transition* (pp. 143–170). IGI Global. DOI: 10.4018/979-8-3693-2667-1.ch008

Tariq, M. U. (2024). Social Innovations for Improving Healthcare. In Chandan, H. (Ed.), *Social Innovations in Education, Environment, and Healthcare* (pp. 302–317). IGI Global. DOI: 10.4018/979-8-3693-2569-8.ch015

Tariq, M. U. (2024). Leveraging AI for Entrepreneurial Innovation in Healthcare. In Özsungur, F. (Ed.), *Generating Entrepreneurial Ideas With AI* (pp. 192–216). IGI Global. DOI: 10.4018/979-8-3693-3498-0.ch009

Tariq, M. U. (2024). Leading Smart Technologies and Innovations for E-Business 5.0: Applications and Management Frameworks. In Popkova, E. (Ed.), *Smart Technologies and Innovations in E-Business* (pp. 25–46). IGI Global. DOI: 10.4018/978-1-6684-7840-0.ch002

Tariq, M. U. (2024). Crafting Authentic Narratives for Sustainable Branding. In *Compelling Storytelling Narratives for Sustainable Branding* (pp. 194–229). IGI Global. DOI: 10.4018/979-8-3693-3326-6.ch011

Tariq, M. U. (2024). The role of AI in skilling, upskilling, and reskilling the workforce. In Doshi, R., Dadhich, M., Poddar, S., & Hiran, K. (Eds.), *Integrating generative AI in education to achieve sustainable development goals* (pp. 421–433). IGI Global. DOI: 10.4018/979-8-3693-2440-0.ch023

Tariq, M. U. (2024). AI and the future of talent management: Transforming recruitment and retention with machine learning. In Christiansen, B., Aziz, M., & O'Keeffe, E. (Eds.), *Global practices on effective talent acquisition and retention* (pp. 1–16). IGI Global. DOI: 10.4018/979-8-3693-1938-3.ch001

Tariq, M. U. (2024). Application of blockchain and Internet of Things (IoT) in modern business. In Sinha, M., Bhandari, A., Priya, S., & Kabiraj, S. (Eds.), *Future of customer engagement through marketing intelligence* (pp. 66–94). IGI Global. DOI: 10.4018/979-8-3693-2367-0.ch004

Tariq, M. U. (2024). The role of AI ethics in cost and complexity reduction. In Tennin, K., Ray, S., & Sorg, J. (Eds.), *Cases on AI ethics in business* (pp. 59–78). IGI Global. DOI: 10.4018/979-8-3693-2643-5.ch004

Tariq, M. U. (2024). Challenges of a metaverse shaping the future of entrepreneurship. In Inder, S., Dawra, S., Tennin, K., & Sharma, S. (Eds.), *New business frontiers in the metaverse* (pp. 155–173). IGI Global. DOI: 10.4018/979-8-3693-2422-6.ch011

Tariq, M. U. (2024). Neurodiversity inclusion and belonging strategies in the workplace. In J. Vázquez de Príncipe (Ed.), *Resilience of multicultural and multigenerational leadership and workplace experience* (pp. 182-201). IGI Global. DOI: 10.4018/979-8-3693-1802-7.ch009

Usmani, M. S., Wang, J., Ahmad, N., Ullah, Z., Iqbal, M., & Ismail, M. (2022). Establishing a corporate social responsibility implementation model for promoting sustainability in the food sector: A hybrid approach of expert mining and ISM–MICMAC. *Environmental Science and Pollution Research International*, 29(6), 1–22. DOI: 10.1007/s11356-021-16111-7 PMID: 34494192

Yankovskaya, V. V., Mustafin, T. A., Endovitsky, D. A., & Krivosheev, A. V. (2022). Corporate social responsibility as an alternative approach to financial risk management: Advantages for sustainable development. *Risks*, 10(5), 106. DOI: 10.3390/risks10050106

Zhao, J. (2021). Reimagining corporate social responsibility in the era of COVID-19: Embedding resilience and promoting corporate social competence. *Sustainability (Basel)*, 13(12), 6548. DOI: 10.3390/su13126548

ADDITIONAL READING

Ashfaq, M., Khan, I., Alzahrani, A., Tariq, M. U., Khan, H., & Ghani, A. (2024). Accurate wheat yield prediction using machine learning and climate-NDVI data fusion. *IEEE Access : Practical Innovations, Open Solutions*, 12, 40947–40961. DOI: 10.1109/ACCESS.2024.3376735

Iqbal, N., Shahzad, M. U., Sherif, E.-S. M., Tariq, M. U., Rashid, J., Le, T.-V., & Ghani, A. (2024). Analysis of Wheat-Yield Prediction Using Machine Learning Models under Climate Change Scenarios. *Sustainability (Basel)*, 16(16), 6976. DOI: 10.3390/su16166976

Kaleem, S., Sohail, A., Babar, M., Ahmad, A., & Tariq, M. U. (2023). Ensemble learning for multi-class COVID-19 detection from big data. *PLoS One*, 18(10), e0292587. DOI: 10.1371/journal.pone.0292587 PMID: 37819992

Kaleem, S., Sohail, A., Tariq, M. U., & Asim, M. (2023). An improved big data analytics architecture using federated learning for IoT-enabled urban intelligent transportation systems. *Sustainability (Basel)*, 15(21), 15333. DOI: 10.3390/su152115333

Raimi, L., Kah, J. M., & Tariq, M. U. (2022). The discourse of blue economy definitions, measurements, and theories: Implications for strengthening academic research and industry practice. In Raimi, L., & Kah, J. (Eds.), *Implications for entrepreneurship and enterprise development in the blue economy* (pp. 1–17). IGI Global. DOI: 10.4018/978-1-6684-3393-5.ch001

Raimi, L., Tariq, M. U., & Kah, J. M. (2022). Diversity, equity, and inclusion as the future workplace ethics: Theoretical review. In Raimi, L., & Kah, J. (Eds.), *Mainstreaming diversity, equity, and inclusion as future workplace ethics* (pp. 1–27). IGI Global. DOI: 10.4018/978-1-6684-3657-8.ch001

Tariq, M. U., & Ismail, M. U. S. B. (2024). AI-powered COVID-19 forecasting: A comprehensive comparison of advanced deep learning methods. *Osong Public Health and Research Perspectives*, 15(2), 2210–9099. DOI: 10.24171/j.phrp.2023.0287 PMID: 38621765

Tariq, M. U., & Ismail, S. B. (2024). Deep learning in public health: Comparative predictive models for COVID-19 case forecasting. *PLoS One*, 19(3), e0294289. DOI: 10.1371/journal.pone.0294289 PMID: 38483948

Tariq, M. U., Ismail, S. B., Babar, M., & Ahmad, A. (2023). Harnessing the power of AI: Advanced deep learning models optimization for accurate SARS-CoV-2 forecasting. *PLoS One*, 18(7), e0287755. DOI: 10.1371/journal.pone.0287755 PMID: 37471397

Tsietso, D., Yahya, A., Samikannu, R., Tariq, M. U., Babar, M., Qureshi, B., & Koubaa, A. (2023). Multi-input deep learning approach for breast cancer screening using thermal infrared imaging and clinical data. *IEEE Access : Practical Innovations, Open Solutions*, 11, 52101–52116. DOI: 10.1109/ACCESS.2023.3280422

KEY TERMS AND DEFINITIONS

Corporate Social Responsibility (CSR): A strategy involving the integration of ethical, sustainable practices into business operations.

Economic Pillar of CSR: A focus within CSR that aims to provide equitable access to healthcare while ensuring the financial sustainability of healthcare services.

Environmental Pillar of CSR: The aspect of CSR that emphasizes reducing environmental impact through practices like waste management, energy efficiency, and reducing carbon footprints.

Resilience in Healthcare: The ability of healthcare systems to maintain and improve operations during crises.

Social Pillar of CSR: The CSR component that promotes inclusivity, diversity, and community engagement.

Stakeholder Engagement in CSR: The process of involving key groups such as patients, employees, and the community in CSR initiatives to ensure their relevance and effectiveness.

Sustainability in Healthcare: The practice of integrating environmentally responsible strategies into healthcare operations.

Telemedicine: A digital health technology that facilitates remote medical consultations, aligning with CSR goals by improving accessibility and reducing environmental impacts.

Chapter 4
Corporate Social Responsibility in Healthcare:
An Empirical Observation

Anna Maria Melina
http://orcid.org/0000-0001-6725-7992
University of Messina, Italy

Concetta Lucia Cristofaro
http://orcid.org/0009-0000-5157-5128
University E-Campus, Italy

Marzia Ventura
http://orcid.org/0000-0001-6339-7103
University of Catanzaro, Italy

Walter Vesperi
University of Palermo, Italy

ABSTRACT

Contemporary society requires every organization to operate with a sense of social responsibility. Many organizations, including those in the healthcare sector, now include corporate social responsibility (CSR) activities in their work programs. Today, healthcare organizations have different choices and tools to communicate their CSR activities. The use of traditional means of communication of CSR (social, sustainability and integrated reports, codes of ethics, certification standards, etc.) is often integrated with the implementation of interactive communication technologies (internet, websites, social media, social networks, mobile apps) that have gained

DOI: 10.4018/979-8-3693-5991-4.ch004

ground year after year. This paper analyzes how new technologies support the development and attention of CSR in the healthcare sector.

INTRODUCTION

Contemporary society demands that every organization operates with a sense of social responsibility, so many include Corporate Social Responsibility (CSR) activities in their work programs. CSR, today, is a topic of broad global interest that impacts all types of sectors. The literature on the topic has grown rapidly in recent years, but the definition of the concept continues to be a matter of debate (Peloza and Falkenberg, 2009; Aguinis and Glavas, 2013). The European Commission itself in 2021 stated that "companies of all types voluntarily decide to contribute to a better society and a cleaner environment and integrate social and environmental concerns into their business operations and their interaction with their stakeholders on a voluntary basis". Thus, there is substantial agreement that CSR refers to the responsibility of companies towards their impact on society, the environment and the various stakeholders (Carrol,1979; Shamir, 2005; EU Commission, 2011; Tomaselli et al., 2018). CSR, therefore, can be seen as the responsibility of companies that goes beyond the economic aspect and refers to the "type and scope of social obligations that companies must consider in the course of their routine business practices" (Chaundri & Wang, 2007).

In the last decade, in this context, there is also healthcare organizations that, due to the numerous public controls to which they are continuously subjected, have paid greater attention to issues of CSR (Collins, 2010). The interest of the healthcare sector in CSR is of recent birth (Russo, 2016), in fact in literature the topic is scarcely covered especially with reference to digital Health.

Although CSR should concern organizations in all sectors, it is crucial for the healthcare sector, which is facing challenges, especially rapid technological advances and financial, economic and sustainability pressures.

The continuous increase in healthcare costs, the expansion of market demands, the emergence of new diseases and treatments, technological advances, public awareness, growing customer dissatisfaction and media attention are as highlighted by Orlikoff and Pointer (1999), the challenges that healthcare organizations have to face.

To achieve greater awareness, the healthcare sector is paying more and more attention to different methods of CSR and, in particular, to the use of technologies.

In this regard, technologies are commonly used in the healthcare sector to communicate CSR activities. The importance of communicating CSR lies in the fact that it can influence leaders and public opinions as well as their behavior (Tomaselli and Melia, 2014).

Today, healthcare organizations have different choices and tools to communicate their CSR activities. The use of traditional means of communication of CSR (social, sustainability and integrated reports, codes of ethics, certification standards, etc.) is often integrated with the implementation of interactive communication technologies (internet, websites, social media, social networks, mobile apps) that have gained ground year after year.

This research aims on the one hand to evaluate the impact of CSR on the healthcare sector, trying to increase the little literature on the topic, on the other hand it analyzes how new technologies, such as apps, support the development and attention of CSR in the healthcare sector.

On these premises, the work presents the results of an exploratory and descriptive study in order to understand and define the framework of the general dynamics of the phenomenon (Yin, 2015). This study can be divided into two phases. The first step - Theoretical Background - explores the little literature on the development and impact that CRS has in the healthcare context. In this on the desk analysis, scientific documents were identified and filtered using keywords, language and abstracts. This phase allowed us to theoretically frame the phenomenon according to our research questions. The second step – Empirical Observation – explores some mApps officially identified as new interactive communication technologies in the healthcare sector, trying to understand whether they can be tools with an impact on CSR.

1 THEORETICAL FRAMEWORK

1.1 Corporate Social Responsibility Over Time

The business environment, the outside world have changed, which is precisely why CSR is beginning to take on very specific connotations. For several years, CSR has considered the long-term effects of organizations on social, cultural and environmental spheres (Campra et al., 2023). The impact that an organization's activity can have on the social context in the short and long terms must be considered and managed for collective well-being (Esposito and Antonucci, 2022). It must be configured as an investment capable of contributing to the competitiveness and development of the company itself and not as an additional cost. first of all, it is necessary to attribute the right meaning to the term CSR. This is a concept that, to date, is not yet well defined and above all is seen as a way to meet the expectations of stakeholders, fulfill legal obligations and level with competitors. Such a vision leads to a wrong inclusion of CSR in organizations as it is not well integrated into strategic and operational management. The assumption of social responsibility is not an element that is added, but represents a structural dimension of the company which must be part of the culture and fit into the entire company system. CSR is a transversal, innovative and constantly developing concept, but it is not new, in fact, the cultural roots of CSR can be found in the Anglo-Saxon world and the dawn of the debate date back to the 20s. To date, there is no unambiguous definition of what CSR is. There are many management studies and various definitions that have certainly contributed to enriching the contents of the topic, developing numerous practices, more or less standardized, on what are the issues of CSR.

The first attempts to reinterpret the nature of corporate obligations date back to 1932 in America and Europe with Berle and Means. In Italy it began to be reflected in the business economics school through Zappa in 1962 who argued that "the interests and needs of individuals operating in companies are not only mere material and economic needs, but also include moral, social, political, religious aspects, etc." the concept of common good "not attributable to a sum of particular interests" was developed. The ongoing discussion on how the logic of sustainability, shared value and corporate citizenship contribute to the creation of value and the common good is thus anticipated. Between the '50s and '60s, the awareness of the need for a social and proactive role on the part of companies began to assert itself widely, thus opening the line of research on business ethics. The first significant contribution starts from Bowen in 1953 where the vision of the company is changed as it begins to see a philanthropic company oriented towards the financing of social causes towards employees and the community of reference. The affirmation of CSR finds its highest expression in the academic community, in particular among the economists of the neoclassical school through Friedman who in 1962 defines "... The responsibility for the company is to use its resources in activities capable of increasing profit in compliance with the rules of the game, i.e. in a context of free and open competition free of deception or fraud". Subsequently, in the '70s and early '80s, a phase of great ferment flourished, in which the thought on CSR began to consolidate and diversify considerably. The logic of social responsibility converges in various contributions of American and European schools, outlining multiple approaches.

In 1978 Friederick paved the way for Corporate Social Responsiveness, according to which companies are not only responsible for the social obligations deriving from their activity, but this must be accompanied by a proactive orientation thanks to which companies adapt to the demand expressed by the various social partners, enrich themselves and complete the logic of corporate philanthropy by trying to anticipate changes in values and cultures. In 1979 Carrol introduced the concept of Corporate Social Performance. The author defines the social performance of the firm as the result of 4 factors: 1. The economic dimension 2. The legal dimension 3. The ethical dimension: conformity to social values and the duty to operate according to criteria of justice, equity and impartiality 4. Philanthropic discretion: the possibility that the company chooses to make social investments without there being specific expectations in this sense from the community. And it is precisely Carrol that explicitly introduces the concept of a company of "be a good corporate Citizen" as an integrated actor in the community in which it operates, developing social capital. The social strategy of the company clearly explains the relevance of legitimation strategies, based on the identification of the raison d'être of the company, also recognizes the role of proactive and anticipatory behavior of social interlocutors, thus the concept of stakeholder management emerges, one of the areas characterizing CSR in the 80s. Also, at the beginning of the 80s, the focus from the analysis progressively shifted from the defining aspects to the relationship between CSR and economic performance and Porter and Kramer highlighted the positive relationship between competitive advantage, CSR and productivity variables in a competitive context.

In the transition from the 80s to the 90s, the environmental emergency and the widespread attention in Western countries to the protection and enhancement of environmental resources went to raise awareness and stimulate growing attention from civil society and it is precisely in this period that the concept of sustainability and sustainable development was born, understood as "an approach aimed at creating value in the long term, not only for shareholders and company ownership, but also for other stakeholders, based on the ability to seize opportunities and manage risks arising from changes in the environment." Also in this period, an approach was reached that is still valid and discussed today: the Triple Bottom Line which considers not only economic areas but also the social and environmental aspect. With the beginning of the 90s, the phase of the institutionalization of CSR began at the level of international agencies (UN, ILO, etc.), supranational organizations (European Union) and individual governments. Major supranational organizations such as the UN are beginning to issue guidelines to link the concepts of CSR and sustainability to public policies. In the 2000s there was a further evolution and various evolutionary logics of CSR took hold and we arrive at Global Corporate Citizenship. From this point of view, the company is seen as a citizen holder of rights and duties, a fundamental agent for the improvement of global practices that supports the already existing institutions. Moving from a CSR approach to a GCC approach means moving from a vision in which the purpose is the satisfaction of individual shareholders, to one in which the good of society is to be achieved by integrating different types of initiatives. This means that the company, in addition to engaging in the classic CSR logics such as reporting, the triple bottom line, attention to external stakeholders; it also has the task of carrying out actions in favor of the community by developing the logic of so-called social entrepreneurship. To date, the focus is on the evaluation of performance related to CSR strategies, measuring what the results and impact are; and in terms of costs and revenues related to the various activities that the company carries out and which will subsequently have an impact on the environment and on society itself. In addition to this, the concept of creating shared value begins to become predominant, so the organization is part of a broader, broader concept in which all the players in the value chain are involved, such as: suppliers, customers, the community and the territory, with attention also to the decentralization of production at an international level, which today has become predominant to reduce costs.

Another trend currently underway are the ISO 26000 standards, which have represented a significant turning point compared to the standards developed previously: here the different areas of responsibility are added together also according to the Triple Bottom Line logic, but also going to consider organizational performance, Corporate Governance, fair trade, respect for human rights, the level and conditions of work, the protection and safeguarding of the environment, consumer protection and related environmental development.

1.2 Corporate Social Responsibility: Theories and Definitions

The concept of CSR has been discussed for years, not only because of a lack of a clear definition accepted by all, but also because of disagreement regarding the regulations and mechanisms for implementing CSR within the organization itself. There is no single definition regarding CSR, therefore, rules and regulations may differ from one country to another, as well as monitoring and compliance with current regulations. Some research has shown that the absence of international standards on environmental and social issues leads to the application of CSR in an illegitimate, wrong way, without a logical sense that does not amalgamate what the company system is and make it so inconsistent and in doing so it generates uselessness and low profitability. In addition, CSR implemented within an organization sometimes does not leverage it as it is not used as a tool to achieve eco-sustainable development and societal improvement, but is only used as a way to avoid a negative impact.

According to Kolk and Pinkse (2010), CSR is used by companies to their advantage only and exclusively to improve their financial, image, brand and reputation performance and through these practices they make them more sensitive to environmental and social concerns. Different theories and concepts revolve around CSR that connect and amalgamate with each other. They give and have given the basis of the various theories in the environmental and social spheres. Freeman (1984) emphasizes that corporations have as their purpose the interests of all its stakeholders to meet their needs. The organization, in fact, is part of a network of interactions and exchange relationships with multiple social interlocutors capable of influencing its fate in a positive or negative sense. Only a careful management of this complex system of relationships allows the company to obtain the resources and contributions essential for the continuation of the activity over time and the realization of its mission or purpose. The ultimate goal of the organization is to create value for stakeholders. The concept of value creation has progressively shifted towards the Triple Bottom Line. This concept was made known in 1997 by John Elkington who argues that the company must perform its functions not only in the economic dimension, but also in the social and environmental one. Lozano (2015) continues on this path by inserting a further evolutionary step and declaring that sustainability at the corporate level requires a "holistic" vision: it is necessary to consider all three dimensions and how they impact and interact with each other. CSR is one of the tools to achieve sustainable development, but at the same time it is not enough for a complete implementation, which requires society, states, the local community and environmental development. With Porter and Kramer (2007) a further step forward is taken by outlining a different definition of CSR by including it as an important element in the corporate strategy. The two authors maintain as a basic principle that there is an interrelationship between a company and society, as they need each other. Therefore, the more a social cause is linked to the business of the company, the greater the opportunity to leverage the commitment and skills of the company and just as great, consequently, the opportunity to benefit society.

Another definition of CSR is provided by Molteni (2007) who intends: "the tension of the company – and therefore first and foremost of the top management – to satisfy to an ever-increasing extent, going beyond legal obligations, the legitimate social and environmental, as well as economic expectations of the various internal and external stakeholders, through the performance of its activities". Molteni's definition takes up in some respects the essential features of the one contained in the European Commission's Green Paper which states that: "social responsibility is the voluntary integration, by companies, of social and environmental issues in their activities and in relations with interested parties (stakeholders)". Therefore, being socially responsible means going beyond the applicable legal obligations by "investing more" in human capital, the environment and relations with stakeholders. The two definitions are very similar and substantially the advantage that social responsibility brings is that of bringing out questions that are structurally inherent in corporate choices and that are nevertheless often silenced in business processes. The commission emphasizes that social responsibility is not an additional element to the fundamental activities of the company, but on the contrary correlated with the type of integrated management of companies themselves, this is because they must be socially responsible and to do this they define and consider within their strategy, in their policies, in their daily management the interests of all its stakeholders and the impacts that their work can have both at the level of economic, environmental and social.

Although there is no unambiguous definition of CSR, the literature highlights how social responsibility is a sort of "umbrella" under which a changing set of elements relating to the different business areas and stakeholders is gathered. It can change in time and space and lead to a new business model that appears in the social reality, where the company places itself in an active, participatory way, trying to solve problems, challenging and promoting continuous and evolutionary interaction both with itself and with other companies and the surrounding environment. Beyond positive returns, CSR can help the company build a strong, positive and long-term reputation. But at the same time, it cannot be used only as a tool to achieve easy consensus and cultivate clientele and the interests of the various stakeholders since it is a radical innovation of which we are witnessing today of the evolution taking place and which has important effects on the current and future context.

1.3 Corporate Social Responsibility in Healthcare Sector

From what has been reported above, it can therefore be said that CSR is concerned with the commitment of business organizations to contribute to sustainable development, stakeholder issues/concerns and improvement of societal (Jamali et al., 2010). Although an exact definition of CSR remains elusive, the term is generally used to refer to a mode of business engagement and value creation which fulfills legal, ethical and public societal expectations (Matten & Moon, 2008; Luetkenhorst, 2004). In simple terms, Snider et al. (2003) states that CSR can be defined as the obligation of a firm to use its resources in ways to benefit society. The World Business Council for Sustainable Development (2001) defines CSR as the commitment of business to contribute to the sustainable economic development of employees, families and the local communities. More generally, CSR is a set of policies, practices and programs that are integrated throughout business operations and decision-making processes, and intended to ensure that the company maximizes the positive impacts of its operations on society. In the healthcare sector, CSR is a key element in promoting an ethical and sustainable business model, centred on the well-being of the community and the environment. The literature lacks research on CSR issues in healthcare (Uyar,et al, 2021). Despite this, the limited existing literature outlines that healthcare organizations that adopt CSR practices not only improve their reputation, but actively contribute to public health and sustainability. A responsible approach starts with the accessibility of services: ensuring high-quality care at affordable costs and promoting equality in access to treatment is crucial for the well-being of the population. In addition, healthcare facilities can reduce their environmental impact through efficient resource management, recycling materials, reducing emissions, and using renewable energy sources. Employee training and well-being are another pillar of CSR in healthcare: investing in human capital through professional development programs, promoting inclusive work environments, and ensuring worker safety are essential to creating a responsible corporate culture. Finally, healthcare organizations should be transparent in their operations and governance practices, engaging stakeholders in an open dialogue and building partnerships with the community to address local health challenges. By adopting these principles, healthcare institutions can become agents of positive change, contributing to a more equitable, sustainable and resilient healthcare system.

The development of CSR in the healthcare sector takes place through a structured process involving different phases and strategic actions. The first step is to carry out a thorough analysis of the needs and expectations of internal and external stakeholders, including patients, employees, providers, local communities and regulators. This analysis helps to identify key areas of social and environmental impact, as well as provide the basis for setting clear and measurable CSR goals. Once you've identified your CSR goals, it's critical to integrate them into your overall business strategy. This means aligning CSR practices with the healthcare organization's mission, values, and long-term goals, ensuring that every department and business function understands and contributes to CSR goals. Healthcare organizations develop and implement a number of programs and initiatives designed to address CSR priorities. These can include accessibility to care programs, prevention and health promotion campaigns, environmental sustainability initiatives such as efficient waste management and the use of renewable energy, as well as ethical and inclusive labor practices. Stakeholder engagement is essential for successful CSR in healthcare. Organizations should engage in an ongoing dialogue with their stakeholders, gathering feedback and collaborating to improve CSR programs. This involvement can take place through forums, surveys, community meetings and strategic partnerships. Measuring the impact of CSR initiatives is crucial to assess the effectiveness of the actions taken and to make continuous improvements. Healthcare organizations use key performance indicators (KPIs) to monitor progress toward CSR goals, as well as conduct internal and external audits to ensure compliance and effectiveness of CSR practices. Transparency is a fundamental aspect of CSR. Healthcare organizations must clearly and transparently communicate their CSR activities, using different channels such as annual reports, company websites, press releases, and social media. This helps to build trust with stakeholders and strengthen the reputation of the organization.

CSR is a dynamic process that requires a continuous improvement approach. Healthcare organizations must periodically review their CSR strategies and practices in light of changes in the social, economic, and regulatory environment, as well as in response to stakeholder feedback. Through this process, healthcare organizations can develop effective CSR that contributes to people's well-being, environmental sustainability, and economic prosperity, while strengthening their reputation and stakeholder trust. CSR tools are key to implementing and managing social responsibility strategies effectively in the healthcare sector. These tools help organizations plan, monitor, measure and communicate their CSR activities.

The main CSR tools used in the healthcare sector:

1. Codes of Conduct and Ethical Guidelines: These documents outline the core principles and values that guide the organization's decisions and actions. They are key tools for ensuring that all business operations are conducted ethically and responsibly.
2. Training and Awareness Programs: Continuous training of staff on CSR, professional ethics, sustainability and patient care is essential to integrate CSR into the corporate culture. These programs can be delivered through workshops, online courses, seminars, and other educational activities.
3. Environmental Management Systems (EMS): These systems help healthcare organizations monitor and manage their environmental impact. EMS can include measures to reduce energy consumption, manage waste, recycle, and use renewable resources.
4. Communication and Stakeholder Engagement Plans: Tools such as questionnaires, patient and employee satisfaction surveys, and meetings with local communities are used to engage stakeholders and gather feedback on CSR initiatives.
5. Sustainability Reports: These reports provide a detailed overview of the organization's CSR activities, the progress made towards sustainability goals, and the challenges faced. Reports can be published annually and are often structured according to international standards such as the Global Reporting Initiative (GRI).
6. Quality Standards and Certifications: Many healthcare organizations pursue certifications such as ISO 14001 (environmental management), ISO 45001 (occupational health and safety), and Joint Commission International (JCI) for quality of care. These certifications provide a framework for implementing CSR practices and ensure compliance with globally recognized standards.
7. Partnership and Collaboration Programs: Organizations can use strategic partnerships with other healthcare institutions, non-governmental organizations (NGOs), government agencies, and private companies to develop and implement CSR programs. These collaborations can lead to joint initiatives to address local or global health issues.
8. Measurement and Evaluation Tools: These include KPIs (Key Performance Indicators), social and economic impact metrics, and life cycle analysis tools. They help organizations evaluate the effectiveness of their CSR initiatives and identify areas for improvement.

By using these tools, healthcare organizations can more effectively manage their CSR initiatives, ensuring a positive impact on society and the environment, while improving their reputation and stakeholder satisfaction.

2. HEALTH TECHNOLOGIES

The health care sector is in the process of transformation, this can also be demonstrated by the increasingly widespread use of Health Technology. Health Technology can be defined as what science and research make available to all health professionals (Francesconi, 2007). The evolution of the health context thanks to health technologies has inevitably led to a new clinical management (Buccoliero and Nasi, 2004). Health technologies, therefore, do not only refer to the devices necessary for medical practices but also to all the procedures necessary to obtain the satisfaction of the demand for health care. On the other hand, the use of new technologies in health requires greater accuracy of information because they support patients in their clinical procedures. In order to do this, it is necessary that the technologies used have certain characteristics such as reliability, real-time availability and everywhere of the information necessary for health professionals to be able to intervene promptly in patient care. More generally, in the world of healthcare, the trends determined by the introduction of health technologies and the Web can be summarized as follows: 1. greater transparency and accountability in the public sector with new governance models (new partnerships, involvement of intermediaries, recognition of new roles of stakeholders); 2. greater choice and accessibility of public services and attention to efficiency and quality; 3. a strengthening of data- and evidence-based policies that allow for correct decisions to be made; 4. an improvement in digital skills in healthcare professionals (Reina et al., 2017). Health technologies include a wide range of tools and solutions that improve the efficiency and effectiveness of healthcare services. These may include: medical devices, i.e. diagnostic tools, therapeutic equipment, and monitoring tools; healthcare software, i.e. health information management systems (EHR), telemedicine, and mobile health applications (mHealth); biotechnologies involving gene therapies, advanced diagnostics, and vaccine development; and finally Artificial Intelligence, i.e. machine learning algorithms for diagnosis and personalization of treatments. Software, artificial intelligence and telemedicine have an origin that dates back to the 1950s, the use of APPs in the healthcare sector, however, is a much more recent topic. These categories are not to be considered perfectly distinct from each other, there are many sectors that can embrace two or more types of technologies. Just think, for example, of m-health ("mobile health"), now replaced by the term IoMT ("Internet of Medical Thing"), which is exponentially gaining the attention of researchers thanks to its wide applicability in Smart

Healthcare systems for monitoring patients via devices that they always carry with them. With respect to these digital solutions in healthcare, there are two aspects to take into consideration: on the one hand, the identification of clinically effective and efficient solutions compared to the myriad of solutions developed and ensuring that consumers choose the best solution for specific needs (Chelagat et al, 2021). All the tools identified can be used both individually and combined with each other in a synergistic way.

2.1 The Relationship Between Health Technologies and CSR

There is an increasingly relevant relationship between health technologies and CSR, especially in the field of public health and business management. However, few studies demonstrate that these two highly topical areas are intertwined, creating significant impacts and common practices. In fact, CSR concerns the commitment of companies to operate ethically and to contribute positively to society, while health technologies involve the use of technological innovations to improve diagnosis, treatment and health management. The integration of health technologies with CSR practices can have multiple benefits such as improving public health, in fact through the use of advanced technologies, companies can improve access to and quality of care; sustainability and efficiency, since health technologies can help reduce waste and inefficiencies in the health system, contributing to environmental sustainability; inclusive innovation because companies can develop solutions that consider the needs of vulnerable groups, such as the elderly and people with disabilities, promoting social inclusion and finally education and awareness as technologies can be used to educate the public on preventive health practices and management of chronic diseases, improving the general health of the population. Some practical examples can be represented by Telemedicine in Rural Areas as there are companies that provide telemedicine platforms to offer remote consultations in areas where access to doctors is limited. Another example could be low-cost devices i.e. the development of low-cost medical devices for the diagnosis and treatment of common diseases in developing countries; or Vaccination programs for collaboration with non-governmental organizations and local governments to implement mass vaccination programs; and finally, the reduction of environmental impact through the implementation of green technologies for the management of hospital waste and the use of renewable energy. All the examples presented want to be the demonstration that the link between health technologies and CSR is continuously strengthening (table 1).

Table 1. Link between CSR and health technologies

CSR Aspects	Healthcare Technologies
Accessibility and Inclusivity	**Telemedicine Technologies:** Companies can invest in telemedicine platforms to reach patients in remote areas or with limited access to traditional healthcare services. This improves accessibility to care and reduces health disparities.
	Low-Cost Medical Devices: The development and distribution of low-cost medical devices, such as portable diagnostic tests, can make care more accessible to underserved populations.
Environmental Sustainability	**Waste Management:** The implementation of technologies for sustainable management of healthcare waste reduces the environmental impact of hospitals and clinics.
	Renewable Energy: Using renewable energy sources in healthcare facilities helps reduce carbon emissions and promote environmental sustainability.
Ethics and Transparency	**Blockchain Technologies:** The use of blockchain can provide transparency in clinical trials and management of medical records, ensuring that patient data is protected and that information is accurate and accessible.
	Artificial Intelligence: AI algorithms can be used to analyze large amounts of health data in an ethical manner, ensuring the correct and safe use of information.
Responsible Innovation	**Research and Development:** Invest in R&D to develop new therapies and technologies that address global health needs, such as infectious diseases and chronic conditions, promoting sustainable and accessible solutions.
	Partnerships with NGOs: Work with non-governmental organizations to deploy innovative health technologies in communities that need them, improving public health globally.

Source: our elaboration

3. METHODOLOGY

The methodology, linked to the purpose of the research (Silverman, 2016), implemented in this work is qualitative exploratory and descriptive study in order to understand and define the framework of the general dynamics of the phenomenon (Yin, 2015). This study is based on two-step:

1. Theoretical Framework
2. Empirical Observation

Figure 1. Steps of research (Authors' elaboration)

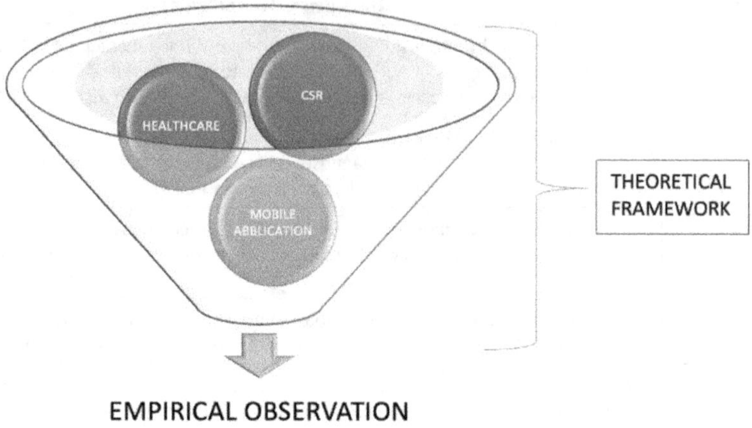

The first step - Theoretical Framework - explores the scarce literature on the development and impact that CRS has in the healthcare context and the link that it has with healthcare technologies as innovative tools.

This research, in fact, started with the definition of a theoretical framework built using CSR, healthcare, technology and mobile application (M-App) as keywords. This phase was necessary to understand how to analyze the observed phenomenon. In this on-the-desk analysis, scientific documents were identified and filtered using keywords, language and abstracts. This phase allowed us to theoretically frame the phenomenon. After trying to understand the connection that can exist between CSR and healthcare through M-apps, we move on to the next phase.

The second part of the research - Empirical Observation - focused on a taxonomy of apps officially identified as new interactive communication technologies in the healthcare sector, focusing in particular on those apps that support CSR in the healthcare sector.

A total of 8 M-apps were observed on the two most popular operating platforms (Play Store and iTunes) were analyzed, using search terms such as: "CSR and healthcare". All the M-Apps identified were classified according to type, technical functionality, description, number of downloads.

3.1 Context

Mobile apps have become a new long-term commodity as consumers are more open to paying for their services. The app market has been impacted by the global COVID-19 pandemic. After accelerating in 2021, consumer spending declined to US$167 billion in 2022. In 2023, annual app spending returned to track, generating

US$171 billion, with China and the United States ranking as the leading markets based on consumer spending on mobile apps. After declining in 2022, consumer spending per user recovered to exceed five US dollars in the second quarter of 2023.

App installs and user time followed similar trends. In 2022, app engagement increased by only three percent year-over-year, while between 2019 and 2022, time spent using mobile apps for global users increased by about 46 percent. Similarly, app downloads saw a slowing growth trend between 2022 and 2023, reaching 257 billion installs, up less than one percent year-over-year.

The Apple App Store and Google Play Store were the most common discovery hubs for mobile apps, according to nearly half of global consumers. Word of mouth and advertising were less effective, as 35 percent of consumers and 25 percent of consumers said they discovered apps through these two methods, respectively. Health-related M-Apps are often classified as "Health & Fitness" or "Medical" M-Apps. Typically, M-Apps designed for health, fitness, and medicine are intended for everyday use by patients, performing functions such as calorie and diet trackers, assisting patients with exercise and diaries, or as support for patients with a medical condition.

4. RESULTS AND DISCUSSION

The use of mobile applications (Apps) in medicine has transformed the way in which health professionals and patients interact, manage and monitor health. Medical apps, in fact, offer a wide range of functions that go from the management of medical records to telemedicine, up to specific tools for the diagnosis and treatment of various medical conditions. While on the one hand the world of mobile applications (APPs) is very versatile and very easy to use for the end user, on the other hand the production phase and placing them on the market presents difficulties and critical issues for the manufacturer. In the healthcare sector there are APPs that analyze physiological parameters, others are used in the clinical field, which demonstrates how there is a global trend towards the development of a digital therapy for patients. In this context, Italy is trying to develop an orientation very similar to the German one. In fact, Germany, through legislative regulation, has identified a list of "certified apps" for which prescription by healthcare personnel is permitted (Mageit, 2000). They can be divided into two categories: Wellness, which includes more than half of iOS and Android apps. This area includes all those APPs for fitness, lifestyle and nutrition, and is placed in the phase of behavioral change and preventive wellness. The other category concerns Disease and Treatment Management. This typology includes APPs useful in the management of a specific pathology, which support all the phases ranging from diagnosis to treatment and control of the same (Bhavnani et.al., 2016). The branch of digital health that deals with these applications is m-Health more commonly known as IoMT ("Internet of Medical Thing"). The main purpose of medical APPs is the empowerment of the patient who is responsible for his/her own care. This type of solutions lead to huge health economic savings since investments are made in prevention and the only cost of these solutions is that relating to the creation of the APP and possibly the necessary wearable sensors. On the other hand, mobile applications are becoming a powerful tool for healthcare companies that want to integrate CSR practices into their daily operations.

In this exploratory research, the authors analyzed some types of healthcare apps for CSR management. They noticed that they mainly focused on how healthcare organizations can integrate ethical and sustainable practices into their operations. These apps can facilitate various aspects of CSR, from environmental sustainability initiatives to public health and employee well-being campaigns. In particular, these apps help companies monitor, manage and improve their social and environmental impact. In Table 2 below, we have identified, on IOS and Android operating systems, some types of apps that can support and amplify companies' CSR efforts.

Table 2. Types of apps by CSR areas

CSR Area	App Types
Health and Wellness	**Employee Wellness Apps**: Companies can develop apps that promote the physical and mental well-being of employees through fitness programs, meditation, and health monitoring.
	Telemedicine Apps: Facilitate access to medical care for employees and local communities by offering remote medical consultations and health monitoring.
Environmental Sustainability	**Waste Reduction Apps:** Apps can help monitor and reduce the company's carbon footprint by tracking resource consumption and promoting recycling practices.
	Sustainable Mobility Apps: Promote the use of sustainable transportation among employees, such as carpooling, cycling, and public transportation.
Education and Awareness	**Educational Apps:** Offer educational resources on sustainable practices and public health issues, raising awareness among employees and the public on crucial issues.
	Volunteer Apps: Facilitate employee participation in volunteer activities, with event calendars, registration, and tracking of service hours.
Community and Social Inclusion	**Diversity and Inclusion Apps**: Create platforms that promote diversity and inclusion within the company, offering resources and support for underrepresented groups.
	Community Support Apps: Connect companies with local communities through support initiatives such as donating goods, services, and funds.

Source: our elaboration

In the second part of the research, the authors analyzed and explored those apps, available on both IOS and Android, that could be used by healthcare organizations to apply the principles of CSR. The following Table 3 reports the apps studied and the type of support they offer.

Table 3. Apps to support CSR

App	Features
Virgin Pulse	Corporate Wellness app that helps companies promote employee wellness through fitness programs, health monitoring and healthy lifestyle incentives.
Apple Health	Health Monitoring app that helps people monitor their health, encouraging a healthy lifestyle.
Teladoc	Telemedicine app that offers remote medical consultations, improving access to medical care in remote areas or for people with mobility difficulties.
JouleBug	Corporate Sustainability app that encourages sustainable behaviors through challenges and rewards, helping employees reduce their environmental impact
RecycleCoach	Recycling app that provides information to companies on how to recycle properly, reducing waste and promoting sustainability.
JouleBug	Carbon Tracking app that helps companies monitor and reduce their carbon footprint, promoting eco-friendly behaviors.
InHerSight	Diversity and Inclusion app that allows companies to monitor and improve the work environment for women, through feedback and ratings.
Benevity	Volunteering app that facilitates corporate volunteering, donations and charity campaigns, with tools to engage and motivate employees

Source: our elaboration

Every healthcare and non-healthcare organization can decide to implement CSR apps in different ways. Among these implementation methodologies we have the development of proprietary apps as companies can develop their own apps to promote specific CSR initiatives, such as corporate wellness programs or corporate volunteering platforms; collaboration with existing apps as companies can collaborate with existing app developers to integrate CSR features into their services, such as partnerships with telemedicine apps or recycling platforms; promoting the use of CSR apps among employees and customers through awareness campaigns and incentives can amplify the positive impact of CSR initiatives.

5. THEORETICAL AND PRACTICAL IMPLICATIONS

Corporate Social Responsibility (CSR) in the healthcare sector concerns the commitment of organizations to promote ethical and sustainable practices that go beyond simple profit, including environmental protection, employee well-being, and community responsibility. From a theoretical point of view, CSR in the healthcare context implies a reconfiguration of the role of companies, which are no longer seen only as providers of services, but as social actors with a significant impact on public health and equity in access to care.

Uyar et al (2021) underlined that CSR activities help healthcare organizations to gain a good reputation, to strengthen their stakeholder relations, to enhance their brand advocacy and to improve their competitive position in the marketplace, by which to achieve favorable business results, such as increased social and financial performance motivated staff, enhanced job satisfaction. Practically, healthcare organizations can implement CSR policies by reducing the environmental impact of their operations, adopting ethical work practices, and improving accessibility to healthcare services for disadvantaged communities. For example, the use of green technologies, the promotion of prevention programs, and investment in public health projects are concrete actions that strengthen corporate social responsibility. Mobile health applications (Mobile Health Apps) represent a technological innovation that can have a significant impact on CSR. These apps improve accessibility to health information, promote patient education and facilitate self-monitoring of health conditions, thus reducing the pressure on traditional health systems. Furthermore, the responsible use of health apps, with a focus on data protection and transparency, reflects the commitment of companies to protecting consumer rights, a key element of CSR. In short, Mobile Health Apps can amplify the positive impact of CSR in the healthcare sector, promoting a more inclusive and sustainable approach to health management.

6. CONCLUSION

Limbu et al (2020) states that the pressure on healthcare organizations to act responsibly and consider their ethical obligations toward society is increasing. In according with Uyar et al (2021) and Limbu et al (2020), to survive in a competitive sector like healthcare, building a good reputation, establishing strong relations with stakeholders have become crucial.

CSR is a key activity for today's healthcare organizations (Tomaselli et al, 2016), which are faced with everyday challenges: technological advances, economic and financial crisis, sustainability and social pressures (Tomaselli et al, 2018). Furthermore, healthcare organizations are required to provide optimal and cost-effective quality care with the limited resources they have available or allocated, therefore healthcare organizations should pay special attention to CSR and the extent to which they make it visible and accessible to their stakeholders.

This research work, of an exploratory nature, aimed to support the scarce literature on CSR and healthcare. Specifically, the study tried to identify some apps that could support healthcare organizations to become increasingly “sustainable”. We know that the continuous evolution of mobile technology and connection capabilities is directed towards further innovations in the way in which health and well-being are managed. Medical apps, in fact, represent an important resource to improve access to care, personalize treatments and support both patients and healthcare professionals. However, the synergy between healthcare technologies and CSR also represents a promising path to improve global health, while promoting sustainability and social responsibility. Investing in innovative and sustainable solutions not only improves public health, but also promotes a responsible and ethical business model. Companies that embrace this synergy can contribute to achieving the United Nations Sustainable Development Goals (SDGs), promoting health and well-being for all. Healthcare companies have the opportunity to make a significant difference by adopting CSR practices integrated with technological innovation. Such practices can be developed through mobile applications that represent a powerful and versatile means to integrate CSR actions into business operations. By using apps to promote sustainability, employee well-being, social inclusion and community involvement, companies can amplify the impact of their CSR initiatives and contribute to a more sustainable and inclusive future. Another important consideration is that the use of CSR Apps by healthcare organizations only brings benefits in terms of: Improved social impact as apps can amplify CSR efforts, making it easier for companies to implement and monitor their initiatives; Employee Engagement as apps can increase employee engagement by offering interactive and accessible tools to participate in CSR programs; Efficiency and monitoring as apps allow tracking and analyzing data related to CSR initiatives, improving effectiveness and accountability; visibility and communication In fact, apps can improve the communication of CSR initiatives, increasing transparency and building a positive reputation for the company.

REFERENCES

Aguinis, H., & Glavas, A. (2013). Embedded versus peripheral corporate social responsibility: Psychological foundations. *Industrial and Organizational Psychology: Perspectives on Science and Practice*, 6(4), 314–332. DOI: 10.1111/iops.12059

Berle, A. A., & Means, G. C. (1932). *The Modern Corporation and Private Property*. Transaction Publishers.

Bhavnani, S. P., Narula, J., & Sengupta, P. P. (2016). Mobile technology and the digitization of healthcare. *European Heart Journal*, 37(18), 28. DOI: 10.1093/eurheartj/ehv770 PMID: 26873093

Bowen, H. R. (1953). *Social Responsibility of the Businessman*. Harper and Row.

Buccoliero, L., & Nasi, G. (2004). Il sistema informativo delle aziende sanitarie italiane: stato dell'arte e prospettive evolutive dell'area clinica. In *Rapporto OASI 2004. L'aziendalizzazione della sanità in Italia* (pp. 559–578). Egea.

Campra, M., Esposito, P., & Brescia, V. (2023). Corporate social responsibility and technological perspectives in healthcare: An exploratory analysis of the evolution of the anti-corruption system through multiple case studies. *Corporate Social Responsibility and Environmental Management*, 30(6), 2816–2829. DOI: 10.1002/csr.2517

Carrol, A. B. (1979). A tree-dimensional model of corporate social performance. *Academy of Management Review*, 4.

Chaudhri, V., & Wang, J. (2007). Communicating corporate social responsibility on the internet: A case study of the top 100 information technology companies in India. *Management Communication Quarterly, 21*(2), 232-247. .DOI: 10.1177/0893318907308746

Chelagat, T., Kokwaro, G., Onyango, J., & Rice, J. (2021). Sustainability drivers and inhibitors for the health system performance improvement projects in selected health facilities in Kenya: a qualitative study. *BMJ Open, 11*(7). .DOI: 10.1136/bmjopen-2019-035475

Cohen, T. A., Patel, V. L., & Shortliffe, E. H. (2021). Intelligent Systems in Medicine and Health. *The Role of AI.*

Collins, P. (2010). *CSR and ethical issues in operations management. Organizational Immunity to Corruption: Building Theoretical and Research Foundations, 225.* DOI: 10.4018/JGIM.2018100104

EU Commission (2001). Green Paper - Promoting a European framework for Corporate Social Responsibility. COM (2001).

EU Commission (2002). Corporate Social Responsibility: A business contribution to sustainable development. COM (2002). 347.

Commission, E. U. (2006). *Implementing the Partnership for Growth and Jobs: Making Europe a Pole of Excellence on Corporate Social Responsibility*. E. Commission.

Commission, E. U. (2010). A strategy for smart, sustainable and inclusive growth. *Europe*.

EU Commission (2011). Comunicazione al Parlamento europeo, al Consiglio, al Comitato economico e sociale europeo e al Comitato delle Regioni, Strategia rinnovata dell'UE per il periodo 2011-2014 in materia di responsabilità sociale delle imprese, Bruxelles, 25.10.2011 COM (2011).

Elkington, J., & Rowlands, I. H. (1999). Cannibals with forks: The triple bottom line of 21st century business. *Alternatives Journal*, 25(4), 42.

Esposito, P., & Antonucci, G. (2022). NGOs, corporate social responsibility and sustainable development trajectories in a new reformative spectrum: 'New wine in old bottles or old wine in new bottles?'. *Corporate Social Responsibility and Environmental Management*, 29(3), 609–619. DOI: 10.1002/csr.2223

Francesconi, A. (2007). *Innovazione organizzativa e tecnologica in sanità. Il ruolo dell'health technology assessment* (Vol. 29). FrancoAngeli.

Freeman, R. E. (2010). *Strategic management: A stakeholder approach*. Cambridge university press. DOI: 10.1017/CBO9781139192675

Friederick, W. C. (1978). From CSR to CRS. *Business & Society*, 33(2), 1994.

Friedman, M., & Friedman, R. D. (1962). *Capitalism and freedom. [By] M. Friedman, with the assistance of Rose D. Friedman*. University of Chicago Press.

Hart, S. M. (2010). Self-regulation, corporate social responsibility, and the business case: Do they work in achieving workplace equality and safety? *Journal of Business Ethics*, 92(4), 585–600. DOI: 10.1007/s10551-009-0174-1

Jamali, D., Hallal, M., & Abdallah, H. (2010). Corporate governance and corporate social responsibility: evidence from the healthcare sector. *Corporate Governance: The international journal of business in society, 10*(5), 590-602. DOI: 10.1108/14720701011085562

Kim, S. T., Lee, H. H., & Lim, S. (2021). The effects of green SCM implementation on business performance in SMEs: A longitudinal study in electronics industry. *Sustainability (Basel)*, 13(21), 11874. DOI: 10.3390/su132111874

Kolk, A., & Pinkse, J. (2010). The integration of corporate governance in corporate social responsibility disclosures. *Corporate social responsibility and environmental management, 17*(1), 15-26. DOI: 10.1002/csr.196

Kramer, M. R., & Porter, M. E. (2006). Strategy and society: The link between competitive advantage and corporate social responsibility. *Harvard Business Review*, 84(12), 78–92. PMID: 17183795

Limbu, Y. B., Pham, L., & Mann, M. (2020). Corporate social responsibility and hospital brand advocacy: Mediating role of trust and patient-hospital identification and moderating role of hospital type. *International Journal of Pharmaceutical and Healthcare Marketing*, 14(1), 159–174. DOI: 10.1108/IJPHM-04-2019-0029

Lozano, R. (2015). A holistic perspective on corporate sustainability drivers. *Corporate Social Responsibility and Environmental Management, 22*(1), 32-44. DOI: 10.1002/csr.1325

Luetkenhorst, W. (2004). Corporate social responsibility and the development agenda: The case for actively involving small and medium enterprises. *Inter Economics*, 39(3), 157–166. DOI: 10.1007/BF02933583

Mageit, S. (2020). *Two healthcare apps available for prescription in Germany for f first time*. Healthcare IT News.

Matten, D., & Moon, J. (2008). Implicit and explicit CSR: A conceptual framework for a comparative understanding of corporate social responsibility. *Academy of Management Review*, 33(2), 404–424. DOI: 10.5465/amr.2008.31193458

Molteni, M. (2007). Gli stadi di sviluppo della CSR nella strategia aziendale. *Impresa Progetto-Electronic Journal of Management*, (2).

Orlikoff, J. E., & Pointer, D. D. (1999). Board Work: Governing Health Care Organizations.

Peloza, J., & Falkenberg, L. (2009). The role of collaboration in achieving corporate social responsibility objectives. *California Management Review, 51*(3), 95-113. DOI: 10.2307/41166495

Piekkari, R., & Welch, C. (2018). The case study in management research: Beyond the positivist legacy of Eisenhardt and Yin. *The SAGE handbook of qualitative business and management research methods*, 345-358.

Reina, R., Ventura, M., & Ingrassia, R. (2017). M-App & Health Knowledge Management–Virtual Artfacts between Doctor & Patient. In *organizing for digital economy: societies communities and individual*. ItAIS 2017.

Russo, F. (2016). What is the CSR's Focus in Healthcare? *Journal of Business Ethics, 134*, 323-334. DOI: 10.1007/s10551-014-2430-2

Shamir, R. (2005). Mind the gap: The commodification of corporate social responsibility. *Symbolic Interaction*, 28(2), 229–253. DOI: 10.1525/si.2005.28.2.229

Silverman, D. (2016). Introducing qualitative research. *Qualitative Research*, 3(3), 14–25.

Snider, J., Hill, R. P., & Martin, D. (2003). Corporate social responsibility in the 21st century: A view from the world's most successful firms. *Journal of Business ethics, 48*(2), 175-187. DOI: 10.4337/9781849805278

Tomaselli, G., Garg, L., Gupta, V., Xuereb, P. A., Buttigieg, S. C., & Vassallo, P. (2018). Healthcare systems and corporate social responsibility communication: A comparative analysis between Malta and India. *Journal of Global Information Management*, 26(4), 52–66. DOI: 10.4018/JGIM.2018100104

Tomaselli, G., & Melia, M. (2014). The role of interactive technologies for CSR communication. *Journal of International Scientific Publications: Economy & Business*, 8, 324–340.

Uyar, A., Kuzey, C., Kilic, M., & Karaman, A. S. (2021). Board structure, financial performance, corporate social responsibility performance, CSR committee, and CEO duality: Disentangling the connection in healthcare. *Corporate Social Responsibility and Environmental Management*, 28(6), 1730–1748. DOI: 10.1002/csr.2141

World Business Council for Sustainable Development. (2001). *The Business Case for Sustainable Development: Making a Difference toward the Johannesburg Summit 2002 and Beyond*. World Business Council for Sustainable Development.

Yin, R. K. (2015). *Qualitative research from start to finish*. Guilford publications.

Zappa, G. (1962). *L'economia delle aziende di consumo*. Giuffrè.

KEY TERMS AND DEFINITIONS

Corporate Social Responsibility (CSR): CSR refers to the responsibility of businesses towards their impact on society, the environment and different stakeholders. It can be defined as the obligation of a firm to use its resources in ways to benefit society.

CSR in Healthcare Sector: It concerns the commitment of organizations to promote ethical and sustainable practices that go beyond simple profit, including environmental protection, employee well-being, and community responsibility.

Health Technology: It can be defined as what science and research make available to all health professionals. It involves the use of technological innovations to improve diagnosis, treatment and health management

Internet of Medical Things: (IoMT) is the collection of medical devices and applications that connect to healthcare information technology systems through online computer networks.

Key Performance Indicators: They help organizations evaluate the effectiveness of their CSR initiatives and identify areas for improvement.

Mobile Application: It is a new technological system able to transmit, create and share knowledge and improve an open innovation model. M-Apps in healthcare sector is an interactive tool among patients and doctors, able to facilitate the monitoring and highlighting of alerts by developing combinations of know-how among the nodes of healthcare networks.

Public Health: Public Health is a multidisciplinary field whose goal is to assure conditions in which people can be healthy. It aims to provide maximum benefit for the largest number of people.

Sustainability: It entails three interdependent dimensions: i) economic; ii) environmental; and iii) social, in pursuit of sustainable objectives. Sustainability in healthcare sector involves a system maintaining itself and constantly adapting to a changing social, economic and environmental context, making sure that limited resources (physical, financial and human) are being used efficiently and responsibly in order to permanently maintain or improve the health and wellbeing of the population as a whole and of each individual.

Chapter 5
Corporate Social Responsibility in the Health Sector:
A 2023 Case Study of Canon and Sony, RepTrak Leaders

Mohamed Boulesnam
http://orcid.org/0009-0003-9677-7788
Yahia Fares University of Medea, Algeria

Ouissam Hocini
http://orcid.org/0009-0009-9658-5595
Yahia Fares University of Medea, Algeria

ABSTRACT

Corporate Social Responsibility (CSR) has become a cornerstone of contemporary business practices, embodying a company's dedication to ethical conduct, sustainable development, and social welfare. The healthcare sector, due to its essential role in society and the increasing demand for enhanced healthcare services, has recently gained prominence as a focal point for CSR initiatives. This study aims to investigate the contributions of leading companies, specifically Canon and Sony, as ranked by the RepTrak platform for corporate reputation, to the healthcare sector as part of their CSR activities. By analyzing their annual and sustainability reports from 2023, this research seeks to identify their tangible contributions to healthcare and evaluate the correlation between CSR practices and corporate reputation.

DOI: 10.4018/979-8-3693-5991-4.ch005

INTRODUCTION

Corporate Social Responsibility (CSR) has become a core aspect of contemporary business practices, embodying a company's dedication to ethical conduct, sustainable development, and social welfare. The healthcare sector, due to its significant role in society and the increasing demand for enhanced healthcare services, has recently gained prominence as a major priority for CSR initiatives. This study aims to investigate the contributions of leading companies, mainly Canon and Sony, as ranked by the RepTrak platform for corporate reputation, to the healthcare sector as part of their CSR activities. By analyzing their sustainability reports, this research seeks to identify their tangible contributions to healthcare and evaluate the correlation between CSR practices and corporate reputation.

RepTrak is a global platform that ranks companies based on their reputation using various indicators and criteria such as company performance, leadership, innovation, citizenship, governance, and corporate social responsibility commitment. This platform provides a comprehensive view of how companies are perceived by their stakeholders and the public. Understanding the role of CSR in shaping corporate reputation is crucial, mainly in sectors like healthcare, where the impact on human lives is direct and critical.

The healthcare sector is pivotal and highly sensitive due to its significant impact on a diverse range of stakeholders, including patients, healthcare professionals, communities, and governments. Companies that excel in CSR within this sector not only enhance their reputation but also contribute to the overall well-being of society. Given the growing importance of CSR in addressing both societal needs and business sustainability, this study is essential for exploring how CSR activities in healthcare by leading companies like Canon and Sony not only meet societal expectations but also ensure long-term benefits for both the community and the companies themselves. By providing a comprehensive examination of the CSR activities of Canon and Sony as ranked at the top of companies by RepTrak, this research focuses on their contributions to the healthcare sector and explores how these activities influence their reputation, ultimately offering insights that can guide future corporate strategies and policies in healthcare.

OBJECTIVES

The primary objectives of this study are:

- To examine the CSR activities of Canon and Sony in the healthcare sector.

- To analyze the sustainability reports of these companies to assess quantitatively and qualitatively their commitment to healthcare.
- To explore the correlation between the adoption of CSR practices and the companies' reputations.

METHODOLOGY

The study employs a mixed-methods approach, incorporating both quantitative and qualitative analyses. The quantitative analysis involves examining specific indicators of CSR commitment, such as those related to employees, customers, the environment, and the community. The qualitative analysis focuses on content analysis of the sustainability reports to understand the depth and nature of CSR activities.

LITERATURE REVIEW OF CORPORATE SOCIAL RESPONSIBILITY IN THE HEALTH SECTOR

Social responsibility has become an increasingly important concept in modern organizational practices, mainly in the healthcare sector. This section explores the theoretical foundations of social responsibility, its various areas, and its specific applications within healthcare institutions, providing a comprehensive overview of existing research and literature.

1. Corporate Social Responsibility Background

The concept of Corporate Social Responsibility (CSR) has experienced significant evolution since its inception, expanding to encompass various dimensions that were not originally considered integral to CSR. This broadening perspective now incorporates economic, legal, ethical, and discretionary aspects, reflecting the growing expectations of society towards business entities.

Bowen et al. (1953), widely regarded as the founder of this concept, posited that CSR is the obligation of businessmen to formulate policies and make decisions that align with societal objectives and values. Building upon this foundation, Davis (1960) conceptualized CSR as the business's priority beyond profit-making to address social issues, irrespective of their causation. In contrast, Friedman (1970) propounded a more limited view, asserting that the sole mission of corporate social responsibility was profit maximization.

Jones (1980) further expanded the scope of CSR, defining it as an obligation towards various societal groups beyond shareholders and those stipulated by law or union contracts. Subsequently, Carroll (1991) proposed a multidimensional framework, arguing that CSR includes the economic, legal, ethical, and discretionary expectations that society holds for organizations at any given time.

Wood (1991) introduced a process-oriented perspective, characterizing CSR as a reflective process wherein organizational managers contemplate their relationships with stakeholders and their roles in advancing the common good. Hopkins (2003) further improved this notion, positing CSR as the process by which companies manage their business operations to produce a positive impact on society as a whole.

Sheehy (2014) conceptualized CSR as a set of strategic initiatives undertaken by businesses to evaluate and assume responsibility for their environmental and social impact.

A recent study by Fatima and Elbanna (2023) defines Corporate Social Responsibility (CSR) as a business approach that contributes to sustainable development by integrating economic, social, and environmental benefits for all stakeholders into corporate strategies. This integration not only enhances corporate reputation but also attracts and retains talent, fostering long-term business sustainability by addressing essential social and environmental challenges. This corresponds with the comprehensive definition of CSR provided by Goyal & Routroy (2021), who emphasize the importance of sustainable practices in achieving more extensive corporate and societal goals.

Several international organizations have also contributed to the theoretical discourse on CSR:

The Commission of the European Communities (2001) framed CSR as a voluntary integration of social and environmental considerations into business operations and stakeholder interactions. The World Business Council for Sustainable Development (2003) emphasized the ongoing nature of CSR, defining it as a sustained commitment by businesses to behave ethically and contribute to economic development while improving the quality of life for their workforce, their families, and society at large.

United Nations Industrial Development Organization, (2018) offered a management-oriented definition, depicting CSR as an approach that integrates social and environmental considerations into business operations and stakeholder interactions. Consequently, The European Commission (2011) provided a clear and concise explanation, stating that CSR is the responsibility of businesses for their impacts on community.

In conclusion, Corporate Social Responsibility has evolved into a multifaceted management concept that integrates economic, legal, ethical, and discretionary dimensions into business operations and stakeholder interactions. This theoretical progression reflects an increasing recognition of businesses' role in addressing social and environmental issues, going beyond mere profit-making to enhance the quality of life for employees, their families, and the broader community. The evolution of CSR definitions underscores the growing societal expectations for businesses to contribute positively to sustainable development and collective well-being.

2. The Evolution of Corporate Social Responsibility (CSR) Areas

The concept of Corporate Social Responsibility (CSR) has undergone a significant transformation over the decades, reflecting the evolving expectations and values of society.

Primarily, in the 1950s, CSR was mostly focused on philanthropy, with corporations engaging in charitable giving and community investment (Bowen et al., 1953). Subsequently, the 1960s witnessed the emergence of social and environmental movements that heightened awareness of issues such as civil rights, consumerism, and environmentalism (Davis, 1960). Thus, this period marked the inception of a more comprehensive understanding of CSR beyond mere charity.

In the 1970s, environmental responsibility became a main focus as concerns about pollution and resource depletion intensified, leading to the establishment of environmental regulations(Friedman, 1970). Following this, the 1980s introduced stakeholder theory, which expanded the scope of CSR to encompass various stakeholders such as employees, customers, suppliers, and the community, thereby emphasizing that businesses have responsibilities beyond profit maximization (Freeman, 1984).

Moreover, the 1990s introduced the concept of sustainability and the triple bottom line, which combines social, environmental, and economic performance into corporate strategy (Elkington, 1997). On top of that, this decade highlighted the importance of sustainable development and the necessity for businesses to balance their operations with environmental impact and social equity.

Eventually, the early 2000s witnessed a surge in attention to corporate governance and ethical conduct, driven by numerous corporate scandals. Therefore, companies began to prioritize transparency, accountability, and ethical behavior (Carroll, 2009).

In the current decade, the focus on Environmental, Social, and Governance (ESG) factors has become increasingly pronounced. Consequently, businesses are integrating ESG criteria into their strategies and investment decisions, with particular attention to climate action, diversity, equity, and inclusion (DEI) (Eccles et al., 2014).

In conclusion, this evolution reflects a more holistic and strategic approach to CSR, recognizing its critical role in sustainable business practices and long-term value creation.

3. Corporate Social Responsibility in the Health Sector

Corporate Social Responsibility (CSR) in the health sector has evolved significantly over time, reflecting broader changes in societal expectations and business practices. Primarily, CSR in healthcare was often limited to philanthropic activities, such as donations to medical research or community health initiatives (Carroll, 1999). Nevertheless, as the concept of CSR matured, healthcare organizations began to adopt more comprehensive approaches.

In the late 20th and early 21st centuries, there was an increasing recognition of the distinctive social obligations of healthcare organizations and pharmaceutical firms, emerging from their profound influence on public health outcomes (Lee & Kohler, 2010). This realization motivated a broadening of CSR initiatives within the health sector. Companies began to implement more comprehensive programs aimed at enhancing healthcare accessibility in marginalized populations and tackling widespread health issues on a global level. Lee & Kohler (2010) observe that this shift signifies an increasing recognition of the health industry's ability to drive positive change beyond its primary business activities, especially in tackling health disparities and enhancing global health outcomes. This evolution in Corporate Social Responsibility (CSR) practices marked a transition towards a more proactive stance on social responsibility within the healthcare sector, progressing from conventional philanthropic efforts to more strategic and impactful interventions.

The rise of stakeholder theory in management literature also influenced CSR in the health sector. Freeman's (1984)work on stakeholder management emphasized the importance of considering the interests of all groups affected by a company's operations, not just shareholders. In healthcare, this translated to a broader consideration of patients, employees, local communities, and the environment in decision-making processes.

The growing inequality in global health outcomes has placed pharmaceutical companies under increasing pressure regarding their pricing strategies and accessibility of medicines in low-income countries (Leisinger, 2009). As a reaction, many firms implemented CSR programs, including differential pricing schemes and medication donation initiatives. However, these attempts to address health inequities were frequently regarded inadequate by critics, stressing the intricate dilemma faced by the pharmaceutical industry in reconciling commercial interests with ethical obligations to improve global health. Leisinger (2009) also argues that this tension reflects a broader challenge within the sector: How to maintain profitability and innovation while simultaneously meeting societal expectations for accessible healthcare in resource-limited settings is an ongoing debate. This issue emphasizes the necessity for more comprehensive and sustainable approaches to corporate social responsibility (CSR) in the pharmaceutical industry, aimed at effectively bridging the gap between business goals and global health needs.

Recently, there has been a shift towards more strategic approaches to CSR in healthcare. Porter's and Kramer's (2006) concept of "Creating Shared Value" has impacted many organizations to seek ways to integrate their CSR activities with their core business strategies. This has resulted in initiatives that not only address social needs but also contribute to long-term business sustainability.

The COVID-19 pandemic has further emphasized the critical role of CSR in the health sector. Across various regions, CSR efforts have focused on enhancing public health, addressing social inequalities, and promoting environmental sustainability. In Taiwan, CSR initiatives have targeted health disparities and leveraged technology for improved outcomes (Chu & Chu, 2024). In Greece, the pandemic spurred a significant increase in CSR activities within the pharmaceutical and biomedical sectors (Liopa et al., 2022). Similarly, in India, CSR efforts have focused on hospitals services, which were crucial during the pandemic (Reddy & Mariyappan, 2023). In Algeria, CSR initiatives led by startups have introduced digital solutions to offer essential services and price reductions, promoting electronic payments to support quarantine measures and strengthen efforts against the pandemic. (Boulesnam et al., 2021), while in Brazil, the focus has been on health equity and environmental sustainability (Cé et al., 2024). These initiatives highlight CSR's vital role in addressing both immediate and long-term health challenges, contributing to societal well-being and sustainable development.

Looking forward, CSR in the health sector is expected to continue evolving, with increased emphasis on addressing global health challenges, promoting health equity, and contributing to sustainable development goals (Droppert & Bennett, 2015). The growing expectation for healthcare companies to demonstrate their commitment to public health beyond their core operations will likely shape future CSR strategies (Crane & Matten, 2021).

In conclusion, Corporate Social Responsibility in the health sector has developed from simple philanthropy to strategic initiatives integrated with core business operations. The COVID-19 pandemic has further highlighted the critical role of healthcare organizations in the community. Looking ahead, CSR in healthcare is anticipated to increasingly concentrate on tackling global health challenges, promoting health equity, and supporting sustainable development goals.

CSR Activities and Health Contribution in Canon and Sony: Leaders 2023 RepTrak

In this section, the initial phase involves identifying RepTrak methodology, followed analyzing the most significant corporate social responsibility (CSR) activities in both companies using the 2023 sustainability reports. This requires identifying key activities within each of the four CSR areas. In the second phase, quantitative indicators disclosed by Canon and Sony during 2023 will be examined. Finally, content analysis methodology will be employed to evaluate the qualitative disclosure of health-related activities, based on the 2023 sustainability reports of both companies.

1. Reptrak Platform and Methodology

RepTrak is a platform and a company that specializes in measuring and analyzing corporate reputations. The company publishes an annual Global RepTrak 100 report, which ranks the world's 100 most reputable companies based on a comprehensive analysis of public sentiment and corporate reputation data.

The ranking process involves collecting and analyzing data from more than 243,000 survey responses across 14 major economies. These surveys assess various dimensions of corporate reputation, including Products & Services, Innovation, Workplace, Governance, Citizenship, Leadership, and Performance. The company reputation is scored on a scale, and the aggregate scores determine their ranking (RepTrak, 2023).

RepTrak uses a combination of advanced reputation monitoring software and expert analysis to compile the rankings. This process includes evaluating how stakeholders perceive companies' conduct, citizenship efforts, corporate social responsibility initiatives, willingness to invest, and brand communications. The goal is to provide actionable insights that help companies enhance their reputation, align with stakeholder expectations, and improve their overall business performance (RepTrak, 2023).

The RepTrak methodology calculates a reputation score known as the RepTrak Pulse score, which typically ranges from 0 to 100. This score is derived from survey data that captures public perceptions of a company across various reputation dimensions, such as products and services, innovation, workplace, governance, citizenship, leadership, and financial performance. A higher RepTrak Pulse score indicates a stronger overall reputation, with scores above 80 considered excellent, 70-79 strong, 60-69 average, and below 60 weak. These scores are used to rank companies in the annual RepTrak 100 list, identifying the most reputable companies globally. The methodology provides companies with detailed insights into their reputation, helping them understand their strengths and identify areas for improvement, thus enabling them to manage and enhance their corporate reputation effectively.

Table 1. Reptrak top 10 in 2023

Rank	Company	Score
01	The Lego Group	78.9
02	The Bosch Group	78.1
03	Rolls-Royce Aerospace	77.3
04	Harley-Davidson	76.8
05	Canon	76.5
06	Rolex SA	76.3
07	Miele	75.9
08	Sony	75.5
09	Nintendo	75.3
10	Mercedes-Benz	75.0

Source: 2023 Global RepTrak 100 Most Reputable Companies.

Table 01 shows the top 10 leaders in 2023, The LEGO Group was ranked as the most reputable company in the world according to the Global RepTrak 100 report, with a score of 78.9. Following LEGO, the Bosch Group secured the second position with a score of 78.1, while Rolls-Royce Aerospace came in third with a score of 77.3. Harley-Davidson ranked fourth with a score of 76.8, and Canon rounded out the top five with a score of 76.5. Other companies in the top ten included Rolex SA in sixth place with a score of 76.3, Miele in seventh with 75.9, Sony in eighth with 75.5, Nintendo in ninth with 75.3, and Mercedes-Benz in tenth place with a score of 75.0. These scores highlight the reputation of these companies based on various drivers such as Products & Services, Innovation, Governance, and Citizenship.

Canon and Sony, leaders of electronics and imaging industries, are ideal case in this study due to their substantial contributions and innovative CSR practices, mainly in the health sector. Canon excels with its advanced medical imaging technologies like X-ray systems and MRI machines, enhancing diagnostic accuracy and patient care. Their "Kyosei" philosophy underscores a commitment to global health initiatives and sustainable practices. Sony, with its cutting-edge developments in telemedicine, wearable health devices, and medical imaging, drives healthcare innovation while prioritizing sustainability and global health partnerships. Both companies exemplify how technology leaders can positively impact healthcare through dedicated CSR efforts.

2. CSR KEY ACTIVITIES IN CANON AND SONY

The focus will be on the four fundamental areas of social responsibility, which are primarily concerned with the community, the environment, employees, and customers.

2.1 Consumers

Customers, or product interest, are considered one of the most important areas of social responsibility that can be of concern to institutions of various types. It encompasses numerous aspects and activities, such as attention to product quality, product safety, and after-sales services.

Table 2. Canon and Sony consumers key activities

CSR Key Activities	Consumers Key Activities
Canon	• Quality department • Iso 9001 • Education of quality awareness • Production quality • Production safety • Safety department • Security measures • Product reliability • After sales supports • Providing information about the product
Sony	• Designing recyclability and reparability to the product • Edge AI solutions to help solve problems • Responsible ai (research and development of the product) • Product safety • Product quality • Product reliability • Customer services • Consumer satisfaction • Quality department • After sales • Security measures • Training for customer staff • Testing products before purchase

Source: Canon and Sony Sustainability Report 2023.

2.2 Employees

Concern for employees is considered one of the oldest areas of corporate social responsibility focus. Major institutions prioritize clear strategies to improve workers' lives, ensure their safety, provide training, and achieve fairness in their selection processes.

Table 3. Canon and Sony employees key activities

CSR Key Activities	Employees Key Activities
Canon	• Respecting human rights • Hiring and treatment of human resources • Diversity and inclusion • Occupational safety and health management • Human resource development and personal growth • Employees training and learning • Diversity and inclusion
Sony	• Responsible AI • Promoting greater opportunities for individuals with disabilities • Safe work place • Learning and training • Well-being • Health care of employee's children • Occupational safety • Reduce workers accident • Measuring new risks • Mental health • Woman health • Helping employees stop smoking

Source: Canon and Sony Sustainability Report 2023.

2.3 Community

Socially responsible institutions are those that prioritize the communities in which they operate. Based on this principle, many institutions undertake various community activities such as improving education, health, culture, and the arts.

Table 4. Canon and Sony community key activities

CSR Key Activities	Community Key Activities
Canon	• support the arts • support culture • support sports • providing humanitarian aid and disaster relief • enrich local communities • taking care of the global environment • donation • education
Sony	• Responsible AI • Education • Sport • Local community donations • Health welfare • Arts • Disasters

Source: Canon and Sony Sustainability Report 2023.

2.4 Environment

In recent decades, institutions have become far removed from social responsibility if they fail to address their environmental impacts. Socially responsible institutions are those that strive to optimize the use of natural resources, increase the use of renewable energies, and improve their products to be more environmentally friendly.

Table 5. Canon and Sony environment key activities

CSR Key Activities	Environment Key Activities
Canon	• Designing energy-efficient products • Improving energy efficiency at operational sites • Reducing CO2 emissions from logistics • Expanding use of renewable energy • Designing more compact, lighter weight products • Reducing waste through prevention, reuse and recycling • Remanufacturing products • Recycling consumables • Using sustainable water resources • Chemical substances • Managing chemicals contained in products • Meeting international standards • Managing chemical substances in production processes • Reducing discharge into air, water, and soil • Green supply chain • Biodiversity Policy • Basic Policy on the Procurement of Timber Products • Canon Bird Branch Project • Preservation of natural habitats and biodiversity, forest conservation • Tree-planting initiatives
Sony	• Climate change • Resources • Chemical substances • Biodiversity • Reducing Waste • Recycling • Renewable energy use • Iso 140001 • Environmental audit • GHG emission • Development of environmental technologies • Environmentally beneficial products and services • Conserving resources • Reducing plastic packaging • Reducing paper • Environmental promotion • Efficient use of energy • Responsible AI

Source: Canon and Sony Sustainability Report 2023.

3. CANON AND SONY CSR INDICATORS DURING 2023

Canon and Sony will focus on the most important quantitative indicators related to corporate social responsibility activities. These indicators primarily include environmental aspects, labor-related metrics, and community contributions.

3.1 Environmental Indicators

Based on the sustainability reports of the two studied companies, common environmental indicators were selected, which included CO2 emissions, water usage, and the extent of renewable energy utilization.

- **Co2 Emission**

Measuring CO2 emissions is crucial for assessing a company's environmental impact and climate change contributions. This metric helps identify areas for reduction and demonstrates commitment to sustainability goals.

Table 6. Total Co2 emission

	2018	2019	2020	2021	2022
Canon (t. co2)	1090991	1043238	945981	1060382	1021327
Sony (t. co2)	10600000	12010000	13860000	11960000	11800000

Source: Canon and Sony Sustainability Reports 2018-2023

Figure 1. Canon vs. Sony CO2 emissions (2018-2022) (Canon and Sony Sustainability Reports 2018-2023)

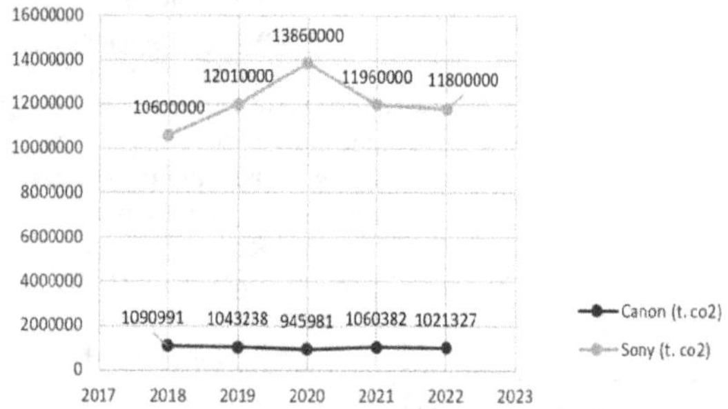

Canon has demonstrated a consistent effort to reduce CO2 emissions over the years. Starting from 1,090,991 tons in 2018, the company managed to bring it down to 1,021,327 tons by 2022. This reduction is indicative of Canon's commitment to improving its environmental impact.

Sony's CO2 emissions have shown significant fluctuations, peaking at 13,860,000 tons in 2020 before decreasing to 11,800,000 tons in 2022. Despite the reduction in the last two years, Sony's emissions remain significantly higher compared to Canon, reflecting the larger scale of its operations.

While both companies are making efforts to reduce CO2 emissions, Canon's emissions are substantially lower than Sony's. This difference highlights Canon's more effective strategies in controlling emissions relative to the size of its operations compared to Sony.

- **Water Use**

Tracking water consumption reflects a company's resource efficiency and conservation efforts. It's especially important in water-stressed regions and industries with high water dependency.

Table 7. Canon vs. Sony water use (2018-2022)

	2018	2019	2020	2021	2022
Canon (m^3)	9725000	9212000	8426000	8578000	8397000
Sony (m^3)	13600000	15300000	18700000	19550000	19970000

Source: Canon and Sony Sustainability Reports 2018-2023

Figure 2. Canon vs. Sony water usage (2018-2022) (Canon and Sony Sustainability Reports 2018-2023)

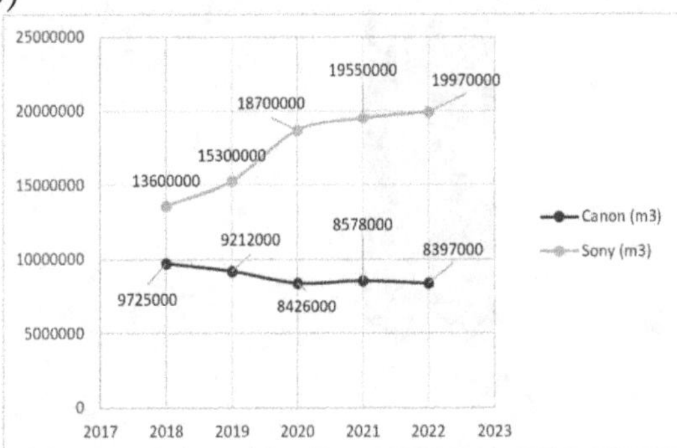

Canon's water usage has shown a decreasing trend from 9,725,000 m^3 in 2018 to 8,397,000 m^3 in 2022. This decline demonstrates Canon's efficient water management practices and its commitment to reducing water consumption.

Sony's water usage has been on the rise, increasing from 13,600,000 m^3 in 2018 to 19,970,000 m^3 in 2022. This upward trend indicates Sony's growing operational needs and highlights the challenges it faces in managing water resources efficiently.

Comparatively, Sony's water usage is significantly higher than Canon's, reflecting the larger scale of its operations. Canon's steady reduction in water use contrasts with Sony's increasing consumption, suggesting different approaches and challenges in water resource management.

- **Renewable Energies**

Solar power generation showcases a company's investment in clean energy and reduced reliance on fossil fuels. It indicates long-term commitment to sustainability and potentially lower energy costs.

Table 8. Canon vs. Sony renewable energy generation (2023)

	Total solar power
Sony	758.953 MW
Canon	94.793MW

Source: Canon and Sony Sustainability Reports 2023

Figure 3. Renewable energy generation by Canon and Sony (Total Solar Power) (Canon and Sony Sustainability Reports 2023)

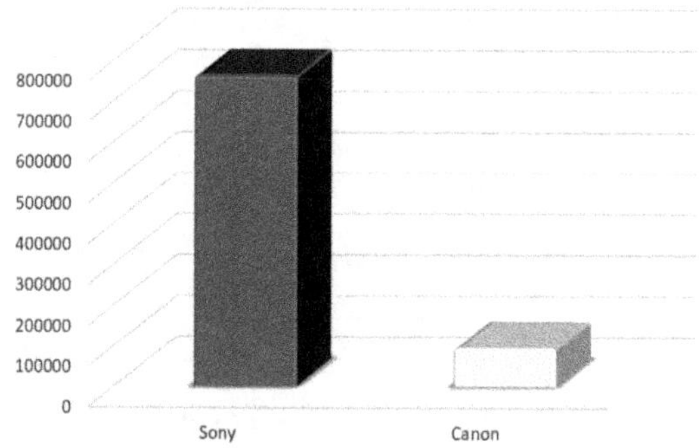

Canon's utilization of renewable energy is represented by a total solar power generation of 94.793 MW. This reflects the company's efforts to incorporate sustainable energy sources into its operations.

Sony's renewable energy usage is much higher, with a total solar power generation of 758.953 MW. This substantial figure highlights Sony's major investment in renewable energy infrastructure.

Sony's renewable energy generation is considerably higher than Canon's, indicating a stronger emphasis on renewable energy adoption. This comparison underscores the scale and intensity of Sony's commitment to sustainable energy compared to Canon.

3.2 Employees Indicators

Regarding employee-related indicators, the following were selected: the annual number of worker injuries, the number and percentage of employees resigning during the year, the proportion of female employees in both companies, as well as the percentage of employees with disabilities out of the total workforce. All these statistics covered the period from 2018 to 2022.

- **Injuries**

Monitoring worker injuries is essential for ensuring employee safety and well-being. It reflects the effectiveness of safety protocols and highlights the company's prioritization of worker health.

Table 9. Canon vs. Sony workers injuries (2018- 2022)

	2018	2019	2020	2021	2022
Canon (number)	130	114	112	96	78
Sony (number)	105	74	71	75	57

Source: Canon and Sony Sustainability Reports 2018-2023

Figure 4. Canon vs. Sony worker injuries (2018-2022) (Canon and Sony Sustainability Reports 2018-2023)

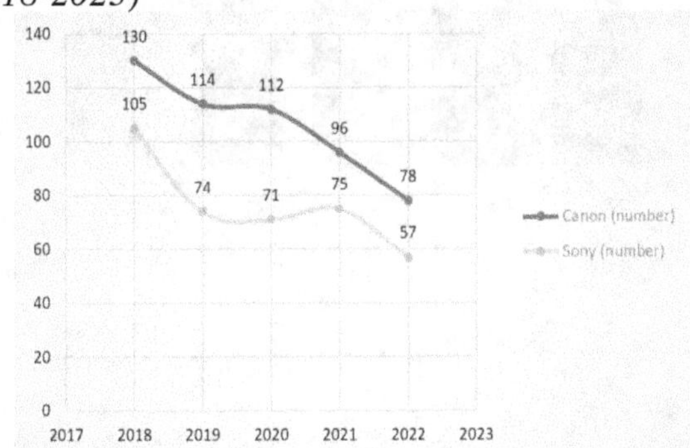

Canon has shown a reduction in the number of worker injuries from 130 in 2018 to 78 in 2022. This improvement demonstrates Canon's effective health and safety measures and its commitment to protecting employees.

Sony has also reduced worker injuries from 105 in 2018 to 57 in 2022. This indicates Sony's efforts to enhance workplace safety and reduce the risk of accidents.

Both companies have successfully reduced the number of worker injuries over the years. However, Canon started with a higher number of injuries compared to Sony, but both have shown significant improvements, reflecting their commitment to employee safety.

- **Turnover**

High turnover can indicate workplace issues and dissatisfaction, while low rates suggest employee loyalty and satisfaction. This metric reflects the company's ability to retain talent and maintain a positive work environment.

Table 10. Number and rate of employee's turnover (2018-2022)

	2018	2019	2020	2021	2022
Canon (number)	409	491	462	448	474
Sony (%)	11%	9.55%	5.3%	6.4%	7.37%

Source: Canon and Sony Sustainability Reports 2018-2023

Figure 5. Employees turnover rates for Canon (2018-2022) (Canon Sustainability Reports 2018-2023)

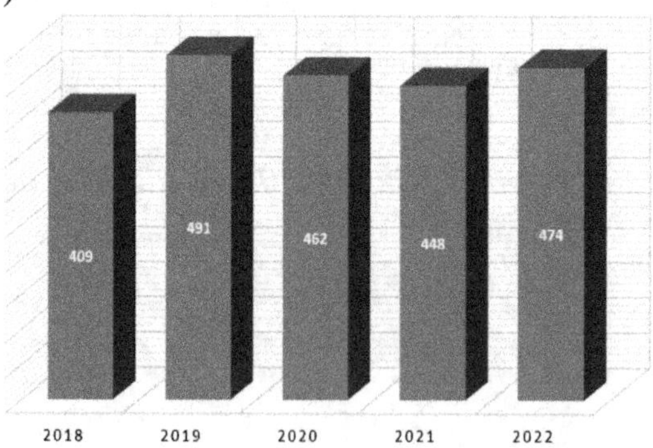

Figure 6. Employees turnover rates for Sony (2018-2022) (Sony Sustainability Reports 2018-2023)

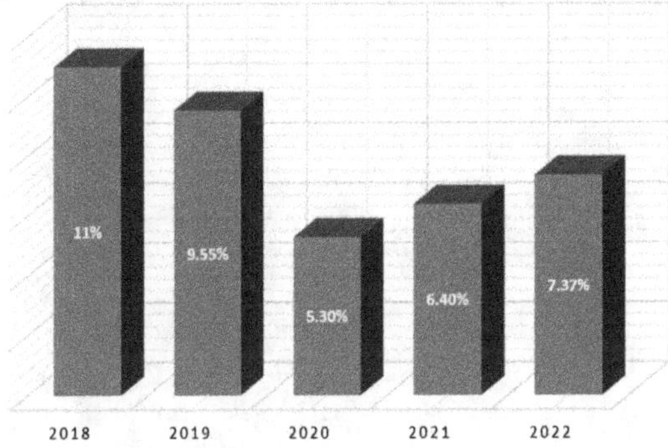

Canon's employee turnover numbers have fluctuated slightly, with a peak of 491 in 2019 and 474 in 2022. This variation indicates a relatively stable but slightly increasing trend in employee turnover.

Sony's employee turnover rate has varied, with a notable decrease to 5.3% in 2020 but increasing to 7.37% in 2022. This fluctuation highlights the challenges Sony faces in retaining employees.

Canon's employee turnover numbers show less variation compared to Sony's turnover rate. While Canon has maintained relatively stable turnover numbers, Sony's rates have fluctuated more significantly, indicating different dynamics in employee retention strategies.

- **Women Workforce**

This metric demonstrates a company's commitment to gender diversity and equal opportunities. It can highlight efforts to create an inclusive workplace and tap into diverse talent pools.

Table 11. Rate of women workforce

	2018	2019	2020	2021	2022
Canon (%)	**15.8**	**16.1**	**16.5**	**16.6**	**16.8**
Sony (%)	**32.94**	**34.57**	**38.98**	**38.72**	**37.82**

Source: Canon and Sony Sustainability Reports 2018-2023

Figure 7. Rate of women workforce at Canon and Sony (2018-2022) (Canon and Sony Sustainability Reports 2018-2023)

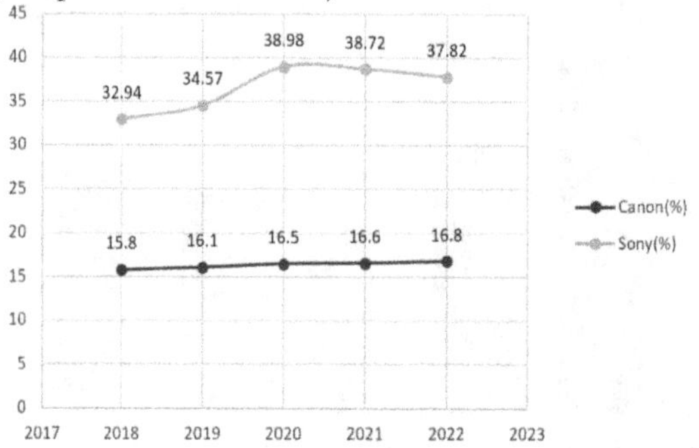

The percentage of women in Canon's workforce has gradually increased from 15.8% in 2018 to 16.8% in 2022. This steady increase reflects Canon's efforts to promote gender diversity.

Sony has a higher and more fluctuating percentage of women in its workforce, peaking at 38.98% in 2020 and slightly decreasing to 37.82% in 2022. This shows Sony's strong emphasis on gender diversity.

Sony consistently has a higher percentage of women in its workforce compared to Canon. While both companies are promoting gender diversity, Sony's figures indicate a more substantial presence of women in its workforce.

- **Disabilities**

Tracking this rate shows dedication to inclusive hiring practices and workplace accessibility. It reflects a company's efforts to provide equal opportunities for all individuals, regardless of ability.

Table 12. Canon vs. Sony rate of disabilities (2018-2022)

	2018	2019	2020	2021	2022
Canon (%)	2.22	2.30	2.34	2.39	2.44
Sony (%)	2.57	2.61	2.65	2.68	2.61

Source: Canon and Sony Sustainability Reports 2018-2023

Figure 8. Rate of employees with disabilities at Canon and Sony (2018-2022) (Canon and Sony Sustainability Reports 2018-2023)

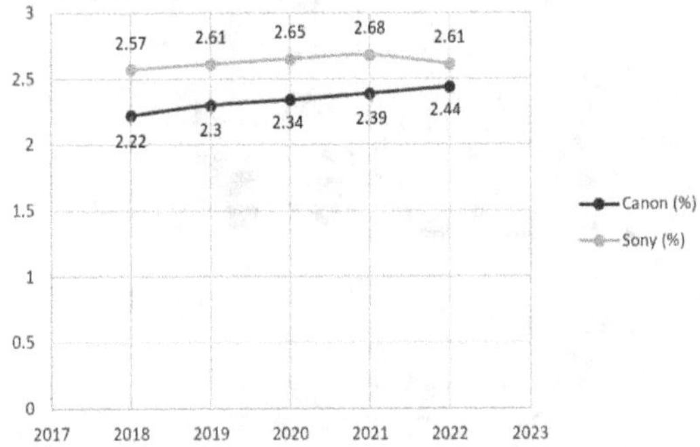

Canon's percentage of employees with disabilities has slightly increased from 2.22% in 2018 to 2.44% in 2022, indicating a commitment to inclusivity and diversity.

Sony also shows an increase in the rate of employees with disabilities, from 2.57% in 2018 to 2.61% in 2022, demonstrating its efforts to support and include employees with disabilities.

Both companies show a commitment to employing people with disabilities. Sony maintains a slightly higher percentage compared to Canon, reflecting a marginally greater emphasis on inclusivity.

3.3 Community Indicators

Within the limits of the statistics available in the sustainability reports of both companies, community contributions were analyzed for the years 2018 to 2022.

- **Community Engagement**

This metric quantifies a company's financial investment in local communities. It demonstrates commitment to social responsibility and positive impact beyond immediate business operations.

Table 13. Canon vs. Sony community engagement (2018-2022)

	2018	2019	2020	2021	2022
Canon (billion Yen)	1.14	/	/	1.7	1.8
Sony (billion Yen)	2.5	2.6	2	3.5	5.1

Source: Canon and Sony Sustainability Reports 2018-2023

Figure 9. Community engagement spending by Canon and Sony (2018-2022) (Canon and Sony Sustainability Reports 2018-2023)

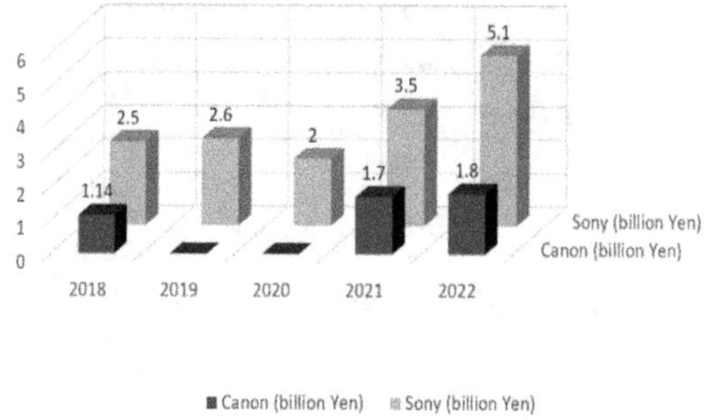

Canon's community engagement spending fluctuated, with notable contributions in 2021 (1.7 billion Yen) and 2022 (1.8 billion Yen). This indicates Canon's targeted approach to community investments.

Sony's community engagement spending increased significantly, reaching 5.1 billion Yen in 2022. This upward trend shows Sony's growing commitment to community development.

Sony's community engagement spending is consistently higher than Canon's, reflecting a more extensive investment in community initiatives. This comparison highlights Sony's broader impact on community support and development.

- **Health Engagement**

Measuring health-related contributions shows a company's investment in employee and community well-being. It reflects a holistic approach to CSR that extends beyond societal concerns.

Regarding the analysis of both companies' contributions in the health sector, and according to the information available in the sustainability reports of the two companies, financial contributions to the health aspect were obtained for Sony company only.

Table 14. Sony health engagement (2018-2022)

	2018	2019	2020	2021	2022
Sony (Million Yen)	175	234	240	560	663

Source: Sony Sustainability Reports 2018-2023

Figure 10. Health financial contributions by Sony (2018-2022) (Sony Sustainability Reports 2018-2023)

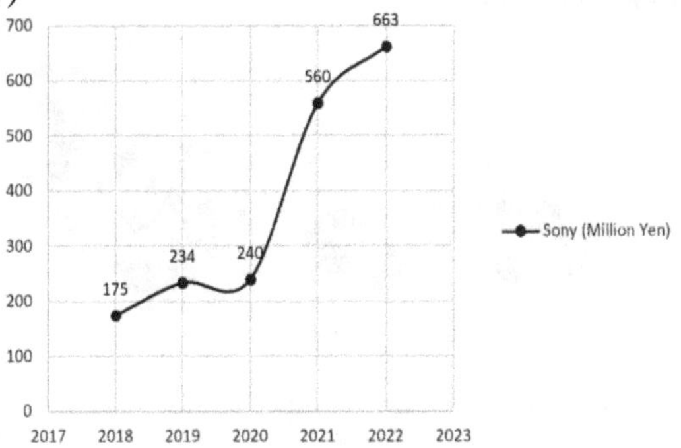

Sony's financial contributions to health-related activities increased from 175 million Yen in 2018 to 663 million Yen in 2022. This significant rise underscores Sony's growing focus on health initiatives.

Data for Canon's health engagement was not available, making a direct comparison difficult. However, the available information for Sony highlights its substantial and increasing investment in health-related activities.

4. CANON AND SONY HEALTH QUALITATIVE DISCLOSURE IN 2023

In order to understand the importance of health-related activities in both companies under study, content analysis method was used, relying on the sentence unit. The focus on health was divided into two categories: employee health and general health.

Table 15. Canon vs. Sony health qualitative disclosure (2023)

	Health of employees	Health in General	Total
Canon (number of sentences)	60	53	113
Sony (number of sentences)	71	59	130

Source: Canon and Sony Sustainability Reports 2023

Figure 11. Health qualitative disclosures by Canon and Sony (2023) (Canon and Sony Sustainability Reports 2023)

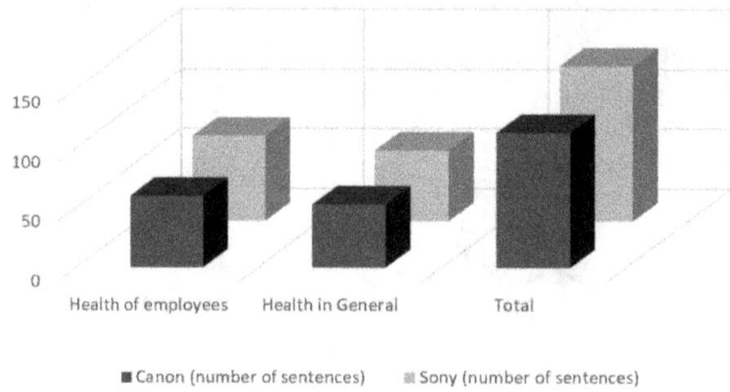

Canon's focus on health-related activities includes 60 mentions of employee health and 53 mentions of general health, totaling 113 mentions. This indicates a balanced approach to health-related CSR activities.

Sony recorded 71 mentions of employee health and 59 mentions of general health, totaling 130 mentions. This suggests a slightly greater emphasis on health-related CSR activities compared to Canon.

Both companies show a strong focus on health-related CSR activities. Sony's higher number of mentions indicates a marginally greater emphasis on these activities compared to Canon.

CONCLUSION

This chapter has provided a comprehensive examination of the Corporate Social Responsibility (CSR) activities of Canon and Sony, with a particular focus on their contributions to the healthcare sector and the impact of these activities on their corporate reputation as ranked by the RepTrak platform. Through a mixed-methods approach that included both quantitative and qualitative analyses, several key insights have been uncovered.

Canon and Sony, as leaders in the electronics and imaging industries, have demonstrated substantial commitment to CSR, particularly in the areas of community support, environmental sustainability, employee welfare, and consumer satisfaction. Their advanced medical imaging technologies, telemedicine innovations, and wearable health devices underscore their contributions to healthcare, enhancing diagnostic accuracy, patient care, and overall health outcomes.

The quantitative analysis revealed significant efforts by both companies to reduce CO2 emissions, manage water usage efficiently, and invest in renewable energy sources. Canon's consistent reduction in CO2 emissions and Sony's substantial investment in solar power generation highlight their dedication to environmental sustainability. Additionally, both companies have shown improvements in worker safety, gender diversity, and inclusivity, with increasing percentages of women and employees with disabilities in their workforce.

The qualitative analysis of their sustainability reports further emphasized their commitment to health-related CSR activities. Both companies have prioritized health initiatives, with a balanced approach towards employee health and general health contributions. Sony's substantial financial contributions to health-related activities and Canon's emphasis on health engagement activities reflect their strategic integration of CSR into their core business operations.

The linkage between CSR practices and corporate reputation is evident in the high rankings of Canon and Sony in the RepTrak 100 report. Their commitment to CSR not only enhances their reputation but also contributes to long-term business sustainability by fostering trust and loyalty among stakeholders, attracting and retaining talent, and aligning with societal expectations for ethical and responsible business conduct.

In sum, the evolution of CSR in the healthcare sector, as exemplified by Canon and Sony, underscores the significant role of businesses in addressing social and environmental problems. Their proactive and strategic approaches to CSR highlight the importance of integrating ethical considerations into business practices to achieve sustainable development and collective well-being. As societal expectations continue to evolve, the focus on CSR, particularly in sensitive sectors like healthcare, is likely to intensify, with increasing emphasis on addressing global health challenges, promoting health equity, and supporting sustainable development goals. This chapter confirms the significance of CSR in shaping corporate reputation and underscores the need for continuous innovation and commitment to ethical practices in achieving long-term business success and societal impact.

REFERENCES

Boulesnam, M., Seguiri, S., & Kebtan, C. (2021). The role of startups in the age of COVID-19 pandemic: Evidence from the world. *Administrative and Financial Sciences Review*, 5(2), 494–505. DOI: 10.37644/1939-005-002-026

Bowen, H. R. (1953). *Social responsibilities of the businessman*. Harper & Row.

Carroll, A. B. (1991). The pyramid of corporate social responsibility: Toward the moral management of organizational stakeholders. *Business Horizons*, 34(4), 39–48. DOI: 10.1016/0007-6813(91)90005-G

Carroll, A. B. (1999). Corporate social responsibility: Evolution of a definitional construct. *Business & Society*, 38(3), 268–295. DOI: 10.1177/000765039903800303

Carroll, A. B. (2009). A history of corporate social responsibility: Concepts and practices. In Crane, A., Matten, D., McWilliams, A., Moon, J., & Siegel, D. S. (Eds.), *The Oxford handbook of corporate social responsibility* (pp. 19–46). Oxford University Press. DOI: 10.1093/oxfordhb/9780199211593.003.0002

Cé, F. R., da Silva, B. G., de Britto, R. E. D., & Fernandes, A. S. (2024). Corporate social responsibility communication during the COVID-19 pandemic: Comparison between Brazilian and British companies. *Revista Contemporânea*, 4(5), e4079. DOI: 10.56083/RCV4N5-047

Chu, W., & Chu, N.-F. (2024). Corporate social responsibility and social needs in health care sectors—A critical analysis of social innovation in the health sector in Taiwan. *Health Care*, 12(1543), 1543. Advance online publication. DOI: 10.3390/healthcare12151543 PMID: 39120246

Commission of the European Communities. (2001). Green paper: Promoting a European framework for corporate social responsibility.

Crane, A., & Matten, D. (2021). COVID-19 and the future of CSR research. *Journal of Management Studies*, 58(1), 280–284. DOI: 10.1111/joms.12642

Davis, K. (1960). Can business afford to ignore social responsibilities? *California Management Review*, 2(3), 70–76. DOI: 10.2307/41166246

Droppert, H., & Bennett, S. (2015). Corporate social responsibility in global health: An exploratory study of multinational pharmaceutical firms. *Globalization and Health*, 11(1), 1–8. DOI: 10.1186/s12992-015-0100-5 PMID: 25886175

Eccles, R. G., Ioannou, I., & Serafeim, G. (2014). The impact of corporate sustainability on organizational processes and performance. *Management Science*, 60(11), 2835–2857. DOI: 10.1287/mnsc.2014.1984

Elkington, J. (1997). *Cannibals with forks: The triple bottom line of 21st century business*. Capstone.

European Commission. (2011). A renewed EU strategy 2011-14 for corporate social responsibility.

Fatima, T., & Elbanna, S. (2022). Corporate social responsibility (CSR) implementation: A review and a research agenda towards an integrative framework. *Journal of Business Ethics*, •••, 1–17. DOI: 10.1007/s10551-022-05000-2 PMID: 35125567

Freeman, R. E. (1984). *Strategic management: A stakeholder approach*. Pitman.

Friedman, M. (1970, September 13). The social responsibility of business is to increase its profits. The New York Times Magazine, 32-33.

Goyal, S., & Routroy, S. (2023). Analyzing environmental sustainability enablers for an Indian steel manufacturing supply chain. Journal of Engineering. *Design and Technology*, 21(1), 1–22. DOI: 10.1108/JEDT-03-2021-0118

Hopkins, M. (2003). *The planetary bargain: Corporate social responsibility matters*. Tailor and Francis.

Jones, T. M. (1980). Corporate social responsibility revisited, redefined. *California Management Review*, 22(3), 59–67. DOI: 10.2307/41164877

Lee, K., & Kohler, J. (2010). Benchmarking and transparency: Incentives for the pharmaceutical industry's corporate social responsibility. *Journal of Business Ethics*, 95(4), 641–658. DOI: 10.1007/s10551-010-0444-y

Leisinger, K. M. (2008). Corporate responsibilities for access to medicines. *Journal of Business Ethics*, 85(1), 3–23. PMID: 23535994

Liopa, M., Latsou, D., & Geitona, M. (2022). Corporate social responsibility in health technology industry prior and during the COVID-19 pandemic in Greece. *Health (Irvine, Calif.)*, 14(11), 1161–1172. DOI: 10.4236/health.2022.1411082

Porter, M. E., & Kramer, M. R. (2006). Strategy and society: The link between competitive advantage and corporate social responsibility. *Harvard Business Review*, 84(12), 78–92. PMID: 17183795

Reddy, R. R., & Mariyappan, R. (2023). The impact of CSR in hospitals: Study of beneficiaries. *Journal of Informatics Education and Research*, 3, 859–865.

RepTrak. (2023). 2023 global RepTrak 100 most reputable companies. https://ri.reptrak.com/2023-global-reptrak

Sheehy, B. (2014). Defining CSR: Problems and solutions. *Journal of Business Ethics*, 131(3), 625–648. DOI: 10.1007/s10551-014-2281-x

United Nations Industrial Development Organization. (2010). What is CSR?

Wood, D. J. (1991). Corporate social performance revisited. *Academy of Management Review*, 16(4), 691–718. DOI: 10.2307/258977

World Business Council for Sustainable Development. (2003). Corporate social responsibility: The WBCSD's journey.

KEY TERMS AND DEFINITIONS

Corporate Reputation: Is the integrated perception of a company's trust, credibility, and respect held by its customers, employees, investors, and the public.

Corporate Social Responsibility: Corporate Social Responsibility has developed into a multiple aspects management concept that integrates economic, legal, ethical, and discretionary dimensions into business operations and stakeholder interactions. It reflects an increasing recognition of businesses' role in addressing social and environmental issues, going beyond mere profit-making to enhance the quality of life for employees, their families, and the broader community.

Corporate Social Responsibility Areas: Include different dimensions such as customers, environment, community, and employees. Recently, these areas have been increasingly focusing on creating value and sustainability.

Health Engagement: All the activities undertaken companies within the framework of its social responsibility and directly related to the health sector, whether they concern the health of the workers or public health.

Health Sector: Includes all services and organizations dedicated to maintaining and improving health, including hospitals, clinics, pharmaceuticals, public health initiatives, and health insurance.

RepTrak: Is a reputation platform and measurement tool used by companies to assess and analyze their corporate reputation. It provides insights into how stakeholders perceive a company across various dimensions such as trust, respect, innovation, corporate social responsibility commitment.

Sustainability Reporting: Is an annual accounting practice of companies disclosing qualitatively and quantitatively their environmental, social, and governance (ESG) performance and impact.

Chapter 6
Fusion of Social Responsibility and Digital Health:
An Indian Scenario

Nalini R.
SASTRA University (Deemed), India

Alamelu R.
Srinivasa Ramanujan Centre, SASTRA University (Deemed), India

Dinesh S.
http://orcid.org/0000-0003-1751-7973
Sri Ramachandra Institute of Higher Education and Research, India

ABSTRACT

In the present era, the digital revolution permeates every aspect of life, greatly bolstering the health and well-being of individuals, communities, and populations to an unprecedented extent. Recent technological advancements have transformed clinical practice, encompassed prevention, diagnosis, monitoring, and disease management, while also fostered unprecedented public interest and engagement in self-management and wellness. Digital health involves the use of information and communications technologies to enhance human health, healthcare services, and wellness for both individuals and population. This paper examines potential ways in which businesses could positively impact social well-being and health, as well as their perceptions of their role in promoting health. It also explores how CSR projects can utilize cutting-edge technologies such as mHealth and eHealth.

DOI: 10.4018/979-8-3693-5991-4.ch006

INTRODUCTION

The healthcare system in India operates on a three-tier structure, with sub-centres at the base. Over 68% of the rural population lacks access to adequate medical facilities. There is a significant disparity in healthcare services between urban and rural areas due to insufficient resources and infrastructure in rural regions. The rural populace relies heavily on government-funded medical facilities because of limited financial means.

According to the Planning Commission (2011), the three main challenges facing India's healthcare system are accessibility, availability, and affordability. The importance of healthcare in a sustainable economy has compelled developing countries, including India, to increase healthcare expenditure. Despite these efforts, modern healthcare remains inaccessible and unaffordable for a large segment of the Indian population due to socio-economic factors. The NITI Aayog Action Agenda 2017-2020 emphasized the need for data-driven and decentralized health planning to enhance population health effectively. Developing a healthcare system based on readily retrievable data is gaining importance for its long-term planning advantages at the national level. India is increasingly adopting new technologies to bridge this gap. Personal Health Information (PHR) is emerging as a crucial tool for documenting health information using cloud-based computer technology.

Cloud computing is a technology that delivers applications and services through pooled resources over the Internet, offering greater flexibility and reduced costs. Public-Private Partnerships (PPP), a collaboration between the public and private sectors to achieve common goals, have become a popular approach globally, particularly in the health sector. In India, many PPP schemes are successfully operating in healthcare across various states.

Under the provisions of Section 135 of the Companies Act 2013 and the requirements outlined in the Companies (CSR Policy) Rules, 2014, all corporate sectors are required to allocate 2% of their average profit, calculated based on the preceding three financial years, to CSR activities. This significant opportunity for substantial funding in the form of social investment by corporate houses, in alignment with the UNO's Millennium Development Goals (MDGs), provides a substantial advantage in terms of resources. Researchers have examined the rural health sector and analyzed various CSR activities undertaken by select Indian companies across different thematic areas.

The WHO released new recommendations 10 ways countries can use digital health technology—accessible via mobile phones, tablets, and computers—to enhance people's health and essential services.

"Harnessing digital technologies is crucial for achieving universal health coverage," says WHO Director-General Dr. Tedros Adhanom Ghebreyesus. "Ultimately, digital technologies are not goals in themselves; they are essential tools to promote health, ensure global safety, and support the vulnerable."

One digital intervention that has already shown positive effects in some areas is sending reminders to pregnant women for antenatal care appointments and for children to return for vaccinations. Other reviewed digital approaches include decision-support tools to assist health workers in delivering care and systems that enable individuals and health workers to communicate and consult on health issues from different locations.

"Digital health is not a silver bullet" says Bernardo Mariano, WHO's Chief Information Officer. "The WHO is focused on ensuring it is used as effectively as possible. This involves making sure it provides value to both health workers and individuals, considers infrastructural limitations, and is well-coordinated."

Digital Health in India During the Pandemic

The COVID-19 pandemic has had a significant global impact, compelling businesses, governments, and individuals to adopt digital technologies to stay connected and access essential services. The medical field is no exception. Throughout the pandemic, digital technologies have been employed to support public health interventions, facilitate medical diagnoses, and deliver healthcare services worldwide.

Governments are leveraging data visualization techniques, machine learning, advanced data analytics, and telecommunication technologies to track contacts, identify cases, conduct epidemiological surveillance, and forecast infection waves in specific regions. They are also using social media channels for public communication. The pandemic has underscored the critical importance of national IT infrastructure to generate accurate real-time estimates of disease incidence. This capability enables the effective allocation of limited medical resources and facilitates the tracking, tracing, and quarantining of affected individuals during public health emergencies.

In response to the COVID-19 pandemic, healthcare professionals are increasingly relying on clinical informatics. They are focusing on telemedicine initiatives, such as training clinicians on existing telehealth systems and developing new workflows for video triage of COVID-19 patients. Additionally, they are prioritizing reporting and analytics, which includes creating dashboards and electronic contact tracing.

Emerging digital health innovations for COVID-19 diagnosis harness AI and data from wearable IoT devices. These include using cough recordings for diagnosis with 98% sensitivity and 94% specificity, detecting pre-symptomatic cases through elevated heart rates recorded by smartwatches, and employing CRISPR-Cas13a with mobile phones for SARS-CoV-2 detection. AI applications, such as Babylon Health's symptom-checking app featuring a dedicated COVID-19 decision algorithm, and deep-learning neural networks analyzing chest X-rays to differentiate COVID-19 from other types of pneumonia, exemplify these advancements.

A digital health platform serves as a forum that provides health information services accessible via various channels, including the web. Several start-ups have developed applications within these platforms to connect users directly with healthcare providers. The rise of digital health platforms has significantly eased access to healthcare services, particularly during the Covid-19 pandemic, when many people opted for virtual consultations over visiting physical health facilities. Various stakeholders are involved in the operation of these platforms, including doctors, patients, start-ups, pharmaceutical companies, drug delivery service providers, electronic payment companies, and insurance companies, each playing a distinct role in delivering services.

A start-up is the creator and manager of a digital health platform. A start-up is defined as a developing business that leverages technology, often in the form of an application, as its primary tool or product. According to Halodoc's official website, their platform is available as an application for both Android and iOS, and can also be accessed via the web. The platform acts as a bridge between users and third-party service providers, which include doctors, veterinarians, psychologists, laboratories, pharmacies, hospitals, delivery services, and insurance providers. These entities are collectively referred to as service providers. Halodoc's website clearly states that digital health platforms are technology companies, not healthcare providers, a distinction that is also emphasized by other platforms like Alodokter.

Digital health platforms such as Alodokter, Halodoc, Getwell, KlikDokter, Good Doctor, GrabHealth, and KlinikGo are electronic systems developed by PSE. These platforms provide electronic health-related information, online consultation services with doctors via chat, medication purchase services, appointment scheduling for in-person consultations with specialist doctors, and laboratory test arrangements.

The operator of a digital health platform is classified as a Private Scope PSE, which refers to the organizers of PSEs by individuals, business entities, and the community. Private Scope PSEs are required to register with the Ministry of Communication and Informatics through the system. Service users access digital health platforms based on their needs. They can use the platform to read health articles by doctors and other health professionals, and take advantage of features such as paid consultations with selected doctors. Users who seek medical services from doctors through the platform are also referred to as patients.

The platform organizer partners with third parties to enhance the services offered on the platform. For example, collaborations with pharmacies facilitate the acquisition of prescribed medications for patients. Additionally, the platform organizers work with delivery service providers to handle orders for drugs and medical devices.

Some platforms also partner with online payment service providers (e-wallets) to offer users convenient payment options for transactions. Both delivery and payment service providers working with digital health platforms are classified as private PSEs. Furthermore, platforms like Halodoc and GetWell collaborate with insurance companies, allowing users to link their insurance with the applications to access health services at no additional cost.

CSR Initiatives for Digital Health in India During the Pandemic

Corporate Social Responsibility (CSR) played a crucial role in supporting digital health initiatives during the pandemic, providing essential technological assistance for threat validation, risk assessment, and mitigation efforts. As the world moved towards online risk communication through social media, many companies stepped up to help public health agencies better utilize these channels to engage citizens and disseminate critical information about health risks. By 2018, it was projected that 75 million wireless-connected health and fitness devices would be shipped, a significant increase from the 23 million shipped in 2011.

Several CSR-backed initiatives were launched to develop COVID-19 epidemiology models. Examples include the SUTRA model from IIT Kanpur and IIT Hyderabad, and the INDSCI-SIM model by the Indian Scientists' Response to COVID-19 group. Through partnerships and collaborations, corporations helped fund and support these models, which were vital in forecasting infection spread and guiding government policies on lockdowns, testing, and quarantines.

In addition, private sector companies contributed significantly to telemedicine and digital health advancements during the pandemic. CSR funding enabled the development of e-Sanjeevani, a teleconsultation platform that conducted over 300,000 consultations within six months. The app AarogyaSetu, supported by both public and private sector partnerships, saw 114 million downloads and became an essential tool for contact tracing. CSR initiatives also aided startups like Nocca Robotics, which developed ICU ventilators, and Modulus Housing, which created portable hospital units.

The digital health sector's growth has been fueled by CSR contributions, with companies supporting innovation in telehealth services, AI-driven diagnostics, and accessible healthcare platforms. These efforts have not only advanced healthcare access but have also built integrated ecosystems involving business-to-business collaborations, innovative insurance models, and digital solutions, laying the groundwork for a sustainable and inclusive digital health infrastructure in India.

Indian researchers undertook several initiatives to detect COVID-19. Researchers from ISI Kolkata developed a deep learning tool for COVID-19 screening, while DRDO's Centre for Artificial Intelligence & Robotics (CAIR) created ATMAN

AI, an AI-based application that uses chest X-rays (CXRs) to classify images into categories of normal, COVID-19, and pneumonia.

The government introduced AarogyaSetu, a contact tracing app designed to track individuals with COVID-19 and their contacts. Within just over a month of its launch, the app was downloaded by 114 million users. It proved effective: among those recommended for testing via the app, nearly 24% tested positive for COVID-19, compared to the overall positive rate of around 5% in May 2020. Additionally, the CoWin digital app/portal was developed to support the vaccination drive.

In April 2020, the Health Ministry launched the e-Sanjeevani platform, which facilitated over 300,000 consultations within just six months. Private healthcare providers have also significantly adopted telemedicine, with Apollo Hospitals introducing its telehealth program, 'Apollo 24/7'. Additionally, several innovative startups have emerged with cutting-edge digital health solutions. For example, Nocca Robotics, an IIT Kanpur-incubated company, developed the Noccarc V310, a fully-functioning ICU ventilator, while Modulus Housing, an IIT Madras-incubated startup, created a rapidly deployable portable hospital unit.

In an article in The Economic Times, Priyanka Aggarwal from BCG explains that, following the pandemic, digital access to healthcare has become a new norm for Indian consumers. Joint research by BCG and B Capital projects that India's digital healthcare sector could generate $37 billion in revenue by 2030, up from $2.7 billion in 2022. Aggarwal notes that partnerships on the supply side, including business-to-business collaborations and innovative insurance models, have fostered the development of integrated ecosystems rather than isolated business models across the industry. (https://www.bcg.com/news/1november2023-digital-health-care-on-rise-in-india)

Software Systems in Healthcare

India is rapidly adopting software systems in healthcare, including:

1. **Electronic Medical Records (EMR)**: These systems are used within hospitals or clinics to support patient diagnosis and treatment, focusing on transactions. The National Digital Health Mission (NDHM) requires these systems to be updated to adhere to standards and allow patient access to their data.

2. **Electronic Health Records (EHR):** EHRs contain comprehensive records of a patient from multiple doctors and providers, used within a healthcare system (such as a state government) to improve patient care.

3. **Personal Health Records (PHR):** PHRs allow patients to compile, update, and maintain their own health records, helping them manage their care more effectively and focusing on the individual.

Federated Architecture of Health Data

1. **The National Digital Health Mission (NDHM)** will implement a federated health records exchange system, allowing patient data to be stored at the point of care or as close as possible to where it was created. Patients will be able to access and share their records with appropriate consent, while retaining full control over their data. A digital consent framework, in line with NDHM standards and leveraging the DigiLocker consent management framework where possible, will be used for consent management.
2. Healthcare providers will need to adopt software that qualifies them as **Health Information Providers (HIPs)**, also known as Health Data Fiduciaries. These entities will create and share health information digitally, in compliance with NDHM standards and policies. HIPs must maintain digital copies of both inpatient and outpatient records they issue, as per current Ministry of Health and Family Welfare (MoHFW) guidelines, which require the indefinite digital storage of medical records.
3. Until digital services become mandatory, maintaining physical records will still be required. While a **digital Health ID** option will be available, treatment should not be denied to individuals who choose not to have a Health ID.
4. HIPs will need to request a Health ID from patients, assist in creating Health IDs as needed, link the Health ID with medical documents, and issue medical documents only with patient consent. Healthcare facilities must **enroll in the NDHM** Healthcare Facilities' Registry to become HIPs.
5. **Health Information Users (HIUs)** can request access to patient health records with the individual's consent, using compliant software. EMR systems, doctors, and applications providing advice based on health records must adhere to HIU specifications. HIUs cannot access data without patient consent.
6. Many entities serving as HIPs may also act as HIUs. However, their responsibilities are distinct: **HIPs are responsible for storing health records**, while HIUs request access to this data with patient consent. Entities taking on either role must follow the specific guidelines for HIPs or HIUs.

NATIONAL DIGITAL HEALTH MISSION: CORE SERVICES IN SUBSEQUENT PHASES

1.Health Claims Platform

The National Health Claims Platform will be developed to handle claims for various government health schemes, such as PM-JAY, ESIS, BoCWs, and CAPF. The platform will eventually include public and private health insurance schemes with support from the Ministry of Health and Family Welfare (MoHFW), other ministries, and IRDAI or related bodies. All outpatient and inpatient claims under NDHM's purview will be processed through this centralized platform, which will be regularly monitored for efficiency and accuracy.

2.Telemedicine

The telemedicine system will be developed in compliance with the Telemedicine Practice Guidelines 2020, the Indian Medical Council (Professional Conduct, Etiquette, and Ethics Regulation, 2002), and other relevant laws and regulations. This system may either be custom-built or utilize an existing product, with the government maintaining full ownership and control. Following legal and regulatory clearance, NDHM will pilot the telemedicine system before a nationwide rollout, involving private sector participation to enhance service delivery and access.

3. e-Pharmacy

The e-Pharmacy system will be technically prepared and phased in following legal and regulatory approvals. The platform will integrate all Jan Aushadhi Kendras to promote the use of generic medicines. Private sector e-Pharmacy providers will also have opportunities to collaborate with the platform. Their involvement will be secured before the service platform launches to ensure active participation.

4. Anonymizer as-a-Service

NDHM will develop an Anonymizer service that will process data from Health Lockers and other health data sources, removing personally identifiable information to ensure privacy. The anonymizer will handle both structured and unstructured data. Once complete, this service will be shared publicly for transparency and access, and integrated with existing and new NDHM schemes where necessary.

5. Health Analytics

Initially, NDHM will focus on six key areas: quality of care, data quality, wellness, public health, fraud and abuse, and policy support. These themes will largely depend on integration with other government schemes, and the Steering Committee will guide NDHM to ensure widespread integration.

6. **GIS/Visualization**

NDHM will implement a multi-layered approach to leverage GIS services. The system will generate outputs from health analytics data that can be used by various applications. GIS services will assist in regional and state-level health planning and monitoring, and will be made publicly available with appropriate identification, authentication, and authorization.

National Digital Health Mission: Stakeholder Engagement Plan

NDHM will integrate architectural and design capabilities with coordination efforts to ensure effective implementation and avoid duplication across states and organizations. The mission will focus on creating reusable, multi-tenant, open-source, and standards-compliant services. The stakeholder engagement strategy for NDHM includes the following:

1. **Individuals**

As the central focus of NDHM, individuals must be actively engaged and supportive of the initiative. The mission will adopt a people-centric approach, incorporating user feedback and ensuring a positive user experience in the development and enhancement of systems.

2. **Government**

Given that health is a state subject under the Indian Constitution, the successful implementation of NDHM requires collaboration between the Central and State Governments. A coordinated approach will be designed to facilitate the widespread adoption of health informatics standards and NDHM components. This coordination is crucial for the effective operation of the federated architecture and ensuring compliance with data security and protection requirements. The mission will work closely with public healthcare schemes and related ministries to integrate NDHM with existing and new programs, providing technical and management support as needed.

3. **Private Ecosystem**

NDHM's large-scale implementation necessitates a comprehensive and interoperable digital architecture involving the private sector. The mission will work with private stakeholders, including hospitals and labs, to adopt federated architecture and comply with NDHM standards. Guidelines and a certification process for Health Information Providers (HIPs) will be established, with certification conducted by MeitY through empanelled service providers. NDHM will support and encourage the development of innovative applications and services by startups and entrepreneurs to enhance value for all stakeholders.

4. **Leveraging Emerging Technologies**

NDHM will explore and adopt emerging technologies to advance digital health services. This includes investigating the use of blockchain for health data management and leveraging innovations from India's startup sector. An Innovation Wing within NDHM will oversee the following:

- Monitoring emerging technologies, especially their applicability in health.
- Conducting proof-of-concept (PoC) projects for these technologies.
- Creating sandbox environments for startups to test new technologies.
- Developing a policy for Value-Added Services (VAS), including identifying viable areas, registering startups, and publishing APIs for service development.
- Focusing on the use of AI for enhancing rural healthcare services and developing user-friendly clinical decision support systems.

In accordance with the Agile IndEA Framework, NDHM will engage stakeholders through five levels of involvement: Inform, Consult, Involve, Collaborate, and Empower. A Stakeholder Engagement Plan (SEP) will outline the strategy for engaging and communicating with stakeholders, ensuring they are informed, consulted, involved, and empowered in the adoption and expansion of NDHM, while addressing their concerns promptly.

A digital health platform serves as a forum that provides health information services accessible via various channels, including the web. Several start-ups have developed applications within these platforms to connect users directly with healthcare providers. The rise of digital health platforms has significantly eased access to healthcare services, particularly during the Covid-19 pandemic, when many people opted for virtual consultations over visiting physical health facilities. Various stakeholders are involved in the operation of these platforms, including doctors, patients, start-ups, pharmaceutical companies, drug delivery service providers, electronic payment companies, and insurance companies, each playing a distinct role in delivering services.

A start-up is the creator and manager of a digital health platform. A start-up is defined as a developing business that leverages technology, often in the form of an application, as its primary tool or product. According to Halodoc's official website, their platform is available as an application for both Android and iOS, and can also be accessed via the web. The platform acts as a bridge between users and third-party service providers, which include doctors, veterinarians, psychologists, laboratories, pharmacies, hospitals, delivery services, and insurance providers. These entities are collectively referred to as service providers. Halodoc's website clearly states that digital health platforms are technology companies, not healthcare providers, a distinction that is also emphasized by other platforms like Alodokter.

Digital health platforms such as Alodokter, Halodoc, Getwell, KlikDokter, Good Doctor, GrabHealth, and KlinikGo are electronic systems developed by PSE. These platforms provide electronic health-related information, online consultation services with doctors via chat, medication purchase services, appointment scheduling for in-person consultations with specialist doctors, and laboratory test arrangements.

The operator of a digital health platform is classified as a Private Scope PSE, which refers to the organizers of PSEs by individuals, business entities, and the community. Private Scope PSEs are required to register with the Ministry of Communication and Informatics through the system. Service users access digital health platforms based on their needs. They can use the platform to read health articles by doctors and other health professionals, and take advantage of features such as paid consultations with selected doctors. Users who seek medical services from doctors through the platform are also referred to as patients.

The platform organizer partners with third parties to enhance the services offered on the platform. For example, collaborations with pharmacies facilitate the acquisition of prescribed medications for patients. Additionally, the platform organizers work with delivery service providers to handle orders for drugs and medical devices. Some platforms also partner with online payment service providers (e-wallets) to offer users convenient payment options for transactions. Both delivery and payment service providers working with digital health platforms are classified as private PSEs. Furthermore, platforms like Halodoc and GetWell collaborate with insurance companies, allowing users to link their insurance with the applications to access health services at no additional cost.

Technological support for threat validation and verification, risk assessment, and evaluation can greatly reduce the manual efforts currently undertaken by public health experts. Additionally, risk communication during emergencies and about health threats is increasingly conducted online and through social media, rather than through traditional, controlled health communication channels. However, public health agencies are still lagging in effectively utilizing these new channels for citizen engagement and risk communication compared to the rapid advancements in technology.

By 2018, it was projected that 75 million wireless-connected health and fitness devices would be shipped, a significant increase from the 23 million shipped in 2011. Mobile technology, including self-monitoring/tracking apps and wearable devices that interact directly with social media, has significantly enhanced citizens' engagement with healthy lifestyles and well-being. It has also transformed how patients are empowered to independently monitor and manage their conditions. For example, companies like MC10, HealBe, and Proteus are innovating with sensors and wearables to improve health outcomes.

Corporate Social Responsibility in the Changing Business Environment

In recent decades, corporate social responsibility (CSR) has become a standard practice in the operations of socially sustainable businesses in both developed and developing countries. While numerous definitions have been proposed, the European Commission defines CSR as "the responsibility of enterprises for their impact on society."

To fully meet their corporate social responsibility (CSR) obligations, companies should establish a process that integrates social, environmental, ethical, and human rights concerns into their business operations and core strategies, working closely with their stakeholders. The definition also underscores the importance of aligning core business strategies with the creation of shared value and the explicit recognition of human rights and ethical considerations, alongside environmental and consumer interests, particularly focusing on the well-being of key stakeholders, especially employees. CSR represents the social pillar of the triple bottom line of sustainable development—people, planet, and profit. Garriga et al. propose categorizing CSR into four sets of theories that encompass various perspectives: ethical, political, integrative, and instrumental theories. Ethical theories of CSR emphasize the moral expectations, obligations, and relationships between businesses and society, with a focus on universal rights, sustainable development, and the common good as foundational elements of the business-society relationship. Political theories examine the power dynamics between businesses and society, as well as the responsibilities, duties, and rights that arise from the social power held by businesses. These political theories manifest in several forms, including corporate constitutionalism, which addresses the social power of businesses and the responsible use of this power; integrative social contract theory, which considers the implicit macro-social and micro-social contracts between business and society and their associated obligations; and corporate citizenship, which views businesses as societal citizens. With nation-states increasingly unable to meet social needs due to globalization, deregulation, and market externalities, there has been a renewed interest in corporate citizenship, as businesses are increasingly called upon to take a more active social role in the communities—both local and global—in which they operate.

Corporate social responsibility presents a chance for businesses to tackle global health challenges by making a case for stakeholder health. This can be accomplished by creating a platform that aligns CSR with global health promotion as part of sustainable development. However, further research is needed to determine which interventions would be most effective in achieving this goal.

Role of Corporate Social Responsibility in Healthcare

This study aims to contribute to the literature on Corporate Social Responsibility (CSR). It begins by introducing the concept of CSR and the extended stakeholder model, then explores whether health should be considered a CSR stakeholder. The research examines how companies perceive their role in health promotion, investigates how they can contribute positively to social well-being and health, and explores the potential use of emerging technologies like digital Health and mHealth in these initiatives.

Emily Senay (2018) studied that, Sustainability practices by large corporations are essential for reducing environmental and social impacts. The health care sector, which is a major part of the US economy, plays a significant role in these efforts. However, this sector lags behind others in sustainability reporting, which is crucial for measuring and improving environmental performance. By publicly reporting their sustainability activities, health care organizations could better track their environmental impact, reduce costs, and enhance public health.

Daú G, Scavarda A, Scavarda LF (2019) analysed that, Increasing concern about the circular economy and Industry 4.0 is emerging in developing countries. This study aims to analyze the sustainable healthcare supply chain 4.0 by proposing a conceptual framework for transitioning to a circular economy, using corporate social responsibility (CSR) as a guiding principle. The authors collected empirical data from a private healthcare institution in Rio de Janeiro, which has been investing in new technologies within its operations, with observations conducted between January and April 2017. The findings reveal that the glass structure of the facility can serve as a channel for lighting resources, solar energy via photovoltaic panels, and water management. CSR links the social role of healthcare institutions with sustainable practices and enhances the use of smart technologies. The integration of the Internet of Things (IoT) and the Internet of Services (IoS) adds value to these sustainable practices. The study concludes that combining the triple bottom line, Industry 4.0, and CSR facilitates the transition from a linear to a circular model, thereby improving the sustainable healthcare supply chain 4.0.

Ahmad, N., Ullah, Z., Ryu, H. B., Ariza-Montes, A., & Han, H. (2023). While extensive research has explored the effects of corporate social responsibility (CSR) on employee outcomes, there is limited focus on its impact on healthcare employees' burnout (BUO). Additionally, the mechanisms through which CSR may help reduce burnout are not fully understood. To address these gaps, we examined the relationship between CSR and BUO, as well as the potential mediating roles of subjective well-being (SW) and compassion (CM). We also investigated whether employee admiration (AM) moderates this relationship.

The study collected data from 335 healthcare employees in Pakistan, including nurses, doctors, paramedics, and administrative staff, using a paper-pencil questionnaire. Participants' perceptions of CSR practices, burnout, admiration, subjective well-being, and compassion within their organizations were assessed using standardized scales validated in previous research. Analysis using AMOS software revealed that CSR is negatively associated with burnout, indicating that strong CSR practices can help reduce burnout among healthcare employees. Moreover, the relationship between CSR and burnout was mediated by both subjective well-being and compassion, highlighting the pathways through which CSR can influence employee burnout. Additionally, employee admiration was found to buffer the relationship between CSR and burnout. Burnout is an increasing concern in healthcare, with significant implications for patient care, staff morale, and organizational success. Implementing effective CSR strategies can be a powerful tool in addressing burnout in healthcare settings. These strategies should be meaningful to employees and offer opportunities for them to engage in activities that resonate with their values and interests.

Saxena, K., Balani, S. and Srivastava, P. (2021) explained that, this study aims to review existing literature in the pharmaceutical sector on corporate social responsibility (CSR), sustainability, and organizational performance to determine if a relationship exists among these three elements. A total of 301 research articles were collected from online databases and classified under CSR, sustainability, and organizational performance using a new ECG framework representing environment, community, and growth.

Droppert, H., Bennett, S (2015). studied that, As pharmaceutical companies face growing pressure from civil society to act responsibly in an increasingly globalized world, many are expanding or reforming their corporate social responsibility (CSR) strategies. This study aimed to understand how multinational pharmaceutical companies are currently engaging in CSR activities in developing countries, their motivations, and how their strategies are evolving to impact global health.

CSR approaches varied significantly across firms, particularly in how CSR is defined, the organizational structures managing CSR, the specific activities undertaken, and the motivations behind them. Common CSR activities included differential pharmaceutical pricing, strengthening drug distribution infrastructure in developing countries, mHealth initiatives, and targeted research and development. Key motivations for CSR engagement were reputational benefits, recruitment and employee satisfaction, higher rankings in sustainability indices, access to new markets, long-term economic returns, and improved population health. Firms were at different stages on a spectrum from philanthropic donations to integrated systemic shared value business models. CSR is becoming increasingly important for multinational pharmaceutical companies, but the understanding of the range of CSR strategies and their effects is still emerging. Our study highlights the need to (i) develop clearer and more standardized definitions of CSR in global health, (ii) strengthen indices to track CSR strategies and their impact on public health in developing countries, and (iii) conduct more country-level studies to examine how CSR interacts with national health systems.

Oftedal EM, Foss L, Iakovleva T.(2019) explored that, Responsible innovation (RI) has gained significant attention from policymakers and academics as a solution to grand challenges and is considered a key driver of innovation. The United Nations has proposed 17 Sustainable Development Goals, and responsible innovation is seen as a tool that can help society move toward reducing inequality, addressing environmental challenges, and sustaining economic and societal development. However, our understanding of how businesses act responsibly in addressing these challenges is limited. An inductive analysis of 14 e-health startups in Norway reveals that responsibility is highly prevalent. Entrepreneurs have direct contact with users (patients or healthcare professionals), which enhances inclusiveness, anticipation, and reflection as key elements of responsibility. However, these firms show limited contextual and strategic awareness of responsibility, resulting in a lack of focused strategies to exercise it. As a result, entrepreneurial startups struggle to engage with broader stakeholders and fully integrate the knowledge they gain. Additionally, RI activities are often integrated with other activities along the path to successful commercialization. This paper contributes to the current understanding of RI from a firm perspective and offers implications for practitioners and policymakers to promote sustainable development in the healthcare sector.

Faggini M, Cosimato S, Nota FD, Nota G.(2019) explained that, sustainability, along with the sustainable use of resources and related issues, has sparked an ongoing and vibrant debate among scholars from various disciplines. Given the under-exploration of many sustainability-related challenges, this paper seeks to deepen our understanding of the system dynamics that, with the support of digital enablers such as digital technologies and platforms, enhance the sustainability of complex service systems like healthcare. To achieve this, the paper presents a theoretical meta-model of interaction types that inspired the development of a prototype digital platform for delivering health-related services online. Additionally, several healthcare usage scenarios based on the prototype's functions are analyzed and discussed. This analysis highlights the crucial role of technologies, particularly digital platforms, in empowering actors and encouraging them to interact and share their resources in continuously innovative ways. This process facilitates ongoing value co-creation, which is vital for the sustainability of healthcare systems.

Rodrigues S, Kanduri A, Nyamathi A, Dutt N, Khargonekar P, Rahmani (2022) explored that, Digital health–enabled community-centered care (D-CCC) represents a groundbreaking approach to future community health. By integrating a novel AI-driven closed-loop digital health platform specifically designed for community health workers, D-CCC enhances their digital capabilities, leading to more timely, supported, and personalized interventions. This approach has the potential to advance community-centered care into a digitally interconnected and collaborative ecosystem, supported by a strong and digitally empowered community health workforce.

Recent global health trends are driving a shift from a patient-centered medical care model to an upstream health promotion approach that addresses the health and social needs within the communities where people live. A community-centered health and social care ecosystem, supported by a strong community health worker (CHW) workforce, aligns with this necessary shift. Across the United States, states are focusing on expanding their CHW workforces and launching initiatives to complement the work of registered healthcare professionals and enhance home-delivered services. For instance, the California Employment Development Department estimates that an additional 200,000 CHWs will be required by 2024 to sustain current levels of home care service coverage. As the COVID-19 pandemic continues to escalate health and social support needs worldwide, there is a critical need to rapidly expand the CHW presence to prevent these needs from escalating into costly medical crises, especially in vulnerable communities.

The D-CCC platform is designed to address the diverse needs of clients, community health workers (CHWs), and registered providers (RPs) by facilitating communication, data collection and analysis, training, and intelligent decision-making. Its design includes the following modules:

Multichannel Stakeholders Module: Facilitates smart communication among stakeholders via various channels (client-CHW, CHW-CHW, CHW-supervisor).

Monitoring Module: Provides continuous monitoring and updating of both subjective and objective physiological and contextual information.

Health Estimation Module: Analyzes data from clients, CHWs, and medical histories in real time to assess client health status.

Knowledge Base Module: Manages the storage, access, and retrieval of knowledge derived from client, CHW, and supervisor data to enable personalized model development.

Personal Models Module: Constructs cognitive learning models from client data to make autonomous, intelligent intervention recommendations tailored to each client.

Smart Recommendation Module: Predicts and delivers personalized health care and lifestyle recommendations to CHWs or directly to clients, based on the context and risk level.

Smart Supervision Module: Assists RPs in supervising CHWs by automating repetitive tasks and reflecting on personal models and the knowledge base.

Smart Assistance Module: Enhances the quality of health care services by supporting CHWs in making interventional, educational, or procedural decisions in the field.

Smart Training Module: Provides training for CHWs on new digital technologies and offers web-based training modules to supplement traditional in-person training.

D-CCC's AI-enabled platform seamlessly integrates these modules to form a comprehensive, data-driven system that connects clients, CHWs, and supervisors in an ongoing cycle of measurement, estimation, guidance, and influence.

The D-CCC model facilitates multi-way communication among key stakeholders in community-centered care delivery networks via digital channels. This model explain the various combinations of these communication channels among clients, CHWs, and supervisors, which can be categorized as follows:

Client-CHW Channel: This channel enables communication between clients and their assigned CHWs, who provide community health-related services. Traditionally, interactions occur during scheduled appointments or as needed. D-CCC transforms this into continuous, on-demand communication available to all clients served.

CHW-Supervisor Channel: This channel facilitates communication between CHWs and their supervisors, who provide oversight and feedback. While traditionally each CHW has a designated supervisor, D-CCC enhances this by enabling real-time, on-demand interactions, and allows for additional supervisors (e.g., RPs) with specialized expertise as service demands evolve.

CHW-CHW Channel: This channel supports communication among CHWs, fostering knowledge transfer and information exchange tailored to specific community challenges. D-CCC transforms this into an on-demand, real-time interaction through digital means.

Monitoring Module

This module oversees the continuous tracking of client physiological signs, contextual information, lifelogs, surveys, and ecological momentary assessments. Utilizing advanced wearable devices (e.g., smart rings, watches, patches), portable sensors (e.g., smart ECG sensors, stethoscopes, BP monitors), stationary sensors (e.g., smart beds, fall detection cameras), and mobile health (mHealth) solutions (e.g., smartphone apps), D-CCC centralizes data collection from these diverse sources. This integration enables comprehensive data synthesis and the delivery of intelligent recommendations and support to stakeholders.

Health Estimation Module

This module assesses the client's health status using high-dimensional and holistic information. It processes various data modalities to estimate health variables and determines a client's current health state relative to their desired, safe state. By continuously comparing the current health status with the desired state, this module evaluates overall health safety. The health status information informs personal model development and guides recommendations for decision-making.

Knowledge Base Module

This module encompasses CCC-related facts, information, and skills gained from the experiences of stakeholders (CHWs, supervisors, and clients), as well as theoretical and practical knowledge within the field. It evolves by continuously learning from new data generated by clients, CHWs, and supervisors. The knowledge base constructs knowledge graphs to represent meaningful connections between cause-and-effect pairs, such as linking specific physiological data readings to health criticality. These graphs support the development of population models and personal models. By incorporating individual insights, the knowledge base facilitates the creation of comprehensive personal models for other clients. Figure 3 illustrates the process of deploying a generic learning analytics model, which is updated with person-specific data to produce personalized models. Data includes continuously monitored physiological parameters, contextual information from lifelogging, past intervention procedures, and health estimation logs for clients, as well as CHW intervention logs and effectiveness, along with supervision and training details. This module underpins the development of learning analytics and cognitive models in subsequent modules.

Samuel, L. (2021). This research article aims to highlight the disparity in availability and utilization between public and private healthcare, particularly in the context of the National Digital Health Mission (NDHM) recently announced by the Indian government. Despite the intention of digital health initiatives to provide affordable healthcare access, especially in rural areas, their success will depend on the healthcare system's response and effective state control and regulation. In India, where over 70% of the population relies on the private medical sector and a comprehensive state-sponsored healthcare system is lacking, the implementation of the NDHM becomes crucial.

Leveraging Corporate Social Responsibility to Advance Digital Health Initiatives

Corporate social responsibility and digital health are among the most crucial elements of global competitiveness in today's world. The modern business landscape is constantly evolving, significantly shaped by technological progress. Technology is now a fundamental driver of both societal and civilizational change.

Every year on April 7, the World Health Organization and other pertinent organizations host World Health Day, highlighting the value of preserving health and strengthening healthcare systems. The ongoing fight against the COVID-19 pandemic emphasizes how vital it is to take preventative action in these areas. The World Health Organization has selected "Health for All" as the theme for its 75th anniversary, which falls on this historic day in 2023. As we commemorate World Health Day, let's take a look at some of India's best healthcare CSR efforts.

Recent advancements in technology, including the development of real-time big data streams, social media, and infectious disease modelling are central to the field of public health computer science. This discipline aims to bolster disease surveillance, early warning systems, preparedness, and response by integrating traditional surveillance methods with new data sources. Improvements in the reliability and accuracy of medical devices, alongside the rise of personalized technology and wearable tracking devices (MedTech), have rapidly become mainstream. These advancements offer opportunities for personalized care, enhancing self-management practices, and fostering behaviour change. The widespread adoption of mobile phones, with over 4.55 billion users globally in 2023, has paved the way for mHealth apps and interventions. By 2024, this trend continued to grow, with an even higher number of users embracing mobile technology for health-related purposes. Utilizing technology to capture, understand, and disseminate knowledge is crucial for realizing this vision. Recent research in web science, data mining, medical ontologies, and recommender systems presents further opportunities for improving evidence dissemination, medical advice, and the development of personalized intelligent systems. Serious games for health and game-based learning have transitioned from entertainment to educational and health intervention tools. However, the rapid pace of data sharing technologies necessitates policy discussions to safeguard individual privacy, regulate the commercial use of data, and promote transparent data sharing for research purposes. Digital health is inherently a multidisciplinary field encompassing areas such as computer science, engineering, information science, journalism, economics, clinical medicine, public health, epidemiology, and more. While technology and computer science explore new frameworks and algorithms of significant theoretical value, successful digital health research must address real-world medical challenges, solve clinical or public health problems, and meet patients' needs. Clinical IT solutions should enhance the management of conditions and the delivery of care by leveraging advanced computer science innovations. This requires a collaborative effort between healthcare professionals, medical scientists, and computer scientists, ensuring equal contributions from both fields. The Digital Health section, associated with Frontiers in Public Health and Frontiers in ICT, promotes this collaborative approach by providing a unique interdisciplinary publication platform for both professional communities. This facilitates cross-fertilization and the cultivation of a new generation of researchers who comprehend the language, methods, needs, and challenges of different disciplines. This growing momentum highlights the need for interdisciplinary training in health and public health computer science. Additionally, closer partnerships between researchers, industry/start-ups, and policymakers are crucial for driving meaningful change.

Finance Minister, Nirmala Sitharaman highlights today's robust GDP data, showcasing growth rates of 8.2% for FY 2023-24 and 7.8% for Q4 of FY 2023-24, the highest among major economies. Notably, the Manufacturing sector saw significant growth of 9.9% in 2023-24, underscoring the success of government efforts. Despite global challenges, high-frequency indicators suggest India's economy remains resilient and buoyant. India's economy continues to show resilience, boasting a GDP growth rate of 8.7% in FY 2022. Nonetheless, despite this robust economic growth, the nation grapples with persistent multi-dimensional inequalities, despite the burgeoning middle class and ambitious goals to achieve a $5 trillion economy by FY 2025. As India navigates its recovery from the Covid-19 pandemic, it is imperative for stakeholders within the ecosystem to prioritize investments aimed at fortifying the philanthropic infrastructure, thereby enhancing community resilience. While social sector spending in India as a percentage of GDP increased from 8.6% in FY 2021 to 9.6% in FY 2022, propelled by a 35% surge in public spending, it still falls significantly short of NITI Aayog's recommended estimate (13% of GDP) for annual funding required to fulfill the United Nations Sustainable Development Goals (SDGs) by 2030. CSR spending has witnessed a growth rate of 13% over the past five years, reaching $3.3 billion (INR 27,000 crore) in FY 2022. While experiencing a slower pace of growth in FY 2022, it is anticipated to maintain its historical trajectory and attain $6.4 billion (INR 52,000 crore) by FY 2027.

The exceptional CSR endeavour shines brightly as a symbol of positive transformation, as Rambus and Aahwahan Foundation combine their skills and resources to enhance the health infrastructure of a government maternity hospital. This overhaul goes beyond mere physical renovations; it revitalizes the core of maternal care in rural areas. Rambus has transformed healthcare by introducing an advanced ultrasound machine to the hospital, significantly enhancing laboratory capabilities to unprecedented standards. This state-of-the-art equipment, often unattainable for the underprivileged, demonstrates the duo's forward-thinking approach. In a pioneering step, they have not only brought in advanced medical technology but have also broken-down economic barriers, ensuring that even the economically disadvantaged can avail themselves of high-quality healthcare. Rambus and Aahwahan Foundation recognize that genuine transformation transcends mere physical infrastructure. Their initiative encompasses community outreach programs, health education campaigns, and supportive networks that empower mothers to make informed choices regarding their and their newborns' well-being. This joint endeavor not only enhances a maternity hospital but also raises the standard of living for the entire community. It underscores the transformative potential of corporate social responsibility fueled by a unified vision and steadfast commitment.

Since initiating services through Mobile Public Health Units (mPHUs), Tata Steel Foundation (TSF), dedicated to comprehensive community development, has been revolutionizing primary healthcare services in the outlying villages of the Tata Steel Meramandali plant in Dhenkanal district. These units have catered to 29 peripheral villages spanning seven panchayats in the area, namely Mangalpur, Sibapur, Khadagprasad, Nuagaon, Kusupanga, Nuahata, and Paika Puruna Kote. The primary objective of the mPHUs is to provide convenient, top-tier primary healthcare directly to the doorsteps of peripheral villages, offering regular check-ups, screenings, and complimentary medications. Equipped with a committed team comprising a certified MBBS doctor, nurses, pharmacists, technicians, and coordinators, they adhere to a structured schedule, conducting four visits per village every month. These visits encompass health camps that provide check-ups, consultations, and complimentary basic diagnoses and medications. Last year, around 41,000 patients received healthcare services through these mPHUs. Acknowledging the necessity for doorstep primary healthcare facilities in the region, the TSF launched the operation of two Mobile Public Health Units (mPHUs) in 2019. Since then, thousands have benefited from this initiative. These endeavors have notably improved health awareness and encouraged the adoption of healthier practices, paving the way for a healthier future for these communities.

The Pfizer Foundation, established in 1953, aims to "help build healthier communities around the world" by supporting community-based innovations, safety net healthcare providers, and promoting health equity, with a focus on ensuring equitable access to vaccines.

Additionally, the foundation provides grants in response to natural disasters, such as after Hurricane Matthew in Haiti and during the global refugee crisis in Europe and the Middle East. These funds are distributed in collaboration with NGOs to maximize their impact.

Through Pfizer's Global Health Innovation Grants program, $100,000 is awarded annually to twenty organizations to develop solutions that address vaccine-preventable diseases in their communities. One such grant recipient is the North Star Alliance in Uganda.

The Spoken Tutorial Health and Nutrition project by IIT Bombay provides expert guidance on Maternal Nutrition, Child Nutrition, General Nutrition, and COVID-related information, delivered by a team of experienced doctors, nutritionists, and field officers with over a decade of expertise. With more than 300 videos translated into over 18 recognized national languages in India, this initiative has become a vital resource.

These tutorials are available online and are being utilized in the ongoing training programs in the Nashik District. Additionally, plans are in place to extend training to health workers in the districts of Jashpur, Washim, and potentially Thane. This initiative will significantly benefit newborns, their mothers, and entire families in these regions of Maharashtra.

During the year, 16,636 women of reproductive age were screened for anemia, with over 10,000 diagnosed as anemic. These women received nutrition counseling and health awareness, and those with moderate to severe anemia were treated with hematinic and deworming medications according to protocol. Those needing specialized treatment were referred to RFH. In 2018-19, more than 11,500 children under five were screened, and 550 were identified as malnourished and given free treatment and counseling. In the area of Non-Communicable Disease Control and Prevention, over 35,000 individuals were screened for hypertension, with around 10% newly diagnosed as hypertensive. Out of 21,000 individuals screened for diabetes, approximately 5,000 were diagnosed with the condition. At-risk patients were advised to make lifestyle changes, while diagnosed patients were promptly started on treatment and are regularly followed up to prevent, identify early, and control complications. The cancer prevention and control program screened about 15,000 individuals for oral, breast, and cervical cancers. Comprehensive health awareness sessions were TCS has undertaken several key health initiatives, including disaster relief, technological support for hospitals (including cancer institutes), and financing for hygienic sanitation.

Key Implementations by TCS Under These Health Initiatives Include

Hospital Management System for Cancer Research Institute, Chennai: TCS provided a comprehensive, fully integrated, web-based IT solution free of charge.

Hospital Management System for Tata Medical Center (TMC), Kolkata: TCS implemented the IT infrastructure and provided pro bono IT services valued at 4.2 crore in FY 14.

CSR Tech Team: In FY 14, the CSR Tech Team focused on various health-based initiatives for organizations such as Retina India Foundation (Indian Retina Repository) and Operation Smile (Patient Management System). The team also developed a Case MONGC, in collaboration with Help Age India, continues its efforts to deliver healthcare directly to the elderly through Mobile Medicare Units (MMUs). In this initiative, nearly 1.9 lakh treatments were administered across eight states and one Union Territory. The MMUs provide essential medical services to the elderly, including medical consultations, medicine distribution, basic diagnostic tests, special health camps, and palliative care at their doorsteps. A total of 20 MMUs are deployed to offer basic healthcare across nine states, 17 districts, 35 blocks, 131 Gram Panchayats, and 240 villages in India. In total, 11,86,020 beneficiaries received treatment for chronic conditions such as hypertension, diabetes, osteoarthritis, dyspepsia, and skin problems.

This project, launched as a CSR initiative in the financial year 2014-15, operates on a PAN India basis, focusing on ONGC's operational areas and backward districts across various states. Management System for Justice and Care to track human trafficking cases and a tracking system for Childline India Foundation. held in the communities, and individuals suspected of having cancer were referred for further evaluation, confirmation, and, if necessary, treatment at higher centers.

ONGC's Contribution to PM CARES Fund for Healthcare Infrastructure

On March 31, 2023, Oil and Natural Gas Corporation Limited (ONGC), India's Energy Maharatna, donated 100 crore to the Prime Minister's Citizen Assistance and Relief in Emergency Situations Fund (PM CARES Fund). This contribution will support the government's ongoing efforts to strengthen healthcare infrastructure, particularly in combating COVID-19 and the H3N2 influenza virus.

Previously, ONGC contributed 300 crore to the PM CARES Fund in April 2020 during the first wave of the COVID-19 pandemic and an additional 70 crore in FY 2021-22 to maintain medical equipment purchased by Oil Public Sector Enterprises (PSEs) during the two waves of the pandemic.

BPCL and Tata Memorial Centre Partner to Support Cancer Treatment and Research in Punjab

Bharat Petroleum Corporation Limited (BPCL) recently announced a Memorandum of Understanding (MoU) with Tata Memorial Centre to provide CSR support to the Homi Baba Cancer Hospital in Sangrur and the Homi Baba Cancer Hospital & Research Centre in Mullanpur, both units of Tata Memorial Centre in Punjab.

As part of its commitment to improving health and community development, BPCL will invest 1,84,87,300 towards procuring advanced surgical equipment for these hospitals. This will make high-end reconstructive surgeries and advanced cancer treatments accessible to the underprivileged population at affordable costs, significantly improving the quality of life for cancer patients.

Greenply Industries Ltd's Mobile Medical Van in Nagaland

Greenply Industries Ltd, a leading plywood manufacturer, is running an ongoing healthcare project through a Mobile Medical Van (MMV) in Tizit and nearby villages in Mon district, Nagaland, where the company operates a factory. The mobile van offers essential diagnostic services, medicines, treatment, referrals, and counseling to the rural population. This initiative aims to improve access to healthcare in remote areas and raise community awareness about healthy and hygienic living.

Greenply's Mobile Medical Van in Tizit, Nagaland

STL's Digital Healthcare Program

STL, a leading optical and digital solutions company, has launched a Mobile Telehealth and Social Behavior Change program across more than 1,200 villages in Maharashtra's Aurangabad, Nandurbar, Gadchiroli, and other districts, where it operates its flagship glass, optical fiber, and cable facilities.

In the tribal areas of Nandurbar and Gadchiroli, where healthcare awareness is low and medical facilities are scarce, STL is ensuring free, accessible healthcare through a hybrid program. The initiative combines 24/7 teleconsultation, video consultations, and diagnoses with physical onsite check-ups, on-call doctors, health awareness campaigns, and specialist health camps for primary ailments. Additionally, digital health records are maintained for all patients, enabling instant access to health information. STL has partnered with nearby hospitals to provide patients with advanced treatments when needed.

SBI Foundation and NSDL's Clinics-on-Wheels

The SBI Foundation and National Securities Depository Limited (NSDL) are addressing the high rates of non-communicable, air-borne, and vector-borne diseases in Mumbai's slum settlements—Govandi, Sion, and Kurla—by offering free doorstep healthcare through Mobile Medical Units under the SBIF Sanjeevani program. The program, implemented by Doctors For You, a non-profit organization focused on improving healthcare access in India, has so far deployed 24 Mobile Medical Units (MMUs) across 18 states and 2 union territories.

With NSDL's funding support and the addition of three new MMUs, SBIF Sanjeevani will expand to three wards in Mumbai and further scale up to Uttar Pradesh's Hardoi district, in partnership with Gramin Vikas Trust, and Assam's Baksa district, in partnership with the Assam Centre for Rural Development.

In addition to screening and treatment, the MMUs will hold daily camps focusing on maternal and child health, as well as WASH (Water, Sanitation & Hygiene) practices. OPD services will be available 22 days a month. The project will also collaborate with public healthcare stakeholders, including Health and Development officers from the BMC, ICDS, Block Development Program, CHCs, PHCs, Anganwadis, ASHA workers, and ANMs.

LG India, a leading consumer durables brand, has taken a significant step toward fostering a healthier and brighter future for the country's youth. In a landmark partnership with Akshaya Patra and Annapoorna Trust, LG India has launched the "Life's Good Nutrition Program," an initiative focused on ensuring the well-being and proper nutrition of school children in government schools across India. The program will cover an impressive 808 schools, benefiting over 59,202 children.

With a steadfast commitment to promoting holistic growth and development, LG India is addressing the pressing issue of childhood malnutrition and contributing to a healthier generation. The "Life's Good Nutrition Program" involves collaboration with two renowned organizations: Akshaya Patra, known for its transformative Midday Meal program, which provides nutritious lunches to millions of schoolchildren, and Sri Sathya Sai Annapoorna Trust, which offers a Morning Nutrition Program to ensure children start their day with a healthy meal.

Through this expansive initiative, LG India is not only tackling the immediate challenge of malnutrition but also supporting the cognitive and physical development of the nation's future leaders.

Hong Ju Jeon, MD of LG Electronics India, stated, “At LG, we believe that a brighter future begins with a healthy foundation. We are committed to supporting the government and have aligned our CSR initiatives accordingly. Through the ‘Life’s Good Nutrition Program,’ we are taking concrete steps to ensure every child has access to nutritious meals, empowering them to reach their full potential. We are proud to partner with Akshaya Patra and Annapoorna Trust on this noble mission.”

Previously, LG India had pledged its support in the fight against hunger by providing mid-day meals to 33,334 students across the country, ensuring their nutrition and right to education.

LG India, a leading consumer durables brand, has taken a significant step toward fostering a healthier and brighter future for the country’s youth. In a landmark partnership with Akshaya Patra and Annapoorna Trust, LG India has launched the “Life’s Good Nutrition Program,” an initiative focused on ensuring the well-being and proper nutrition of school children in government schools across India. The program will cover an impressive 808 schools, benefiting over 59,202 children.

With a steadfast commitment to promoting holistic growth and development, LG India is addressing the pressing issue of childhood malnutrition and contributing to a healthier generation. The “Life’s Good Nutrition Program” involves collaboration with two renowned organizations: Akshaya Patra, known for its transformative Midday Meal program, which provides nutritious lunches to millions of schoolchildren, and Sri Sathya Sai Annapoorna Trust, which offers a Morning Nutrition Program to ensure children start their day with a healthy meal.

Through this expansive initiative, LG India is not only tackling the immediate challenge of malnutrition but also supporting the cognitive and physical development of the nation’s future leaders.

Hong Ju Jeon, MD of LG Electronics India, stated, “At LG, we believe that a brighter future begins with a healthy foundation. We are committed to supporting the government and have aligned our CSR initiatives accordingly. Through the ‘Life’s Good Nutrition Program,’ we are taking concrete steps to ensure every child has access to nutritious meals, empowering them to reach their full potential. We are proud to partner with Akshaya Patra and Annapoorna Trust on this noble mission.”

Previously, LG India had pledged its support in the fight against hunger by providing mid-day meals to 33,334 students across the country, ensuring their nutrition and right to education.

The Union Cabinet, chaired by Prime Minister Narendra Modi, has approved a landmark proposal to extend health coverage under the Ayushman Bharat Pradhan Mantri Jan Arogya Yojana (AB PM-JAY) to all senior citizens aged 70 and above, regardless of income. This decision will bring approximately 4.5 crore families, including six crore senior citizens, under the scheme, providing them with free health insurance coverage of 5 lakh per year on a family basis.

This initiative fulfills one of the key promises made by the BJP in its agenda. Eligible senior citizens will receive a new, distinct AB PM-JAY card to access their benefits.

Senior citizens aged 70 and above who are part of families already covered under AB PM-JAY will receive an additional top-up of 5 lakh per year for their healthcare needs, separate from the family's total coverage. Meanwhile, those aged 70 and above who are not yet enrolled will receive 5 lakh coverage per family annually.

Senior citizens who are already benefiting from other public health insurance schemes such as the Central Government Health Scheme (CGHS), Ex-Servicemen Contributory Health Scheme (ECHS), and Ayushman Central Armed Police Force (CAPF) may choose to continue with their current schemes or switch to AB PM-JAY. Those covered under private health insurance or the Employees' State Insurance Scheme (ESI) are also eligible to benefit from AB PM-JAY.

According to a government release, AB PM-JAY is the world's largest publicly funded health assurance scheme, providing 5 lakh in annual coverage per family for secondary and tertiary hospital care to 55 crore individuals, representing 12.34 crore families. So far, the scheme has supported 7.37 crore hospital admissions, including 49% women beneficiaries, resulting in benefits worth over 1 lakh crore.

The Health Ministry noted that the AB PM-JAY has steadily expanded its beneficiary base. Initially launched to cover 10.74 crore poor and vulnerable families, representing the bottom 40% of India's population, the scheme was later expanded in January 2022 to include 12 crore families, reflecting India's 11.7% population growth since 2011.

The scheme was further extended to provide healthcare coverage to 37 lakh ASHA, Anganwadi, and Auxiliary Nurse Midwife workers (ASHAs/AWWs/AWHs) and their families. Now, with the inclusion of all citizens aged 70 and above, AB PM-JAY will offer free healthcare coverage of 5 lakh per year to senior citizens across the country.

Challenges and Opportunities for CSR in Digital Healthcare in India

Digital Infrastructure: Many regions in India, especially rural areas, still face gaps in reliable internet connectivity and basic digital infrastructure. Corporate Social Responsibility (CSR) initiatives can play a critical role in bridging this divide by investing in infrastructure projects that enhance digital connectivity and access to healthcare services in underserved regions.

Digital Literacy: A significant portion of the population, particularly in rural areas and among older demographics, lacks the digital literacy needed to navigate digital healthcare platforms. CSR programs can contribute by offering educational initiatives that train individuals on how to use technology for healthcare, empowering them to access telemedicine and other digital health services.

Data Privacy and Security: Ensuring the protection of sensitive medical information is a critical issue in digital healthcare. Companies can leverage their CSR resources to develop secure systems, raise awareness about data privacy, and implement robust safeguards to protect patient data.

Telemedicine Regulations: Telemedicine has expanded rapidly, but clear regulations are still lacking, particularly around cross-state consultations and prescriptions. CSR initiatives can support policy advocacy and the development of regulatory frameworks to ensure the safe and effective use of telemedicine.

CONCLUSION

In conclusion, Corporate Social Responsibility (CSR) can play a pivotal role in advancing digital health by fostering innovation and supporting crucial healthcare developments. By investing in blockchain technology for secure health record management, companies can empower patients with control over their medical data while ensuring safety and seamless collaboration among healthcare providers. CSR-driven initiatives in data analytics can enhance public health by predicting disease patterns, optimizing resource allocation, and designing targeted interventions. Additionally, through online training and skill development programs, corporations can equip healthcare professionals with the necessary tools and knowledge to adapt to emerging digital health trends. Furthermore, by collaborating with governments and stakeholders, CSR efforts can help shape ethical digital health policies, ensuring robust regulations around data privacy and security. Ultimately, CSR's involvement in digital health can lead to a more efficient, equitable, and secure healthcare system that benefits society as a whole.

REFERENCES

Ahmad, N., Ullah, Z., Ryu, H. B., Ariza-Montes, A., & Han, H. (2023). From corporate social responsibility to employee well-being: Navigating the pathway to sustainable healthcare. *Psychology Research and Behavior Management*, 16, 1079–1095. DOI: 10.2147/PRBM.S398586 PMID: 37041962

Daú, G., Scavarda, A., Scavarda, L. F., & Portugal, V. J. T. (2019). The healthcare sustainable supply chain 4.0: The circular economy transition conceptual framework with the corporate social responsibility mirror. *Sustainability (Basel)*, 11(12), 3259. DOI: 10.3390/su11123259

Droppert, H., & Bennett, S. (2015). Corporate social responsibility in global health: An exploratory study of multinational pharmaceutical firms. *Globalization and Health*, 11(1), 15. DOI: 10.1186/s12992-015-0100-5 PMID: 25886175

Faggini, M., Cosimato, S., Nota, F. D., & Nota, G. (2019). Pursuing sustainability for healthcare through digital platforms. *Sustainability (Basel)*, 11(1), 165. DOI: 10.3390/su11010165

Kostkova, P. (2015). Grand challenges in digital health. *Frontiers in Public Health*, 3, 134. DOI: 10.3389/fpubh.2015.00134 PMID: 26000272

Luosta, J. (2015). eHealth in corporate social responsibility: Explorative study on extended stakeholder value for health.

Nanda, W. M., Cahyani, P., & Abarran, M. A. E. F. (2024). Responsibilities of medical practice through digital health platforms. *Yuridika*, 39(1), 97–110. DOI: 10.20473/ydk.v39i1.43150

Oftedal, E. M., Foss, L., & Iakovleva, T. (2019). Responsible for responsibility? A study of digital e-health startups. *Sustainability (Basel)*, 11(19), 5433. DOI: 10.3390/su11195433

Orbik, Z., & Zozuľaková, V. (2019). Corporate social and digital responsibility. *Management Systems in Production Engineering*, 27(2), 79–83. DOI: 10.1515/mspe-2019-0013

Rodrigues, S., Kanduri, A., Nyamathi, A., Dutt, N., Khargonekar, P., & Rahmani, A. (2022). Digital health–enabled community-centered care: Scalable model to empower future community health workers using human-in-the-loop artificial intelligence. *JMIR Formative Research*, 6(4), e29535. DOI: 10.2196/29535 PMID: 35384853

Samuel, L. (2021). Transforming the healthcare system: The public-private healthcare dichotomy in India in the era of digital health. *Proceedings of the International Conference on Public Health*, 6(1), 18–31. DOI: 10.17501/24246735.2020.6103

Saxena, K., Balani, S., & Srivastava, P. (2021). The relationship among corporate social responsibility, sustainability and organizational performance in pharmaceutical sector: A literature review. *International Journal of Pharmaceutical and Healthcare Marketing*, 15(4), 572–597. DOI: 10.1108/IJPHM-12-2020-0104

Senay, E., & Landrigan, P. J. (2018). Assessment of environmental sustainability and corporate social responsibility reporting by large health care organizations. *JAMA Network Open*, 1(4), e180975. DOI: 10.1001/jamanetworkopen.2018.0975 PMID: 30646093

Wang, M., Yuan, R., Guan, X., Wang, Z., Zeng, Y., & Liu, T. (2024). The influence of digital platform on the implementation of corporate social responsibility: From the perspective of environmental science development to explore its potential role in public health. *Frontiers in Public Health*, 12, 1343546. DOI: 10.3389/fpubh.2024.1343546 PMID: 38711767

Chapter 7
User Perceptions in Measuring the Impact of Digital Health Platforms on Social Care

Dinesh Sathasivam
http://orcid.org/0000-0003-1751-7973
Sri Ramachandra Institute of Higher Education and Research, India

Renuka Vidyashankar
Sri Ramachandra Institute of Higher Education and Research, India

Nalini R.
SASTRA University (Deemed), India

ABSTRACT

The present study aims to measure the perception of users towards digital health platforms and its benefits to society. Researcher has collected 282 responses from the respondents. Notably, younger adults, particularly those aged 21 to 40 years, are the predominant users, reflecting a strong inclination towards digital health applications within this demographic. The trend of using these platforms for both personal and family healthcare underscores a preference for family-inclusive solutions. The preference for mobile devices among 97.3% of respondents emphasized the need for mobile-optimized digital health platforms. Apollo 24/7's prominence as the most used application suggests its strong market presence and user satisfaction. The factor analysis identifies four main factors influencing the use of digital health platforms, accounting for a substantial proportion of the variance in the dataset. These factors highlight the significant trends and characteristics affecting users' en-

DOI: 10.4018/979-8-3693-5991-4.ch007

gagement, proactive health management, trust in security, and barriers to adoption.

1. INTRODUCTION

Digital health Digital health has evolved from the early days of digitized records to the current era of Artificial Intelligence and Internet of Things, and telehealth. The evolution of digital health has been driven by technological advancements and a growing emphasis on patient-centric care. Some milestones in the evolution of digital health are as follows - In 1959, The University of Nebraska used two-way video communication for telemedicine for the first time in the United States. Clinicians used interactive video to transmit neurological examinations across campus to medical students. In Late 1990s, Studies showed that teleradiology reduced transports for head injuries out of rural areas and that teleconsultation with a radiologist significantly affected diagnosis and treatment plans. Prior to the pandemic, Some services used telehealth routinely, such as remote monitoring for implantable cardiac devices.

Now in Current era, Digital health is leveraging AI, IoT, and telehealth to enhance patient care and accessibility. For example, AI is currently used in oncology, including FDA-approved AI used in support of care for breast, lung, and prostate cancer

Digital platforms are essential in today's technologically evolved society, where everything changes rapidly. Digital health, or digital healthcare, is a wide, interdisciplinary term that encompasses ideas from the integration of technology and innovation in the healthcare system. Digital health refers to the effective and stable digital transformation of the healthcare industry, which includes software, hardware, and services. Digital health platforms reduce healthcare expenditures while meeting the needs of a large number of patients in a timely manner. Technology and healthcare innovations are constantly enhancing the delivery and quality of health services by assisting in diagnosis in preventive care, and treatment in curative, and palliative settings.

India has many digital health platforms, including telemedicine apps, healthtech startups, and initiatives. Telemedicine apps include Tata 1mg, Practo, MFine, Netmeds, and PharmEasy. Tata 1mg is a leading online healthcare platform that offers doctor on demand and an online pharmacy. Practo is an integrated healthcare app founded in 2007. Healthtech startups include HealthifyMe, cult.fit, Innovaccer, Tata Health, Docplexus, and Ekincare. Initiatives include Ayushman Bharat Digital Mission (ABDM), CoWIN App, Aarogya Setu, e-Sanjeevani, and e-Hospital. The ABDM was launched in 2021 to strengthen the digital health ecosystem by integrating health data records and registries. It also focuses on registering health providers and beneficiaries. Another key facet of the digital health mission is creating the Ayushman Bharat Health Account (ABHA) for individuals and establishing a unique identity (ABHA ID) across healthcare providers. This allows seamless access to unified benefits from insurance schemes and public health programs.

Government, as well as the World Health Organization, prioritize accessible and inexpensive health services and goods such as medications, vaccines, and public health services. Health technology is a crucial driver in meeting health-related sustainable development goals. Following the pandemic, the availability of digital health platforms boosted remote patient support and virtual care. Digital health systems have helped diagnose fatal diseases like cancer earlier and more precisely than people alone. Spending on digital healthcare solutions is expected to total EUR 232 billion by 2025.

2. STATEMENT OF THE PROBLEM

Digital healthcare platforms are transforming traditional healthcare procedures, which can lead to several benefits for both citizens and the government's contribution to society. These advantages are especially clear during pandemics like Covid-19, when the majority of healthcare services are delivered digitally. Though the digital platform is gaining inroads into healthcare institutions, there is still some skepticism due to worries about data security and, more specifically, the ability to connect with a doctor in person. There have been very few studies that look at how people perceive digital healthcare systems. The research aims to better understand the reach of digital apps and the problems that users confront when utilizing the facility and how they are affected by health consciousness and motivation.

3. OBJECTIVES OF THE STUDY

To scrutinize the socioeconomic profile of the respondents

To measure the health consciousness and its impact on intention to use healthcare applications

To understand the relationship between health motivation and perceived privacy protection

To find out factors influencing the perception of digital health platforms among users of healthcare platforms.

4. HYPOTHESES OF THE STUDY

H_1: There is a significant difference between health consciousness and its impact on intention to use healthcare applications

H_0: There is no significant difference between health consciousness and its impact on intention to use healthcare applications

H_2: There is a significant relationship between health motivation and perceived privacy protection

H_0: There is no significant relationship between health motivation and perceived privacy protection

5. REVIEW OF LITERATURE

Mobile health (mHealth) tools have emerged as a promising health care technology that may contribute to better access to health services, enhanced quality of care, and cost savings. These novel technologies may also present an opportunity to enhance communication between patients and their health care providers and facilitate self-monitoring and self-management, leading to better treatment outcomes. Patients' adoption is a key factor for mHealth success; however, it has been recognized as one of the key challenges. (Christine Jacob et al 2022). Digital health technologies have changed the way healthcare is experienced by patients. Research highlights the disconnect between the development and implementation of digital health tools and the patients they are created for. (Samaneh Madanian 2023) Remote monitoring and consultations are examples of online health services made possible by technological improvements. Technology and services have increased, access to treatments regardless of geographic location, while also allowing patients to take a more active part in their clinical care. The active role can be defined as patient engagement, involvement, compliance and adherence, (Menichetti J. et al., 2016). Few research has focused on consumers' or patients' perceptions on digital health solutions, despite poor patient adoption and acceptability (Park JI et al, 2021). Patient portals, smartphone applications, and wearable technology are examples of digital solutions that provide convenience, give patients access to their health information and professional knowledge, and make health data collection less invasive. This might result in improved patient experiences (Perakslis E, 2021) and perhaps transform the patient-provider interaction from a paternalistic to a patient-centric approach. Despite the fact that digital health solutions are created to meet the perceived requirements of patients, it appears that patients have seldom been included in the design process from the beginning, and their opinions are not taken into consideration.

Panggabean. Bungarana, Suharjo. Budib, Sumarwan. Ujangc, Yuliati. Lilik Noorc. (2023). Telemedicine characteristics include mobile consultation, electronic diagnosis, electronic prescription, and electronic pharmacy. The major objective of this study is to investigate human perceptions of perceived value as well as social impacts on intention to utilize digital healthcare services. A Google Forms web link is used to distribute a collection of four-point Likert scale surveys. A total of 364 full replies were obtained. The data is processed using a descriptive technique with Microsoft Excel and SPSS software. The Cronbach's Alpha coefficient and the item total-correlation approach are used to assess validity and reliability. 87 respondents out of 364 (24%) have utilized digital healthcare services, with Halodoc (92%) being most desired application, and mobile consultation becoming the most popular option to use. The average score for perceived value is 3.16 out of four, while for social influence, it is 2.86. Another conclusion of this study shows that some social factors from family, friends, and mass media have an effect on amplifying the intention to use. A lack of trust is thought to be the root reason of a small number of users.

Many studies advocate a collaborative approach to designing future digital health solutions [Hanna L, et al. 2017, Monaco A, 2021]. However, research reflect on several elements and criteria influencing patients' perceptions of digital health technologies. In this study, we intend to examine and combine existing evidence about patients' perceptions on digital health tools and apps. This enabled us to extract and comprehend existing research trends, identify gaps, and consider future options. This study also attempted to uncover barriers and variables that promote the use of digital health technologies.

6. RESEARCH DESIGN

The researcher outlines the features of variables affecting the use of digital apps in healthcare. As a result, the descriptive research design is appropriate for this study. The data was collected via an online structured, self-administered questionnaire. A sample of 23 respondents was used in the pilot study to verify, assess reliability, validity, and identify the optimal sample size for the study. Out of 23 replies, three were not appropriately responded to. As a result, the error rate is predicted to be 13.04%. The researcher opted on a 95% confidence level and a standard z value of 1.96. The average variance estimated across the variables impacting user perceptions of digital health platforms is 1.248. A minimum of 282 samples are required, and the researcher collected survey data from 293 respondents. The researcher employed purposive sampling to acquire data.

Cronbach alpha is used to assess the dependability of research instruments. There are seventeen functional factors used to quantify consumers' perceptions of digital health platforms. The current study's Cronbach alpha value is 0.940. It implies that there is a 94% consistency in measuring consumers' perceptions of digital health platforms. The significance value of the F-test demonstrates the internal validity of the research instrument. The present study has a significance level of 0. As a result, the research instrument has been determined to be internally valid.

7. DATA ANALYSIS AND DISCUSSIONS

Table 1. Demographic profile of the respondents

Variable	Measurement	Frequency	Percent
Gender	Female	167	57.0
Age wise classification of the respondents	21-40 years	164	56.0
Healthcare Application is frequently used for	Myself & Spouse	131	44.7
	My parents / in-laws	102	34.8
Residence	Urban	275	93.9
Education level	Post-graduation	214	73.0
Occupation	Employed in private concerns	154	52.6
Monthly Income	Less than Rs. 30000	96	32.8
Family Type	Nuclear family	165	56.3
Device preferred by you to use healthcare platform	Mobile	285	97.3
Applications used	Apollo 24/7	126	43.0

The table above illustrates the demographic profile of respondents and their perceptions towards digital health platforms. Compared to males, a higher proportion of females are utilizing digital health platforms. Out of 282 respondents, 167 (57%) are using digital health applications. These users predominantly belong to the younger demographic, with 56% of respondents aged between 21 and 40 years. A significant portion (44.7%) of these users employ digital health applications for themselves and their spouses, while 34.8% use them primarily for their parents or in-laws. Additionally, the majority (93.9%) of respondents reside in urban areas. Furthermore, 214 respondents, accounting for 73%, have completed post-graduate. A significant portion of the respondents, 154 out of 282 (52.6%), are employed in private sector jobs. This suggests that a large portion of the users of digital health platforms are likely to be working professionals, possibly indicating a need for accessible and convenient healthcare options due to their busy schedules. A considerable number of respondents, 96 out of 282 (32.8%), have a monthly income of less than Rs. 30,000. This indicates that nearly one-third of the users of digital health platforms come from lower-income brackets, highlighting the potential affordability and cost-effectiveness of these platforms as a significant factor in their adoption. The majority of respondents, 165 out of 282 (56.3%), live in nuclear families. This could imply that the primary decision-makers and users of digital health platforms are likely to be from smaller family units, which might influence their healthcare choices and preferences for more individualized healthcare solutions. An overwhelming majority of respondents, 275 out of 282 (97.3%), prefer using mobile devices to access healthcare platforms. This underscores the importance of mobile-friendly interfaces and the widespread reliance on smartphones for healthcare management, making mobile optimization a critical aspect for digital health services. Among the various healthcare applications available, Apollo 24/7 is the most popular, with 126 out of 282 respondents (43%) reporting its usage. This suggests that Apollo 24/7 has a significant market presence and user base, indicating its effectiveness and reliability in providing healthcare services digitally.

Table 2. Exploratory factor analysis

Total Variance Explained			
Component	**Rotation Sums of Squared Loadings**		
	Total	**% of Variance**	**Cumulative %**
1	5.979	35.169	35.169
2	3.923	23.077	58.246
3	2.595	15.266	73.512
4	2.030	11.939	85.451

The first factor explains 35.169% of the total variance in the dataset. This suggests that this factor accounts for a substantial portion of the variability among the respondents. It is likely capturing the most significant underlying trend or pattern in the data, which might be related to a major demographic characteristic or common behavior regarding the use of digital health platforms.

The second factor explains an additional 23.077% of the variance, bringing the cumulative variance explained to 58.246%. This factor is also significant and may represent another key trend or demographic characteristic that influences how respondents use digital health platforms, distinct from the first factor.

The third factor accounts for 15.266% of the total variance, with a cumulative variance of 73.512%. This indicates another important but less dominant trend or characteristic influencing the dataset.

The fourth factor explains an additional 11.939% of the variance, making the cumulative explained variance 85.451%. This factor, while smaller, still represents a meaningful aspect of the dataset's variability.

Interpretation based on the rotated component matrix

Factor 1: Engagement and Satisfaction with Digital Health Applications

This factor represents the respondents' overall engagement with and satisfaction in using digital health applications. It includes their willingness to invest time in learning about new health-related technologies (.857), confidence in the diagnostic capabilities of digital health technologies (.637), and the belief that these platforms improve their ability to track health (.591). Additionally, respondents feel that using digital health applications enhances their healthcare experience (.803), plan to incorporate these platforms into their daily routine (.655), expect to continue using them in the future (.891), have already started using them (.778), and are satisfied with the digital health applications (.797).

Factor 2: Proactive Health Management

This factor highlights the respondents' proactive approach to managing their health using digital platforms. It encompasses their habits of actively seeking health information (.821), regularly monitoring health indicators like blood pressure and cholesterol (.860), being motivated to use technology that helps manage their health better (.672), and believing that digital health platforms provide reliable health information (.770).

Factor 3: Security and Trust in Digital Health Platforms

This factor focuses on the respondents' perceptions of security and trust when using digital health platforms. It indicates their confidence that personal health information is secure on digital health platforms (.840) and their comfort in sharing health information with these applications (.771).

Factor 4: Barriers to Adoption

This factor addresses the barriers to adopting digital health platforms. It includes concerns that digital healthcare cannot replace physical consultation (.701), discomfort with the way healthcare services are consumed digitally (.944), and mixed feelings regarding data security (.633).

Figure 1. AMOS graphically represents the user perceptions in measuring the impact of digital health platforms on social care

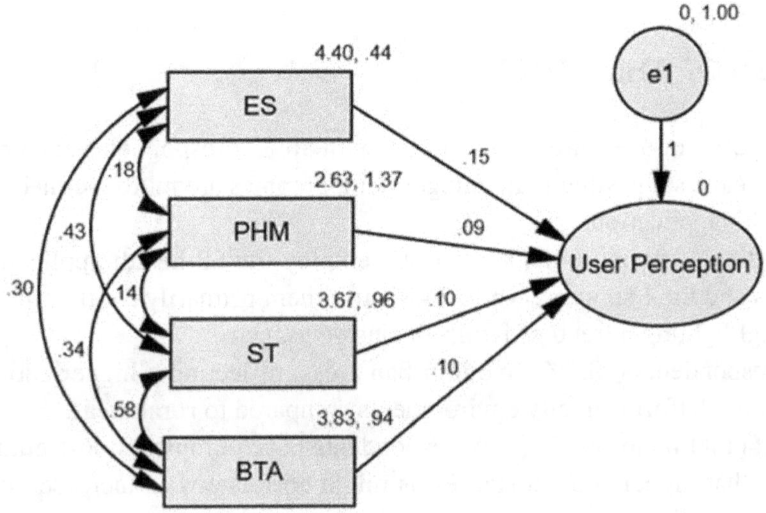

The AMOS graphical representation of the study illustrates the relationships between the key factors influencing User Perceptions in Measuring the Impact of Digital Health Platforms on Social Care (UP). The diagram typically includes arrows pointing from the independent variables—Engagement and Satisfaction with Digital Health Applications (ES), Proactive Health Management (PHM), Security and Trust in Digital Health Platform (ST), and Barriers to Adoption (BTA)—toward the dependent variable, User Perceptions (UP). The thickness and direction of these arrows represent the strength and direction of the relationships, with the regression weights indicating how much each factor contributes to changes in user perceptions. For example, Engagement and Satisfaction (ES) would have the thickest arrow due to its stronger positive impact (0.151) on user perceptions compared to the other factors.

Additionally, the AMOS model includes covariances between the independent variables, shown as double-headed arrows between them. These covariances illustrate how these factors interrelate, such as the moderate positive relationship between Barriers to Adoption (BTA) and Security and Trust (ST) (0.578), suggesting that higher perceived barriers are associated with increased concerns about security and trust. The graphical representation, therefore, provides a visual summary of the study's findings, demonstrating the interconnectedness of the factors and their collective influence on how users perceive the impact of digital health platforms on social care.

FINDINGS OF THE STUDY

The majority of users are young adults, with 56% of respondents aged between 21 and 40 years, suggesting that younger demographics are more inclined towards digital health applications.

A significant portion (44.7%) of users employ digital health applications for themselves and their spouses, while 34.8% use them primarily for their parents or in-laws, highlighting a trend of family-inclusive usage.

Most respondents (93.9%) live in urban areas, reflecting a higher adoption of digital health platforms in city environments compared to rural areas.

A substantial majority (73%) of respondents have completed post-graduation, suggesting that higher educational levels might correlate with increased usage of digital health applications.

Over half (52.6%) of the respondents are employed in private sector jobs, indicating that busy professionals are likely to seek convenient digital health solutions.

About 32.8% of respondents have a monthly income of less than Rs. 30,000, suggesting that affordability and cost-effectiveness of digital health platforms are important factors for a significant segment of users.

The majority (56.3%) of respondents live in nuclear families, which may influence their preference for individualized healthcare solutions.

An overwhelming majority (97.3%) prefer using mobile devices to access healthcare platforms, highlighting the critical need for mobile-optimized health applications.

Apollo 24/7 is the most used healthcare application among respondents, with 43% reporting its usage, indicating its strong market presence and user satisfaction.

The first factor explains 35.169% of the total variance in the dataset. This suggests that this factor accounts for a substantial portion of the variability among the respondents. It is likely capturing the most significant underlying trend or pattern in the data, which might be related to a major demographic characteristic or common behavior regarding the use of digital health platforms.

The second factor explains an additional 23.077% of the variance, bringing the cumulative variance explained to 58.246%. This factor is also significant and may represent another key trend or demographic characteristic that influences how respondents use digital health platforms, distinct from the first factor.

The third factor accounts for 15.266% of the total variance, with a cumulative variance of 73.512%. This indicates another important but less dominant trend or characteristic influencing the dataset.

The fourth factor explains an additional 11.939% of the variance, making the cumulative explained variance 85.451%. This factor, while smaller, still represents a meaningful aspect of the dataset's variability.

Engagement and Satisfaction as a Primary Driver: Among the factors analyzed, *Engagement and Satisfaction with Digital Health Applications (ES)* emerged as the most influential in shaping *User Perceptions (UP)*. With a regression weight of 0.151, this factor demonstrates that users who are more engaged and satisfied with digital health applications tend to have more positive perceptions regarding the impact of these platforms on social care. This suggests that enhancing user engagement and satisfaction could be a crucial strategy for improving perceptions of digital health platforms' effectiveness in social care.

Interconnectedness of Barriers, Security, and Trust: The covariances between the independent variables highlight significant interrelations, particularly between *Barriers to Adoption (BTA)* and *Security and Trust (ST)*, with a covariance of 0.578. This finding indicates that as users perceive more barriers to adopting digital health platforms, their concerns about security and trust also increase. This relationship underscores the importance of addressing barriers to adoption in tandem with enhancing security measures to build trust among users, which could, in turn, positively influence their overall perception of the platform's impact on social care.

Suggestions of the study

- Given the high preference for mobile devices, digital health platforms should prioritize developing and optimizing mobile-friendly interfaces to improve user experience and accessibility.
- Develop targeted marketing and feature sets to address the needs and preferences of female users, who exhibit a higher usage rate of digital health platforms compared to males.
- Integrate features that support proactive health management, such as tools for tracking health indicators and providing reliable health information, to cater to users who actively seek to manage their health.

- Strengthen data security protocols and transparently communicate these measures to enhance user trust and address concerns regarding the security of personal health information.
- Develop affordable pricing models or offer tiered services to cater to users from lower-income brackets, ensuring that cost does not hinder access to essential digital health services.

CONCLUSION

The study reveals significant insights into the usage patterns and perceptions of digital health platforms among respondents. Notably, younger adults, particularly those aged 21 to 40 years, are the predominant users, reflecting a strong inclination towards digital health applications within this demographic. The trend of using these platforms for both personal and family healthcare underscores a preference for family-inclusive solutions. Urban residents represent a vast majority, indicating a higher adoption rate in city environments, likely due to better infrastructure and accessibility. Educational background plays a role, as higher levels of education correlate with increased usage of digital health applications. Busy professionals, particularly those employed in the private sector, demonstrate a clear demand for convenient digital health solutions. Additionally, affordability is a key factor, with a substantial portion of users having lower monthly incomes, highlighting the importance of cost-effective solutions.

The preference for mobile devices among 97.3% of respondents emphasizes the need for mobile-optimized digital health platforms. Apollo 24/7's prominence as the most used application suggests its strong market presence and user satisfaction. The factor analysis identifies four main factors influencing the use of digital health platforms, accounting for a substantial proportion of the variance in the dataset. These factors highlight the significant trends and characteristics affecting users' engagement, proactive health management, trust in security, and barriers to adoption.

The study highlights the significant influence of user engagement and satisfaction on positive perceptions of digital health platforms' impact on social care. Addressing barriers to adoption and enhancing security and trust are also crucial for improving user perceptions. The interconnectedness of these factors suggests a holistic approach is needed to optimize the effectiveness of digital health platforms in social care settings.

REFERENCES

Gilbert, R. M. (2022). Reimagining digital healthcare with a patient-centric approach: The role of user experience (UX) research. *Frontiers in Digital Health*, 4, 899976. DOI: 10.3389/fdgth.2022.899976 PMID: 36016600

Hanna, L., Gill, S. D., Newstead, L., Hawkins, M., & Osborne, R. H. (2017). Patient perspectives on a personally controlled electronic health record used in regional Australia: 'I can be like my own doctor'. *The HIM Journal*, 46(1), 42–48. DOI: 10.1177/1833358316661063 PMID: 27486184

Jacob, C., Sezgin, E., Sanchez-Vazquez, A., & Ivory, C. (2022, January). Sociotechnical Factors Impacting Patients' Adoption of Mobile Health Tools: Systematic Literature Review and Narrative Synthesis. *JMIR mHealth and uHealth*, 10(5), e36284. Advance online publication. DOI: 10.2196/36284 PMID: 35318189

Madanian, S., Nakarada-Kordic, I., Reay, S., & T'heniel, C. (2023, December). Patients' perspectives on digital health tools. *PEC Innovation*, 2, 100171. DOI: 10.1016/j.pecinn.2023.100171 PMID: 37384154

Menichetti, J., Libreri, C., Lozza, E., & Graffigna, G. (2016). Giving patients a starring role in their own care: A bibliometric analysis of the on-going literature debate. *Health Expectations*, 19(3), 516–526. DOI: 10.1111/hex.12299 PMID: 25369557

Monaco, A., Palmer, K., Faber, N. H. R., Kohler, I., Silva, M., & Vatland, A.. (2021). Digital health tools for managing noncommunicable diseases during and after the COVID-19 pandemic: Perspectives of patients and caregivers. *Journal of Medical Internet Research*, 23(1), 23. DOI: 10.2196/25652 PMID: 33464206

Panggabean, B., Suharjo, B., Sumarwan, U., & Yuliati, L. N. (2023). Panggabean. Bungarana, Suharjo. Budib, Sumarwan. Ujangc, Yuliati. Lilik Noorc, (2023), Perception study of perceived value and social influence of digital health services in Indonesia. *International Journal of Risk & Safety in Medicine*, 34(4), 367–377. DOI: 10.3233/JRS-220058 PMID: 37302043

Park, J. I., Lee, H. Y., Kim, H., Lee, J., Shinn, J., & Kim, H. S. (2021). Lack of acceptance of digital healthcare in the medical market: Addressing Old problems raised by various clinical professionals and developing possible solutions. *Journal of Korean Medical Science*, 36(37), e253. DOI: 10.3346/jkms.2021.36.e253 PMID: 34581521

Perakslis, E., & Ginsburg, G. S. (2021). Digital health—The need to assess benefits, risks, and value. *Journal of the American Medical Association*, 325, 127–128. PMID: 33369627

Chapter 8
Patient-Centered Care for TB Patients: An Effective Approach to Corporate Social Responsibility

S. Srinivasan
http://orcid.org/0009-0002-0179-9849
Department of Humanities and Social Sciences, Graphic Era University (Deemed), India

Prabha Lama
Department of Humanities and Social Sciences, Graphic Era University (Deemed), India

ABSTRACT

The research study emphasized patient-centred care using a community assessment tool for persons with TB. The main objective was to identify the timeliness of healthcare services, access to TB services, quality of information from TB patients, and attitudes of healthcare providers, communities, and families towards TB patients. Conducted in the Trichy district across nearly 10 TUs, site selection was based on TB champions, high caseload, and District TB Officer suggestions. The study had a descriptive design with convenient sampling and used a mixed-method approach. The sample size was nearly 1,223 TB patients, including in-patients, current patients, and those who completed treatment within 6 months. The study aims to promote corporate social responsibility, provide better treatment for all patients, enhance their lives, and effectively eliminate TB.

DOI: 10.4018/979-8-3693-5991-4.ch008

INTRODUCTION

Patient-centric care is one of the core and central points for TB patients, benefiting them with all the services provided in PCC. It encompasses all services, including those from healthcare providers, to deliver high-quality healthcare for TB patients. It ensures continuous health improvement services (Tamil & Sain, 2023). PCC consistently offers better assessment for healthcare providers and its service quality to improve the health of TB patients. There is no universally accepted definition for PCC; it is referred to as patient-centeredness or patient-centricity (Alkhaibari et al., 2023). This study aims to demonstrate how comprehensive PCC can effectively benefit TB patients. It introduces a novel approach that emphasizes the patients' roles and the feasible implementation of healthcare delivery support for their benefit in a sustainable manner. TB champions play a vital role in supporting patient access to PCC on a regular, periodic basis. The study focuses on providing a better health system to identify the most effective PCC models and achieve the goal of systematic improvement. The study is based on interventions designed to provide better education for people affected by TB and to offer psychosocial support (Myburgh et al., 2023). PCC can play an important role in supporting the diagnosis, treatment, and prevention of TB, including early diagnosis. PCC provides early intervention services for TB patients, addressing all aspects of care and treatment adherence to ensure better healthcare services (Mahmud et al., 2020).

The study involves CSR activities to support healthcare delivery, particularly in improving the well-being and health services of TB patients. CSR takes accountability for supporting TB patients and providing better health services. CSR plays an important role in developing the social, economic, environmental, and societal aspects of TB patients' lives (Fallah Shayan et al., 2022).

CSR can support by contributing 2% of the company's average net profit. This 2% can lead to tremendous changes in vulnerable communities, benefiting health-affected individuals and those in need. It also helps to enhance the industry's reputation among employees and the community (Erhemjamts et al., 2013). The significance of the study is to provide TB patients with effective services through CSR activities and to improve their lives (Katsanis et al., 2021). CSR focuses on philanthropic activities and volunteerism, as well as environmental sustainability, to enhance human life (Saz-Gil et al., 2020). The proposed chapter incorporates CSR and PCC to effectively support TB patients and provide better services for health-affected individuals. Primary data can be used to evaluate various aspects of TB patients' utilization of services, including the timeliness of health services in PCC, access to TB services, the quality of information received from health centers, and attitudes among health workers. This data can help address and support CSR activities (Macq et al., 2005). The study clearly indicates the attitudes of healthcare workers, general communities, and family members. The study highlights the significant approach that CSR can take to support various aspects of addressing health issues in the future (Boukouvalas et al., 2020).

The study addresses TB patient treatment adherence and the loneliness felt by TB patients, and it supports CSR activities by adopting various strategies. PCC can support TB patients' wellness and treatment adherence throughout the entire course of treatment. CSR can enhance the well-being of TB patients by including physical support, emotional support, and social aspects. PCC, when incorporated with CSR, can improve the overall quality of life for TB patients (Rajeswari et al., 2005). CSR can provide additional support to contribute to TB patients' wellness through CSR initiatives and activities. CSR can support various aspects, including engaging TB patients in health education and awareness campaigns to enhance the well-being of TB patients and community members (Agyemang-Duah et al., 2024). CSR plays an important role in providing services and combating aging TB disease. PCC can incorporate CSR initiatives to address the complete treatment and surveillance of TB patients and provide successful treatment (Munro et al., 2007).

The research study emphasized patient-centred care through the use of a community assessment tool to evaluate its effectiveness for persons with TB. The main objective of the study was to identify the timeliness of healthcare services in providing diagnostic services, access to TB services for better treatment during and after TB, the quality of information obtained from TB patients, the behaviour and attitude of healthcare providers, and local communities and families' attitudes towards TB patients to improve service identification. The research study was conducted in the India, Tamil Nadu state and Trichy district, covering nearly 10 TUs. The selection was based on the availability of TB champions, the high caseload, and suggestions from the District TB Officer. The research design was descriptive, and the sampling method was convenient sampling. A mixed-method approach, combining qualitative and quantitative methods, was used. The sample size of the study was nearly 1,223 TB patients, including in-patients (IP), current patients (CP), and patients who completed treatment within 6 months. The study plays a significant role in promoting corporate social responsibility to adopt the village, provide better treatment for all the patients, enhance their lives, and effectively eliminate TB diseases.

BACKGROUND OF THE STUDY

The significance of the study on PCC and CSR lies in enhancing TB patients' lives, which includes the following themes to understand their profiles and needs for effective PCC approaches. The study emphasizes the diagnosis and treatment process, assessing how effectively they are utilized and how timely health services are followed. It assesses the availability of TB services for patients and ensures equitable healthcare provision. The quality of information TB patients receives from healthcare workers are also evaluated for clarity. Effective treatment adherence in daily routine life during the treatment period is examined. The study assesses TB patients' behavior and the attitude of healthcare providers during interactions to ensure compassionate, respectful, and supportive care. Local communities' and family members' attitudes and behavior are investigated to understand their perceptions of TB patients, supporting the reduction of stigma in society. The study highlights CSR as a crucial part of healthcare initiatives, demonstrating how businesses can contribute to public health goals, improve patient outcomes, and build strong community relations through responsible and ethical practices.

Patient-centric care is healthcare that involves treating the affected individual to provide physical health, emotional support, and social support for those in need, including psychological aspects. TB patients' treatment in PCC emphasizes the quality of care. It involves the patient's treatment and plans to ensure quality service, quality care, and support services in clinical aspects. The study provides important aspects of a better partnership between patients and healthcare providers (Kallon, 2018).

On the other hand, CSR plays a significant role in PCC for TB patients to enhance effective implementation. CSR mainly focuses on health and aims to improve health for TB patients, increasing better outcomes and the success or cure rate of the patients. It is the role of these activities to reduce health disparities and provide community support to needy patients (John et al., 2024). To adopt the PCC approach in CSR activities to support and commit to enhancing TB patients' well-being and preventing TB diseases. The CSR approach can provide additional support to improve the global effort for TB patients' outcomes, reduce the transmission rate, and promote public health (Uduji et al., 2019).

PCC and CSR Involve Various Health Activities to Reduce the TB Diseases

Community Engagement activities: CSR can involve local healthcare workers and support National Tuberculosis Elimination Program (NTEP) team members in organizing community-based interventions to ensure that TB patients' needs are identified and supported with necessary resources (WHO, 2023). This approach can increase various resources, such as funding mobile clinics, providing educational materials, and supporting healthcare workers.

Personalized Support: CSR can improve the effectiveness of strategies through PCC support by identifying needy individuals who can assist with medicine arrangements, ensure regular treatment adherence, and provide Adverse Reaction Support (ADR). Most prominently, to provide services such as counseling, social services, nutritional arrangements, and socio-economic assistance (Li, 2010). After successful treatment, arrange job opportunities, support TB patients' family members, and provide livelihood training for affected people.

Innovation and Technology Support: Digital health enhances technology improvements and PCC for TB patients. Digital health tools support TB patient interventions through mobile health apps, telemedicine options, and enhanced e-health records (Mezzalira et al., 2024). These tools can monitor and track patient details, such as drug adherence, loss to follow-up, treatment defaults, and post-treatment failures. Patients can be identified, and regular follow-up visits can be scheduled to improve success rates and cure TB. The technology can include reminders for medication, which can facilitate support for both patients and healthcare workers (Tadesse et al., 2021).

Education and Awareness program support: CSR provides additional support for PCC. It can improve awareness programs and implement TB prevention, treatment, and adherence support for TB patients. It can reduce TB levels and help achieve universal global health. Conducting regular and routine health campaigns in crowded public places is essential (Levine, 2007). This way, public awareness creation and workplaces, such as industries and places with high noise and dust, can conduct contact screening and wellness programs through educational awareness programs. We can protect against TB and identify it through early diagnosis.

A CSR strategy that supports PCC for TB patients to address individual needs can contribute to the greater social good and reduce the burden of TB in society. CSR has healthcare goals that make a difference in the fight against TB and supports additional help for the NTEP team and health workers' collaboration to fulfill CSR goals and objectives (Suseela & Shannawaz, 2023).

Conceptual Clarification

PCC focuses on TB patients as a better way to emphasize the affected individuals, their needs and values, and patients' preferences. It can address the TB patients' health behavior and support corporate efforts through emotional, psychological, and social and cultural support for the well-being of TB patients. PCC can ensure patients' involvement in drug consumption and promote the health and support of TB patients. The affected TB patients' PCC health care workers provide care and respect to respond to identified individual needs and improve the TB patients' outcomes.

Corporate Social Responsibility (CSR): The role of CSR is to enhance the society in the surrounding area, provide services, and focus on profit-making services. CSR adversely affects activities such as the environment, social equity, and public health in the nation and society. For a company, engaging in CSR activities is mandatory. It is a requirement to fulfill legal obligations, enhance the company's reputation and responsibility, and support the welfare of employees, customers, and the community.

Conceptual Clarification: Linking Patient-Centered Care for TB Patients to Corporate Social Responsibility

Ethical Response: Implementing PCC and CSR can increase responsibility for TB patients' care and support services. It can enhance the company's reputation, positively impact the company, and benefit society. The corporation aims to strengthen the focus on TB patients' health care services and support. It particularly aims to prevent health issues and ensure easy access to TB services.

Improve Public Health: Major health issues are present in all low-income countries, especially in Africa and India. PCC and CSR can initiate support for public health. They can provide support for eradicating TB disease. It not only supports TB patients but also provides overall support to the general public. It reduces the public health burden and contributes to a healthier community and a TB-free society.

The reputation of Corporate Image: PCC is involved with TB patients, and through CSR, it can improve corporate reputation and increase social responsibility within society and the corporate sector. This can improve industry loyalty and attract customers and employees who are retained by the corporation. These are the initiatives that are building a good reputation among stakeholders and funders, such as investors, partners, and the general community.

Long-term Economic Benefits: The PCC and CSR collaborative approach supports the economic aspects of TB patients, reduces the cost of healthcare, and promotes a healthier society. Two sets of follow-ups for the TB patients' innovation ideas aim to support TB patients, increase community health, and sustain improved healthcare services.

Collaboration Support: The collaboration fosters more innovation and provides additional support for eradicating TB. PCC and CSR collaboration with government, non-profit organizations, and healthcare voluntary organizations to support TB patients. This type of collaboration is more effective in enhancing the TB patients' lives and improving their quality of life after TB. This can enhance the benefits people receive from public health policies.

PCC for TB patients in CSR effective strategically plan to various activities to improve the public health and community support. It is a corporate responsibility to uphold ethical and social values to improve the quality of life for individuals. This type of initiative can improve CSR obligations and contribute to the global fight against TB. It supports a healthy society and enhances the well-being of TB patients.

Research Gap, Research Questions and Research Objectives

The study aims to find out if the healthcare service benefits people with TB, how effectively it functions in primary care centres (PCC), and how TB patients receive TB services in PCC. It examines the quality of information provided to TB patients from the PCC, and the behavior and attitude of healthcare providers, assessing their impact on TB patients and how they cope with the situation. Additionally, the study considers the feelings of family members and society towards TB patients. It identifies the problems faced by TB patients to assess the major gaps and address the issues.

Developing Frameworks for PCC-CSR Integration

The framework aims to improve research development and integrate PCC by incorporating CSR initiatives to promote TB care services. The framework involves various aspects of TB patients' engagement, cultural sensitivity, and collaboration with healthcare workers.

Experimental Study: A longitudinal study to enhance the PCC and CSR initiative and conduct experimental research should focus on pilot projects in these areas. It can improve TB patients' treatment adherence, patient satisfaction, and their quality of life. It compares studies between CSR and PCC, examining how CSR models can effectively promote TB patients' well-being and quality of life.

Corporate Motivation and Perceptions: There is no proper study on the aspects of PCC, making a focus on CSR initiatives essential. Qualitative research can help improve CSR leaders' motivation and their perception of benefits and challenges. It can enhance CSR strategies and increase interest in implementing public health aspects.

Analyze the Scalability and Adaptability: The research gap in PCC and CSR investigation methods is quite challenging and involves healthcare settings in both rural and urban contexts. Identifying the factors involved in the implementation of successful CSR activities.

Case Studies and Best Practices: There are no proper case studies and quite a few best practices in CSR initiatives. TB care improves practical experience, and further research is needed on patient lessons learned, PCC experience, and CSR best practices. These can enhance future research studies. It can enhance the new innovative approach to engaging stakeholders and achieving sustainable outcomes.

The research gap addresses patient-centered care for TB treatment, and CSR can play a significant role in public health outcomes. PCC and CSR play a vital role in improving TB care and enhancing social responsibilities. These above-mentioned strategies can explore the gaps and provide significant insights into practical aspects to improve effective patient treatment, enhance patient-centered care, and increase social responsibility in health care activities.

Hence, this chapter is an attempt to reduce the ambiguity of previous literature and it considers the following research questions:

- How to approach after symptoms through reaching the health facility or PCC?
- How to access the treatment start time and what are the processes and problems faced by TB Patients?
- What are the problems faced during the treatment and how do TB patients overcome them?
- How to reduce the ADR issues and what remedies are available for TB patients?
- What are the timelines for the health services?
- How to get TB services and benefit TB patients?
- How do they get quality information?
- What are the merits and demerits of health workers in supporting TB patients?
- What are the problems faced by the local community and family members of TB patients?

Literature Review

PCC provides personalized healthcare for individual patients' needs and preferences. This study highlights the effective management of TB by improving patient outcomes and ensuring treatment adherence. The study mentions that PCC for TB patients can serve as a viable CSR strategy for healthcare organizations. TB is one of the world's major health problems, especially in low- and middle-income countries (Igbo, 2023). The study provides comprehensive support through PCC, which can address TB patients' health services and reduce the costs associated with medical and treatment support (Albareda, 2010; Googins et al., 2007). PCC provides health services to TB patients and achieves higher satisfaction, even though PCC alone cannot support all TB patients. Through additional support, treatment time can be optimized, leading to better treatment adherence, improved outcomes, and higher success rates among TB patients. This approach ensures a better standard of treatment for TB patients (Waweru et al., 2020). The study reveals that PCC enhances TB patients' lifestyles through CSR activities, contributing to improved community health. The findings from the longitudinal study provide comprehensive support for the long-term impact of CSR outcomes on TB patients (Ekman et al., 2011).

The Hospital Consumer Assessment of Healthcare Providers and Systems (HCAHPS) patient satisfaction surveys show that physician-owned hospitals (POHs) receive more top 5-star ratings than other hospitals (Sharma, 2018). The Affordable Care Act (ACA) regulated physician-owned hospitals, positively impacting patient benefits. The quality of care and services is high in both corporate-owned and not-for-profit hospitals. PCC practices are implemented in all types of hospitals, but ownership affects preferences in some practices. The outcome measures include patient perceptions of the quality of care and service (Sharma, 2018). The study presents several questions from its viewpoint, such as how CSR demonstrates its commitment to stakeholders and identifies them, how stakeholders engage with and support CSR efforts, and how stakeholders are managed. It also explores how CSR and stakeholders support health improvements in nations and assist vulnerable people (Macias, 2016). CSR mainly concentrates on affected populations, prioritizing children, the elderly, ANC patients, and individuals with disabilities, to provide enhanced service quality (Srinivasan et al., 2023).

A recent study conducted the CSR and PCC linkage between the health and well-being of TB patients. CSR supports the delivery of PCC through vehicles within healthcare organizations. The findings show that CSR and PCC are interrelated in health aspects, particularly focusing on PCC as part of the CSR strategy. There are two features involved in the quality of care for health-affected people and in providing health education promotion. CSR can support PCC in giving patients rights and dignity, as both explicitly emphasize PCC characteristics (Buttigieg et al., 2019). Social responsibility can be attributed to health professionals within health systems, as it can create effective and equitable support for a sustainable system. The present paper emphasizes the role of health professionals and communities in identifying problems and implementing a patient-centred vision. It can improve the health and well-being of patients (Lopez, 2022).

CSR can be adopted for patient communication support. Communication strategies are not only important for corporations but also crucial for healthcare support. This study emphasizes how CSR can improve the healthcare industry by highlighting the hypocrisy of hospitals and empowering patients with informed clinical support and healthcare advancements in socially and politically meaningful ways. Health communication provides patients and physicians with patient-friendly medical support to better understand medical procedures (Student, 2023). The research explores CSR findings and the interconnections between non-profit and for-profit entities in acting socially responsible for global firms. The study mainly focused on firms and the consequences of social support for community needs; highlighting how social responsibility applies to the various groups they serve (Smith, 2011).

From the author's point of view, PCC clinical ethics in nutrition practice promote healthcare and a clinical ethics model. Nutritional support for affected individuals is incorporated with PCC in clinical aspects. It can improve the cultural elements for health care professionals to provide nutritional support for affected individuals, patients, and their family members. CSR ensures interconnection with the PCC team and supports medical and life-sustaining treatment, nutritional support for PCC, prevention, clinical ethics, religious/spiritual and cultural diversity, and care planning. CSR is part of the support activities to involve patient care and empower patients and their family members (Schwartz, 2013).

PCC can be practiced in holistic care involving various components such as physicians, healthcare providers, and social workers to implement efficiency for the affected community and to provide holistic care support for physicians. PCC can enhance patients' health through various human resources, such as physicians, nurses, and healthcare workers, to provide responsive care. CSR can interlink with PCC and support the shared work for health concerns to influence professional practices in implementing patient health care support, including PCC practices in acute care for hospitals (Sidani et al., 2018).

The study highlights the CSR policy to promote the importance of health care implementation and support for medical clinics, including mobile clinics, in unprivileged and peripheral areas where people benefit. It can provide various ways to improve and implement CSR policies and the importance of enhancing health and well-being for affected communities through the use of mobile medical clinics (Bhardwaj, 2023).

PCC and CSR play a role in social responsibility to reduce health inequalities based on race and ethnicity, provide support for socioeconomic status, and address the inescapable reality of racism in America. To reduce discrimination in accessing treatment and provide balanced medicine and well-being for patients, it is important to foster a strong relationship between patients and physicians to meet the healthcare needs of society. There are challenges faced in the medical profession to establish an equilibrium between the quality of health care and individual patients, to effect social changes, and to achieve health goals for all (Francis, 2001).

The study discussed the relevant and recent trends in PCC and CSR collaboration, emphasizing patient health and well-being. The study provides comprehensive information on the status of TB patients, identifying the timeline for receiving patient health services, how they access TB services, and the roles and responsibilities of CSR and PCC support services. Patients need to receive quality information from the health sector, such as the role of PCC in providing valuable information. How behavioral health staff and physicians provide support for TB patients, and how CSR plays a role in empowering and treating TB patients. Additionally, how community attitudes and family members support patients, and the role of CSR in enhancing campaign modes and creating awareness programs. CSR can provide additional support to PCC for implementing services for TB patients who are entitled to CSR.

CSR-PCC APPROACHES

There are four different approaches a company can take to be socially responsible. CSR activities can be classified into four different categories based on the company's engagement in social and environmental responsibilities. These approaches can link with PCC in various ways.

Obstructive CSR

Industries in various categories tend to resist changes and may only engage in CSR activities when forced by regulation or public pressure. This links to PCC as the impact on industries or companies might result in minimal terms of PCC improvements (Alharbi et al., 2012). It is often seen as a requirement rather than a genuine commitment to patient welfare. Compliance-based initiatives may include basic compliance with health and safety regulations. CSR will play a vital role in improving patient health education and supporting community health activities (Pillai et al., 2022).

Defensive CSR

Industries can adopt a defensive mechanism to engage in CSR primarily to avoid criticism or legal issues, rather than out of a proactive commitment to social responsibility. PCC might provide practical implementation to improve PCC in the face of negative publicity or legal challenges. In response to poor patient services, industries might start offering better patient amenities and support services (Kenagy et al., 1999; Rathert et al., 2013). CSR can be linked with basic TB patient support programs or campaigns to enhance healthcare services, protect the company's reputation, and support patients' health and well-being.

Accommodating

Examine the study to address CSR's main role is to acknowledge their social responsibilities and to link with CSR activities that address community needs, including patients' needs, though it is not the primary focus. CSR also plays an active role in supporting sustainable development goals. CSR supports health programs and community health screenings, patient education, and partnerships with other local stakeholders. It encourages employees to support volunteer-based healthcare-related CSR activities and advocates for TB patient support groups to actively participate. CSR plays a crucial role in improving patient care, hospital facilities, and PCC, supporting patient well-being, and enhancing communication to support additional health services (Russo, 2016; Wofford et al., 2016; Bertiz Colomer, 2022).

Proactive CSR

CSR activities are proactive and integrate social responsibility into core business activities. This approach leads to innovation and sets industry standards. PCC invests in cutting-edge healthcare services to improve patient outcomes. This study includes various technologies and innovations to enhance health services, such as telemedicine, personalized medicine, and advanced medical support. CSR activities support health promotion and enhance PCC services through patient support programs (Duggirala et al., 2008; Kvedar et al., 2014). These programs focus not only on health but also on the social, emotional, and financial aspects of patient care. Regular support includes leading community health initiatives, large-scale vaccination drives, chronic disease management, and public health awareness programs for PCC beneficiaries. These services also aim to support environmental sustainability and healthcare facilities, promoting a healthy lifestyle and reducing the healthcare sector's carbon footprint.

The different types of CSR approaches support healthcare and help companies better align strategies and enhance PCC. These joint efforts impact patient health, improve outcomes, reduce deaths, and increase patient well-being.

Rule of Law

The CSR rule of 7 Companies policy rules, 2014 (1) The board shall ensure that the administrative overheads shall not exceed five percent of the total CSR expenditure for the financial year.

The Companies Act, of 2013 it is providing CSR under section 135. It is mandatory for companies covered under section 135 to comply with the CSR provision. The companies must spend a minimum of 2% of their net profit over the preceding three years as CSR.

Rule of Law in HealthCare

The rule of law in PCC for TB patients and CSR represents a unique approach to addressing public health issues.

The censure protected everyone's rights and evolved medical practices. The law was implemented to include health and care for everyone, ensuring that patient care meets legal standards. TB is an infectious disease that requires proper and regular adherence to support public health laws. It can maintain confidentiality and protect the law to help manage healthcare complications. TB patients receive the appropriate care without any discrimination.

Patient-Centered Care for TB Patients: PCC can focus on the TB patient's needs, preferences, and values. Healthcare workers should support and respect the patients. They have the right to change the treatment options and methods of operation; they have these rights. They have the decision-making power to continue or discontinue the treatment (Gebremariam et al., 2010). They have the right to know about the medicine and to receive care that is respectful and tailored to their unique conditions. TB patients regularly face stigma and isolation; PCC can provide crucial care and support. Understanding the patient's social, emotional, and psychological aspects to treat through PCC and support CSR initiatives (Buttigieg et al., 2019).

Corporate Social Responsibility (CSR) in Healthcare: CSR aims to improve the company's earnings and responsibility to impact society. CSR can involve health-care and contribute to several activities. CSR can effectively utilize TB awareness campaigns to support research for better treatments; it can improve TB access and enhance healthcare services. A CSR initiative is part of the healthcare providers' efforts to enhance PCC initiatives (Chilaka & Nwaneke, 2016).

Rule of Law PCC and CSR

Legal Supporting CSR Initiatives: CSR initiatives promote TB care support and engage in the government's legal activities. They relate to income tax, and companies benefit from strict regulations that ensure patients' rights.

Patient-Centered Approaches through CSR: CSR can support healthcare workers involved with PCC. It can improve the quality of care and service, which may help increase the number of TB patients served. The law can protect TB patients by ensuring respectful and empathetic treatment in the workplace, general places, and family support. It supports the PCC (Adepoju et al., 2022).

Collaborative Models: Multilevel partnerships involving government agencies, private companies, and NGOs can combat TB disease. This collaboration can support TB patients in their care in a holistic, legally supportive, and socially responsible way.

Legal Challenges and Recommendation

There is a challenge in legal ways, insufficient healthcare infrastructure, and lack of awareness; TB patients face stigma and isolation, which complicates the implementation of PCC for TB. To ensure that CSR activities can improve public health goals, enhance patient rights, and support legal aspects. The law can support the protection of TB patients and their rights in PCC. CSR can adopt policies to promote TB patients' health outcomes (Ekman et al., 2011). PCC staff members and CSR supporters can enhance legal support for patients and improve PCC approaches to the care of TB patients. PCC and CSR can improve effective strategies for TB patients' lives. To ensure the legal and ethical aspects of health goals, they can increase health outcomes for TB patients. CSR requirements are fulfilled to protect vulnerable communities (Buhmann, 2006).

The PCC Benefits Through the CSR Benefits

CSR activities are a volunteer effort and significantly enhance PCC in several ways. The study efforts focus on patients' needs and healthcare support to create a more supportive, inclusive, and effective healthcare environment (Luxfod et al., 2011). Some key aspects of the benefits of incorporating PCC can be achieved through CSR activities.

Improved access to care for patients through CSR

CSR plays a significant role in conducting free health camps and screenings in nearby adopted villages, providing treatment for underserved communities, and improving medical care. It supports healthcare facilities and increases access to medical services for people in underserved areas (Ram, 2012; Barbosa et al., 2021).

Enhance Quality of Care

The study highlights the importance of continuous education to provide training for healthcare professionals, ensuring they are up to date with the latest medical practices and technologies. CSR activities in adopted villages create health awareness and conduct educational programs on health, hygiene, and disease prevention to empower patients to take control of their health and minimize diseases (Agyemang-Duah et al., 2019).

Patient Support Program

CSR activities can enhance the lifestyle of TB patients by providing emotional and psychosocial support through proper counseling services. Conducting peer group meetings and patient-provider support meetings can help make patient treatment more effective. CSR supports affected individuals or their family members by providing grants, scholarships, and financial assistance to patients who cannot afford their treatment (Davidson et al., 1999).

Community Engagement

CSR supports services to enhance community health drives and vaccination campaigns and provides health education at the grassroots level to promote overall community health services. It also aims to collaborate with other stakeholders and NGOs to reach wider communities and provide comprehensive healthcare support (London & Morfopoulos, 2009).

Patient Feedback and Involvement

Patient feedback regarding PCC support and health services includes input from patient representatives who provide feedback on healthcare services and suggest improvements. The study uses patient feedback to understand their needs and preferences and to make necessary adjustments to care delivery (Crow et al., 2002).

Sustainability Initiatives

The CSR role includes promoting environmental practices within healthcare facilities, reducing waste, conserving energy, and using sustainable materials. Patient healthy lifestyle promotion focuses on well-being through nutrition and exercise, which can prevent disease and improve overall patient health (Fallah Shayan et al., 2022).

Incorporating PCC initiatives into CSR strategies allows healthcare organizations to make a significant impact on the well-being of individuals and communities. This leads to better health outcomes and more sustainable healthcare practices. Through CSR programs, organizations conduct various philanthropic and volunteer efforts that have a positive social impact and boost their business brands. Businesses should essentially self-regulate and address issues such as climate change, poverty, equality, diversity, and inclusion in their practices.

Major Objective of the Study

- To know the details of TB patients respondents
- To identify timelines in health services
- To access TB services
- To find out the quality of Information
- To assess the behavior and attitude of healthcare providers
- To know the attitudes of local communities and family members
- TB patients are entitled to corporate responsibility accountability.

Research Methodology

The research study was conducted in the Trichy district, covering nearly 10 TUs. The names of the TUs are Ponmalai, Thiruvarambur, K. Abishekapuram, Thuraiyur, Manachanallur, Lalgudi, T. Puthur, Musiri, Pullambadi, and Srirangam. The selection was based on the availability of TB champions, the high caseload, and suggestions from the District TB Officer. The research design was descriptive, and the sampling method was convenient sampling. A mixed-method approach, combining qualitative and quantitative methods, was used. The sample size of the study was nearly 1223 TB patients, including in-patients (IP), current patients (CP), and patients who completed treatment within 6 months. The study was analyzed using SPSS software to obtain the results.

Result and Discussion

The result of the study mainly focused on Patient-Centered Care (PCC) for TB patients: an effective approach to Corporate Social Responsibility (CSR). It identified the status of TB patients and how PCC provides comprehensive health services on time and access to TB services. PCC aims to provide quality information, and PCC healthcare providers' behavior and attitude influence access to care and help reduce stigma among TB patients, as well as the attitudes of local communities and family members. CSR plays a vital role in addressing these challenges and overcoming related issues. The adoption of villages by each industry to support health services can enhance TB patients' lives, reduce the TB burden, decrease TB disease globally, and eliminate TB through CSR initiatives.

Table 1. Background of the respondents

Background of Respondent		No of the Respondents	%
Sex	Male	987	80.7
	Female	236	19.3
	Total	1223	100
Age	1-14	8	0.7
	15-30	51	4.2
	31-45	193	15.8
	46-60	490	40.1
	61-75	424	34.7
	Above 75	57	4.7
	Total	1223	100
TU	Ponmalai	73	6
	Thiruvarambur	124	10.1
	Srirangam	138	11.3
	K. Abishekapuram	118	9.6
	Thuraiyur	136	11.1
	Manachanallur	161	13.2
	Lalgudi	137	11.2
	Pullambadi	137	11.2
	Musiri	120	9.8
	T. Puthur	79	6.5
	Total	1223	100
Interview being held	Respondent's House	416	34
	Facility -Tuberculosis Unit	160	13.1
	Facility-DMC	135	11
	Facility-DOT centre	114	9.3
	In a public Place Other (Specify)	398	32.5
	Total	1223	100
On Treatment	Diagnosed < 2 months back	76	3.85
	Diagnosed 2-6 months back	421	21.4
	Diagnosed 7-12 months back	351	17.85
	More than 12 months back	135	6.85

continued on following page

Table 1. Continued

Background of Respondent		No of the Respondents	%
Recovered TB	<2 months back	57	11.9
	2-6 months back	133	27.7
	More than 6 months back	50	10.4
	Total	1223	100
DS TB	Pulmonary TB	805	78.5
	Extra-Pulmonary TB	221	21.5
DR TB	Pulmonary TB	15	71.4
	Extra-Pulmonary TB	6	28.6

Table 1 indicates that the majority of TB patients, 80.7%, are male, while females constitute 19.3%. The age distribution of the respondents shows that 0.7% are between 1 to 14 years old, and 4.2% are young adults aged 15 to 30. Among TB patients, 15.8% are aged between 31-45 years, and the largest age group, 46-60 years, accounts for 40.1% of those affected by TB. This reflects that a more protective age group is also affected by the disease. Additionally, 34.7% of elderly persons aged between 61 to 75 years are affected, while 4.7% of super seniors above 75 years old are affected by TB. The findings suggest that children and elderly people are highly vulnerable, even as the more active and typically protective age group is also affected by TB. The study conducted across various TUs, such as Ponmalai, Thiruvarambur, Srirangam, K. Abishekapuram, Thuraiyur, Manachanallur, Lalgudi, Pullambadi, Musiri, and T. Puthur, found that the majority of TB cases were in the TU of Srirangam (11.3%), while the lowest percentage of TB cases was in the TU of Ponmalai (6%).

The interview was conducted at various locations of TB patients concerned and various places Patients' households, TB units, DMC centres, and DOT facility places, and public places. The majority of respondents 34% comfortable with their household hold and the least area was the DOT centre facility 9.3% of the TB patients. The treatment duration Diagnosed < 2 months back: 3.85% (76 individuals), Diagnosed 2-6 months back: 21.4% (421 individuals), Diagnosed 7-12 months back: 17.85% (351 individuals), More than 12 months back: 6.85% (135 individuals). The treatment duration recovered TB patients < 2 months back: 11.9% (57 individuals), 2-6 months back: 27.7% (133 individuals), and more than 6 months back: 10.4% (50 individuals), The total number of respondents is 1,223. DS TB (Drug-Susceptible TB) Pulmonary TB: 78.5% (805 individuals) and Extra-Pulmonary TB: 21.5% (221 individuals). DR TB (Drug-Resistant TB) Pulmonary TB: 71.4% (15 individuals), Extra-Pulmonary TB: 28.6% (6 individuals). The above table provides the compressive status of the respondent's demographic details, location of the distribution and interview places, treatment duration, recovery status and Type of TB details.

Table 2. Timeliness

Respondents Details		No of the Respondents	%
In how many days from the time you came to the health facility with symptoms did you get a sputum test or an X-ray	0-3 days	126	10.5
	4-7 days	237	19.7
	7-15 days	428	35.6
	>15 days	412	34.2
	Total	**1203**	**100**
How many days after testing were you given your diagnosis	4-7 days	6	30
	7-15 days	10	50
	>15 days	4	20
	Total	**20**	**100**
How many days after diagnosis were you started on treatment Result out of DS TB	0-3 days	71	5.8
	4-7 days	223	18.2
	7-15 days	472	38.6
	>15 days	457	37.2
	Total	**1223**	**100**
After you were started on treatment, how many days did it take to link your bank account to the NPY	Less than a week	673	55.4
	2-4 weeks	237	19.5
	More than one month	286	23.5
	I don't have a bank account	19	1.6
	Total	**1215**	**100**
Did a relative link their bank account to the NPY	Yes	38	82.6
	No	8	17.4
	Total	**46**	**100**
you have completed treatment, Did you receive NPY funds in full	Yes	216	17.7
	No	1007	82.3
	Total	**1223**	**100**
What did you use the money	For medicines	181	14.8
	Others (Specify)	1042	85.2
	Total	**1223**	**100**

Table 2 provides the information Timeline for the TB patient's initial diagnosis test in a health facility 1 to 3 days, 4 to 7 days and 7 to 15 days and more than 15 days the majority of respondents 34.4% more than 15 days because the reason they said sputum difficult get and after result it takes more time to collect the information from the health facility. After diagnosis get the result 4-7 days: 30% (6 respondents) received their diagnosis in this period, 7-15 days: 50% (10 respondents) were diagnosed within 7-15 days. >15 days: 20% (4 respondents) waited more than 15 days for a diagnosis. Starting treatment for DS and DR TB majority of the respondents 37.2% said after 15 days only starting the treatment reflects the slow process from the health facility. Link with Bank account number for NPY post-treatment strat majority of the respondents said when they come for treatment health staff collect the bank account details and link with NPY less than a week linked 55.4% responded.

The majority of the respondent 8.2.6% said their account linkage with an NPY account. The majority of them said 74.4% did not receive their NPY payment. The majority of the TB patients 85.2% use the NPY payment for nutritional purposes and family expenses. Diagnostic Test Timing: The majority of respondents (69.8%) waited more than a week for initial diagnostic tests. Diagnosis Timing: Half of the respondents (50%) received their diagnosis within 7-15 days of testing. Treatment Start Timing: Most respondents (75.8%) began treatment within 7-15 days or later. Bank Account Linkage: Over half (55.4%) linked their bank accounts to NPY within a week after starting treatment, but a significant portion (23.5%) took more than a month. Relative Bank Account Linkage: The majority (82.6%) had a relative link to their bank account. NPY Fund Receipt: Only a quarter (25.6%) received NPY funds, with a smaller fraction (17.7%) receiving the full amount post-treatment. Use of NPY Funds: A small percentage (14.8%) used the funds for medicines, while the majority used them for other unspecified purposes.

Table 3. Access to TB services

General experience in reaching the TB facility nearest	I have no difficulty at all	232	19
	There is no public transport to reach the TB diagnostic facility, so I use my own or borrowed vehicle	406	33.2
	There is no public transport nor do I have my own transport, so I walk	286	23.4
	I had to go to multiple facilities before I reached this one	299	24.4
	Total	**1223**	**100**

continued on following page

Table 3. Continued

Did you find it convenient during your first visit to the health facility to locate the doctor, lab technician, X-ray technician or pharmacies	Yes, it was convenient as it was well explained	38	3.1
	I took the help of signage to locate them	294	24
	I took help from other health staff to locate them	544	44.5
	I took help from other patients in the facility	309	25.3
	No, I was confused and went back without seeing anyone	38	3.1
	Total	**1223**	**100**
Do you remember seeing signage to reach the TU and the DMC nearby to help you reach there	Yes	118	9.6
	No	1105	90.4
	Total	**1223**	**100**
Find the timings at the TU convenient	Yes	407	33.3
	No	696	56.9
	Not always	120	9.8
	Total	**1223**	**100**
quickly did the staff see you at the TU after you arrived at the TU	Below 30 min	737	60.3
	1-2 hours	457	37.4
	More than 2 hours	29	2.4
	Total	**1223**	**100**
regular drug intake interrupted at any time during the course of treatment	Yes	128	10.5
	No	1095	89.5
	Total	**1223**	**100**
Reason for interrupted	Drugs were not available	575	47
	Due to side effects of medicine	448	36.6
	Because I stopped taking the medicines	110	9
	Other Reasons	90	7.4
	Total	**1223**	**100**
During your treatment, did you have to spend money out of pocket	Nothing	38	3.1
	< 500	279	22.8
	About 500 to 1000	293	24
	About 1000 to 1500	377	30.8
	About 1500 to 2000	236	19.3
	Total	**1223**	**100**

In terms of waiting time at the TB unit, the majority (60.3%) of respondents had a positive experience, receiving services within 30 minutes. During the treatment period, 89.5% of respondents reported no interruptions in their regular drug intake.

However, 47% of those who did not continue treatment stated that the non-availability of drugs or medicine was a key issue.

Adverse drug reactions were one of the major problems during the treatment time there was majority of the patients said 30.8% of the respondents Rs. 1000 to Rs. 1500 expenses during the period of treatment out of pocket expenses. The above table 3 summarizes the details of transportation issues: A significant portion (56.6%) faced transportation challenges, either using personal vehicles (33.2%) or walking (23.4%). Initial Facility Navigation Many respondents (69.8%) needed assistance from staff or other patients to navigate the facility during their first visit. Lack of Signage: A large majority (90.4%) did not notice any signage to help them reach the TU and DMC. Inconvenient TU Timings: More than half (56.9%) found the TU timings inconvenient. Prompt Attention most respondents (60.3%) were seen within 30 minutes of arrival at the TU. Drug Intake Interruption is a small portion (10.5%) that experienced interruptions, primarily due to drug unavailability (47%) and side effects (36.6%). This interpretation highlights the challenges faced by respondents in accessing TB services, including transportation issues, navigation difficulties within health facilities, inconvenient timings, and financial burdens.

Table 4. Quality of information

How helpful was the guidance before and after the collection of the sputum sample	It was clearly explained to me – that a sputum test was required, that it would tell me if I had TB,	482	39.4
	No one explained this to me – I was just told to give my sample	344	28.1
	It was partially explained to me but I still had many questions	278	22.7
	It was clearly explained to me – that a sputum test was required, that it would tell me if I had TB,	119	9.7
	Total	**1223**	**100**
At the time you were diagnosed with lung TB, how helpful was the counselling on cough hygiene	Very helpful, I was told how to practice cough hygiene at home to protect my family	1017	83.2
	I was told about it but not how to do it	163	13.3
	I did not get any information about cough hygiene	43	3.5
	Total	**1223**	**100**
After being diagnosed with any kind of TB, were you also counseled to take/ offered a HIV test	Yes	833	68.1
	No	289	23.6
	Don't remember	101	8.3
	Total	**1223**	**100**

continued on following page

Table 4. Continued

Has it been entered into your treatment card	Yes	969	79.2
	No	254	20.8
	Total	**1223**	**100**
Are you diabetic	Yes	492	40.2
	No	603	49.3
	Don't know	128	10.5
	Total	**1223**	**100**
After being diagnosed with any kind of TB, were you also counseled to take/ offered a blood sugar test for diabetes	Yes	851	69.6
	No	289	23.6
	I was told about it but did not get a test	83	6.8
	Total	**1223**	**100**
Did you have a habit of using tobacco	Yes	87	7.1
	No	1136	92.9
	Total	**1223**	**100**
After being diagnosed with any kind of TB, were you also counselled to take/ offered any support with quitting tobacco use	Yes	85	98.8
	No	1	1.2
	Total	**86**	**100**
consider quitting use of tobacco after counselling	I have quit use of tobacco	37	3
	I have considered quitting	1186	97
	Total	**1223**	**100**
follow-up visits after completion of the intensive phase of treatment	Yes	1181	96.6
	No	42	3.4
	Total	**1223**	**100**
How useful did you find the displays at the TU or the educational materials given to you, if any	Yes, very useful	798	65.2
	I saw some materials and displays but could not understand them because I cannot read	171	14
	I saw some materials and displays but they were difficult to understand	218	17.8
	I don't remember seeing or receiving any materials	36	2.9
	Total	**1223**	**100**

The quality of information received from the health facility regarding guidance before and after sputum sample collection was clear, with 39.4% of TB patients agreeing that they received clear explanations. During treatment and the initiation of treatment, counseling on cough hygiene and the impact of lung TB was found to be useful by 83.2% of respondents. Regarding counseling on other diseases, 68.1%

of respondents received an HIV test after a TB diagnosis. The treatment card for TB patients was reported to contain all necessary information by 79.02% of respondents. However, 49.3% of respondents noted that their diabetes test status was not mentioned. After TB diagnosis, 69.6% of respondents confirmed that they had a blood sugar test. Additionally, 92.9% of respondents reported not having a tobacco habit, while 7.1% did, which is alarming given the potential for TB side effects and other complications. Counseling was effective in supporting tobacco cessation after TB diagnosis, with 98.8% of respondents agreeing that they were offered support to quit tobacco. Following counseling, 97% of respondents considered quitting tobacco, while 3% quit.

Follow-up visits after completion of the Intensive phase of treatment there are 96.6% of them had follow-up visits. There was the usefulness of display and education materials used fully at the TU level 65.2% of them said very useful. Summarize the table provides valuable information about TB patients. Guidance and counseling quality a majority of respondents received clear or helpful guidance and counseling, and a significant portion experienced inadequate explanations or partial information. Health information and tests most of the respondents were counseled and offered relevant health tests (HIV and blood sugar), but a notable minority were not. Diabetes awareness a substantial number of respondents are either unaware of their diabetes status or are not diabetic. Tobacco uses a small percentage had tobacco habits, with nearly all receiving support to quit, and many considering or succeeding in quitting. Follow-up and educational materials follow-up visits after treatment were largely adhered to, and educational materials were generally found useful, though some respondents faced challenges in understanding them due to illiteracy or complexity.

Table 5. Attitude of care providers

Overall, during treatment, how would you rate the behavior of TU staff towards you	Unsatisfactory	54	4.4
	Average	791	64.7
	Satisfactory	378	30.9
	Total	**1223**	**100**
Describe in how well did the TU staff ensure your confidentiality and privacy	Unsatisfactory	66	5.4
	Average	871	71.2
	Satisfactory	286	23.4
	Total	**1223**	**100**
Were you ever denied access to TB services at the facility	Yes	82	6.7
	No	1141	93.3
	Total	1223	100

The attitude of care providers in the health facility: The overall rating of TU staff behavior showed that the majority of respondents (64.7%) rated staff behavior as average. Additionally, 4.4% of respondents rated staff behavior as unsatisfactory, while 30.9% found it satisfactory. This indicates room for improvement in staff-patient interactions. Regarding the maintenance of confidentiality and privacy by TU staff, 71.2% of respondents rated it as average, 5.4% found it unsatisfactory, and 23.4% rated it satisfactory. In terms of access to TB services, 93.3% of respondents said they were not denied access, while 6.7% reported being denied services at the health facility. Overall, respondents rated TU staff behavior and the maintenance of confidentiality as satisfactory or average. However, there are opportunities to improve and ensure consistently high standards of patient care and access.

Table 6. Local communities and family attitudes towards TB patients

Have you shared your status of TB with your friends /community members	Yes	528	43.2
	No	695	56.8
	Total	**1223**	**100**
How respectful are friends/community attitudes towards you	They treat me kindly	1100	89.9
	They are indifferent	87	7.1
	They avoid me as much as possible	36	2.9
	Total	**1223**	**100**
How accepting and caring are your family members towards you	Very caring	753	61.6
	They take care but make me feel miserable	460	37.6
	They mistreated me	10	0.8
	Total	**1223**	**100**
working for an employer, how does he/she treat you, after you informed her or him about being treated for TB	My employer is supportive	818	66.9
	My employer is indifferent	398	32.5
	I lost my job/ trying to fire me	3	0.2
	Not Applicable	4	0.3
	Total	**1223**	**100**

Local communities and family attitudes towards TB Patients: Family attitudes have positive aspects, with 43.2% of respondents stating that their family takes care of them and is ready to share their TB status. However, 56.8% of respondents have not shared their TB status due to stigma or fear of discrimination. Regarding community attitudes, 89.9% of respondents reported being treated kindly, indicating positive community support. On the other hand, 7.1% of respondents said they were treated indifferently or avoided, and 2.9% said that friends and community members avoided them, showing that stigma still exists within the community. Family attitudes show that 61.6% of respondents felt their family members were very caring, while 37.6% reported feeling miserable due to their family members' attitudes, and 0.8% said they were occasionally mistreated by family members. At the workplace, 66.9% of respondents found their employers highly supportive; while 32.5% reported that their employers were indifferent, highlighting a need for better employer education and support. Additionally, 0.2% of respondents lost their jobs due to TB, indicating some degree of workplace discrimination. The table results show strong indications from family, friends, and employers, but there are areas where stigma and indifference still exist. Providing health education and support to both the community and workplaces could further improve and enhance the experience of TB patients.

Policy Implications

Implementing PCC for TB aims to improve policy levels and various healthcare systems. PCC incorporates several strategic framework approaches, including patient care, patient education, and psychosocial support services. It enhances care and practices based on patient experiences. Policy implications support healthcare workers in PCC, encompassing communication skills, cultural competence, and involving patients in the decision-making process. PCC helps healthcare workers adopt best practices and equips them for professional development. It involves not only patients and health workers but also a multidisciplinary team, including doctors, nurses, TB champions, community volunteers, social workers, and healthcare workers, to address the comprehensive needs of TB patients. The study focuses on improving the social determinants of health that impact TB patients, such as poverty, housing conditions, and nutritional status, and recognizing and addressing these issues. It aims to raise awareness about the importance of PCC in TB care, improving healthcare providers and the general public's understanding and leading to effective policy-making. CSR grants can be utilized to develop innovative approaches for PCC initiatives, adopting new technologies and creating models to improve TB care centers. There are challenges and barriers to implementing CSR approaches to PCC, which may include the need for regulatory support for new care models and the removal of bureaucratic obstacles. PCC can protect the well-being of TB patients through collaboration between governments, healthcare providers, voluntary organizations, and multilevel stakeholders, coordinating efforts to align PCC and CSR activities.

Innovation of the Chapter

The innovation of the proposed study to provide comprehensive patient-centered care for tuberculosis significantly enhances the TB care framework. This study provides for the TB patient's needs and critical assessment. The study provides the for TB patients treatment in the following aspects psychological, social and economic affected patients. The study identified a significant improvement in the patient's well-being. The concurrent research study to provide better implementation and navel approach for TB patients care and need to provide patient-centric care. This makes good attention for the health care workers, social workers, and community organizations to implement to support for comprehensive care and support. To provide education and empower TB patients through awareness and regular motivation important of drugs to provide knowledge regarding TB symptoms causes and during the treatment follow the diet. The study's significant community-based approach to decrease the TB patient's burden and provide care and support to home-based treatment is to reduce the TB patient's barriers decrease the stigma level and enhance treatment adherence to increase the treatment success. There are various innovative support for the psychological aspects such as counseling support, and peer counseling support, to provide mental health service support for severely emotionally affected patients. The study mainly concentrates on policy-level improvement such as advocacy efforts. It provides patient rights and advocacy for patient support. The innovation of the present research paper on PCC for TB patients as an effective approach to CSR incorporates the following ways. Supporting the integration of new technologies, such as digital health technologies, can enhance PCC for TB patients. Tools like telemedicine, mobile health apps, and e-health records can significantly improve care. Advanced technologies like AI can aid in the early detection and prevention of TB.

CONCLUSION

The outcome of the study can emphasize the importance of treatment adherence for TB patients, which can be supported through CSR activities. PCC and CSR play a vital role in improving the successful treatment completion of TB patients. The concurrent research study focuses on TB patients' satisfaction and their individual experiences to enhance the success rate of treatment. The study aims to address how TB patients can benefit from PCC and how CSR can be implemented in future research. TB patients suffer from stigma and isolation, lack proper health education, and have limited awareness. The role of CSR in improving the lives of TB patients is crucial. PCC healthcare workers and additional CSR manpower can protect and enhance the quality of life and wellness services for TB patients. CSR-driven PCC programs require careful planning and effective implementation with ongoing evaluation. Successful programs involve collaboration between healthcare providers, government agencies, and NGOs, supporting TB patients throughout their treatment duration and contributing to a healthier life.

Limitations and Further Future Research Directions

In patient-centered care in the health system, there are so many barriers such as a lack of coordination from various health care providers. Difficult to engage highly vulnerable patients elderly people and ANC mothers, differently-abled persons. Longitudinal studies provide a sustainable model for the PCC for the treatment outcome of patients and utilize the health care facilities. The study provides comprehensive benefits for challenges faced by PCC. The community engagement activities better TB care for the needed TB patients. It will provide various successful models of education, and communication and empower the patients and communities. PCC reduce the stigma for TB patients.

The further research direction on patient-centered care for TB patients as an effective approach to CSR can consider various aspects. The impact of PCC on TB success rate outcomes includes improving treatment adherence, reducing the rate of last follow-up loss, and increasing patient health and life expectancy. To enhance TB patients' long-term health and well-being, PCC can be incorporated with CSR strategies to support services for TB patients and community health. CSR can involve healthcare and TB care services to impact community health. CSR can address the economic aspects of TB patients, improving their lifestyle. CSR can focus on supporting health-affected communities throughout the entire treatment duration, including support for rehabilitation and livelihood aspects. CSR should place more emphasis on the sustainability of TB care services. CSR can ensure TB patients receive long-term health services and continuous treatment until completion. CSR should prioritize patient satisfaction through its activities. CSR can play a vital role in TB patient welfare and establish best practices. CSR can involve multiple stakeholders, including governments and NGOs, to enhance TB patient care. In this way, TB care can demonstrate how CSR addresses successful TB treatment and improves public health.

Recommendations for Future Research

Multilevel Collaboration: Future research may focus on collaboration between corporate strategists, legal researchers, social scientists, sociologists, public health experts, and governments to effectively integrate PCC TB care services into the CSR approach.

Public-Private Partnerships (PPM): Research may be conducted in partnership with government health departments, non-governmental organizations, and the Lion Department to evaluate the effectiveness of PCC based on CSR initiatives.

Policy and Advocacy Improvement: A policy framework can enhance PCC and CSR initiatives, helping to improve environmental sustainability and advance the program.

TB Champion Involvement: The study highlights crucial aspects and suggests further research to involve TB patients who have successfully completed treatment in PCC and CSR activities. This engagement aims to eradicate TB through various strategies, such as storytelling, experience sharing, peer groups, motivation, and encouragement to maintain regular treatment. Fundraising and support for nutrition, along with additional team efforts, are also essential in the fight against TB.

Declarations

Ethics approval and consent to participate Participants gave their informed consent, and the experimental protocol was developed by the S. Srinivasan Declaration's ethical criteria.

REFERENCES

Adepoju, V. A., Oladimeji, K. E., Adejumo, O. A., Adepoju, O. E., Adelekan, A., & Oladimeji, O. (2022). Knowledge of international standards for tuberculosis care among private non-NTP providers in Lagos, Nigeria: A cross-sectional study. *Tropical Medicine and Infectious Disease*, 7(8), 192. DOI: 10.3390/tropicalmed7080192 PMID: 36006284

Agyemang-Duah, W., Arthur-Holmes, F., Sobeng, A. K., Peprah, P., Dokbila, J. M., Asare, E., & Okyere, J. (2019). Corporate social responsibility in public health provision: Community members' assessment. *Cogent Medicine*, 6(1), 1622999. Advance online publication. DOI: 10.1080/2331205X.2019.1622999

Albareda, L. (2010). Mapping the novel arrangements adopted to build the corporate responsibility institutional setting. *Journal of Corporate Citizenship*, 40(40), 75–100. DOI: 10.9774/GLEAF.4700.2010.wi.00007

Alharbi, T. S. J., Ekman, I., Olsson, L. E., Dudas, K., & Carlström, E. (2012). Organizational culture and the implementation of person centered care: Results from a change process in Swedish hospital care. *Health Policy (Amsterdam)*, 108(2-3), 294–301. DOI: 10.1016/j.healthpol.2012.09.003 PMID: 23069131

Alkhaibari, R. A., Smith-Merry, J., Forsyth, R., & Raymundo, G. M. (2023). Patient-centered care in the Middle East and North African region: a systematic literature. DOI: 10.1186/s12913-023-09132-0

Barbosa, W., Zhou, K., Waddell, E., Myers, T., & Dorsey, E. R. (2021). Improving access to care: Telemedicine across medical domains. *Annual Review of Public Health*, 42(1), 463–481. DOI: 10.1146/annurev-publhealth-090519-093711 PMID: 33798406

Bértiz Colomer, A. (2022). Nursing Homes: The Person-Centred Care (PCC) Model. In *Humanistic Perspectives in Hospitality and Tourism, Volume II: CSR and Person-Centred Care* (pp. 167-184). Cham: Springer International Publishing. DOI: 10.1007/978-3-030-95585-4_9

Bhardwaj, B. (2023). Impact of Corporate Social Responsibility on the Social Well-Being of Unprivileged with Mobile Medical Clinics. In *PRIMA* (Vol. 11, No. 1, p. 21). Publishing India Group. https://www.proquest.com/openview/d019c0321377064d1f449deae31f6210/1?pq-origsite=gscholar&cbl=2030962

Boukouvalas, E., El-Den, S., Murphy, A. L., Salvador-Carulla, L., & O'Reilly, C. L. (2020). Exploring health care professionals' knowledge of, attitudes towards, and confidence in caring for people at risk of suicide: A systematic review. *Archives of Suicide Research*, 24(sup2), S1–S31. Advance online publication. DOI: 10.1080/13811118.2019.1586608 PMID: 30856366

Buhmann, K. (2006). Corporate social responsibility: what role for law? Some aspects of law and CSR. *Corporate Governance: The International Journal of Business in Society, 6*(2), 188-202.

Buttigieg, S. C., Tomaselli, G., Byers, V., Cassar, M., Tjerbo, T., & Rosano, A. (2019). Corporate social responsibility and person-centered care: A scoping review. *Journal of Global Responsibility*, 10(4), 289–306. DOI: 10.1108/JGR-01-2019-0006

Chilaka, M. A., & Nwaneke, P. K. (2016). Integrating corporate social responsibility, health improvement, and community support in development programmes: A case for enhancing the application of health impact assessment in programme implementation in the Niger Delta region. *Local Environment*, 21(3), 383–395. DOI: 10.1080/13549839.2014.1000287

Crow, H., Gage, H., Hampson, S., Hart, J., Kimber, A., Storey, L., & Thomas, H. (2002). Measurement of satisfaction with health care: Implications for practice from a systematic review of the literature. *Health Technology Assessment*, 6(32). Advance online publication. DOI: 10.3310/hta6320 PMID: 12925269

Davidson, L., Chinman, M., Kloos, B., Weingarten, R., Stayner, D., & Tebes, J. K. (1999). Peer support among individuals with severe mental illness: A review of the evidence. *Clinical Psychology : a Publication of the Division of Clinical Psychology of the American Psychological Association*, 6(2), 165–187. DOI: 10.1093/clipsy.6.2.165

Duggirala, M., Rajendran, C., & Anantharaman, R. N. (2008). Patient-perceived dimensions of total quality service in healthcare. *Benchmarking*, 15(5), 560–583. DOI: 10.1108/14635770810903150

Ekman, I., Swedberg, K., Taft, C., Lindseth, A., Norberg, A., Brink, E., Carlsson, J., Dahlin-Ivanoff, S., Johansson, L.-I., Kjellgren, K., Liden, E., Ohlen, J., Olsson, L. E., Rosen, H., Rydmark, M., & Sunnerhagen, K. S. (2011). Person-centered care—Ready for prime time. *European Journal of Cardiovascular Nursing*, 10(4), 248–251. DOI: 10.1016/j.ejcnurse.2011.06.008 PMID: 21764386

Erhemjamts, O., Li, Q., & Venkateswaran, A. (2013). Corporate social responsibility and its impact on firms' investment policy, organizational structure, and performance. *Journal of Business Ethics*, 118(2), 395–412. DOI: 10.1007/s10551-012-1594-x

Fallah Shayan, N., Mohabbati-Kalejahi, N., Alavi, S., & Zahed, M. A. (2022). Sustainable development goals (SDGs) as a framework for corporate social responsibility (CSR). *Sustainability (Basel)*, 14(3), 1222. DOI: 10.3390/su14031222

Francis, C. K. (2001). Medical ethos and social responsibility in clinical medicine. *Journal of Urban Health*, 78(1), 29–45. DOI: 10.1093/jurban/78.1.29 PMID: 11368201

Gebremariam, M. K., Bjune, G. A., & Frich, J. C. (2010). Barriers and facilitators of adherence to TB treatment in patients on concomitant TB and HIV treatment: A qualitative study. *BMC Public Health*, 10(1), 1–9. oi.org/10.1186/1471-2458-10-651. DOI: 10.1186/1471-2458-10-651 PMID: 21029405

Googins, B. K., Mirvis, P. H., & Rochlin, S. A. (2007). *Beyond good company: Next generation corporate citizenship*. Palgrave Macmillan. DOI: 10.1057/9780230609983

Igbo, F. I. (2023). *Determining Strategies for Cost Effectiveness in Sustainable Healthcare Delivery–An Emerging Market Study* (Doctoral dissertation, Walden University).

John, J., Smiju, I. S., Thampi, K., & Joseph, M. K. (2024). Environmental, Social, and Governance (ESG) Sustainability Through Corporate Social Responsibility: A Scoping Review. *ESG Frameworks for Sustainable Business Practices*, 31-52. DOI: 10.4018/979-8-3693-3880-3.ch002

Kallon, I. I. (2018). Influences on the continuity of care for patients with Mycobacterium tuberculosis referred from tertiary and district hospitals. https://open.uct.ac.za/items/0c494162-92b1-43dd-a9e6-f9e29bb02bc8

Katsanis, L. P., Pitta, D., & Morinville, A. (2021). Patient centricity: Lip service or genuine commitment? A qualitative examination of the pharmaceutical industry. *International Journal of Pharmaceutical and Healthcare Marketing*, 15(1), 106–133. DOI: 10.1108/IJPHM-02-2020-0010

Kenagy, J. W., Berwick, D. M., & Shore, M. F. (1999). Service quality in health care. *Journal of the American Medical Association*, 281(7), 661–665. DOI: 10.1001/jama.281.7.661 PMID: 10029131

Kumar, V., Verma, M. A., & Jain, M. D. (2014). National Corporate Social Responsibility Hub, Research Team. https://thdc.co.in/sites/default/files/ImpactAssessmentReport_TISS2014.pdf

Kvedar, J., Coye, M. J., & Everett, W. (2014). Connected health: A review of technologies and strategies to improve patient care with telemedicine and telehealth. *Health Affairs*, 33(2), 194–199. DOI: 10.1377/hlthaff.2013.0992 PMID: 24493760

Levine, R. (2007). *Case studies in global health: millions saved.* Jones & Bartlett Publishers. https://www.google.co.in/books/edition/Case_Studies_in_Global_Health/fafpHV26iK8C?hl=en&gbpv=0

Li, D. S. (2010). *Patient centered care approach to adherence with cardiovascular medications: Self-determination theory integration.* Old Dominion University. https://www.proquest.com/openview/9a71d4e519a81d3e2e4e81234ea59072/1?pq-origsite=gscholar&cbl=18750

London, M., & Morfopoulos, R. G. (2009). *Social entrepreneurship: How to start successful corporate social responsibility and community-based initiatives for advocacy and change.* Routledge., DOI: 10.4324/9780203878149

Lopez, M., Pérez-Villalobos, C., Suárez, D., & Ar, A. Y. (2022). The training of a new social-responsible generation of health professionals with a patient-centered vision. *Ciencia & Saude Coletiva,* 27(8), 3043–3051. DOI: 10.1590/1413-81232022278.07392021 PMID: 35894317

Luxford, K., Safran, D. G., & Delbanco, T. (2011). Promoting patient-centered care: A qualitative study of facilitators and barriers in healthcare organizations with a reputation for improving the patient experience. *International Journal for Quality in Health Care : Journal of the International Society for Quality in Health Care,* 23(5), 510–515. DOI: 10.1093/intqhc/mzr024 PMID: 21586433

Macias, J. J. (2016). *Espoused and practiced stakeholder engagement in support of corporate social responsibility within the United States healthcare sector.* Pepperdine University.

Macq, J., Solis, A., & Martinez, G. (2005). Can we make TB control more pro-poor by addressing the sticky business of stigma? In *36th Union World Conference on Lung Health-" Scaling up TB control to meet the needs of the poor"((France) Paris, du 18/10/2005 au 22/10/2005).The International Journal of Tuberculosis and Lung Disease,* 9(11, Suppl 1), S17.

Mahmud, A., Rahim, A. A., & Zaidi, N. A. A. (2020). Primary health care as a pillar of the end-tb strategy: A scoping review. *International Journal of Public Health and Clinical Sciences,* 7(5), 13–27.

Mezzalira, E., Canzan, F., Marini, G., Longhini, J., Leardini, C., Saiani, L., & Ambrosi, E. (2024). Introduction of novel complex integrated care models supported by digital health interventions in European primary settings: A scoping review. *Health Policy and Technology,* 100896(4), 100896. Advance online publication. DOI: 10.1016/j.hlpt.2024.100896

Munro, S. A., Lewin, S. A., Smith, H. J., Engel, M. E., Fretheim, A., & Volmink, J. (2007). Patient adherence to tuberculosis treatment: A systematic review of qualitative research. *PLoS Medicine*, 4(7), e238. DOI: 10.1371/journal.pmed.0040238 PMID: 17676945

Myburgh, H., Baloyi, D., Loveday, M., Meehan, S. A., Osman, M., Wademan, D., Hesseling, A., & Hoddinott, G. (2023). A scoping review of patient-centred tuberculosis care interventions: Gaps and opportunities. *PLOS Global Public Health*, 3(2), e0001357. DOI: 10.1371/journal.pgph.0001357 PMID: 36963071

Pillai, R. D., Wang, P., & Kuah, A. T. (2022). Unlocking corporate social responsibility in smaller firms: Compliance, conviction, burden, or opportunity? *Thunderbird International Business Review*, 64(6), 627–646. DOI: 10.1002/tie.22315

Rajeswari, R., Muniyandi, M., Balasubramanian, R., & Narayanan, P. R. (2005). Perceptions of tuberculosis patients about their physical, mental and social well-being: A field report from south India. *Social Science & Medicine*, 60(8), 1845–1853. DOI: 10.1016/j.socscimed.2004.08.024 PMID: 15686814

Ram, K. (2012). Corporates and Rural Development: A Study of TVS Group's CSR Initiatives in Padavedu, Tamilnadu. *CSR and Competitiveness—Essential of the Corporate India and its. Sustainability*, 88.

Rathert, C., Wyrwich, M. D., & Boren, S. A. (2013). Patient-centered care and outcomes: A systematic review of the literature. *Medical Care Research and Review : MCRR*, 70(4), 351–379. DOI: 10.1177/1077558712465774 PMID: 23169897

Russo, F. (2016). What is the CSR's Focus in Healthcare? *Journal of Business Ethics*, 134(2), 323–334. DOI: 10.1007/s10551-014-2430-2

Saz-Gil, M. I., Cosenza, J. P., Zardoya-Alegría, A., & Gil-Lacruz, A. I. (2020). Exploring corporate social responsibility under the background of sustainable development goals: A proposal to corporate volunteering. *Sustainability, 12*(12), 4811. /DOI: 10.3390/su12124811

Schwartz, D. B. (2013). Integrating patient-centered care and clinical ethics into nutrition practice. *Nutrition in Clinical Practice*, 28(5), 543–555. DOI: 10.1177/0884533613500507 PMID: 24046190

Sharma, A. (2018). Patient-centric care in the US-A comparative study of patient satisfaction and quality care among for-profit physician-owned, corporate-owned, and not-for-profit hospitals. https://vtechworks.lib.vt.edu/items/87c5c1a1-3ab9-4154-81f6-d5313a50ca09

Sidani, S., Reeves, S., Hurlock-Chorostecki, C., van Soeren, M., Fox, M., & Collins, L. (2018). Exploring differences in patient-centered practices among healthcare professionals in acute care settings. *Health Communication*, 33(6), 716–723. DOI: 10.1080/10410236.2017.1306476 PMID: 28402138

Smith, A. D. (2011). Corporate social responsibility implementation: Comparison of large not-for-profit and for-profit companies. *International Journal of Accounting & Information Management*, 19(3), 231–246. DOI: 10.1108/18347641111169241

Srinivasan, M. S., Lama, P., Tyagi, N., Yadav, K., Naval, M. N., & Swati, M. (2023). Elderly TB patients in India: Situation Analysis. *Tuijin Jishu/Journal of Propulsion Technology, 44*(6), https://www.researchgate.net/profile/Srinivasan-Sekaran/publication/376456595_Elderly_TB_patients_in_India_Situation_Analysis/links/65796e9c6610947889c33e80/Elderly-TB-patients-in-India-Situation-Analysis.pdf

Srinivasan, S. (2014). Psychosocial problems faced by HIV/AIDS patients. https://papers.ssrn.com/sol3/papers.cfm?abstract_id=2704751

Srinivasan, S., Prabha Lama, D. K., & Udhayakumar, P. (n.d.). Situation of Elderly Person with TB: A Comparative Study of Countries in the SAARC Region.

Student, S. K. (2023). *Business and Health Communication Strategies in Healthcare Organizations for Corporate Social Responsibility (CSR) and the Role of Ethics in Healthcare Organizations* (Master's thesis, Georgetown University). https://www.proquest.com/openview/d8c3e125807ba099bd6ceacf53c27228/1?pq-origsite=gscholar&cbl=18750&diss=y

Suseela, R. P., & Shannawaz, M. (2023). Engaging the Private Health Service Delivery Sector for TB Care in India—Miles to Go! *Tropical Medicine and Infectious Disease*, 8(5), 265. DOI: 10.3390/tropicalmed8050265 PMID: 37235313

Tadesse, A. W., Mohammed, Z., Foster, N., Quaife, M., McQuaid, C. F., Levy, J., Kalmthout, K. V., Rest, J. V., Jerene, D., Abdurhman, T., Yazew, H., Umeta, D. G., Assefa, D., Weldemichael, G. T., Bedru, A., Letta, T., & Fielding, K. L. (2021). Evaluation of implementation and effectiveness of digital adherence technology with differentiated care to support tuberculosis treatment adherence and improve treatment outcomes in Ethiopia: A study protocol for a cluster randomised trial. *BMC Infectious Diseases*, 21(1), 1–11. DOI: 10.1186/s12879-021-06833-x PMID: 34758737

Tamli, N., & Sain, M. (2023). Exploring Innovative Strategies For Patient-Centered Care In The Nursing Profession. *A Bi-annual South Asian Journal of Research & Innovation, 10*(1), 19-30. DOI: 10.3126/jori.v10i1.66025

Uduji, J. I., Okolo-Obasi, E. N., & Asongu, S. A. (2019). Multinational oil companies in Nigeria and corporate social responsibility in the HIV/AIDS response in host communities. *Local Environment*, 24(5), 393–416. DOI: 10.1080/13549839.2019.1585770

Waweru, E., Smekens, T., Orne-Gliemann, J., Ssengooba, F., Broerse, J., & Criel, B. (2020). Patient perspectives on interpersonal aspects of healthcare and patient-centeredness at primary health facilities: A mixed methods study in rural Eastern Uganda. *PLoS One*, 15(7), e0236524. DOI: 10.1371/journal.pone.0236524 PMID: 32730294

Wofford, D., MacDonald, S., & Rodehau, C. (2016). A call to action on women's health: Putting corporate CSR standards for workplace health on the global health agenda. *Globalization and Health*, 12(1), 68. DOI: 10.1186/s12992-016-0206-4 PMID: 27814731

World Health Organization. (2016). WHO Country Cooperation Strategy 2016-2021: Seychelles.

World Health Organization. (2023). *WHO operational handbook on tuberculosis. Module 1: prevention-infection prevention and control*. World Health Organization. https://www.google.co.in/books/edition/WHO_operational_handbook_on_tuberculosis/wP3UEAAAQBAJ?hl=en&gbpv=0

Chapter 9

Towards a Person-Centered Care Approach in Community Mental Health Services

Michael Galea
http://orcid.org/0000-0002-3459-5992
University of Malta, Malta

Frankline Zammit Galea
University of Malta, Malta

ABSTRACT

Person-centered care presents a welcoming change towards a more holistic healthcare model. Rather than restricting its scope to the deficiencies and challenges that the individual may have, PCC widens its view to the autonomy of the person. Pertinent to this scope, it is the intention of this study to investigate the value and contribution of PCC to community mental health services. As noted by WHO, these services locate social inclusion and participation within the community life. Research suggests a dearth of studies on PCC within community mental health services. This applies to Malta as well. In fact, Galea and Mallia in their leading study on this reality strongly recommended more knowledge, practice and research from the perspective of a person-centered approach among mental healthcare services. This includes continuous professional development among HCPs in line with the latest PCC principles. Transitioning to a person-centered approach within community mental health services benefits the community because it empowers the person and improves clinical outcomes.

DOI: 10.4018/979-8-3693-5991-4.ch009

INTRODUCTION

A shift from a traditional medical model of care, which has long been the dominant approach in healthcare, towards a more holistic and inclusive approach known as person-centered care (PCC) is increasingly reflected in literature. According to Lauver et al. (2002), PCC marks a significant and positive change by acknowledging that patients are not just passive recipients of healthcare but are active participants in their own healing journey. This model emphasizes the importance of giving individuals a voice in their care, ensuring they are heard, and empowering them to take an active role in their health recovery. Central to PCC is the concept of informed decision-making, where patients are equipped with the necessary information to make decisions about their health in collaboration with their healthcare providers (Tanvi et al., 2016).

This transition towards PCC represents a broader understanding of healthcare, one that values the individual's experience and involvement as critical to achieving better health outcomes.

In this context, the current study seeks to examine the impact and significance of PCC on community mental health services. This highlights the need for further research and ongoing professional development for HCPs, which not only empowers individuals but also enhances clinical outcomes.

Mental health problems can escalate into mental illness, a pathological condition characterized by disruptions in a person's thoughts, feelings, actions, and relationships, leading to significant suffering and impaired functioning. According to the World Health Organization's International Classification of Diseases 11th Revision (ICD-11, 2019), mental illness represents a serious health concern. The Global Burden of Disease (GBD) further highlights the severity of this issue, revealing that mental health disorders are among the leading causes of disease burden worldwide, largely due to demographic shifts.

Currently, eight out of ten people globally experience mental illness, making it the most common cause of years lived with disability. Mental illness accounts for one in six years lived with disability worldwide. Compounding this issue, severe mental health disorders are associated with premature death due to related physical conditions. Additionally, suicide ranks as the fourth most common cause of death among young people and adolescents aged 15-29. The COVID-19 pandemic in 2020 exacerbated these challenges, significantly increasing the number of individuals affected by anxiety and depression (WHO, 2022).

According to the WHO's Comprehensive Mental Health Action Plan 2013–2030, mental health services are highly recommended to prioritize good practices and implement person-centered care. This approach is crucial for integrating human rights perspectives, promoting equality, non-discrimination, ensuring legal capacity, and fostering community inclusion. Policymakers, healthcare professionals (HCPs), communities, and individuals with lived experience of mental health conditions all play essential roles in ensuring that community mental health services adhere to international human rights standards (WHO, 2012; WHO, 2021). Consequently, an increasing number of countries are developing mental health strategies aimed at creating a more positive and rights-based healthcare system, in line with the WHO's Comprehensive Mental Health Action Plan 2013–2030.

According to the WHO (2015), healthcare professionals play a crucial role in addressing global health challenges. The WHO's Executive Summary emphasizes that "people-centered health services" adopt the perspectives of individuals, families, and communities, treating them as active participants in trusted health systems that respond to their needs and preferences in humane and holistic ways (WHO, 2015, p. 7). Consequently, integrating Person-Centered Care (PCC) into mental healthcare, particularly within Community Mental Health Services (CMHS), is essential. This approach has become even more critical in the wake of the COVID-19 pandemic, which has significantly exacerbated mental health challenges worldwide (Wang et al., 2021).

Rogers and Person-Centered Care

Person-centered care has its roots in the field of psychology, particularly through the pioneering work of Carl Rogers (1902-1987). Rogers developed the client-centered theory, which shifted the responsibility of healthcare onto the client, emphasizing their active role in the process. Over time, Rogers refined this approach, renaming it the person-centered approach. This change in terminology underscored his belief that those seeking help are more than just 'clients' or 'patients'; they are active individuals within the healthcare system, engaged in addressing their own needs (Rogers, 1967).

This approach represented a significant paradigm shift in healthcare. Instead of focusing solely on individuals as passive recipients of care or as people with difficulties, Rogers emphasized their autonomy. He shifted the focus from the disease or problems presented to the person seeking help. In doing so, Rogers placed the individual at the center of the healthcare system. He argued that people possess inherent resources for self-knowledge and self-healing, and that personality change and development are possible when a specific climate of facilitative conditions is present (Rogers, 1992).

To achieve this significant transformation, Rogers (1967) urged healthcare professionals to adopt and excel in several key therapeutic attitudes: congruence, unconditional positive regard, and empathic understanding of the individual's internal frame of reference. Building on this, Ekman et al. (2011) noted that person-centered care embodies a paradigm shift from the traditional biomedical model to a biopsychosocial approach in healthcare delivery. This approach fundamentally asserts that patients are individuals who should be valued and cared for beyond their diseases or the immediate challenges they face.

Next, we will examine the relationship between family- and society-centered patient-centered care (PCC) and mental health services.

Family and Society-Focused PCC Mental Health Nursing

The shift from a predominant medical model to a more holistic approach in healthcare is notably reflected in nursing, a field profoundly influenced by Florence Nightingale (1820-1910). Nightingale emphasized the importance of addressing patients' needs and experiences rather than solely focusing on the diseases they suffer from (Lauver et al., 2002).

Tanvi et al. (2016) identified six key themes in defining person-centered care (PCC): establishing therapeutic relationships, sharing power and responsibility, understanding the individual, empowering the person, fostering trust and mutual respect, and ensuring clear, genuine communication. These themes are consistent with findings by Youssef et al. (2020).

According to the World Health Organization (WHO, 2015), all healthcare professionals are crucial in addressing global health challenges. PCC is one of thirteen essential attributes for healthcare professionals, emphasizing the creation of effective therapeutic relationships and collaboration with patients and their families. It empowers individuals to take an active role in their care, promoting self-autonomy rather than passivity (WHO, 2015; McCormack & McCance, 2017). PCC is grounded in respect for individuals, their right to self-determination, mutual respect, and understanding (McCormack et al., 2010).

The Person-Centered Practice Framework (PCPF), updated by McCormack and McCance in 2017, offers a structured approach to understanding and implementing person-centered care (PCC) in nursing. This framework is designed to address the complexity of PCC by breaking it down into five interrelated domains, each crucial for fostering effective and compassionate healthcare practices:

1. Macro Context: This domain encompasses the broader environment and societal factors that influence healthcare delivery, such as policy, cultural norms, and economic conditions.
2. Influence Research: This involves integrating evidence from research to inform and improve person-centered care practices. Research helps to validate and refine approaches to ensure they align with the principles of PCC.

3. Workforce Developments: This domain focuses on the need for continual development and education of healthcare professionals to equip them with the skills necessary for delivering person-centered care. It highlights the importance of updating curricula and training programs to reflect current best practices.
4. Strategic and Policy Levels: Leadership and policy-making play a critical role in embedding person-centered principles into healthcare systems. This domain emphasizes the need for strategic influence to drive the adoption and sustainability of PCC practices.
5. Effective Interpersonal Practice: At the core of PCC is the therapeutic relationship between healthcare providers and patients. This domain underscores the significance of building strong, empathetic, and respectful relationships to achieve positive outcomes.

McCormack and McCance (2006) originally conceptualized the PCPF to highlight the dynamic interactions between various stakeholders in healthcare, focusing on the therapeutic relationship as the foundation of effective care. The updated 2017 framework continues to emphasize the importance of understanding individual needs, respecting personal convictions, and involving both the person seeking care and their family in the decision-making process.

PCC is predicated on the belief that each person is unique, with their own set of needs, preferences, and values. Therefore, care should be tailored to align with the individual's specific circumstances, ensuring that their perspectives and wishes are central to the care process. This approach fosters a collaborative and responsive healthcare experience, where decisions are made in partnership with the person receiving care.

Person centered care is all about placing the patient—and often their family—at the heart of the healthcare process. This approach emphasizes collaboration and respect for the patient's personal values, preferences, and needs. In PCC, healthcare providers actively involve the patient in decision-making, ensuring that care plans are tailored to the individual's unique circumstances and preferences. This might mean considering not just medical factors, but also the patient's lifestyle, goals, and any specific concerns they have. The idea is to create a partnership where the patient's voice is heard and their needs are central to the care process.

By prioritizing the individual's perspective, PCC aims to enhance the quality of care, improve patient satisfaction, and ultimately lead to better health outcomes.

It is clear that the terminology and conceptual framework matter significantly in healthcare. Patient-Centered Care focuses primarily on the individual patient within the clinical context. PCC's approach emphasizes the patient's specific needs, preferences, and values regarding their health and treatment. The scope is typically centered on interactions within healthcare settings and the immediate needs of the patient. Person-centered care focuses on a broader than just the patient, incorporating their entire context, including family, social, and community aspects. The approach considers the whole person, including their physical, psychological, emotional, social, and spiritual needs. The scope extends beyond clinical encounters to encompass the individual's life and relationships within their broader environment.

The World Health Organization (WHO) and other sources emphasize that person-centered care integrates the idea of caring for the whole person rather than just their illness. This holistic approach acknowledges that healthcare impacts and is impacted by the individual's broader life context, including family and community relationships. This wider lens not only aims to improve the individual's overall quality of life but also enhances the effectiveness and satisfaction of care provided.

Starfield's perspective reinforces this view by indicating that person-centered care is a development from patient-centered care, reflecting a more inclusive understanding of the patient's context and relationships. As you mentioned, Ekman et al. (2011) support the idea that this holistic approach results in better health outcomes and higher satisfaction for those involved.

In summary, while patient-centered care focuses on the individual within a clinical context, person-centered care expands to include the individual's entire life situation, aiming for a more comprehensive and satisfying healthcare experience (Starfield, 2011). The World Health Organization (2020b, p.12) defines people-centered care as being organized around the needs of 'people…rather than on diseases.' This approach extends beyond the individual to include all people with whom they have interpersonal relationships, whether formal or informal, direct or indirect (WHO, 2020b). Thus, 'person-centered care' encompasses not just clinical interactions but also holistic care, addressing the physical, psychological, emotional, social, and spiritual dimensions of individuals as members of families and communities. This comprehensive approach leads to stronger healthcare outcomes and greater satisfaction for those involved (Ekman et al., 2011).

Bacha et al. (2020) highlighted that while mental health service-users historically had limited opportunities to voice their experiences and opinions about mental health care, recent studies continue to show their marginalization and undervaluation within mental health research communities. Their research underscored the critical need to incorporate patients' perspectives into evidence-based medicine (EBM), advocating for the integration of patient views into clinical guidelines and other aspects of mental health care.

In a qualitative co-production study, Trevillion et al. (2022) demonstrated the potential for enhancing community care for individuals with mental health conditions. Co-production research involves collaborating with individuals who have lived experience alongside researchers, fostering an equal partnership throughout the study. Similarly, Moore et al. (2017) recommended that researchers adapt strategies to encourage patient involvement in research, thereby supporting the implementation of person-centered care (PCC). One effective approach to achieving this is through community mental health services (CMHS).

Our next focus will be on community mental health services, exploring their impact and what they involve in the context of PCC-inspired health care.

Community Mental Health Services

According to the World Health Organization (WHO), the purpose of community mental health services is to offer diverse types of care and support through centers located within residential areas, rather than relying solely on hospitals and traditional institutions. This approach enhances social inclusion and community engagement (WHO, 2021).

These centers are designed to promote individual health and well-being while adhering to international, evidence-based mental health practices and policies (WHO, 2022). They are expected to lead to improved long-term outcomes.

In line with this, the WHO's Comprehensive Mental Health Action Plan 2020-2030 (2013) advocates for the prioritization of best practices and person-centered care (PCC) in mental health services. This approach advances human rights, equality, non-discrimination, and community inclusion. Inspired by the International Strategy Framework Action Plan 2020-2030, many communities have developed mental health strategies aimed at creating a more sustainable and inclusive mental health system.

Patient-Centered Care (PCC) emphasizes the importance of active individual participation and a proactive approach in care settings. The World Health Organization (WHO, 2022) identifies PCC as a fundamental principle for delivering high-quality care in community mental health services, highlighting its critical role in achieving universal mental health coverage.

However, despite this understanding, WHO (2019) notes that individuals using mental health services, whether in community settings or as inpatients, continue to face significant challenges. These include difficulties in accessing care, receiving high-quality services, and encountering coercive practices. Such issues persistently undermine their rights and dignity (WHO, 2022).

Strengths and Growing Edges of PCC Within CMHC

Despite a growing body of literature highlighting the value of person-centered care (PCC) in healthcare, the evidence remains mixed, indicating both positive and negative outcomes. This is particularly important when considering its application to guide community mental health services. On the positive side, PCC has been shown to enhance health and wellness (Edvardsson et al., 2011), foster mutual interaction in interpersonal relationships (Hansson, 2017; Fors et al., 2015), improve the work environment (Brownie & Nancarrow, 2013), and be economically beneficial (Ulin et al., 2016).

However, there are also paradoxical findings. For instance, PCC has sometimes excluded certain groups, such as those with limited decision-making capacity, leading to increased dependency (Britten et al., 2017), despite its aim to be inclusive. Additionally, it has been associated with higher personal and financial costs, such as increased risks of patient falls (Blom et al., 2016). There are concerns that PCC may overlook the staff's personhood (Buber, 1971) and result in unequal treatment due to varying levels of empathy, where some patients receive more attention than others, or caregivers risk becoming excessively empathetic (Batson, 2011). Furthermore, empathy-based care can lead to unfair treatment if carers prioritize feelings over fairness (Hakansson et al., 2018).

Meranius et al. (2020) highlighted that person-centered care (PCC) can produce paradoxical outcomes, warranting further exploration. They identified four key paradoxes: a) for patients, PCC can offer both benefits and drawbacks to individual wellbeing; b) in terms of relationships, while PCC can enhance mutual interactions, it may also create imbalances by favoring some individuals over others; c) from a staff perspective, PCC can improve the work environment but might also undermine staff's personal identity and contribute to compassion fatigue; and d) organizationally, PCC can be cost-effective in some contexts while being resource-intensive in others.

When applied to Community Mental Health Services (CMHS), the impact of PCC varies. Tejada (2019) observed that higher salaries, reduced competition, and more targeted resources benefit these services. However, challenges such as stigma, isolation, limited training opportunities, and inadequate resources for interventions persist.

Fai Ma et al. (2023) argued that CMHS should be adapted dynamically to meet the diverse needs of different populations and socioeconomic contexts. Health authorities are encouraged to regularly revise and enhance CMHS strategies to address the specific needs of their participants. In line with this, Choy-Brown et al. (2020) suggested that increased training and support are necessary to consistently implement PCC across community mental health programs, especially given the mixed outcomes in mental health management highlighted by Tejada (2019).

A study focused on improving PCC in South Australia's community mental health services emphasized the concept of 'relational recovery'. This approach advocates for a systematic and holistic method that collaborates with the individual, their family, and their community. It underscores the importance of considering recovery within the broader context of personal development, family dynamics, relationships, life roles, and social connections (Loughhead et al., 2023).

This underscores the ongoing need for further research in this area to better understand the true value of PCC in healthcare, including its benefits and potential limitations. It also highlights the importance of incorporating the recovery model, which adds complexity but also strengthens the robustness of this new PCC-inspired approach to healthcare.

The Recovery Model

Hummelvoll et al. (2015) argued that recovery centers on individuals maintaining control over their own situations and making informed decisions through collaboration with relevant stakeholders, including family and service providers. Their research highlights a common foundation between the recovery model and person-centered care, despite their differences. The recovery model is rooted in service user and activist organizations as well as disability movements, while person-centered care draws from Carl Rogers' work and humanistic-existential movements. According to Hummelvoll et al. (2015), recovery is viewed as a spontaneous and natural process, resulting from active treatment, that occurs despite impairments. They describe recovery as comprising personal, social, and spiritual dimensions.

The personal dimension involves transitioning from being a patient to reclaiming one's identity. The social dimension emphasizes the importance of relationships between individuals and their environments. The spiritual dimension pertains to what imbues one's life with meaning, transforming everyday reality into a purposeful and significant existence. Hummelvoll et al. (2015) further break down the spiritual aspects of recovery into: a) restoring hope and commitment to life (Davidson et al., 2005); b) engaging in spiritual practices (Timms, 2010); c) experiencing growth through adversity (Culliford, 2005); and d) finding recovery in nature (Mayer et al., 2009).

Despite advancements in healthcare, individuals seeking mental health support are often still treated as mere 'cases'. To shift from this outdated, medically-focused approach, significant changes are necessary. Hummelvoll et al. (2015) argue that a fundamental shift is required to place the individual at the center of the process, rather than focusing solely on the services provided. Additionally, mental health issues should be viewed through both personal and social lenses. This means meeting individuals where they live and belong, which is a core principle of Community Mental Health Services (CMHS). Furthermore, life should not be viewed solely as an outcome (Davidson et al., 2012). Recovery involves hope and continuing with life despite daily physical, emotional, and other challenges. This approach requires a move from relying solely on randomized controlled trials as the gold standard to incorporating practice-based evidence that values the lived experiences of individuals, their families, and healthcare professionals (Hummelvoll et al., 2015).

Research introduces a crucial fourth dimension for effecting a significant paradigm shift in the recovery process: genuine attention to spirituality. Incorporating spirituality into recovery is essential as it fosters hope (Murphy et al., 2000) and empowers individuals to remain committed to life despite challenges (Galea, 2008, 2014). Hope often thrives within interpersonal relationships.

The connection between spirituality and mental and physical health has ancient roots. However, in the 19th and 20th centuries, religious involvement became less emphasized in psychiatry, leading to poorer outcomes (Moreira-Almeida et al., 2014). It wasn't until the 1970s and 1980s that research began to highlight the benefits of integrating spirituality and religiosity into mental health care, showing improved outcomes (Koenig, 2012).

Moreira-Almeida et al. (2016) underscore the World Psychiatry Association's recommendation to include spirituality and religiosity in clinical practice for a more holistic approach to mental health care. While the exact mechanism by which spirituality acts as a buffer remains unclear, it appears that religious beliefs, rather than behaviors, provide a cognitive framework that may help counter feelings of hopelessness (Murphy et al., 2000). Spirituality might mitigate the negative effects of trauma by enhancing emotional well-being in those with a history of trauma. Baumeister (1991) argues that "suffering stimulates the need for meaning" as people tend to scrutinize their suffering more deeply than their joys (p. 232). Consistent with this, Galea et al. (2007) found that transcendence or spirituality was significantly correlated with subjective well-being and positive affect, though no direct link to negative affect was observed.

The recovery model of mental health promotes a comprehensive approach to healthcare, focusing on the overall well-being of individuals. According to the Substance Abuse and Mental Health Services Administration (SAMHSA), recovery from mental and substance use disorders is viewed as a developmental journey aimed at achieving one's full potential (2024). SAMHSA outlines ten guiding principles for recovery, which include being hopeful, person-driven, diverse in methods, holistic, supported by peers and relationships, culturally grounded, involving family and community, based on respect, and responsive to trauma (SAMHSA, 2024). While the recovery model is sometimes seen as contrasting with the medical model—which attributes mental disorders to bio-physiological causes and seeks medical treatment—researchers argue that the two models can be complementary (Jacob, 2015). The recovery model's core belief is that recovery from mental illness is both possible and self-determined.

However, the recovery model does have limitations. Its broad and individualized nature can make it difficult to measure its outcomes or effectiveness. Additionally, because it relies on the person's commitment and active participation, it may not be suitable for everyone. Some individuals may struggle with engagement due to their conditions, while others might require more immediate medical intervention (Jacob, 2015). Harvey et al. (2023) suggest that further research and innovation in service delivery, with a focus on inclusion, are needed.

The recovery model's principles—hope, dignity, self-determination, and responsibility—align closely with the goals of community mental health. However, since the recovery model is tailored to individual needs and lacks a standardized approach, assessing its effectiveness can be challenging (Leamy et al., 2023).

Challenges to a PCC Approach Within CMHS

To fully embrace person-centered care, it's important to assess and measure its impact. De Silva (2014) identified four key areas of focus in related studies: definitional measures, the preferences of those involved, their experiences, and the outcomes.

Adopting person-centered planning necessitates a cultural shift within institutions or organizations towards a recovery-oriented person-centered care approach. This shift involves developing new skills for those seeking help, as well as a learning curve for healthcare professionals (HCPs) who must adapt to this approach. A significant challenge in this transition is the need for a standardized method of patient engagement, even though person-centered care often calls for a more flexible and individualized approach tailored to each person's stage in their recovery journey (Miller et al., 2017).

Byrne (2020) highlighted that Person-Centered Care (PCC) remains fundamentally conceptual, with no single, universally accepted definition. This lack of consensus often leads to variations in how PCC is interpreted and implemented, a challenge noted in other literature with potentially negative outcomes. For instance, Kogan et al. (2016) found that a definitive, agreed-upon definition of PCC is still elusive.

Despite these challenges, SAMHSA (2024) outlines four essential dimensions to support recovery: a) holistic health (encompassing both physical and mental well-being, which may require informed choices and a lifestyle free from addiction), b) a safe and nurturing environment, c) purposeful and meaningful activities (such as work, education, and family routines), and d) supportive social relationships.

The authors of this article believe that several related characteristics are crucial for achieving a person-centered, holistic approach to recovery, especially within community mental healthcare.

First, using appropriate language is crucial. Person-centered language prioritizes the individual rather than their mental health condition. The words we choose reflect our attitudes. As highlighted by the Mental Health Coordinating Council's Recovery Oriented Language Guide (2020), our language indicates whether we value and respect people. Person-centered care language should be respectful, non-judgmental, clear, consistent with non-verbal communication, genuine, open to opportunities, and trauma-informed. It should work to reduce stigma and be sensitive to cultural diversity, age, sexual orientation, and grief. Recovery language must be carefully considered in written communication, notes, and conversations with colleagues. It's important to note that simply offering community mental health services does not automatically address the specific needs of individuals seeking help. Therefore, using appropriate language is essential for ensuring that community mental health services truly meet their intended goals.

Secondly, there is a need to move beyond the current cultural competence framework and focus on developing cultural partnerships (Galea & Galea, 2023). Research and practice should evolve to embrace this approach, particularly in areas like healthcare where cross-cultural interactions are often not value-neutral. The traditional 'competence approach' tends to favor the perspective of the provider over the recipient of help and fails to account for the dynamic nature of culture (Gopalkrishnan, 2018). Additionally, integrating Culturally and Mechanistically Sensitive (CMHS) practices should enhance the connection to the cultural realities of those seeking assistance.

Thirdly, ethical considerations are crucial in person-centered care during recovery. Hansson and Froding (2020) acknowledge that some person-centered care (PCC) practices can raise ethical concerns. Issues such as privacy, autonomous decision-making, safeguarding medical quality, professional integrity, fairness, and non-discrimination are key examples. It is essential to be vigilant not only to prevent ethical issues but also to maintain and enhance the focus on the needs and potential of individuals seeking help. Given the rapid advancement of technology and artificial intelligence, this aspect warrants significant attention. Liegeois and Van Audenhove (2005) provide a comprehensive approach to the ethical dilemmas that may arise in community mental health services, addressing issues like autonomy and privacy, support and safety, justice and participation, and trust and solidarity.

To truly embody a holistic recovery effort, a person-centered approach must integrate a rights-based perspective. The World Health Organization's 2021 guidance on Community Mental Health Services underscores the importance of consistently addressing connections with housing, education, job security, and social protection to genuinely uphold this approach. The WHO guidance offers specific recommendations for developing community mental health services grounded in human rights with a focus on recovery. Mann, Bradley, and Sahakian (2016) emphasize that human rights-based approaches are essential both legally and morally, as they underpin principles of justice and civilization, and their inclusion is crucial for achieving positive therapeutic outcomes.

Person-Centered care and Recovery in CMHS in Small Countries

When addressing person-centered care and recovery in small communities and nations, several factors need to be considered. Firstly, it's important to recognize the evolving nature of the healthcare system. According to Galea and Mallia (2014), Malta is currently transitioning towards a person-centered care (PCC) model, moving away from a predominantly medical approach, with a strong emphasis on community mental health systems (CMHS). Individuals using community mental health clinics (CMHCs) in Malta have a range of mental health needs, from mild issues to more complex disorders. These clinics are staffed by a variety of professionals, including psychiatrists, doctors, charge nurses, senior staff nurses, registered mental health nurses, social workers, psychologists, and counselors. Additionally, all public health and mental health services in Malta are government-funded, ensuring that these services are free for Maltese citizens and residents with a valid residence permit.

Secondly, there is always a need for ongoing research in this area. Galea and Mallia (2014) highlighted a lack of studies on Person-Centered Care (PCC) within Community Mental Health Centers (CMHCs), with no research specifically addressing the situation in Malta. From the existing studies, most emphasize the importance of the therapeutic relationship between mental health service users and healthcare professionals. Key factors in this relationship include empathic listening, respecting patients' identities, providing non-judgmental and stigma-free acceptance, fostering less hierarchical interactions, and promoting education about mental health issues to prevent severe illness (Maassen et al., 2016; Erin et al., 2018; Youssef et al., 2020).

Implementing PCC is crucial because involving individuals actively in decision-making and addressing their holistic needs can lead to improved clinical outcomes. Benefits include reduced use of emergency hospital services, better management of chronic conditions (De Silva, 2011), improved medication adherence (De Silva, 2012; Scerri, 2020), earlier engagement with community services, lower anxiety and stress, and shorter hospital stays (De Silva, 2012). Consequently, adopting PCC not only enhances individual health and well-being but also mitigates economic losses at both global and national levels.

In a groundbreaking qualitative study on Malta's community mental health services and their alignment with a person-centered approach, Galea and Mallia (2024) emphasized the need for enhanced knowledge, practice, and research in person-centered care (PCC). They highlighted the importance of ongoing professional development for healthcare professionals to stay updated with the latest PCC principles.

Galea and Mallia (2024) identified three key domains necessary for delivering truly person-centered and recovery-focused care within the Maltese healthcare system. First, the need for quality care was emphasized. This entails care that is effective, people-centered, timely, equitable, integrated, and efficient, in accordance with World Health Organization (2023) recommendations. Crucial to this is mutual respect, attention to individual values, and a deep understanding of participants. Second, the study highlighted the necessity of emotional support, where empathy from healthcare professionals was essential for those seeking help. The third domain focused on partnership and collaborative care, which includes active engagement in care, patient education, family involvement, and comprehensive, integrated care.

Based on these findings, several key recommendations were proposed: a) increase awareness of rights and responsibilities within the therapeutic process to strengthen relationships between patients and healthcare professionals, b) improve integration into decision-making and ensure patients are well-informed about their treatment, and c) create a more user-friendly healthcare system with enhanced follow-up procedures.

Next we focus on the importance of corporate social responsibility in the context of health and social care. The reasons for its incorporation include increased patient trust and satisfaction, better community relations, the ability to attract and retain talent, effective compliance and risk management, improved operational efficiency, distinct brand differentiation, and long-term sustainability.

CSR in Health and Social Care

According to the United Nations Industrial Development Organization (UNIDO), Corporate Social Responsibility (CSR) is a management approach that integrates social and environmental concerns into business operations and interactions with key stakeholders (2024). It is often viewed as a balancing act between economic, environmental, and social dimensions while addressing the needs of major stakeholders. This approach is sometimes referred to as the 'Triple-Bottom-Line-Approach'. Although CSR differs from philanthropy, charity, or sponsorships, it goes beyond these activities by contributing more significantly to poverty reduction and enhancing a company's reputation.

Schwartz and Carroll (2003) expanded on Carroll's earlier models of CSR (1979, 1991) to define three core domains: economic, legal, and ethical responsibility, which are illustrated using a Venn diagram framework. Corporate Social Responsibility (CSR) is a complex concept that blends theoretical perspectives with practical legal principles.

The theoretical aspects of CSR include: a) Stakeholder Theory: Proposed by Edward Freeman, this theory argues that companies have responsibilities beyond just shareholders, extending to all stakeholders. b) Shareholder Theory: Milton Friedman's perspective that a company's primary duty is to maximize financial returns for shareholders. c) Triple Bottom Line: Introduced by John Elkington, this approach evaluates CSR by assessing a company's performance in three areas: social, environmental, and economic (People, Planet, Profit). d) Corporate Citizenship: This view sees corporations as 'citizens' with responsibilities to contribute to society and uphold ethical standards. e) Ethical Theories: these include i) Utilitarianism, which suggests CSR actions should aim to maximize overall happiness, and ii) Deontology, which emphasizes businesses' duty to follow ethical principles and respect human rights, regardless of outcomes.

The practical aspects of CSR involve: a) Legal Frameworks: Regulations and laws that shape CSR practices; b) Corporate Governance: The systems and processes that oversee company conduct; c) Judicial Interpretation: How courts interpret CSR-related laws; d) Regulatory Oversight: Monitoring and enforcement of CSR compliance; and e) Human Rights: Ensuring that corporate practices respect and promote human rights.

In essence, CSR is a dynamic interplay of ethical theories, stakeholder expectations, and legal requirements. Theoretical approaches provide the underlying principles and justifications for CSR, while legal frameworks and regulations offer the practical means for implementation and enforcement.

Collins (2010) notes that the global importance of CSR is increasingly recognized, yet the healthcare sector remains slow to systematically embrace it (Tommaselli et al., 2018). In healthcare, CSR can enhance patient and community well-being, promote environmental sustainability, foster diversity and inclusion, and advance ethical business practices (Singh, 2024).

In their study investigating whether corporate social responsibility could enhance person-centered care (PCC) in healthcare organizations, Buttigieg et al. (2019) discovered that while CSR and PCC are interconnected, only two CSR aspects—quality of care and health communication—directly align with PCC features. Other CSR areas are not fully utilized in this context. The study calls for further research to explore how CSR can be more effectively leveraged to improve PCC, particularly in mental health services.

Doherty et al. (2020) highlighted that inconsistent clinical outcomes of PCC might stem from its conceptual and operational ambiguities. They emphasized that the core of PCC lies in the consumer-provider relationship, suggesting that resolving conflicts within this relationship is crucial for effective PCC. Epstein et al. (2011) noted that since PCC focuses on interpersonal relationships, communication, and patient involvement, merely making infrastructural changes may not be enough. Doherty et al. (2020) recommend incorporating both provider and consumer perspectives to better advance PCC in mental healthcare.

Moore et al. (2022) identified funding as a major barrier to sustainability in mental health services, particularly within community mental health services (CMHS), while connectedness emerged as a significant facilitator. They called for more research into macro-level factors, such as government policies, to address these challenges.

A number of case studies further the inherent importance of CSR to healthcare. Lubis (2018) explored the influence of Corporate Social Responsibility (CSR) on the health sector, focusing on government hospitals. The study found that CSR had a positive effect on the hospital's reputation, patient loyalty, and overall value. It suggests that CSR should be used strategically to enhance the value of hospitals.

Additionally, Kim, Kim, and Lee (2023) provided evidence indicating that CSR can alleviate employee depression. As a result, they suggested that CSR should be considered a valuable and effective 'investment,' rather than simply a 'moral obligation and expense.'

The following section of this study will explore the synergies of CSR, with a focus on its impact on mental health both broadly and within the community.

Synergies of CSR and Mental Health

Corporate Social Responsibility (CSR) and mental health intersect in ways that can amplify positive outcomes for both employees and communities. When companies integrate mental health support into their CSR strategies, they not only foster a more inclusive and supportive work environment but also enhance their overall brand reputation and employee satisfaction.

1. Employee Well-being: CSR initiatives that prioritize mental health can lead to improved employee morale, productivity, and retention (Kim, Kim, and Lee, 2023). Programs such as mental health days, counseling services, and stress management workshops demonstrate a company's commitment to its workforce, reducing absenteeism and burnout.
2. Community Impact: Companies that extend mental health support beyond their workforce contribute to broader societal well-being (Doherty et al. 2020). By funding mental health programs, partnering with mental health organizations, or raising awareness, businesses can address mental health issues in the communities they serve, reinforcing their role as responsible corporate citizens.
3. Brand Reputation: Integrating mental health into CSR can enhance a company's reputation, making it an employer of choice and a trusted partner. It shows that the company values the holistic well-being of both its employees and the community, which can attract talent and foster customer loyalty (Lubis, 2018).
4. Legal and Ethical Alignment: Proactively addressing mental health aligns with legal and ethical expectations around employee welfare (Singh, 2024). By integrating these practices into their CSR framework, companies can stay ahead of regulations and build a culture of respect and care.

In summary, the integration of CSR and mental health initiatives forms a positive feedback loop, boosting employee satisfaction, amplifying community impact, and strengthening brand reputation, all while meeting ethical and legal obligations.

CONCLUSION

Inspired by Rogers, healthcare professionals are encouraged to embrace person-centered care (PCC), marking a shift from the traditional medical model. PCC focuses on tailoring care to the unique needs, preferences, and values of each individual, placing the patient at the core of the healthcare process. This approach emphasizes active patient participation and a proactive care strategy, though its effectiveness requires further study, particularly in integrating the recovery model, which adds complexity to PCC.

To successfully implement PCC, it's essential to measure its impact, focusing on appropriate language, cultural partnerships beyond mere competence, ethical considerations, and a rights-based approach. Recognizing the evolving nature of healthcare is crucial, and ongoing research is necessary to support this shift. Quality care, emotional support for healthcare providers, and collaboration are key to achieving this goal, with corporate social responsibility playing a vital role in aligning ethical practices, stakeholder expectations, and legal requirements, particularly in mental health.

REFERENCES

Bacha, K., Hanley, T., & Winter, L. A. (2020). 'Like a human being, I was an equal, I wasn't just a patient': Service users' perspectives on their experiences of relationships with staff in mental health services. *Psychology and Psychotherapy: Theory, Research and Practice*, 93(2), 367–386. DOI: 10.1111/papt.12218 PMID: 30720230

Batson, C. D. (2011). *Altruism in Humans*. Oxford University Press.

Baumeister, R. F. (1991). *Meanings of Life*.

Blom, J., den Elzen, W., van Houwelingen, A. H., Heijmans, M., Stijnen, T., Van den Hout, W., & Gussekloo, J. (2016). Effectiveness and cost-effectiveness of a proactive, goal-oriented, integrated care model in general practice for older people. A cluster randomized controlled trial: Integrated Systematic Care for older People—the ISCOPE study. *Age and Ageing*, 45(1), 30–41. DOI: 10.1093/ageing/afv174 PMID: 26764392

Britten, N., Moore, L., Lydahl, D., Naldemirci, O., Elam, M., & Wolf, A. (2017). Elaboration of the Gothenburg model of person-centred care. *Health Expectations*, 20(3), 407–418. DOI: 10.1111/hex.12468 PMID: 27193725

Brownie, S., & Nancarrow, S. (2013). Effects of person-centered care on residents and staff in aged-care facilities: A systematic review. *Clinical Interventions in Aging*, 8, 1–10. DOI: 10.2147/CIA.S38589 PMID: 23319855

Buber, M. (1971). *I and Thou*. Charles Scribner's Sons.

Buttigieg, S. C., Tomaselli, G., Byers, V., Cassar, M., Tjerbo, T., & Rosano, A. (2019). Corporate social responsibility and person-centered care: A scoping review. *Journal of Global Responsibility*, 10(4), 289–306. Advance online publication. DOI: 10.1108/JGR-01-2019-0006

Byrne, A. L., Baldwin, A., & Harvey, C. (2020). Whose centre is it anyway? Defining person-centred care in nursing: An integrative review. *PLoS One*, 15(3), e0229923. Advance online publication. DOI: 10.1371/journal.pone.0229923 PMID: 32155182

Choy-Brown, M., Stanhope, V., & Bond, L. (2020). Delivering Person-centered care in community mental health programs. *Research on Social Work Practice*, 30(8), 8. DOI: 10.1177/1049731520944568

Collins, S. K. (2010). Corporate social responsibility and the future health care manager. *The Health Care Manager*, 29(4), 339–345. DOI: 10.1097/HCM.0b013e3181fa050e PMID: 21045586

Culliford, L. (2005). *Healing from Within: Spirituality and Mental Health*. Royal College of Psychiatrists, Spirituality and Psychiatry Special Interest Group.

Davidson, L., O'Connell, M., Tondora, J., Staeheli, M., & Evans, A. (2005). Recovery in serious mental illness: A new wine or just a new bottle? *Professional Psychology, Research and Practice*, 36(5), 480–487. DOI: 10.1037/0735-7028.36.5.480

Davidson, L., Tondora, J., & Ridgway, P. (2012). Life is not an 'outcome': Reflections on recovery as an outcome and as a process. *Journal of Psychiatric Rehabilitation*, 13(1), 1–8.

de Silva, D. (2011). *Evidence: Helping people help themselves.* The Health Foundation. https://www.health.org.uk/publications/evidence-helping-people-help-themselves

de Silva, D. (2012). *Helping people share decision making.* The Health Foundation. https://www.health.org.uk/publications/helping-people-share-decision-making

de Silva, D. (2014). *Helping measure person-centred care*. The Health Foundation.

Doherty, M., Bond, L., Jessel, L., Tennille, J., & Stanhope, V. (2020). Transitioning to Person-Centered Care: A Qualitaive Study of Provider Perspectives. *The Journal of Behavioral Health Services & Research*, 47(3), 399–408. DOI: 10.1007/s11414-019-09684-2 PMID: 31820326

Edvardsson, D., Fetherstonhaugh, D., McAuliffe, L., Nay, R., & Chenco, C. (2011). Job satisfaction amongst aged care staff: Exploring the influence of person-centered care provision. *International Psychogeriatrics*, 23(8), 1205–1212. DOI: 10.1017/S1041610211000159 PMID: 21320379

Ekman, I., Swedberg, K., Taft, C., Lindseth, A., Norberg, A., Brink, E., Carlsson, J., Dahlin-Ivanoff, S., Johansson, I. L., Kjellgren, K., Lidén, E., Öhlén, J., Olsson, L.-E., Rosén, H., Rydmark, M., & Sunnerhagen, K. S. (2011). Person-centered care—Ready for prime time. *European Journal of Cardiovascular Nursing*, 10(4), 248–251. DOI: 10.1016/j.ejcnurse.2011.06.008 PMID: 21764386

Epstein, R. M., & Street, R. L. (2019, October 21). The values and value of patient-centered care. *Annals of Family Medicine*, 2011. https://www.annfammed.org/content/9/2/100.shorton PMID: 21403134

Erin, L., Karen, R. F., Reppermunc, S., & Troller, J. (2018). Access to mental health services: The experiences of people with intellectual disabilities. *Journal of Applied Research in Intellectual Disabilities*, 32(2), 2. DOI: 10.1111/jar.12533 PMID: 30306674

Fai Ma, C., Luo, H., & Fong, L. (2023). Impact of community mental health services on the adult psychiatric admission through the emergency unit: A 20-year population-based study. *Lancet*, 39, 100814. DOI: 10.1016/j.lanwpc.2023.100814 PMID: 37927999

Fors, A., Ekman, I., Taft, C., Björkelund, C., Frid, K., Larsson, M. E., Thorn, J., Ulin, K., Wolf, A., & Swedberg, K. (2015). Person-centered care after acute coronary syndrome, from hospital to primary care—A randomized controlled trial. *International Journal of Cardiology*, 187, 693–699. DOI: 10.1016/j.ijcard.2015.03.336 PMID: 25919754

Galea, M. (2008). The Impact of Child Abuse on the Psycho-Spiritual and Religious Status of Maltese College Students. *Pastoral Psychology*, 57(3-4), 147–159. DOI: 10.1007/s11089-008-0159-5

Galea, M. (2014a). The Progressive Impact of Burnout on Maltese Nurses. *SOP Transactions on Psychology*, 1(1), 1–12. DOI: 10.15764/STP.2014.01001

Galea, M. (2014c). Assessing the Incremental Validity of Spirituality in Predicting Nurses' Burnout. *Archiv für Religionspsychologie*, 36(1), 118–136. DOI: 10.1163/15736121-12341276

Galea, M., Ciarrocchi, J. W., Piedmont, R. L., & Wicks, R. J. (2007). Child Abuse, Personality, and Spirituality as Predictors of Happiness in Maltese College Students. *Research in the Social Scientific Study of Religion*, 18, 141–154. DOI: 10.1163/ej.9789004158511.i-301.57

Galea, M., & Galea, F. Z. (2023). Mental Health's address to the challenging cultural reality of Malta. *Humanities and Social Science Research*, 6(1), p22. Advance online publication. DOI: 10.30560/hssr.v6n1p22

Galea, M. & Mallia. N. (2024). Towards a person-centered care model among community mental health services. *European Journal of Psychotherapy & Counseling*.

Gopalkrishnan, N. (2018). Cultural diversity and Mental Health. Considerations for Policy and Practice. *Frontiers in Public Health*, 6, 179. DOI: 10.3389/fpubh.2018.00179 PMID: 29971226

Håkansson Eklund, J., Holmström, I. K., Kumlin, T., Kaminsky, E., Skoglund, K., Höglander, J., Sundler, A. J., Condén, E., & Summer Meranius, M. (2018). "Same same or different?" A review of reviews of person-centered and patient-centered care. *Patient Education and Counseling*, 102(1), 3–11. DOI: 10.1016/j.pec.2018.08.029 PMID: 30201221

Hansson, E., Carlström, E., Olsson, L.-E., Nyman, J., & Koinberg, I. (2017). Can a person-centred-care intervention improve health-related quality of life in patients with head and neck cancer? A randomized, controlled study. *BMC Nursing*, 16(1), 9. DOI: 10.1186/s12912-017-0206-6 PMID: 28239295

Hansson, S. O., & Froding, B. (2020). Ethical conflicts in patient-centered care. *Clinical Ethics*, 16(2), 55–66. Advance online publication. DOI: 10.1177/1477750920962356

Harvey, C., Zirnsak, T. M., Brasier, C., Ennals, P., Fletcher, J., Hamilton, B., Killaspy, H., McKenzie, P., Kennedy, H., & Brophy, L. (2023). Community-based models of care facilitating recovery of people living with persistent and complex mental health needs: A systematic and narrative synthesis. *Frontiers in Psychiatry*, 14, 1259944. Advance online publication. DOI: 10.3389/fpsyt.2023.1259944 PMID: 37779607

Hemmelvoll, J. K., Karlsson, B., & Borg, M. (2015). Recovery and person-centredness in mental health services: roots of the concepts and implications for practice. *International Practice Development Journal,* 5(7). https://www.fons.org/Resources/Documents/Journal/Vol5Suppl/IPDJ_05(suppl)_07.pdf

Jacob, K. S. (2015). Recovery model of mental illness: A complementary approach to psychiatric care. *Indian Journal of Psychological Medicine*, 37(2), 117–119. DOI: 10.4103/0253-7176.155605 PMID: 25969592

Kim, B., Kim, M., & Lee, D. (2023). The mental health implications of Corporate Social Responsibility: The significance of the sense-making process and prosocial motivation. *Behavioral Sciences (Basel, Switzerland)*, 13(10), 10. DOI: 10.3390/bs13100870 PMID: 37887520

Koenig, H. G. (2012). Religion, spirituality, and health: The research and clinical implications. *ISRN Psychiatry*, 2012, 278730. DOI: 10.5402/2012/278730 PMID: 23762764

Kogan, A. C., Wilber, K., & Mosqueda, L. (2015). Person-centered care for older adults with chronic conditions and functional impairment: A systematic literature Review. *Journal of the American Geriatrics Society*, 64(1). Advance online publication. DOI: 10.1111/jgs.13873 PMID: 26626408

Lauver, D. R., Ward, S. E., Heidrich, S. M., Keller, M. L., Bowers, B. J., Brennan, P. F., Kirchhoff, K. T., & Wells, T. J. (2002). Patient-centred interventions. *Research in Nursing & Health*, 25(4), 246–255. DOI: 10.1002/nur.10044 PMID: 12124719

Leamy, M., Foye, U., Hirrich, A., Bjorgen, D., Silver, J., Simpson, A., Ellis, M., & Johan-Johanson, K. (2023). A systematic review of measures of the personal recovery orientation of mental health services and staff. *International Journal of Mental Health Systems*, 17(1), 33. DOI: 10.1186/s13033-023-00600-y PMID: 37849003

Liegeois, A., & Van Audenhove, C. (2005). Ethical dilemmas in community mental health care. *Journal of Medical Ethics*, 31(8), 452–456. DOI: 10.1136/jme.2003.006999 PMID: 16076969

Loughhead, M., McDonough, J., Baker, K., Rhodes, K., Macedo, D., Ferguson, M., McKellar, L., & Procter, N. Person-centred and Consumer Directed Mental Health Care: Transforming Care Experiences, prepared for the National Mental Health Commission, University of South Australia; 2023. DOI: 10.25954/jkqx-ay14

Lubis, A. N. (2018). Corporate social responsibility in health sector: A case study in the government hospitals in Medan, Indonesia. *Business: Theory and Practice*, 19(0), 25–36. DOI: 10.3846/btp.2018.04

Maassen, E. F., Schrevel, S. J. C., Dedding, C., Broerse, J. E. W., & Regeer, B. J. (2017b). Comparing patients' perspectives of "good care" in Dutch outpatient psychiatric services with academic perspectives of patient-centred care. *Journal of Mental Health (Abingdon, England)*, 26(1), 84–94. DOI: 10.3109/09638237.2016.1167848 PMID: 27067671

Mann, S. P., Bradley, V. J., & Sahakian, B. J. (2016). Human rights=based approaches to mental health. *Health and Human Rights*, 18(1), 263–276. PMID: 27781015

Mayer, S., Bruehlman-Senecal, E., & Dolliver, K. (2009). Why is nature beneficial? The role of connectedness to nature. *Environment and Behavior*, 41(5), 607–643. DOI: 10.1177/0013916508319745

McCormack, B., & McCance, T. (2017). *Person-Centred Practice in Nursing and Health Care: Theory and Practice*. John Wiley & Sons. DOI: 10.1002/9781119099635

Mental Health Coordinating Council. (2020). *Recovery Oriented Language Guide: words matter*. https://mhcc.org.au/wp-content/uploads/2022/10/Recovery-Oriented-Language-Guide-3rd-edition.pdf

Meranius, M. S., Holmstrom, I. K., Hakansson, J., Breitholtz, A., Moniri, F., Skogevall, S., Skoglund, K., & Rasoal, D. (2020). Paradoxes of person-centred care: A discussion paper. *Nursing Open*, 7(5), 1321–1329. DOI: 10.1002/nop2.520 PMID: 32802352

Miller, E., Stanhope, V., Restrepo-Toro, M., & Tondora, J. (2017). Person-centered planning in mental health: A transatlantic collaboration to tackle implementation barriers. *American Journal of Psychiatric Rehabilitation*, 20(3), 251–267. DOI: 10.1080/15487768.2017.1338045 PMID: 31632212

Moore, A., Bertotti, M., Hanafiah, A., & Hayes, D. (2022). Factors affecting the sustainability of community mental health assets: A systematic review. *Health & Social Care in the Community*, 30(6), 6. DOI: 10.1111/hsc.13929 PMID: 35900123

Moreira-Almeida, A., Koenig, H. G., & Lucchetti, G. (2014). Clinical implications of spirituality to mental health: Review of evidence and practical guidelines. *The British Journal of Psychiatry*, 36(2), 176–182. DOI: 10.1590/1516-4446-2013-1255 PMID: 24839090

Moreira-Almeida, A., Sharma, A., van Rensburg, B. J., Verhagen, P. J., & Cook, C. C. W. P. A. (2016). Position Statement on Spirituality and Religion in Psychiatry. *World Psychiatry; Official Journal of the World Psychiatric Association (WPA)*, 15(1), 87–88. DOI: 10.1002/wps.20304 PMID: 26833620

Murphy, P. E., Ciarrocchi, J. W., Piedmont, R. L., Cheston, S., Peyrot, M., & Fitchett, G. (2000). The Relation of Religious Belief and Practices, Depression, and Hopelessness in Persons with Clinical Depression. *Journal of Consulting and Clinical Psychology*, 68(6), 1102–1106. DOI: 10.1037/0022-006X.68.6.1102 PMID: 11142544

Recovery and Recovery Support. (2024). *SAMHSA*. https://www.samhsa.gov/find-help/recovery

Rogers, C. R. (1967). *On Becoming a Person: A Therapist's View of Psychotherapy*. Constable and Robinson Ltd.

Rogers, C. R. (1992). The necessary and sufficient conditions of therapeutic personality change. *Journal of Consulting Psychology*, 21(2), 95–103. DOI: 10.1037/h0045357 PMID: 13416422

Scerri, J., Churchill, J., Banks, D., & Sultana, J. (2021). Advocating a person-centered care approach to drug safety. *Expert Opinion on Drug Safety*https://www.um.edu.mt/library/oar/handle/123456789/90465

Schwartz, M. S., & Carroll, A. B. (2003). Corporate Social Responsibility: A Three-Domain Approach. *Business Ethics Quarterly*, 13(4), 503–530. Advance online publication. DOI: 10.5840/beq200313435

Singh, R. R. (2012). *Corporate Social Responsibility in Healthcare: The Way Forward*. https://www.vantagefit.io/blog/corporate-social-responsibility-in-healthcare/

Starfield, B. (2011). Is patient-centered care the same as person-focused care? *The Permanente Journal*, 15(2), 63–69. DOI: 10.7812/TPP/10-148 PMID: 21841928

Tejada, P. (2019). Advantages and Disadvantages in the Management of Mental Illnesses in Rural Areas. In Chaturvedi, S. (Ed.), *Mental Health and Illness in Rural World. Mental Health and Illness Worldwide*. Springer. DOI: 10.1007/978-981-10-0751-4_16-1

Timms, P. (2010). *Spirituality and Mental Health*. The Royal College of Psychiatrists Spirituality and Psychiatry Special Interest Group.

Tomaselli, G., Garg, L., Gupta, V., Xuereb, P., Buttigieg, S. C., & Vassallo, P. (2018). Healthcare systems and corporate social responsibility communication: A comparative analysis between Malta and India *Journal of Global Information Management*, 26(4), 52–66. DOI: 10.4018/JGIM.2018100104

Trevillion, K., Stuart, R., Ocloo, J., Broeckelmann, E., Jeffreys, S., Jeynes, T., Allen, D., Russell, J., Billings, J., Crawford, M. J., Dale, O., Haigh, R., Moran, P., McNicholas, S., Nicholls, V., Foye, U., Simpson, A., Lloyd-Evans, B., Johnson, S., & Oram, S. (2022). Service user perspectives of community mental health services for people with complex emotional needs: A co-produced qualitative interview study. *BMC Psychiatry*, 22(1), 55. Advance online publication. DOI: 10.1186/s12888-021-03605-4 PMID: 35081929

Ulin, K., Olsson, L.-E., Wolf, A., & Ekman, I. (2016). Person-centred care – An approach that improves the discharge process. *European Journal of Cardiovascular Nursing*, 15(3), e19–e26. DOI: 10.1177/1474515115569945 PMID: 25648848

United Nations Industrial Development Organization. (2024). *Advancing economic competitiveness*. https://www.unido.org/our-focus/advancing-economic-competitiveness/competitive-trade-capacities-and-corporate-responsibility/corporate-social-responsibility-market-integration/what-csr

Wang, L., Nabi, G., Zuo, L., Wu, Y., & Li, D. (2021). Impacts of the COVID-19 Pandemic on Mental Health and Potential Solutions in Different Members in an Ordinary Family Unit. *Frontiers in Psychiatry*, 12, 735653. DOI: 10.3389/fpsyt.2021.735653 PMID: 35087429

World Health Organisation (2013). *Comprehensive Mental Health Action Plan 2013–2030*. 9789240031029-eng.pdf (who.int)

World Health Organisation. (2015). *Interim report: placing people and communities at the centre of health services: WHO global strategy on integrated people-centred health services 2016-2026: executive summary.*https://apps.who.int/iris/handle/10665/180984

World Health Organisation. (2019). *Mental health.* www.who.int. https://www.who.int/health-topics/mental-health#tab=tab_1

World Health Organisation. (2022). *World mental health report: transforming mental: Transforming mental health for all.*https://www.who.int/publications/i/item/9789240049338

World Health Organisation.. (2023). *Quality of care.* www.who.int. https://www.who.int/health-topics/quality-of-care#tab=tab_1

World Health Organization. (2020b). *World Health Organization health systems strengthening glossary.* World Health Organization.

World Health Organization. (2021). *Mental health.*https://www.who.int/publications/i/item/9789240025769

World Health Organization. (2021). *Guidance on community mental health services: Promoting person-centered and rights-based approaches.* https://www.who.int/publications/i/item/9789240025707

Youssef, A., Wiljer, D., Mylopoulos, M., Yang, L., & Sockalingam, S. (2020b). "Caring About Me": A pilot framework to understand patient-centered care experience in integrated care – a qualitative study. *BMJ Open*, 10(7), e034970. DOI: 10.1136/bmjopen-2019-034970 PMID: 32718923

KEY TERMS AND DEFINITIONS

Community Mental Health Services (CMHS): Provide accessible, comprehensive mental health support within local communities, making it easier for individuals to receive care close to home.

Holistic Healthcare: Holistic healthcare is an approach that considers the whole person, not just their symptoms or illnesses. It integrates physical, emotional, mental and spiritual aspects of health and well-being.

Person-Centered Care (PCC): PCC is an approach to healthcare and support that prioritizes the individual needs, preferences, and values of the person receiving care. It emphasizes treating people with respect and dignity and involves them in decisions about their own care.

Chapter 10
Healthcare Professionals' Attitudes Towards Digital Technology to Support Their Mental Wellbeing

Stephanie Bonello
University of Malta, Malta

Sandra Buttigieg
http://orcid.org/0000-0002-0572-2462
University of Malta, Malta

ABSTRACT

Digital mental health therapies have been suggested to improve the accessibility and use of psychological treatment. However, little information is available about the attitudes and behavioural intentions of healthcare professionals towards such treatments for personal use. Poor attitudes and negative behavioural intentions can cause a significant barrier to the uptake and utilisation of this form of therapy. Therefore, this study sought to explore the attitudes and intentions of healthcare professionals towards digital mental health services. The relationships between attitudes, intentions, mental health status, and demographics were also investigated. The present study took the form of a quantitative cross-sectional needs analysis by distributing an online questionnaire to the targeted population. The findings from this study suggest a neutral attitude towards digital therapy, while maintaining openness to its utilization. Additionally, the findings highlight the need to enhance healthcare professionals' knowledge about digital therapy's empirical effectiveness.

DOI: 10.4018/979-8-3693-5991-4.ch010

1. INTRODUCTION

A responsive and productive healthcare workforce is essential for a health system to perform well and provide access to high-quality care. To maintain long-term productivity, supporting healthcare workers' physical and mental well-being has been identified as critical (World Health Organisation [WHO], 2007). The stressful nature of the profession, the continuous interaction with people, coping with the patients' demands, ethical dilemmas and the necessity to make rapid major decisions, are just a few of the factors that render the healthcare sector as one of the most stressful professions (Koinis et al., 2015).

Besides the personal burden caused by mental health issues, research observes that the mental health of professionals working in the healthcare industry is also connected to the quality of patient care provided and the number of medical errors that may occur (Suzuki et al., 2004). Therefore, it stands to reason that the mental health status of healthcare professionals is increasingly becoming a focus of attention in research (Apap, 2018; Portoghese et al., 2014; Talaee et al., 2020). Various studies have revealed that healthcare professionals are prone to experience an array of mental health issues, such as anxiety (Kim et al., 2018), depression (Weaver et al., 2018), burnout (Apap, 2018) and stress (Talaee et al., 2020). This has only been exacerbated with the recent COVID-19 pandemic (Talaee et al., 2020; Temsah et al., 2020; Vizheh et al., 2020). Therefore, it is critical to be proactive in supporting the mental health status of healthcare professionals, as globally, the treatment rate for mental health issues is disturbingly low, ranging from 35%-50% and there is a worldwide limitation on human resources for mental health treatment (Rebello et al., 2014). Moreover, there is a large time gap from the primary onset of mental illness to the initial treatment occurring. Studies across countries have all found similar results, showing that the delay in treatment universally approaches a decade (Wang et al., 2005).

As the world becomes more digitalised, various mental health services are being transcribed to the internet. With the evolution of technology and psychotherapy, this led to the development of digital therapies, such as internet-delivered CBT (Andersson et al., 2016). This form of intervention can be described as a predominantly self-guided intervention program (Andersson et al., 2016). Generally, the treatment content is provided by means of an online program or website, via a computer or mobile. The programs typically consist of written texts, audio files and/or videos. The intervention attempts to promote a positive change, improve the individual's knowledge and awareness through the delivery of health-related information and immersive web components (Barak et al., 2009). There are many forms of internet-delivered mental health services, they can differ in duration, intensity and treatment. Some digital mental health services are free of charge and only present automated advice, while others, based on the client's progress within the program, offer some form of support and guidance through text and feedback by an identified therapist (Andersson, 2014).

Hedman et al. (2012) revealed in their study, that the limited therapist time required in digital therapy suggests that the treatment is significantly cost effective, is not impacted by the geographical distances between therapist and patient and is not limited to a clinic's opening hours. Additionally, since the individual can partake in digital therapy from the comfort of their own home, the stigma implicated when visiting a therapist is significantly reduced. However, there are a few limitations to digital therapy, the first being that the therapist's feedback in face-to-face therapy is more direct and likely to be more efficient (Andersson, 2014).

Nonetheless, since the founding of digital therapy, numerous clinical trials have taken place to test its clinical effectiveness and it has proven to have short and long-term beneficial effects for several mental health issues. These included job stress and burnout (Smoktunowicz et al., 2019), depression (Berking et al., 2019), anxiety (Rollman et al., 2018), alcohol use disorder (Eriksson et al., 2017), insomnia (Buntrock et al., 2016) and psychosomatic disorders (De Zwaan et al., 2017). It allows for the deliverance of low threshold treatment options on a mass scale, reaching even individuals who do not have the option for face-to-face treatment, at a faster rate (Apolinário-Hagen, Fritsche, et al., 2018). Despite numerous random controlled trials proving the efficacy of digital mental health services, some studies have still observed a low rate of adherence (O. Johansson et al., 2019; Persson Asplund et al., 2018). Therefore, for the successful implementation of such services one must look at the theory and evidence behind the behavioural intentions of health care professionals when seeking mental health services (Godin et al., 2008).

1.1 Objective

In line with the background above, the study took the form of a needs analysis, with the objective to explore the relationships between the attitudes and behavioural intentions of healthcare professionals working within an acute teaching hospital in Malta towards digital mental health services. The study poses an emphasis on their perception of its usefulness and relative advantages in comparison with conventional psychotherapy, and also reveals the influence of their mental health status and sociodemographic characteristics on their attitude towards these services.

2. THEORY

The difficulty of understanding why healthcare professionals adopt a given behaviour or not, has led to the development of social psychological theories that are able to predict moderate discrepancies of intention and behaviour (Godin et al., 2008). Research on the determinants of intention to use digital mental health services, however, is still quite limited (Apolinário-Hagen, Harrer, et al., 2018). Nonetheless, there are a few potential factors that are commonly discussed as predictors of acceptance and intentions to use digital psychotherapy. This entails the 'attitudes' of the intended users towards the intervention (Casey et al., 2013; March et al., 2018). An individual's attitude is generally recognised as a method to understand and predict that individual's behaviour (Ajzen, 2001):

A positive attitude could indicate acceptance and adoption of new technology or services, such as internet-delivered/digital therapy.

A negative attitude could be a more pertinent factor for low utilisation of such services than actual structural barriers (Hennemann et al., 2016).

This review will adopt a triangulated approach in the theoretical backing of the present research. The Theory of Reasoned Action (TRA) and its extension, the Theory of Planned Behaviour (TPB), suggest that a person's behaviour is determined through their intention. However, a persons' behavioural intention is a function of their beliefs, and the theory maintains that people act on their intentions depending on their attitude in relation to the behaviour, subjective norm and perceived behavioural control (Fishbein & Ajzen, 1975; Luxton, 2016). While in accordance with the Innovation Diffusion Theory (IDT) and the Unified Theory of Acceptance and Use of Technology (UTAUT), the individual's attitude plays a crucial role on the acceptance and utilisation of digital mental health services (M.D. Williams et al., 2015). In lieu of these conceptual models, by assessing the attitudes of healthcare professionals, this research may be able to predict the illness behaviour of healthcare professionals and the value they place on the utilisation of digital mental health care services to support their mental well-being. However, Ajzen (2001) suggests that, in terms of health behaviour, there are indications of ambivalent attitudes. This is important to consider when assessing attitudes towards topics or innovations related to health, as, generally, attitudes are believed to be unidimensional. Nevertheless, it can be that a person experiences both negative and positive attitudes towards the same item. Insight about possible ambivalent attitudes towards digital mental health services can facilitate a more thorough understanding behind the lack of use of these services and how to improve utilisation (Apolinário-Hagen, Fritsche et al., 2018).

The mental health status of an individual is considered an antecedent to their health-related behaviours and has been utilised in research to inform the development of interventions (Morales-Rodríguez et al., 2020). Most of the research suggests that a poorer mental health status is associated with a higher intention to use mental health services (Yu et al., 2015). Some researchers examined the effects of specific psychological factors such as Scheier and Carver, (1985) who delved into the impact of optimistic attitudes on the regulation of health behaviour. As claimed by the theory of stress and coping that was developed by Lazarus and Folkman (1984), perceived stress and coping mechanisms can influence an individual's attitude and behaviour towards an event. Vogel and Wei (2005) found that an individual's perceived stress plays a vital role in motivating the utilisation of mental health services. It is suggested that the severity of the individual's perceived distress is significantly influential on their willingness to seek help and use mental health services (Norcross & Prochaska, 1986; Robbins & Greenley, 1983).

The transactional model of stress suggests that a possible stressful situation is mediated by various factors. These include the primary and secondary states of appraisal, followed by the choice and application of a coping strategy (Lazarus & Folkman, 1984). The individual's perceived control of internal states can affect all stages of this model; since individuals with a high control of their internal states would appraise and respond to a possibly stressful situation quite differently than someone who has limited control over their internal states. A person with a greater level of control is less likely to be hindered by the emotional and physical stress from the situation and is capable of choosing an appropriate coping strategy quickly. While a person with low control, is more likely to view the situation as a threat and feel a lack of internal resources to adequately handle the stressful event (Pallant, 2000). A recent study found that an individual's perceived control of internal states and perceived stress are strongly associated, and can influence behaviour, psychological and physical health (Rezaei & Mousanezhad, 2020). This is supported by the findings of Klein and Cook (2010) and Apolinário-Hagen, Vehreschild et al. (2017), who discovered that the respondents in their studies that held a greater positive attitude towards digital mental health services and were more willing to utilise such services, had a lower control of their internal states.

Good mental health is also dependent on a person's level of affect. Affect is a general term to denote emotions, stress responses, impulses and mood. A person may experience a mixture of levels of positive affect and negative affect (Gross et al., 2019). A person with a high-level control of internal states is likely to feel greater levels of positive affect and less levels of negative affect (Russell et al., 2011). This is supported by previous research, which suggested that an individual who experiences higher levels of negative affect is more probable to experience high levels of perceived stress and have poor coping strategies (D. Watson et al., 1988). Previous research demonstrates that individuals who experience more negative affect are more likely to perceive the usefulness and relative advantages of digital mental health services as a positive association was found between high levels of negative affect and seeking help online (Apolinário-Hagen, Vehreschild, et al., 2017; Klein & Cook, 2010; Ryan et al., 2010). The authors suggested that this was likely due to the respondents experiencing higher levels of negative affect, have a greater need for support and are therefore more willing to try unconventional sources.

A significant amount of research has been conducted specifically on the value of optimism as a psychological phenomenon. For instance, Scheier and Carver (1985), theorised that 'dispositional optimism' is a trait of a balanced personality. In the authors' study, individuals with this trait were found to positively correlate with a better mental well-being, as they are more resilient to stress and make use of coping strategies. Therefore, people encompassing this cognitive bias tend to handle stressful situations better than pessimists (Weinstein, 1980). Research has also indicated that optimism takes a pivotal role in the severity of depressive symptoms, specifically with individuals who work in a highly stressful job, such as healthcare professionals (Romswinkel et al., 2018). Moreover, Spendelow and Jose (2010) found that optimism plays a mediating role in help-seeking. Within their study, optimistic individuals reported a lower need for help and were hopeful for a positive prognosis without any official treatment in comparison to others with equivalent symptoms of mental disorders. Higher levels of optimism are, in fact, linked with better mental and physical health in various studies (Galatzer-Levy & Bonanno, 2014). This has led to the development of several psychological interventions that strive to enhance a patient's optimism, in order to reduce their mental issues and increase their life quality and satisfaction (Malouff & Schutte, 2017). Therefore, according to the theory, people who are prone to high levels of optimism are less likely to have a positive attitude towards digital mental health services (Klein & Cook, 2010)

Some demographic variables have also been linked with digital mental health services attitudes and engagement and have been investigated in several studies concerning digital therapy (Apolinário-Hagen, Harrer, et al., 2018; Eichenberg et al., 2013; Linardon et al., 2020; March et al., 2018). According to an internet intervention model created by Ritterband et al. (2009), user characteristics is one of the main components that influences the uptake and utilisation of digital mental health services. This is in compliance with both the UTAUT and the TPB, that describe the possible influence of demographic differences, such as gender, age and experience, as moderators that affect the use of technology (Ajzen, 1991; Venkatesh et al., 2003). The developers of the internet intervention model state that user characteristics are the most complicated set of variables to evaluate. Some characteristics may be fixed and not prone to manipulation, such as age and gender, while others can be modified, such as knowledge, computer abilities and self-efficacy. However, these demographic differences are crucial to studies as they may serve as predictor variables or assist in identifying barriers to utilising digital mental health services (Ritterband et al., 2009).

This research study tested a theoretical framework addressing the relationship between the behavioural intentions of individuals in utilising digital mental health services and their attitude towards such services, influenced by their mental health status. Associations between their attitudes and various demographic variables, which included the following: age, gender, sex, level of education, number of years employed at the hospital, living status, ethnicity, occupation, previous experience with mental health services, frequency of internet usage and previous knowledge of digital therapy, were explored. The dimensions for measuring the respondents' attitude towards digital mental health services included the perceived usefulness and relative advantages in accordance with previous literature. Whereas mental health status was measured as perceived stress levels over the 4 weeks prior to the completion of the survey, current perceived stress levels, perceived control of internal state, optimism level and levels of positive and negative affect. The development of the hypotheses for this research was based on theoretical models and the results from other research studies.

3. METHODS

3.1 Research Setting

The Maltese healthcare system consists of public and private sectors. This study focuses on employees at Malta's main acute teaching hospital, which provides secondary and tertiary care. The hospital employs around 4,127 staff, including clinical and support personnel. Given the importance of maintaining the physical and mental health of public health workers, this setting is ideal for studying occupational stress and mental health (Azzopardi-Muscat et al., 2017).

3.2 Target Population

Healthcare professionals in acute hospital settings face numerous occupational stressors, which increase their risk of developing mental health issues (Al-Meerza et al., 2012; Hall et al., 2016). Those who work directly with patients are at an even higher risk due to the nature of their work, which involves dealing with suffering, conflicts, emotional suppression, and legal concerns (Firth-Cozens & Greenhalgh, 1997; Ruotsalainen et al., 2008). For this study, the target population was clinical staff working full-time at the main teaching hospital in Malta. A number of inclusion criteria were set by the researchers, referring to key characteristics that participants must exhibit if they were to be included in the research study (Polit & Beck, 2013). It was determined that 3086 individuals were deemed eligible to partake in this study. A purposive sampling method, specifically total population sampling, was used to conduct the study (Polit & Beck, 2013).

3.3 Research Tool

A 7-part questionnaire was used to collect data, incorporating validated psychometric tools to measure various psychological constructs. The E-Therapy Attitudes Measure (ETAM), originally a 14-item scale and later expanded to 17 items, evaluates attitudes toward digital mental health services, focusing on perceived benefits, comparisons with face-to-face therapy, and subjective beliefs using a 5-point Likert scale (Apolinário-Hagen et al., 2017; 2018). This tool is used to gauge users' general approval and adoption of digital interventions, aligning with the UTAUT (Venkatesh et al., 2003). The Visual Analogue Scale (VAS) measures self-reported stress through a simple 10-cm line ranging from 'not at all' to 'maximal' stress (McCormack et al., 1988; Hasson & Arnetz, 2005). Despite its simplicity, it provides a quick and effective assessment of stress (Lesage et al., 2012). The Perceived Stress Questionnaire (PSQ-20), a 20-item version derived from the original 30-item scale, assesses stress perceptions using a 5-point Likert scale (Levenstein et al., 1993; Fliege et al., 2005). This tool is used due to its reliability and comprehensive coverage of stress reactions and stressors. The Perceived Control of Internal State Scale (PCOISS) evaluates individuals' perceptions of their ability to manage internal states and emotions through an 18-item scale, developed based on extensive research and pilot studies (Pallant, 2000). This scale is relevant for understanding how perceived control over internal states influences preferences for mental health care. The Life Orientation Test-Revised (LOT-R) measures optimism and its impact on help-seeking behaviour using a 6-item scale (Scheier et al., 1994). It is included to explore how optimism affects attitudes toward mental health care. Lastly, the Positive and Negative Affect Scale (PANAS), which consists of two 10-item scales, captures mood dimensions by assessing the extent of positive and negative affects over recent weeks (Watson et al., 1988). This tool is utilised to understand mood fluctuations and their relation to mental health issues and help-seeking behaviours. Each tool is chosen for its specific ability to measure relevant psychological constructs and attitudes, contributing to a comprehensive understanding of participants' responses and behaviour.

Table 1. Overview of Questionnaire Sections, Items, and Objectives

Section	Number of Items	Objective of the questionnaire
Section A: Demographic Data	10	Collect basic information about participants to understand their background.
Section B: E-Therapy Attitudes Measure (ETAM)	17	Assess attitudes towards e-therapy to understand acceptance and identify potential barriers to digital mental health services
Section C: Visual Analogue Scale (VAS).	1	Measure participants' overall stress levels, providing a quick assessment of their current mental state
Section D: Perceived Stress Questionnaire (PSQ-20)	20	Evaluate perceived stress, a key factor influencing mental health, to gauge stress levels among healthcare workers.
Section E: Perceived Control of Internal State Scale (PCOISS)	8	Measure the degree of control participants feel they have over their emotions, important for understanding resilience and stress management.
Section F: Life Orientation Test-Revised (LOT-R)	10	Assess optimism, a psychological trait that influences how stress and mental health issues are experienced.
Section G: Positive and Negative Affect Scale (PANAS).	20	Assess mood by measuring both positive and negative emotions, providing a balanced view of participants' emotional states

3.4 Ethical Considerations

Ethical approval was obtained from relevant health authorities, including the hospital's CEO, Data Protection Officer, and Medical Director, as well as the Faculty Research Ethics Committee. Special attention was given to the sensitive nature of mental health topics. For example, permission was secured from the Richmond Foundation, a non-profit mental health organization, to include their contact details for participants needing support.

For this research study anonymity was deemed vital as it is centred on a sensitive topic, mental health, and in order to gain valuable data, it was important to collect honest and reliable data from the targeted population. Therefore, alongside the questionnaire, participants were provided with a letter of informed consent that included a brief explanation on what digital therapy entails and the aims of the study. Participation was voluntary, with the option to withdraw at any time. To maintain anonymity, an intermediary sent the questionnaire to potential participants, ensuring the researcher had no direct contact with them.

3.5 Data Collection

Data was collected via a self-administered online questionnaire. An intermediary, using the hospital's email system, sent the questionnaire to eligible participants. Responses were collected securely on the researcher's password-protected computer, ensuring no personal identifiers were linked to the data. To maximise response rates, reminder emails were sent on two occasions, each after a four-week interval.

3.6 Data Analysis

Data were analysed using the Statistical Package for the Social Sciences (SPSS) Version 27. An exploratory factor analysis (EFA) was conducted on the 17-item ETAM scale to identify underlying theoretical constructs. Items that did not load onto any components were removed based on previous research recommendations. The final analysis identified two components, which were labelled according to the UTAUT, consistent with prior studies (Apolinário-Hagen, Harrer, et al., 2018; Apolinário-Hagen, Vehreschild, et al., 2017). The results revealed by means of this analysis endorse the use of these two constructs for further analysis.

Descriptive statistics summarised the data, and Pearson correlation coefficients identified relationships between attitudes, moods, perceived stress, control, and optimism. Analysis of variance (ANOVA) tests explored how these variables predicted attitudes toward digital mental health services, with post hoc tests examining mean differences.

4. RESULTS

4.1 Descriptive Results

A total of 491 submissions were received. After performing data cleaning, 486 submissions were deemed suitable for data analysis. This provided a response rate of 16%. Most respondents were female (314/486, 64.61%), married (310/486, 63.92%) and maltese (458/486, 94.24%). The most common highest education achieved was a bachelor's degree (86/486 38.27%) and the respondents' age varied from under 25 to over 65 years. The age group '25-34 years' had the highest response rate (158/486, 32.51%). Only 92 (18.93%) of the respondents had previously made use of mental health services, however most made use of the internet daily (457/486, 94.03%) and 215/486 respondents (44.24%), were aware of the existence of digital mental health services.

Table 2. Sample characteristics (N = 486)

Variable		Sample n = 486
Gender	Male n (%)	170 (34.98%)
	Female n (%)	314 (64.61%)
	Non-binary n (%)	1 (0.21%)
Age	Less than 25 n (%)	47 (9.67%)
	25-34 n (%)	158 (32.51%)
	35-44 n (%)	86 (17.70%)
	45-54 n (%)	112 (23.05%)
	55-64 n (%)	80 (16.46%)
	65 + n (%)	3 (0.62%)
Education Level	Bachelor's Degree n (%)	186 (38.27%)
	Master's Degree n (%)	135 (27.78%)
	Diploma n (%)	71 (14.61%)
	Doctoral Degree n (%)	57 (11.37%)
	Doctor of Medicine n (%)	12 (2.47%)
	Post Grad Diploma n (%)	6 (1.23%)
Years of Employment	less than 5 years n (%)	137 (28.19%)
	5-10 n (%)	93 (19.14%)
	11-20 n (%)	104 (21.40%)
	21-30 n (%)	71 (14.61%)
	30+ n (%)	81 (16.67%)
Ethnicity	Maltese n (%)	458 (94.24%)
	Foreign n (%)	18 (3.7%)
Marital Status	Single n (%)	148 (30.52%)
	Married or living in a close relationship n (%)	310 (63.92%)
	Divorced or separated n (%)	27 (5.57%)
Occupation	Doctor n (%)	98 (20.41%)
	Nurse n (%)	183 (37.73%)
	Allied Health Professional n (%)	167 (34.43%)
	Other n (%)	36 (7.42%)
Experience with Psychotherapy	No n (%)	182 (37.45%)
	Yes, as a professional n (%)	147 (30.25%)
	Yes, as a patient n (%)	92 (18.93%)
	Yes, as a relative n (%)	63 (12.96%)

continued on following page

Table 2. Continued

Variable		Sample n = 486
Frequency of Internet Use	Daily n (%)	457 (94.03%)
	Several times a week n (%)	22 (4.53%)
	Several times a month n (%)	4 (0.82%)
	Rarely or Occasionally n (%)	3 (0.62%)
Awareness of Digital Mental Health Therapy	Yes, Aware n (%)	215 (44.24%)
	No, Not Aware n (%)	192 (39.51%)
	Not Sure n (%)	79 (16.26%)

Descriptive statistics were also obtained from the ETAM scores, this allowed for the classification of the participants' attitudes towards digital mental health services. Analysis of the data collected from the ETAM tool indicated an overall neutral attitude towards digital mental health services. A summary of the overall mean score, standard deviation and median for each item within the ETAM scale is illustrated in Table 3. Additionally, each item is listed under their respective factor in accordance with the conducted Exploratory Factor Analysis explained previously. The two factors were labelled 'perceived usefulness' and 'relative advantages and comparability'. However, three items from the scale were excluded from these two factors due to significant cross-loading or non-loading on either component.

Table 3. ETAM scale items measured using a 5-point Likert scale, ranging from strongly disagree to strongly agree

ETAM Scale Items:		Mean	95% Confidence Interval for Mean (Lower Bound)	95% Confidence Interval for Mean (Upper Bound)	Median
1./PU	**Internet-based therapies are modern and in line with our modern times.**	**3.69**	**3.62**	**3.77**	**4.0**
2./RA	Internet-based therapies will replace conventional face-to-face psychotherapy in the future.	2.39	2.30	2.48	2.0
3.	Internet-based therapy is more compatible with work and private life than conventional face-to-face therapy.	3.06	2.98	3.15	3.0
4./RA	It makes no difference to me whether psychotherapy is conducted through the internet or in a practice in a clinic.	2.25	2.16	2.35	2.0
5./PU	Internet-based therapies will reach more individuals with mental health problems.	3.52	3.43	3.61	4.0

continued on following page

Table 3. Continued

ETAM Scale Items:		Mean	95% Confidence Interval for Mean (Lower Bound)	95% Confidence Interval for Mean (Upper Bound)	Median
1./PU	**Internet-based therapies are modern and in line with our modern times.**	**3.69**	**3.62**	**3.77**	**4.0**
6./PU	Employers should offer Internet-based therapies free of charge	3.94	3.86	4.03	4.0
7./RA	Internet-based therapy programs are as effective as conventional face-to-face psychotherapies.	2.54	2.46	2.62	3.0
8./RA	Trust in a therapist can be just as easily built over the internet as in conventional face-to-face psychotherapy.	2.38	2.29	2.46	2.0
9./RA	Internet-based therapies are an appropriate alternative to conventional face-to-face psychotherapy.	2.98	2.88	3.07	3.0
10./RA	In case of mental health problems, I would attend internet-based therapy.	2.94	2.84	3.03	3.0
11./RA	I would prefer internet-based therapy to conventional face-to-face psychotherapy.	2.36	2.27	2.44	2.0
12./PU	Internet-based therapies will reach more patients and help them.	3.54	3.45	3.63	4.0
13.	I'm not particularly worried about data security in internet therapies.	2.62	2.52	2.71	2.0
14./PU	The anonymity in internet therapies decreases the threshold to speak openly and honestly about important issues.	3.16	3.07	3.25	3.0
15./PU	Through the dissemination of internet therapies, persons will get professional help earlier.	3.57	3.49	3.64	4.0
16.	Misunderstandings occur in internet therapies as often as in conventional psychotherapies.	3.14	3.05	3.23	3.0
17./RA	Internet therapies are suitable for most patients, regardless of their personal background (age, sex, education, etc.).	2.46	2.36	2.56	2.0

PU – Perceived Usefulness
RA – Relative Advantages and Comparability

Generally, participants classified 5 items from the scale to be positive. These included modernism (item 1), ease of access (item 5), coverage of expenses by employers (item 6), helpfulness (item 12) and enabling access to therapy earlier (item 15).

However, participants held a negative attitude towards 5 items within the scale. Participants disagreed with the following items, the prospect of digital therapy replacing conventional therapies (item 2), the comparability of both delivery modes (item 4), the establishment of therapeutic relationships (item 8), personal preference for digital therapy (item 11) and its appropriateness for various populations (item 17).

5 items were classified as neutral by the participants. These items addressed the compatibility of digital therapy with everyday life (item 3), equivalence of effectiveness between the two modes (item 7), the appropriateness of using digital therapy as a replacement to conventional therapies (item 9), their inclination to use digital therapy (item 10), data protection (item 13), the possibility of anonymity in digital therapy (item 14) and the possibilities of misunderstandings (item 16).

In congruence with previous research, the overall mean score was then grouped according to predefined cut-offs:

negative attitude: 1-2.49,

neutral attitude: 2.5-3.49,

positive attitude: 3.5-5 (Apolinário-Hagen, Harrer, et al., 2018).

The number of participants grouped within the predefined cut-offs, for overall attitude, perceived usefulness and relative advantages and comparability is shown in Table 4.

Table 4. Classification of ETAM scores

*ETAM	Negative attitude (%)	Neutral Attitude (%)	Positive Attitude (%)
Overall mean score	86 (16.9)	327 (67.3)	68 (14)
Perceived usefulness	38 (5.8)	144 (29.6)	312 (64.2)
Relative advantages and Comparability	224 (46.8)	216 (45.1)	39 (8.1)

*ETAM – E-therapy Attitude Measure

Overall, as shown in Table 4, the study identified that the majority of the sample, 327 (67.3%), held a neutral attitude. 86 (16.9%) held predominantly a negative attitude, while only 68 (14%) had a positive attitude towards digital therapy. Further descriptive analysis showed that most participants, 312 (64.2%), perceived digital mental health services as useful, however, only a few, 39 (8.1%), also indicated that this form of psychotherapy was comparable or held relative advantages over more conventional approaches, such as face-to-face therapy.

The attitudes of the participants were analysed further by investigating their preferences of mode to receive psychotherapy and their intentions to use these services. One single item within the tool asked participants to indicate their preference of using digital mental health over face-to-face psychotherapy while another was used to investigate an individual's intention to use digital therapy if required (March et al., 2018). The results were then dichotomised as yes or no for analysis:

1-3 were categorised as no, representing the participants with a preference for more conventional means of therapy, while 4-5 'Yes', representing those who prefer digital therapy. The same method was utilised for the second single item, where 'No' represented those who had no intentions to use digital therapy in the future, while 'Yes' represented the participants with intentions to utilise digital mental health services in the future if required.

Only 62 (12.8%) of the participants revealed a preference for digital therapy over conventional face-to-face therapy, while 423 (87.2%) primarily prefer face-to-face therapy, while 313 (64.7%) of the population showed limited intentions to use digital therapy, if available, however, 171 (35.3%) affirmed their intention to use such services if readily available.

4.2 Correlation of Mental Health Status

For this study different variables evaluating the participant's mental health status were measured as possible attitude predictors The independent variables analysed included, respondents' current perceived stress (as measured by the VAS), total perceived stress (as measured by the PSQ-20) control of internal states (as measured by the PCOISS), level of optimism (as measured by the LOT-R), and finally their levels of negative and positive effects (as measured by the PANAS). Association between the independent variables and both components encompassing attitudes towards digital therapy, i.e., 'perceived usefulness' and 'relative advantage and comparability', were investigated using Pearson correlation coefficient.

There were no significant correlations between the two attitude scores and the scores of the psychological variables. However, in accordance with Cohen (1988) guidelines, there was a strong positive correlation between both attitude scores, while all the psychological variables were correlated to one another.

Table 5. Correlation matrix between e-therapy attitude factors and mental health status variables

Variable	1	2	3	4	5	6	7	
1. Total Perceived Usefulness	-							
2. Total Relative Advantages and Comparability	.526**	-						
3. Current Perceived Stress	.000	-.028	-					
4. Total Perceived Stress	.054	-.017	.693**	-				
5. Total PCOISS	-.020	.013	-.430**	-.631**	-			
6. Total LOT	.010	.008	-.296**	-.483**	.530**	-		
7. Total Positive Affect	-.021	.004	-.321**	-.399**	.478**	.443**	-	

continued on following page

Table 5. Continued

Variable	1	2	3	4	5	6	7	
1. Total Perceived Usefulness	-							
8. Total Negative Affect	.008	-.053	.478**	.671**	-.526**	-.476**	-.264**	-

Correlation is significant at the 0.01 level (2-tailed)

4.3 Sociodemographic Predictors

Prior to conducting the follow-up analysis of variance (ANOVA) and post-hoc comparisons, Multivariate Analysis of Variance (MANOVA) was carried out to compare the mean scores as it can help reduce the inflation of Type 1 error. Through this test, the researcher was able to compare the groups and reveal the mean differences between the groups on the combination of dependent variables. Therefore, the independent variables analysed using ANOVA were age, career length, occupation, and frequency of internet use.

Due to the ethnicity variable being made up of only two groups, it was investigated utilising the MANOVA results, which proved a statistically significant difference, $F(2, 465) = 2.70, p = .011$; Wilks' Lambda = .981; partial eta squared = .02. Therefore, the dependent variables were considered separately and the only differences to reach statistical significance were the relative advantages and comparability variable, $F(1, 466) = 7.39, p = .007$, partial eta squared = .02. The mean scores were inspected and revealed that the Maltese participants perceived the relative advantages and comparability of digital therapy less than the foreigners that partook in this study.

The effect of age was investigated by initially dividing the participants into six groups according to their age (Group 1: Less than 25; Group 2: 25-34; Group 3: 35-44; Group 4: 45-54; Group 5: 55-64; Group 6: 65 and above). A statistically significant difference was revealed at the $p < .05$ level in perceived usefulness scores for the age groups, $F(5, 22.18) = 3.68; p = .01$. The effect size was calculated using eta squared, with a resulting value of .04, hence, it is considered a small effect in accordance with Cohen's (1988) guidelines. Post-hoc comparisons using the Tukey HSD test revealed that the mean score for Group 1 ($M = 22.91$, $SD = 3.99$) was significantly different from Group 3 ($M = 20.33$, $SD = 4.9$) and Group 4 ($M = 20.79$, $SD = 4.16$). While Group 2 ($M = 22.21$, $SD = 3.82$) was also significantly different to group 3 ($M = 20.33$, $SD = 4.9$). Group 5 ($M = 21.13$, $SD = 3.12$) and Group 6 ($M = 21.33$, $SD = 2.31$) did not differ significantly.

A statistically significant difference in mean scores for perceived usefulness was also revealed between the different levels of career length. Participants were initially divided into groups according to the number of years working within the national hospital (Group 1: Less than 5 years; Group 2: 5-10 years, Group 3: 11-20 years, Group 4: 21-30 years; Group 5: 30+ years). The ANOVA test showed a statistically significant difference, $F (4, 479) = 3.85$, $p = .00$. The effect size, calculated using eta squared, was .03, and is, therefore, considered a small effect. Post-hoc comparisons were conducted using the Tukey HSD test. These revealed that the mean score for Group 4 (M = 20.06, SD = 4.49) was significantly different from Group 1 (M = 22.15, SD = 3.91) and Group 2 (M = 22.00, SD = 4.20). While Group 3 (M = 21.01 SD = 4.27) and Group 5 (M = 21.44 SD = 3.30), did not vary significantly from the other groups.

The impact of different occupations on perceived usefulness and relative advantages and comparability, as measured by the ETAM scale, was also explored. Participants were divided according to their profession (Group 1: doctor; Group 2: nurse; Group 3: allied health professionals; Group4: other). According to the ANOVA results, there was a statistically significant difference at the $p < .05$ level for the relative advantages and comparability scores between the groups, $F (3, 474) = 3.09$ $p = .03$. However, the effect size was calculated using eta squared and at a value of .02 is considered a small effect. Post-hoc comparisons conducted using the Tukey HSD test indicated that the means score for Group 3 (M = 21.18, SD = 5.29) was significantly different from Group 4 (M = 18.44, SD = 4.99). Group 1 (M = 19.81, SD = 5.18) and Group 2 (M = 20.26, SD = 5.74) did not differ significantly from either Group 3 or 4. Similar results were obtained for the perceived usefulness variable. A statistically significant difference was found across the groups, $F (3, 479) = 3.35$ $p = .02$; effect size = .02. The post-hoc comparisons revealed that again, the mean score for Group 3 (M = 22.05, SD = 3.71) was significantly different from Group 4 (M = 20.08, SD = 4.63). Group 1 (M = 21.72, SD = 3.89) and Group 2 (M = 21.04, SD = 4.30) did not differ significantly from either Group 3 or 4.

Lastly, the influence of frequency of internet use was also explored. Participants were divided into predefined groups (Group 1: daily; Group 2: several times a week; Group 3: several times a month; Group4: rarely or occasionally). The ANOVA results revealed a statistically significant difference at the $p < .05$ level for the relative advantage scores between the groups, $F (3, 478) = 3.08$ $p = .03$. However, the effect size resulted in a value of .02, hence, it is considered a small effect. Using the Tukey HSD test, post-hoc comparisons were conducted. The multiple comparisons test did not indicate where the differences among the groups occur, which could be due to some groups having small sizes (Pallant, 2016). However, the generated mean plot provided an easy method to compare the mean scores. It was noted that Group 4 (M = 19.00, SD = 5.47) perceived the relative advantages and comparability of digital therapy the least. Group 3 (M = 26.75, SD = 2.06) had the highest scores, while Group 1 (M = 20.18, SD = 5.49) and Group 2 (M = 22.43, SD = 4.20) mean scores placed between the two other groups.

5. DISCUSSION

5.1 Summary of Main Findings and Implications

In summary, the present study findings revealed the presence of ambivalent attitudes, the convergence of negative and positive feelings towards an intervention, which in this case was towards the utilisation of digital mental health services.

Despite an overall neutral attitude, the participants for this current study identified several positive factors for digital mental health services. The items with the highest agreement were the suitability of digital therapy in today's modern society and the provision of free digital mental health services by employers. Simultaneously, the majority of the respondents within this study disagreed on the effectiveness of digital therapy and the building of therapeutic relationships. This is akin to the results observed in previous studies (Apolinário-Hagen, Vehreschild, et al., 2017; Musiat et al., 2014).

Revealing these results are vital when implementing a new service because it is of utmost importance to consider the intended consumers' behavioural intentions. Whether an intention is translated into action has become a pivotal challenge when implementing interventions and is usually referred to as the 'intention-behaviour gap'. This entails the underlying psychological process that shifts an intention to action (Sniehotta et al., 2005). Research has suggested that misconstructions, low expectations, and negative attitudes can hinder the uptake or efficacy of digital mental health services (Hennemann et al., 2016). If there is the presence of ambivalent attitudes, a person may identify positive factors on the perceived usefulness of digital therapy, however that same person may also indicate low behavioural intentions to utilise this novel service for personal use. From the results observed in this study, it seems that the participants do not agree with the efficacy of digital mental health services, its comparability with face-to-face therapy and respondents who preferred digital mental health services over face-to-face psychotherapy was limited. Similarly, a previous study (Klein and Cook, 2010), revealed comparable results. The study highlights a crucial 'intention-behaviour gap,' where despite recognizing the potential benefits of digital mental health services, there is a reluctance to act on these intentions. Managers must address this gap by not only promoting digital mental health services but also by actively working to convert positive attitudes into actual usage. This could involve, customised marketing strategies, developing targeted campaigns that address specific concerns and misconceptions about digital therapy. Education and training would also be beneficial, implementing educational programs to increase understanding of digital mental health services and demonstrate their effectiveness.

This is in line with previous studies, which have proven that education (Hennemann et al., 2016) and providing brief information via text (Apolinário-Hagen, Fritsche, et al., 2018; Casey et al., 2013) has increased positive attitudes and strengthened intentions to make use of digital mental health services. However, research is still limited, hence, Batterham and Calear (2017) recommend the examination of additional factors that are associated with preference, with the aim to identify any barriers limiting the acceptance of digital therapy. Despite the repeated results of preferences for conventional therapy, the fact that the majority of this study's participants have a neutral attitude towards digital mental health services is a lifeline. This study points out that knowledge and understanding play a key role in user acceptance. Therefore, increasing awareness about the available services and ensuring clarity about data confidentiality can help in reducing hesitations and fostering a more positive outlook towards digital mental health solutions (Apolinário-Hagen, Fritsche, et al., 2018) .

The results gained from this study supported this plan of action, as the healthcare professionals' preferences for digital mental health services appear to be distinct from their reported intentions to utilise this form of service, since over double the number of respondents who indicated a preference for digital therapy, reported an intention to use these services. This discovery is important in the context of previous research data, which revealed the number of individuals who suffer from mental health issues who do not receive treatment is on the rise, while simultaneously there is a global decrease in human resources for mental health services (Rebello et al., 2014; Wainberg et al., 2017). Therefore, a willingness to use digital therapy could prove to be vital to reducing the existing 'treatment gap', while broadening the reach of treatment for those with limited access (Hedman et al., 2012).

It is also crucial for future research to pinpoint the reasons as to why few people report an intention to utilise digital therapy for future use and even fewer indicate a preference for digital therapy. The TPB does offer a plausible explanation as to why many researchers report a negative assessment of digital therapy when compared to face-to-face therapy despite a positive attitude towards its perceived usefulness. The theory suggests that uncertainties in relation to digital therapy could be caused by a lack of knowledge on this form of treatment, which would result in few preferring digital therapies or willing to utilise this form of service in the future (Ajzen, 1985). In the current study, less than half of the sample of the population was aware of the existence of digital psychotherapy, which is comparable to a study that found similar results in relation to attitudes, preferences and intentions to use digital therapy (Apolinário-Hagen, Fritsche, et al., 2018). However, as the world advances in technology, it is likely to be accompanied by an increasing demand for digital psychotherapy. Therefore, health politics, research and practice need to be prepared for these possible developments (Eichenberg, et al., 2013).

5.2 Effects of Mental Health Status in Attitudes Towards Digital Mental Health Services

From the present study, no association was revealed between the participants' mental health status level and their attitude towards digital mental health services. Despite these results not being in line with the mainstream of research, similar results were found in a study performed by Apolinário-Hagen et al. (2020). The authors revealed that perceived stress was not statistically significant as a predictor of attitudes in their research. They explain that this could be caused by the 'feeling healthy' barrier, which is an established motivational barrier that influences participation in health programmes (Borghouts et al., 2021). Researchers have previously stated that healthcare professionals associate a lower level of mental health status, including high levels of stress and negative affect, as a part of the norm when working within a hospital (Portoghese et al., 2014). Therefore, it could be possible that the participants within this study were not conscious of their mental distress. Apolinário-Hagen et al. (2020) recommend screening tools for stress and mental health distress to be provided, as in due time this could lead to an increase in intentions to use psychological interventions. This process has been proven to be an effective approach to improve utilisation of digital mental health services in previous research (Ebert, et al., 2017).

5.3 Sociodemographic Differences in Attitudes Towards Digital Mental Health Services

In the present study, the sociodemographic differences and attitude scores towards digital therapy were scrutinised to identify relationships amongst them. As explained previously, the attitude scores were divided into two components labelled 'perceived usefulness' and 'relative advantage and comparability', in accordance with the exploratory factor analysis conducted and previous research data (Apolinário-Hagen, Harrer, et al., 2018). Therefore, the results gained from the current study will be discussed in reference to the scores of the two components.

This study observed a relationship between younger age and higher scores for the perceived usefulness of digital mental health services. This is similar to the results of other studies (Batterham and Calear, 2017, Apolinário-Hagen et al. 2020, and Eichenberg et al. 2013). This discrepancy may be due to older adults' technology skills and understanding, since younger people tend to be more comfortable in making use of technology (Chudy-Onwugaje et al., 2018). The results from the study suggest that additional support might be needed for those with lower technological skills or less confidence in using digital tools. This could include training programs, offering workshops or online tutorials to enhance digital literacy, providing accessible helpdesks or user support to assist with any technical issues that may arise. Therefore, further research is warranted on what hinders the older population from accessing digital mental health services, and how their attitudes towards such services can be improved.

The current study found a positive association between working for a shorter duration of time and higher perceived usefulness scores and more positive attitudes toward digital therapy, as demonstrated in previous research (Cliffe et al. 2020). However, limited research has explored the impact of career length on attitudes toward digital therapy, nevertheless certain studies have examined the link between perceived stress and years of professional experience (Skakon et al., 2011; Tabak & Orit, 2007). These studies demonstrated that longer professional experience correlated with lower stress levels and reduced likelihood of seeking mental health support, possibly attributed to lower expectations and improved coping strategies over time. Accordingly, individuals with longer careers might experience lower perceived stress, leading to less positive attitudes toward digital mental health services. Sukums et al. (2014) also noted that, despite no significant link between career length and attitude toward digital therapy, healthcare workers with more years of experience lacked confidence in learning to use digital therapy and held lower expectations of its benefits. Consequently, this lack of confidence and low expectations could explain their more negative attitudes. This is interconnected with the previously mentioned age factor.

The study identified an association between ethnicity and perceived advantages and comparability of digital mental health services. The results supported the hypothesis that foreign healthcare professionals held more positive attitudes toward digital therapy. This connection mirrors prior research (Liem et al., 2021), prompting a recommendation for implementing digital mental health services for all migrant workers at MDH. However, the results from this study must be interpreted with caution, due to unequal group sizes in the sample.

Moreover, diverse occupations displayed associations with perceived usefulness and relative advantage and comparability. This aligns with prior studies (Wells et al., 2007; Topooco et al., 2017), even though limited research delves into the impact of different occupations on attitudes. Some studies (Koinis et al. 2015; Vizheh et al. 2020) unveiled varied distress levels among professions, which in turn could shape their attitudes toward digital mental health services, as reported in earlier research (Apolinário-Hagen, Harrer, et al., 2018). Nevertheless, further research is necessary to identify the drivers and barriers influencing attitudes and intentions regarding digital mental health services across diverse occupations.

An association was found between internet usage frequency and participants' perception of the advantages and comparability of digital mental health services in this study. Those using the internet less often, reported lower scores in these areas, aligning with the study's initial hypothesis. This trend mirrors findings in similar studies that link frequent internet use to positive attitudes toward digital therapy (Eichenberg et al., 2013; Horgan & Sweeney, 2010; March et al., 2018). Increased internet usage suggests better digital and health literacy, which is tied to positive attitudes and engagement with digital mental health services (Berry et al., 2019; Borghouts et al., 2021; Feijt et al., 2018). Consequently, it's advisable to enhance digital literacy through training before service implementation. However, it's important to exercise caution regarding these results due to unequal participant distribution among predefined internet usage groups.

Contrary to previous studies, this research found no correlation between gender or education level and attitude scores. This surprising finding challenges the established pattern seen in literature, suggesting that the overrepresentation of women and highly educated individuals in digital intervention assessments might not solely result from negative attitudes toward digital therapy among men and those with lower education. Instead, additional barriers could be at play. For instance, men might experience greater reluctance to seek help (Sagar-Ouriaghli et al., 2019), while individuals with lower education levels might lack technological confidence and easy access to digital therapy (Batterham & Calear, 2017). Addressing these barriers and improving the acceptance of digital mental health services among men and less educated individuals requires further research to comprehend their distinct technological and structural challenges and develop customised interventions accordingly.

Social implications of the study suggest both opportunities and challenges in the realm of digital mental health services. While these services hold promise for reducing disparities by reaching diverse populations, they also risk widening existing equity gaps if barriers like technological confidence and digital literacy are not addressed (Chudy-Onwugaje et al., 2018). In workplace settings, the positive response to free digital mental health services provided by employers indicates potential benefits, such as enhanced employee well-being (Weisel et al., 2019) and improved accessibility (Andrews et al., 2018). However, cultural sensitivity is crucial, as differences in attitudes based on ethnicity highlight the need for culturally relevant content and the involvement of multicultural teams in service development (Liem et al., 2021). Future research should focus on understanding specific barriers to digital mental health service utilisation and evaluating the long-term impacts of these services on usage patterns and overall mental health outcomes. Addressing these areas will be essential for ensuring that digital mental health solutions effectively meet diverse needs and contribute to more equitable access to mental health support.

5.4 Limitations

This research did encompass various limitations. The first major limitation being that this study took an exploratory approach using a cross-sectional design, which restricts the reliability of cause and effect from simple relationship causality (Bowling, 2014). Due to time limitations, the theoretical grounding for the research question on the effect of mental health status on attitudes towards digital mental health services was based solely on the theory of stress, developed by Lazarus and Folkman, (1984). However, healthcare workers are commonly reported in literature to experience burnout syndrome (Buttigieg et al., 2015; Galea, 2014; Portoghese et al., 2014; E. S. Williams et al., 2019), therefore, it is recommended that future studies consider other constructs. When conducting the exploratory factor analysis, the author of this study noted multiple items cross-loading on both factors, which has also been observed in previous research using the same tool (Apolinário-Hagen, Fritsche, et al., 2018; Apolinário-Hagen et al., 2017). Nevertheless, the author decided to remain faithful to the original tool, as the items cross-loading were essential to the study. Non-probability sampling is a common technique in digital mental health services research (Apolinário-Hagen, Harrer, et al., 2018; Apolinário-Hagen, Vehreschild, et al., 2017; Linardon et al., 2020; March et al., 2018), however it increases the possibility of the results being influenced by selection bias and non-response bias (Sharma, 2014). Nonetheless, due to the online distribution of the questionnaire, the pandemic's impact on healthcare professionals, and the limited study sample, purposive sampling was chosen for this study, to boost responses and facilitate data analysis. Another limitation vital to mention, would be the limited response rate, which after data cleansing the received submissions, a response rate of 16% was achieved. Previous research has found that online questionnaires typically do suffer from limited responses in comparison to other data collection methods (Nulty, 2008). Van Mol (2017) observed that it is not uncommon for online surveys to receive even a response rate of below 10%, however the data collected can still prove to be trustworthy if analysed appropriately. The researcher tried to combat a low response rate, by forwarding two reminders at pre-set time intervals in an attempt to encourage a larger response over the course of three months. However, one must keep in mind the extreme circumstances that healthcare professionals were undergoing due to the pandemic and forcing the study to be conducted purely online.

6. CONCLUSION

This research study provided a better understanding of the current attitudes and behavioural intentions held by healthcare professionals, working within the national acute hospital of Malta, towards digital mental health services. It revealed high levels of unawareness or uncertainty of digital mental health services; hence it was suggested that more resources are made available on the efficacy of digital therapy. It also presented the results of a needs analysis, identifying the different cohorts of healthcare professionals more likely to utilise digital therapy, whilst observing a lack of literature revolving around the motives behind negative attitudes towards digital therapy of certain cohorts. Therefore, further research, identifying additional barriers, was recommended, in an attempt to increase the uptake and adherence of digital mental health services.

REFERENCES

Ajzen, I. (1991). The Theory of Planned Behavior. In Organizational Behavior and Human Decision Processes (Vol. 50). DOI: 10.1016/0749-5978(91)90020-T

Ajzen, I. (2001). Nature and operation of attitudes. *Annual Review of Psychology*, 52(1), 27–58. DOI: 10.1146/annurev.psych.52.1.27 PMID: 11148298

Al-Meerza, A., Al-Sayegh, S. F. Y., Al-Sayrafy, L. M., Alkoot, E. M., El-Shazly, M. K., & Kamel, M. I. (2012). Comparison of sources and expressions of stress among hospital and primary health care physicians. *Alexandria Journal of Medicine*, 48(4), 367–371. DOI: 10.1016/j.ajme.2012.02.001

Andersson, G. (2014). The Internet and CBT: A Clinical Guide. CRC Press. https://books.google.com.mt/books?hl=en&lr=&id=ColqBAAAQBAJ&oi=fnd&pg=PP1&dq=Andersson+G.+The+internet+and+CBT:+A+clinical+guide+2014+CRC+Press+Boca+Raton+&ots=bbFvMwOLpf&sig=1OJd30x3lKbWjZ2u6btdnhzSGKY&redir_esc=y#v=onepage&q&f=false

Andersson, G. (2016). Internet-Delivered Psychological Treatments. *Annual Review of Clinical Psychology*, 12(1), 157–179. DOI: 10.1146/annurev-clinpsy-021815-093006 PMID: 26652054

Andrews, G., Basu, A., Cuijpers, P., Craske, M. G., McEvoy, P., English, C. L., & Newby, J. M. (2018). Computer therapy for the anxiety and depression disorders is effective, acceptable and practical health care: An updated meta-analysis. *Journal of Anxiety Disorders*, 55, 70–78. DOI: 10.1016/j.janxdis.2018.01.001 PMID: 29422409

Apap, B. (2018). Levels of burnout amongst nursing and caring staff in Maltese long-term care facilities [University Of Malta]. https://www.um.edu.mt/library/oar/bitstream/123456789/40365/4/18MGER001.pdf

Apolinário-Hagen, J., Fritsche, L., Bierhals, C., & Salewski, C. (2018). Improving attitudes toward e-mental health services in the general population via psychoeducational information material: A randomized controlled trial. *Internet Interventions : the Application of Information Technology in Mental and Behavioural Health*, 12, 141–149. DOI: 10.1016/j.invent.2017.12.002 PMID: 30135778

Apolinário-Hagen, J., Harrer, M., Kählke, F., Fritsche, L., Salewski, C., & Ebert, D. D. (2018). Public attitudes toward guided internet-based therapies: Web-based survey study. *Journal of Medical Internet Research*, 20(5), e10735. Advance online publication. DOI: 10.2196/10735 PMID: 29764797

Apolinário-Hagen, J., Hennemann, S., Kück, C., Wodner, A., Geibel, D., Riebschläger, M., Zeißler, M., & Breil, B. (2020). Exploring User-Related Drivers of the Early Acceptance of Certified Digital Stress Prevention Programs in Germany. *Health Services Insights*, 13. Advance online publication. DOI: 10.1177/1178632920911061 PMID: 32206013

Apolinário-Hagen, J., Vehreschild, V., & Alkoudmani, R. M. (2017). Current Views and Perspectives on E-Mental Health: An Exploratory Survey Study for Understanding Public Attitudes Toward Internet-Based Psychotherapy in Germany. *JMIR Mental Health*, 4(1), e8. DOI: 10.2196/mental.6375 PMID: 28232298

Armstrong, R. A. (2014). When to use the Bonferroni correction. In Ophthalmic & physiological optics : the journal of the British College of Ophthalmic Opticians (Optometrists) (Vol. 34, Issue 5, pp. 502–508). Ophthalmic Physiol Opt. DOI: 10.1111/opo.12131

Azzopardi-Muscat, N., Buttigieg, S., Calleja, N., & Merkur, S. (2017). Health Systems in Transition: Malta (Vol. 19 No. 1 2017). In Malta. *Health Systems Review*, 19(1).

Barak, A., Klein, B., & Proudfoot, J. G. (2009). Defining internet-supported therapeutic interventions. In Annals of Behavioral Medicine (Vol. 38, Issue 1, pp. 4–17). DOI: 10.1007/s12160-009-9130-7

Batterham, P. J., & Calear, A. L. (2017). Preferences for Internet-Based Mental Health Interventions in an Adult Online Sample: Findings From an Online Community Survey. *JMIR Mental Health*, 4(2), e26. DOI: 10.2196/mental.7722 PMID: 28666976

Berking, M., Eichler, E., Luhmann, M., Diedrich, A., Hiller, W., & Rief, W. (2019). Affect regulation training reduces symptom severity in depression – A randomized controlled trial. *PLoS One*, 14(8), e0220436. DOI: 10.1371/journal.pone.0220436 PMID: 31465443

Berry, N., Lobban, F., & Bucci, S. (2019). A qualitative exploration of service user views about using digital health interventions for self-management in severe mental health problems. *BMC Psychiatry*, 19(1), 35. Advance online publication. DOI: 10.1186/s12888-018-1979-1 PMID: 30665384

Borghouts, J., Eikey, E., Mark, G., De Leon, C., Schueller, S. M., Schneider, M., Stadnick, N., Zheng, K., Mukamel, D., & Sorkin, D. H. (2021). Barriers to and facilitators of user engagement with digital mental health interventions: Systematic review. In Journal of Medical Internet Research (Vol. 23, Issue 3). JMIR Publications Inc. DOI: 10.2196/24387

Bowling, A. (2014). *Research methods in health: investigating health and health services* (4th ed.). Open University Press. https://eprints.soton.ac.uk/371922/

Buntrock, C., Ebert, D. D., Lehr, D., Smit, F., Riper, H., Berking, M., & Cuijpers, P. (2016). Effect of a web-based guided self-help intervention for prevention of major depression in adults with subthreshold depression a randomized clinical trial. *Journal of the American Medical Association*, 315(17), 1854–1863. DOI: 10.1001/jama.2016.4326 PMID: 27139058

Buttigieg, S., Cachia, D., & Gauci, D. (2015). Stress, Burnout and Coping Strategies in the Emergency and Intensive Care Hospital Departments. In C. R. Hopkins (Ed.), Job Stress: Risk Factors, Health Effects and Coping Strategies (pp. 49–82). Nova Publisher. https://www.researchgate.net/publication/274256556_Stress_Burnout_and_Coping_Strategies_in_the_Emergency_and_Intensive_Care_Hospital_Departments

Casey, L. M., Joy, A., & Clough, B. A. (2013). The impact of information on attitudes toward e-mental health services. *Cyberpsychology, Behavior, and Social Networking*, 16(8), 593–598. DOI: 10.1089/cyber.2012.0515 PMID: 23679567

Cattell, R. B. (1966). The scree test for the number of factors. *Multivariate Behavioral Research*, 1(2), 245–276. DOI: 10.1207/s15327906mbr0102_10 PMID: 26828106

Chudy-Onwugaje, K., Abutaleb, A., Buchwald, A., Langenberg, P., Regueiro, M., Schwartz, D. A., Kathleen Tracy, J., Ghazi, L., Patil, S. A., Quezada, S., Russman, K., Horst, S., Beaulieu, D., Quinn, C., Jambaulikar, G., & Cross, R. K. (2018). Age modifies the association between depressive symptoms and adherence to self-testing with Telemedicine in Patients with inflammatory bowel disease. *Inflammatory Bowel Diseases*, 24(12), 2648–2654. DOI: 10.1093/ibd/izy194 PMID: 29846623

Cliffe, B., Croker, A., Denne, M., & Stallard, P. (2020). Clinicians' use of and attitudes towards technology to provide and support interventions in child and adolescent mental health services. *Child and Adolescent Mental Health*, 25(2), 95–101. DOI: 10.1111/camh.12362 PMID: 32307835

Cohen, J. (1988). Statistical Power Analysis for the Behavioral Sciences. In *Statistical Power Analysis for the Behavioral Sciences*. Routledge. DOI: 10.4324/9780203771587

De Zwaan, M., Herpertz, S., Zipfel, S., Svaldi, J., Friederich, H. C., Schmidt, F., Mayr, A., Lam, T., Schade-Brittinger, C., & Hilbert, A. (2017). Effect of internet-based guided self-help vs individual face-to-face treatment on full or subsyndromal binge eating disorder in overweight or obese patients: The INTERBED randomized clinical trial. *JAMA Psychiatry*, 74(10), 987–995. DOI: 10.1001/jamapsychiatry.2017.2150 PMID: 28768334

Ebert, D. D., Cuijpers, P., Muñoz, R. F., & Baumeister, H. (2017). Prevention of mental health disorders using internet- and mobile-based interventions: A narrative review and recommendations for future research. *Frontiers in Psychiatry*, 8(AUG), 1. DOI: 10.3389/fpsyt.2017.00116 PMID: 28848454

Eichenberg, C., Wolters, C., & Brähler, E. (2013). The internet as a mental health advisor in Germany - Results of a national survey. *PLoS One*, 8(11), 79206. DOI: 10.1371/journal.pone.0079206 PMID: 24278121

Feijt, M. A., De Kort, Y. A. W., Bongers, I. M. B., & IJsselsteijn, W. A. (2018). Perceived drivers and barriers to the adoption of eMental health by psychologists: The construction of the levels of adoption of eMental health model. *Journal of Medical Internet Research*, 20(4), e153. Advance online publication. DOI: 10.2196/jmir.9485 PMID: 29691215

Firth-Cozens, J., & Greenhalgh, J. (1997). Doctors' perceptions of the links between stress and lowered clinical care. *Social Science & Medicine*, 44(7), 1017–1022. DOI: 10.1016/S0277-9536(96)00227-4 PMID: 9089922

Fishbein, M. A., & Ajzen, I. (1975). Belief, attitude, intention and behaviour: An introduction to theory and research. https://www.researchgate.net/publication/233897090_Belief_attitude_intention_and_behaviour_An_introduction_to_theory_and_research

Fliege, H., Rose, M., Arck, P., Walter, O. B., Kocalevent, R. D., Weber, C., & Klapp, B. F. (2005). The Perceived Stress Questionnaire (PSQ) reconsidered: Validation and reference values from different clinical and healthy adult samples. *Psychosomatic Medicine*, 67(1), 78–88. DOI: 10.1097/01.psy.0000151491.80178.78 PMID: 15673628

Galatzer-Levy, I. R., & Bonanno, G. A. (2014). Optimism and Death: Predicting the Course and Consequences of Depression Trajectories in Response to Heart Attack. *Psychological Science*, 25(12), 2177–2188. DOI: 10.1177/0956797614551750 PMID: 25298294

Galea, M. (2014). The Progressive Impact of Burnout on Maltese Nurses. *SOP Transactions on Psychology*, 2(1), 1–12. Advance online publication. DOI: 10.15764/STP.2014.01001

Godin, G., Bélanger-Gravel, A., Eccles, M., & Grimshaw, J. (2008). Healthcare professionals' intentions and behaviours: A systematic review of studies based on social cognitive theories. In Implementation Science (Vol. 3, Issue 1, pp. 1–12). BioMed Central. DOI: 10.1186/1748-5908-3-36

Gross, J. J., Uusberg, H., & Uusberg, A. (2019). Mental illness and well-being: An affect regulation perspective. *World Psychiatry; Official Journal of the World Psychiatric Association (WPA)*, 18(2), 130–139. DOI: 10.1002/wps.20618 PMID: 31059626

Hall, L. H., Johnson, J., Watt, I., Tsipa, A., & O'Connor, D. B. (2016). Healthcare staff wellbeing, burnout, and patient safety: A systematic review. In PLoS ONE (Vol. 11, Issue 7). Public Library of Science. DOI: 10.1371/journal.pone.0159015

Hedman, E., Ljótsson, B., & Lindefors, N. (2012). Cognitive behavior therapy via the Internet: A systematic review of applications, clinical efficacy and cost-effectiveness. In Expert Review of Pharmacoeconomics and Outcomes Research (Vol. 12, Issue 6, pp. 745–764). DOI: 10.1586/erp.12.67

Hennemann, S., Beutel, M. E., & Zwerenz, R. (2016). Drivers and barriers to acceptance of web-based aftercare of patients in inpatient routine care: A cross-sectional survey. *Journal of Medical Internet Research*, 18(12), e337. Advance online publication. DOI: 10.2196/jmir.6003 PMID: 28011445

Horgan, Á., & Sweeney, J. (2010). Young students' use of the internet for mental health information and support. *Journal of Psychiatric and Mental Health Nursing*, 17(2), 117–123. DOI: 10.1111/j.1365-2850.2009.01497.x PMID: 20465756

Johansson, O., Bjärehed, J., Andersson, G., Carlbring, P., & Lundh, L. G. (2019). Effectiveness of guided internet-delivered cognitive behavior therapy for depression in routine psychiatry: A randomized controlled trial. *Internet Interventions : the Application of Information Technology in Mental and Behavioural Health*, 17, 100247. Advance online publication. DOI: 10.1016/j.invent.2019.100247 PMID: 31249791

Kaiser, H. F. (1974). An Index of Factorial Simplicity. Psycometrika, 39(1). http://cda.psych.uiuc.edu/psychometrika_highly_cited_articles/kaiser_1974.pdf

Kim, M. S., Kim, T., Lee, D., Yook, J., Hong, Y.-C., Lee, S.-Y., Yoon, J.-H., & Kang, M.-Y. (2018). Mental disorders among workers in the healthcare industry: 2014 national health insurance data. *Annals of Occupational and Environmental Medicine*, 30(1), 31. Advance online publication. DOI: 10.1186/s40557-018-0244-x PMID: 29755753

Klein, B., & Cook, S. (2010). Preferences for e-mental health services amongst an online Australian sample. *E-Journal of Applied Psychology : Clinical and Social Issues*, 6(1), 27–38. DOI: 10.7790/ejap.v6i1.184

Koinis, A., Giannou, V., Drantaki, V., Angelaina, S., Stratou, E., & Saridi, M. (2015). The impact of healthcare workers job environment on their mental-emotional health. Coping strategies: The case of a local general hospital. *Health Psychology Research*, 3(1). Advance online publication. DOI: 10.4081/hpr.2015.1984 PMID: 26973958

Lazarus, R. S., & Folkman, S. (1984). Stress, Appraisal, and Coping. Springer. https://books.google.com.mt/books?hl=en&lr=&id=i-ySQQuUpr8C&oi=fnd&pg=PR5&ots=DgDTqugfRa&sig=egcnoJlciYaOn6g-BSUyW5367II&redir_esc=y#v=onepage&q&f=false

Lesage, F. X., Berjot, S., & Deschamps, F. (2012). Clinical stress assessment using a visual analogue scale. *Occupational Medicine*, 62(8), 600–605. DOI: 10.1093/occmed/kqs140 PMID: 22965867

Liem, A., & Natari, R. B. Jimmy, & Hall, B. J. (2021). Digital Health Applications in Mental Health Care for Immigrants and Refugees: A Rapid Review. In Telemedicine and e-Health (Vol. 27, Issue 1, pp. 3–16). Mary Ann Liebert Inc. DOI: 10.1089/tmj.2020.0012

Linardon, J., Shatte, A., Tepper, H., & Fuller-Tyszkiewicz, M. (2020). A survey study of attitudes toward, and preferences for, e-therapy interventions for eating disorder psychopathology. *International Journal of Eating Disorders*, 53(6), 907–916. DOI: 10.1002/eat.23268 PMID: 32239725

Luxton, D. D. (2016). *Artificial Intelligence in Behavioral and Mental Health Care*. Elsevier Inc. DOI: 10.1016/B978-0-12-420248-1.00001-5

Malouff, J. M., & Schutte, N. S. (2017). Can psychological interventions increase optimism? A meta-analysis. *The Journal of Positive Psychology*, 12(6), 594–604. DOI: 10.1080/17439760.2016.1221122

March, S., Day, J., Ritchie, G., Rowe, A., Gough, J., Hall, T., Yuen, C. Y. J., Donovan, C. L., & Ireland, M. (2018). Attitudes toward e-mental health services in a community sample of adults: Online survey. In Journal of Medical Internet Research (Vol. 20, Issue 2). Journal of Medical Internet Research. DOI: 10.2196/jmir.9109

Morales-Rodríguez, F. M., Espigares-López, I., Brown, T., & Pérez-Mármol, J. M. (2020). The relationship between psychological well-being and psychosocial factors in university students. *International Journal of Environmental Research and Public Health*, 17(13), 1–21. DOI: 10.3390/ijerph17134778 PMID: 32630816

Musiat, P., Goldstone, P., & Tarrier, N. (2014). Understanding the acceptability of e-mental health - attitudes and expectations towards computerised self-help treatments for mental health problems. *BMC Psychiatry*, 14(1), 109. DOI: 10.1186/1471-244X-14-109 PMID: 24725765

Norcross, J. C., & Prochaska, J. O. (1986). Psychotherapist heal thyself. I. The psychological distress and self-change of psychologists, counselors, and laypersons. *Psychotherapy (Chicago, Ill.)*, 23(1), 102–114. DOI: 10.1037/h0085577

Nulty, D. D. (2008). The adequacy of response rates to online and paper surveys: What can be done? *Assessment & Evaluation in Higher Education*, 33(3), 301–314. DOI: 10.1080/02602930701293231

Pallant, J. (2000). Development and validation of a scale to measure perceived control of internal states. *Journal of Personality Assessment*, 75(2), 308–337. DOI: 10.1207/S15327752JPA7502_10 PMID: 11020147

Pallant, J. (2016). *SPSS Survival Manual* (6th ed.). Open University Press. https://smdbooks.com/en/shop/textbooks-fall-2020-2021-ieseg-en/masters-ieseg-en/spss-survival-manual/

Persson Asplund, R., Dagöö, J., Fjellström, I., Niemi, L., Hansson, K., Zeraati, F., Ziuzina, M., Geraedts, A., Ljótsson, B., Carlbring, P., & Andersson, G. (2018). Internet-based stress management for distressed managers: Results from a randomised controlled trial. *Occupational and Environmental Medicine*, 75(2), 105–113. DOI: 10.1136/oemed-2017-104458 PMID: 28855344

Polit, D. F., & Beck, C. T. (2013). Essentials of Nursing Research: Appraising Evidence for Nursing Practice. In Wolters Kluwer Health (8th ed.). Wolters Kluwer Health. https://books.google.com.mt/books?id=N4TpwETZYPQC&dq=essentialsofnursingresearch&lr&source=gbs_similarbooks

Portoghese, I., Galletta, M., Coppola, R. C., Finco, G., & Campagna, M. (2014). Burnout and workload among health care workers: The moderating role of job control. *Safety and Health at Work*, 5(3), 152–157. DOI: 10.1016/j.shaw.2014.05.004 PMID: 25379330

Rebello, T. J., Marques, A., Gureje, O., & Pike, K. M. (2014). Innovative strategies for closing the mental health treatment gap globally. In Current Opinion in Psychiatry (Vol. 27, Issue 4, pp. 308–314). Lippincott Williams and Wilkins. DOI: 10.1097/YCO.0000000000000068

Rezaei, A., & Mousanezhad Jeddi, E. (2020). Relationship between wisdom, perceived control of internal states, perceived stress, social intelligence, information processing styles and life satisfaction among college students. *Current Psychology (New Brunswick, N.J.)*, 39(3), 927–933. DOI: 10.1007/s12144-018-9804-z

Ritterband, L. M., Thorndike, F. P., Cox, D. J., Kovatchev, B. P., & Gonder-Frederick, L. A. (2009). A behavior change model for internet interventions. In Annals of Behavioral Medicine (Vol. 38, Issue 1, pp. 18–27). DOI: 10.1007/s12160-009-9133-4

Robbins, J. M., & Greenley, J. R. (1983). Thinking about what's wrong: Attributions of severity, cause, and duration in the problem definition stage of psychiatric help-seeking. *Research in Community and Mental Health*, 3, 209–232. https://psycnet.apa.org/record/1984-21016-001

Rollman, B. L., Belnap, B. H., Abebe, K. Z., Spring, M. B., Rotondi, A. J., Rothenberger, S. D., & Karp, J. F. (2018). Effectiveness of online collaborative care for treating mood and anxiety disorders in primary care: A randomized clinical trial. *JAMA Psychiatry*, 75(1), 56–64. DOI: 10.1001/jamapsychiatry.2017.3379 PMID: 29117275

Romswinkel, E. V., König, H. H., & Hajek, A. (2018). The role of optimism in the relationship between job stress and depressive symptoms. Longitudinal findings from the German Ageing Survey. *Journal of Affective Disorders*, 241, 249–255. DOI: 10.1016/j.jad.2018.08.005 PMID: 30138809

Russell, A., Bergeman, C. S., Deboeck, P., Baird, B., Montpetit, M., & Ong, A. (2011). Emotion control during later life: The relationship between global perceptions and daily experience. *Personality and Individual Differences*, 50(7), 1084–1088. DOI: 10.1016/j.paid.2011.01.030 PMID: 24860206

Ryan, M. L., Shochet, I. M., & Stallman, H. M. (2010). Universal online interventions might engage psychologically distressed university students who are unlikely to seek formal help. *Advances in Mental Health*, 9(1), 73–83. DOI: 10.5172/jamh.9.1.73

Sagar-Ouriaghli, I., Godfrey, E., Bridge, L., Meade, L., & Brown, J. S. L. (2019). Improving Mental Health Service Utilization Among Men: A Systematic Review and Synthesis of Behavior Change Techniques Within Interventions Targeting Help-Seeking. *American Journal of Men's Health*, 13(3). Advance online publication. DOI: 10.1177/1557988319857009 PMID: 31184251

Scheier, M. F., & Carver, C. S. (1985). Optimism, coping, and health: Assessment and implications of generalized outcome expectancies. *Health Psychology*, 4(3), 219–247. DOI: 10.1037/0278-6133.4.3.219 PMID: 4029106

Scheier, M. F., Carver, C. S., & Bridges, M. W. (1994). Distinguishing optimism from neuroticism (and trait anxiety, self-mastery, and self-esteem): A reevaluation of the Life Orientation Test. *Journal of Personality and Social Psychology*, 67(6), 1063–1078. DOI: 10.1037/0022-3514.67.6.1063 PMID: 7815302

Sharma, S. K. (2014). Nursing Research and Statistics (2nd ed.). Reed Elsevier-India Private Limited. https://books.google.com.mt/books?id=9RyMBgAAQBAJ&printsec=frontcover&dq=define+target+population&hl=en&sa=X&ved=0ahUKEwjLr6Hz_NPnAhXQAxAIHeirBH0Q6AEIUTAF#v=onepage&q=definetargetpopulation&f=false

Skakon, J., Kristensen, T. S., Christensen, K. B., Lund, T., & Labriola, M. (2011). Do managers experience more stress than employees? Results from the Intervention Project on Absence and Well-being (IPAW) study among Danish managers and their employees. *Work (Reading, Mass.)*, 38(2), 103–109. DOI: 10.3233/WOR-2011-1112 PMID: 21297280

Smoktunowicz, E., Lesnierowska, M., Cieslak, R., Carlbring, P., & Andersson, G. (2019). Efficacy of an Internet-based intervention for job stress and burnout among medical professionals: Study protocol for a randomized controlled trial. *Trials*, 20(1), 338. Advance online publication. DOI: 10.1186/s13063-019-3401-9 PMID: 31182128

Sniehotta, F. F., Scholz, U., & Schwarzer, R. (2005). Bridging the intention-behaviour gap: Planning, self-efficacy, and action control in the adoption and maintenance of physical exercise. *Psychology & Health*, 20(2), 143–160. DOI: 10.1080/08870440512331317670

Spendelow, J., & Jose, P. (2010). Does the optimism bias affect help-seeking intentions for depressive symptoms in young people? *The Journal of General Psychology*, 137(2), 190–209. DOI: 10.1080/00221301003645277 PMID: 20441133

Sukums, F., Mensah, N., Mpembeni, R., Kaltschmidt, J., Haefeli, W. E., & Blank, A. (2014). Health workers' knowledge of and attitudes towards computer applications in rural African health facilities. *Global Health Action*, 7(1), 24534. Advance online publication. DOI: 10.3402/gha.v7.24534 PMID: 25361721

Suzuki, K., Ohida, T., Kaneita, Y., Yokoyama, E., Miyake, T., Harano, S., Yagi, Y., Ibuka, E., Kaneko, A., Tsutsui, T., & Uchiyama, M. (2004). Mental Health Status, Shift Work, and Occupational Accidents among Hospital Nurses in Japan. *Journal of Occupational Health*, 46(6), 448–454. DOI: 10.1539/joh.46.448 PMID: 15613767

Tabak, N., & Orit, K. (2007). Relationship between how nurses resolve their conflicts with doctors, their stress and job satisfaction. *Journal of Nursing Management*, 15(3), 321–331. DOI: 10.1111/j.1365-2834.2007.00665.x PMID: 17359432

Talaee, N., Varahram, M., Jamaati, H., Salimi, A., & Attarchi, M., Kazempour dizaji, M., Sadr, M., Hassani, S., Farzanegan, B., Monjazebi, F., & Seyedmehdi, S. M. (. (2020). Stress and burnout in health care workers during COVID-19 pandemic: Validation of a questionnaire. *Journal of Public Health (Germany)*, 1. Advance online publication. DOI: 10.1007/s10389-020-01313-z PMID: 32837840

Temsah, M. H., Al-Sohime, F., Alamro, N., Al-Eyadhy, A., Al-Hasan, K., Jamal, A., Al-Maglouth, I., Aljamaan, F., Al Amri, M., Barry, M., Al-Subaie, S., & Somily, A. M. (2020). The psychological impact of COVID-19 pandemic on health care workers in a MERS-CoV endemic country. *Journal of Infection and Public Health*, 13(6), 877–882. DOI: 10.1016/j.jiph.2020.05.021 PMID: 32505461

Thompson, B. (2004). Exploratory and Confirmatory Factor Analais: Understanding Concepts and Applications. American Psychological Association. www.apa.org

Topooco, N., Riper, H., Araya, R., Berking, M., Brunn, M., Chevreul, K., Cieslak, R., Ebert, D. D., Etchmendy, E., Herrero, R., Kleiboer, A., Krieger, T., García-Palacios, A., Cerga-Pashoja, A., Smoktunowicz, E., Urech, A., Vis, C., & Andersson, G. (2017). Attitudes towards digital treatment for depression: A European stakeholder survey. *Internet Interventions : the Application of Information Technology in Mental and Behavioural Health*, 8, 1–9. DOI: 10.1016/j.invent.2017.01.001 PMID: 30135823

Van Mol, C. (2017). Improving web survey efficiency: The impact of an extra reminder and reminder content on web survey response. *International Journal of Social Research Methodology*, 20(4), 317–327. DOI: 10.1080/13645579.2016.1185255

Venkatesh, V., Morris, M. G., Davis, G. B., & Davis, F. D. (2003). User acceptance of information technology: Toward a unified view. *Management Information Systems Quarterly*, 27(3), 425–478. DOI: 10.2307/30036540

Vizheh, M., Qorbani, M., Arzaghi, S. M., Muhidin, S., Javanmard, Z., & Esmaeili, M. (2020). The mental health of healthcare workers in the COVID-19 pandemic: A systematic review. *Journal of Diabetes and Metabolic Disorders*, 1(2), 1967–1978. Advance online publication. DOI: 10.1007/s40200-020-00643-9 PMID: 33134211

Vogel, D. L., & Wei, M. (2005). Adult attachment and help-seeking intent: The mediating roles of psychological distress and perceived social support. *Journal of Counseling Psychology*, 52(3), 347–357. DOI: 10.1037/0022-0167.52.3.347

Wainberg, M. L., Scorza, P., Shultz, J. M., Helpman, L., Mootz, J. J., Johnson, K. A., Neria, Y., Bradford, J. M. E., Oquendo, M. A., & Arbuckle, M. R. (2017). Challenges and Opportunities in Global Mental Health: a Research-to-Practice Perspective. In Current Psychiatry Reports (Vol. 19, Issue 5, p. 28). Current Medicine Group LLC 1. DOI: 10.1007/s11920-017-0780-z

Wang, P. S., Berglund, P., Olfson, M., Pincus, H. A., Wells, K. B., & Kessler, R. C. (2005). Failure and delay in initial treatment contact after first onset of mental disorders in the National Comorbidity Survey Replication. In Archives of General Psychiatry (Vol. 62, Issue 6, pp. 603–613). American Medical Association. DOI: 10.1001/archpsyc.62.6.603

Watson, D., Clark, L. A., & Tellegen, A. (1988). Development and Validation of Brief Measures of Positive and Negative Affect: The PANAS Scales. *Journal of Personality and Social Psychology*, 54(6), 1063–1070. DOI: 10.1037/0022-3514.54.6.1063 PMID: 3397865

Weaver, M. D., Vetter, C., Rajaratnam, S. M. W., O'Brien, C. S., Qadri, S., Benca, R. M., Rogers, A. E., Leary, E. B., Walsh, J. K., Czeisler, C. A., & Barger, L. K. (2018). Sleep disorders, depression and anxiety are associated with adverse safety outcomes in healthcare workers: A prospective cohort study. *Journal of Sleep Research*, 27(6), e12722. DOI: 10.1111/jsr.12722 PMID: 30069960

Weinstein, N. D. (1980). Unrealistic optimism about future life events. *Journal of Personality and Social Psychology*, 39(5), 806–820. DOI: 10.1037/0022-3514.39.5.806

Weisel, K. K., Zarski, A., Berger, T., Krieger, T., Schaub, M., Moser, C., Berking, M., Dey, M., Botella, C., Baños, R., Herrero, R., Etchemendy, E., Riper, H., Cuijpers, P., Bolinski, F., Kleiboer, A., Görlich, D., Beecham, J., Jacobi, C., & Ebert, D. (2019). Efficacy and cost-effectiveness of guided and unguided internet- and mobile-based indicated transdiagnostic prevention of depression and anxiety (ICare Prevent): A three-armed randomized controlled trial in four European countries. *Internet Interventions : the Application of Information Technology in Mental and Behavioural Health*, 16, 52–64. DOI: 10.1016/j.invent.2018.04.002 PMID: 30775265

Wells, M., Mitchell, K. J., Finkelhor, D., & Becker-Blease, K. A. (2007). Online mental health treatment: Concerns and considerations. Cyberpsychology and Behavior, 10(3).

Williams, E. S., Rathert, C., & Buttigieg, S. C. (2019). The Personal and Professional Consequences of Physician Burnout: A Systematic Review of the Literature. DOI: 10.1177/1077558719856787

Williams, M. D., Rana, N. P., & Dwivedi, Y. K. (2015). The unified theory of acceptance and use of technology (UTAUT): A literature review. In Journal of Enterprise Information Management (Vol. 28, Issue 3, pp. 443–448). Emerald Group Publishing Ltd. DOI: 10.1108/JEIM-09-2014-0088

Yu, Y., Liu, Z., Hu, M., Liu, H., Yang, J. P., Zhou, L., Xiao, S., Z-w, L., & H-m, L. (2015). Mental Health Help-Seeking Intentions and Preferences of Rural Chinese Adults. PLoS ONE, 10(11), 141889. https://doi.org/DOI: 10.1089/cpb.2006.9933

KEY TERMS AND DEFINITIONS

Attitudes: An individual's feelings or opinions towards a particular object, person, or situation.

Behavioural Intentions: A person's plans or motivations to engage in particular behaviours in the future.

Coping Mechanisms: Strategies or techniques individuals use to manage stress and deal with challenging situations.

Customised Interventions: Tailored or personalised strategies or approaches designed to address specific needs or preferences.

Digital Therapy: Therapeutic interventions delivered through digital platforms such as websites, mobile applications, or virtual sessions.

Exploratory Approach: Investigative method aimed at exploring or discovering new information or insights.

Intention-Behaviour Gap: Discrepancy between individuals' intentions to perform a behaviour and their actual behaviour.

Occupational Stressors: Factors within the workplace that cause stress, strain, or pressure on individuals.

Sociodemographic Differences: Variances or distinctions in characteristics such as age, gender, ethnicity, occupation, education, income, etc., within a population.

Chapter 11
Bridging Gaps in Palliative Care Through Corporate Social Responsibility:
Emerging Trends in India

Maya M.
http://orcid.org/0000-0002-8289-9587
Christ University, India

Priya Joseph
http://orcid.org/0009-0003-9484-1459
Christ University, India

ABSTRACT

The National Programme for Palliative Care (NPPC) in India was launched in 2012 with the aim of enhancing the quality of life of patients and their families affected with life limiting illness. Along with interventions at the government level, voluntary and community based models are also implemented through non-governmental organisations (NGOs). However, there is a dearth of adequate palliative care services in the country. The growing demand for robust palliative care systems requires coordinated efforts from all stakeholders. This chapter explores the trends and patterns of corporate social responsibility (CSR) spending for palliative care in India based on the CSR reports submitted by companies and analyses the potential of corporate contributions to ensure a meaningful palliative care management system. The study aims to establish possible linkages between Government's interventions, NGO involvement and CSR funding which could ensure a robust palliative care

DOI: 10.4018/979-8-3693-5991-4.ch011

system in India which would help the country to achieve Sustainable Development Goals (SDG 3).

INTRODUCTION

Palliative care is an approach that improves the quality of patients and gives total care to the patient as well as family (WHO, 2014). The ultimate aim of palliative care is to build an atmosphere where people with the morbid condition spend their days with complete ease, at a place where they are most comfortable. Palliative care encompasses a multidisciplinary approach where an array of stakeholders come together with symptom management, spiritual support, family support and maximum support to the patient and family during the last stages of the patient's life. Such an approach respects the cultural and religious aspects of people. With advancement in medical care and increased longevity, more people tend to live with chronic illness both at the global and national levels.

At the global level only 14 percent of those who require palliative care services receive it (WHO, 2020). As per WHO estimates, out of the 40 million people who need palliative care, 78 percent of adults are from Low and Middle Income Countries (LMIC) (Aregay et al., 2020). Vallath et al. (2022) notes that 84 percent of low- and middle-income countries have very little access to palliative care. This is a challenge in Low- and Middle-Income Countries and the case of India is not different. Bottlenecks to LMIC countries include poverty, lack of infrastructure, lack of awareness and lack of effective palliative care model. Sundara and Poalo (2004) opine that palliative care in developing countries is to be delivered and implemented according to the feasibility of resources available in that area. In the context of limited resources, evidence on costs and cost-effectiveness of alternative methods of delivering health-care services is increasingly important to facilitate appropriate resource allocation (Smith et al., 2014). Lack of awareness about the need for affordable palliative care support systems and lack of fundings are the major challenges the country faces. Lack of support, lack of research and insufficient budget allocation from the government also delay the implementation of palliative care in the country.

Palliative care policy as well as policies on corporate social responsibility (CSR) evolved in India almost at the same time period. India is the first country to have a clear CSR policy (Companies Act, 2013) where it is mandatory for companies with a turnover of rupees one thousand crore or above to spend a minimum of two percent of their net profit in the preceding three years. This chapter explore the ways in which CSR funds are used for providing palliative care services in India and the future possibilities with a potential to positively contribute towards achieving Sustainable Development Goal- SDG 3.

Methodology

This is a conceptual paper which explores the possibility of CSR funding in India to create an effective palliative care system. Arguments were built on data collected through secondary resources. Books, articles, and newspaper reports are used to discuss the status of palliative care in India and the need for collaborative efforts. Trends and patterns of CSR spending in India were collected from the reports submitted by corporates to the Ministry of Corporate Affairs. The government's dashboard was used to collect details of CSR initiatives in the area of palliative care and have analyzed based on the type of interventions and the regions covered.

Need for Palliative Care

The goal of palliative care is to help people with terminal illnesses feel better. Palliative care needs arise when a person is affected with diseases like cancer, kidney dysfunction, lung disease, cardiovascular issues, stroke, dementia, or HIV/AIDS. The need can also arise in case of accidents, post-surgery or comorbidities and decline of general health during old age. People who may suffer from pain, sleeplessness, shortness of breath, mobility issues, wounds etc. might require support at different stages from diagnosis to treatment and post treatment period. A disease is not just affecting the body. It has its impact on the emotional, social, and spiritual dimensions of a person and his or her family. Palliative care services take into account these wider aspects too. According to the requirement, palliative care can be provided by a team of doctors, nurses, nursing assistants, dietitians, social workers, psychologists, physiotherapists, and chaplains. Palliative care is offered by hospitals, home care agencies, cancer centers, and long-term care facilities. However, the availability of adequate palliative care support systems as well as access and utilization of the existing services are greater concerns to be addressed.

Traditionally, family is considered as the significant social unit having the primary responsibility of caring for the ill and disabled persons. Changes in the occupational structure and women's participation in the labor force necessitated the need for professional institutions like palliative care (Patel, 2012). In countries like India, where public health programs are yet to become more effective and accessible to the masses, palliative care is still in the initial phase (Chandra,2023). Even though palliative care was formally introduced in India in the 1960s, it has not yet become common outside its urban centers (Kumar, 2013). Even in cities, its presence has a marginal presence and impact. India is the most populous country as well as the seventh largest country. The spatial distribution of population is yet another challenge which poses issues of access and utilization.

Enhancement of quality of life is the core tenant of palliative care. Palliative care is not restricted to certain sections of population or individuals in particular life stages. It is the right of every individual to receive adequate support to manage their health condition. Patients requiring palliative care support in India are not homogeneous. Socio-economic status, age, caste, gender is some of the signifiers having impact on access and utilization of palliative care services. Based on the Global Burden of Disease (GBD) report 2019, around 7.5 million people in India require palliative care services and among them, 2.7 percent are below 15 years, and the rest are adults. According to Nair and Ghoshal (2023), there are around 1.6 million children in India who require pediatric palliative care, compared to 20 million people worldwide. Increase in the number of people requiring palliative care support necessitates the need to evolve systems that ensure affordable and accessible services to people irrespective of class, caste, gender dimensions.

Palliative Care in India

The Constitution of India has listed health as a state subject, where the states or the subnational governments become the primary actors in providing healthcare services. The National Program for Palliative Care (NPPC) in India was launched in 2012 to enhance the quality of life of patients and their families affected by life-limiting illnesses. Funding to scale up palliative care support programs by the states is earmarked from the flex pool of the National Health Mission. Along with interventions at the government level, voluntary and community-based models are implemented through non-governmental organizations (NGOs) and the private sector. However, the country has a dearth of adequate palliative service care services. The country's significant challenges are the lack of awareness about the need for affordable palliative care support systems and funding. Lack of support, lack of research and insufficient budget allocation from the government also delay the implementation of palliative care in the country.

Palliative care in India is a growing need of the population as the number of people with chronic diseases and the ageing population with age-related illnesses which require palliative care has increased. (Rocker et al., 2016). Even though a significant portion of the population lives in rural areas, there is a shortage of palliative care facilities in rural areas than in urban areas (Ferman et al., 2024). Lack of awareness is one of the primary reasons for the slow growth of palliative care (Fliger et al., 2020). People are unaware of when to get palliative care assistance and think it is support given only to dying people (Bergman et al., 2023). There is limited support from the government. Even though the National Health Policy (2017) still approved palliative care, the execution level remains in its infancy (NPPC,2024). This ever-increasing requirement for more robust palliative care systems demands coordinated efforts from all stakeholders, including the government, NGOs, and corporations.

Corporate Social Responsibility (CSR) in India

Corporate Social Responsibility (CSR) as a modern phenomenon emerged during the post second world war period. Carroll (2015) discusses the socio-political situations made the corporations to think beyond maximizing wealth to a much greater cause of giving back to the society and environment along with making profits. Over a period in time, different models of CSR emerged and most of the framework consider Corporate Social Responsibility as a voluntary set of initiatives by the corporates. Cooperation of social responsibility or shared social responsibility brings overall development as it helps communities to get support locally and globally (Hamann, 2009). The history of CSR in India can be traced back to the ancient concept of 'seva' and 'daan', which made the wealthier communities to serve the community and provide support for the needy (Garg & Agarwal, 2022). India is the first country to have a clear CSR policy (Sheikh, 2013), where companies with a turnover of rupees one thousand crores or above must spend a minimum of two per cent of their net profit in the preceding three years.

This policy decision is based on the vision shared by the then Prime Minister of India Mr Manmohan Singh on the larger responsibility of corporates to be an active agent in transforming India. The National Voluntary guidelines was launched initially by taking feedback from all stakeholders including the small and medium industries and later got crystalized through the Section 135 of Companies Act in 2013. With a clarity on what is CSR and what is not, corporates started contributing the priority areas set by the government through part 7 of the companies act. The priority areas were based on the expected industry support that the government requires to address issues of poverty, rural development, women empowerment, educational requirements etc. India's commitment to achieve Sustainable Development Goals SDG had its impact on the CSR initiatives too. Today, corporates started linking their CSR initiatives to one or more SDG goals too.

SDG 3 Good Health and Wellbeing aims to ensure healthy lives and promote well being for all at all ages. This SDG can be linked to various scheduled activities of the companies act 2013. For instance, activities related to eradicating hunger and ensuring sanitation and drinking water; promotion of gender equality and senior citizen wellbeing; slum area development; rural development; support to armed forces veteran's widows and prime minister's relief fund.

In order to achieve SDG 3, the government of India has launched many programs and policies and like Pradhan mantri Swasthya Suraksha Yojna and strengthens programs offered under National Health Mission, National Mission on Ayush, National AIDS & STD control program and Integrated Child Development Service (ICDS). The private contribution is expected to support an effective and inclusive national health system and also in providing accessible and affordable healthcare to communities (SDGCC,2000). Healthcare and WASH (Water, Sanitation and Hygiene) is an area that the companies are contributing to in a very consistent manner. CSRBOX report 2023, has given the trend from 2014-15 where 32% of the CSR funds were spent in the area of Healthcare and WASH.In 2015-16, it was 33% and in subsequent years there was a dip: 2016-17 (25%); 2017-18 (27%); 2018-19 (26%); 2019-20 (28%). In 2020-21 and 2021-2022 the contribution again rose back to 36%. During the post covid period, the percentage Even though the contribution of CSR funds to the other domains of the healthcare sector is much less, its impact on society is enormous. Mukherjee (2024) discusses the findings of a study by SoulAce on the health-related CSR spending of 70 companies, both public and private in India during the financial year 2022-23. The study analyzed the impact of over 100 projects and argue that the CSR initiatives have reduced the burden on public health care institutions. CSR funds are spent on the vulnerable section of society, which helps to raise their companies' marketing strategies and goodwill activities (Avadhani, 2024). CSR aims to render modern healthcare benefits to the primary section of society (Health, 2024).

CSR and Palliative Care

Palliative care policy as well as policies on corporate social responsibility (CSR) evolved in India almost at the same time period. Part 7 of Companies Act provisions under section 135 of Companies Act 2013, lists out areas where a company can invest their CSR funds. Although a single activity does not cover dimensions of health, we have used the key words to identify projects from the government dashboard on CSR reports submitted by the companies.

CSR projects show how palliative care is increasingly recognized in India as a critical area of need and a means of bringing positive change. By funding palliative care, CSR helps patients live longer and contribute to developing a humane and compassionate healthcare system. A few noteworthy projects and initiatives include HDFC Bank's CSR Initiative where they partnered with the Cipla Palliative Care and Training Centre in Pune, Maharashtra. The partnership improved community knowledge of palliative care, trained medical professionals in palliative care, and improved infrastructure. Tata Group's contribution offers cancer patients services emphasizing quality of life enhancement, psychosocial support, and pain control.

They additionally carry out a great deal of research and offer training courses on palliative care.

Infosys Foundation's support for Palliative Care provides grants to various palliative care centers and funding for infrastructure, medical equipment, and operational costs. Biocon Foundation's Palliative Care Programs has set up mobile palliative care units; they provide home-based palliative care services, including pain management, counselling, and emotional support and bring palliative care to create awareness among communities who do not have access to palliative services. Wipro Cares Palliative Care Initiative has partnered with various non-profit organizations, including the Cankids Kidscan organization, which provides holistic care for children and their families, including medical, nutritional, psychological, and educational support. Godrej Group's Support for Palliative Care supports the Jaslok Hospital in Mumbai, Maharashtra. The trust funds palliative care services, aids education of medical professionals, and organizes public awareness campaigns.

Glenmark Foundation's Palliative Care Initiative partnered with various NGOs to provide palliative care services in rural areas, and they focus on training healthcare workers in palliative care and setting up community-based palliative care programs. Dr Reddy's Foundation supports the Pallium India initiative, which works to improve access to palliative care nationwide.

Larsen & Toubro (L&T) Health Initiatives support the Shanti Avedna Sadan in Mumbai, one of the first hospices in India which focuses on providing free palliative care to terminally ill cancer patients, assuring them dignified healthcare in their last days. Apollo Foundation's Palliative Care Program provides palliative care services at several Apollo Hospitals across India, including pain management, counselling, spiritual care for patients with serious illnesses, and training programs for healthcare professionals in palliative care.

Vedanta group of companies has Nand Ghat palliative care outreach programs which is a novel initiative to integrate palliative care into Nand Ghars, which are modern Anganwadis or Integrated Child care centers, offering community-based care. The program is implemented in the rural areas of Rajasthan and Uttar Pradesh. The Swasthya Initiative of Reliance Foundation is implemented in teh states of Maharashtra, Gujarat, and Andhra Pradesh. In this initiative, palliative care services are part of a broader health initiative focusing on marginalized communities.

Aditya Birla group promotes Palliative Care at Aditya Birla Memorial Hospital and ensures support for a dedicated palliative care unit providing end-of-life care, counselling, and pain management. This is located in Pune, Maharashtra. ICICI Foundation runs the project 'Sukoon' in Chennai, Tamil Nadu. It provides palliative care for terminally ill patients, primarily focusing on pain management and psychological support. Mahindra and Mahindra have Samriddhi Program of palliative care in teh states of Maharashtra, Tamil Nadu and Punjab. It is a part of a holistic health initiative, focusing on providing palliative care to rural communities.

GAIL (India) Ltd. runs a significant project to provide home-Based Palliative Care in Northeast India covering states of Assam, Manipur, and Meghalaya. Supporting home-based palliative care programs in the Northeastern states, where healthcare access is limited, is an indicator of the impacts that the private sector can contribute. Hero Motor corporation has a rural health initiative with palliative care focus. In the states of Haryana and Rajasthan, they provide palliative care as part of rural health camps and mobile health services in remote areas. Ashok Leyland provides community-based palliative care for workers and their families, particularly in industrial areas covering the states of Tamil Nadu, Gujarat. In the states of Maharashtra, West Bengal, Axis bank foundation has campaigns and support services focused on spreading awareness and providing care to terminally ill patients.

Challenges and Opportunities for CSR in Palliative Care

There are currently significant gaps in palliative care in India, which Corporate Social Responsibility (CSR) intends to address (Roa & Simha, 2011). By participating in palliative care programs under Corporate Social Responsibility (CSR), companies can contribute to a noble cause and enhance their corporate image and employee morale (Ahmad et al.,2023). A significant obstacle to enlisting firms in such programs is the general ignorance of the importance of palliative care. Many companies are not aware of the significant impact they can make in helping people with terminal illnesses live better lives. Even though palliative care is crucial for the comfort of patients who are near death, it is frequently eclipsed by more well-known and acknowledged healthcare concerns, such as infectious diseases, child nutrition, maternity health, and sanitation (Sampson & Dening, 2013). Companies usually direct their corporate social responsibility (CSR) funds on projects like infrastructure development, primary healthcare, or education that have a substantial impact right away and can be easily measured. Palliative care has a lower profile due to a lack of public activism and media attention, which makes firms overlook it as a potential CSR option (Hawley, 2017). Palliative care is often associated with end-of-life situations. However, its enormous significance in managing chronic ailments, cancer, and the pain and symptoms of incurable illnesses across all age groups is often underestimated by corporates (Yu et al., 2023).

The widespread misperception that palliative care is solely about managing death rather than enhancing the quality of life for patients and their families is another factor preventing corporations from getting involved (Shalev, 2017). Businesses may be reluctant to fund causes seen as exclusively morbid or incompatible with the upbeat image they wish to present. Healthcare programs that prioritize treatment and recovery and have measurable results, like saved lives or successfully treated patients, are typically backed by businesses. Palliative care is often misunderstood and underestimated in terms of its beneficial effects on patient well-being since it prioritizes easing suffering over treating illness (Senderovich & Macdayden, 2020). Corporations tend to remove themselves from topics that are emotionally and culturally uncomfortable, such as death, pain, and terminal disease.

Palliative care is becoming more and more in demand in India due to the growing burden of non-communicable diseases (NCDs), which include cancer, heart disease, and respiratory disorders. Nonetheless, many corporations are ignorant of the scope and urgency of this demand, especially in neglected and rural areas. Companies might not be aware of the full extent of the benefits of palliative care, which extends beyond the elderly and terminally sick to include a wide range of patients with chronic illnesses, children with life-threatening ailments, and people with incapacitating pain (Bajwah et al., 2020). The necessity for palliative care is becoming more widely acknowledged in metropolitan areas. Corporate engagement is further hampered by the public's and firms' lack of understanding in rural India, where access to healthcare is already scarce.

A contributing factor to businesses' reluctance to invest in palliative care is the dearth of thorough data and metrics that demonstrate the benefits of this treatment in terms of more remarkable health outcomes (Pastrana & Murray, 2020). As a result of the lack of complex data supporting the benefits of palliative care, many businesses depend on data-driven strategies to defend their CSR spending. Palliative care is not typically a prominent topic in CSR assessments or national healthcare reports, which makes it more difficult for businesses to understand the entire scope of the problem and possible initiatives. Palliative care may seem less appealing to firms looking for quantifiable results since it can be challenging to measure its long-term societal and economic benefits, which include fewer hospital admissions, better chronic disease management, and enhanced family well-being (Khandelwal et al.,2017).

A notable obstacle to involving firms in palliative care via corporate social responsibility (CSR) is the inadequate comprehension of its enduring consequences and advantages. Although palliative care interventions aim to enhance the quality of life for patients facing terminal illnesses, companies that prioritize measurable, short-term outcomes sometimes misunderstand or underestimate the significance of these advantages (Bredley et al., 2018). Corporates frequently give priority to CSR projects that produce rapid, quantifiable returns. Examples of these projects include the construction of schools, hospitals, or clean water sources, all of which provide fast, transparent results. Palliative care, on the other hand, provides long-term, intangible advantages that are harder to measure, such as pain relief, emotional support, and an improvement in quality of life. Comfort, dignity, and alleviation from pain are the main goals of palliative care, which may not necessarily translate into the kinds of metrics businesses are used to track, such as the number of lives saved or treatments given (Chandra et al., 2023). Instead of producing quick fixes or spectacular results, palliative care measures frequently have a gradual and cumulative effect that improves the lives of patients and their families over time. This long-term view might not match the company's demands for quick outcomes.

Many healthcare CSR initiatives are assessed using standard healthcare measures, like the number of patients treated, surgeries completed, or illnesses cured. Palliative care, however, emphasizes the general well-being of patients with terminal illnesses, which complicates its assessment. Improved pain control, mental health, and family support are common indicators of the effectiveness of palliative care interventions—outcomes that are challenging to measure with conventional healthcare measurements (Luyten et al., 2015). When these softer, quality-of-life gains are the primary results, corporations could find it difficult to show ROI (Return on Investment). Numerous corporations prioritize interventions aimed at curing or preventing illnesses while focusing less on care that improves the quality of life in cases when a cure is not possible. Because palliative care's objectives conflict with a cure-centric approach to healthcare, it is underestimated as a result of this curative perspective.

In contrast to other healthcare initiatives that can call for a one-time payment, palliative care frequently necessitates ongoing assistance over an extended period of time. Businesses looking to engage in limited-event, short-term projects may find it challenging to maintain this level of engagement. Palliative care patients frequently need long-term assistance, such as consistent pain management, emotional support, and social services. Business executives could be reluctant to commit to ongoing funding or involvement if they are used to projects with defined start and finish dates. In addition to assisting patients, palliative care supports families in overcoming bereavement and the stress of providing care. Businesses could overlook these interventions' broader, community-wide effects, concentrating solely on the immediate results for patients and ignoring the trickle-down effects on family members and caregivers.

Palliative care can have a positive social and economic impact and directly affect patient well-being. These benefits can include a decrease in hospital readmissions, a reduction in medical expenses, and an improvement in the mental health of patients and their families. Corporations, however, frequently ignore these long-term systemic benefits. Palliative care aids in the efficient management of chronic illnesses, hence lowering the need for needless hospital stays, Emergency Room visits and, eventually, healthcare expenditures. Many companies, however, are focused on high-profile, infrastructure-driven initiatives and are unaware of this potential for cost savings. Better mental health outcomes, less stress on caregivers, and increased productivity when caregivers return to the workforce are all benefits of supporting families during the palliative care process (Bijnsdorp et al.,2022). A lack of knowledge about the broader social effects of palliative care often means that these indirect advantages are overlooked when making corporate social responsibility decisions.

Numerous businesses frequently concentrate on CSR projects that provide quick, noticeable results that can improve public relations and brand image. Palliative care may not be in line with these objectives because it is more discreet and less noticeable to the public (Flieger et al., 2020). Palliative care CSR initiatives might not receive as much media attention as those in other sectors, such as disaster assistance or infrastructure development. As a result, businesses could be reluctant to fund palliative care because they believe there are not many opportunities to raise brand awareness (Cardenas et al., 2021). Proof of the effectiveness of palliative care through nuanced storytelling that emphasizes care's psychological and emotional components rather than complex data is frequently needed for CSR efforts. Corporates, however, might not know or have the means to inform stakeholders and the general public about these subtler effects.

A notable obstacle to properly leveraging Corporate Social Responsibility (CSR) to close gaps in palliative care is the fragmented practice of distributing cash among multiple local organizations (French et al., 2023). Although these little initiatives might support palliative care initiatives, their overall influence is frequently diminished by their lack of coordination and size. Due to this fragmentation, there is less efficiency, effort duplication, and difficulties in enacting systemic, long-term change. While many small-scale palliative care programs are helpful locally, they fall short of the scale required to address the more significant gaps in access and quality throughout the nation (Ghoshal et al., 2022). As a result, many firms allocate their corporate social responsibility (CSR) contributions to these initiatives. Numerous small-scale palliative care initiatives are beneficial locally, but they do not reach the size needed to close the more serious disparities in quality and access across the country. Because of this, many businesses donate to these programs as part of their corporate social responsibility (CSR) efforts. Rather than focusing on a few well-designed, large-scale programs that may serve as models for national development, CSR funds are dispersed too widely, making it difficult to overhaul India's palliative care services and infrastructure (Sharma et al., 2023).

Numerous firms frequently provide uncoordinated funding for palliative care programs of a similar nature in the same area or industry. This results in unnecessary work and resource waste. Without being aware of one another's involvement, corporations may separately support comparable services in the same geographic areas, such as home-based palliative care or pain management centers (Salikhanov et al., 2023). Instead of addressing new or underdeveloped areas, this lack of collaboration results in redundant services and resources. Some aspects of palliative care, like public awareness campaigns, emotional counselling, and healthcare worker training, continue to receive inadequate funding. In contrast, other aspects, like physical care, could attract undue attention because efforts are not adequately coordinated or consolidated.

A lot of palliative care programs supported by CSR are only in place for a year or so, depending on the project's duration (Seow & Bainbridge, 2018). These initiatives struggle to make a lasting difference or develop sustainable service models without consistent funding. Because CSR contributions are frequently linked to annual budgets, help is piecemeal and might not last past the original funding cycle. Many of these small-scale projects cannot continue on their own if financing stops, which results in service closures or a drop in quality. Long-term investments in infrastructure, education, and service delivery are necessary for palliative care. These continuous demands are challenging for small, dispersed projects with short timescales to meet, which hinders the creation of palliative solid care systems that can survive beyond individual CSR donations (Hawley, 2017).

A disjointed approach frequently results from a lack of cooperation amongst government agencies, non-profits, and businesses providing palliative care. Even if each of these organizations has the capacity to make a substantial contribution to the field, ineffective cooperation and communication result in inefficiency (Rosen et al., 2018). Corporates may unilaterally launch projects without fully utilizing well-established NGOs' resources and reach or coordinating their actions with palliative care-related government policies and activities. Vital, cooperative ecosystems that can improve the efficacy and scalability of interventions are prevented from developing as a result. Corporates frequently lack direction on where to devote resources in the absence of defined frameworks that drive CSR financing into areas of highest need, which leads to a disorganized approach rather than a concerted effort to meet specific shortages (Ruggiero & Cupertino, 2022).

Case Studies and Examples

This section presents case studies of effective corporate social responsibility (CSR) projects in palliative care in India. It also illustrates how PPPs and businesses have helped close gaps in the sector. These illustrations offer perceptions of successful models and procedures that are replicable for more significant influence.

Case Study 1: Cipla Foundation's Palliative Care Initiative

Background

India's pioneer in palliative care is the Cipla Foundation, the corporate social responsibility division of Cipla Ltd. The Cipla Foundation has been actively supporting palliative care services since the 1990s, realizing the increasing need for patients with terminal illnesses, particularly cancer, to receive compassionate care. Cipla's contribution is distinct because of its extensive participation in healthcare and its heritage in pharmaceuticals.

Goals of Cipla's CSR Initiatives for Palliative Care

Providing all-encompassing palliative care that takes into account a patient's emotional, social, and spiritual needs in addition to their physical pain is Cipla's primary goal. Cipla's goal is to train medical professionals—physicians, nurses, and caregivers—in order to create a robust system capable of providing high-quality palliative care in various geographical areas. Cipla guarantees that patients, particularly those residing in rural and semi-urban areas, have access to essential treatments by establishing palliative care facilities and working in conjunction with hospitals.

Outcomes

A premier CSR initiative of Cipla, this center offers free care to patients nearing the end of their lives and sets an example for palliative care in India. The center's priorities are end-of-life care, emotional support, and pain management. By providing palliative care training to over 1,500 physicians, nurses, and social workers, Cipla has improved the ability of India's healthcare system to treat terminal illnesses with compassion. In order to help families understand palliative care and to support caregivers during trying times, the foundation has conducted awareness campaigns and community outreach activities.

Case Study 2: Tata Trusts and Their Palliative Care Approach

Background

Tata Trusts, one of India's oldest and most prominent philanthropic organizations, has a broad portfolio of health-related CSR initiatives, including a strong focus on palliative care. Tata Trust's involvement has raised awareness about palliative care, especially in low-resource settings.

Goals of Tata Trusts' Involvement in Palliative Care

Tata Trusts aims to create a long-lasting system that incorporates palliative care into the current healthcare offerings, particularly for marginalized groups. Promoting home-based palliative care is a significant priority since it allows patients to get treatment in the comfort of their own homes, which lessens the strain on hospitals. In order to guarantee that palliative care is incorporated into the public health system, Tata Trusts concentrate on forming alliances with governmental organizations and medical facilities.

Outcomes

One of India's top cancer hospitals, Tata Memorial Hospital in Mumbai, features palliative care departments because of the assistance of Tata Trusts. Patients with cancer can receive integrated palliative care because of this partnership. In addition to helping to create palliative care guidelines for Indian healthcare systems, Tata Trusts have been instrumental in campaigning for the inclusion of palliative care in national healthcare policies. Tata Trusts have expanded home-based palliative care services throughout different regions, providing care to patients who cannot attend institutional facilities by partnering with NGOs and healthcare providers.

Case Study 3: Public-Private Partnerships (PPP) in Palliative Care

Background

In India, PPPs—public-private partnerships—have become a cutting-edge strategy for increasing access to palliative care. PPP models, particularly in areas with limited access to healthcare, have offered sustainable palliative care solutions by utilizing corporate resources and government infrastructure.

Examples of PPP Models

Kerala's Neighborhood Palliative Care Network (NNPC): Many people consider Kerala's PPP model among the world's most effective palliative care efforts. Palliative care services are provided to both rural and urban populations through the NNPC, a community-based model that combines government assistance, private money (CSR), and local volunteers.

Apollo Hospitals' collaboration with government agencies: Apollo Hospitals and the Tamil Nadu government collaborated to establish palliative care facilities in many government hospitals. The government supplies healthcare experts and facilities, while CSR financing from private firms covers operating costs.

Outcomes

Palliative care services are now much more accessible because of PPP models, especially in rural and isolated locations. By integrating government and corporate funding, PPPs have established a more sustainable palliative care delivery structure. Many PPP projects concentrate on training medical staff and raising the standard of palliative care offered by public and private organizations. PPPs have allowed communities to take charge of palliative care and include volunteers and neighborhood organizations in providing care, improving the caliber and accessibility of services.

Discussion

India's expenditure on health is way less than 2.5% of its GDP. The subsequent budget allocation on health is inclusive of ensuring clean drinking water and sanitation facilities. Disease profile of India highlights the urgent need to have collaborative efforts to address a diverse range of health issues including non-communicable disease, tropical disease, rare genetic disorders, and the rising number of accidents. Another challenge is the health expenditure where more than 90% of the financial burden has to be spent out of pocket. This raises concerns over health becoming a priority for people irrespective of their caste, class identities. So, it is obvious that palliative care services may not be a priority while the states plan their health intervention strategies. India is a country with massive socio-economic diversity. Since the government is helpless in addressing these diversities, it seeks the support of corporate houses to address the issues (Chapparia & Jha, 2021). The significant problems that palliative care institutions face are a lack of palliative care units, funds, non-visibility, and awareness among many companies (Sinha, 2024). The companies support organizations with the same interest in making palliative care available for as many people as possible (Cipla, 2018). By practicing corporate social responsibility, also called corporate citizenship, companies can impact all aspects of society, including economic, social, and environmental (Sneha, 2023).

The increasing burden of non-communicable diseases and the increase in the number of elderly population necessitates the need for palliative care at the global level and this is significant in the case of India too. According to Worldwide Palliative Care Alliance (WPCA) and the World Health Organization (WHO), only a few countries have quality palliative care. The Worldwide Hospice Palliative Care Alliance (WHPCA) is an international non-governmental organization focusing exclusively on hospice and palliative care development worldwide. Although more than 100 million people worldwide need hospice and palliative care annually, only less than eight percent of those in need access it (Oliver, 2017). In India 'health' being a matter of state list, each state designs its health priorities, and most states are in the nascent stage to include palliative care as a significant priority. However, institutionalization of palliative care services is an urgent requirement to ensure the well being of all.

Davies and Higginson (2004) mention in their article that the persons living with illness will have their own physical and social uncertainties, and, they have their experiences and values. These uncertainties will be different from person to person. For that, palliative care should be an integral part of the person and family members who receive care. Palliative care should help a person make decisions and express their wish on what sort of care they want. In turn, this will help palliative care professionals have better control of ill-person and their families. Palliative care emphasizes general palliative home care improvement in terms of around-the-clock staff availability, increased competence in effective symptom control, and skillful communication (Schelin et al., 2018). Awareness creation among medical professionals and educational interventions can bridge this gap.

A community attitude, a society, to the dying elderly who constitute the majority of global deaths, and the chronically ill are more critical for a good death than the purely medical approach (Stjernsward 2005). Along with providing palliative care services among different sections of the population, it is equally important to create awareness among the larger public about the need and significance of palliative care. CSR initiatives can contribute towards this in a very significant way.

The cases discussed in this study shows an interesting pattern where most of the initiatives are confined to a very few states and the largest number of projects are in the state of Maharashtra probably because it is home to the headquarters of most of the corporations. We need a system in place to help the corporations to channalise their funds towards areas or regions that require special attention. Currently, most of the corporations are implementing their CSR activities by partnering with NGOs. The government or institutions lille Palliaum India can take an initiative to support the corporation-NGO partnership about taking care of the immediate requirements for palliative care support especially in the remote areas. The current CSR policy also supports collaboration among corporations and for this we need a nodal agency at the center to ensure such collaborations and dialogues.

CONCLUSION

This study examined the need and relevance of partnerships among government, Corporations and NGOs to provide better palliative care services in India. Considering the miniscule budgetary allocation for health in India and a diverse array of health intervention requirements, palliative care services, to get a priority is difficult unless through industry collaborations. Corporations have the resources and willingness to support this cause. What we require is a vision at the national level and a mechanism to direct the interest corporations about the needs of the community. A community led action plan which is decentralized can provide micro plans to the state governments and the master plan of the state governments can be shared with the corporations so as to take a meaningful decision. CSR landscape in India is reaching its mature phase and has a great potential in helping India to achieve SDG 3, if managed meaningfully.

REFERENCES

Ahmad, N., Ullah, Z., Ryu, H. B., Ariza-Montes, A., & Han, H. (2023). From corporate social responsibility to employee well-being: Navigating the pathway to sustainable healthcare. *Psychology Research and Behavior Management*, 16, 1079–1095. DOI: 10.2147/PRBM.S398586 PMID: 37041962

Aregay, A., O'Connor, M., Stow, J., Ayers, N., & Lee, S. (2020). Strategies used to establish palliative care in rural low- and middle-income countries: An integrative review. *Health Policy and Planning*, 35(8), 1110–1129. DOI: 10.1093/heapol/czaa051 PMID: 32577766

Avadhani. (2024). Corporate social responsibility and Indian healthcare sector: An analysis. GSC Advanced Research and Reviews, 18(1), 235-265. https://doi.org/ DOI: 10.30574/gscarr.2024.18.1.0496

Bajwah, S., Oluyase, A. O., Yi, D., Gao, W., Evans, C. J., Grande, G., Todd, C., Costantini, M., Murtagh, F. E., & Higginson, I. J. (2020). The effectiveness and cost-effectiveness of hospital-based specialist palliative care for adults with advanced illness and their caregivers. Cochrane Database of Systematic Reviews, 2020(9). DOI: 10.1002/14651858.CD012780.pub2

Bergman, T. D., Van der Plas, A. G., Pasman, H. R., & Onwuteaka-Philipsen, B. D. (2023). Awareness and actual knowledge of palliative care among older people: A Dutch national survey. *Journal of Pain and Symptom Management*, 66(3), 193–202. e2. DOI: 10.1016/j.jpainsymman.2023.05.005 PMID: 37207787

Bijnsdorp, F. M., Onwuteaka-Philipsen, B. D., Boot, C. R., Van der Beek, A. J., & Pasman, H. R. (2022). Caregiver's burden at the end of life of their loved one: Insights from a longitudinal qualitative study among working family caregivers. *BMC Palliative Care*, 21(1), 142. Advance online publication. DOI: 10.1186/s12904-022-01031-1 PMID: 35945558

Bradley, N., Lloyd-Williams, M., & Dowrick, C. (2018). Effectiveness of palliative care interventions offering social support to people with life-limiting illness-A systematic review. *European Journal of Cancer Care*, 27(3), e12837. DOI: 10.1111/ecc.12837 PMID: 29573500

Braveman, P., & Gottlieb, L. (2014). The social determinants of health: It's time to consider the causes of the causes. *Public Health Reports*, 129(1, suppl2), 19–31. DOI: 10.1177/00333549141291S206 PMID: 24385661

Cardenas, V., Rahman, A., Zhu, Y., & Enguidanos, S. (2021). Reluctance to accept palliative care and recommendations for improvement: Findings from semi-structured interviews with patients and caregivers. *The American Journal of Hospice & Palliative Care*, 39(2), 189–195. DOI: 10.1177/10499091211012605 PMID: 33896233

Carroll, A. B. (2015). Corporate social responsibility. *Organizational Dynamics*, 44(2), 87–96. DOI: 10.1016/j.orgdyn.2015.02.002

Chandra, A., Debnath, A., & Nongkynrih, B. (2023). Palliative care need in India: A systematic review and meta-analysis. *Indian Journal of Palliative Care*, 29, 375–387. DOI: 10.25259/IJPC_140_2023 PMID: 38058486

Chhaparia, P., & Jha, M. (2021). The role of CSR in skilling India. Corporate Social Responsibility and Sustainable Development, 153-165. DOI: 10.4324/9780429295997-13

Cipla. (2018). CSR Projects India, Companies and CSR, NGO partners, CSR funding India. https://csrbox.org/India_CSR_Project_Palliative-Healthcare-Maharashtra_11034

CSRBOX. (2023). India CSR Outlook Report. Source: https://indiacsr.in/wp-content/uploads/2023/10/India-CSR-Outlook-Report-2023.pdf

Davies, E., & Higginson, I. J. (2004). *Better palliative care for older people*. World Health Organization. Regional Office for Europe.

Flieger, S. P., Chui, K., & Koch-Weser, S. (2020). Lack of awareness and common misconceptions about palliative care among adults: Insights from a national survey. *Journal of General Internal Medicine*, 35(7), 2059–2064. DOI: 10.1007/s11606-020-05730-4 PMID: 32157652

Freeman, J. Q., Scott, A. W., & Akhiwu, T. O. (2024). Rural–urban disparities and trends in utilization of palliative care services among US patients with metastatic breast cancer. *The Journal of Rural Health*, 40(4), 602–609. Advance online publication. DOI: 10.1111/jrh.12826 PMID: 38375950

French, M., Hansford, L., & Moeke-Maxwell, T. (2023). Reflecting on choices and responsibility in palliative care in the context of social disadvantage. *Palliative Care and Social Practice*, 17. Advance online publication. DOI: 10.1177/26323524231193037 PMID: 37654731

Garg, V., & Agarwal, S. (2021). An empirical study on the corporate social responsibility regime in India: Pre-COVID and COVID times. *Review of Market Integration*, 13(2-3), 124–153. DOI: 10.1177/09749292221093835

Gautam, R., & Singh, A. (2010). Corporate social responsibility practices in India: A study of top 500 companies. *Global Business and Management Research*, 2(1), 41–56.

Ghoshal, A., Khan Joad, A., Spruijt, O., Nair, S., Rajagopal, M., Patel, F., Damani, A., Deodhar, J., Goswami, D., Joshi, G., Butola, S., Singh, C., Rao, S. R., Bhatwadekar, M., Muckaden, M. A., & Bhatnagar, S. (2022). Situational analysis of the quality of palliative care services across India: A cross-sectional survey. ecancermedicalscience, 16. DOI: 10.3332/ecancer.2022.1486

Hamann, R. (2009). An academic's perspective on the role of academics in corporate responsibility. Professionals' Perspectives of Corporate Social Responsibility, 347-361. DOI: 10.1007/978-3-642-02630-0_19

Harsha Kumar, H., & Pai, U. (2015). A study on corporate social responsibility for the health care of the elderly by private health care providers of Mangalore city: A health systems research. *International Journal of Medicine and Public Health*, 5(2), 157. DOI: 10.4103/2230-8598.153826

Hawley, P. (2017). Barriers to access to palliative care. *Palliative Care*, 10, 117822421668888. DOI: 10.1177/1178224216688887 PMID: 28469439

Health. (n.d.). Service Unavailable. https://www.bharatpetroleum.in/social-responsibility/csr-thrust-areas/health.aspx https://indiacsr.in/csr/

Khandelwal, N., Brumback, L. C., Halpern, S. D., Coe, N. B., Brumback, B., & Curtis, J. R. (2017). Evaluating the economic impact of palliative and end-of-life care interventions on intensive care unit utilization and costs from the hospital and healthcare system perspective. *Journal of Palliative Medicine*, 20(12), 1314–1320. DOI: 10.1089/jpm.2016.0548 PMID: 28972860

Kumar, S. (2013). Models of delivering palliative and end-of-life care in India. *Current Opinion in Supportive and Palliative Care*, 7(2), 216–222. DOI: 10.1097/SPC.0b013e3283610255 PMID: 23635881

Luyten, J., Kessels, R., Goos, P., & Beutels, P. (2015). Public preferences for prioritizing preventive and curative health care interventions: A discrete choice experiment. *Value in Health*, 18(2), 224–233. DOI: 10.1016/j.jval.2014.12.007 PMID: 25773558

Ministry of Corporate Affairs (MCA). (2020). The Companies Act 2013 (18 OF 2013 amended in 2020). Source: https://www.mca.gov.in/content/mca/global/en/acts-rules/ebooks/acts.html?act=NTk2MQ==

Mukherjee, R. (2024). CSR health initiaves by corporates strengthened healthcare framework. https://timesofindia.indiatimes.com/india/csr-health-initiatives-by-corporates-strengthened-healthcare-framework/articleshow/108685492.cms

Nair, M., & Ghoshal, A. (2023). Hospice Care in India—A Pediatrician's Perspective. *South Asian Journal of Cancer*, 12(03), 303–308. DOI: 10.1055/s-0043-1771407 PMID: 38047051

NPPC. Ministry of Health & Family Welfare-Government of India. (n.d.). Home: National Health Mission. https://nhm.gov.in/

Oliver, D. (2017). Palliative care for people with neurological disease. *Palliative Medicine in Practice*, 11(2), 41–47.

Pastrana, T., & Murray, S. A. (2024). The value and economic benefits of palliative care in primary care: An international perspective. *Annals of Palliative Medicine*, 13(2), 445–451. DOI: 10.21037/apm-23-270 PMID: 38509650

Patel, F., Sharma, S., & Khosla, D. (2012). Palliative care in India: Current progress and future needs. *Indian Journal of Palliative Care*, 18(3), 149. DOI: 10.4103/0973-1075.105683 PMID: 23439559

Radbruch, L., De Lima, L., Knaul, F., Wenk, R., Ali, Z., Bhatnaghar, S., Blanchard, C., Bruera, E., Buitrago, R., Burla, C., Callaway, M., Munyoro, E. C., Centeno, C., Cleary, J., Connor, S., Davaasuren, O., Downing, J., Foley, K., Goh, C., & Pastrana, T. (2020, October). Redefining Palliative Care—A New Consensus-Based Definition. *Journal of Pain and Symptom Management*, 60(4), 754–764. DOI: 10.1016/j.jpainsymman.2020.04.027 PMID: 32387576

Rao, K., & Simha, N. (2011). Networking of palliative care at the corporate level. *Indian Journal of Palliative Care*, 17(4), 20. DOI: 10.4103/0973-1075.76235 PMID: 21811363

Rocker, G., Downar, J., & Morrison, R. S. (2016). Palliative care for chronic illness: Driving change. *Canadian Medical Association Journal*, 188(17-18), E493–E498. DOI: 10.1503/cmaj.151454 PMID: 27551031

Salikhanov, I., Katapodi, M. C., Kunirova, G., & Crape, B. L. (2023). Improving palliative care outcomes in remote and rural areas of LMICs through family caregivers: Lessons from Kazakhstan. *Frontiers in Public Health*, 11, 1186107. Advance online publication. DOI: 10.3389/fpubh.2023.1186107 PMID: 37601198

Sampson, E., & Dening, K. H. (2013). *Palliative care and end of life care*. Oxford Medicine Online., DOI: 10.1093/med/9780199644957.003.0028

Schelin, M. E., Sallerfors, B., Rasmussen, B. H., & Fürst, C. J. (2018). Quality of care for the dying across different levels of palliative care development: A population-based cohort study. *Palliative Medicine*, 32(10), 1596–1604. DOI: 10.1177/0269216318801251 PMID: 30229696

Senderovich, H., & McFadyen, K. (2020). Palliative care: Too good to be true? *Rambam Maimonides Medical Journal*, 11(4), e0034. DOI: 10.5041/RMMJ.10394 PMID: 32213278

Shalev, A., Phongtankuel, V., Kozlov, E., Shen, M. J., Adelman, R. D., & Reid, M. C. (2017). Awareness and misperceptions of hospice and palliative care: A population-based survey study. *The American Journal of Hospice & Palliative Care*, 35(3), 431–439. DOI: 10.1177/1049909117715215 PMID: 28631493

Sharma, M., Sarkar, S., Adinarayanan, S., & Karunanithi, G. (2023). Mapping of palliative care services and challenges in implementation of national program for palliative care in Puducherry. *Indian Journal of Palliative Care*, 29, 266–278. DOI: 10.25259/IJPC_146_2022 PMID: 37700898

Sheikh, S. (2013). A guide to the Companies Act 2006. DOI: 10.4324/9780203885871

Sinha. (2024). Bridging gaps in palliative care through innovative technology solutions in India. LinkedIn. https://www.linkedin.com/pulse/bridging-gaps-palliative-care-through-innovative-technology-sinha-jy0xf/

Sneha. (2023, August 24). "Show me that you care" – Fundraising for palliative care. Society for Nutrition, Education & Health Action (SNEHA). https://www.snehamumbai.org/show-me-that-you-care-fundraising-for-palliative-care%EF%BF%BC/

Stjernsward, J. (2005). Community participation in palliative care. *Indian Journal of Palliative Care*, 11(2), 111. DOI: 10.4103/0973-1075.19190

Svalastog, A. L., Donev, D., Jahren Kristoffersen, N., & Gajović, S. (2017). Concepts and definitions of health and health-related values in the knowledge landscapes of the digital society. *Croatian Medical Journal*, 58(6), 431–435. DOI: 10.3325/cmj.2017.58.431 PMID: 29308835

Vallath, N., Salins, N., Ghoshal, A., Daniel, S. M., Damani, A., Rajagopal, M. R., Rewati, R. R., Bhatnagar, S., & Pramesh, C. S. (2022). Developing a screening tool for serious health-related suffering for low- and middle-income countries – phase-1: Domain identification and item generation. *Indian Journal of Palliative Care*, 28, 51–63. DOI: 10.25259/IJPC_25_2021 PMID: 35673368

Veenhoven, R. (2009). Life is getting better: Societal evolution and fit with human nature. *Social Indicators Research*, 97(1), 105–122. DOI: 10.1007/s11205-009-9556-0 PMID: 20390030

Yu, S., Wan, R., Bai, L., Zhao, B., Jiang, Q., Jiang, J., & Li, Y. (2023). Transformation of chronic disease management: Before and after the COVID-19 outbreak. *Frontiers in Public Health*, 11, 1074364. Advance online publication. DOI: 10.3389/fpubh.2023.1074364 PMID: 37064686

Chapter 12
Promoting Equality Through CSR Practices:
Legal Imperatives for Disability Rights and Inclusive Business Strategies for a Sustainable Society

Anuttama Ghose
http://orcid.org/0000-0002-7210-4074
School of Law, Dr. Vishwanath Karad MIT-World Peace University, India

Hartej Singh Kochher
http://orcid.org/0000-0002-4979-4951
Vinayaka Mission's Law School, Chennai, India

S. M. Aamir Ali
http://orcid.org/0000-0002-8686-0217
Symbiosis Law School, Symbiosis International University (Deemed), Pune, India

ABSTRACT

The complex relationship between human rights, corporate social responsibility (CSR), and global sustainability is explored in this chapter, with a particular emphasis on the intersection of disability rights and inclusive business practices. Examining both Indian domestic legislation and international agreements, the study finds that there are obstacles to enforcing policies that demand equal treatment and the elimination of bias against people with disabilities. A cornerstone of CSR, inclusive business practices are also examined, with an emphasis on the need for major changes to company policy and culture. In order to achieve genuine inclusion

DOI: 10.4018/979-8-3693-5991-4.ch012

and fair job chances, it delves into holes in political theory, examines theories of capacities and social mobilization, and argues for a strategic strategy that aligns CSR with inclusive practices. In order to better understand disability rights, this chapter delves further into the existing domestic and international legal frameworks and makes the case for a more all-encompassing legal framework that is in line with CSR policies.

INTRODUCTION

The convergence of Disability Rights and Inclusive Business Practices brings to light a complex collection of challenges that arise from the interdependence of human rights, Corporate Social Responsibility (CSR), and global sustainability. This academic endeavor delves into the intricate challenges and possible benefits that arise from the interplay of many legal factors. According to Oware (2023), eliminating discrimination and providing equitable treatment to those with disabilities are mandated by the legal criteria of Disability Rights, as set forth in international accords and Indian domestic legislation. Implementation of the aforementioned legislation is fraught with difficulty due to the fact that people with disabilities continue to encounter barriers to education, employment, and full social participation despite the clarity of its basic principles (Blanck, 2020). These issues draw attention to the persistent gap between the goal and implementation of the law.

At the same time, a wide range of ethical obligations for companies are included in Inclusive Business Practices, which are an essential part of CSR. However, a number of challenges arise when trying to carry out these duties within the context of corporations (Cordero et al., 2014). Getting to real inclusiveness isn't just about lip service; it calls for major changes to company policy, procedures, and culture. The study's overarching goal is to provide a critical analysis of the complex legal framework controlling disability rights and the actual execution of inclusive business practices. The overarching goal of this effort is to shed light on the many complications that arise when these two theoretical frameworks are considered together, complications that extend beyond mere compliance with regulations (Gould et al., 2020). Additionally, the chapter assesses the setting of CSR programs that seek to educate the public about disabilities, empower society, provide fellowships, harness talents, and provide vocational training, among other related endeavors. The urgent need to address these challenges in the corporate world is emphasized by its persuasive appeal. Not only does the study lay out a plan to reduce current inequalities, but it also calls for a more equitable and environmentally aware world community to be built. In addition, it aims to motivate companies to fulfill their ethical obligations while still complying with legal requirements, with a focus on

India. This study utilizes a thorough analysis of legal principles to investigate the obstacles and factors businesses encounter when implementing Disability Rights and Inclusive Business Practices. The study specifically concentrates on the Indian legal framework and the international commitments outlined in the Convention on the Rights of Persons with Disabilities (CRPD). The chapter intends to perform a comprehensive examination of legislative and regulatory frameworks, as well as important case law pertaining to Disability Rights and Inclusive Business Practices in India, with a specific focus on doctrinal analysis. The technique starts by conducting a thorough examination of the existing body of literature, which includes academic publications, legislative documents, and judicial judgments. This process aims to provide a strong theoretical foundation and identify crucial legal concepts and precedents. This study aims to analyze legal provisions and court decisions in order to gain a deeper understanding of the legal methods that businesses can utilize to advance Disability Rights and inclusivity in their operations in India. Additionally, it will explore practical approaches for implementing these strategies.

This research aims to address gaps in the current literature by comprehensively examining all relevant papers in this field. Current regional and international legal requirements have been the center of the author's in-depth examination of Gauthier de Beco's work within the framework of Capabilities theory and Social Mobilization Theory (De Beco, 2021). The goal is to highlight the areas where political philosophy is lacking and where handicapped people are not given equal moral treatment. The author also delves into possible ways forward in this domain. The author has also assessed the evolving dynamics of the modern business world and consulted Marco Fasciglione's research to better comprehend the relationship between corporate social responsibility and the right to employment of persons with disabilities (Fasciglione, 2015). In their examination of global issues, the writers drew on the work of Michael Ashley Stein, who, with a meticulous approach, highlighted the importance of human rights, particularly those of people with disabilities (Stein & Bantekas, 2021). According to Jackie Shaw and Chi Kin Kwan, organizations must take a strategic approach that combines corporate social responsibility with inclusive business practices if they want to help people with disabilities find meaningful work and live their full potential (Shaw et al., 2022; Kwan, 2020). For his part, Peter Blanck continues to fight for disabled people's rights in the business world by promoting disability-inclusive employment policies and practices (Blanck, 2020). A basic understanding of how stakeholders globally seek to facilitate Person with Disability (hereinafter, PWD) integration into society, especially in the domain of employment and CSR activities, is demonstrated by the existing literature on efforts to integrate persons with disabilities into mainstream employment.

The paper emphasizes on the critical role that businesses play in promoting inclusivity, especially for individuals with disabilities. Managers can leverage the legal frameworks around disability rights to develop and implement CSR policies that not only comply with legal requirements but also advance social equality. From a managerial perspective, this paper highlights how integrating disability inclusion into CSR initiatives can enhance the company's reputation, attract a diverse workforce, and foster innovation. Businesses that prioritize disability inclusion can tap into the talents of a broader talent pool, offering them a competitive advantage. The paper underscores the importance of managers aligning business strategies with global sustainability goals, focusing on inclusivity as a key driver for long-term success. The legal imperatives discussed in the paper guide managers on how to structure CSR policies that align with national and international regulations. By ensuring legal compliance, companies can avoid potential litigation and enhance stakeholder trust. Moreover, the paper encourages managers to view disability inclusion not as a compliance obligation but as a strategic opportunity to contribute to societal progress while driving business growth. In conclusion, the paper serves as a blueprint for managers to implement inclusive business strategies, making a positive impact both socially and economically.

Disability Rights and CSR: A Fusion of Concepts and Theories

Corporate Social Responsibility (CSR) refers to the responsibility of corporations to acknowledge and address their impact on the economy, environment, society, human rights, and corporate governance. This paper highlights the impacts and possible risks to the rights and interests of the stakeholders within a certain group (Tilt, 2016). The company's CSR strategy actively involves and acknowledges these stakeholders. The notion of Corporate Social Responsibility (CSR) emerged in the United States during the 1950s and 1960s, when industrial entrepreneurs were more concerned about the living circumstances of their workers, notably in terms of housing and general social welfare. The author, Celma, describes this as a paternalistic approach towards their staff. This marks the beginning of the movement, which later spread far throughout Europe and eventually reached Asia (Celma et al., 2018). The full realization of social cohesion and job promotion policies and practices in enterprises did not occur until the 1990s when the European Commission aggressively lobbied for their adoption. Under the CSR framework outlined earlier, corporations target their corporate responsibility activities towards addressing human rights that are universally recognized as international rights, led by the application of the Guiding Principles. The Universal Declaration of Human Rights (UDHR), situated in the center, expresses in its first article that "*all human beings are born free and equal in dignity and rights.*" Further, according to Article 2, "*Everyone is entitled to all the rights and freedoms set forth in the Universal Declaration without distinction of any kind, such as race, color, sex, language, religion, political or other opinions, national or social origin, property, birth or another status."* Article 4 of the convention also, states that "*equality of opportunity and treatment for disabled men and women workers shall be respected.*" As per the aforementioned Articles and the 2006 UN Convention on the Rights of Persons with Disabilities, it is a basic human right to guarantee that persons with disabilities are not subjected to discrimination. This right should be included in the corporate social responsibility (CSR) policies of all firms, particularly multinational corporations.

Promoting diversity is a fundamental problem on the contemporary CSR agenda, and the importance of socially responsible or sustainable HR practices is becoming more acknowledged. Corporate social responsibility (CSR) in the field of human rights goes beyond the usual scope of corporate activities and charity contributions to be seen as fundamental to the proper operation of a firm in line with its declared goals. If companies are serious about being sustainable, they will behave ethically and put money into their local communities and economies. The current financial crisis has shown that companies' actions driven by short-term profit may have far-reaching consequences. A key component of inclusive corporate culture and successful CSR programs is disability inclusion, which is a rising trend in MNE practices. In any case, "disability" remains a delicate issue in CSR, and companies deal with it in different ways due to workers' differing levels of understanding of the needs and benefits of such programs. This chapter explores the concept of Capabilities Theory as a framework for comprehending and promoting the integration of impaired persons. The theoretical framework, developed by Nobel laureate Amartya Sen, highlights the significance of improving people's ability to live a life that they consider valuable rather than just concentrating on resources and money (Sen, 1999). Unlike social contract theory, capacities theory prioritizes desired results above procedural considerations. The notion of capabilities is a significant foundation for improving the quality of life for those with impairments (Sen, 1992). The allocation of resources is dynamic and varies depending on the extent to which resources may be transformed into essential human tasks. Sen argues that persons with disabilities often need more resources in order to properly perform fundamental human tasks. According to Rawls, the capabilities theory recognizes that an individual's "natural primary goods" will impact their capacity to use "social primary goods" (Sen, 1992). A more sophisticated strategy is used to accommodate the range of human differences by using resource allocation systems that empower persons with disabilities to enhance their abilities. The concept explores the realistic opportunities accessible to those with impairments while considering their distinct situations. Nussbaum's concept of 'combined capacities' pertains to the cultivation of capabilities via the creation of appropriate political, social, and economic conditions (Nussbaum, 2007).

One should contemplate the degree to which capabilities theory corresponds with the social model of disability and, thus, the fundamental philosophy of the *UN Convention on the Rights of Persons with Disabilitie*s (hence referred to as CRPD). In order to advocate the idea that disability is a consequence of social structure, capacity theory must address the need to remove barriers that impede the involvement of impaired persons in society (Sandel, 1998, p. 27). A crucial inquiry to contemplate is whether the capacities theory provides a foundation for promoting the inclusion of impaired persons via campaigning for environmental alterations to accomplish this objective. It is important to consider the extent to which capabilities theory aligns with the social model of disability and, as a result, the underlying philosophy of the CRPD. To promote the notion that disability is a result of social structure, it is crucial for capability theory to concentrate on eliminating obstacles that hinder the participation of impaired persons in society (Burchardt, 2004). One should contemplate if the capacities theory might serve as a basis for promoting the inclusion of impaired persons by pushing for environmental improvements to attain this goal. The capacities theory does not entirely align with the purposes of the Convention, but there may be some degree of congruence in this regard. The approach examines the interplay between impairments and other obstacles, leading to a reassessment of social frameworks via the redistribution of resources. The capabilities hypothesis, in contrast to the Convention's mandate for States Parties to raise knowledge of the abilities of individuals with disabilities, fails to sufficiently address the enhancement of societal attitudes (Wong, 2009). The theory also takes a generally gloomy view of these talents, emphasizing the need to remedy their absence rather than recognizing their importance. Overall, it is consistent with the CRPD's interpretation of disability, although it does not fully accomplish the objectives of the Convention.

Additionally, an examination using Legal Mobilization Theory and Critical Legal Studies (hereinafter referred to as CLS) within the framework of Inclusive Business Practices and Corporate Social Responsibility (CSR) uncovers the complex interaction between legal requirements and profound societal transformation (Lejeune & Ringelheim, 2019). This introduction provides a detailed study that highlights the complex legal aspects that influence the techniques used to create a more inclusive and socially responsible environment for people with disabilities. The Rights of Persons with Disabilities Act, 2016 is a significant legal foundation in India that establishes a strong framework for safeguarding the rights of individuals with disabilities. From a legal mobilization perspective, this Act serves as a central focus for strategic litigation, using the concepts of Legal Mobilization Theory to contest discriminatory practices and promote the effective implementation of inclusive policies (Lejeune & Ringelheim, 2019). A study using Critical Legal Studies (CLS) of this Act examines its effect on wider legal principles, providing guidance for legal advocacy activities to scrutinize and modify elements that may unintentionally sustain systematic discrimination. The Equal Opportunities, Protection of Rights and Full Participation Act, 1995, has a crucial role in influencing techniques for legal mobilization. From a legal perspective, this Act provides a means to contest unfair employment practices and pursue legal action based on concepts of Critical Legal Studies (CLS) in order to address broader concerns within its legal structure. The CLS perspective encourages a thorough analysis of how this Act interacts with wider legal standards, leading to attempts to mobilize the law in order to deconstruct entrenched systems that contribute to systemic discrimination. The Companies Act 2013 includes the National CSR Policy, which presents distinct legal options and highlights the need for ethical and socially responsible company behavior. From a legal perspective, attempts to mobilize the law may strategically use corporate social responsibility (CSR) policies to guarantee that CSR programs actively contribute to the well-being of persons with disabilities.

An Overview of Worldwide Legal Standards Protecting Persons with Disabilities

Including people with disabilities in the workforce should be a priority for states, according to the UN. International accords also compel them to respect and protect the human rights of people with disabilities on the job. These duties are in line with the constantly changing CSR rules. According to Stein and Stein (2007), some states have passed or amended domestic laws that are in accordance with the CRPD. The use of existing criteria to recognize and encourage the inclusion of persons with impairments is endorsed by many non-binding rules. A number of significant resolutions and recommendations have been issued by various organizations, including the United Nations General Assembly in 1982 regarding a World Programme of Action Concerning Disabled Persons, the International Labor Organization in 1983 regarding Recommendation No. 168, the United Nations General Assembly in 1994 regarding Standard Rules on the Equalization of Opportunities for Persons with Disabilities, and the International Labor Organization in 1998 regarding Fundamental Principles and Rights at Work. Despite the fact that these elements had a significant role in developing the arguments and wording of Article 27 CRPD, they have failed to influence the internal policies of MNCs or to include disability rights into voluntary monitoring systems such as the UNGC or the OECD Guidelines on Multinational Enterprises. The International Covenant on Economic, Social, and Cultural Rights (ICESCR, 1966) and its explanatory General Comment No. 5 on Persons with Disabilities place substantial obligations on states regarding the hiring of individuals with disabilities (ILO, 2006). International human rights agreements such as these also impose certain requirements on states. Convention

No. 159 of the International Labor Organization on the Employment and Rehabilitation of People with Disabilities, which was adopted in 1983, is also of great importance. According to the United Nations Department of Economic and Social Affairs (2015), the Sustainable Development Goals (SDGs) will remain in force until 2030. They were put into action in 2015. As a consequence of effective lobbying for disability rights, the SDGs have included eleven references to those with disabilities. One such mention is in SDG 8, which seeks to ensure that all people, especially youths and persons with disabilities, have access to full and meaningful work with equitable compensation. Target 10 of the Sustainable Development Goals seeks to ensure that all people, irrespective of their age, gender, handicap, race, ethnicity, origin, religion, or socioeconomic level, are fully empowered and fully included in all social, economic, and political arenas. At the same time, the CRPD undeniably altered the legal rights of people with disabilities, requiring their full participation in society (De Beco, 2020).

The CRPD is groundbreaking because it is the first legally enforceable international agreement guaranteeing full rights for those with disabilities. It has the potential to initiate a significant shift in how disability policies and practices are developed and put into action (Saul, 2010). The CRPD's conceptual foundation rests on the tenets of the social model of disability. Pre-existing ideas of human rights, including the basic concept of non-discrimination, form the basis of the CRPD, which must be acknowledged (Saul, 2010). Everyone, regardless of ability, should be able to fully participate in society without fear of discrimination, and this concept guarantees that people with disabilities have the same rights and obligations as everyone else. There have been major policy shifts since the CRPD was passed and almost universally adopted, benefiting groups who were previously persecuted, disadvantaged, and cut off from mainstream society. One reason for this is that governments are now faced with the unprecedented challenge of guaranteeing equal treatment for their greatest minority population (Weber, 2011). Article 5 of the CRPD, which contains fifty substantive provisions, makes it clear that refusing to provide reasonable accommodation is a kind of discrimination that cannot be tolerated (UNCRPD, 2006). State parties are obligated to aggressively encourage the recognition of the talents and skills of disabled workers according to Article 8 of the UNCRPD (2006). State governments are obligated to ensure that people with disabilities are treated fairly in the workplace, according to Article 27. Article 27 of the UNCRPD (2006) not only outlaws discrimination but also offers state parties a non-exhaustive list of positive activities they may take to close the participation gap and inequality in the workplace.

CSR and Disability Legislation in India: An In-Depth Analysis

The corporate social responsibility (CSR) framework under the Companies Act 2013 represents a pivotal development in India's corporate governance landscape. Enacted to institutionalize corporate philanthropy, Section 135 of the Companies Act mandates that certain companies, based on their financial thresholds, allocate at least two percent of their average net profits over the preceding three years towards CSR activities. These activities, outlined in the seventh schedule of the Act, span a wide array of social welfare initiatives, including education, healthcare, environmental sustainability, and rural development. There is also a significant focus on disability, inclusion, and welfare.

Legislative Framework of CSR under the Companies Act in India

Section 135 of the Companies Act 2013 specifies that every company with a net worth of INR 500 crore or more, a turnover of INR 1000 crore or more, or a net profit of INR 5 crore or more during the immediately preceding financial year must constitute a corporate social responsibility committee on the board consisting of three or more directors, including at least one independent director.

The CSR committee is responsible for formulating and recommending a CSR policy, specifying the activities to be undertaken in the area as mentioned in schedule seven, recommending the expenditure to be incurred, monitor the CSR policy periodically. The board, after considering the CSR committee's recommendation, must approve the CSR policy, disclose its content in the annual report, and ensure its implementation. Companies must spend at least 2% of their average net profits on CSR activities, with preference given to local areas of operation. Penalties are also prescribed for non-compliance.

Provisions Pertaining to CSR and Disability Inclusion

A notable aspect of the CSR mandate is to focus on the welfare of differently abled individuals. Schedule seven of the act explicitly includes the promotion of education, special education, and employment, as well as enhancing vocational skills, particularly for children, women, the elderly, and definitely abled individuals. This inclusion underscores the acts and commitment to fostering an inclusive society where the needs of differently-abled persons are comprehensively addressed (Gautam & Singh, 2010).

The emphasis in Entry II of Schedule VII is on promoting education, including special education and employment-enhancing vocational skills, especially for vulnerable groups like children, women, the elderly, and people with disabilities. This directive seeks to improve livelihood opportunities and address educational disparities (Gautam & Singh, 2010). Through the prioritization of inclusive education and vocational training, companies can make a substantial contribution to the socio-economic development and empowerment of marginalized communities, including the differently abled. Under this mandate, projects frequently involve opening schools, giving scholarships, running skill-development courses, and developing jobs that are specifically designed to meet the needs of people with disabilities. These initiatives not only enhance educational attainment and employability but also promote a more just and inclusive society by allowing marginalized groups to engage more fully in economic activities (Ghose et al., 2024).

Sustainable Development Goal (SDG) and Corporate Social Responsibility (CSR)

A 2018 report by the high-level committee on CSR recommended further alignment of Schedule Seven with sustainable development goals, which emphasize the welfare of differently-abled persons as well. This alignment aims to create a holistic approach to CSR, encouraging companies to integrate disability welfare into their broader CSR strategies. The sustainable development goals emphasize the importance of inclusivity, particularly for differently-abled individuals. Goals such as Goal 4 (inclusive and equitable quality education) and Goal 11 (sustainable citizen communities) explicitly reference disability. These goals call for equal access to education, employment, and public spaces, emphasizing the need for accessible infrastructure and inclusive policies. This global framework supports and complements the CSR initiatives under the Companies Act, highlighting the intersection of corporate responsibility and sustainable development in promoting disability rights (Ghose et al., 2024).

According to Mitra and Chatterjee (2020), there is a substantial overlap between the Sustainable Development Goals (SDGs) set forth by the United Nations in 2016 and the Corporate Social Responsibility (CSR) mandate in India as stated in the Companies Act, 2013. The Act's Schedule VII, which outlines the priority areas for CSR initiatives, includes references to 15 of the 17 SDGs, as noted by the authors. These areas include, but are not limited to, ending hunger, advancing education, maintaining environmental sustainability, and improving vocational skills. Under the Companies Act of 2013, the goals of Corporate Social Responsibility (CSR) are closely aligned with the Rights of Persons with Disabilities Act of 2016 (RPWD Act). Sections 16 and 19 of the RPWD Act place a strong emphasis on inclusive education and vocational training for people with disabilities. In line with Entry 2 of Schedule VII of the Companies Act, CSR initiatives can advance these by constructing easily accessible educational facilities, offering scholarships, conducting specialized skill development programs, and developing opportunities for tailored employment (Jumde, 2021).

Section 20 prohibits employment, discrimination and mandates, reasonable accommodations, and barrier-free environments. CSR efforts can include creating inclusive workplace policies, conducting accessibility audits, and offering training programs to sanitize employers and employees about disability, rights, and inclusion. Companies can make a substantial contribution to the inclusion and empowerment of people with disabilities, as well as to meeting legal requirements and fostering an inclusive society, by coordinating their CSR strategies with the RPWD Act (Jumde, 2021).

Challenges Pertaining to Inclusive Business Practices and Equal Opportunities

People with disabilities in Indian society have serious challenges, including societal prejudice and a feeling of being ignored. The lack of healthcare, educational opportunities, and jobs is making life even more difficult for most people with disabilities in India. Together with private companies and non-governmental organizations (NGOs), the government has launched a number of programs to boost their economic and physical capacities. However, a major challenge for people in this scenario is the lack of physical accessibility to buildings, transit, and services (Wohl, 2014). Because of this, the unemployment rate for those with impairments is much greater. People with disabilities may gain financial independence via increased mobility, access to technical education and training, and the ability to hold down a job or launch their own company. Nevertheless, many people with disabilities face many challenges while trying to get a job, keep one, or advance in their current position. Perceptions regarding the rights and qualifications of people with disabilities for work are deeply ingrained and provide significant obstacles to implementing disability-inclusive employment practices. Consequently, those who are successful in navigating restrictive recruitment processes often feel undervalued and stigmatized in their corporate settings (Wohl, 2014). Disregarding the subjective, social, and dynamic variables that maintain unequal power relations and, thus, prolong workplace exclusion, current approaches to promote disability-inclusive employment often fail to have substantial impacts. Companies often see disability inclusion as difficult, potentially detrimental to revenues, or only a charitable endeavor to fulfill their corporate social responsibility (CSR) duties; this misinformation just makes the issues worse.

Employment Equity: Ensuring Equal Opportunities

A basic obligation stated in Article 27 of the CRPD is to guarantee equality and non-discrimination. Third parties, including companies, are also bound by these responsibilities, not just people. They are relevant at all points in the employment life cycle, including but not limited to job hunting, interviewing, hiring, training, progression, and termination. To attain genuine equality under the CRPD, it is essential for states to eradicate any kind of discrimination based on disability in regard to employment and labor, as stated in the CRPD's jurisprudence. International human rights practice recognizes several types of discrimination, any of which may exist alone or in combination. The refusal to provide a reasonable accommodation is one example of this category, along with direct and indirect forms of discrimination. Although it might be challenging to put these rules into effect, it is critical for business success to create an atmosphere that promotes support and inclusion. Striking a balance between accommodating varying talents and maintaining seamless operations may be quite a challenge. Promoting inclusive policies and assisting businesses in effectively integrating them into organizational culture are the primary goals of CSR projects. People with impairments are more likely to thrive in such an atmosphere (Weber, 2009).

Barriers to Societal Prejudices and Biases

Misconceptions and preconceptions about people with disabilities' skills lead to social stigmatization. To this day, prejudice and bigotry persist because most people see disability as a limitation rather than a range of skills. Social inclusion is illusory because this prejudice prevents people with disabilities from fully participating in all aspects of communal life. In the context of disabilities, the fight for social inclusion is made more difficult by discrimination. Discrimination creates obstacles that hinder the social, economic, and cultural engagement of people with disabilities. These barriers might be in the form of accessibility locations, discrepancies in employment, or subtle prejudices. Uneven chances and the harsh reality of systematic discrimination persist for many despite legal protections; this undermines the core principle of social inclusion. The illusion of social inclusion is further distorted by ableism, which is defined as the systematic devaluing of people with disabilities. People with disabilities face societal obstacles when they want to fully participate due to a combination of non-accommodation and negative attitudes. A significant change in public attitudes, acknowledging the unique qualities and accomplishments of people with disabilities, is necessary to overcome ableism, in addition to physical accessibility. The fight against prejudice and stigma frequently takes place in the workplace, an important setting for social inclusion. Disabled people face a number of obstacles that prevent them from advancing in their careers, including discrimination in employment and inadequate accommodations. Inclusive policies, accessibility programs, and a dedication to cultivating a diverse workplace culture are proactive steps that companies may take to break down these obstacles (Wohl, 2014).

Identifying the Barriers to Educational and Vocational Training

Understanding the complex nature of the obstacles that prevent different learners from engaging in inclusive learning and improving their skills is crucial for finding effective solutions. The absence of inclusive teaching strategies and curricular modifications is a major obstacle in education. People with disabilities are frequently left out of mainstream education because traditional methods do not adequately address their unique learning styles and demands (Pullum, 2005). To overcome this obstacle, educational practices must undergo a sea change, encouraging the creation and adoption of inclusive pedagogies that accommodate a variety of learning styles and abilities. This includes developing inclusive education-focused teacher training programs, accessible learning resources, and flexible curriculum.

Another major obstacle in the field of education is the lack of accessible adaptive tools and assistive technology. Adaptive keyboards for those with mobility difficulties and screen readers for the visually impaired are just two examples of the specific tools that many people with disabilities need to help them study. To overcome this obstacle, we must do more than just make sure that current educational technologies are accessible; we must also encourage the creation and use of new assistive technologies that may improve the educational experiences of people with a wide range of abilities (Truter, 1996).

The lack of accessible vocational training programs that specifically address the requirements of people with disabilities is a major barrier to skill development. There is a disparity between the skills people have and the skills needed for stable work since these programs have a hard time changing their teaching methods to accommodate students from different backgrounds (Truter, 1996). To overcome this obstacle, inclusive vocational training programs that take into account the specific talents and difficulties of people with disabilities are needed so that they may be prepared for jobs that are both meaningful and long-lasting. In addition, widespread cultural attitudes and misunderstandings about disability might serve as educational roadblocks. There may be less mutual support and understanding in settings where people are learning new skills because of prejudices and negative preconceptions. In order to overcome this obstacle, we must work together to dispel myths, promote understanding, and create a welcoming environment for people with disabilities (Pullum, 2005).

Infrastructure and Standards: Bridging Gaps

Fostering fair job opportunities for those with disabilities hinges on creating a work environment that is inclusive and accessible. However, there are substantial obstacles stemming from physical infrastructure that must be overcome on the road to inclusive workplaces. Even though accessibility regulations have come a long way, many companies still lack the tools disabled workers need. The lack of accessible facilities, including ramps, elevators, bathrooms, and signs, creates an essentially exclusive atmosphere (Pugh, 2000). To overcome these obstacles, we need to closely examine the current infrastructure and make smart changes to ensure everyone can use it. Access to reliable transportation is still a major barrier for people with impairments when looking for work. Public transportation and business places that are not accessible might be quite challenging (Rudolph, 2022).

The availability of assistive technology in the workplace is another critical component. Specialized equipment is essential for many people with impairments to carry out daily activities. From modified keyboards for those with movement impairments to screen readers for the visually impaired, employers should provide and invest in these assistive technologies. Not only does this investment show that you care about including people with impairments, but it also improves their work experience. Government laws and incentives may also greatly aid in Addressing physical infrastructure difficulties. Businesses must pursue inclusive infrastructure by creating a legal framework that enforces workplace accessibility requirements. Additional incentives for enterprises to engage in inclusive physical infrastructure might include tax breaks or public acknowledgment of businesses with outstanding accessibility policies (Pugh, 2000).

Promoting Cultural Shifts for a More Inclusive Workplace

Achieving a fully accessible workplace for people with disabilities necessitates tackling issues related to physical infrastructure and triggering significant cultural transformations inside businesses. A cultural shift is necessary to establish a setting that welcomes and even celebrates variety, including disability, by altering long-held beliefs, values, and practices. The change starts at the top when leaders demonstrate their commitment to diversity and inclusion by actively promoting these principles across the company. Cultural transformations towards inclusive behaviours are driven in large part by CSR activities (Karin & Bollinger, 2020). Corporate social responsibility (CSR) is an effective means of advancing equality, inclusiveness, and diversity when it is ingrained in the values of a firm. Businesses may make a difference by directing their corporate social responsibility (CSR) funds into accessible projects, disability advocacy groups, and programs that help businesses adapt to and be inclusive of all employees. In doing so, CSR objectives are brought into harmony with the larger social need to ensure that people with disabilities have equal access to opportunity. It is in efforts that go beyond mere legal compliance that the synergy between workplace adaptability and CSR becomes most apparent, revealing a dedication to social responsibility. Digital platforms, assistive technology, and goods and services that adhere to universal design principles may all be made more accessible by companies. Customers and the community at large also get the advantages, in addition to the company's own personnel. When it comes to promoting adaptability in the workplace, cultural transformations are incomplete without training and awareness activities. Creating a more inclusive workplace begins with teaching staff members proper disability etiquette, which in turn increases tolerance and acceptance of individuals with a wide range of abilities. As part of their dedication to the well-being of society, CSR efforts may lend a hand to these programs by highlighting the importance of education and awareness (Karin & Bollinger, 2020).

Workplace adaptation and corporate social responsibility (CSR) work together even better when disability advocacy groups and organizations are involved. To make sure their programs are responsive to people with disabilities' real needs, businesses should include these communities in the process of creating and evaluating inclusive policies. By working together, we can strengthen the social responsibility component of CSR and create a more welcoming work environment for all employees.

Case Studies to Evaluate the Effectiveness of CSR in Promoting Disability Rights

A country thrives when every one of its members is given an equitable chance to contribute to its progress. This may be achieved by proactive efforts to construct an inclusive society where persons with disabilities are equitably treated and provided with equal opportunities and remuneration as their counterparts. Business Social Responsibility (BSR) is crucial in advancing good social change and inclusion, especially in relation to the rights of those with disabilities. This section examines impactful case examples where corporations have adopted BSR efforts, acting as drivers for significant changes in the lives of persons with disabilities.

Indian Oil Corporation Limited (IOCL) has significantly contributed to the empowerment of differently abled individuals, known as Divyangjans, through various CSR initiatives (Indian Oil, n.d.). Their efforts focus on providing essential aids and assistive devices, enhancing accessibility, and promoting skill development, thereby fostering an inclusive society. One of the cornerstone initiatives by IOCL is the provision of AIDS and assistive devices to Divyangjans across India. This initiative addresses the needs of the individual with a disability, including movement, hearing, and visual impairments (Indian Oil, n.d.). IOCL organizes an assessment campus in collaboration with the Artificial Limbs Manufacturing Corporation (ALIMCO) and local administration to evaluate the specific needs of the beneficiaries. Based on these assessments, aids such as tricycles, wheelchairs, crutches, walking sticks, braille kits, hearing aids, and artificial limbs are distributed. In a report available on this website, IOCL says that from 2018-2023, approximately 50,000 Divyangjans from 23 states have benefitted from this initiative, significantly improving their mobility and quality of life (Indian Oil, n.d.).

Project Drishti is another notable initiative aimed at empowering the visually impaired community. This project introduces AI-powered smart vision glasses designed to enhance the independence and accessibility of visually impaired individuals. These glasses come equipped with features that enable users to identify objects, read books and manuscripts in multiple languages, provide walking assistance, recognize faces, and include an emergency button for safety. By incorporating advanced technology, this project has improved the lives of the beneficiaries, showcasing the potential of innovation solutions to address the needs of the visually impaired. IOCL has partnered with the Skill Council for Persons with Disability (SCPwD) to provide vocational training for differently abled individuals. One such project in Ernakulam District focuses on training individuals with locomotor disabilities to become proficient Data Entry Operators. This initiative aims to enhance their self-reliance, boost family incomes, and elevate their overall quality of life. The project has successfully trained, assessed, and certified job opportunities for several individuals. This helps to integrate the differently abled individuals into the broader economy (Indian Oil, n.d.).

Through focused skill development and vocational training, the Tech Mahindra Foundation's SMART+ initiative provides a model for empowering Persons with Disabilities (PwDs). SMART+, which was introduced in 2013, aims to bridge the gap between disability and employability by offering specialized training tailored to the unique needs of PwDs. The SMART+ initiative operates 13 centers across India, offering a range of courses tailored to the needs of PwDs (Mahindra Rise, n.d.). It has a specially created curriculum and well-equipped classrooms to support productive dialogue and education. In order to improve employment prospects, the program integrates workplace readiness skills and basic English language proficiency with vocational training catered to different types of disabilities. The Tech Mahindra Foundation's ARISE+ (All Round Improvement in School Education) program aims to integrate 3- to 18-year-old children with disabilities into the regular school system. It assists institutions and groups committed to special needs education, enabling kids with physical limitations to realize their full potential (Mahindra Rise, n.d.).

Early disability detection, integrating assistive technology into the classroom, and parent and caregiver counseling are important approaches. The initiative delivered close to 400 tablets for online learning during the pandemic and had an impact on 3,792 students in FY 2021–22 and 2,776 in FY 2020–21 (Nehanaayar, 2023). The ARISE+ program is concentrated in a number of important areas:

1) Early Disability Detection: Recognizing impairments in children at an early age allows for prompt intervention and support.
2) Assistive technology and educational support: Providing children with disabilities with educational resources and utilizing assistive technologies to enhance their learning.
3) Counseling for Caregivers: Offering guidance and instruction on how to properly support children with special needs to parents, educators, and other caregivers.

Through its partner organizations, ARISE+ supported 2,776 students in the 2020–21 financial year while reaching 3,792 students in the 2021–22 financial year (Nehanaayar, 2023).

It is commonly acknowledged that persons with impairments still face substantial prejudice. Blindness leads to a harmful cycle in which illiteracy, poverty, and social isolation become interconnected for blind children, making them one of the most vulnerable groups worldwide. Only a limited number of individuals have the opportunity to get any kind of education. Bajaj Finserv Limited, the parent company of the financial services enterprises of the Bajaj Group, a well-known and established conglomerate in India, partnered with Sightsavers India to launch the Social Inclusion and Inclusive Education Programs in the districts of Raisen, Khagariya, Kasganj, and Pratapgarh in Madhya Pradesh, Bihar, Uttar Pradesh, and Rajasthan, respectively (Sightsavers India, 2022). Bajaj Allianz General Insurance Company Limited is dedicated to enhancing the well-being of persons with disabilities and delivering exceptional education to visually impaired children as part of their continuous corporate social responsibility (CSR) efforts targeting children and young people. Sightsavers, in collaboration with Bajaj Finserv, will provide support to those aged 18 and above with disabilities in obtaining social security benefits and employment opportunities (CSR Journal, 2022). The program aims to eradicate discrimination against individuals with disabilities in the domains of education, healthcare, and income. Additionally, it endeavors to foster their social inclusion and ensure their equitable rights. At the completion of the project, about 1,260 impaired persons will be able to benefit from a range of social security services (CSR Journal, 2022). These programs include disability pensions, child financial aid, aids and appliances, housing loans, and other benefits.

The Flipkart Foundation, a division of the Flipkart Group, which is India's domestic e-commerce marketplace, seeks to promote an all-encompassing, equitable, empowered, and environmentally responsible society in India. In pursuit of its objective, the foundation collaborated with Mitti Cafe, a network of cafes that provides hands-on training and job prospects for persons with physical and intellectual impairments (Flipkart Foundation, n.d.). The Flipkart Foundation has offered monetary support for the initial setup costs of a Mitti Cafe in Bengaluru. Furthermore, the Flipkart Foundation is providing sponsorship to Mitti café in order to educate 249 persons with disabilities (PWDs) at their training centers in Bengaluru and Kolkata. This initiative aims to provide long-term and viable employment opportunities for people from underprivileged areas (CSR Journal, 2023). The Flipkart Foundation seeks to provide assistance to persons with disabilities (PwD) via a collaboration with Mitti Café (India CSR, 2023). The objective of this collaboration is to enhance the autonomy and skill development of persons with disabilities (PwD) via the provision of financial resources. This will also help raise awareness about inclusive workplaces that may be run by individuals with disabilities. The newly built Mitti café will be supervised by persons with disabilities, with the goal of improving their career opportunities and, therefore, their ability to support themselves, by promoting their skill growth. His endeavor will bolster equity, inclusivity, and consciousness about the inclusion of those with disabilities via the provision of training and professional opportunities. The Flipkart Foundation aims to have a positive impact on 20 million lives, both directly and indirectly, in the next ten years. It focuses on rural areas and ensuring equal access to development opportunities for women and other disadvantaged groups.

Hero MotoCorp gifted Hero Destini 125 bikes to Indian Army veterans who suffered infirmities while doing their duty in April 2022 (Harshith, 2022). The Company has disseminated these scooters to the military personnel of the Indian Army throughout several states in India. In August 2022, the company introduced a range of social incentives for former employees and their families. The 'Hero Salutes Heroes of the Nation' program, carried out under the Company's corporate social responsibility (CSR) platform 'Hero We Care', included supplying modified Hero Destini 125 scooters to former members of the Central Reserve Police Force (CRPF) (CSR Journal, 2023). The scooters are equipped with two modified rear auxiliary wheels to accommodate the specific riding requirements of disabled former servicemen who sustained injuries during their service.

The establishment of a facility named 'Dialogue in the Dark' has been initiated by SBI Foundation in partnership with ACE Social Foundation, as reported by the Times of India (Times of India, 2022). The main goal of this effort is to promote empathy and increase public knowledge of the skills of individuals with disabilities, including those who have visual impairments (The Print 2022). The 'Dialogue in the Dark' center in Mumbai is open to both corporate organizations and the general population. The thorough examination of these situations highlights the concrete advantages that result from strategic BSR activities, which include bolstering business reputation, fostering a better workplace culture, and promoting innovation. The results highlight the versatility of BSR in many business contexts, demonstrating its effectiveness in both large multinational firms and small to medium-sized businesses. The reported achievements provide persuasive proof that a dedication to disability inclusion not only corresponds to ethical obligations but also yields demonstrable benefits for both individuals and companies. The knowledge acquired from these instances drives us towards a future where companies have a crucial role in breaking down obstacles, advocating for equality, and making meaningful contributions to a society that is more inclusive and fair.

Recommendations for fostering inclusivity and Equality Through CSR Practices

A strategy approach that harmoniously combines inclusive business practices with CSR is necessary to propel firms toward true inclusion and fair job opportunities for those with disabilities. Building a culture of diversity and inclusion that is pervasive across the company begins with a commitment to these principles from the top down. A commitment like this from upper management sends a powerful message about the importance of diversity and inclusion and sets the tone for the whole company. When culturally integrated principles shape an organization's policies, procedures, and communication, inclusive practices become an integral part of the organization's DNA (Karin & Bollinger, 2020).

To find and remove digital and physical obstacles in the workplace, thorough accessibility audits are an important part of this strategy moving ahead. If we want to build places that everyone can enjoy, we must invest in infrastructural improvements. These enhancements, which may be either digital or physical in nature, provide the groundwork for a welcoming workplace that can easily accommodate a wide range of talents. Educational opportunities might spark a new societal shift toward tolerance and compassion. It is critical to establish specialized training programs and sensitization seminars that emphasize proper behavior and understanding of people with disabilities. Making sure that workers at all levels take part in continuing education programs makes for a more understanding and welcoming workplace, which in turn helps to remove obstacles and promote an atmosphere that values diversity (Karin & Bollinger, 2020). Flexible work rules and reasonable accommodations are essential for firms to properly meet varied requirements. Empowerment and equitable employment opportunities are aided by the inherent flexibility of policy, which includes flexible scheduling and the ability to work remotely. Equally important is making sure that workers with disabilities achieve their maximum potential by providing them with appropriate accommodations that are customized to their specific needs. Important corporate social responsibility (CSR) efforts should be in line with the larger aims of disability inclusion and assistance. Corporate social responsibility (CSR) initiatives are multiplied in their beneficial effect by strategic investments in initiatives that affect accessibility, education, and job prospects. By aligning CSR programs with inclusive aims, they may have a significant impact, benefiting both the enterprise and society as a whole in the pursuit of diversity and equality. Organizations may further demonstrate their dedication to diversity by forming relationships with disability advocacy organizations. Organizations get priceless insights and direction when these groups are involved in creating and evaluating inclusive policies and practices. The authenticity and relevance of inclusive business practices are fostered via collaborative efforts that guarantee organizational plans are inspired by real-world experiences.

Organizations should set quantifiable goals to track the success of inclusive business practices in order to track development and promote responsibility. Transparently communicating success and difficulties on a regular basis promotes a learning and improvement culture inside the company. A persistent commitment to inclusion may be achieved via the use of metrics and reporting methods, which provide a concrete means of evaluating the results of projects. This allows for the improvement of policies over time. Organizations may help bring about a social movement towards diversity and fairness by adopting these strategic ideas and setting out on a path towards true inclusion, which in turn helps to provide equitable job prospects.

CONCLUSION

Human rights and Corporate responsibility encompasses more than just a company's main operations and donations to charity. It is considered a crucial component of doing business, based on the corporate principles ingrained in the organization's strategy and daily activities. Moreover, the current financial crisis has shown the substantial global consequences of economic activities motivated only by the desire for quick financial profit. In order to build sustainable practices, corporations must give priority to ethical behaviour and devote resources to local communities and economies. Recognizing the importance of successful corporate social responsibility (CSR) practices and the promotion of an inclusive corporate culture, the inclusion of disability in CSR strategies is increasingly acknowledged as a critical factor for Multinational Enterprises (MNEs). There is a rising need for a greater number of 'disability champions': persons who provide persuasive business justifications and demonstrate exemplary methods in advocating for the employment of those with disabilities. The importance of the issue is shown by the rise of specialized organizations and networks that aim to improve the underemployment of persons with disabilities and work together with both public and private companies to broaden their corporate social responsibility (CSR) initiatives. Organizations face substantial obstacles when attempting to go beyond surface-level efforts and implement reforms that really promote the meaningful participation of individuals with disabilities. The emphasized concerns include a range of problems, including guaranteeing accessibility and accommodation, as well as advocating for fair work opportunities. It is essential for corporations, politicians, and society as a whole to understand that Disability Rights go beyond just following the law. It is essential to protect and achieve basic human rights within the legal and operational structures of enterprises.

In conclusion, the fusion of corporate social responsibility and disability rights within the Indian context underscores our transformative approaches to corporate governance and social inclusivity. The legislative framework established by the Companies Act 2013 and the Rights of Persons with Disabilities Act 2016 mandate companies to actively engage in initiatives that promote the welfare and employment of differently abled individuals. Through the implementation of CSR policy, companies are not only adhering to legal requirements but also contributing to societal progress. The case studies of Indian Oil Corporation and Tech Mahindra vividly illustrate the positive impacts of targeted CSR initiatives. Indian Oil Corporation's provision of aids, assistive devices, and skill training programs, along with Tech Mahindra SMART + and ARISE+ initiatives, highlight successful models of enhancing accessibility, vocational training, and educational support for persons with disabilities. These efforts demonstrate the potential of corporate interventions to bridge the gap between disability and employability. Despite the successes, challenges such as societal prejudices, infrastructure, inadequacies, and the need for cultural shifts remain. Addressing these requires a collaborative effort across sectors. By aligning CSR activities with sustainable development goals and disability legislation, companies can drive change, fostering a more inclusive and equitable society where individuals with disabilities are empowered to participate in economic and social life.

REFERENCES

Bajaj Finserv collaborates with Sightsavers to bring inclusive education and promote disability rights across four districts in India. (2022, September 15). *The CSR Journal*.https://thecsrjournal.in/bajaj-finserv-collaborates-with-sightsavers-to-bring-inclusive-education-and-promote-disability-rights-across-four-districts-in-india/

Bajaj Finserv collaborates with Sightsavers to bring inclusive education and promote disability rights across three districts in India. (2022, October 14). *Sightsavers India*. https://www.sightsaversindia.org/news/2022/10/bajaj-finserv-collaborates-with-sightsavers-to-bring-inclusive-education-and-promote-disability-rights-across-three-districts-in-india/

Blanck, P. (2020). Disability inclusive employment and the accommodation principle: Emerging issues in research, policy, and law. *Journal of Occupational Rehabilitation*, 30(4), 505–510. DOI: 10.1007/s10926-020-09940-9

Burchardt, T. (2004). Capabilities and disability: The capabilities framework and the social model of disability. *Disability & Society*, 19(7), 735–751. DOI: 10.1080/0968759042000284213

Celma, D., Martinez-Garcia, E., & Raya, J. M. (2018). Socially responsible HR practices and their effects on employees' wellbeing: Empirical evidence from Catalonia, Spain. *European Research on Management and Business Economics*, 24(2), 82–89. DOI: 10.1016/j.iedeen.2017.12.001

Complete CSR report of hero motocorp. (2023, July 31). *The CSR Journal*. https://thecsrjournal.in/corporate-social-responsibility-complete-csr-report-hero-motocorp/

Cordero, J., De Zúñiga, T. O., & Rueda, M. (2014). *Disability and corporate social responsibility reporting: An analysis comparing reporting practices of 40 selected multinational enterprises*. (Working Paper No. 8). https://www.ilo.org/wcmsp5/groups/public/---ed_emp/---ifp_skills/documents/publication/wcms_316814.pdf

CSR. Flipkart Foundation supports MITTI Cafe to catalyze mainstream inclusion, through skilling and sustainable livelihood opportunities for persons with disabilities. (2023, March 23). *The CSR Journal*. https://thecsrjournal.in/corporate-social-responsibility-csr-news-flipkart-foundation-supports-mitti-cafe-to-catalyze-mainstream-inclusion-through-skilling-and-sustainable-livelihood-opportunities-for-persons-with-disabilitie/

CSR. Flipkart Foundation supports Mitti Cafe to train and employ persons with disabilities. (2023, March 24). *India CSR*. https://indiacsr.in/csr-flipkart-foundation-supports-mitti-cafe-to-train-and-employ-persons-with-disabilities/

De Beco, G. (2020). Intersectionality and disability in international human rights law. *International Journal of Human Rights*, 24(5), 593–614. DOI: 10.1080/13642987.2019.1661241

De Beco, G. (2021). Theoretical background: The inclusion of disabled people. In De Beco, G. (Ed.), *Disability in International Human Rights Law* (pp. 46–63). Oxford University Press. DOI: 10.1093/oso/9780198824503.003.0004

Fasciglione, M. (2015). Corporate social responsibility and the right to employment of persons with disabilities. In Della Fina, V., & Cera, R. (Eds.), *Protecting the Rights of People with Autism in the Fields of Education and Employment: International, European and National Perspectives* (pp. 171–193). Springer International Publishing. DOI: 10.1007/978-3-319-13791-9_7

Flipkart Foundation. (n.d.). Flipkart Foundation supports MITTI Cafe to catalyze mainstream inclusion, through skilling and sustainable livelihood opportunities for persons with disabilities. https://storiesflistgv2.blob.core.windows.net/stories/2023/03/Flipkart-Foundation-X-Mitti-Cafe-21032023.pdf

Gautam, R., & Singh, A. (2010). Corporate Social Responsibility Practices in India: A Study of Top 500 Companies. *Global Business and Management Research*, 2(1), 41–56.

Ghose, A., Kochher, H. S., & Ali, S. M. A. (2024). Towards equity and inclusion: Legal exploration for inclusive business practices integrating CSR and disability rights in India. In Pucelj, M., & Bohinc, R. (Eds.), Advances in Human and Social Aspects of Technology. DOI: 10.4018/979-8-3693-2325-0.ch006

Gould, R., Harris, S. P., Mullin, C., & Jones, R. (2020). Disability, diversity, and corporate social responsibility: Learning from recognized leaders in inclusion. *Journal of Vocational Rehabilitation*, 52(1), 29–42. DOI: 10.3233/JVR-191058

Harshith, K. N. (2022, August 2). Hero Motocorp partners with CRPF to present retro fitted scooters to the specially-abled ex-personnel. *The Times of India*. https://timesofindia.indiatimes.com/auto/bikes/hero-motocorp-partners-with-crpf-to-present-retro-fitted-scooters-to-the-specially-abled-ex-personnel/articleshow/93294989.cms?from=mdr

Indian Oil. (n.d.). Corporate Social Responsibility Reaching out, Touching Lives. https://iocl.com/uploads/IndianOil_CSR_in_Aspirational_Districts.pdf

Jumde, A. (2021). The law on CSR in India: An analysis of its compliance by companies through corporate disclosures. *Journal of Corporate Law Studies*, 21(1), 253–282. DOI: 10.1080/14735970.2020.1834265

Karin, M., & Bollinger, L. (2020). Disability rights: past, present, and future: roadmap for disability rights. *University of the District of Columbia David A.Clarke School of Law Review*, 23(1), 1–22.

Kwan, C. K. (2020). Socially responsible human resource practices to improve the employability of people with disabilities. *Corporate Social Responsibility and Environmental Management*, 27(1), 1–8. DOI: 10.1002/csr.1768

Lejeune, A., & Ringelheim, J. (2019). Workers with disabilities between legal changes and persisting exclusion: How contradictory rights shape legal mobilization. *Law & Society Review*, 53(4), 983–1015. DOI: 10.1111/lasr.12439

Mahindra Rise. (n.d.). *Empowered to rise: Smart academies*. https://www.mahindra.com/blogs/en/empowered-to-rise-smart-academies

Mitra, N., & Chatterjee, B. (2020). India's contribution to the sustainable development goals (SDGs) with respect to the CSR mandate in the Companies Act, 2013. In Idowu, S. O., Schmidpeter, R., & Zu, L. (Eds.), *The Future of the UN Sustainable Development Goals* (pp. 383–396). Springer International Publishing. DOI: 10.1007/978-3-030-21154-7_19

Nehanaayar. (2023, September 27). Empowerment through education with Tech Mahindra Foundation. *Medium*. https://techmahindr.medium.com/empowerment-through-education-with-tech-mahindra-foundation-b41ff38d44d5

Nussbaum, M. (2007). *Frontiers of Justice: Disability, Nationality, Species Membership*. The Belknap Press., DOI: 10.2307/j.ctv1c7zftw

Oware, K. M. (2023). Mandatory CSR reporting and disability employment. Evidence from India. *Cogent Business & Management.Taylor & Francis Online*, 10(2), 1–15.

Pugh, K. J. (2000). Disability rights. *Human Rights (Chicago, Ill.)*, 27(1), 2–2.

Pullum, M. E. (2005). Public Employment: ADA, Disability. *Stetson Law Review*, 34(3), 941–964.

Rudolph, K. (2022). Comparative disability policy in employment. *Emory International Law Review*, 36(4), 833–863.

Sandel, M. (1998). *Liberalism and the Limits of Justice*. Cambridge University Press., DOI: 10.1017/CBO9780511810152

Saul, B. (2010). Waiting for Dignity in Australia: Migrant Rights to Social Security and Disability Support under International Human Rights Law. *UCL Human Rights Review*, 3, 72–108.

SBI Foundation launches 'dialogue in the dark' centre in Mumbai. (2022, October 1). *The Print*. https://theprint.in/ani-press-releases/sbi-foundation-launches-dialogue-in-the-dark-centre-in-mumbai/1150671/

SBI Foundation launches 'dialogue in the dark' centre in Mumbai. (2022, October 1). *The Times of India*. https://timesofindia.indiatimes.com/sbi-foundation-launches-dialogue-in-the-dark-centre-in-mumbai/articleshow/94580643.cms?from=mdr

Sen, A. (1992). *Inequality Re-examined*. Clarendon Press.

Shaw, J., Wickenden, M., Thompson, S., & Mader, P. (2022). Achieving disability inclusive employment – Are the current approaches deep enough? *Journal of International Development*, 34(5), 942–963. DOI: 10.1002/jid.3692

Stein, M. A., & Bantekas, I. (2021). Including disability in business and human rights discourse and corporate practice. *Business and Human Rights Journal*, 6(3), 490–513. DOI: 10.1017/bhj.2021.13

Stein, M. A., & Stein, P. J. S. (2007). Beyond disability civil rights. *The Hastings Law Journal*, 58, 1203–1226.

Tilt, C. A. (2016). Corporate social responsibility research: The importance of context. *International Journal of Corporate Social Responsibility*, 1(1), 2. DOI: 10.1186/s40991-016-0003-7

Truter, L. (1996). Disability rights: Employment developments in Britain. *Journal of South African Law*, 1996(4), 658–668.

Weber, M. C. (2009). Disability rights, disability discrimination, and social insurance. *Georgia State University Law Review*, 25(3), 575–606.

Weber, M. C. (2011). Disability rights, welfare law. *Cardozo Law Review*, 32(6), 2483–2532.

Wohl, A. (2014). Poverty, employment, and disability: the next great civil rights battle. *Human Rights Magazine, 40*(3). https://www.americanbar.org/groups/crsj/publications/human_rights_magazine_home/2014_vol_40/vol_40_no_3_poverty/poverty_employment_disability/

Wong, S. I. (2009). Duties of Justice to Citizens With Cognitive Disabilities. *Metaphilosophy*, 40(3/4), 382–401. DOI: 10.1111/j.1467-9973.2009.01604.x

KEY TERMS AND DEFINITIONS

Corporate Social Responsibility: Corporate Social Responsibility (CSR) refers to the intentional measures taken by firms as part of their corporate governance to guarantee that their operations are carried out in an ethical way and have a good impact on society.

Disability Rights: Promoting the rights of persons with disabilities and facilitating their inclusion in society, in various roles such as leaders, workers, providers, and consumers, yields a threefold advantage: it enhances the well-being of individuals with disabilities, it boosts the performance of enterprises, and it contributes to the overall welfare of society.

Equal Employment Opportunity: Employment Equal Opportunity refers to the principle of providing equal chances for individuals within an organization to attain or sustain equitable employment. The fundamental concept of EEO (Equal Employment Opportunity) is that all workers should get equitable treatment in various employment choices, including hiring, promotion, termination, salary, and others.

Human Rights: Human rights are a collection of ideas that recognize and protect every person's inherent value and dignity. Human rights govern the conduct and relationships of people in society, including their contacts with the State and the associated obligations that the State has towards them.

Inclusive Business Practice: Inclusion refers to the cultural environment where a diverse group of individuals may feel at ease and self-assured to express their true selves and operate in a manner that aligns with their preferences while effectively meeting your company's or service's requ. By promoting inclusion, we can guarantee that every individual is recognized for their worth and significantly contributes to the overall value.

Chapter 13
Corporate Social Responsibility (CSR) of Pharmaceutical Companies:
Evidence From Antibiotic Resistance Tackling Strategies in Bangladesh

Md. Golam Rabbani
University of Rajshahi, Bangladesh

Asif All Mahmud Akash
http://orcid.org/0009-0002-6167-2938
University of Rajshahi, Bangladesh

ABSTRACT

Apart from its defined contribution, the role of CSR in addressing health-related issues is not without criticisms. It is given critical weight, particularly about the CSR practices led by the pharmaceutical companies owing to its outright linkage with health outcomes. Thus, shedding light on pharmaceutical companies involved in dealing with a major public health threat associated with antibiotic resistance (ABR) through some forms of CSR practice is of greater importance. This chapter explores CSR practice backed by the evidence from ABR tackling strategies in Bangladesh. Recruiting a case study method, this chapter resorts to some broader theoretical underpinnings of CSR. Primary findings indicate that while CSR is viewed as a self-regulatory mechanism is inadequate in the ground reality. Pharmaceutical

DOI: 10.4018/979-8-3693-5991-4.ch013

companies maintaining legal and ethical standards in antibiotic promotion fall short. Such unethical practices largely became visible with participants reporting taking antibiotics indiscriminately. It worsens due to the lax drug regulation at the field- level in Bangladesh.

1. INTRODUCTION

The pharmaceutical industry is a major contributor to both the global and national economies. It plays a critical role in the economy, shaping health outcomes worldwide. In 2017, the global pharmaceutical industry accounted for 532 billion U.S. dollars of the world's Gross Domestic Product (GDP) (Ostwald et al., 2020, p.7). That same year, the industry employed over 74.5 million workers (IFPMA, 2022, p.16). Additionally, the pharmaceutical sector represented 8% of the global health economy in 2014 (Ostwald et al., 2020, p.4). Given this context, the economic impact of the pharmaceutical sector is undeniably significant. Progress in the health sector would be hard to imagine without the contributions of the pharmaceutical industry. In addition, the pharmaceutical industry plays a critical role in innovating new drugs and producing and distributing them globally to ensure sustainable access to essential medications for people from diverse socio-economic backgrounds. However, the industry faces contention for prioritizing profit maximization while neglecting health and environmental concerns, engaging in unethical production and promotion practices, and perpetuating unequal distribution. It is criticized for failing to adequately promote the core values of corporate social responsibility (CSR) in the health sector (Droppert & Bennett, 2015; Yıldırım & Dinçer, 2020; Bae et al., 2022).

CSR is an old age issue. Researchers have tried to analyze the relationship between religious philosophy and business principles. The focus of their discussion descends to a sense of responsibility of the business enterprises and their ethical practices for ensuring the betterment of the wider society. Accordingly, CSR is mentioned in basic texts of Hinduism, Christianity, and Islam (Zinkin & Williams, 2006; Epstein, 2002; Muniapan, 2014; Amer, 2023). Historical explorations inform that the CSR practice of South Asia, more specifically in ancient India was founded more than 50 centuries ago (Muniapan, 2014, p.19). This ancient concept has got a mature shape after more than two centuries long theoretical and real life-centered practices (Yu & Hu, 2014). CSR initiatives mostly are adopted to solve social problems and bring positive social changes. It is a much-talked issue in academia, more specifically in business management and its allied disciplines. It is mentioned at the beginning of this chapter that the pharmaceutical industry is a dynamic global business player.

Therefore, its CSR initiatives are essential in addressing the challenges within the health sector.

Relying on CSR-related pieces of literature coming out in Scopus from 2021 to 2024, Gallo and Serluca (2024) conducted a systematic review "*to investigate the integration of economic and social goals within a business framework, focusing on how corporate social responsibility can align with sustainable competitive advantage*" (Gallo & Serluca, 2024, p.196). The review identified that outcome and the strategies of CSR are linked to "corporate contexts and stakeholder needs". It also highlighted that renewed attention is needed to explore the financial impact of CSR on business enterprises while huge attention is given to maintaining environmental and social compliance. Concerns of Gallo and Serluca (2024) are partially addressed by another systematic review, such as Mostepaniuk et al., (2022). It underscored that there is a positive relationship between CSR initiatives and the attainment of sustainable development. However, the relationship depends on some social, public policy, organizational (internal issues of an enterprise), and market-related issues (Mostepaniuk et al., 2022). Thus, contemporary scholarships on CSR inform us that the meanings of CSR initiatives vary from context to context. One of the key targets of CSR initiatives, at least in terms of policy commitment, is improving the health of stakeholders, as 'health' is one of the foundational pillars of society. Low et al., (2014) edited a book titled *Corporate Social Responsibility in Asia: Practice and Experience*, which includes chapters that address various aspects of CSR. While the chapters cover different dimensions of CSR, a common theme is the promotion of quality healthcare and the importance of addressing social determinants of health. Antimicrobial resistance (AMR), including antibiotic resistance (ABR), is a complex and pressing issue, often referred to as a 'future pandemic' and a current public health threat, attributing to seven million global deaths annually (Otaigbe & Elikwu, 2023, p.1). As key stakeholders in the health sector, pharmaceutical companies are expected to play a pivotal role in addressing this challenge. CSR initiatives in the pharmaceutical industry could be viewed as one potential avenue for tackling this public health threat.

Contemporary scholarship has evaluated the CSR activities of the pharmaceutical industry in promoting healthcare services to its stakeholders. However, much of this research approaches CSR from a narrow perspective, focusing on issues such as pricing, product licensing, voluntary initiatives by multinational companies, and economic contributions (for more details, see Droppert and Bennett, 2015). To the best of our knowledge, there is a lack of studies that examine the activities of pharmaceutical companies through the broader lens of CSR, which emphasizes a firm's commitment to maximizing the benefits for society and its stakeholders (Yu & Hu, 2014; Muniapan, 2014). Mitema (2010) is one of the few who highlighted those weaknesses in the health system—such as the inadequate capacity of state-led regulatory agencies and a lack of awareness about antibiotic resistance—contribute to the unethical sale and irrational use of antibiotics, both of which are linked to AMR. A similar situation has been observed in Bangladesh (Bepari et al., 2023). Furthermore, it is rare to find studies that focus on the role of CSR efforts in addressing ABR-related challenges at the grassroots or 'field level' led by pharmaceutical companies in Bangladesh. Against this backdrop, this chapter evaluates the CSR initiatives of pharmaceutical companies in Bangladesh, where ABR is a growing concern (see Box 1), the capacity of regulatory agencies is weak (Hoque et al., 2020), and the pharmaceutical sector is vibrant (Bonna et al., 2022). Yet, CSR practices remain underdeveloped and are not widely adopted (Kabir & Chowdhury, 2023). Bangladesh is considered a representative case for other developing countries that share similar healthcare and regulatory challenges, including weak antibiotic regulation, low awareness of AMR, and the rapid growth of pharmaceutical companies. To achieve the objective of this study, a conceptual framework has been developed based on the theoretical foundations of CSR.

2. THEORIES AND CONCEPTUAL FRAMEWORK

Yu and Hu (2014) mentioned that the concept of CSR has a mature shape by offering clearer definitions that has been found as a result of two centuries long theoretical and real life-centered practices. Our writing disagrees with Yu and Hu (2014)'s understating. It shows different opinions because existing theories of CSR do not consider the recent social changes (such as rapid globalization of business enterprises, and technology-mediated social changes) put a question mark on the definitions of stakeholder (Awa et al., 2024), societal, ethical and moral (Knox, 2020, professional (Brès et al., 2019) perspectives. Considering this theoretical concern, this writing presents a short description of the theoretical understanding of CSR. Relying on the theoretical understating of CSR, a conceptual framework has been offered to investigate the role of pharmaceutical companies in tackling problems stemming from ABR.

Scholarships explored the dynamics of CSR by applying different theoretical perspectives. Risi et el., (2022) shed light on the role of value-driven institutional perspectives in implementing CSR initiatives. This analysis offers how value-driven institutional initiatives influence CSR outcomes. Brammer et al., (2012) considered institutional analysis as "[...] *a promising avenue to explore how the boundaries between business and society are constructed in different ways* [...]" (Brammer et al., 2012, p.3). In determining the state of CSR and its impact on society or the lives of stakeholders, some institutional factors of business enterprises, society, government, and international regimes play a significant role (Brammer et al., 2012; Risi et al.,

2022). The connection or disconnection between business and society is very much linked to value-driven institutional decisions (Risi et.al, 2022). The institutional perspective of CSR relies on the core understanding of institutional theory that considers an organization as a sub-set of a society and influenced by dominating social norms and values (Zampone et al., 2023). Thus, it can be noted that Risi et.al (2022)'s value-driven institutional approach is not a new one. The understanding is deeply rooted in the learning of 'institutional theory'. The introductory section of this chapter describes how advocates of CSR trace the root of the philosophical understanding of CSR to the core understanding of religious texts or normative practices (Zinkin & Williams, 2006; Epstein, 2002; Muniapan,2014; Amer, 2024). Though it is argued that understanding CSR is influenced by religious norms and practices, "the literature in this field yields conflicting results" (Aaken & Buchner, 2020, p.917). Thus, institutional, value-driven institutional, and religious perspectives of CSR do not conclude how and to what extent the perspective individually or collectively resulted in the need of all stakeholders.

A good deal of scholarship defines CSR through the lens of stakeholder theory (Freeman et al., 2010). Advocates of this theory posit that "*CSR is obligatory and aims at higher responsiveness to stakeholders" (*cited in Awa et al., 2024, p.3). Stakeholder theory loosely defines the boundary of stakeholders and how the interests of stakeholders are measured and transmitted into practices. To solve this problem Awa et al., (2024) offer a list of stakeholders and they view CSR from a broader perspective. They define it as, "*CSR is a self-regulatory mechanism whereby an organization actively monitors society, the environment, global trends, ethical principles, and legal standards for compliance*" (Awa et al., 2024, p.5). This definition of CSR offers a broader framework for investigating the CSR activities of an enterprise.

First, CSR scholarship (Alavi et al., 2016, p.1121) mostly defines self-regulation as the "*frameworks for monitoring, codification, and certification of firm's compliance with different environmental, labor, human rights, and anticorruption standards*". Based on the given definition of 'self-regulation', this chapter investigates the role of pharmaceutical companies in tackling social problems, more specifically the CSR initiatives of selected pharmaceutical companies in tackling the ABR burden at the grass-root level of Bangladesh. More specifically, it focuses on how self-induced CSR practices of the companies consider the ABR tackling strategies.

Second, as per the understanding of Awa et al., (2024), CSR practices are supposed to include a state of legal compliance. In this regard, this chapter sheds light on to what extent the pharmaceutical industry of Bangladesh ensures compliance with legal provisions in managing ABR-related challenges at the grassroots level.

Third, monitoring the social problems considering both the local and global trends is considered an emerging dimension of CSR (Awa et al., 2024; Alavi et al., 2016). This dimension adds new issues with CSR knowledge breaking the traditional boundary of CSR of pharmaceutical companies where CSR was considered from a legal compliance perspective. Depending on the contemporary theoretical understanding, this chapter unveils how and to what extent the promotional activities of pharmaceutical companies are proactive in monitoring the irrational use of antibiotics and its impact on health.

Fourth, translating ethical principles into practices is found as the core element of CSR. Mostly, social, religious, and professional norms and values are found as the normative roots of ethical practices (Risi et al., 2022; Zampone et al., 2023). To explore the ethical part of CSR of pharmaceutical companies, this chapter stresses: i) incentives given to doctors to encourage antibiotic prescriptions, (ii) promotional activities and perception of medicine shop staff (iii) prescription monitoring by the pharmaceutical companies.

3. METHODOLOGICAL ISSUES

A descriptive and exploratory case study approach was adopted to achieve the objectives of the study. The exploratory method was chosen to gather information from selected pharmaceutical companies, as publicly available data is scarce in Bangladesh. Consequently, this chapter relied on websites, social media, and other publicly accessible information regarding antibiotic use and misuse in the country. Ten leading pharmaceutical companies in Bangladesh were selected for analysis (see Table 1). The case under consideration is the 'CSR activities of the companies to tackle ABR-related challenges in Bangladesh' (Yin, 1994).

The study relied on both primary and secondary data. Primary data were collected through key informant interviews (KII) with the district drug superintendent, focus group discussions (FGD), and semi-structured interviews. KII was conducted using predefined open-ended guidelines, while two FGDs were held with community members. Each FGD lasted approximately one hour and focused on exploring community perceptions of antibiotic availability and use. At the household level, semi-structured interviews were conducted with 50 respondents. These interviews included both closed and open-ended questions. In addition, 10 drug retailers and pharmacists were interviewed. Each semi-structured interview lasted, on average, about 30 minutes. In total, 61 respondents (excluding those in FGDs) from Rajshahi district, Bangladesh, were interviewed to achieve the study's objectives. Primary evidence was organized thematically, and an argumentative link between the primary findings and relevant theories was established in the discussion of the results.

Secondary data were gathered by consulting policy documents, grey literature, scholarly articles, and the websites of relevant stakeholders.

4. HEALTHCARE NEEDS, EMINENT GROWTH OF PHARMACEUTICAL INDUSTRY, AND ABR IN BANGLADESH

Bangladesh is a developing country in South Asia that has achieved several international development goals, including the Millennium Development Goals (MDGs), despite facing challenges related to transparency and accountability. The country frequently encounters climate change-induced disasters but has successfully reduced its poverty rate. However, these changes may not be sustainable due to social disparities, the institutionalization of corruption, the threats posed by climate change, and the social changes brought about by COVID-19. Within this socio-economic context, approximately 170 million people in Bangladesh are receiving healthcare services (BBS, 2023).

Health is recognized as a basic human right globally by international policies. These policy documents view health as an instrument of welfare, highlighting the interrelatedness of health, human rights, and development (Ahmed, 2022). In addition to being a signatory to various international health treaties, covenants, and declarations, Bangladesh has incorporated specific provisions for health improvement in its Constitution. Article 15(1) of the Constitution of the People's Republic of Bangladesh declares medical care to be a basic human necessity. Therefore, ensuring the affordability and accessibility of medicinal drugs is of great importance, and the pharmaceutical industry plays a key role in this regard.

Over the years, the pharmaceutical sector in Bangladesh has demonstrated significant growth. From 2014 to 2018, the sector recorded an impressive average annual growth rate of 8.3% (Pradhan & Jubayer, 2021). Previously, multinational companies dominated the pharmaceutical sector in Bangladesh. Before 1971, about 60-70% of drugs were collected from former West Pakistan (now Pakistan), as most pharmaceutical industries were located there (cited in Murshid and Haque, 2019, p.105). The Government of Bangladesh faced enormous challenges in ensuring the accessibility and availability of essential medicines for its population. Currently, 273 local companies meet 98% of the country's drug demand. In addition to fulfilling domestic needs, Bangladeshi pharmaceuticals are exported to 147 countries, significantly contributing to the national economy through foreign currency earnings (Munir, 2023).

However, the rapid growth of the pharmaceutical industry and the resulting increased access to drugs have raised public health concerns. This issue is particularly evident in the rising consumption of antimicrobial drugs, including antibiotics, leading to antibiotic resistance (ABR). A recent global survey involving 76 countries, including Bangladesh, found a significant 65% increase in antibiotic use. The rise in antibiotic consumption, especially in low and middle-income countries (LMICs), accounted for a 35% increase in the overall consumption rate (cited in Hossain et al., 2023, p.2). Consequently, the increased consumption of antibiotics has inevitably contributed to the growth of drug-resistant bacteria in these countries, posing a serious threat to public health. Bangladesh is no exception. We would like to mention some recent trade of AMR growth in Bangladesh (see Box: 1) to underscore its alarming state.

Box 1: State of AMR in Bangladesh

- The resistance to five of the most critical medications recommended by the World Health Organization (WHO) has been on the rise in Bangladesh year after year.
- In Bangladesh, a minimum of 10 types of bacteria have developed increased resistance to 17 vital antibiotics used to treat patients with various infectious diseases.
- According to data from the World Health Organization, nearly 90% of patients in Bangladesh show resistance to ciprofloxacin, a prominent antibiotic, in contrast to only 11.5% of patients in the United Kingdom.
- Approximately 70% of fatalities in Bangladesh's Intensive Care Units (ICUs) are attributed to Antimicrobial Resistance (AMR).
- Research has identified elevated levels of antibiotic-resistant bacterial infections in children under the age of 5 with pneumonia in Bangladesh.
- Within the Intensive Care Unit (ICU) at BSMMU, 52% of admitted patients exhibit resistance to multiple antibiotics, and this figure is steadily increasing.
- Around 40% of adults aged 15 and above in Bangladesh display resistance to at least three different antibiotics, and 70% of the population demonstrates resistance to at least one antibiotic.

Source: One Health Trust (2018); Kingsland (2021); Jamil (2022); Islam (2023)

Thus, in Bangladesh, an unbidden growth of ABR has become evident with recent trends. An orchestrated effort supposedly could be expensed to fight the ABR. However, the regulatory capacities of the national drug regulatory authority are not sufficient in this regard. As a result, the sale and dispensing of antibiotics are found to be largely unregulated in Bangladesh (Orubu et al. 2021; Saha & Promite, 2017; Johora & Rahman, 2018). However, because of health sector weakness and unfavorable social determinants of health, people rely on the informal healthcare sector composed of unqualified healthcare providers and unqualified drug dispensers or retailers. This sector is a well-known source of non-prescription and over-the-counter (OTC) antibiotics. In this situation, CSR practices of the pharmaceutical industry might be an avenue to tackle the antibiotic resistance-related challenges in Bangladesh.

5. IMPERATIVE OF CSR PRACTICE TO DEAL WITH ABR

Responding to the concurrent threats posed by antibiotic resistance (ABR) and addressing the foreseeable consequences has garnered global attention. International and regional commitments to tackle ABR-related threats have been prioritized in various policy interventions and strategies. The WHO has introduced a Global Action Plan (GAP) on AMR, and many countries have formulated National Action Plans (NAPs) based on this framework, which are considered blueprints for combating AMR (Patel et al., 2023). The engagement of relevant stakeholders is crucial for the effective implementation of these actions, with the pharmaceutical industry playing a key role. The availability of essential medicines, including antibiotics, largely depends on the flourishing of the pharmaceutical sector. However, the compliance of pharmaceutical companies with regulations regarding the production and distribution of medicines like antibiotics significantly influences public health outcomes.

A critical question remains regarding the extent to which the CSR practices of pharmaceutical companies address the challenges of ABR and impact health outcomes in low and middle-income countries (LMICs). Health is intrinsically linked to social and economic progress, and the CSR initiatives of the pharmaceutical industry have long been recognized as essential for promoting social, economic, and environmental advancement. It has been argued that *"pharmaceutical companies should be more sensitive to CSR than other industries, and to gain social recognition, they must effectively cooperate to respond to social, economic, and environmental obligations"* (Bae et al., 2022, p.3). Thus, CSR initiatives within the pharmaceutical industry hold manifold importance.

As discussed in the theoretical section of this chapter, this writing is grounded in the works of Awa et al. (2024) and other scholars, exploring the self-regulatory mechanisms of pharmaceutical companies at the field level. CSR through self-regulatory mechanisms is particularly critical in Bangladesh for several specific reasons. First, the pharmaceutical industry is more vibrant than the regulatory authority. Therefore, compliance with legal provisions through the initiatives of pharmaceutical companies themselves is an important aspect of CSR that can significantly contribute to tackling antibiotic resistance (ABR) at the grassroots level in Bangladesh. Second, as part of their CSR responsibilities, pharmaceutical companies are expected to monitor the state of ABR and the factors contributing to its increasing prevalence. Third, promoting ethical practices is considered a cornerstone of CSR initiatives. The promotional activities of pharmaceutical companies should prioritize ethical principles, as unethical promotional practices have been identified as contributing factors to the rising risk of ABR at the grassroots level in Bangladesh.

6. COMPLIANCE WITH LEGAL PROVISIONS: UNDERSTANDING FROM A CSR PERSPECTIVE

Pharmaceutical companies often engage in promotional activities to boost the market share of their products. The World Health Organization (WHO) established the Ethical Criteria for Medicinal Drug Promotion (ECMDP) in 1988. This guide is intended to help countries shape their regulations and practices regarding medicinal drugs. The primary goal of these ethical criteria is to enhance healthcare by promoting the sensible use of medicinal drugs. Different parts of the world and societies may have varying interpretations of what is considered ethical. The key concern everywhere is determining what constitutes proper behavior. Ethical criteria for drug promotion should establish a basis for appropriate conduct in promoting medicinal drugs, aligning with principles of truthfulness and righteousness. These criteria are not mandatory by law, but governments and other groups may choose to create legislation or adopt measures based on them. Oversight and enforcement of these standards should be carried out by the respective bodies implementing them (Johora & Rahman, 2018).

Table 1. Key contents of Ethical Criteria for Medicinal Drug Promotion (ECMDP)

Promotion	• Drug promotion should only be carried out for drugs that are legally available in the country. • Promotion should adhere to national health policies and comply with national regulations and voluntary standards where applicable. • Promotional material should be truthful, reliable, and not contain misleading statements.
Advertising	• Advertisements to healthcare professionals must align with approved scientific data and contain essential product information. • Advertisements to the general public should provide information for rational drug decisions, avoid exploiting health concerns, and not generally be allowed for prescription drugs.
Medical Representative	• Medical representatives should have an appropriate educational background, training, medical knowledge, and integrity. • They must provide complete and unbiased information about products and be responsible for their statements and activities. • Employers are responsible for training and conduct. Incentives should not be based directly on sales volume to prevent over-promotion.

[Ethical Criteria for Medicinal Drug Promotion (WHO, 1988)]

By following these ethical standards, pharmaceutical companies and healthcare industry stakeholders are obliged to showcase their dedication to conducting responsible drug promotion. This commitment guarantees that healthcare professionals and the general public receive truthful and impartial information about medicinal drugs. Failure to adhere to these standards can lead to regulatory measures and legal repercussions.

Primarily relying on the ECMDP and IFPMA, CPMP has been introduced as a crucial instrument for ensuring the rational use of medicines in Bangladesh. It places responsibility on pharmaceutical manufacturers to implement the code's principles. The code expects doctors and pharmacists to adhere to professional standards. The main objective of the Code of Pharmaceutical Marketing Practices is to support and encourage the improvement of health care through the rational use of medicinal substances. The Code serves as a form of self-regulation and is a request directed towards pharmaceutical makers, distributors, the promotion sector, healthcare professionals engaged in prescribing and distributing drugs, universities, educational institutions, professional groups, patient and consumer organizations, media professionals (including those overseeing medical publications), and the public.

According to Johora and Rahman (2018), In Bangladesh, the CPMP is the primary regulatory document addressing pharmaceutical promotion. The authors suggested that besides the CPMP, other regulatory documents in Bangladesh, such as the NDP, Drug Control Ordinance, and Consumer Protection Act, do not cover essential aspects related to promotion such as:

- Form of promotion
- Monitoring of promotion
- Interpretation and implementation procedure for regulation of promotion

  Johora and Rahman (2018) in their study stated that CPMR suffers from certain loopholes:

- Absence of clearly defined ethical and legal prohibitions
- Absence of specific legal provisions for violations
- Absence of clearly defined authority

In addition, non-compliance with the defined rules and regulations is prevalent among these entities. For instance, two official orders are mentioned below as issued by the DGDA:

- Letter no-*DGDA/miscellaneous/03/03/425* issued by the director general of DGDA to the Chair of BCDS on May 31, 2020. Since OTC drugs were reported to be sold without the prescriptions of registered physicians to treat COVID-19-related illnesses, the DGDA urged BCDS to take the initiative and inform its members of society regarding the concern (DGDA, 2020).
- DGDA also issued an official order *(DGDA/Law/2019/18)* on February 4, 2020, for the concerned officials of the drug administration to take required initiatives against the retail sale of antibiotics without the prescriptions of

drug-registered physicians. The order mentioned taking legal steps based on the Drug Act 1940 (DGDA, 2020).

Some previous studies have uncovered that pharmaceutical companies often do not exhibit a positive attitude toward self-compliance with legal provisions when the capacity of regulatory agencies is weak (Matin et al., 2020; Rousham et al., 2019). At times, field-level officers face the burden of "selling targets", which compels them to overlook compliance with legal provisions. A report from a newspaper describes the situation of non-compliance as follows.

Pharmaceutical companies often set unattainable sales targets for their representatives, knowing full well the pressure it exerts on them [...]. The stress and fear of these repercussions drive representatives to cut corners, engage in unethical practices, and prioritize sales over patient welfare (Mamun, 2024).

This strategy of pharmaceutical companies is linked to ABR. Promotional activities and the influence of 'medical representatives' act as the influencing factors of irrational sales and use of antibiotics. As per the research, '*the influence of pharmaceutical representatives and advertisers contribute to inappropriate sales of antibiotics*' (Matin et al., 2020, p.5.).

The evidence noted above shows that the profit maximization policy of the pharmaceutical industry often ignores self-compliance with legal provisions. Additionally, target-oriented promotional practices can trigger unethical behavior. This profit maximization approach encourages companies to overlook social problems, such as the irrational production and distribution of antibiotics, framing antibiotic sales as a profitable option while disregarding the health impacts associated with the irrational use of these medications.

7. MONITORING OF ABR-RELATED CHALLENGES

Pharmaceutical companies in Bangladesh are supposed to play a self-regulatory role in monitoring their antibiotic promotion and sale since monitoring business-related problems is considered a key activity of CSR initiatives. This chapter investigates how ABR-related business and social problems are recognized by pharmaceutical companies. Apart from this, this chapter includes how and to what extent pharmaceutical companies recognized the health impact of irrational promotion and sale of antibiotics.

7.1 Recognition of ABR as Health and Social Problems

It has been mentioned earlier that the state of antibiotic resistance in Bangladesh is alarming. Considering this situation, pharmaceutical companies should be rational and ethical in promoting antibiotics. The state of the sale of antibiotics indicates that antibiotic promotion ignores the present state of antibiotic availability. A recent investigation stated the share of antibiotics in the market as,

Share of 'acidity'-related accounted for more than 13 percent of the total marketed drugs. In the case of antibiotics, this rate is more than 6 percent. After acidity, antibiotics are the most sold diabetes drugs in the country. The share of this drug used in the form of injection is 3.5 percent of the total market. Thus, acidity, antibiotics, and diabetes collectively represent about 23 percent of the total sold drugs in the country [Translated from The Daily Bonikbatra[1], January 3, 2023].

Why do antibiotics remain at the top of the sales list? First, selling antibiotics is considered profitable. One seller mentioned, "*We find antibiotic sales to be a profitable product*" (Interview, 2023). A similar observation was reported in an investigation by a national English daily in Bangladesh. According to the investigation, a drug shop owner stated, "Since antibiotics work better and are more profitable, we sometimes suggest them" (Sujan, 2020). Second, the general population in Bangladesh tends to believe that more expensive antibiotics are more effective. This perception, coupled with higher profit margins, contributes to the popularity of antibiotics (Matin et al., 2020).

Pharmaceutical companies are expected to recognize issues related to ABR. To investigate these issues, the websites of the top ten pharmaceutical companies in Bangladesh (as identified by Awal & Saidy, 2021) were reviewed. More specifically, this review explores the role of these selected companies in addressing ABR as part of their CSR practices. Table 2 highlights the CSR activities of some dominant pharmaceutical companies. With increased production, distribution, and importation of drugs, these companies significantly contribute to the economic landscape of Bangladesh. It is also desirable for larger companies to carry out their CSR initiatives more effectively to benefit the wider society. When it comes to combating ABR, CSR plays a critical role, as it is linked to the well-being of the population.

Table 2. CSR activities of selected pharmaceutical companies

Name of the Company	CSR Activities	Focus on AMR
Square Pharmaceuticals Ltd	The company claimed the CSR initiatives include some social issues (for more details please refer: www .squarepharma.com.bd	The company published an AMR awareness poster on World AMR Awareness Week 2023
Opsonin Pharmaceuticals Ltd	The CSR focus of the company: Increase health awareness; individual and social health care and emphasis on preventive health care. (www.opsonin-pharma.com/)	While promoting a herbal product the company recognized the issue of AMR.
Incepta Pharmaceuticals Ltd.	This company mentioned that it distributed 5% of the company profit among the employees. However, it takes necessary steps to operate day-care centers. (www.inceptapharma.com)	The company highlighted its integrity and honesty to ensure compliance with ethical and policy issues.
Aristopharma Ltd.	It performs CSR through a set of social activities. For instance, bearing the expenses of poor patients, donating free medicines to the vulnerable strata of society, and the like. (www.aristopharma.com)	Addressing ABR as a major threat to human health in Bangladesh, this company introduced Zavicef. It is considered a better option for physicians to treat bacterial infections.
Beximco Pharmaceuticals Ltd.	Building a sustainable society and meeting the evolving needs of the population are the core CSR philosophy of this company. It does so through working together with non-profit organizations, supporting youth-based organizations, assisting AIDS patients with drugs, and so on. (www.beximcopharma.com)	Introduced a revolutionary antibiotic Lefamulin to treat community-acquired bacterial pneumonia Mulina.
Healthcare Pharmaceuticals Ltd.	To ensure people live a healthy life, the CSR of this company includes addressing healthcare needs, infrastructural development, effective agricultural farming, and the like. (www.hplbd.com)	No certain activities relating to AMR containment are found.
ACME Laboratories Ltd	As a part of CSR activities, this company claims commitment attention in three major areas including employees, society, and the environment. (www.acmeglobal.com)	Under the One Health banner, carried out AMR awareness campaigns with, and partnered with animal health companies to collectively fight against AMR in Bangladesh.
Renata Limited	Under CSR activities, this company puts major emphasis on environmental activism and bioequivalent products. (renata-ltd.com)	No certain activities relating to AMR containment are found.

continued on following page

Table 2. Continued

Name of the Company	CSR Activities	Focus on AMR
Eskayef Bangladesh Ltd.	No certain section of CSR is found on its website.	No certain activities relating to AMR containment are found.
ACI Ltd.	This company is involved in CSR activities of different kinds. For instance, village development, ensuring safe drinking water, skill development, and the like. (www.aci-bd.com)	No certain activities relating to AMR containment are found.

[Websites and social media of relevant stakeholders]

As mentioned earlier this chapter views the CSR of pharmaceutical companies as a self-regulatory mechanism aimed at helping these companies better monitor their practices and meet ethical and legal standards in antibiotic production and distribution. However, a review of the CSR activities of pharmaceutical companies reveals that they often lack focus on ensuring AMR (antimicrobial resistance) initiatives as part of their activities. While most companies showcase their CSR efforts on their respective websites, more detailed actions regarding AMR remain ambiguous. Some companies, such as ACME, Beximco, Square, and Aristopharma, have been found to engage in AMR-focused interventions as part of their CSR activities.

7.2 Monitoring the Health Impact: Focus on ABR

Driven by limited healthcare access and financial constraints patients are involved in self-care or taking advice from the informal sector. They tend to use antibiotics except under the supervision of healthcare experts. Patients seek healthcare from informal sectors (See Table 3). Primary data revealed that respondents (81.25%) mostly took antibiotics by following the advice of drug shop retailers. Self-medication with antibiotics was also found among the respondents. (50%).

Table 3. Sources of taking antibiotics in the last six months

Indicator/s	Response
Advice from local drug shops retailers (n=13)	81.25%
Village doctor (n=9)	69.21%
Self-medication (n=8)	50.0%
Registered physicians (n=6)	46.15%

[multiple responses counted]
Field Data (2023)

Qualitative data, however, expressed similar findings. FGD participants expressed that

The initial outbreak of COVID-19 was frightening for us. We were worried about what if we were infected by the virus. When we had minor illnesses like cough or mild fever, we used to take medicines like NAPA extra or antibiotics. More or less we all know about the efficacy of these medicines. Our family members often went nearer to drug shops where they bought these medicines (FGD, September 4, 2023).

As cited in the study by Bepari et al., (2023), approximately 62% of Bangladeshi people live in rural areas. The number of unqualified healthcare practitioners in rural areas outweighs the number of existing qualified healthcare practitioners in Bangladesh. Matin et al., (2020) also focused on antibiotic sales in rural Bangladesh. Dispensing of antibiotics without seeking a physician's prescription was largely found in the study. The authors claimed that misuse of antibiotics is largely triggered by rural drug dispensers. The injudicious use of antibiotics is prompted by self-medication practices among people in Bangladesh. Self-medication of antibiotics is highly prevalent in Bangladesh. Biswas et al., (2014) in their investigation found that out of 1300 participants, 26.69% experienced self-medication with antibiotics. Likewise, studies found that during the COVID-19 pandemic, self-medication behavior increased up to 88%. Self-medication for symptoms such as SARS-CoV-2 without doing a COVID-19 test was found to be widespread in Bangladesh during the pandemic period where ivermectin (77%) and azithromycin (54%) were the most commonly self-medicated medicines during the COVID-19 pandemic time (cited in Mahadi, 2021).

The irrational antibiotic is very much influenced by the promotional activities of the medical representatives and promotional documents. Primary data indicate that drug sellers act as the source of antibiotics. The earlier research identified that promotional sources of pharmaceutical industries acted as a source of the 'drug shop sellers' who mostly recommend antibiotics. The availability of antibiotics, people's inclination to antibiotics, and recommendations of the drug shop sellers are the dominant causes of the irrational use of antibiotics. Table 4 showcases, that out of 34 respondents who took medicines in the last six months, 47.06% of them took antibiotics. Whereas 38.24% of respondents did not take any antibiotic and 14.71% found that they were not sure about it. In a different research study on people's antibiotic usage habits, it was revealed that approximately 46.6% of the participants had used antibiotics in the preceding six months (Ahmed et al., 2020). The study also indicated that out of all the respondents, only 56.1% possessed knowledge about antibiotic resistance, while the remaining participants lacked awareness of antimicrobial resistance (AMR).

This writing also would like to disclose the state of antibiotic dosage completion behavior. Our field data uncovered that among 16 respondents, 56.25% of them completed the dosage of antibiotics. By turn, 43.75% of total respondents reported that they had not fulfilled the dosage. It is regarded as a risky behavior that triggers antibiotic resistance.

Table 4. Antibiotic taking history in the last six months

Issues	Indicator	Response
Antibiotic Taking History in the Last Six Months	Yes (n=16)	47.06%
	No (n=13)	38.24%
	Not sure (n=5)	14.71%
State of Complete of Dosage	Yes (n=9)	56.25%
	No (n=7)	43.75%

Field Data (2023)

Also, the first-hand qualitative data of this study revealed that the practice of incomplete antibiotic dosage is common among the respondents. They tend to cease the course when the symptoms start alleviating. A major share of the respondents has reported the same practice. One respondent opined:

We stop taking antibiotics when the symptoms are alleviated. Doctors advise to take the full course of antibiotics. However, the unit price of an antibiotic is high. Intending to save money, we usually cease the antibiotic course midway (FGD, September 4, 2023).

8. ETHICAL PERSPECTIVE OF CSR

Prominent pharmaceutical companies engage in aggressive marketing practices to establish a dominant presence in the pharmaceutical market. Medical representatives and field field-level promotional staff play a pivotal role in executing these strategies (Mohiuddin et al., 2015). Ahmed et al., (2020) in their study revealed that pharmaceutical firms tend to spend more on marketing activities. The same study found that among the selected firms, medical representatives are the most recruited number of staff (46%) among the other types of staff. A study by Unicomb et al. (2021) identified the behavioral patterns of Medical Representatives (MR) as significant contextual drivers influencing antibiotic sales, purchases, consumption, and promotion in Bangladesh. The study highlighted several practices observed among medical representatives:

- MRs offer incentives to doctors to encourage antibiotic prescriptions.
- Providing incentives to drug shop staff to boost antibiotic sales.
- Monitoring prescriptions and meeting monthly as part of their marketing strategies.

8.1 Incentives to Doctors to Encourage Antibiotic Prescriptions

Medical representatives establish communication channels with healthcare practitioners, with most of them receiving monthly targets to promote their companies' drugs. MRs provide registered physicians with information about the latest generation of antibiotics and related prescribing guidelines (Interview, 2023). Ahmed et al. (2020) in their study found that medical representatives (MRs) maintain regular visits to MBBS doctors in urban areas for pharmaceutical promotion, allowing physicians to gather information about various drugs. These MRs offer samples of different drug types to physicians. Physicians often yield to the influence of MRs, leading them to recommend medications from the MRs' companies to their patients. The physicians' commissions, which are tied to their agreements with MRs, increase as medication sales rise. Due to economic incentives, some physicians stray from their ethical standards and make unethical prescription decisions. It is not only pharmaceutical companies that benefit from what their medical representatives do. Doctors and hospitals ask pharmaceutical companies to support events like medical conferences or picnics for medical school students. The companies that respond positively with financial support get preference in the prescriptions. In 2018, five doctors from Bangabandhu Sheikh Mujib Medical University and Northern International Medical College studied the morality of the relationship between doctors and pharmaceutical companies. They found that companies reward doctors handsomely with financial support, trip allowances, workshop sponsorships, chamber decorations, medicine samples, and many other professional and non-professional gifts (Tanjim, 2019).

8.2 Promotional Activities and Perception of Medicine Shop Staff

MRs also offer antibiotic prescribing guidelines to drug sellers, even though this practice is not authorized (Nizame et al., 2021). The pharmaceutical companies mostly target the bigger medicine shops where most of the buyers go to buy medicine. In this regard an owner of a drug shop describes,

You can see my pharmacy is not spacious compared to the other pharmacies in this place. So, I never received any offer from the medical representatives. They know, that a smaller number of patients come to my shop to buy medicines. They usually target pharmacies where they can accrue profits (Interview, September 6, 2023).

This statement means that promotional activities are focused on profit maximization. However, the medical representatives provide information to the medicine sellers. Relying on their directions, medicine shop owners sell different types of medicine, including antibiotics. In this connection, medicine shop owners who are mostly known as "village doctors" would like to make a friendly relationship with medical representatives (Mohiuddin et al., 2015). This relationship promotes benefit-sharing opportunities. The list of benefits includes: "[...] *special discounts to sell a particular product, financial incentives, gift boxes, and invitations to attend commercial medical education sessions* (Matin, 2020, p.6).

A few drug sellers also found the practices harmful to the health system, including AMR. While interviewing a pharmacy owner (drug seller) about the promotional activities of pharmaceutical companies, he expressed his view in the following way:

Unless the company's rigorous promotional activities stop, the medical system won't develop in Bangladesh. Although the unit price of antibiotics is high, patients tend to buy antibiotics from their nearest pharmacies. For instance, the unit price of Zimax is 40 BDT. Patients take it initially. When they feel better, they do not complete the full dosage. I usually do not sell antibiotics without seeing prescriptions. But in many drug shops, antibiotics are sold indiscriminately. Since antibiotics are promoted as profitable drugs (Interview, September 6, 2023).

8.3 Monitoring Prescriptions

Pharmaceutical companies closely monitor the prescribing habits of these physicians to assess their prescription volumes. Mostly, assigned persons take pictures of prescriptions of patients immediately after they visit doctors' chambers. While talking with the assigned person about the ethical issue of this kind of photo taking, he mentioned that,

"This is my job. We are taking pictures with the consent of the concerned persons. [...] Most of the people of Bangladesh do not think about ethical practices. So, we do not bother about the ethical practices while we monitor the prescription (Interview, 2023)".

This kind of monitoring puts pressure on the ethical practices of physicians. Another study highlighted an MR's perception in the following way:

"When we visit a doctor, we check whether the doctor who agreed to prescribe our product did so...sometimes our company buys prescription survey data from other companies. We usually check the prescription from the patient...if our product is not prescribed, we keep reminding them through frequent visits..."(MR's Perception, Cited in Mohiuddin et al., 2015)

It can be assumed that because of this kind of pressure, including the intention to get benefits from the industry, the physicians prescribe the drug of the specific company ignoring the ethical issues.

9. DISCUSSION AND CONCLUSION

The role of pharmaceutical companies in boosting the economy is significant worldwide, including in Bangladesh. In terms of public health, these companies are expected to play a critical role in ensuring the health and environmental sectors in any geographical location, as they are key stakeholders in the health sector. CSR initiatives are one of the strategies that contribute to society through social enterprise. Theoretical discussions and practical issues related to CSR raise several concerns, and the CSR initiatives of pharmaceutical companies are connected to these concerns. First, contextual factors influence decisions regarding CSR practices, including those of specific enterprises.

Bangladesh is a country where pharmaceutical companies are dominant actors in the health and economic sector. It played a key role in improving health-related social indicators, such as access to medicine and generating huge employment opportunities (Islam et al., 2018). This sector is very often criticized for unethical promotion (Awal and Saidy, 2021; Mohiuddin, 2019, Mohiuddin et al., 2015). This writing attempted to explore CSR activities as part of self-regulation. Findings including primary and secondary data signify a distressed picture of CSR of pharmaceutical companies in tackling ABR in Bangladesh. It was noted earlier that CSR-led outcomes can be determined by the engagement and responsiveness of stakeholders. Also, it denotes the self-regulatory mechanism posed by the business enterprises that ensure legal and ethical compliance (Awa et al., 2024; Zhao, 2021; Parmer et al., 2016).

Our findings indicate that most of the pharmaceutical companies of Bangladesh are engaged in different kinds of social development-related activities which are known as corporate social responsibilities. However, the websites of the top ten selected pharmaceutical companies do not disclose the details of their CSR initiatives. The companies do not include the ABR-related challenges in the list of CSR initiatives. However, most of the companies recognized the problem of antibiotic resistance in Bangladesh. CSR initiatives of the pharmaceutical industry are not isolated from the broader society. Regarding the practices of CSR in Bangladesh, "[...] MNCs in Bangladesh are moving toward strategic CSR and away from the conventional altruistic (philanthropic) CSR (Roy and Quazi, 2021). This situation is not similar in national-level companies. The overall CSR practice of this country is regarded as "low". Less effective self-governance of corporate houses, lack of ethical practice, and poor level of stakeholder engagement are found as key factors behind the poor performance of CSR efforts (Hossain, 2021). This situation in Bangladesh is very much linked to the theoretical understanding of institutional theory. This means that both societal and enterprise-related norms and values influence CSR practices (Risi et al., 2022). Lack of stakeholder engagement is also found in this sector which is highlighted by the stakeholder theory (Freeman et al., 2010).

It has been mentioned earlier that the antibiotics regulation of the Government of Bangladesh is weak. The institutional weakness cannot be transformed into a strong regulatory organization within a very short time. On the contrary, the state of ABR and the risk factors of ABR are alarming in this country. Since the 'pharmaceutical industry' is one of the key stakeholders and well-equipped to deal with ABR-related challenges, then ethical promotional activities of the industry as a part of CSR might be an alternative option. The findings of this study uncovered that due to lack of government regulation, the MRs are engaged in some unethical practices:(i) prescription monitoring (ii) putting pressure on physicians or doctors to prescribe the drugs of a specific company & (iii) unethical and illegal benefit giving to registered doctors, medicine shop staffs and village doctors. The unethical practices promote illegal sales and promotions of antibiotics. Not only this research but earlier studies also highlighted those illegal pharmaceutical practices are closely linked to antibiotic resistance in Bangladesh (Olivier et al., 2010; Islam et al., 2019; Hoque et al., 2020). This practice is not only found in Bangladesh. A similar situation is found in Jordan. Altawalbeh et al., (2020) found that promotional activities of pharmaceutical companies influence the medicine prescribing practices of doctors in this country. Relying on review findings, Marmat et al., (2020) uncovered unethical practices of pharmaceutical companies are found both in Western and non-western country contexts but most of the studies are focused on Western context. The review highlighted that "*The organizational variables appeared to be the dominant cause of these ethical issues and unethical practices along with other determinants such as environmental and stakeholders*" (Marmat et al., 2020, p.367). Keeping resemblance with the findings of the review, this study would like to note that field-level staff of the pharmaceutical companies are aware of the unethical practices. They mostly perform their jobs to meet the policy decisions of pharmaceutical companies, such as meeting periodic targets. However, pharmaceutical companies do not give job security to the field-level staff that are linked to unethical practices. Thus, central-level policy decisions are connected to the state of ethical practices and lack of compliance with government rules or regulations at the field level. A good number of studies (Alssageer & Kowalski, 2013; Hsu et al., 2009; Murshid & Mohaidin, 2017), throughout the world found unethical practices of medical representatives.

To illustrate, pharmaceutical promotion reaches down to the grassroots levels in Bangladesh. Such promotion lacks ethical standards as it is manifested by the rapacious selling and purchasing of antibiotics among the selected respondents. The indiscriminate use of antibiotics that is prompted by rapid promotional activities became evident with 47.06% of respondents taking antibiotics. Among them, 50.0% of total respondents were involved in self-medication with antibiotics. Studies revealed that self-medication is highly prevalent in South Asian countries including Pakistan (61.2%), and Nepal (59.0%) (cited in Saha et al., 2023). One study conducted by Saha et al. (2023) found antibiotic self-medication based on previous prescriptions (68%) and local drug stores (51%) were high among the respondents in Bangladesh.

The monitoring role of the pharmaceutical industry is compromised by its profit motive. It is manifested by the economic contribution made by the pharmaceutical companies. Thus, it won't be an overstatement that economic success often supersedes health concerns in the context of Bangladesh. Meanwhile, health system-induced factors and socioeconomic backgrounds of people mostly provoke them to take antibiotics indiscriminately. Community people were found largely dependent on local drug stores (81.25%) where they sought antibiotics in terms of common illnesses like fever, cough, cold, or throat pain. Ahmed et al., (2017) in their study found that 65% of patients visited drug shops to seek healthcare without any prescriptions. Another study carried out by Do et al., (2021) states that in Bangladesh, healthcare services provided at the district level or lower are offered for free but are perceived as of low quality, with only a limited variety of antibiotics accessible. Consequently, residents predominantly turn to nearby drug vendors for minor health issues. In Ghana, the primary and initial choice for antibiotics is licensed chemical sellers, as delays in receiving hospital care led people to seek medication from these licensed vendors instead of public healthcare providers. A similar trend was observed in Vietnam, where a significant presence of private and unlicensed antibiotic suppliers further contributes to this pattern (Do et al., 2021). Similar to this finding, the present study revealed that rural and semi-urban community people tend to rely on drug outlets or pharmacies (52%) as the key healthcare-seeking point.

To sum up, CSR practices of national-level companies are not well institutionalized in Bangladesh. Like other developing countries, organizational factors (such as promotional policy and lack of job security of MRs) play a more dominant role than the environment and stakeholders-related issues. Finally, referring to the findings, it can be envisaged that pharmaceutical companies functioning at the grassroots levels lack self-regulation and nominal engagement of the pharmaceutical industry to combat ABR as a part of its CSR initiatives. The study highlighted that self-regulation-led moral principles of CSR (betterment of the health sector) have not been followed by the Pharmaceutical Industry of Bangladesh. The findings of the study showed a good resemblance with other related studies. Droppert and Bennett (2015) investigated the role of multinational pharmaceutical industries in improving the state of global health and concluded the "effects" are nascent". Considering the context of Korea Bae et al., (2020) uncovered that CSR of national pharmaceutical firms "are now in the early stages". To ensure the quality of care of global health an advocacy is required that will motivate the multinational and domestic pharmaceutical companies to bring their CSR efforts to 'a philanthropic level' where self-regulation principles of CSR may add value to this understanding.

REFERENCES

Ahmed, S. M., Naher, N., Hossain, T., & Rawal, L. (2017). Exploring the status of retail private drug shops in Bangladesh and action points for developing an accredited drug shop model: A facility based cross-sectional study. *Journal of Pharmaceutical Policy and Practice*, 10(1), 21. Advance online publication. DOI: 10.1186/s40545-017-0108-8

Ahmed, S. M., Naher, N., Tune, S. N. B. K., & Islam, B. Z. (2022). The Implementation of National Action Plan (NAP) on Antimicrobial Resistance (AMR) in Bangladesh: Challenges and Lessons Learned from a Cross-Sectional Qualitative Study. *Antibiotics (Basel, Switzerland)*, 11(5), 690. DOI: 10.3390/antibiotics11050690

Alavi, H., Habek, P., & Cierna, H. (2016). Corporate social responsibility and self-regulation. *MM Science Journal*, 2016(04), 1121–1126. DOI: 10.17973/MMSJ.2016_10_201681

Alssageer, M. A., & Kowalski, S. R. (2013). What do Libyan doctors perceive as the benefits, ethical issues and influences of their interactions with pharmaceutical company representatives? *The Pan African Medical Journal*, 14, 14. DOI: 10.11604/pamj.2013.14.132.2598

Altawalbeh, S. M., Ibrahim, I. A., & Al-Shatnawi, S. F. (2020). Influence of pharmaceutical promotion on prescribers in Jordan. *International Journal of Clinical Pharmacy*, 42(2), 744–755. DOI: 10.1007/s11096-020-01006-3

Amer, M. (2023). Systematic review of religiosity and social responsibility. *Journal of Business and Socio-economic Development*. https://doi.org/doi:10.1108/JBSED-02-2023-0007

Awa, H. O., Etim, W., & Ogbonda, E. (2024). Stakeholders, stakeholder theory and Corporate Social Responsibility (CSR). *International Journal of Corporate Social Responsibility*, 9(1), 11. DOI: 10.1186/s40991-024-00094-y

Awal, A., Saidy, S., & Aliullah, M. (2021). The unethical practices of the pharmaceutical industries in Bangladesh in their drug promotion and its impacts. *International Journal of Engineering and Management Research*, 11(4), 1–5. DOI: 10.31033/ijemr.11.4.1

Bae, G., Ahn, J., Lim, K., & Bae, S. (2022). Corporate social responsibility of pharmaceutical industry in Korea. *Frontiers in Pharmacology*, 13, 950669. Advance online publication. DOI: 10.3389/fphar.2022.950669

Bepari, A. K., Rabbi, G., Shaon, H. R., Khan, S. I., Zahid, Z. I., Dalal, K., & Reza, H. M. (2023). Factors Driving Antimicrobial Resistance in Rural Bangladesh: A Cross-Sectional Study on Antibiotic Use-Related Knowledge, Attitude, and Practice among Unqualified village medical Practitioners and pharmacy shopkeepers. *Advances in Therapy, 40*(8), 3478–3494. doi:DOI: 10.1007/s12325-023-02547-5

Biswas, M., Roy, M. N., Manik, M. I. N., Hossain, M. S., Tapu, S. T. A., Moniruzzaman, M., & Sultana, S. (2014). Self medicated antibiotics in Bangladesh: A cross-sectional health survey conducted in the Rajshahi City. *BMC Public Health*, 14(1), 1–7. DOI: 10.1186/1471-2458-14-847

Bonna, A. S., Pavel, S. R., Ferdous, J., Khan, S. A., & Ali, M. (2022). Antibiotic resistance: An increasingly threatening but neglected public health challenge in Bangladesh. *International Journal of Surgery Open*, 49, 100581. DOI: 10.1016/j.ijso.2022.100581

Brammer, S., Jackson, G., & Matten, D. (2012). Corporate Social Responsibility and institutional theory: New perspectives on private governance. *Socio-economic Review*, 10(1), 3–28. DOI: 10.1093/ser/mwr030

Brès, L., Mosonyi, S., Gond, J., Muzio, D., Mitra, R., Werr, A., & Wickert, C. (2019). Rethinking professionalization: A generative dialogue on CSR practitioners1. *Journal of Professions and Organization*, 6(2), 246–264. DOI: 10.1093/jpo/joz009

Do, N. T., Vu, H. T. L., Nguyen, C. T. K., Punpuing, S., Khan, W. A., Gyapong, M., Asante, K. P., Munguambe, K., Gómez-Olivé, F. X., John-Langba, J., Tran, T. K., Sunpuwan, M., Sevene, E., Nguyen, H. H., Ho, P. D., Matin, M. A., Ahmed, S., Karim, M. M., Cambaco, O., & Wertheim, H. (2021). Community-based antibiotic access and use in six low-income and middle-income countries: A mixed-method approach. *The Lancet. Global Health*, 9(5), e610–e619. DOI: 10.1016/S2214-109X(21)00024-3

Droppert, H., & Bennett, S. (2015). Corporate social responsibility in global health: An exploratory study of multinational pharmaceutical firms. *Globalization and Health*, 11(1), 1–8. DOI: 10.1186/s12992-015-0100-5

Epstein, E. M. (2002). Religion and business–the critical role of religious traditions in management education. *Journal of Business Ethics*, 38(1/2), 91–96. DOI: 10.1023/A:1015712827640

Freeman, R. E., Harrison, J. S., Wicks, A. C., Parmar, B. L., & De Colle, S. (2010). Stakeholder theory: The state of the art.

Gallo, A. M., & Serluca, M. C. (2024). Corporate Social Responsibility and Stakeholders: a Systematic Literature Review. *Accounting and Taxation (IWAT2024)*, 196.

Hoque, R., Ahmed, S. M., Naher, N., Islam, M. A., Rousham, E. K., Islam, B. Z., & Hassan, S. (2020). Tackling antimicrobial resistance in Bangladesh: A scoping review of policy and practice in human, animal and environment sectors. *PLoS One*, 15(1), e0227947. DOI: 10.1371/journal.pone.0227947

Hossain, M. J., Jabin, N., Ahmmed, F., Sultana, A., Abdur Rahman, S. M., & Islam, M. R. (2023). Irrational use of antibiotics and factors associated with antibiotic resistance: Findings from a cross-sectional study in Bangladesh. *Health Science Reports*, 6(8), e1465. DOI: 10.1002/hsr2.1465

Hsu, Y. H., Fang, W., & Lee, Y. (2009). Ethically questionable behavior in sales representatives–An example from the Taiwanese pharmaceutical industry. *Journal of Business Ethics*, 88(S1), 155–166. DOI: 10.1007/s10551-008-9823-z

International Federation of Pharmaceutical Manufacturers & Associations. (2022). The Pharmaceutical Industry and Global Health.

Islam, M. S., Sikdar, K. Y. K., Hossain, A. M. A., & Faroque, A. B. M. (2019). Study on the pattern of antibiotic use including the resistance episodes in Bangladesh. *Dhaka University Journal of Pharmaceutical Sciences*, 18(2), 135–143. DOI: 10.3329/dujps.v18i2.43255

Islam, S., Rahman, A., & Al Mahmood, A. K. (2018). Bangladesh pharmaceutical industry: Perspective and the prospects. *Bangladesh Journal of Medical Science*, 17(4), 519–525. DOI: 10.3329/bjms.v17i4.38306

Johora, F., & Rahman, M. S. (2018). Pharmaceutical promotion in Bangladesh: Assessing the strength of regulatory documents. *Bangladesh Journal of Bioethics*, 9(3), 1–10. DOI: 10.3329/bioethics.v9i3.48911

Kabir, M. A., & Chowdhury, S. S. (2023). Empirical analysis of the corporate social responsibility and financial performance causal nexus: Evidence from the banking sector of Bangladesh. *Asia Pacific Management Review*, 28(1), 1–12. DOI: 10.1016/j.apmrv.2022.01.003

Kingsland, J. (2021, July 19). Antibiotic-resistant infections in Bangladeshi kids deemed 'very worrying.' *Medical News Today*. https://www.medicalnewstoday.com/articles/antibiotic-resistant-infections-in-bangladeshi-kids-deemed-very-worrying

Knox, B. D. (2018). Employee Volunteer Programs are Associated with Firm-Level Benefits and CEO Incentives: Data on the Ethical Dilemma of Corporate Social Responsibility Activities. *Journal of Business Ethics*, 162(2), 449–472. DOI: 10.1007/s10551-018-4005-0

Mahadi, A. R. (2021). Post COVID antimicrobial resistance threat in Lower- and Middle-Income Countries: Bangladesh. *Frontiers in Public Health*, 9, 770593. Advance online publication. DOI: 10.3389/fpubh.2021.770593

Mamun, M. R. (2024, June 19). Unveiling the struggles of Bangladesh's pharmaceutical representatives. *The Daily Star*. https://www.thedailystar.net/opinion/views/news/unveiling-the-struggles-bangladeshs-pharmaceutical-representatives-3635606

Marmat, G., Jain, P., & Mishra, P. N. (2020). Understanding ethical/unethical behavior in pharmaceutical companies: A literature review. *International Journal of Pharmaceutical and Healthcare Marketing*, 14(3), 367–394. DOI: 10.1108/IJPHM-03-2018-0016

Matin, M. A., Khan, W. A., Karim, M. M., Ahmed, S., John-Langba, J., Sankoh, O. A., Gyapong, M., Kinsman, J., & Wertheim, H. (2020). What influences antibiotic sales in rural Bangladesh? A drug dispensers' perspective. *Journal of Pharmaceutical Policy and Practice*, 13(1), 20. DOI: 10.1186/s40545-020-00212-8

Mitema, E. S. (2010). The role of unregulated sale and dispensing of antimicrobial agents on the development of antimicrobial resistance in developing countries. *Antimicrobial Resistance in Developing Countries*, 403-411.

Mohiuddin, A. K. (2019). An AZ pharmaceutical industry: Bangladesh perspective. *Asian Journal of Research in Pharmaceutical Science*, 9(1), 17–28. DOI: 10.5958/2231-5659.2019.00004.3

Mohiuddin, M., Rashid, S. F., Shuvro, M. I., Nahar, N., & Ahmed, S. M. (2015). Qualitative insights into promotion of pharmaceutical products in Bangladesh: How ethical are the practices? *BMC Medical Ethics*, 16(1), 1–9. DOI: 10.1186/s12910-015-0075-z

Muniapan, B. (2013). The roots of Indian corporate social responsibility (CSR) practice from a Vedantic perspective. In Corporate Social Responsibility in Asia: Practice and Experience (pp. 19–33). Springer International Publishing.

Munir, M. M. H. (2023, August 12). Affordable medicines in Bangladesh in post TRIPS regime. *The Business Standard*. https://www.tbsnews.net/thoughts/affordable-medicines-bangladesh-post-trips-regime-680282

Murshid, M. A., & Mohaidin, Z. (2017). A systematic review of the influence of medical representatives and promotional tools on prescribing: A comparison between developed and developing countries. *International Journal of Pharmaceutical and Healthcare Marketing*, 11(4), 361–394. DOI: 10.1108/IJPHM-09-2016-0047

Murshid, M. E., & Haque, M. (2019). Bangladesh national drug policy 1982-2016 and recommendations in policy aspects. *Eurasian journal of emergency medicine, 18*(2), 104.

Nizame, F. A., Shoaib, D. M., Rousham, E. K., Akter, S., Islam, M. A., Khan, A. A., Rahman, M., & Unicomb, L. (2021). Barriers and facilitators to adherence to national drug policies on antibiotic prescribing and dispensing in Bangladesh. *Journal of Pharmaceutical Policy and Practice*, 14(S1), 85. Advance online publication. DOI: 10.1186/s40545-021-00342-7

Olivier, C., Williams-Jones, B., Doize, B., & Ozdemir, V. (2010). Containing global antibiotic resistance: ethical drug promotion in the developing world. *Antimicrobial resistance in developing countries*, 505-524.

One Health Trust. (2018). *Antibiotic use and resistance in Bangladesh: Situation analysis and recommendations*. https://onehealthtrust.org/ publications/reports / antibiotic-use-and-resistance-in-bangladesh/

Orubu, E. S. F., Samad, M. A., Rahman, M. T., Zaman, M. H., & Wirtz, V. J. (2021). Mapping the antimicrobial supply chain in Bangladesh: A Scoping-Review-Based Ecological Assessment Approach. *Global Health, Science and Practice*, 9(3), 532–547. DOI: 10.9745/GHSP-D-20-00502

Ostwald, D., Cramer, M., Albu, N., & Tesch, J. (2020). The global economic impact of the Pharmaceutical Industry. Retrieved February 25, 2022 from https:// www. ifpma. org/wp-content/uploads/2021/04/WifOR_Global_Economic_Footprint_Study_September_2020. pdf

Otaigbe, I., & Elikwu, C. J. (2023). Drivers of inappropriate antibiotic use in low- and middle-income countries. *JAC-Antimicrobial Resistance*, 5(3), dlad062. Advance online publication. DOI: 10.1093/jacamr/dlad062

Patel, J., Harant, A., Fernandes, G., Mwamelo, A. J., Hein, W., Dekker, D., & Sridhar, D. (2023). Measuring the global response to antimicrobial resistance, 2020–21: A systematic governance analysis of 114 countries. *The Lancet. Infectious Diseases*, 23(6), 706–718. DOI: 10.1016/S1473-3099(22)00796-4

Pradhan & Zubayer. (2021, February 6). An emerging global player of the pharmaceutical industries: Challenges and prospects for Bangladesh. *The Business Standard*. https://www.tbsnews.net/thoughts/emerging-global-player-pharmaceutical-industries-challenges-and-prospects-bangladesh-197476

Rishi, P. (2022). Integrating CSR with Climate Change and Sustainability. In *Managing climate change and sustainability through behavioural transformation* (pp. 105–135). Springer Singapore., DOI: 10.1007/978-981-16-8519-4_5

Roy, T. K., Al-Abdin, A., & Quazi, A. (2021). Examining the CSR strategy of MNCs in Bangladesh. *Sustainability Accounting.Management and Policy Journal*, 12(2), 467–490.

Saha, A., Marma, K. K. S., Rashid, A., Tarannum, N., Das, S., Chowdhury, T., Afrin, N., Chakraborty, P., Emran, M., Mehedi, H., Hussain, M. I., Barua, A., & Mistry, S. K. (2022). Risk factors associated with self-medication among the indigenous communities of Chittagong Hill Tracts, Bangladesh. *PLoS One*, 17(6), e0269622. DOI: 10.1371/journal.pone.0269622

Saha, S. K., & Promite, S. (2017). Factors influencing clinician's antibiotic prescribing behaviors (APB) in Bangladesh: An in-depth review using COMB Model. *Open Access Journal of Translational Medicine & Research*, 1(4), 00019. DOI: 10.15406/oajtmr.2017.01.00019

Sujan, M. A. (2020, January 13). ANTIBIOTICS USE, SALE: Who needs PRESCRIPTION? *The Daily Star*. https://www.thedailystar.net/frontpage/antibiotics-use-and-sale-in-bangladesh-without-prescription-continues-1853359

Tajmim, T. (2019, November 16). Aggressive drug promotion practices bane for patients. *The Business Standard*. https://www.tbsnews. net/bangladesh/ health/aggressive-drug-promotion-practices-bane-patients

Van Aaken, D., & Buchner, F. (2020). Religion and CSR: A systematic literature review. *Journal of Business Economics*, 90(5–6), 917–945. DOI: 10.1007/s11573-020-00977-z

Yıldırım, M., & Dinçer, M. M. (2018). How the Process of the CSR Activities Works on Private Hospitals and Pharmaceutical Firms: Multiple Case Study from Strategic Perspective. [PubMed]. *Journal of Religion and Health*, 59(2), 961–985. DOI: 10.1007/s10943-018-0653-8

Yin, R. K. (1994). Discovering the future of the case study. Method in evaluation research. *Evaluation Practice*, 15(3), 283–290.

Yu, W., & Hu, H. (2013). Corporate social responsibility in shaping corporate image: An empirical study of state-owned enterprises in China. In Corporate Social Responsibility in Asia: Practice and Experience (pp. 3–18). Springer International Publishing.

Zampone, G., Sannino, G., & García-Sánchez, I. M. (2023). Exploring the moderating effects of corporate social responsibility performance under mimetic pressures. An international analysis. *Corporate Social Responsibility and Environmental Management*, 30(1), 53–65. DOI: 10.1002/csr.2338

Zhao, J. (2021). Reimagining corporate social responsibility in the era of COVID-19: Embedding resilience and promoting corporate social competence. *Sustainability (Basel)*, 13(12), 6548. DOI: 10.3390/su13126548

Zinkin, J., & Williams, G. (2006). Islam and CSR: A study of the compatibility between the tenets of Islam and the UN Global Compact. *Available atSSRN* 905201. doi:DOI: 10.2139/ssrn.905201

KEY TERMS AND DEFINITIONS

Antibiotic Resistance: Antibiotics are medicines that inhibit the growth of or destroy microorganisms. Over the years, the irrational, excessive, and misuse of antimicrobials or antibiotics across humans, agriculture, and poultry led pathogen-like bacteria to develop their ability to defeat the drugs supposed to kill them. Thus, the injudicious use of antibiotics has come out as drug-resistant microorganisms known as antimicrobial resistance or AMR (see Coates, 2012; Boutin et al., 2017).

Corporate Social Responsibility (CSR): CSR may refer to a theory that posits that business should function in a way that benefits the well-being of society and the environment. Such responsibilities of the business enterprises and their ethical practices for ensuring the betterment of the wider society (see Brejning 2016; Singh and Mishra, 2022).

Demand and Supply-Side Factors: As per the economic theory, the demand side is linked to the consumer or target group-related factors that generate demand for goods or services. On the other hand, supply-side factors are opposite to demand-side and connected to offering the services to a target group or individuals.

Drug Regulation: Drug regulation denotes controlling drug use through a set of policies and drug regulatory authorities. The ways drugs are regulated may vary from country to country depending on different factors and cotexts (see Snow, 2016; Abraham, 2023).

Health Systems: Health systems encapsulate institutional structures and resources that provide healthcare services, healthcare interventions, and people who opt to avail of them. Accordingly, the decision to seek healthcare is influenced by dynamic factors, such as health needs, available health resources, and socioeconomic, cultural, political, and situational elements. The interplay of these various aspects collectively shapes individuals' choices in pursuing medical care (see Tomson and Vlad, 2014).

Self-Medication: Self-medication simply implies selecting and using any medicines by themselves relying on their own identified symptoms for a disease. In a broader sense, it involves seeking suggestions or pieces of advice from others in case of an ailment, using non-prescription medicines, and over-the-counter (hereinafter OTP) drugs (see Baracaldo-Santamaría et al., 2022).

Self-Regulation: Self-regulation involves managing and controlling one's behavior, particularly in aligning oneself with desired or standard expectations (see D Vhos and Baumeister, 2004).

Chapter 14
Socially Responsible Marketing and Children's Health:
Preliminary Insights

Joana Maria Duarte Lima
Polytechnic Institute of Cávado and Ave, Portugal

Bruno Barbosa Sousa
http://orcid.org/0000-0002-8588-2422
Polytechnic Institute of Cávado and Ave, Portugal & Applied Management Research Unit (UNIAG), Portugal & Centre for Tourism Research, Development and Innovation (CiTUR), Portugal

ABSTRACT

In a world where children's health and well-being are non-negotiable priorities, this research emerges completely at the intersection between socially responsible marketing and the promotion of children's health, meticulously focusing its attention on the pharmaceutical sector, notably the involving the field of dermocosmetics. The analysis addresses in detail the fundamentals of socially responsible marketing, examining how ethical communication strategies and sustainable practices influence consumer perception and behavior. Consumer behavior is explored identically, investigating the role of brand attachment and examining how the emotional connection between consumers and brands can be strengthened or compromised, through the marketing strategies adopted. It is imperative to highlight quality management as the foundation on which consumer trust is built. This study includes a detailed review of academic and professional literature relevant to understanding the key concepts and practices of socially responsible marketing in the context of children's health.

DOI: 10.4018/979-8-3693-5991-4.ch014

INTRODUCTION

The need to understand how ethical and sustainable marketing strategies can positively influence children's health, one of the most vulnerable segments of the population, fully justifies this study. The proposal is to explore the intersection between corporate social responsibility and child health promotion, evaluating how socially responsible marketing can act as a catalyst for behavioral and consumption changes, which benefit both individual health and the environment. The choice of dermocosmetics as the focus of this study is based on its duality of integrating dermatological and cosmetic knowledge, aiming to promote skin health. This area is particularly relevant when applied to children's health, given that children's skin is so sensitive and vulnerable, requiring specific and rigorous care. Thus, dermocosmetics emerges as an ideal field for implementing sustainable and responsible practices. The analysis addresses in detail the fundamentals of socially responsible marketing, examining how ethical communication strategies and sustainable practices influence consumer perception and behavior. The valorization and integration of ingredients produced organically, and on national soil, stands out as key elements in promoting practices in this industry, including product labeling, where transparency and clarity of information become essential for consumers.

THEORETICAL BACKGROUND

Dermocosmetics

The narrative of cosmetics dates back to ancient times, as evidenced by archaeological finds that reveal the habits of prehistoric civilizations. Records dating back to around 30,000 years ago suggest the application of pigments for body ornamentation and the practice of body marking through tattoos, in addition to the use of essential oils in funeral ceremonies and for preservation purposes. Evidence in graves reveals varied artifacts, such as censers, vases with oil and balm contents, and clay tablets engraved with instructions regarding asepsis and body aesthetics, testifying to the magnitude attributed to such rituals since the dawn of humanity. An extensive succession of eras preceded the period of Ancient Egypt, standing out as the heyday of cosmetics, where attention to personal appearance assumed extreme importance. To this day, Cleopatra and Nefertiti remain iconic symbols of beauty. During the Greek era, personal care was frequent, which, naturally, included the use of cosmetic products, according to Draelos (2006) During the period of the Roman Empire, the eminent Greek physician Galen of Pergamum (129 BC) 199 AD) designed a formulation for skin care, by amalgamating beeswax, olive oil and rose water, creating Unguentum Refrigerans, popularly recognized as cold cream. This product, an emollient that provides a refreshing and pleasant sensation, continues to be used today in water-in-oil emulsions. During the Middle Ages, there was a significant decline in the use of cosmetics, due to the change in the perception of the human body as an entity that did not require aesthetic attention. During the Renaissance, we witnessed an emergence of cosmetics, a trend that lasted until the period of the French Revolution. However, in this historical context, cosmetic procedures suffered a new decadence, marked by moderation in aesthetic exaggerations (Stewart, 2017). Interest in it was revived later, mainly influenced by Napoleon, whose consort, Josephine, played a crucial role in this germination. From this turnaround, exponential growth was observed in this industry and in beauty treatments. This growth was so remarkable that in 1938, the Food and Drug Administration (FDA) assigned a distinction and classified topical products as cosmetics or medicines, reflecting their growing importance, both in the market and in society. A cosmetic product was formally defined as any substance used to enhance aesthetics and improve appearance, without inducing adverse effects on the skin (Gupta et al., 2022). However nowadays, this conception is a mere illusion), while pharmaceuticals were categorized as substances used to treat, mitigate and prevent illnesses, demonstrating safety and efficiency. This classification proved to be highly relevant in that period, however, over the years, dermatological research has gained more and more prominence, showing that all substances applied to the skin exert some type of effect, considering its permeability. During this period, the methods used to investigate the impact of exogenous substances on the physiology and anatomy of the skin evolved to extreme sophistication, adopting increasingly sensitive and precise approaches. These broad and extensive definitions are in accordance with what seems to be the main objective of cosmetics, for thousands of years in history: to promote attractiveness, or change the appearance of the human body (Grammer et al., 2003), as well as to guarantee health and well-being. In the 20th century, dermocosmetics experienced an era of transformation, marked by the introduction of renowned beauty treatments and innovative formulations, often acclaimed as true miracles in combating signs of aging, such as the dreaded wrinkles. This period saw a fervent exploration for products that met the aesthetic demands of the time, driving notable advances in research and cosmetic development. At the same time, makeup has evolved, closely following haute couture trends, offering palettes rich in colors and textures (Becker, 2016).

The skin, one of the largest organs of the human body, performs a variety of vital functions, acting as a defensive barrier and external covering, with different characteristics and purposes, in various areas of the body (Menon, 2014). Composed of multiple layers and specialized structures, adult skin generally covers around $2m^2$, and has an average weight of 2kg. Its thickness varies considerably, being higher in places such as the palm of the hands, and lower in areas such as the area surrounding the eyes. The structure of the skin comprises three main layers: the epidermis, made up of epithelial tissue and located more externally; the dermis, composed of connective tissue; and the hypodermis, the deepest layer, composed of adipose tissue. In the interval between birth and maturity, an increase in the surface area of children's skin is observed, accompanied by anatomical and functional changes in various skin structures. Children's skin is characterized by ease of peeling and greater water loss, due to less cohesion between cells, resulting in a different texture compared to adult skin. Children's skin stands out for its delicacy and sensitivity, attributes influenced by a series of factors. It is characterized by having a surface with a neutral pH, which compromises its ability to defend against the excessive proliferation of microorganisms (Akinsemolu & Onyeaka, 2024). Furthermore, the low activity of the sebaceous glands results in a lower lipid content, although it maintains a high hydration rate. The smooth texture of the skin in childhood is due to the thinner stratum corneum, as well as the thinner dermis and epidermis, in contrast to adult skin. Children's dermis has a lower amount of mature collagen, but a high concentration of proteoglycans, which increases its water content (Thiboutot, 2004). Particularly in infants, the skin is extremely delicate due to the immaturity of the structures that make it up, making it more susceptible to the penetration of potentially harmful substances, and less able to maintain homeostasis. It becomes uniquely sensitive to excess glandular secretions, dust mites (Fernandes et al., 2011), environmental bacteria, impurities accumulated in diaper areas, occlusion caused by diaper material and extreme weather conditions. Skin permeability is higher during the first two weeks of life, gradually decreasing during chronological succession, although characterized as lower, when compared to adult skin. In addition to the above, children's skin becomes more susceptible to mechanical attacks, such as friction with diapers or the use of wet wipes, which can result in the repetitive and localized removal of cells from the stratum corneum, thus increasing skin permeability. In terms of body surface area, newborns have a smaller area, around three times, equivalent to that of an adult, resulting in a higher tissue concentration for the same area of application (Holford et al., 2013).

In the pediatric population, the occurrence of several dermatological conditions, including dermatitis, is common, which share similar therapeutic approaches, despite their different causes (Akdis et al., 2006). The most common forms of dermatitis in this age group include atopic, seborrheic, contact and diaper dermatitis, with the latter representing a significant group. Other common skin conditions include miliaria and acne, with dermatitis being the most prevalent. Due to the specificities of children's skin, cosmetic products developed for its hygiene and protection require meticulous formulations. They must be designed with the same delicacy reserved for products intended for sensitive or very sensitive skin, in order to minimize any risk of irritation, allergies or other adverse effects. This implies the exclusion of potentially aggressive ingredients, such as preservatives and fragrances, and the careful selection of raw materials of high quality, purity and microbiological stability. During the development process of these products, several criteria are taken into consideration, including minimizing skin irritation and sensitization, controlling the risk of comedogenesis, maintaining a pH close to neutrality, appropriate selection of surfactants and use of antioxidants to protect lipids (Nohynek et al., 2010). of the skin. In addition to the above, safety measures are established, such as risk assessment, and special attention is paid to the concentration of dyes, natural substances, solvents and preservatives. Cosmetic products intended for the pediatric population can be classified into hygiene and protection products. Adequate hygiene is essential for the health of newborn and child's skin, requiring the use of appropriate products, such as soaps, shampoos, oils and cleansing lotions. For skin protection, emollient and protective products are preferable, such as barrier creams, pediatric oils and moisturizing emulsions. The use of powders, sunscreens and colognes is recommended, with special attention to the formulation to avoid potential adverse effects, such as dehydration caused by the alcohol present (Brown & Fardell, 2000).

The sector with the largest production area that reaches the organic market is olive groves, where there are several mills working well, in the best olive growing regions of the country.

Socially Responsible Marketing and Children's Health

As globalization increases, environmental issues are also growing rapidly (Suryavanshi & Agrawal, 2023; Santos et al., 2023). However, it is essential to recognize that global interconnection is not limited to environmental issues alone, but similarly encompasses a complex range of social responsibilities. These transcendental concerns encompass the preservation of the environment, but also the guarantee of equity, social justice and respect for human rights (Juss, 1997). Therefore, as we navigate the currents of globalization, it becomes imperative to holistically address the issues of social responsibility that shape our contemporary world. Currently, there is a great cultural revolution guided by changes in social values and current paradigms, due to the flow of events witnessed in the near past. The most obvious result is the ease of access to information in real time, whether by companies or consumers and, therefore, human beings are more demanding because they are better informed. Therefore, understanding this trend and meeting customer expectations has become a crucial factor in the good health of organizations (Barros & Sousa, 2021). From this new perspective of the responsible consumer, there is an increase in interest in the origin of products, their production and manufacturing processes, in compliance with global standards of fair work and human rights. On the other hand, there is an increase in concern about the growth of the military industry, state corruption and animal cruelty, among many aspects that impact the decision to purchase and use any good or service (Nibert, 2013). Faced with this scenario of cultural changes and growing demands for transparency and social responsibility, companies are increasingly pressured to align their commercial practices with the well-being of society, recognizing the importance of meeting customers' informed expectations. As Trkulja reports et al., (2024) the concept of Socially Responsible Marketing (MSR), emerged as a strategy, whose scope transcends the mere improvement of brand reputation and consumer loyalty, extending to the resolution of pressing social issues, especially those related to diversity, equity and inclusion. In contemporary society, companies are urged to demonstrate their social responsibility through a series of initiatives. They are urged to produce safer products, protect and respect the environment, promote the inclusion of minorities, create employment opportunities for unemployed youth, combat racial discrimination and maintain a high standard of integrity in all their practices. The growing attention devoted to promoting diversity, equity and inclusion in organizational environments reflects a paradigm shift in contemporary business discourse. In this context, the role of socially responsible marketing emerges as an essential catalyst to drive significant and sustainable changes in society. Kamila & Jasrotia (2023) observe that the incorporation of ethical and responsible principles in marketing is becoming progressively crucial in business operations, as organizations seek to align their commercial objectives with their ethical and social responsibilities. Trkulja et al., (2024) further detail socially responsible marketing as a strategy that aims to integrate ethical and social values into marketing activities, establishing transparent communication between companies and consumers. This approach aims to establish a more meaningful connection between brands and their audiences, providing a means to express shared moral and social values. A central element of Socially Responsible Marketing is cause-related marketing, in which companies align their marketing strategies with specific social or environmental issues, demonstrating their commitment to social responsibility while promoting their products or services. This form of marketing reinforces the brand's image, but also attracts conscious consumers who value brands that contribute to the well-being of society (Aydon Simmons, 2009). Additionally, the MSR encompasses sustainability initiatives aimed at minimizing the environmental impact of marketing activities, from product design to distribution and disposal. This focus on sustainability reflects a growing awareness of environmental issues, and a response to consumer demand for more responsible business practices. Another relevant aspect of this aspect of marketing is ethical advertising, which focuses on promoting products or services in a transparent, honest and socially responsible way, including avoiding misleading advertising practices and ensuring that marketing messages are accurate and ethical, building trust with consumers and fostering lasting relationships. Social identity theory suggests that individuals' self-esteem is influenced by group associations, affecting their consumption decisions and market direction. In this context, companies can design marketing strategies that resonate with a variety of audiences, promoting inclusion and representation. Inclusive marketing is a strategic approach that prioritizes the creation of campaigns, products and services capable of serving a wide range of profiles, considering aspects such as cultural origin, skills, gender, age and socioeconomic position (Daykin, 2022). Furthermore, inclusive marketing plays a crucial role in MSR, ensuring that marketing campaigns reflect the diversity of society and are inclusive in their representation of different groups. This approach expands the reach of marketing campaigns, but also promotes inclusion and equality, contributing to a fairer and more diverse society. A notable example of Socially Responsible Marketing was provided by the Baby Dove brand, which captured the essence of the tumultuous journey of motherhood. There is no escaping the impact of these brands' ads when we enter the world of socially responsible marketing. In the tumultuous journey of motherhood, between dirty diapers and sleepless nights, one truth resonates: there is no manual for being a mother. There is no predefined script, no magic formula. And that's okay. Baby dove decided to celebrate each mother in her authenticity, without judgement, without unrealistic expectations. Because the true beauty of motherhood lies in the imperfections, the chaotic moments and the sincere smiles. While other brands paint an idealized portrait of motherhood, Baby Dove has embraced reality. They understood the tears of tiredness, the moments of uncertainty and the hugs that heal any wound. Because being a mother is a journey of ups and downs, of unconditional love and unexpected challenges. The brand claims that the products in this campaign are not just for cleaning and soothing babies' delicate skin. They are a reminder that every mother is unique, with her own struggles and triumphs. They claim to be a silent support in the midst of chaos, a beacon of hope in times of doubt. In a world that demands perfection, they chose to celebrate authenticity. Because there is no perfect mother, only real mothers, navigating the wonderful and tumultuous world of motherhood. And they affirm their presence for every moment, for every tear and for every laugh. Johnson & Johnson also took a significant step by launching a campaign that celebrates family diversity and promotes values of social responsibility. When we look at the concept of family, we see more than simply blood ties. We see deep connections, unconditional love, and shared joy. For Bayer, the "Skin with Skin" campaign is not just about promoting products, but about celebrating the precious moments and deep bonds between parents/caregivers and children. Nothing compares to the comforting feeling of "skin-to-skin" contact between a newborn and their parents/caregivers. These moments, full of love and tenderness, are essential for strengthening family bonds, but also for promoting physical and mental health (Koo et al.,

2024). By highlighting the importance of these intimate moments, Bayer reminds us that physical touch is a universal language of love and care. Consumers increasingly request to associate with brands that demonstrate an authentic commitment to their customer base, but also to the general well-being of the community. As companies recognize that genuine competitiveness cannot be achieved at the expense of collective well-being, it becomes crucial that they integrate this social responsibility into their marketing strategies (Hess & Story, 2005). This goal can only be truly realized when companies are sensitive to the adverse impacts of inappropriate targeting practices and marketing messages. Unfortunately, marketing and commercial communication practices persist that lack this social commitment. From deceptive advertising campaigns to unethical tactics in promoting fashion, cosmetics and even social causes, there is a moral demand for companies to reevaluate and adjust their marketing approaches, thereby reflecting a heightened awareness and true commitment to collective well-being. Challenges arise when companies seek to gain unjustified advantages at the expense of targeted individuals. Marketers must understand that socially responsible marketing requires segmentation and targeting that meet the interests of both the company and target individuals without causing harm to the latter, respecting the diversity and individual values of target consumers, without promoting stereotypes or discrimination. And it is equally imperative to understand that, in the practice of segmentation, it is crucial to respect the diversity and values of target consumers, avoiding the promotion of stereotypes or any form of discrimination, whether based on gender, ethnicity, or other characteristic. Over the decades, we have been the audience of a dazzling and sometimes disconcerting spectacle: countless marketing campaigns that transport us to a fantasy world, full of extravagant promises and unrealistic images. Behind this facade of glamour, however, we often find unethical practices that challenge our conscience. This narrative, unfortunately, is not restricted to a single industry; it spans a vast spectrum, from the realms of fashion to the realms of cosmetics. It is a saga that reminds us of the importance of remaining vigilant, questioning not only the veracity of the messages that surround us, but also the underlying moral values.

Kamila & Jasrotia (2023) show that over time, companies in the tobacco sector have resorted to misleading marketing strategies to promote cigarette consumption, generating devastating consequences for public health and affecting millions of people. At the same time, in recent years, technology companies have faced criticism for neglecting to protect their users' data and for contributing to the spread of misinformation through their platforms. Furthermore, the fast fashion industry has been the target of severe questioning due to its contribution to environmental damage and unfavorable working conditions in the countries in which it operates. These examples highlight the importance of a proactive approach by companies to ethics and responsibility in marketing, carefully considering the long-term implications of their actions. By integrating ethical and responsibility principles into their business strategy, organizations can avoid exposure to negative publicity and strengthen the construction of a more sustainable and trustworthy brand (Van de Ven, 2008).

GREEN MARKETING

Within the scope of socially responsible marketing, Green Marketing emerges as a powerful and essential aspect, offering an additional approach intrinsically linked to ethical and sustainable practice (Huang et al., 2024). By embracing this aspect, companies recognize their responsibility towards society, but also make a tangible commitment to preserving the environment and promoting sustainability, highlighting their role as agents of positive change for a more balanced and prosperous future (Machado et al., 2022). Companies must, in addition to delivering value to customers, satisfying their needs and desires, be concerned with considering ethics, society and the environment. According to Nadanyiova et al. (2020), the natural environment constitutes a fundamental component of a company's marketing environment, highlighting the imperative need for its preservation to be integrated cohesively into the company's marketing strategy. The consideration of companies as physical systems embedded in a finite and vulnerable natural environment has been largely neglected as a management and marketing concern until very recently. Concern for the environment mobilizes the global market, affecting organizations that wish to continue in the current commercial market. However, it is essential to incorporate social responsibility, economic situation and sustainability to provide the services and products demanded by consumers. Green Marketing appears as a tool that can facilitate and inform about issues that are decisive for conscious consumption (Sousa et al., 2020). National economies and companies have recognized the value of green marketing in meeting consumer needs and demands, in addition to serving as an incentive for the growth and expansion of economic activities (Popović et al., 2023). Khan et al., (2022) observe that the continuous degradation of the environment is a significant factor in the growth of environmental awareness among consumers. The rise of environmental sensitivity among consumers opens horizons for companies to adopt green marketing strategies. The insertion of this approach provides a competitive advantage to companies, but also allows them to contribute in a beneficial way to the environment (Cronin et al. 2011). The importance attributed by the media to the topic of ecology and sustainability has led to a growing concern among the population. This concern results in greater environmental awareness, which ends up influencing the purchasing decision, that is, people check whether a product is ecological and sustainable. As a consequence, companies need to act immediately to respond to this demand, being able to use this factor as a competitive differentiator

(Sousa et al., 2020). Consumers with greater environmental awareness tend to adopt more sustainable consumption patterns (Tanner & Wölfing Kast, 2003). Currently, consumers demonstrate a significant commitment to environmental issues, choosing to avoid products that cause harm to the environment or are unhealthy. They are actively involved in the selection of brands, and studies reveal that sustainable practices and the preference for environmentally friendly products play a decisive role in their choices. Consumers show preference for brands that promote products and contribute positively to the environment. The beliefs of these consumers are fundamental to guide the development of effective marketing strategies for products that value environmental sustainability. Research also indicates that consumers' perception of sustainability results in more favorable attitudes towards brands that adopt environmentally responsible practices and communicate them effectively to target consumers. Popović et al., (2023) highlight that the concept of green pricing plays a crucial role in consumers' purchasing decisions in relation to sustainable products. In general, green products tend to have a higher price compared to conventional products. While sustainability should not be the sole determinant of higher pricing, it is important to recognize that the production, distribution and promotion of environmentally friendly products involve significant costs. Consumers are increasingly willing to pay a premium for green products, as they perceive that these products offer added value and are beneficial to the environment. Green marketing denotes the adoption of strategies, which are based on preserving the environment. It is a process of promoting, endorsing, marketing and providing products and services so that they are environmentally responsible. In addition to the aforementioned, it involves educating the consumer regarding ecologically beneficial products, highlighting their positive environmental attributes. It is, therefore, a marketing approach that is based on offering ecologically sustainable products and services, aiming to minimize environmental impact. The responsibility of the industrial sector plays a fundamental role in promoting Green Marketing and raising consumer awareness about sustainable products. This challenge requires a joint effort from companies and consumers (Sarkar, 2013). It is imperative that companies develop high-quality products that meet consumer expectations in order to spread awareness about green products. Although Green Marketing involves additional costs for companies, the long-term benefits for all stakeholders are evident. Therefore, it is essential that everyone gets involved in this process to preserve the environment from degradation. The commitment to Green Marketing must be seen as a duty and a responsibility shared by everyone involved. It is essential that all activities related to this aspect are ecologically correct, resulting in the offering of products and services that promote environmental sustainability. During the 1970s, the physical environment assumed a crucial role in the realm of marketing, giving rise to the concept of “ecological marketing”. Initially, ecological marketing was focused on industrial sectors with a high environmental impact, exploring new technologies to mitigate specific issues. However, in the 1980s, there was a resurgence of environmental awareness in response to landmark events such as the Exxon -Valdez oil spill and the chemical disaster in Bhopal. These incidents triggered consumer boycotts, led to the enactment of new environmental legislation, and drove a growing demand for "green" products. These occurrences have stimulated debates about the implications of environmental marketing, highlighting the responsibility of marketers to mitigate negative impacts on the environment. At the beginning of the 21st century, even more radical concepts emerged about the integration of marketing with the environment, proposing a practical approach that aimed to transform marketing into a closed cycle system, in which there is no generation of waste or degradation of natural resources.

These approaches represent a fundamental change in the paradigm of economic, business, marketing, consumption and production thinking, committed to finding greater harmony between commercial activities and environmental preservation. As highlighted by Sousa et al., (2020), the challenge of mitigating environmental damage, such as contamination caused by the release of substances such as oils, is becoming increasingly costly and, in certain cases, extremely complex. Thus, companies capable of reducing their harmful waste can reap significant financial savings. In this quest to minimize waste, companies often find themselves forced to reevaluate their production processes, resulting, in many cases, in the development of more efficient methods that not only reduce waste production, but also reduce dependence on certain materials. -cousins. On the other hand, in some situations, companies choose to find post-production solutions, rather than focusing on reducing waste. In these circumstances, companies look for markets or applications for their waste, transforming them into necessary inputs for other companies in their production processes. By emphasizing the characteristics of products that do not harm the environment and communicating the importance of a green lifestyle, the company seeks to inform consumers about the need to protect and preserve the environment through marketing activities. Bearing in mind that the benefits of green products are intangible, and that consumers cannot perceive them in the short term, communicating their benefits is a challenge for the company. Through advertising and public relations activities, the company can effectively inform consumers about the advantages of green products and, at the same time, can create the image of a socially responsible company in the eyes of the public.

FINAL CONSIDERATIONS

Understanding consumers' needs and aspirations, as well as identifying strategies to satisfy them and establishing solid relationships with them, has become progressively more crucial and, at the same time, challenging. In the current fierce competition scenario, understanding consumption patterns becomes essential for survival in the business world. "The customer is the reason for being for any company. One of the objectives of entrepreneurs or marketers is to understand customer decisions, how and why they buy or stop buying something, their motivations, etc. Such understanding has become a necessity for organizations, which, consequently, becomes a subject of interest for any company, whatever its activity or function." Considering the intricate complexity of the topic, the analysis of consumer behavior emerges as an interdisciplinary area, which integrates a variety of concepts and methods, originating from different fields of knowledge, such as sociology, psychology, economics, cultural anthropology, semiotics, history and demography. Values, structured in a hierarchy, are sets of principles or beliefs that direct people's choices and behaviors, serving individual and collective interests. These values are abstractions that represent desired goals, and have cognitive and motivational dimensions, influencing people's perception and desires. Furthermore, they perform a social function, serving as a basis for judgments and justifications of behavior. Thus, values have the function of guiding people's conduct, determining their priorities and making distinctions between what is considered primary or secondary. This interaction between studies on human values and the analysis of consumer behavior reflects the breadth of influences that shape individuals' purchasing decisions. Throughout the development of marketing as a consolidated discipline, these conceptual contributions were gradually amalgamated, weaving an intricate background for current theories. Understanding consumer behavior goes beyond simple commercial transactions. It is an interdisciplinary field that incorporates a variety of concepts, from economic theories to sociological and psychological studies on human values. As discussed, values play a key role in guiding consumer choices, reflecting individual preferences but also broader social and cultural influences. The analysis of consumer behavior assumes a central position in the design and implementation of socially responsible marketing strategies in the pharmaceutical dermocosmetics sector, particularly in the context of promoting children's health. Consumers, increasingly informed and sensitive, express growing concern about issues relating to health, safety, sustainability and corporate responsibility. Within this context, pharmaceutical companies have the opportunity to positively influence consumer behavior through transparent and educational communication approaches. By providing detailed information about the benefits and impacts of children's dermatology products, organizations empower consumers to make informed, ethical decisions regarding their children's health. In addition to the above, proactive involvement with the community emerges as an effective socially responsible marketing strategy. By sponsoring initiatives aimed at education and prevention of childhood dermatological diseases, companies promote children's well-being, but also consolidate their reputation as entities committed to the common good and sustainable development. Finally, innovation and the design of innovative and sustainable children's dermatological products are fundamental elements to satisfy consumer demands for safe, effective and ecologically conscious products. By adopting ethical and responsible practices at all stages of the product life cycle, companies can generate value for consumers and contribute to the promotion of children's health and environmental preservation. Consumer behavior is explored identically, investigating the role of brand attachment and examination how the emotional connection between consumers and brands can be strengthened or compromised, through the marketing strategies adopted. It is imperative to highlight quality management as the foundation on which consumer trust is built. This study includes a detailed review of academic and professional literature relevant to understanding the key concepts and practices of socially responsible marketing in the context of children's health, providing a solid basis for analysis .

REFERENCES

Abratt, R., & Sacks, D. (1988). The marketing challenge: Towards being profitable and socially responsible. *Journal of Business Ethics*, 7(7), 497–507. DOI: 10.1007/BF00382596

Akdis, C. A., Akdis, M., Bieber, T., Bindslev-Jensen, C., Boguniewicz, M., Eigenmann, P., Hamid, Q., Kapp, A., Leung, D. Y. M., Lipozencic, J., Luger, T. A., Muraro, A., Novak, N., Platts-Mills, T. A. E., Rosenwasser, L., Scheynius, A., Simons, F. E. R., Spergel, J., Turjanmaa, K., & Zuberbier, T. (2006). Diagnosis and treatment of atopic dermatitis in children and adults: European Academy of Allergology and Clinical Immunology/American Academy of Allergy, Asthma and Immunology/PRACTALL Consensus Report. *The Journal of Allergy and Clinical Immunology*, 118(1), 152–169. DOI: 10.1016/j.jaci.2006.03.045

Akinsemolu, A. A., & Onyeaka, H. N. (2024). Microorganisms Associated with Food Spoilage and Foodborne Diseases. In Food Safety and Quality in the Global South (pp. 489–531). Springer Nature Singapore. doi:DOI: 10.1007/978-981-97-2428-4_16

Aydon Simmons, J. (2009). "Both sides now": Aligning external and internal branding for a socially responsible era. *Marketing Intelligence & Planning*, 27(5), 681–697. DOI: 10.1108/02634500910977890

Barros, C., & Sousa, BB (2021). The importance of Corporate Social Responsibility in consumer purchasing decisions: an exploratory study. European Journal of Applied Business and Management.

Becker, D. (2016). *Color trends and selection for product design: Every color sells a story*. William Andrew.

Boas, L. H. D. B. V., de Souza Sette, R., & de Brito, M. J. (2006). Consumer behavior of organic products: An application of the means-ends chain theory. *Rural & Agroindustrial Organizations*, 8(1), 25–39.

Borges, M. S., Peres, F. I. G., Oliveira, D. M., Berretta, A. A., & Hori, J. I. (2021). Using honey as a complementary therapy: A review of the biological properties associated with honey. *Brazilian Applied Science Review*, 5(2), 1027–1045.

Brown, M., & Fardell, N. (2000). Sun damage and sunscreen preparations. In Poucher's Perfumes, Cosmetics and Soaps (pp. 467–503). Springer Netherlands. doi:DOI: 10.1007/978-94-017-2734-1_16

Cadiz-Gurrea, M. D. L., Pinto, D., Delerue-Matos, C., & Rodrigues, F. (2021). Olive fruit and leaf wastes as bioactive ingredients for cosmetics—A preliminary study. [PubMed]. *Antioxidants*, 10(2), 245. DOI: 10.3390/antiox10020245

Cronin, J. J.Jr, Smith, J. S., Gleim, M. R., Ramirez, E., & Martinez, J. D. (2011). Green marketing strategies: An examination of stakeholders and the opportunities they present. *Journal of the Academy of Marketing Science*, 39(1), 158–174. DOI: 10.1007/s11747-010-0227-0

Daykin, J. (2022). *Inclusive Marketing: Why Representation Matters to Your Customers and Your Brand*. Kogan Page Publishers.

Draelos, Z. D. (2006). The effect of a daily facial cleanser for normal to oily skin on the skin barrier of subjects with acne. *Cutis*, 78(1, Suppl), 34–40.

Fernandes, J. D., Machado, M. C. R., & Oliveira, Z. N. P. D. (2011). Children and newborn skin care and prevention. *Anais Brasileiros de Dermatologia*, 86, 102–110. DOI: 10.1590/S0365-05962011000100014

Ghorbanzadeh, D., & Rahehagh, A. (2021). Emotional brand attachment and brand love: The emotional bridges in the process of transition from satisfaction to loyalty. *Rajagiri Management Journal*, 15(1), 16–38. DOI: 10.1108/RAMJ-05-2020-0024

Grammer, K., Fink, B., Møller, A. P., & Thornhill, R. (2003). Darwinian aesthetics: Sexual selection and the biology of beauty. *Biological Reviews of the Cambridge Philosophical Society*, 78(3), 385–407. DOI: 10.1017/S1464793102006085

Gupta, V., Mohapatra, S., Mishra, H., Farooq, U., Kumar, K., Ansari, M. J., Aldawsari, M., Alalaiwe, A., Mirza, M., & Iqbal, Z. (2022). Nanotechnology in cosmetics and cosmeceuticals—A review of latest advancements. *Gels (Basel, Switzerland)*, 8(3), 173. DOI: 10.3390/gels8030173

Hess, J., & Story, J. (2005). Trust-based commitment: Multidimensional consumer-brand relationships. *Journal of Consumer Marketing*, 22(6), 313–322. DOI: 10.1108/07363760510623902

Holford, N., Heo, Y. A., & Anderson, B. (2013). A pharmacokinetic standard for babies and adults. *Journal of Pharmaceutical Sciences*, 102(9), 2941–2952. DOI: 10.1002/jps.23574

Huang, S., Qu, H., & Wang, X. (2024). Impact of green marketing on peer-to-peer accommodation platform users' repurchase intention and positive word-of-mouth: Mediation of trust and consumer identification. *International Journal of Contemporary Hospitality Management*, 36(3), 691–712. DOI: 10.1108/IJCHM-10-2022-1300

Juss, S. (1997). Global Environmental Change: Health and the Challenge for Human Rights. *Indiana Journal of Global Legal Studies*, 5, 121.

Kamila, M. K., & Jasrotia, S. S. (2023). Ethics and marketing responsibility: A bibliometric analysis and literature review. *Asia Pacific Management Review*, 28(4), 567–583. DOI: 10.1016/j.apmrv.2023.04.002

Khan, S. A. R., Sheikh, A. A., Ashraf, M., & Yu, Z. (2022). Improving consumer-based green brand equity: The role of healthy green practices, green brand attachment, and green skepticism. *Sustainability (Basel)*, 14(19), 11829. DOI: 10.3390/su141911829

Koo, T. H., Lee, J. K., Grogan, S. P., Ra, H. J., & D'Lima, D. D. (2024). Biocompatibility Study of Purified and Low-Temperature-Sterilized Injectable Collagen for Soft Tissue Repair: Intramuscular Implantation in Rats. *Gels (Basel, Switzerland)*, 10(10), 619. DOI: 10.3390/gels10100619

Lochhead, R. Y., & Huisinga, L. R. (2008). Revolutionary trends in the advancement and integration of cosmetic science: Combinatorial formulation. *International Journal of Cosmetic Science*, 30(1), 77–77. DOI: 10.1111/j.1468-2494.2007.00411_1.x

Machado, A., Vareiro, L., Sousa, B., Figueira, V., & Lavandoski, J. (2022). Green marketing trends in specific contexts of tourism and music festivals: preliminary insights. In Advances in Tourism, Technology and Systems: Selected Papers from ICOTTS 2021 (Vol. 2, pp. 87–96). Springer Nature Singapore. doi:DOI: 10.1007/978-981-16-9701-2_8

Menon, G. K. (2014). Skin basics; structure and function. In *Lipids and skin health* (pp. 9–23). Springer International Publishing.

Nadanyiova, M., Gajanova, L., & Majerova, J. (2020). Green marketing as a part of the socially responsible brand's communication from the aspect of generational stratification. *Sustainability (Basel)*, 12(17), 7118. DOI: 10.3390/su12177118

Nibert, D. (2013). *Animal oppression and human violence: Domesecration, capitalism, and global conflict*. Columbia University Press.

Nohynek, G. J., Antignac, E., Re, T., & Toutain, H. (2010). Safety assessment of personal care products/cosmetics and their ingredients. *Toxicology and Applied Pharmacology*, 243(2), 239–259. DOI: 10.1016/j.taap.2009.12.001

Popović, S., Cvetković, M., & Avramović, M. (2023). Green marketing in the function of sustainable development. *Ekonomika (Nis)*, 69(2), 61–73. DOI: 10.5937/ekonomika2302061P

Rivera Maulucci, M. S. (2023). A History of Ecojustice and Sustainability: The Place Onde Two rivers Meet. In Transforming Education for Sustainability: Discourses on Justice, Inclusion, and Authenticity (pp. 11–37). Springer International Publishing. doi:DOI: 10.1007/978-3-031-13536-1_2

Santos, V., Augusto, T., Vieira, J., Bacalhau, L., Sousa, B. M., & Pontes, D. (2023). E-commerce: issues, opportunities, challenges, and trends. *Promoting organizational performance through 5G and agile marketing*, 224-244.

Sarkar, A. N. (2013). Promoting eco-innovations to leverage sustainable development of eco-industry and green growth. *European Journal of Sustainable Development*, 2(1), 171–171.

Serafim, A., Veloso, C. M., Rivera-Navarro, J., & Sousa, B. (2024). Emotional Intelligence and Internal Marketing as Determinants of Job Satisfaction and Satisfaction with Life among Portuguese Professionals. *Sustainability (Basel)*, 16(5), 1932. DOI: 10.3390/su16051932

Shimul, A. S. (2022). Brand attachment: A review and future research. *Journal of Brand Management*, 29(4), 400–419. DOI: 10.1057/s41262-022-00279-5

Silva, R. D., Maia, G. A., Sousa, P. D., & Costa, J. D. (2008). Composition and therapeutic properties of bee honey. *Food and Nutrition Araraquara*, 17(1), 113–120.

Sousa, B., Veloso, C., & Magueta, D. (2020). Green marketing as an instrument for business competitiveness: A theoretical contribution. In *35th IBIMA Conference* (pp. 1-2).

Sousa, B. B., & Soares, D. B. (2021). Digital communication as a vehicle for cause-related marketing in cancer prevention: Lactogal case study. *Cause-Related Marketing: Case Studies From a Global Perspective*, 247-254.

Stewart, S. (2017). *Painted faces: A colourful history of cosmetics*. Amberley Publishing Limited.

Suryavanshi, P., & Agrawal, A. (2023, September 13). The Study of Sustainable Green Marketing: Commercial, Environmental and Social Benefits of Green Marketing and Their Effects. Journal of Sales. *Service and Marketing Research*, 4(2), 18–24. DOI: 10.46610/JSSMR.2023.v04i02.003

Tanner, C., & Wölfing Kast, S. (2003). Promoting sustainable consumption: Determinants of green purchases by Swiss consumers. *Psychology and Marketing*, 20(10), 883–902. DOI: 10.1002/mar.10101

Thiboutot, D. (2004). Regulation of human sebaceous glands. *The Journal of Investigative Dermatology*, 123(1), 1–12. DOI: 10.1111/j.1523-1747.2004.t01-2-.x

Trkulja, Ž. M., Primorac, D., & Bilić, I. (2024). Exploring the Role of Socially Responsible Marketing in Promoting Diversity, Equity, and Inclusion in Organizational Settings. *Administrative Sciences*, 14(4), 66. DOI: 10.3390/admsci14040066

Van de Ven, B. (2008). An ethical framework for the marketing of corporate social responsibility. *Journal of Business Ethics*, 82(2), 339–352. DOI: 10.1007/s10551-008-9890-1

KEY TERMS AND DEFINITIONS

Child Health: Ensuring that children receive essential, life-saving health and nutrition services from an early age and throughout their development supports their growth, learning and long-term economic opportunity. Nutrition affects all aspects of human development.

Dermocosmetics: Is an area that aims to care for the skin in a deeper and more effective way, using pharmacological active ingredients in its composition. Dermocosmetics are products that have a high degree of safety and effectiveness, as they are developed based on rigorous clinical and scientific studies.

Health Marketing: Is a process of strategic outreach and communications designed to attract healthcare consumers, guide them through their healthcare journey, and keep them engaged with the health system.

Socially Responsible Marketing: Socially responsible marketing focuses on internal actions aimed at social issues. Here, company employees are invited to promote difference in their environment, through institutional campaigns and projects that the company supports.

Compilation of References

Abdelhalim, K., & Eldin, A. G. (2019). Can CSR help achieve sustainable development? Applying a new assessment model to CSR cases from Egypt. *The International Journal of Sociology and Social Policy*, 39(9/10), 773–795. DOI: 10.1108/IJSSP-06-2019-0120

Abratt, R., & Sacks, D. (1988). The marketing challenge: Towards being profitable and socially responsible. *Journal of Business Ethics*, 7(7), 497–507. DOI: 10.1007/BF00382596

Adel, H. M., Zeinhom, G. A., & Younis, R. A. A. (2022). From university social responsibility to social innovation strategy for quality accreditation and sustainable competitive advantage during the COVID-19 pandemic. *Journal of Humanities and Applied Social Sciences*, 4(5), 410–437. DOI: 10.1108/JHASS-04-2021-0086

Adepoju, V. A., Oladimeji, K. E., Adejumo, O. A., Adepoju, O. E., Adelekan, A., & Oladimeji, O. (2022). Knowledge of international standards for tuberculosis care among private non-NTP providers in Lagos, Nigeria: A cross-sectional study. *Tropical Medicine and Infectious Disease*, 7(8), 192. DOI: 10.3390/tropicalmed7080192 PMID: 36006284

Aguinis, H., & Glavas, A. (2013). Embedded versus peripheral corporate social responsibility: Psychological foundations. *Industrial and Organizational Psychology: Perspectives on Science and Practice*, 6(4), 314–332. DOI: 10.1111/iops.12059

Agyemang-Duah, W., Arthur-Holmes, F., Sobeng, A. K., Peprah, P., Dokbila, J. M., Asare, E., & Okyere, J. (2019). Corporate social responsibility in public health provision: Community members' assessment. *Cogent Medicine*, 6(1), 1622999. Advance online publication. DOI: 10.1080/2331205X.2019.1622999

Ahmad, N., Ullah, Z., Ryu, H. B., Ariza-Montes, A., & Han, H. (2023). From corporate social responsibility to employee well-being: Navigating the pathway to sustainable healthcare. *Psychology Research and Behavior Management*, 16, 1079–1095. DOI: 10.2147/PRBM.S398586 PMID: 37041962

Ahmed, J. U., Islam, Q. T., Ahmed, A., Faroque, A. R., & Uddin, M. J. (2021). Corporate social responsibility in the wake of COVID-19: Multiple cases of social responsibility as an organizational value. *Society and Business Review*, 16(4), 496–516. DOI: 10.1108/SBR-09-2020-0113

Ahmed, S. M., Naher, N., Hossain, T., & Rawal, L. (2017). Exploring the status of retail private drug shops in Bangladesh and action points for developing an accredited drug shop model: A facility based cross-sectional study. *Journal of Pharmaceutical Policy and Practice*, 10(1), 21. Advance online publication. DOI: 10.1186/s40545-017-0108-8

Ahmed, S. M., Naher, N., Tune, S. N. B. K., & Islam, B. Z. (2022). The Implementation of National Action Plan (NAP) on Antimicrobial Resistance (AMR) in Bangladesh: Challenges and Lessons Learned from a Cross-Sectional Qualitative Study. *Antibiotics (Basel, Switzerland)*, 11(5), 690. DOI: 10.3390/antibiotics11050690

Ajzen, I. (1991). The Theory of Planned Behavior. In Organizational Behavior and Human Decision Processes (Vol. 50). DOI: 10.1016/0749-5978(91)90020-T

Ajzen, I. (2001). Nature and operation of attitudes. *Annual Review of Psychology*, 52(1), 27–58. DOI: 10.1146/annurev.psych.52.1.27 PMID: 11148298

Akdis, C. A., Akdis, M., Bieber, T., Bindslev-Jensen, C., Boguniewicz, M., Eigenmann, P., Hamid, Q., Kapp, A., Leung, D. Y. M., Lipozencic, J., Luger, T. A., Muraro, A., Novak, N., Platts-Mills, T. A. E., Rosenwasser, L., Scheynius, A., Simons, F. E. R., Spergel, J., Turjanmaa, K., & Zuberbier, T. (2006). Diagnosis and treatment of atopic dermatitis in children and adults: European Academy of Allergology and Clinical Immunology/American Academy of Allergy, Asthma and Immunology/PRACTALL Consensus Report. *The Journal of Allergy and Clinical Immunology*, 118(1), 152–169. DOI: 10.1016/j.jaci.2006.03.045

Akinsemolu, A. A., & Onyeaka, H. N. (2024). Microorganisms Associated with Food Spoilage and Foodborne Diseases. In Food Safety and Quality in the Global South (pp. 489–531). Springer Nature Singapore. doi:DOI: 10.1007/978-981-97-2428-4_16

Alavi, H., Habek, P., & Cierna, H. (2016). Corporate social responsibility and self-regulation. *MM Science Journal*, 2016(04), 1121–1126. DOI: 10.17973/MMSJ.2016_10_201681

Albareda, L. (2010). Mapping the novel arrangements adopted to build the corporate responsibility institutional setting. *Journal of Corporate Citizenship*, 40(40), 75–100. DOI: 10.9774/GLEAF.4700.2010.wi.00007

Alharbi, T. S. J., Ekman, I., Olsson, L. E., Dudas, K., & Carlström, E. (2012). Organizational culture and the implementation of person centered care: Results from a change process in Swedish hospital care. *Health Policy (Amsterdam)*, 108(2-3), 294–301. DOI: 10.1016/j.healthpol.2012.09.003 PMID: 23069131

Ali, S. S., & Kaur, R. (2021). Effectiveness of corporate social responsibility (CSR) in implementation of social sustainability in warehousing of developing countries: A hybrid approach. *Journal of Cleaner Production*, 324, 129154. DOI: 10.1016/j.jclepro.2021.129154

Alkhaibari, R. A., Smith-Merry, J., Forsyth, R., & Raymundo, G. M. (2023). Patient-centered care in the Middle East and North African region: a systematic literature. DOI: 10.1186/s12913-023-09132-0

Allen, K., & Smith, J. (2024). Corporate Social Responsibility and health equity: A comprehensive review. *Journal of Sustainable Health*, 12(1), 45–67. DOI: 10.1234/jshe.2024.01234

Allen, M., & Patel, R. (2024). CSR strategies for universal health coverage: An analytical perspective. *Health Coverage Review*, 13(4), 143–159. DOI: 10.2345/hcr.2024.143

Almaqtari, F. A., Elsheikh, T., Hussainey, K., & Al-Bukhrani, M. A. (2024). Country-level governance and sustainable development goals: Implications for firms' sustainability performance. *Studies in Economics and Finance*, 41(3), 684–723. DOI: 10.1108/SEF-05-2023-0272

Al-Meerza, A., Al-Sayegh, S. F. Y., Al-Sayrafy, L. M., Alkoot, E. M., El-Shazly, M. K., & Kamel, M. I. (2012). Comparison of sources and expressions of stress among hospital and primary health care physicians. *Alexandria Journal of Medicine*, 48(4), 367–371. DOI: 10.1016/j.ajme.2012.02.001

Alssageer, M. A., & Kowalski, S. R. (2013). What do Libyan doctors perceive as the benefits, ethical issues and influences of their interactions with pharmaceutical company representatives? *The Pan African Medical Journal*, 14, 14. DOI: 10.11604/pamj.2013.14.132.2598

Altawalbeh, S. M., Ibrahim, I. A., & Al-Shatnawi, S. F. (2020). Influence of pharmaceutical promotion on prescribers in Jordan. *International Journal of Clinical Pharmacy*, 42(2), 744–755. DOI: 10.1007/s11096-020-01006-3

Amer, M. (2023). Systematic review of religiosity and social responsibility. *Journal of Business and Socio-economic Development*. https://doi.org/doi:10.1108/JBSED-02-2023-0007

Andersson, G. (2014). The Internet and CBT: A Clinical Guide. CRC Press. https://books.google.com.mt/books?hl=en&lr=&id=ColqBAAAQBAJ&oi=fnd&pg=PP1&dq=Andersson+G.+The+internet+and+CBT:+A+clinical+guide+2014+CRC+Press+Boca+Raton+&ots=bbFvMwOLpf&sig=1OJd30x3lKbWjZ2u6btdnhzSGKY&redir_esc=y#v=onepage&q&f=false

Andersson, G. (2016). Internet-Delivered Psychological Treatments. *Annual Review of Clinical Psychology*, 12(1), 157–179. DOI: 10.1146/annurev-clinpsy-021815-093006 PMID: 26652054

Andrews, G., Basu, A., Cuijpers, P., Craske, M. G., McEvoy, P., English, C. L., & Newby, J. M. (2018). Computer therapy for the anxiety and depression disorders is effective, acceptable and practical health care: An updated meta-analysis. *Journal of Anxiety Disorders*, 55, 70–78. DOI: 10.1016/j.janxdis.2018.01.001 PMID: 29422409

Apap, B. (2018). Levels of burnout amongst nursing and caring staff in Maltese long-term care facilities [University Of Malta]. https://www.um.edu.mt/library/oar/bitstream/123456789/40365/4/18MGER001.pdf

Apolinário-Hagen, J., Fritsche, L., Bierhals, C., & Salewski, C. (2018). Improving attitudes toward e-mental health services in the general population via psychoeducational information material: A randomized controlled trial. *Internet Interventions : the Application of Information Technology in Mental and Behavioural Health*, 12, 141–149. DOI: 10.1016/j.invent.2017.12.002 PMID: 30135778

Apolinário-Hagen, J., Harrer, M., Kählke, F., Fritsche, L., Salewski, C., & Ebert, D. D. (2018). Public attitudes toward guided internet-based therapies: Web-based survey study. *Journal of Medical Internet Research*, 20(5), e10735. Advance online publication. DOI: 10.2196/10735 PMID: 29764797

Apolinário-Hagen, J., Hennemann, S., Kück, C., Wodner, A., Geibel, D., Riebschläger, M., Zeißler, M., & Breil, B. (2020). Exploring User-Related Drivers of the Early Acceptance of Certified Digital Stress Prevention Programs in Germany. *Health Services Insights*, 13. Advance online publication. DOI: 10.1177/1178632920911061 PMID: 32206013

Apolinário-Hagen, J., Vehreschild, V., & Alkoudmani, R. M. (2017). Current Views and Perspectives on E-Mental Health: An Exploratory Survey Study for Understanding Public Attitudes Toward Internet-Based Psychotherapy in Germany. *JMIR Mental Health*, 4(1), e8. DOI: 10.2196/mental.6375 PMID: 28232298

Aregay, A., O'Connor, M., Stow, J., Ayers, N., & Lee, S. (2020). Strategies used to establish palliative care in rural low- and middle-income countries: An integrative review. *Health Policy and Planning*, 35(8), 1110–1129. DOI: 10.1093/heapol/czaa051 PMID: 32577766

Arli, D., & Cadeaux, J. (2014). Drivers of corporate community involvement and challenges in measuring its impact. *Social Responsibility Journal*, 10(1), 161–183. DOI: 10.1108/SRJ-10-2012-0116

Armstrong, R. A. (2014). When to use the Bonferroni correction. In Ophthalmic & physiological optics : the journal of the British College of Ophthalmic Opticians (Optometrists) (Vol. 34, Issue 5, pp. 502–508). Ophthalmic Physiol Opt. DOI: 10.1111/opo.12131

Arora, B., & Puranik, R. (2004). A review of corporate social responsibility in India. *Development*, 47(3), 93–100. DOI: 10.1057/palgrave.development.1100057

Ashraf, Z., Afshan, G., & Sahibzada, U. F. (2022). Unpacking strategic corporate social responsibility in the time of crisis: A critical review. *Journal of Global Responsibility*, 13(2), 127–156.

Asuata, P. (2024). *Corporate Social Responsibility (CSR) & Corporate Profitability (CP): A Case Study of For-Profit & Non-For-Profit Organizations in the North-East of England* (Doctoral dissertation, The University of Sunderland).

Avadhani. (2024). Corporate social responsibility and Indian healthcare sector: An analysis. GSC Advanced Research and Reviews, 18(1), 235-265. https://doi.org/ DOI: 10.30574/gscarr.2024.18.1.0496

Awa, H. O., Etim, W., & Ogbonda, E. (2024). Stakeholders, stakeholder theory and Corporate Social Responsibility (CSR). *International Journal of Corporate Social Responsibility*, 9(1), 11. DOI: 10.1186/s40991-024-00094-y

Awal, A., Saidy, S., & Aliullah, M. (2021). The unethical practices of the pharmaceutical industries in Bangladesh in their drug promotion and its impacts. *International Journal of Engineering and Management Research*, 11(4), 1–5. DOI: 10.31033/ijemr.11.4.1

Aydon Simmons, J. (2009). "Both sides now": Aligning external and internal branding for a socially responsible era. *Marketing Intelligence & Planning*, 27(5), 681–697. DOI: 10.1108/02634500910977890

Azzopardi-Muscat, N., Buttigieg, S., Calleja, N., & Merkur, S. (2017). Health Systems in Transition: Malta (Vol. 19 No. 1 2017). In Malta. *Health Systems Review*, 19(1).

Bacha, K., Hanley, T., & Winter, L. A. (2020). 'Like a human being, I was an equal, I wasn't just a patient': Service users' perspectives on their experiences of relationships with staff in mental health services. *Psychology and Psychotherapy: Theory, Research and Practice*, 93(2), 367–386. DOI: 10.1111/papt.12218 PMID: 30720230

Bae, G., Ahn, J., Lim, K., & Bae, S. (2022). Corporate social responsibility of pharmaceutical industry in Korea. *Frontiers in Pharmacology*, 13, 950669. Advance online publication. DOI: 10.3389/fphar.2022.950669

Bajaj Finserv collaborates with Sightsavers to bring inclusive education and promote disability rights across four districts in India. (2022, September 15). *The CSR Journal*. https://thecsrjournal.in/bajaj-finserv-collaborates-with-sightsavers-to-bring-inclusive-education-and-promote-disability-rights-across-four-districts-in-india/

Bajaj Finserv collaborates with Sightsavers to bring inclusive education and promote disability rights across three districts in India. (2022, October 14). *Sightsavers India*. https://www.sightsaversindia.org/news/2022/10/bajaj-finserv-collaborates-with-sightsavers-to-bring-inclusive-education-and-promote-disability-rights-across-three-districts-in-india/

Bajwah, S., Oluyase, A. O., Yi, D., Gao, W., Evans, C. J., Grande, G., Todd, C., Costantini, M., Murtagh, F. E., & Higginson, I. J. (2020). The effectiveness and cost-effectiveness of hospital-based specialist palliative care for adults with advanced illness and their caregivers. Cochrane Database of Systematic Reviews, 2020(9). DOI: 10.1002/14651858.CD012780.pub2

Barak, A., Klein, B., & Proudfoot, J. G. (2009). Defining internet-supported therapeutic interventions. In Annals of Behavioral Medicine (Vol. 38, Issue 1, pp. 4–17). DOI: 10.1007/s12160-009-9130-7

Barbosa, W., Zhou, K., Waddell, E., Myers, T., & Dorsey, E. R. (2021). Improving access to care: Telemedicine across medical domains. *Annual Review of Public Health*, 42(1), 463–481. DOI: 10.1146/annurev-publhealth-090519-093711 PMID: 33798406

Barros, C., & Sousa, BB (2021). The importance of Corporate Social Responsibility in consumer purchasing decisions: an exploratory study. European Journal of Applied Business and Management.

Baskin, J. (2006). Corporate responsibility in emerging markets. *Journal of Corporate Citizenship*, 2006(24), 29–47. DOI: 10.9774/GLEAF.4700.2006.wi.00006

Batson, C. D. (2011). *Altruism in Humans*. Oxford University Press.

Batterham, P. J., & Calear, A. L. (2017). Preferences for Internet-Based Mental Health Interventions in an Adult Online Sample: Findings From an Online Community Survey. *JMIR Mental Health*, 4(2), e26. DOI: 10.2196/mental.7722 PMID: 28666976

Baumeister, R. F. (1991). *Meanings of Life.*

Bautista-Bernal, I., Quintana-García, C., & Marchante-Lara, M. (2021). Research trends in occupational health and social responsibility: A bibliometric analysis. *Safety Science*, 137, 105167. DOI: 10.1016/j.ssci.2021.105167

Bebbington, J., & Unerman, J. (2018). Achieving the United Nations Sustainable Development Goals: An enabling role for accounting research. *Accounting, Auditing & Accountability Journal*, 31(1), 2–24. DOI: 10.1108/AAAJ-05-2017-2929

Becker, D. (2016). *Color trends and selection for product design: Every color sells a story*. William Andrew.

Bennett, S., & Moore, K. (2024). Corporate social responsibility and sustainable health systems: Case studies. *Sustainable Health Journal*, 10(1), 22–36. DOI: 10.6789/shj.2024.022

Bepari, A. K., Rabbi, G., Shaon, H. R., Khan, S. I., Zahid, Z. I., Dalal, K., & Reza, H. M. (2023). Factors Driving Antimicrobial Resistance in Rural Bangladesh: A Cross-Sectional Study on Antibiotic Use-Related Knowledge, Attitude, and Practice among Unqualified village medical Practitioners and pharmacy shopkeepers. *Advances in Therapy, 40*(8), 3478–3494. doi:DOI: 10.1007/s12325-023-02547-5

Bergman, T. D., Van der Plas, A. G., Pasman, H. R., & Onwuteaka-Philipsen, B. D. (2023). Awareness and actual knowledge of palliative care among older people: A Dutch national survey. *Journal of Pain and Symptom Management*, 66(3), 193–202. e2. DOI: 10.1016/j.jpainsymman.2023.05.005 PMID: 37207787

Berking, M., Eichler, E., Luhmann, M., Diedrich, A., Hiller, W., & Rief, W. (2019). Affect regulation training reduces symptom severity in depression – A randomized controlled trial. *PLoS One*, 14(8), e0220436. DOI: 10.1371/journal.pone.0220436 PMID: 31465443

Berle, A. A., & Means, G. C. (1932). *The Modern Corporation and Private Property.* Transaction Publishers.

Berry, N., Lobban, F., & Bucci, S. (2019). A qualitative exploration of service user views about using digital health interventions for self-management in severe mental health problems. *BMC Psychiatry*, 19(1), 35. Advance online publication. DOI: 10.1186/s12888-018-1979-1 PMID: 30665384

Bértiz Colomer, A. (2022). Nursing Homes: The Person-Centred Care (PCC) Model. In *Humanistic Perspectives in Hospitality and Tourism, Volume II: CSR and Person-Centred Care* (pp. 167-184). Cham: Springer International Publishing. DOI: 10.1007/978-3-030-95585-4_9

Bhardwaj, B. (2023). Impact of Corporate Social Responsibility on the Social Well-Being of Unprivileged with Mobile Medical Clinics. In *PRIMA* (Vol. 11, No. 1, p. 21). Publishing India Group. https://www.proquest.com/openview/d019c0321377064d1f449deae31f6210/1?pq-origsite=gscholar&cbl=2030962

Bhavnani, S. P., Narula, J., & Sengupta, P. P. (2016). Mobile technology and the digitization of healthcare. *European Heart Journal*, 37(18), 28. DOI: 10.1093/eurheartj/ehv770 PMID: 26873093

Bijnsdorp, F. M., Onwuteaka-Philipsen, B. D., Boot, C. R., Van der Beek, A. J., & Pasman, H. R. (2022). Caregiver's burden at the end of life of their loved one: Insights from a longitudinal qualitative study among working family caregivers. *BMC Palliative Care*, 21(1), 142. Advance online publication. DOI: 10.1186/s12904-022-01031-1 PMID: 35945558

Biswas, M., Roy, M. N., Manik, M. I. N., Hossain, M. S., Tapu, S. T. A., Moniruzzaman, M., & Sultana, S. (2014). Self medicated antibiotics in Bangladesh: A cross-sectional health survey conducted in the Rajshahi City. *BMC Public Health*, 14(1), 1–7. DOI: 10.1186/1471-2458-14-847

Blanck, P. (2020). Disability inclusive employment and the accommodation principle: Emerging issues in research, policy, and law. *Journal of Occupational Rehabilitation*, 30(4), 505–510. DOI: 10.1007/s10926-020-09940-9

Blom, J., den Elzen, W., van Houwelingen, A. H., Heijmans, M., Stijnen, T., Van den Hout, W., & Gussekloo, J. (2016). Effectiveness and cost-effectiveness of a proactive, goal-oriented, integrated care model in general practice for older people. A cluster randomized controlled trial: Integrated Systematic Care for older People—the ISCOPE study. *Age and Ageing*, 45(1), 30–41. DOI: 10.1093/ageing/afv174 PMID: 26764392

Boas, L. H. D. B. V., de Souza Sette, R., & de Brito, M. J. (2006). Consumer behavior of organic products: An application of the means-ends chain theory. *Rural & Agroindustrial Organizations*, 8(1), 25–39.

Bogoviz, A. V., Lobova, S. V., & Alekseev, A. N. (2022). The concept of corporate social responsibility based on integrating the SDGs into corporate strategies: International experience and the risks for profit. *Risks*, 10(6), 117. DOI: 10.3390/risks10060117

Bonna, A. S., Pavel, S. R., Ferdous, J., Khan, S. A., & Ali, M. (2022). Antibiotic resistance: An increasingly threatening but neglected public health challenge in Bangladesh. *International Journal of Surgery Open*, 49, 100581. DOI: 10.1016/j.ijso.2022.100581

Borges, M. S., Peres, F. I. G., Oliveira, D. M., Berretta, A. A., & Hori, J. I. (2021). Using honey as a complementary therapy: A review of the biological properties associated with honey. *Brazilian Applied Science Review*, 5(2), 1027–1045.

Borghouts, J., Eikey, E., Mark, G., De Leon, C., Schueller, S. M., Schneider, M., Stadnick, N., Zheng, K., Mukamel, D., & Sorkin, D. H. (2021). Barriers to and facilitators of user engagement with digital mental health interventions: Systematic review. In Journal of Medical Internet Research (Vol. 23, Issue 3). JMIR Publications Inc. DOI: 10.2196/24387

Boukouvalas, E., El-Den, S., Murphy, A. L., Salvador-Carulla, L., & O'Reilly, C. L. (2020). Exploring health care professionals' knowledge of, attitudes towards, and confidence in caring for people at risk of suicide: A systematic review. *Archives of Suicide Research*, 24(sup2), S1–S31. Advance online publication. DOI: 10.1080/13811118.2019.1586608 PMID: 30856366

Boulesnam, M., Seguiri, S., & Kebtan, C. (2021). The role of startups in the age of COVID-19 pandemic: Evidence from the world. *Administrative and Financial Sciences Review*, 5(2), 494–505. DOI: 10.37644/1939-005-002-026

Bowen, H. R. (1953). *Social responsibilities of the businessman*. Harper & Row.

Bowen, H. R. (1953). *Social Responsibility of the Businessman*. Harper and Row.

Bowling, A. (2014). *Research methods in health: investigating health and health services* (4th ed.). Open University Press. https://eprints.soton.ac.uk/371922/

Bradley, N., Lloyd-Williams, M., & Dowrick, C. (2018). Effectiveness of palliative care interventions offering social support to people with life-limiting illness-A systematic review. *European Journal of Cancer Care*, 27(3), e12837. DOI: 10.1111/ecc.12837 PMID: 29573500

Brammer, S., Jackson, G., & Matten, D. (2012). Corporate Social Responsibility and institutional theory: New perspectives on private governance. *Socio-economic Review*, 10(1), 3–28. DOI: 10.1093/ser/mwr030

Braveman, P., & Gottlieb, L. (2014). The social determinants of health: It's time to consider the causes of the causes. *Public Health Reports*, 129(1, suppl2), 19–31. DOI: 10.1177/00333549141291S206 PMID: 24385661

Brès, L., Mosonyi, S., Gond, J., Muzio, D., Mitra, R., Werr, A., & Wickert, C. (2019). Rethinking professionalization: A generative dialogue on CSR practitioners1. *Journal of Professions and Organization*, 6(2), 246–264. DOI: 10.1093/jpo/joz009

Britten, N., Moore, L., Lydahl, D., Naldemirci, O., Elam, M., & Wolf, A. (2017). Elaboration of the Gothenburg model of person-centred care. *Health Expectations*, 20(3), 407–418. DOI: 10.1111/hex.12468 PMID: 27193725

Brown, M., & Fardell, N. (2000). Sun damage and sunscreen preparations. In Poucher's Perfumes, Cosmetics and Soaps (pp. 467–503). Springer Netherlands. doi:DOI: 10.1007/978-94-017-2734-1_16

Brownie, S., & Nancarrow, S. (2013). Effects of person-centered care on residents and staff in aged-care facilities: A systematic review. *Clinical Interventions in Aging*, 8, 1–10. DOI: 10.2147/CIA.S38589 PMID: 23319855

Brown, R., & Green, T. (2024). Innovations in CSR for advancing SDG 3: Case studies and future directions. Global Health Policy Review, 8(2), 89-105. https://doi.org/DOI: 10.5678/ghpr.2024.089

Buber, M. (1971). *I and Thou*. Charles Scribner's Sons.

Buccoliero, L., & Nasi, G. (2004). Il sistema informativo delle aziende sanitarie italiane: stato dell'arte e prospettive evolutive dell'area clinica. In *Rapporto OASI 2004. L'aziendalizzazione della sanità in Italia* (pp. 559–578). Egea.

Buhmann, K. (2006). Corporate social responsibility: what role for law? Some aspects of law and CSR. *Corporate Governance: The International Journal of Business in Society, 6*(2), 188-202.

Buntrock, C., Ebert, D. D., Lehr, D., Smit, F., Riper, H., Berking, M., & Cuijpers, P. (2016). Effect of a web-based guided self-help intervention for prevention of major depression in adults with subthreshold depression a randomized clinical trial. *Journal of the American Medical Association*, 315(17), 1854–1863. DOI: 10.1001/jama.2016.4326 PMID: 27139058

Burchardt, T. (2004). Capabilities and disability: The capabilities framework and the social model of disability. *Disability & Society*, 19(7), 735–751. DOI: 10.1080/0968759042000284213

Buttigieg, S., Cachia, D., & Gauci, D. (2015). Stress, Burnout and Coping Strategies in the Emergency and Intensive Care Hospital Departments. In C. R. Hopkins (Ed.), Job Stress: Risk Factors, Health Effects and Coping Strategies (pp. 49–82). Nova Publisher. https://www.researchgate.net/publication/274256556_Stress_Burnout_and_Coping_Strategies_in_the_Emergency_and_Intensive_Care_Hospital_Departments

Buttigieg, S. C., Tomaselli, G., Byers, V., Cassar, M., Tjerbo, T., & Rosano, A. (2019). Corporate social responsibility and person-centered care: A scoping review. *Journal of Global Responsibility*, 10(4), 289–306. DOI: 10.1108/JGR-01-2019-0006

Byrne, A. L., Baldwin, A., & Harvey, C. (2020). Whose centre is it anyway? Defining person-centred care in nursing: An integrative review. *PLoS One*, 15(3), e0229923. Advance online publication. DOI: 10.1371/journal.pone.0229923 PMID: 32155182

Cadiz-Gurrea, M. D. L., Pinto, D., Delerue-Matos, C., & Rodrigues, F. (2021). Olive fruit and leaf wastes as bioactive ingredients for cosmetics—A preliminary study. [PubMed]. *Antioxidants*, 10(2), 245. DOI: 10.3390/antiox10020245

Campra, M., Esposito, P., & Brescia, V. (2023). Corporate social responsibility and technological perspectives in healthcare: An exploratory analysis of the evolution of the anti-corruption system through multiple case studies. *Corporate Social Responsibility and Environmental Management*, 30(6), 2816–2829. DOI: 10.1002/csr.2517

Cardenas, V., Rahman, A., Zhu, Y., & Enguidanos, S. (2021). Reluctance to accept palliative care and recommendations for improvement: Findings from semi-structured interviews with patients and caregivers. *The American Journal of Hospice & Palliative Care*, 39(2), 189–195. DOI: 10.1177/10499091211012605 PMID: 33896233

Carrol, A. B. (1979). A tree-dimensional model of corporate social performance. *Academy of Management Review*, 4.

Carroll, A. B. (1991). The pyramid of corporate social responsibility: Toward the moral management of organizational stakeholders. *Business Horizons*, 34(4), 39–48. DOI: 10.1016/0007-6813(91)90005-G

Carroll, A. B. (1999). Corporate social responsibility: Evolution of a definitional construct. *Business & Society*, 38(3), 268–295. DOI: 10.1177/000765039903800303

Carroll, A. B. (2009). A history of corporate social responsibility: Concepts and practices. In Crane, A., Matten, D., McWilliams, A., Moon, J., & Siegel, D. S. (Eds.), *The Oxford handbook of corporate social responsibility* (pp. 19–46). Oxford University Press. DOI: 10.1093/oxfordhb/9780199211593.003.0002

Carroll, A. B. (2015). Corporate social responsibility. *Organizational Dynamics*, 44(2), 87–96. DOI: 10.1016/j.orgdyn.2015.02.002

Carroll, A. B. (2021). Corporate social responsibility: Perspectives on the CSR construct's development and future. *Business & Society*, 60(6), 1258–1278. DOI: 10.1177/00076503211001765

Casey, L. M., Joy, A., & Clough, B. A. (2013). The impact of information on attitudes toward e-mental health services. *Cyberpsychology, Behavior, and Social Networking*, 16(8), 593–598. DOI: 10.1089/cyber.2012.0515 PMID: 23679567

Castillo-Villar, R. G. (2020). Identifying determinants of CSR implementation on SDG 17 partnerships for the goals. *Cogent Business & Management*, 7(1), 1847989. DOI: 10.1080/23311975.2020.1847989

Cattell, R. B. (1966). The scree test for the number of factors. *Multivariate Behavioral Research*, 1(2), 245–276. DOI: 10.1207/s15327906mbr0102_10 PMID: 26828106

Cé, F. R., da Silva, B. G., de Britto, R. E. D., & Fernandes, A. S. (2024). Corporate social responsibility communication during the COVID-19 pandemic: Comparison between Brazilian and British companies. *Revista Contemporânea*, 4(5), e4079. DOI: 10.56083/RCV4N5-047

Celma, D., Martinez-Garcia, E., & Raya, J. M. (2018). Socially responsible HR practices and their effects on employees' wellbeing: Empirical evidence from Catalonia, Spain. *European Research on Management and Business Economics*, 24(2), 82–89. DOI: 10.1016/j.iedeen.2017.12.001

Chandler, D. (2022). *Strategic corporate social responsibility: Sustainable value creation*. Sage Publications.

Chandra, A., Debnath, A., & Nongkynrih, B. (2023). Palliative care need in India: A systematic review and meta-analysis. *Indian Journal of Palliative Care*, 29, 375–387. DOI: 10.25259/IJPC_140_2023 PMID: 38058486

Chaniotakis, E., Siragusa, A., Tzanis, D., & Stamos, I. (2024). Scoping SDG interlinkages and methods to infer them. *International Journal of Sustainable Development*, 27(5), 1–54. DOI: 10.1504/IJSD.2024.140326

Chapple, W., & Moon, J. (2005). Corporate social responsibility (CSR) in Asia: A seven-country study of CSR web site reporting. *Business & Society*, 44(4), 415–441. DOI: 10.1177/0007650305281658

Chaudhri, V., & Wang, J. (2007). Communicating corporate social responsibility on the internet: A case study of the top 100 information technology companies in India. *Management Communication Quarterly, 21*(2), 232-247. .DOI: 10.1177/0893318907308746

Chelagat, T., Kokwaro, G., Onyango, J., & Rice, J. (2021). Sustainability drivers and inhibitors for the health system performance improvement projects in selected health facilities in Kenya: a qualitative study. *BMJ Open, 11*(7). .DOI: 10.1136/bmjopen-2019-035475

Chhaparia, P., & Jha, M. (2021). The role of CSR in skilling India. Corporate Social Responsibility and Sustainable Development, 153-165. DOI: 10.4324/9780429295997-13

Chilaka, M. A., & Nwaneke, P. K. (2016). Integrating corporate social responsibility, health improvement, and community support in development programmes: A case for enhancing the application of health impact assessment in programme implementation in the Niger Delta region. *Local Environment*, 21(3), 383–395. DOI: 10.1080/13549839.2014.1000287

Choy-Brown, M., Stanhope, V., & Bond, L. (2020). Delivering Person-centered care in community mental health programs. *Research on Social Work Practice*, 30(8), 8. DOI: 10.1177/1049731520944568

Christensen, H. B., Hail, L., & Leuz, C. (2019). *Adoption of CSR and sustainability reporting standards: Economic analysis and review* (Vol. 623). National Bureau of Economic Research.

Chudy-Onwugaje, K., Abutaleb, A., Buchwald, A., Langenberg, P., Regueiro, M., Schwartz, D. A., Kathleen Tracy, J., Ghazi, L., Patil, S. A., Quezada, S., Russman, K., Horst, S., Beaulieu, D., Quinn, C., Jambaulikar, G., & Cross, R. K. (2018). Age modifies the association between depressive symptoms and adherence to self-testing with Telemedicine in Patients with inflammatory bowel disease. *Inflammatory Bowel Diseases*, 24(12), 2648–2654. DOI: 10.1093/ibd/izy194 PMID: 29846623

Chu, W., & Chu, N.-F. (2024). Corporate social responsibility and social needs in health care sectors—A critical analysis of social innovation in the health sector in Taiwan. *Health Care*, 12(1543), 1543. Advance online publication. DOI: 10.3390/healthcare12151543 PMID: 39120246

Cipla. (2018). CSR Projects India, Companies and CSR, NGO partners, CSR funding India. https://csrbox.org/India_CSR_Project_Palliative-Healthcare-Maharashtra_11034

Claydon, J. (2011). A new direction for CSR: The shortcomings of previous CSR models and the rationale for a new model. *Social Responsibility Journal*, 7(3), 405–420. DOI: 10.1108/17471111111154545

Cliffe, B., Croker, A., Denne, M., & Stallard, P. (2020). Clinicians' use of and attitudes towards technology to provide and support interventions in child and adolescent mental health services. *Child and Adolescent Mental Health*, 25(2), 95–101. DOI: 10.1111/camh.12362 PMID: 32307835

Cohen, T. A., Patel, V. L., & Shortliffe, E. H. (2021). Intelligent Systems in Medicine and Health. *The Role of AI.*

Cohen, J. (1988). Statistical Power Analysis for the Behavioral Sciences. In *Statistical Power Analysis for the Behavioral Sciences*. Routledge. DOI: 10.4324/9780203771587

Collins, P. (2010). *CSR and ethical issues in operations management. Organizational Immunity to Corruption: Building Theoretical and Research Foundations, 225*. DOI: 10.4018/JGIM.2018100104

Collins, S. K. (2010). Corporate social responsibility and the future health care manager. *The Health Care Manager*, 29(4), 339–345. DOI: 10.1097/HCM.0b013e3181fa050e PMID: 21045586

Commission of the European Communities. (2001). Green paper: Promoting a European framework for corporate social responsibility.

Commission, E. U. (2006). *Implementing the Partnership for Growth and Jobs: Making Europe a Pole of Excellence on Corporate Social Responsibility*. E. Commission.

Commission, E. U. (2010). A strategy for smart, sustainable and inclusive growth. *Europe.*

Complete CSR report of hero motocorp. (2023, July 31). *The CSR Journal*. https://thecsrjournal.in/corporate-social-responsibility-complete-csr-report-hero-motocorp/

Cook, J., & Foster, L. (2024). CSR and healthcare innovation: Driving health equity. Health Innovation Review, 7(2), 78-93. https://doi.org/DOI: 10.5678/hir.2024.078

Cordero, J., De Zúñiga, T. O., & Rueda, M. (2014). *Disability and corporate social responsibility reporting: An analysis comparing reporting practices of 40 selected multinational enterprises*. (Working Paper No. 8). https://www.ilo.org/wcmsp5/groups/public/---ed_emp/---ifp_skills/documents/publication/wcms_316814.pdf

Crane, A., & Matten, D. (2021). COVID-19 and the future of CSR research. *Journal of Management Studies*, 58(1), 280–284. DOI: 10.1111/joms.12642

Cronin, J. J.Jr, Smith, J. S., Gleim, M. R., Ramirez, E., & Martinez, J. D. (2011). Green marketing strategies: An examination of stakeholders and the opportunities they present. *Journal of the Academy of Marketing Science*, 39(1), 158–174. DOI: 10.1007/s11747-010-0227-0

Crow, H., Gage, H., Hampson, S., Hart, J., Kimber, A., Storey, L., & Thomas, H. (2002). Measurement of satisfaction with health care: Implications for practice from a systematic review of the literature. *Health Technology Assessment*, 6(32). Advance online publication. DOI: 10.3310/hta6320 PMID: 12925269

CSR. Flipkart Foundation supports MITTI Cafe to catalyze mainstream inclusion, through skilling and sustainable livelihood opportunities for persons with disabilities. (2023, March 23). *The CSR Journal*. https://thecsrjournal.in/corporate-social-responsibility-csr-news-flipkart-foundation-supports-mitti-cafe-to-catalyze-mainstream-inclusion-through-skilling-and-sustainable-livelihood-opportunities-for-persons-with-disabilitie/

CSR. Flipkart Foundation supports Mitti Cafe to train and employ persons with disabilities. (2023, March 24). *India CSR*. https://indiacsr.in/csr-flipkart-foundation-supports-mitti-cafe-to-train-and-employ-persons-with-disabilities/

CSRBOX. (2023). India CSR Outlook Report. Source: https://indiacsr.in/wp-content/uploads/2023/10/India-CSR-Outlook-Report-2023.pdf

Culliford, L. (2005). *Healing from Within: Spirituality and Mental Health*. Royal College of Psychiatrists, Spirituality and Psychiatry Special Interest Group.

Daú, G., Scavarda, A., Scavarda, L. F., & Portugal, V. J. T. (2019). The healthcare sustainable supply chain 4.0: The circular economy transition conceptual framework with the corporate social responsibility mirror. *Sustainability (Basel)*, 11(12), 3259. DOI: 10.3390/su11123259

Davidson, L., Chinman, M., Kloos, B., Weingarten, R., Stayner, D., & Tebes, J. K. (1999). Peer support among individuals with severe mental illness: A review of the evidence. *Clinical Psychology : a Publication of the Division of Clinical Psychology of the American Psychological Association*, 6(2), 165–187. DOI: 10.1093/clipsy.6.2.165

Davidson, L., O'Connell, M., Tondora, J., Staeheli, M., & Evans, A. (2005). Recovery in serious mental illness: A new wine or just a new bottle? *Professional Psychology, Research and Practice*, 36(5), 480–487. DOI: 10.1037/0735-7028.36.5.480

Davidson, L., Tondora, J., & Ridgway, P. (2012). Life is not an 'outcome': Reflections on recovery as an outcome and as a process. *Journal of Psychiatric Rehabilitation*, 13(1), 1–8.

Davies, E., & Higginson, I. J. (2004). *Better palliative care for older people*. World Health Organization. Regional Office for Europe.

Davis, K. (1960). Can business afford to ignore social responsibilities? *California Management Review*, 2(3), 70–76. DOI: 10.2307/41166246

Davis, M., & Wilson, L. (2024). Leveraging corporate philanthropy for sustainable health systems. *Health Equity Journal*, 15(3), 234–248. DOI: 10.9101/hej.2024.234

Daykin, J. (2022). *Inclusive Marketing: Why Representation Matters to Your Customers and Your Brand*. Kogan Page Publishers.

De Beco, G. (2020). Intersectionality and disability in international human rights law. *International Journal of Human Rights*, 24(5), 593–614. DOI: 10.1080/13642987.2019.1661241

De Beco, G. (2021). Theoretical background: The inclusion of disabled people. In De Beco, G. (Ed.), *Disability in International Human Rights Law* (pp. 46–63). Oxford University Press. DOI: 10.1093/oso/9780198824503.003.0004

de Silva, D. (2011). *Evidence: Helping people help themselves*. The Health Foundation. https://www.health.org.uk/publications/evidence-helping-people-help-themselves

de Silva, D. (2012). *Helping people share decision making*. The Health Foundation. https://www.health.org.uk/publications/helping-people-share-decision-making

de Silva, D. (2014). *Helping measure person-centred care*. The Health Foundation.

De Zwaan, M., Herpertz, S., Zipfel, S., Svaldi, J., Friederich, H. C., Schmidt, F., Mayr, A., Lam, T., Schade-Brittinger, C., & Hilbert, A. (2017). Effect of internet-based guided self-help vs individual face-to-face treatment on full or subsyndromal binge eating disorder in overweight or obese patients: The INTERBED randomized clinical trial. *JAMA Psychiatry*, 74(10), 987–995. DOI: 10.1001/jamapsychiatry.2017.2150 PMID: 28768334

Doherty, M., Bond, L., Jessel, L., Tennille, J., & Stanhope, V. (2020). Transitioning to Person-Centered Care: A Qualitaive Study of Provider Perspectives. *The Journal of Behavioral Health Services & Research*, 47(3), 399–408. DOI: 10.1007/s11414-019-09684-2 PMID: 31820326

Do, N. T., Vu, H. T. L., Nguyen, C. T. K., Punpuing, S., Khan, W. A., Gyapong, M., Asante, K. P., Munguambe, K., Gómez-Olivé, F. X., John-Langba, J., Tran, T. K., Sunpuwan, M., Sevene, E., Nguyen, H. H., Ho, P. D., Matin, M. A., Ahmed, S., Karim, M. M., Cambaco, O., & Wertheim, H. (2021). Community-based antibiotic access and use in six low-income and middle-income countries: A mixed-method approach. *The Lancet. Global Health*, 9(5), e610–e619. DOI: 10.1016/S2214-109X(21)00024-3

Draelos, Z. D. (2006). The effect of a daily facial cleanser for normal to oily skin on the skin barrier of subjects with acne. *Cutis*, 78(1, Suppl), 34–40.

Droppert, H., & Bennett, S. (2015). Corporate social responsibility in global health: An exploratory study of multinational pharmaceutical firms. *Globalization and Health*, 11(1), 1–8. DOI: 10.1186/s12992-015-0100-5 PMID: 25886175

Duggirala, M., Rajendran, C., & Anantharaman, R. N. (2008). Patient-perceived dimensions of total quality service in healthcare. *Benchmarking*, 15(5), 560–583. DOI: 10.1108/14635770810903150

Dutta, P. K., Singh, B., Towfeek, A.-S. K., Adamopoulou, J. P., Bardavouras, A. N., Bamwerinde, W., Turyasingura, B., & Ayiga, N. (2024). IoT Revolutionizes Humidity Measurement and Management in Smart Cities to Enhance Health and Wellness. *Mesopotamian Journal of Artificial Intelligence in Healthcare*, 2024, 110–117. DOI: 10.58496/MJAIH/2024/013

Ebert, D. D., Cuijpers, P., Muñoz, R. F., & Baumeister, H. (2017). Prevention of mental health disorders using internet- and mobile-based interventions: A narrative review and recommendations for future research. *Frontiers in Psychiatry*, 8(AUG), 1. DOI: 10.3389/fpsyt.2017.00116 PMID: 28848454

Ebrahim, A. H., & Buheji, M. (2020). A pursuit for a 'holistic social responsibility strategic framework' addressing COVID-19 pandemic needs. *American Journal of Economics*, 10(5), 293–304. DOI: 10.5923/j.economics.20201005.04

Eccles, R. G., Ioannou, I., & Serafeim, G. (2014). The impact of corporate sustainability on organizational processes and performance. *Management Science*, 60(11), 2835–2857. DOI: 10.1287/mnsc.2014.1984

Edvardsson, D., Fetherstonhaugh, D., McAuliffe, L., Nay, R., & Chenco, C. (2011). Job satisfaction amongst aged care staff: Exploring the influence of person-centered care provision. *International Psychogeriatrics*, 23(8), 1205–1212. DOI: 10.1017/S1041610211000159 PMID: 21320379

Eichenberg, C., Wolters, C., & Brähler, E. (2013). The internet as a mental health advisor in Germany - Results of a national survey. *PLoS One*, 8(11), 79206. DOI: 10.1371/journal.pone.0079206 PMID: 24278121

Ekman, I., Swedberg, K., Taft, C., Lindseth, A., Norberg, A., Brink, E., Carlsson, J., Dahlin-Ivanoff, S., Johansson, L.-I., Kjellgren, K., Liden, E., Ohlen, J., Olsson, L. E., Rosen, H., Rydmark, M., & Sunnerhagen, K. S. (2011). Person-centered care—Ready for prime time. *European Journal of Cardiovascular Nursing*, 10(4), 248–251. DOI: 10.1016/j.ejcnurse.2011.06.008 PMID: 21764386

ElAlfy, A., Palaschuk, N., El-Bassiouny, D., Wilson, J., & Weber, O. (2020). Scoping the evolution of corporate social responsibility (CSR) research in the sustainable development goals (SDGs) era. *Sustainability (Basel)*, 12(14), 5544. DOI: 10.3390/su12145544

Elkington, J. (1997). *Cannibals with forks: The triple bottom line of 21st century business.* Capstone.

Elkington, J., & Rowlands, I. H. (1999). Cannibals with forks: The triple bottom line of 21st century business. *Alternatives Journal*, 25(4), 42.

Elsig, M., & Amalric, F. (2008). Business and public–private partnerships for sustainability: Beyond corporate social responsibility? *Global Society*, 22(3), 387–404. DOI: 10.1080/13600820802090538

Epstein, E. M. (2002). Religion and business–the critical role of religious traditions in management education. *Journal of Business Ethics*, 38(1/2), 91–96. DOI: 10.1023/A:1015712827640

Epstein, R. M., & Street, R. L. (2019, October 21). The values and value of patient-centered care. *Annals of Family Medicine*, 2011. https://www.annfammed.org/content/9/2/100.shorton PMID: 21403134

Erhemjamts, O., Li, Q., & Venkateswaran, A. (2013). Corporate social responsibility and its impact on firms' investment policy, organizational structure, and performance. *Journal of Business Ethics*, 118(2), 395–412. DOI: 10.1007/s10551-012-1594-x

Erin, L., Karen, R. F., Reppermunc, S., & Troller, J. (2018). Access to mental health services: The experiences of people with intellectual disabilities. *Journal of Applied Research in Intellectual Disabilities*, 32(2), 2. DOI: 10.1111/jar.12533 PMID: 30306674

Espinoza, R. (2024). Practices of selected pharmaceutical companies on integration of community empowerment to corporate social responsibility (CSR): Development of holistic and sustainable CSR framework. *Journal of Humanities and Social Sciences Studies*, 6(5), 160–204. DOI: 10.32996/jhsss.2024.6.5.24

Esposito, P., & Antonucci, G. (2022). NGOs, corporate social responsibility and sustainable development trajectories in a new reformative spectrum: 'New wine in old bottles or old wine in new bottles?'. *Corporate Social Responsibility and Environmental Management*, 29(3), 609–619. DOI: 10.1002/csr.2223

EU Commission (2001). Green Paper - Promoting a European framework for Corporate Social Responsibility. COM (2001).

EU Commission (2002). Corporate Social Responsibility: A business contribution to sustainable development. COM (2002). 347.

EU Commission (2011). Comunicazione al Parlamento europeo, al Consiglio, al Comitato economico e sociale europeo e al Comitato delle Regioni, Strategia rinnovata dell'UE per il periodo 2011-2014 in materia di responsabilità sociale delle imprese, Bruxelles, 25.10.2011 COM (2011).

European Commission. (2011). A renewed EU strategy 2011-14 for corporate social responsibility.

Evans, N., & Thompson, G. (2024). Integrating health equity into corporate strategies: Best practices and challenges. *Corporate Social Responsibility Journal*, 20(1), 14–29. DOI: 10.1123/csrj.2024.014

Evans, P., & Smith, C. (2024). Impact assessment of CSR health programs on equity and access. *Journal of Health Impact Assessment*, 9(1), 33–47. DOI: 10.9101/jhia.2024.033

Eze, P., Idemili, C. J., & Lawani, L. O. (2024). Evaluating health systems' efficiency towards universal health coverage: A data envelopment analysis. *Inquiry*, 61, 00469580241235759. DOI: 10.1177/00469580241235759 PMID: 38456456

Faggini, M., Cosimato, S., Nota, F. D., & Nota, G. (2019). Pursuing sustainability for healthcare through digital platforms. *Sustainability (Basel)*, 11(1), 165. DOI: 10.3390/su11010165

Fai Ma, C., Luo, H., & Fong, L. (2023). Impact of community mental health services on the adult psychiatric admission through the emergency unit: A 20-year population-based study. *Lancet*, 39, 100814. DOI: 10.1016/j.lanwpc.2023.100814 PMID: 37927999

Fallah Shayan, N., Mohabbati-Kalejahi, N., Alavi, S., & Zahed, M. A. (2022). Sustainable development goals (SDGs) as a framework for corporate social responsibility (CSR). *Sustainability (Basel)*, 14(3), 1222. DOI: 10.3390/su14031222

Fasciglione, M. (2015). Corporate social responsibility and the right to employment of persons with disabilities. In Della Fina, V., & Cera, R. (Eds.), *Protecting the Rights of People with Autism in the Fields of Education and Employment: International, European and National Perspectives* (pp. 171–193). Springer International Publishing. DOI: 10.1007/978-3-319-13791-9_7

Fatima, T., & Elbanna, S. (2022). Corporate social responsibility (CSR) implementation: A review and a research agenda towards an integrative framework. *Journal of Business Ethics*, •••, 1–17. DOI: 10.1007/s10551-022-05000-2 PMID: 35125567

Feijt, M. A., De Kort, Y. A. W., Bongers, I. M. B., & IJsselsteijn, W. A. (2018). Perceived drivers and barriers to the adoption of eMental health by psychologists: The construction of the levels of adoption of eMental health model. *Journal of Medical Internet Research*, 20(4), e153. Advance online publication. DOI: 10.2196/jmir.9485 PMID: 29691215

Fernandes, J. D., Machado, M. C. R., & Oliveira, Z. N. P. D. (2011). Children and newborn skin care and prevention. *Anais Brasileiros de Dermatologia*, 86, 102–110. DOI: 10.1590/S0365-05962011000100014

Fiandrino, S., Scarpa, F., & Torelli, R. (2022). Fostering social impact through corporate implementation of the SDGs: Transformative mechanisms towards interconnectedness and inclusiveness. *Journal of Business Ethics*, 180(4), 959–973. DOI: 10.1007/s10551-022-05189-9

Firth-Cozens, J., & Greenhalgh, J. (1997). Doctors' perceptions of the links between stress and lowered clinical care. *Social Science & Medicine*, 44(7), 1017–1022. DOI: 10.1016/S0277-9536(96)00227-4 PMID: 9089922

Fishbein, M. A., & Ajzen, I. (1975). Belief, attitude, intention and behaviour: An introduction to theory and research. https://www.researchgate.net/publication/233897090_Belief_attitude_intention_and_behaviour_An_introduction_to_theory_and_research

Fliege, H., Rose, M., Arck, P., Walter, O. B., Kocalevent, R. D., Weber, C., & Klapp, B. F. (2005). The Perceived Stress Questionnaire (PSQ) reconsidered: Validation and reference values from different clinical and healthy adult samples. *Psychosomatic Medicine*, 67(1), 78–88. DOI: 10.1097/01.psy.0000151491.80178.78 PMID: 15673628

Flieger, S. P., Chui, K., & Koch-Weser, S. (2020). Lack of awareness and common misconceptions about palliative care among adults: Insights from a national survey. *Journal of General Internal Medicine*, 35(7), 2059–2064. DOI: 10.1007/s11606-020-05730-4 PMID: 32157652

Flipkart Foundation. (n.d.). Flipkart Foundation supports MITTI Cafe to catalyze mainstream inclusion, through skilling and sustainable livelihood opportunities for persons with disabilities. https://storiesflistgv2.blob.core.windows.net/stories/2023/03/Flipkart-Foundation-X-Mitti-Cafe-21032023.pdf

Fors, A., Ekman, I., Taft, C., Björkelund, C., Frid, K., Larsson, M. E., Thorn, J., Ulin, K., Wolf, A., & Swedberg, K. (2015). Person-centered care after acute coronary syndrome, from hospital to primary care—A randomized controlled trial. *International Journal of Cardiology*, 187, 693–699. DOI: 10.1016/j.ijcard.2015.03.336 PMID: 25919754

Foster, A., & Lee, M. (2024). CSR initiatives addressing maternal and child health disparities. *International Journal of Public Health*, 18(4), 312–327. DOI: 10.3456/ijph.2024.312

Francesconi, A. (2007). *Innovazione organizzativa e tecnologica in sanità. Il ruolo dell'health technology assessment* (Vol. 29). FrancoAngeli.

Francis, C. K. (2001). Medical ethos and social responsibility in clinical medicine. *Journal of Urban Health*, 78(1), 29–45. DOI: 10.1093/jurban/78.1.29 PMID: 11368201

Freeman, R. E., Harrison, J. S., Wicks, A. C., Parmar, B. L., & De Colle, S. (2010). Stakeholder theory: The state of the art.

Freeman, I., & Hasnaoui, A. (2011). The meaning of corporate social responsibility: The vision of four nations. *Journal of Business Ethics*, 100(3), 419–443. DOI: 10.1007/s10551-010-0688-6

Freeman, J. Q., Scott, A. W., & Akhiwu, T. O. (2024). Rural–urban disparities and trends in utilization of palliative care services among US patients with metastatic breast cancer. *The Journal of Rural Health*, 40(4), 602–609. Advance online publication. DOI: 10.1111/jrh.12826 PMID: 38375950

Freeman, R. E. (2010). *Strategic management: A stakeholder approach*. Cambridge university press. DOI: 10.1017/CBO9781139192675

French, M., Hansford, L., & Moeke-Maxwell, T. (2023). Reflecting on choices and responsibility in palliative care in the context of social disadvantage. *Palliative Care and Social Practice*, 17. Advance online publication. DOI: 10.1177/26323524231193037 PMID: 37654731

Friederick, W. C. (1978). From CSR to CRS. *Business & Society*, 33(2), 1994.

Friedman, M. (1970, September 13). The social responsibility of business is to increase its profits. The New York Times Magazine, 32-33.

Friedman, M., & Friedman, R. D. (1962). *Capitalism and freedom. [By] M. Friedman, with the assistance of Rose D. Friedman*. University of Chicago Press.

Galant, A., & Cadez, S. (2017). Corporate social responsibility and financial performance relationship: A review of measurement approaches. *Ekonomska Istrazivanja*, 30(1), 676–693. DOI: 10.1080/1331677X.2017.1313122

Galatzer-Levy, I. R., & Bonanno, G. A. (2014). Optimism and Death: Predicting the Course and Consequences of Depression Trajectories in Response to Heart Attack. *Psychological Science*, 25(12), 2177–2188. DOI: 10.1177/0956797614551750 PMID: 25298294

Galea, M. & Mallia. N. (2024). Towards a person-centered care model among community mental health services. *European Journal of Psychotherapy & Counseling*.

Galea, M. (2008). The Impact of Child Abuse on the Psycho-Spiritual and Religious Status of Maltese College Students. *Pastoral Psychology*, 57(3-4), 147–159. DOI: 10.1007/s11089-008-0159-5

Galea, M. (2014a). The Progressive Impact of Burnout on Maltese Nurses. *SOP Transactions on Psychology*, 1(1), 1–12. DOI: 10.15764/STP.2014.01001

Galea, M. (2014c). Assessing the Incremental Validity of Spirituality in Predicting Nurses' Burnout. *Archiv für Religionspsychologie*, 36(1), 118–136. DOI: 10.1163/15736121-12341276

Galea, M., Ciarrocchi, J. W., Piedmont, R. L., & Wicks, R. J. (2007). Child Abuse, Personality, and Spirituality as Predictors of Happiness in Maltese College Students. *Research in the Social Scientific Study of Religion*, 18, 141–154. DOI: 10.1163/ej.9789004158511.i-301.57

Galea, M., & Galea, F. Z. (2023). Mental Health's address to the challenging cultural reality of Malta. *Humanities and Social Science Research*, 6(1), p22. Advance online publication. DOI: 10.30560/hssr.v6n1p22

Gallo, A. M., & Serluca, M. C. (2024). Corporate Social Responsibility and Stakeholders: a Systematic Literature Review. *Accounting and Taxation (IWAT2024)*, 196.

Gao, Y. (2011). CSR in an emerging country: A content analysis of CSR reports of listed companies. *Baltic Journal of Management*, 6(2), 263–291. DOI: 10.1108/17465261111131848

Garcia, L., & Patel, R. (2024). Corporate partnerships in achieving universal health coverage: A review. *Journal of Global Health*, 22(1), 56–72. DOI: 10.7890/jgh.2024.056

Garg, V., & Agarwal, S. (2021). An empirical study on the corporate social responsibility regime in India: Pre-COVID and COVID times. *Review of Market Integration*, 13(2-3), 124–153. DOI: 10.1177/09749292221093835

Gatti, L., Vishwanath, B., Seele, P., & Cottier, B. (2019). Are we moving beyond voluntary CSR? Exploring theoretical and managerial implications of mandatory CSR resulting from the new Indian companies act. *Journal of Business Ethics*, 160(4), 961–972. DOI: 10.1007/s10551-018-3783-8

Gautam, R., & Singh, A. (2010). Corporate social responsibility practices in India: A study of top 500 companies. *Global Business and Management Research*, 2(1), 41–56.

Gautam, R., & Singh, A. (2010). Corporate Social Responsibility Practices in India: A Study of Top 500 Companies. *Global Business and Management Research*, 2(1), 41–56.

Gebremariam, M. K., Bjune, G. A., & Frich, J. C. (2010). Barriers and facilitators of adherence to TB treatment in patients on concomitant TB and HIV treatment: A qualitative study. *BMC Public Health*, 10(1), 1–9. oi.org/10.1186/1471-2458-10-651. DOI: 10.1186/1471-2458-10-651 PMID: 21029405

Ghorbanzadeh, D., & Rahehagh, A. (2021). Emotional brand attachment and brand love: The emotional bridges in the process of transition from satisfaction to loyalty. *Rajagiri Management Journal*, 15(1), 16–38. DOI: 10.1108/RAMJ-05-2020-0024

Ghose, A., Kochher, H. S., & Ali, S. M. A. (2024). Towards equity and inclusion: Legal exploration for inclusive business practices integrating CSR and disability rights in India. In Pucelj, M., & Bohinc, R. (Eds.), Advances in Human and Social Aspects of Technology. DOI: 10.4018/979-8-3693-2325-0.ch006

Ghoshal, A., Khan Joad, A., Spruijt, O., Nair, S., Rajagopal, M., Patel, F., Damani, A., Deodhar, J., Goswami, D., Joshi, G., Butola, S., Singh, C., Rao, S. R., Bhatwadekar, M., Muckaden, M. A., & Bhatnagar, S. (2022). Situational analysis of the quality of palliative care services across India: A cross-sectional survey. ecancermedicalscience, 16. DOI: 10.3332/ecancer.2022.1486

Gilbert, R. M. (2022). Reimagining digital healthcare with a patient-centric approach: The role of user experience (UX) research. *Frontiers in Digital Health*, 4, 899976. DOI: 10.3389/fdgth.2022.899976 PMID: 36016600

Godfrey, P. C., Merrill, C. B., & Hansen, J. M. (2009). The relationship between corporate social responsibility and shareholder value: An empirical test of the risk management hypothesis. *Strategic Management Journal*, 30(4), 425–445. DOI: 10.1002/smj.750

Godin, G., Bélanger-Gravel, A., Eccles, M., & Grimshaw, J. (2008). Healthcare professionals' intentions and behaviours: A systematic review of studies based on social cognitive theories. In Implementation Science (Vol. 3, Issue 1, pp. 1–12). BioMed Central. DOI: 10.1186/1748-5908-3-36

Gonzalez, E., & Reynolds, A. (2024). Corporate social responsibility and global health goals: Achieving SDG 3. *Industrial Health Review*, 18(2), 102–117. DOI: 10.2345/ihv.2024.102

Googins, B. K., Mirvis, P. H., & Rochlin, S. A. (2007). *Beyond good company: Next generation corporate citizenship*. Palgrave Macmillan. DOI: 10.1057/9780230609983

Gopalkrishnan, N. (2018). Cultural diversity and Mental Health. Considerations for Policy and Practice. *Frontiers in Public Health*, 6, 179. DOI: 10.3389/fpubh.2018.00179 PMID: 29971226

Gordon, R., & Vink, J. (2024). SDG commentary: Services from institutions that offer fair and sustainable living for all humans. *Journal of Services Marketing*, 38(2), 217–226. DOI: 10.1108/JSM-05-2023-0182

Gould, R., Harris, S. P., Mullin, C., & Jones, R. (2020). Disability, diversity, and corporate social responsibility: Learning from recognized leaders in inclusion. *Journal of Vocational Rehabilitation*, 52(1), 29–42. DOI: 10.3233/JVR-191058

Govindan, K. (2022). Theory building through corporate social responsibility 4.0 for achieving SDGs: A practical step toward integration of digitalization with practice-based view and social good theory. *IEEE Transactions on Engineering Management*, 71, 2103–2120. DOI: 10.1109/TEM.2022.3155247

Goyal, S., & Routroy, S. (2023). Analyzing environmental sustainability enablers for an Indian steel manufacturing supply chain. Journal of Engineering. *Design and Technology*, 21(1), 1–22. DOI: 10.1108/JEDT-03-2021-0118

Grammer, K., Fink, B., Møller, A. P., & Thornhill, R. (2003). Darwinian aesthetics: Sexual selection and the biology of beauty. *Biological Reviews of the Cambridge Philosophical Society*, 78(3), 385–407. DOI: 10.1017/S1464793102006085

Gross, J. J., Uusberg, H., & Uusberg, A. (2019). Mental illness and well-being: An affect regulation perspective. *World Psychiatry; Official Journal of the World Psychiatric Association (WPA)*, 18(2), 130–139. DOI: 10.1002/wps.20618 PMID: 31059626

Gulenko, M. (2018, December). Mandatory CSR reporting—literature review and future developments in Germany. In *NachhaltigkeitsManagementForum| Sustainability Management Forum* (Vol. 26, No. 1, pp. 3-17). Berlin/Heidelberg: Springer Berlin Heidelberg.

Guo, H., & Ren, S. (2018). How Do Firms Respond to Corporate Social Responsibility (CSR) Failures? Evidence from Product Recalls in China. *Journal of Business Ethics*, 152(4), 989–1006.

Gupta, A., & Sharma, M. (2019). Consumer perceptions of CSR and its impact on purchasing decisions in India. *Journal of Business Ethics*, 156(3), 671–683. DOI: 10.1007/s10551-017-3598-3

Gupta, V., Mohapatra, S., Mishra, H., Farooq, U., Kumar, K., Ansari, M. J., Aldawsari, M., Alalaiwe, A., Mirza, M., & Iqbal, Z. (2022). Nanotechnology in cosmetics and cosmeceuticals—A review of latest advancements. *Gels (Basel, Switzerland)*, 8(3), 173. DOI: 10.3390/gels8030173

Håkansson Eklund, J., Holmström, I. K., Kumlin, T., Kaminsky, E., Skoglund, K., Höglander, J., Sundler, A. J., Condén, E., & Summer Meranius, M. (2018). "Same same or different?" A review of reviews of person-centered and patient-centered care. *Patient Education and Counseling*, 102(1), 3–11. DOI: 10.1016/j.pec.2018.08.029 PMID: 30201221

Halkos, G. E., & Nomikos, S. N. (2021). Reviewing the status of corporate social responsibility (CSR) legal framework. *Management of Environmental Quality*, 32(4), 700–716. DOI: 10.1108/MEQ-04-2021-0073

Hall, L. H., Johnson, J., Watt, I., Tsipa, A., & O'Connor, D. B. (2016). Healthcare staff wellbeing, burnout, and patient safety: A systematic review. In PLoS ONE (Vol. 11, Issue 7). Public Library of Science. DOI: 10.1371/journal.pone.0159015

Hamann, R. (2009). An academic's perspective on the role of academics in corporate responsibility. Professionals' Perspectives of Corporate Social Responsibility, 347-361. DOI: 10.1007/978-3-642-02630-0_19

Hanna, L., Gill, S. D., Newstead, L., Hawkins, M., & Osborne, R. H. (2017). Patient perspectives on a personally controlled electronic health record used in regional Australia: 'I can be like my own doctor'. *The HIM Journal*, 46(1), 42–48. DOI: 10.1177/1833358316661063 PMID: 27486184

Hansson, E., Carlström, E., Olsson, L.-E., Nyman, J., & Koinberg, I. (2017). Can a person-centred-care intervention improve health-related quality of life in patients with head and neck cancer? A randomized, controlled study. *BMC Nursing*, 16(1), 9. DOI: 10.1186/s12912-017-0206-6 PMID: 28239295

Hansson, S. O., & Froding, B. (2020). Ethical conflicts in patient-centered care. *Clinical Ethics*, 16(2), 55–66. Advance online publication. DOI: 10.1177/1477750920962356

Harris, J., & Martinez, D. (2024). Evaluating the impact of CSR on public health outcomes. *Sustainable Health Systems Journal*, 10(3), 145–160. DOI: 10.6789/shsj.2024.145

Harsha Kumar, H., & Pai, U. (2015). A study on corporate social responsibility for the health care of the elderly by private health care providers of Mangalore city: A health systems research. *International Journal of Medicine and Public Health*, 5(2), 157. DOI: 10.4103/2230-8598.153826

Harshith, K. N. (2022, August 2). Hero Motocorp partners with CRPF to present retro fitted scooters to the specially-abled ex-personnel. *The Times of India*. https://timesofindia.indiatimes.com/auto/bikes/hero-motocorp-partners-with-crpf-to-present-retro-fitted-scooters-to-the-specially-abled-ex-personnel/articleshow/93294989.cms?from=mdr

Hart, S. M. (2010). Self-regulation, corporate social responsibility, and the business case: Do they work in achieving workplace equality and safety? *Journal of Business Ethics*, 92(4), 585–600. DOI: 10.1007/s10551-009-0174-1

Harvey, C., Zirnsak, T. M., Brasier, C., Ennals, P., Fletcher, J., Hamilton, B., Killaspy, H., McKenzie, P., Kennedy, H., & Brophy, L. (2023). Community-based models of care facilitating recovery of people living with persistent and complex mental health needs: A systematic and narrative synthesis. *Frontiers in Psychiatry*, 14, 1259944. Advance online publication. DOI: 10.3389/fpsyt.2023.1259944 PMID: 37779607

Haski-Leventhal, D. (2021). *Strategic corporate social responsibility: A holistic approach to responsible and sustainable business.*

Hawley, P. (2017). Barriers to access to palliative care. *Palliative Care*, 10, 117822421668888. DOI: 10.1177/1178224216688887 PMID: 28469439

Health. (n.d.). Service Unavailable. https://www.bharatpetroleum.in/social-responsibility/csr-thrust-areas/health.aspx https://indiacsr.in/csr/

Hedman, E., Ljótsson, B., & Lindefors, N. (2012). Cognitive behavior therapy via the Internet: A systematic review of applications, clinical efficacy and cost-effectiveness. In Expert Review of Pharmacoeconomics and Outcomes Research (Vol. 12, Issue 6, pp. 745–764). DOI: 10.1586/erp.12.67

Hemmelvoll, J. K., Karlsson, B., & Borg, M. (2015). Recovery and person-centredness in mental health services: roots of the concepts and implications for practice. *International Practice Development Journal,* 5(7). https://www.fons.org/Resources/Documents/Journal/Vol5Suppl/IPDJ_05(suppl)_07.pdf

Hennemann, S., Beutel, M. E., & Zwerenz, R. (2016). Drivers and barriers to acceptance of web-based aftercare of patients in inpatient routine care: A cross-sectional survey. *Journal of Medical Internet Research*, 18(12), e337. Advance online publication. DOI: 10.2196/jmir.6003 PMID: 28011445

Herrera, J., & de las Heras-Rosas, C. (2020). Corporate social responsibility and human resource management: Towards sustainable business organizations. *Sustainability (Basel)*, 12(3), 841. DOI: 10.3390/su12030841

Hess, J., & Story, J. (2005). Trust-based commitment: Multidimensional consumer-brand relationships. *Journal of Consumer Marketing*, 22(6), 313–322. DOI: 10.1108/07363760510623902

Holford, N., Heo, Y. A., & Anderson, B. (2013). A pharmacokinetic standard for babies and adults. *Journal of Pharmaceutical Sciences*, 102(9), 2941–2952. DOI: 10.1002/jps.23574

Hopkins, M. (2003). *The planetary bargain: Corporate social responsibility matters*. Tailor and Francis.

Hopkins, M. (2005). Measurement of corporate social responsibility. *International Journal of Management and Decision Making*, 6(3-4), 213–231. DOI: 10.1504/IJMDM.2005.006549

Hoque, R., Ahmed, S. M., Naher, N., Islam, M. A., Rousham, E. K., Islam, B. Z., & Hassan, S. (2020). Tackling antimicrobial resistance in Bangladesh: A scoping review of policy and practice in human, animal and environment sectors. *PLoS One*, 15(1), e0227947. DOI: 10.1371/journal.pone.0227947

Horgan, Á., & Sweeney, J. (2010). Young students' use of the internet for mental health information and support. *Journal of Psychiatric and Mental Health Nursing*, 17(2), 117–123. DOI: 10.1111/j.1365-2850.2009.01497.x PMID: 20465756

Hossain, M. J., Jabin, N., Ahmmed, F., Sultana, A., Abdur Rahman, S. M., & Islam, M. R. (2023). Irrational use of antibiotics and factors associated with antibiotic resistance: Findings from a cross-sectional study in Bangladesh. *Health Science Reports*, 6(8), e1465. DOI: 10.1002/hsr2.1465

Hsu, Y. H., Fang, W., & Lee, Y. (2009). Ethically questionable behavior in sales representatives–An example from the Taiwanese pharmaceutical industry. *Journal of Business Ethics*, 88(S1), 155–166. DOI: 10.1007/s10551-008-9823-z

Huang, S., Qu, H., & Wang, X. (2024). Impact of green marketing on peer-to-peer accommodation platform users' repurchase intention and positive word-of-mouth: Mediation of trust and consumer identification. *International Journal of Contemporary Hospitality Management*, 36(3), 691–712. DOI: 10.1108/IJCHM-10-2022-1300

Hung Chen, C. (2011). The major components of corporate social responsibility. *Journal of Global Responsibility*, 2(1), 85–99. DOI: 10.1108/20412561111128546

Huy, P. Q., & Phuc, V. K. (2020). Does strategic corporate social responsibility drive better organizational performance through integration with a public sector scorecard? Empirical evidence in a developing country. *Processes (Basel, Switzerland)*, 8(5), 596. DOI: 10.3390/pr8050596

Igbo, F. I. (2023). *Determining Strategies for Cost Effectiveness in Sustainable Healthcare Delivery–An Emerging Market Study* (Doctoral dissertation, Walden University).

Indian Oil. (n.d.). Corporate Social Responsibility Reaching out, Touching Lives. https://iocl.com/uploads/IndianOil_CSR_in_Aspirational_Districts.pdf

International Federation of Pharmaceutical Manufacturers & Associations. (2022). The Pharmaceutical Industry and Global Health.

Islam, M. S., Sikdar, K. Y. K., Hossain, A. M. A., & Faroque, A. B. M. (2019). Study on the pattern of antibiotic use including the resistance episodes in Bangladesh. *Dhaka University Journal of Pharmaceutical Sciences*, 18(2), 135–143. DOI: 10.3329/dujps.v18i2.43255

Islam, S., Rahman, A., & Al Mahmood, A. K. (2018). Bangladesh pharmaceutical industry: Perspective and the prospects. *Bangladesh Journal of Medical Science*, 17(4), 519–525. DOI: 10.3329/bjms.v17i4.38306

Ite, U. E. (2022). Achieving Sustainable Development Goals through Corporate Social Responsibility. In *Business and Sustainable Development in Africa* (pp. 179–202). Routledge. DOI: 10.4324/9781003038078-10

Jacob, C., Sezgin, E., Sanchez-Vazquez, A., & Ivory, C. (2022, January). Sociotechnical Factors Impacting Patients' Adoption of Mobile Health Tools: Systematic Literature Review and Narrative Synthesis. *JMIR mHealth and uHealth*, 10(5), e36284. Advance online publication. DOI: 10.2196/36284 PMID: 35318189

Jacob, K. S. (2015). Recovery model of mental illness: A complementary approach to psychiatric care. *Indian Journal of Psychological Medicine*, 37(2), 117–119. DOI: 10.4103/0253-7176.155605 PMID: 25969592

Jamali, D., Hallal, M., & Abdallah, H. (2010). Corporate governance and corporate social responsibility: evidence from the healthcare sector. *Corporate Governance: The international journal of business in society, 10*(5), 590-602. DOI: 10.1108/14720701011085562

Jamali, D., & Mirshak, R. (2007). Corporate social responsibility (CSR): Theory and practice in a developing country context. *Journal of Business Ethics*, 72(3), 243–262. DOI: 10.1007/s10551-006-9168-4

Jamali, D., Samara, G., & Hossary, M. (2019). Corporate social responsibility and development: The case of international business firms in emerging economies. In *Business and development studies* (pp. 286–309). Routledge. DOI: 10.4324/9781315163338-12

Johansson, O., Bjärehed, J., Andersson, G., Carlbring, P., & Lundh, L. G. (2019). Effectiveness of guided internet-delivered cognitive behavior therapy for depression in routine psychiatry: A randomized controlled trial. *Internet Interventions : the Application of Information Technology in Mental and Behavioural Health*, 17, 100247. Advance online publication. DOI: 10.1016/j.invent.2019.100247 PMID: 31249791

John, J., Smiju, I. S., Thampi, K., & Joseph, M. K. (2024). Environmental, Social, and Governance (ESG) Sustainability Through Corporate Social Responsibility: A Scoping Review. *ESG Frameworks for Sustainable Business Practices*, 31-52. DOI: 10.4018/979-8-3693-3880-3.ch002

Johnson, E., & Carter, H. (2024). Data-driven approaches in CSR for health equity. *Health Technology Innovations*, 5(2), 78–90. DOI: 10.1234/hti.2024.078

Johora, F., & Rahman, M. S. (2018). Pharmaceutical promotion in Bangladesh: Assessing the strength of regulatory documents. *Bangladesh Journal of Bioethics*, 9(3), 1–10. DOI: 10.3329/bioethics.v9i3.48911

Jones, T. M. (1980). Corporate social responsibility revisited, redefined. *California Management Review*, 22(3), 59–67. DOI: 10.2307/41164877

Jumde, A. (2021). The law on CSR in India: An analysis of its compliance by companies through corporate disclosures. *Journal of Corporate Law Studies*, 21(1), 253–282. DOI: 10.1080/14735970.2020.1834265

Juss, S. (1997). Global Environmental Change: Health and the Challenge for Human Rights. *Indiana Journal of Global Legal Studies*, 5, 121.

Kabir, M. A., & Chowdhury, S. S. (2023). Empirical analysis of the corporate social responsibility and financial performance causal nexus: Evidence from the banking sector of Bangladesh. *Asia Pacific Management Review*, 28(1), 1–12. DOI: 10.1016/j.apmrv.2022.01.003

Kaiser, H. F. (1974). An Index of Factorial Simplicity. Psycometrika, 39(1). http://cda.psych.uiuc.edu/psychometrika_highly_cited_articles/kaiser_1974.pdf

Kallon, I. I. (2018). Influences on the continuity of care for patients with Mycobacterium tuberculosis referred from tertiary and district hospitals. https://open.uct.ac.za/items/0c494162-92b1-43dd-a9e6-f9e29bb02bc8

Kamila, M. K., & Jasrotia, S. S. (2023). Ethics and marketing responsibility: A bibliometric analysis and literature review. *Asia Pacific Management Review*, 28(4), 567–583. DOI: 10.1016/j.apmrv.2023.04.002

Karin, M., & Bollinger, L. (2020). Disability rights: past, present, and future: roadmap for disability rights. *University of the District of Columbia David A.Clarke School of Law Review*, 23(1), 1–22.

Katsanis, L. P., Pitta, D., & Morinville, A. (2021). Patient centricity: Lip service or genuine commitment? A qualitative examination of the pharmaceutical industry. *International Journal of Pharmaceutical and Healthcare Marketing*, 15(1), 106–133. DOI: 10.1108/IJPHM-02-2020-0010

Kenagy, J. W., Berwick, D. M., & Shore, M. F. (1999). Service quality in health care. *Journal of the American Medical Association*, 281(7), 661–665. DOI: 10.1001/jama.281.7.661 PMID: 10029131

Khandelwal, N., Brumback, L. C., Halpern, S. D., Coe, N. B., Brumback, B., & Curtis, J. R. (2017). Evaluating the economic impact of palliative and end-of-life care interventions on intensive care unit utilization and costs from the hospital and healthcare system perspective. *Journal of Palliative Medicine*, 20(12), 1314–1320. DOI: 10.1089/jpm.2016.0548 PMID: 28972860

Khan, S. A. R., Sheikh, A. A., Ashraf, M., & Yu, Z. (2022). Improving consumer-based green brand equity: The role of healthy green practices, green brand attachment, and green skepticism. *Sustainability (Basel)*, 14(19), 11829. DOI: 10.3390/su141911829

Khuong, M. N., Truong An, N. K., & Thanh Hang, T. T. (2021). Stakeholders and corporate social responsibility (CSR) programme as key sustainable development strategies to promote corporate reputation—Evidence from Vietnam. *Cogent Business & Management*, 8(1), 1917333. DOI: 10.1080/23311975.2021.1917333

Kim, B., Kim, M., & Lee, D. (2023). The mental health implications of Corporate Social Responsibility: The significance of the sense-making process and prosocial motivation. *Behavioral Sciences (Basel, Switzerland)*, 13(10), 10. DOI: 10.3390/bs13100870 PMID: 37887520

Kim, M. S., Kim, T., Lee, D., Yook, J., Hong, Y.-C., Lee, S.-Y., Yoon, J.-H., & Kang, M.-Y. (2018). Mental disorders among workers in the healthcare industry: 2014 national health insurance data. *Annals of Occupational and Environmental Medicine*, 30(1), 31. Advance online publication. DOI: 10.1186/s40557-018-0244-x PMID: 29755753

Kim, S. T., Lee, H. H., & Lim, S. (2021). The effects of green SCM implementation on business performance in SMEs: A longitudinal study in electronics industry. *Sustainability (Basel)*, 13(21), 11874. DOI: 10.3390/su132111874

Kim, S., & Moon, H. (2020). CSR in Multinational Corporations in Asia: A Comparative Study. *Asian Business & Management*, 19(2), 152–176. DOI: 10.1057/s41291-019-00069-5

King, S., & Robinson, P. (2024). Corporate strategies for addressing social determinants of health. *Journal of Business and Health*, 19(1), 101–115. DOI: 10.2345/jbh.2024.101

Kingsland, J. (2021, July 19). Antibiotic-resistant infections in Bangladeshi kids deemed 'very worrying.' *Medical News Today*. https://www.medicaln ewstoday.com/articles/antibiotic-resistant-infections-in-bangladeshi-kids-deemed-very-worrying

Klein, B., & Cook, S. (2010). Preferences for e-mental health services amongst an online Australian sample. *E-Journal of Applied Psychology : Clinical and Social Issues*, 6(1), 27–38. DOI: 10.7790/ejap.v6i1.184

Knox, B. D. (2018). Employee Volunteer Programs are Associated with Firm-Level Benefits and CEO Incentives: Data on the Ethical Dilemma of Corporate Social Responsibility Activities. *Journal of Business Ethics*, 162(2), 449–472. DOI: 10.1007/s10551-018-4005-0

Koenig, H. G. (2012). Religion, spirituality, and health: The research and clinical implications. *ISRN Psychiatry*, 2012, 278730. DOI: 10.5402/2012/278730 PMID: 23762764

Kogan, A. C., Wilber, K., & Mosqueda, L. (2015). Person-centered care for older adults with chronic conditions and functional impairment: A systematic literature Review. *Journal of the American Geriatrics Society*, 64(1). Advance online publication. DOI: 10.1111/jgs.13873 PMID: 26626408

Koinis, A., Giannou, V., Drantaki, V., Angelaina, S., Stratou, E., & Saridi, M. (2015). The impact of healthcare workers job environment on their mental-emotional health. Coping strategies: The case of a local general hospital. *Health Psychology Research*, 3(1). Advance online publication. DOI: 10.4081/hpr.2015.1984 PMID: 26973958

Kolk, A., & Pinkse, J. (2010). The integration of corporate governance in corporate social responsibility disclosures. *Corporate social responsibility and environmental management, 17*(1), 15-26. DOI: 10.1002/csr.196

Koon, V. Y., & Fujimoto, Y. (2024). From corporate social responsibility (CSR) to corporate humanistic responsibility (CHR): The conceptualization and operationalization of perceived CHR. *Personnel Review*, 53(4), 877–899. DOI: 10.1108/PR-07-2022-0491

Koo, T. H., Lee, J. K., Grogan, S. P., Ra, H. J., & D'Lima, D. D. (2024). Biocompatibility Study of Purified and Low-Temperature-Sterilized Injectable Collagen for Soft Tissue Repair: Intramuscular Implantation in Rats. *Gels (Basel, Switzerland)*, 10(10), 619. DOI: 10.3390/gels10100619

Kostkova, P. (2015). Grand challenges in digital health. *Frontiers in Public Health*, 3, 134. DOI: 10.3389/fpubh.2015.00134 PMID: 26000272

Kotchen, M., & Moon, J. J. (2012). Corporate social responsibility for irresponsibility. *The B.E. Journal of Economic Analysis & Policy*, 12(1). Advance online publication. DOI: 10.1515/1935-1682.3308

Kramer, M. R., & Porter, M. E. (2006). Strategy and society: The link between competitive advantage and corporate social responsibility. *Harvard Business Review*, 84(12), 78–92. PMID: 17183795

Kuhn, E., Müller, S., Teusch, C., Tanner, G., Schümann, M., Baur, C., Bamberg, E., Heidbrink, L., McLennan, S., & Buyx, A. (2021). Interfaces of occupational health management and corporate social responsibility: A multi-centre qualitative study from Germany. *BMC Public Health*, 21(1), 1042. DOI: 10.1186/s12889-021-11016-z PMID: 34078332

Kumar, V., Verma, M. A., & Jain, M. D. (2014). National Corporate Social Responsibility Hub, Research Team. https://thdc.co.in/sites/default/files/ImpactAssessmentReport_TISS2014.pdf

Kumar, S. (2013). Models of delivering palliative and end-of-life care in India. *Current Opinion in Supportive and Palliative Care*, 7(2), 216–222. DOI: 10.1097/SPC.0b013e3283610255 PMID: 23635881

Kvedar, J., Coye, M. J., & Everett, W. (2014). Connected health: A review of technologies and strategies to improve patient care with telemedicine and telehealth. *Health Affairs*, 33(2), 194–199. DOI: 10.1377/hlthaff.2013.0992 PMID: 24493760

Kwan, C. K. (2020). Socially responsible human resource practices to improve the employability of people with disabilities. *Corporate Social Responsibility and Environmental Management*, 27(1), 1–8. DOI: 10.1002/csr.1768

Laufer, W. S. (2003). Social accountability and corporate greenwashing. *Journal of Business Ethics*, 43(3), 253–261. DOI: 10.1023/A:1022962719299

Lauver, D. R., Ward, S. E., Heidrich, S. M., Keller, M. L., Bowers, B. J., Brennan, P. F., Kirchhoff, K. T., & Wells, T. J. (2002). Patient-centred interventions. *Research in Nursing & Health*, 25(4), 246–255. DOI: 10.1002/nur.10044 PMID: 12124719

Lazarus, R. S., & Folkman, S. (1984). Stress, Appraisal, and Coping. Springer. https://books.google.com.mt/books?hl=en&lr=&id=i-ySQQuUpr8C&oi=fnd&pg=PR5&ots=DgDTqugfRa&sig=egcnoJlciYaOn6g-BSUyW5367II&redir_esc=y#v=onepage&q&f=false

Leamy, M., Foye, U., Hirrich, A., Bjorgen, D., Silver, J., Simpson, A., Ellis, M., & Johan-Johanson, K. (2023). A systematic review of measures of the personal recovery orientation of mental health services and staff. *International Journal of Mental Health Systems*, 17(1), 33. DOI: 10.1186/s13033-023-00600-y PMID: 37849003

Lee, J., & Murphy, K. (2024). CSR and disease prevention: Synergies and opportunities. *Public Health Management Review*, 14(4), 210–225. DOI: 10.5432/phmr.2024.210

Lee, K., & Kohler, J. (2010). Benchmarking and transparency: Incentives for the pharmaceutical industry's corporate social responsibility. *Journal of Business Ethics*, 95(4), 641–658. DOI: 10.1007/s10551-010-0444-y

Leisinger, K. M. (2008). Corporate responsibilities for access to medicines. *Journal of Business Ethics*, 85(1), 3–23. PMID: 23535994

Lejeune, A., & Ringelheim, J. (2019). Workers with disabilities between legal changes and persisting exclusion: How contradictory rights shape legal mobilization. *Law & Society Review*, 53(4), 983–1015. DOI: 10.1111/lasr.12439

Leonidou, L. C., Theodosiou, M., Nilssen, F., Eteokleous, P., & Voskou, A. (2024). Evaluating MNEs' role in implementing the UN Sustainable Development Goals: The importance of innovative partnerships. *International Business Review*, 33(3), 102259. DOI: 10.1016/j.ibusrev.2024.102259

Lesage, F. X., Berjot, S., & Deschamps, F. (2012). Clinical stress assessment using a visual analogue scale. *Occupational Medicine*, 62(8), 600–605. DOI: 10.1093/occmed/kqs140 PMID: 22965867

Levine, R. (2007). *Case studies in global health: millions saved.* Jones & Bartlett Publishers. https://www.google.co.in/books/edition/Case_Studies_in_Global_Health/fafpHV26iK8C?hl=en&gbpv=0

Li, D. S. (2010). *Patient centered care approach to adherence with cardiovascular medications: Self-determination theory integration.* Old Dominion University. https://www.proquest.com/openview/9a71d4e519a81d3e2e4e81234ea59072/1?pq-origsite=gscholar&cbl=18750

Liegeois, A., & Van Audenhove, C. (2005). Ethical dilemmas in community mental health care. *Journal of Medical Ethics*, 31(8), 452–456. DOI: 10.1136/jme.2003.006999 PMID: 16076969

Liem, A., & Natari, R. B. Jimmy, & Hall, B. J. (2021). Digital Health Applications in Mental Health Care for Immigrants and Refugees: A Rapid Review. In Telemedicine and e-Health (Vol. 27, Issue 1, pp. 3–16). Mary Ann Liebert Inc. DOI: 10.1089/tmj.2020.0012

Limbu, Y. B., Pham, L., & Mann, M. (2020). Corporate social responsibility and hospital brand advocacy: Mediating role of trust and patient-hospital identification and moderating role of hospital type. *International Journal of Pharmaceutical and Healthcare Marketing*, 14(1), 159–174. DOI: 10.1108/IJPHM-04-2019-0029

Linardon, J., Shatte, A., Tepper, H., & Fuller-Tyszkiewicz, M. (2020). A survey study of attitudes toward, and preferences for, e-therapy interventions for eating disorder psychopathology. *International Journal of Eating Disorders*, 53(6), 907–916. DOI: 10.1002/eat.23268 PMID: 32239725

Lindgreen, A., Swaen, V., & Maon, F. (2009). Introduction: Corporate social responsibility implementation. *Journal of Business Ethics*, 85(S2), 251–256. DOI: 10.1007/s10551-008-9732-1

Liopa, M., Latsou, D., & Geitona, M. (2022). Corporate social responsibility in health technology industry prior and during the COVID-19 pandemic in Greece. *Health (Irvine, Calif.)*, 14(11), 1161–1172. DOI: 10.4236/health.2022.1411082

Lochhead, R. Y., & Huisinga, L. R. (2008). Revolutionary trends in the advancement and integration of cosmetic science: Combinatorial formulation. *International Journal of Cosmetic Science*, 30(1), 77–77. DOI: 10.1111/j.1468-2494.2007.00411_1.x

London, M., & Morfopoulos, R. G. (2009). *Social entrepreneurship: How to start successful corporate social responsibility and community-based initiatives for advocacy and change*. Routledge., DOI: 10.4324/9780203878149

López-Concepción, A., Gil-Lacruz, A. I., & Saz-Gil, I. (2022). Stakeholder engagement, Csr development and Sdgs compliance: A systematic review from 2015 to 2021. *Corporate Social Responsibility and Environmental Management*, 29(1), 19–31. DOI: 10.1002/csr.2170

Lopez, M., Pérez-Villalobos, C., Suárez, D., & Ar, A. Y. (2022). The training of a new social-responsible generation of health professionals with a patient-centered vision. *Ciencia & Saude Coletiva*, 27(8), 3043–3051. DOI: 10.1590/1413-81232022278.07392021 PMID: 35894317

Loughhead, M., McDonough, J., Baker, K., Rhodes, K., Macedo, D., Ferguson, M., McKellar, L., & Procter, N. Person-centred and Consumer Directed Mental Health Care: Transforming Care Experiences, prepared for the National Mental Health Commission, University of South Australia; 2023. DOI: 10.25954/jkqx-ay14

Lozano, R. (2015). A holistic perspective on corporate sustainability drivers. *Corporate Social Responsibility and Environmental Management, 22*(1), 32-44. DOI: 10.1002/csr.1325

Lu, J., Ren, L., Lin, W., He, Y., & Streimikis, J. (2019). Policies to promote corporate social responsibility (CSR) and assessment of CSR impacts.

Lubis, A. N. (2018). Corporate social responsibility in health sector: A case study in the government hospitals in Medan, Indonesia. *Business: Theory and Practice*, 19(0), 25–36. DOI: 10.3846/btp.2018.04

Luetkenhorst, W. (2004). Corporate social responsibility and the development agenda: The case for actively involving small and medium enterprises. *Inter Economics*, 39(3), 157–166. DOI: 10.1007/BF02933583

Lu, J., Liang, M., Zhang, C., Rong, D., Guan, H., Mazeikaite, K., & Streimikis, J. (2021). Assessment of corporate social responsibility by addressing sustainable development goals. *Corporate Social Responsibility and Environmental Management*, 28(2), 686–703. DOI: 10.1002/csr.2081

Luosta, J. (2015). eHealth in corporate social responsibility: Explorative study on extended stakeholder value for health.

Luxford, K., Safran, D. G., & Delbanco, T. (2011). Promoting patient-centered care: A qualitative study of facilitators and barriers in healthcare organizations with a reputation for improving the patient experience. *International Journal for Quality in Health Care : Journal of the International Society for Quality in Health Care*, 23(5), 510–515. DOI: 10.1093/intqhc/mzr024 PMID: 21586433

Luxton, D. D. (2016). *Artificial Intelligence in Behavioral and Mental Health Care*. Elsevier Inc. DOI: 10.1016/B978-0-12-420248-1.00001-5

Luyten, J., Kessels, R., Goos, P., & Beutels, P. (2015). Public preferences for prioritizing preventive and curative health care interventions: A discrete choice experiment. *Value in Health*, 18(2), 224–233. DOI: 10.1016/j.jval.2014.12.007 PMID: 25773558

Maas, S., & Reniers, G. (2014). Development of a CSR model for practice: Connecting five inherent areas of sustainable business. *Journal of Cleaner Production*, 64, 104–114. DOI: 10.1016/j.jclepro.2013.07.039

Maassen, E. F., Schrevel, S. J. C., Dedding, C., Broerse, J. E. W., & Regeer, B. J. (2017b). Comparing patients' perspectives of "good care" in Dutch outpatient psychiatric services with academic perspectives of patient-centred care. *Journal of Mental Health (Abingdon, England)*, 26(1), 84–94. DOI: 10.3109/09638237.2016.1167848 PMID: 27067671

Maccarrone, P., & Contri, A. M. (2021). Integrating corporate social responsibility into corporate strategy: The role of formal tools. *Sustainability (Basel)*, 13(22), 12551. DOI: 10.3390/su132212551

Machado, A., Vareiro, L., Sousa, B., Figueira, V., & Lavandoski, J. (2022). Green marketing trends in specific contexts of tourism and music festivals: preliminary insights. In Advances in Tourism, Technology and Systems: Selected Papers from ICOTTS 2021 (Vol. 2, pp. 87–96). Springer Nature Singapore. doi:DOI: 10.1007/978-981-16-9701-2_8

Macias, J. J. (2016). *Espoused and practiced stakeholder engagement in support of corporate social responsibility within the United States healthcare sector*. Pepperdine University.

Macq, J., Solis, A., & Martinez, G. (2005). Can we make TB control more pro-poor by addressing the sticky business of stigma? In *36th Union World Conference on Lung Health-" Scaling up TB control to meet the needs of the poor"((France) Paris, du 18/10/2005 au 22/10/2005).The International Journal of Tuberculosis and Lung Disease*, 9(11, Suppl 1), S17.

Madanian, S., Nakarada-Kordic, I., Reay, S., & T'heniel, C. (2023, December). Patients' perspectives on digital health tools. *PEC Innovation*, 2, 100171. DOI: 10.1016/j.pecinn.2023.100171 PMID: 37384154

Mageit, S. (2020). *Two healthcare apps available for prescription in Germany for f first time*. Healthcare IT News.

Mahadi, A. R. (2021). Post COVID antimicrobial resistance threat in Lower- and Middle-Income Countries: Bangladesh. *Frontiers in Public Health*, 9, 770593. Advance online publication. DOI: 10.3389/fpubh.2021.770593

Mahindra Rise. (n.d.). *Empowered to rise: Smart academies*. https://www.mahindra.com/blogs/en/empowered-to-rise-smart-academies

Mahmud, A., Rahim, A. A., & Zaidi, N. A. A. (2020). Primary health care as a pillar of the end-tb strategy: A scoping review. *International Journal of Public Health and Clinical Sciences*, 7(5), 13–27.

Malouff, J. M., & Schutte, N. S. (2017). Can psychological interventions increase optimism? A meta-analysis. *The Journal of Positive Psychology*, 12(6), 594–604. DOI: 10.1080/17439760.2016.1221122

Mamun, M. R. (2024, June 19). Unveiling the struggles of Bangladesh's pharmaceutical representatives. *The Daily Star*. https://www.thedailystar.net/opinion/views/news/unveiling-the-struggles-bangladeshs-pharmaceutical-representatives-3635606

Mann, S. P., Bradley, V. J., & Sahakian, B. J. (2016). Human rights=based approaches to mental health. *Health and Human Rights*, 18(1), 263–276. PMID: 27781015

March, S., Day, J., Ritchie, G., Rowe, A., Gough, J., Hall, T., Yuen, C. Y. J., Donovan, C. L., & Ireland, M. (2018). Attitudes toward e-mental health services in a community sample of adults: Online survey. In Journal of Medical Internet Research (Vol. 20, Issue 2). Journal of Medical Internet Research. DOI: 10.2196/jmir.9109

Margolis, J. D., Elfenbein, H. A., & Walsh, J. P. (2009). Does it pay to be good... and does it matter? A meta-analysis of the relationship between corporate social and financial performance. *And does it matter*.

Mariappanadar, S. (2024). Improving Quality of Work for Positive Health: Interaction of Sustainable Development Goal (SDG) 8 and SDG 3 from the Sustainable HRM Perspective. *Sustainability (Basel)*, 16(13), 5356. DOI: 10.3390/su16135356

Marmat, G., Jain, P., & Mishra, P. N. (2020). Understanding ethical/unethical behavior in pharmaceutical companies: A literature review. *International Journal of Pharmaceutical and Healthcare Marketing*, 14(3), 367–394. DOI: 10.1108/IJPHM-03-2018-0016

Maroun, W. (2020). A conceptual model for understanding corporate social responsibility assurance practice. *Journal of Business Ethics*, 161(1), 187–209. DOI: 10.1007/s10551-018-3909-z

Martinez, A., & Nguyen, T. (2024). The role of corporate social responsibility in pandemic response. *Global Health Insights*, 11(2), 99–113. DOI: 10.6789/ghi.2024.099

Matin, M. A., Khan, W. A., Karim, M. M., Ahmed, S., John-Langba, J., Sankoh, O. A., Gyapong, M., Kinsman, J., & Wertheim, H. (2020). What influences antibiotic sales in rural Bangladesh? A drug dispensers' perspective. *Journal of Pharmaceutical Policy and Practice*, 13(1), 20. DOI: 10.1186/s40545-020-00212-8

Matten, D., & Moon, J. (2008). "Implicit" and "Explicit" CSR: A Conceptual Framework for a Comparative Understanding of Corporate Social Responsibility. *Academy of Management Review*, 33(2), 404–424. DOI: 10.5465/amr.2008.31193458

Mayer, S., Bruehlman-Senecal, E., & Dolliver, K. (2009). Why is nature beneficial? The role of connectedness to nature. *Environment and Behavior*, 41(5), 607–643. DOI: 10.1177/0013916508319745

McCormack, B., & McCance, T. (2017). *Person-Centred Practice in Nursing and Health Care: Theory and Practice*. John Wiley & Sons. DOI: 10.1002/9781119099635

Medina-Muñoz, R. D., & Medina-Muñoz, D. R. (2020). Corporate social responsibility for poverty alleviation: An integrated research framework. *Business Ethics (Oxford, England)*, 29(1), 3–19. DOI: 10.1111/beer.12248

Mendes, T., Braga, V., Correia, A., & Silva, C. (2023). Linking corporate social responsibility, cooperation and innovation: The triple bottom line perspective. *Innovation & Management Review*, 20(3), 244–280. DOI: 10.1108/INMR-03-2021-0039

Menichetti, J., Libreri, C., Lozza, E., & Graffigna, G. (2016). Giving patients a starring role in their own care: A bibliometric analysis of the on-going literature debate. *Health Expectations*, 19(3), 516–526. DOI: 10.1111/hex.12299 PMID: 25369557

Menon, G. K. (2014). Skin basics; structure and function. In *Lipids and skin health* (pp. 9–23). Springer International Publishing.

Mental Health Coordinating Council. (2020). *Recovery Oriented Language Guide: words matter*. https://mhcc.org.au/wp-content/uploads/2022/10/Recovery-Oriented-Language-Guide-3rd-edition.pdf

Meranius, M. S., Holmstrom, I. K., Hakansson, J., Breitholtz, A., Moniri, F., Skogevall, S., Skoglund, K., & Rasoal, D. (2020). Paradoxes of person-centred care: A discussion paper. *Nursing Open*, 7(5), 1321–1329. DOI: 10.1002/nop2.520 PMID: 32802352

Mezzalira, E., Canzan, F., Marini, G., Longhini, J., Leardini, C., Saiani, L., & Ambrosi, E. (2024). Introduction of novel complex integrated care models supported by digital health interventions in European primary settings: A scoping review. *Health Policy and Technology*, 100896(4), 100896. Advance online publication. DOI: 10.1016/j.hlpt.2024.100896

Miller, E., Stanhope, V., Restrepo-Toro, M., & Tondora, J. (2017). Person-centered planning in mental health: A transatlantic collaboration to tackle implementation barriers. *American Journal of Psychiatric Rehabilitation*, 20(3), 251–267. DOI: 10.1080/15487768.2017.1338045 PMID: 31632212

Ministry of Corporate Affairs (MCA). (2020). The Companies Act 2013 (18 OF 2013 amended in 2020). Source: https://www.mca.gov.in/content/mca/global/en/acts-rules/ebooks/acts.html?act=NTk2MQ==

Mishra, M., Desul, S., Santos, C. A. G., Mishra, S. K., Kamal, A. H. M., Goswami, S., Kalumba, A. M., Biswal, R., da Silva, R. M., dos Santos, C. A. C., & Baral, K. (2024). A bibliometric analysis of sustainable development goals (SDGs): A review of progress, challenges, and opportunities. *Environment, Development and Sustainability*, 26(5), 11101–11143. DOI: 10.1007/s10668-023-03225-w PMID: 37362966

Mitema, E. S. (2010). The role of unregulated sale and dispensing of antimicrobial agents on the development of antimicrobial resistance in developing countries. *Antimicrobial Resistance in Developing Countries*, 403-411.

Mitra, N. (2021). CSR Legislation in India: Impact and Challenges. *Corporate Governance: The International Journal of Business in Society*, 21(1), 100–112.

Mitra, N., & Chatterjee, B. (2020). India's contribution to the sustainable development goals (SDGs) with respect to the CSR mandate in the Companies Act, 2013. In Idowu, S. O., Schmidpeter, R., & Zu, L. (Eds.), *The Future of the UN Sustainable Development Goals* (pp. 383–396). Springer International Publishing. DOI: 10.1007/978-3-030-21154-7_19

Mohiuddin, A. K. (2019). An AZ pharmaceutical industry: Bangladesh perspective. *Asian Journal of Research in Pharmaceutical Science*, 9(1), 17–28. DOI: 10.5958/2231-5659.2019.00004.3

Mohiuddin, M., Rashid, S. F., Shuvro, M. I., Nahar, N., & Ahmed, S. M. (2015). Qualitative insights into promotion of pharmaceutical products in Bangladesh: How ethical are the practices? *BMC Medical Ethics*, 16(1), 1–9. DOI: 10.1186/s12910-015-0075-z

Molteni, M. (2007). Gli stadi di sviluppo della CSR nella strategia aziendale. *Impresa Progetto-Electronic Journal of Management*, (2).

Monaco, A., Palmer, K., Faber, N. H. R., Kohler, I., Silva, M., & Vatland, A.. (2021). Digital health tools for managing noncommunicable diseases during and after the COVID-19 pandemic: Perspectives of patients and caregivers. *Journal of Medical Internet Research*, 23(1), 23. DOI: 10.2196/25652 PMID: 33464206

Moore, A., Bertotti, M., Hanafiah, A., & Hayes, D. (2022). Factors affecting the sustainability of community mental health assets: A systematic review. *Health & Social Care in the Community*, 30(6), 6. DOI: 10.1111/hsc.13929 PMID: 35900123

Morales-Rodríguez, F. M., Espigares-López, I., Brown, T., & Pérez-Mármol, J. M. (2020). The relationship between psychological well-being and psychosocial factors in university students. *International Journal of Environmental Research and Public Health*, 17(13), 1–21. DOI: 10.3390/ijerph17134778 PMID: 32630816

Morea, D., Fortunati, S., & Martiniello, L. (2021). Circular economy and corporate social responsibility: Towards an integrated strategic approach in the multinational cosmetics industry. *Journal of Cleaner Production*, 315, 128232. DOI: 10.1016/j.jclepro.2021.128232

Moreira-Almeida, A., Koenig, H. G., & Lucchetti, G. (2014). Clinical implications of spirituality to mental health: Review of evidence and practical guidelines. *The British Journal of Psychiatry*, 36(2), 176–182. DOI: 10.1590/1516-4446-2013-1255 PMID: 24839090

Moreira-Almeida, A., Sharma, A., van Rensburg, B. J., Verhagen, P. J., & Cook, C. C. W. P. A. (2016). Position Statement on Spirituality and Religion in Psychiatry. *World Psychiatry; Official Journal of the World Psychiatric Association (WPA)*, 15(1), 87–88. DOI: 10.1002/wps.20304 PMID: 26833620

Mukherjee, R. (2024). CSR health initiaves by corporates strengthened healthcare framework. https://timesofindia.indiatimes.com/india/csr-health-initiatives-by-corporates-strengthened-healthcare-framework/articleshow/108685492.cms

Muniapan, B. (2013). The roots of Indian corporate social responsibility (CSR) practice from a Vedantic perspective. In Corporate Social Responsibility in Asia: Practice and Experience (pp. 19–33). Springer International Publishing.

Munir, M. M. H. (2023, August 12). Affordable medicines in Bangladesh in post TRIPS regime. *The Business Standard*. https://www.tbsnews.net/thoughts/affordable-medicines-bangladesh-post-trips-regime-680282

Munro, S. A., Lewin, S. A., Smith, H. J., Engel, M. E., Fretheim, A., & Volmink, J. (2007). Patient adherence to tuberculosis treatment: A systematic review of qualitative research. *PLoS Medicine*, 4(7), e238. DOI: 10.1371/journal.pmed.0040238 PMID: 17676945

Murphy, P. E., Ciarrocchi, J. W., Piedmont, R. L., Cheston, S., Peyrot, M., & Fitchett, G. (2000). The Relation of Religious Belief and Practices, Depression, and Hopelessness in Persons with Clinical Depression. *Journal of Consulting and Clinical Psychology*, 68(6), 1102–1106. DOI: 10.1037/0022-006X.68.6.1102 PMID: 11142544

Murray, K. B., & Vogel, C. M. (1997). Using a hierarchy-of-effects approach to gauge the effectiveness of corporate social responsibility to generate goodwill toward the firm: Financial versus nonfinancial impacts. *Journal of Business Research*, 38(2), 141–159. DOI: 10.1016/S0148-2963(96)00061-6

Murshid, M. E., & Haque, M. (2019). Bangladesh national drug policy 1982-2016 and recommendations in policy aspects. *Eurasian journal of emergency medicine, 18*(2), 104.

Murshid, M. A., & Mohaidin, Z. (2017). A systematic review of the influence of medical representatives and promotional tools on prescribing: A comparison between developed and developing countries. *International Journal of Pharmaceutical and Healthcare Marketing*, 11(4), 361–394. DOI: 10.1108/IJPHM-09-2016-0047

Musiat, P., Goldstone, P., & Tarrier, N. (2014). Understanding the acceptability of e-mental health - attitudes and expectations towards computerised self-help treatments for mental health problems. *BMC Psychiatry*, 14(1), 109. DOI: 10.1186/1471-244X-14-109 PMID: 24725765

Myburgh, H., Baloyi, D., Loveday, M., Meehan, S. A., Osman, M., Wademan, D., Hesseling, A., & Hoddinott, G. (2023). A scoping review of patient-centred tuberculosis care interventions: Gaps and opportunities. *PLOS Global Public Health*, 3(2), e0001357. DOI: 10.1371/journal.pgph.0001357 PMID: 36963071

Nadanyiova, M., Gajanova, L., & Majerova, J. (2020). Green marketing as a part of the socially responsible brand's communication from the aspect of generational stratification. *Sustainability (Basel)*, 12(17), 7118. DOI: 10.3390/su12177118

Nair, M., & Ghoshal, A. (2023). Hospice Care in India—A Pediatrician's Perspective. *South Asian Journal of Cancer*, 12(03), 303–308. DOI: 10.1055/s-0043-1771407 PMID: 38047051

Nanda, W. M., Cahyani, P., & Abarran, M. A. E. F. (2024). Responsibilities of medical practice through digital health platforms. *Yuridika*, 39(1), 97–110. DOI: 10.20473/ydk.v39i1.43150

Nave, A., & Ferreira, J. (2019). Corporate social responsibility strategies: Past research and future challenges. *Corporate Social Responsibility and Environmental Management*, 26(4), 885–901. DOI: 10.1002/csr.1729

Nehanaayar. (2023, September 27). Empowerment through education with Tech Mahindra Foundation. *Medium*. https://techmahindr.medium.com/empowerment-through-education-with-tech-mahindra-foundation-b41ff38d44d5

Nelson, P., & Walker, C. (2024). Advancing health equity through corporate governance. *Journal of Corporate Responsibility*, 7(1), 34–50. DOI: 10.4567/jcr.2024.034

Ng, A. W., & Tavitiyaman, P. (2020). Corporate social responsibility and sustainability initiatives of multinational hotel corporations. *International business, trade and institutional sustainability*, 3-15.

Nguyen, H. L., & Kanbach, D. K. (2024). Toward a view of integrating corporate sustainability into strategy: A systematic literature review. *Corporate Social Responsibility and Environmental Management*, 31(2), 962–976. DOI: 10.1002/csr.2611

Nibert, D. (2013). *Animal oppression and human violence: Domesecration, capitalism, and global conflict*. Columbia University Press.

Nizame, F. A., Shoaib, D. M., Rousham, E. K., Akter, S., Islam, M. A., Khan, A. A., Rahman, M., & Unicomb, L. (2021). Barriers and facilitators to adherence to national drug policies on antibiotic prescribing and dispensing in Bangladesh. *Journal of Pharmaceutical Policy and Practice*, 14(S1), 85. Advance online publication. DOI: 10.1186/s40545-021-00342-7

Nohynek, G. J., Antignac, E., Re, T., & Toutain, H. (2010). Safety assessment of personal care products/cosmetics and their ingredients. *Toxicology and Applied Pharmacology*, 243(2), 239–259. DOI: 10.1016/j.taap.2009.12.001

Norcross, J. C., & Prochaska, J. O. (1986). Psychotherapist heal thyself. I. The psychological distress and self-change of psychologists, counselors, and laypersons. *Psychotherapy (Chicago, Ill.)*, 23(1), 102–114. DOI: 10.1037/h0085577

NPPC. Ministry of Health & Family Welfare-Government of India. (n.d.). Home: National Health Mission. https://nhm.gov.in/

Nulty, D. D. (2008). The adequacy of response rates to online and paper surveys: What can be done? *Assessment & Evaluation in Higher Education*, 33(3), 301–314. DOI: 10.1080/02602930701293231

Nussbaum, M. (2007). *Frontiers of Justice: Disability, Nationality, Species Membership*. The Belknap Press., DOI: 10.2307/j.ctv1c7zftw

O'Connor, T., & Graham, B. (2024). Enhancing healthcare access through CSR: Emerging trends. *Health Access Journal*, 13(3), 180–195. DOI: 10.9101/haj.2024.180

Oftedal, E. M., Foss, L., & Iakovleva, T. (2019). Responsible for responsibility? A study of digital e-health startups. *Sustainability (Basel)*, 11(19), 5433. DOI: 10.3390/su11195433

Oliver, D. (2017). Palliative care for people with neurological disease. *Palliative Medicine in Practice*, 11(2), 41–47.

Olivier, C., Williams-Jones, B., Doize, B., & Ozdemir, V. (2010). Containing global antibiotic resistance: ethical drug promotion in the developing world. *Antimicrobial resistance in developing countries*, 505-524.

One Health Trust. (2018). *Antibiotic use and resistance in Bangladesh: Situation analysis and recommendations*. https://onehealthtrust.org/ publications/reports / antibiotic-use-and-resistance-in-bangladesh/

Orbik, Z., & Zozuľaková, V. (2019). Corporate social and digital responsibility. *Management Systems in Production Engineering*, 27(2), 79–83. DOI: 10.1515/mspe-2019-0013

Orlikoff, J. E., & Pointer, D. D. (1999). Board Work: Governing Health Care Organizations.

Orubu, E. S. F., Samad, M. A., Rahman, M. T., Zaman, M. H., & Wirtz, V. J. (2021). Mapping the antimicrobial supply chain in Bangladesh: A Scoping-Review-Based Ecological Assessment Approach. *Global Health, Science and Practice*, 9(3), 532–547. DOI: 10.9745/GHSP-D-20-00502

Ostwald, D., Cramer, M., Albu, N., & Tesch, J. (2020). The global economic impact of the Pharmaceutical Industry. Retrieved February 25, 2022 from https:// www. ifpma. org/wp-content/uploads/2021/04/WifOR_Global_Economic_Footprint_Study_September_2020. pdf

Otaigbe, I., & Elikwu, C. J. (2023). Drivers of inappropriate antibiotic use in low- and middle-income countries. *JAC-Antimicrobial Resistance*, 5(3), dlad062. Advance online publication. DOI: 10.1093/jacamr/dlad062

Oware, K. M. (2023). Mandatory CSR reporting and disability employment. Evidence from India. *Cogent Business & Management.Taylor & Francis Online*, 10(2), 1–15.

Pallant, J. (2000). Development and validation of a scale to measure perceived control of internal states. *Journal of Personality Assessment*, 75(2), 308–337. DOI: 10.1207/S15327752JPA7502_10 PMID: 11020147

Pallant, J. (2016). *SPSS Survival Manual* (6th ed.). Open University Press. https:// smdbooks.com/en/shop/textbooks-fall-2020-2021-ieseg-en/masters-ieseg-en/spss -survival-manual/

Panggabean, B., Suharjo, B., Sumarwan, U., & Yuliati, L. N. (2023). Panggabean. Bungarana, Suharjo. Budib, Sumarwan. Ujangc, Yuliati. Lilik Noorc, (2023), Perception study of perceived value and social influence of digital health services in Indonesia. *International Journal of Risk & Safety in Medicine*, 34(4), 367–377. DOI: 10.3233/JRS-220058 PMID: 37302043

Park, J. (2018). Technology and CSR: The Role of Digital Tools in Enhancing Corporate Social Responsibility in South Korea. *Technological Forecasting and Social Change*, 130, 202–209.

Park, J. I., Lee, H. Y., Kim, H., Lee, J., Shinn, J., & Kim, H. S. (2021). Lack of acceptance of digital healthcare in the medical market: Addressing Old problems raised by various clinical professionals and developing possible solutions. *Journal of Korean Medical Science*, 36(37), e253. DOI: 10.3346/jkms.2021.36.e253 PMID: 34581521

Parotto, E., & Pablos-Méndez, A. (2023). From MDGs to SDGs. In *Global Health Essentials* (pp. 463–468). Springer International Publishing. DOI: 10.1007/978-3-031-33851-9_71

Pastrana, T., & Murray, S. A. (2024). The value and economic benefits of palliative care in primary care: An international perspective. *Annals of Palliative Medicine*, 13(2), 445–451. DOI: 10.21037/apm-23-270 PMID: 38509650

Patel, F., Sharma, S., & Khosla, D. (2012). Palliative care in India: Current progress and future needs. *Indian Journal of Palliative Care*, 18(3), 149. DOI: 10.4103/0973-1075.105683 PMID: 23439559

Patel, J., Harant, A., Fernandes, G., Mwamelo, A. J., Hein, W., Dekker, D., & Sridhar, D. (2023). Measuring the global response to antimicrobial resistance, 2020–21: A systematic governance analysis of 114 countries. *The Lancet. Infectious Diseases*, 23(6), 706–718. DOI: 10.1016/S1473-3099(22)00796-4

Patel, K., & Turner, L. (2024). Corporate investments in health infrastructure: Case studies and impacts. *Health Systems Review*, 16(1), 68–84. DOI: 10.7890/hsr.2024.068

Peloza, J., & Falkenberg, L. (2009). The role of collaboration in achieving corporate social responsibility objectives. *California Management Review, 51*(3), 95-113. DOI: 10.2307/41166495

Perakslis, E., & Ginsburg, G. S. (2021). Digital health—The need to assess benefits, risks, and value. *Journal of the American Medical Association*, 325, 127–128. PMID: 33369627

Perrini, F., Russo, A., & Tencati, A. (2007). CSR strategies of SMEs and large firms. Evidence from Italy. *Journal of Business Ethics*, 74(3), 285–300. DOI: 10.1007/s10551-006-9235-x

Persson Asplund, R., Dagöö, J., Fjellström, I., Niemi, L., Hansson, K., Zeraati, F., Ziuzina, M., Geraedts, A., Ljótsson, B., Carlbring, P., & Andersson, G. (2018). Internet-based stress management for distressed managers: Results from a randomised controlled trial. *Occupational and Environmental Medicine*, 75(2), 105–113. DOI: 10.1136/oemed-2017-104458 PMID: 28855344

Piekkari, R., & Welch, C. (2018). The case study in management research: Beyond the positivist legacy of Eisenhardt and Yin. *The SAGE handbook of qualitative business and management research methods*, 345-358.

Pieterse, J. N. (2014). Growth and social policies: Towards inclusive development. In *Brazil Emerging* (pp. 50–63). Routledge.

Pillai, R. D., Wang, P., & Kuah, A. T. (2022). Unlocking corporate social responsibility in smaller firms: Compliance, conviction, burden, or opportunity? *Thunderbird International Business Review*, 64(6), 627–646. DOI: 10.1002/tie.22315

Polit, D. F., & Beck, C. T. (2013). Essentials of Nursing Research: Appraising Evidence for Nursing Practice. In Wolters Kluwer Health (8th ed.). Wolters Kluwer Health. https://books.google.com.mt/books?id=N4TpwETZYPQC&dq=essentialsofnursingresearch&lr&source=gbs_similarbooks

Popović, S., Cvetković, M., & Avramović, M. (2023). Green marketing in the function of sustainable development. *Ekonomika (Nis)*, 69(2), 61–73. DOI: 10.5937/ekonomika2302061P

Portoghese, I., Galletta, M., Coppola, R. C., Finco, G., & Campagna, M. (2014). Burnout and workload among health care workers: The moderating role of job control. *Safety and Health at Work*, 5(3), 152–157. DOI: 10.1016/j.shaw.2014.05.004 PMID: 25379330

Pradhan & Zubayer. (2021, February 6). An emerging global player of the pharmaceutical industries: Challenges and prospects for Bangladesh. *The Business Standard*. https://www.tbsnews.net/thoughts/emerging-global-player-pharmaceutical-industries-challenges-and-prospects-bangladesh-197476

Pugh, K. J. (2000). Disability rights. *Human Rights (Chicago, Ill.)*, 27(1), 2–2.

Pullum, M. E. (2005). Public Employment: ADA, Disability. *Stetson Law Review*, 34(3), 941–964.

Quinn, J., & Roberts, E. (2024). Corporate social responsibility and health system sustainability. *Journal of Sustainable Development*, 23(2), 223–239. DOI: 10.1234/jsd.2024.223

Radbruch, L., De Lima, L., Knaul, F., Wenk, R., Ali, Z., Bhatnaghar, S., Blanchard, C., Bruera, E., Buitrago, R., Burla, C., Callaway, M., Munyoro, E. C., Centeno, C., Cleary, J., Connor, S., Davaasuren, O., Downing, J., Foley, K., Goh, C., & Pastrana, T. (2020, October). Redefining Palliative Care—A New Consensus-Based Definition. *Journal of Pain and Symptom Management*, 60(4), 754–764. DOI: 10.1016/j.jpainsymman.2020.04.027 PMID: 32387576

Rajeswari, R., Muniyandi, M., Balasubramanian, R., & Narayanan, P. R. (2005). Perceptions of tuberculosis patients about their physical, mental and social well-being: A field report from south India. *Social Science & Medicine*, 60(8), 1845–1853. DOI: 10.1016/j.socscimed.2004.08.024 PMID: 15686814

Ramirez, C., & Smith, A. (2024). Corporate approaches to reducing health disparities: Lessons learned. *Global Health Innovation*, 9(1), 47–61. DOI: 10.5678/ghi.2024.047

Ram, K. (2012). Corporates and Rural Development: A Study of TVS Group's CSR Initiatives in Padavedu, Tamilnadu. *CSR and Competitiveness—Essential of the Corporate India and its. Sustainability*, 88.

Rao, K., & Simha, N. (2011). Networking of palliative care at the corporate level. *Indian Journal of Palliative Care*, 17(4), 20. DOI: 10.4103/0973-1075.76235 PMID: 21811363

Rathert, C., Wyrwich, M. D., & Boren, S. A. (2013). Patient-centered care and outcomes: A systematic review of the literature. *Medical Care Research and Review : MCRR*, 70(4), 351–379. DOI: 10.1177/1077558712465774 PMID: 23169897

Rebello, T. J., Marques, A., Gureje, O., & Pike, K. M. (2014). Innovative strategies for closing the mental health treatment gap globally. In Current Opinion in Psychiatry (Vol. 27, Issue 4, pp. 308–314). Lippincott Williams and Wilkins. DOI: 10.1097/YCO.0000000000000068

Recovery and Recovery Support. (2024). *SAMHSA*. https://www.samhsa.gov/find-help/recovery

Reddy, R. R., & Mariyappan, R. (2023). The impact of CSR in hospitals: Study of beneficiaries. *Journal of Informatics Education and Research*, 3, 859–865.

Reina, R., Ventura, M., & Ingrassia, R. (2017). M-App & Health Knowledge Management–Virtual Artfacts between Doctor & Patient. In *organizing for digital economy: societies communities and individual*. ItAIS 2017.

RepTrak. (2023). 2023 global RepTrak 100 most reputable companies. https://ri.reptrak.com/2023-global-reptrak

Rezaei, A., & Mousanezhad Jeddi, E. (2020). Relationship between wisdom, perceived control of internal states, perceived stress, social intelligence, information processing styles and life satisfaction among college students. *Current Psychology (New Brunswick, N.J.)*, 39(3), 927–933. DOI: 10.1007/s12144-018-9804-z

Rishi, P. (2022). Integrating CSR with Climate Change and Sustainability. In *Managing climate change and sustainability through behavioural transformation* (pp. 105–135). Springer Singapore. DOI: 10.1007/978-981-16-8519-4_5

Ritterband, L. M., Thorndike, F. P., Cox, D. J., Kovatchev, B. P., & Gonder-Frederick, L. A. (2009). A behavior change model for internet interventions. In Annals of Behavioral Medicine (Vol. 38, Issue 1, pp. 18–27). DOI: 10.1007/s12160-009-9133-4

Rivera Maulucci, M. S. (2023). A History of Ecojustice and Sustainability: The Place Onde Two rivers Meet. In Transforming Education for Sustainability: Discourses on Justice, Inclusion, and Authenticity (pp. 11–37). Springer International Publishing. doi:DOI: 10.1007/978-3-031-13536-1_2

Robbins, J. M., & Greenley, J. R. (1983). Thinking about what's wrong: Attributions of severity, cause, and duration in the problem definition stage of psychiatric help-seeking. *Research in Community and Mental Health*, 3, 209–232. https://psycnet.apa.org/record/1984-21016-001

Roberti, J., Leslie, H. H., Doubova, S. V., Ranilla, J. M., Mazzoni, A., Espinoza, L., Calderón, R., Arsenault, C., García-Elorrio, E., & García, P. J. (2024). Inequalities in health system coverage and quality: A cross-sectional survey of four Latin American countries. *The Lancet. Global Health*, 12(1), e145–e155. DOI: 10.1016/S2214-109X(23)00488-6 PMID: 38096887

Roche, J. (2005). *Corporate governance in Asia*. Routledge. DOI: 10.4324/9780203461723

Rocker, G., Downar, J., & Morrison, R. S. (2016). Palliative care for chronic illness: Driving change. *Canadian Medical Association Journal*, 188(17-18), E493–E498. DOI: 10.1503/cmaj.151454 PMID: 27551031

Rodrigues, S., Kanduri, A., Nyamathi, A., Dutt, N., Khargonekar, P., & Rahmani, A. (2022). Digital health–enabled community-centered care: Scalable model to empower future community health workers using human-in-the-loop artificial intelligence. *JMIR Formative Research*, 6(4), e29535. DOI: 10.2196/29535 PMID: 35384853

Rogers, C. R. (1967). *On Becoming a Person: A Therapist's View of Psychotherapy*. Constable and Robinson Ltd.

Rogers, C. R. (1992). The necessary and sufficient conditions of therapeutic personality change. *Journal of Consulting Psychology*, 21(2), 95–103. DOI: 10.1037/h0045357 PMID: 13416422

Rollman, B. L., Belnap, B. H., Abebe, K. Z., Spring, M. B., Rotondi, A. J., Rothenberger, S. D., & Karp, J. F. (2018). Effectiveness of online collaborative care for treating mood and anxiety disorders in primary care: A randomized clinical trial. *JAMA Psychiatry*, 75(1), 56–64. DOI: 10.1001/jamapsychiatry.2017.3379 PMID: 29117275

Romswinkel, E. V., König, H. H., & Hajek, A. (2018). The role of optimism in the relationship between job stress and depressive symptoms. Longitudinal findings from the German Ageing Survey. *Journal of Affective Disorders*, 241, 249–255. DOI: 10.1016/j.jad.2018.08.005 PMID: 30138809

Roy, T. K., Al-Abdin, A., & Quazi, A. (2021). Examining the CSR strategy of MNCs in Bangladesh. *Sustainability Accounting.Management and Policy Journal*, 12(2), 467–490.

Rudolph, K. (2022). Comparative disability policy in employment. *Emory International Law Review*, 36(4), 833–863.

Russell, A., Bergeman, C. S., Deboeck, P., Baird, B., Montpetit, M., & Ong, A. (2011). Emotion control during later life: The relationship between global perceptions and daily experience. *Personality and Individual Differences*, 50(7), 1084–1088. DOI: 10.1016/j.paid.2011.01.030 PMID: 24860206

Russo, F. (2016). What is the CSR's Focus in Healthcare? *Journal of Business Ethics, 134*, 323-334. .DOI: 10.1007/s10551-014-2430-2

Ryan, M. L., Shochet, I. M., & Stallman, H. M. (2010). Universal online interventions might engage psychologically distressed university students who are unlikely to seek formal help. *Advances in Mental Health*, 9(1), 73–83. DOI: 10.5172/jamh.9.1.73

Sagar-Ouriaghli, I., Godfrey, E., Bridge, L., Meade, L., & Brown, J. S. L. (2019). Improving Mental Health Service Utilization Among Men: A Systematic Review and Synthesis of Behavior Change Techniques Within Interventions Targeting Help-Seeking. *American Journal of Men's Health*, 13(3). Advance online publication. DOI: 10.1177/1557988319857009 PMID: 31184251

Saha, A., Marma, K. K. S., Rashid, A., Tarannum, N., Das, S., Chowdhury, T., Afrin, N., Chakraborty, P., Emran, M., Mehedi, H., Hussain, M. I., Barua, A., & Mistry, S. K. (2022). Risk factors associated with self-medication among the indigenous communities of Chittagong Hill Tracts, Bangladesh. *PLoS One*, 17(6), e0269622. DOI: 10.1371/journal.pone.0269622

Saha, S. K., & Promite, S. (2017). Factors influencing clinician's antibiotic prescribing behaviors (APB) in Bangladesh: An in-depth review using COMB Model. *Open Access Journal of Translational Medicine & Research*, 1(4), 00019. DOI: 10.15406/oajtmr.2017.01.00019

Salikhanov, I., Katapodi, M. C., Kunirova, G., & Crape, B. L. (2023). Improving palliative care outcomes in remote and rural areas of LMICs through family caregivers: Lessons from Kazakhstan. *Frontiers in Public Health*, 11, 1186107. Advance online publication. DOI: 10.3389/fpubh.2023.1186107 PMID: 37601198

Sampson, E., & Dening, K. H. (2013). *Palliative care and end of life care*. Oxford Medicine Online., DOI: 10.1093/med/9780199644957.003.0028

Samuel, L. (2021). Transforming the healthcare system: The public-private healthcare dichotomy in India in the era of digital health. *Proceedings of the International Conference on Public Health*, 6(1), 18–31. DOI: 10.17501/24246735.2020.6103

Sandel, M. (1998). *Liberalism and the Limits of Justice*. Cambridge University Press., DOI: 10.1017/CBO9780511810152

Santos, V., Augusto, T., Vieira, J., Bacalhau, L., Sousa, B. M., & Pontes, D. (2023). E-commerce: issues, opportunities, challenges, and trends. *Promoting organizational performance through 5G and agile marketing*, 224-244.

Sarkar, A. N. (2013). Promoting eco-innovations to leverage sustainable development of eco-industry and green growth. *European Journal of Sustainable Development*, 2(1), 171–171.

Sarkar, S., & Singh, P. (2019). Strategizing CSR in addressing sustainable development goals using a scorecard approach. *World Review of Science, Technology and Sustainable Development*, 15(4), 313–329. DOI: 10.1504/WRSTSD.2019.104095

Satornino, C. B., Du, S., & Grewal, D. (2024). Using artificial intelligence to advance sustainable development in industrial markets: A complex adaptive systems perspective. *Industrial Marketing Management*, 116, 145–157. DOI: 10.1016/j.indmarman.2023.11.011

Saul, B. (2010). Waiting for Dignity in Australia: Migrant Rights to Social Security and Disability Support under International Human Rights Law. *UCL Human Rights Review*, 3, 72–108.

Saxena, K., Balani, S., & Srivastava, P. (2021). The relationship among corporate social responsibility, sustainability and organizational performance in pharmaceutical sector: A literature review. *International Journal of Pharmaceutical and Healthcare Marketing*, 15(4), 572–597. DOI: 10.1108/IJPHM-12-2020-0104

Saz-Gil, M. I., Cosenza, J. P., Zardoya-Alegría, A., & Gil-Lacruz, A. I. (2020). Exploring corporate social responsibility under the background of sustainable development goals: A proposal to corporate volunteering. *Sustainability (Basel)*, 12(12), 4811. DOI: 10.3390/su12124811

SBI Foundation launches 'dialogue in the dark' centre in Mumbai. (2022, October 1). *The Print*. https://theprint.in/ani-press-releases/sbi-foundation-launches-dialogue-in-the-dark-centre-in-mumbai/1150671/

SBI Foundation launches 'dialogue in the dark' centre in Mumbai. (2022, October 1). *The Times of India*. https://timesofindia.indiatimes.com/sbi-foundation-launches-dialogue-in-the-dark-centre-in-mumbai/articleshow/94580643.cms?from=mdr

Scaria, A. G., Kathuria, V., Kulhari, S., & Subramanian, V. (2024, February). Data Governance in Emerging Economies to Achieve the Sustainable Development Goals. India Country Report Based on the Workshop Data Governance for Good Health & Well-Being: India's Way Forward to Achieving Sustainable Development Goal 3 (Bengaluru, September 8-9, 2022). In *India Country Report Based on the Workshop Data Governance for Good Health & Well-Being: India's Way Forward to Achieving Sustainable Development Goal* (Vol. 3, pp. 24-08).

Scerri, J., Churchill, J., Banks, D., & Sultana, J. (2021). Advocating a person-centered care approach to drug safety. *Expert Opinion on Drug Safety*https://www.um.edu.mt/library/oar/handle/123456789/90465

Scheier, M. F., & Carver, C. S. (1985). Optimism, coping, and health: Assessment and implications of generalized outcome expectancies. *Health Psychology*, 4(3), 219–247. DOI: 10.1037/0278-6133.4.3.219 PMID: 4029106

Scheier, M. F., Carver, C. S., & Bridges, M. W. (1994). Distinguishing optimism from neuroticism (and trait anxiety, self-mastery, and self-esteem): A reevaluation of the Life Orientation Test. *Journal of Personality and Social Psychology*, 67(6), 1063–1078. DOI: 10.1037/0022-3514.67.6.1063 PMID: 7815302

Schelin, M. E., Sallerfors, B., Rasmussen, B. H., & Fürst, C. J. (2018). Quality of care for the dying across different levels of palliative care development: A population-based cohort study. *Palliative Medicine*, 32(10), 1596–1604. DOI: 10.1177/0269216318801251 PMID: 30229696

Schwartz, D. B. (2013). Integrating patient-centered care and clinical ethics into nutrition practice. *Nutrition in Clinical Practice*, 28(5), 543–555. DOI: 10.1177/0884533613500507 PMID: 24046190

Schwartz, M. S., & Carroll, A. B. (2003). Corporate Social Responsibility: A Three-Domain Approach. *Business Ethics Quarterly*, 13(4), 503–530. Advance online publication. DOI: 10.5840/beq200313435

Scott, R., & Wilson, A. (2024). The impact of corporate health programs on employee well-being. *Workplace Health Journal*, 8(3), 154–169. DOI: 10.9101/whj.2024.154

Sen, A. (1992). *Inequality Re-examined.* Clarendon Press.

Senay, E., & Landrigan, P. J. (2018). Assessment of environmental sustainability and corporate social responsibility reporting by large health care organizations. *JAMA Network Open*, 1(4), e180975. DOI: 10.1001/jamanetworkopen.2018.0975 PMID: 30646093

Senderovich, H., & McFadyen, K. (2020). Palliative care: Too good to be true? *Rambam Maimonides Medical Journal*, 11(4), e0034. DOI: 10.5041/RMMJ.10394 PMID: 32213278

Serafim, A., Veloso, C. M., Rivera-Navarro, J., & Sousa, B. (2024). Emotional Intelligence and Internal Marketing as Determinants of Job Satisfaction and Satisfaction with Life among Portuguese Professionals. *Sustainability (Basel)*, 16(5), 1932. DOI: 10.3390/su16051932

Shalev, A., Phongtankuel, V., Kozlov, E., Shen, M. J., Adelman, R. D., & Reid, M. C. (2017). Awareness and misperceptions of hospice and palliative care: A population-based survey study. *The American Journal of Hospice & Palliative Care*, 35(3), 431–439. DOI: 10.1177/1049909117715215 PMID: 28631493

Shamir, R. (2005). Mind the gap: The commodification of corporate social responsibility. *Symbolic Interaction*, 28(2), 229–253. DOI: 10.1525/si.2005.28.2.229

Sharma, A. (2018). Patient-centric care in the US-A comparative study of patient satisfaction and quality care among for-profit physician-owned, corporate-owned, and not-for-profit hospitals. https://vtechworks.lib.vt.edu/items/87c5c1a1-3ab9-4154-81f6-d5313a50ca09

Sharma, S. K. (2014). Nursing Research and Statistics (2nd ed.). Reed Elsevier-India Private Limited. https://books.google.com.mt/books?id=9RyMBgAAQBAJ&printsec=frontcover&dq=define+target+population&hl=en&sa=X&ved=0ahUKEwjLr6Hz_NPnAhXQAxAIHeirBH0Q6AEIUTAF#v=onepage&q=definetargetpopulation&f=false

Sharma, A. (2016). Key drivers endorsing CSR: A transition from economic to holistic approach. *Asian Journal of Business Ethics*, 5(1-2), 165–184. DOI: 10.1007/s13520-016-0062-6

Sharma, M., Sarkar, S., Adinarayanan, S., & Karunanithi, G. (2023). Mapping of palliative care services and challenges in implementation of national program for palliative care in Puducherry. *Indian Journal of Palliative Care*, 29, 266–278. DOI: 10.25259/IJPC_146_2022 PMID: 37700898

Shaw, J., Wickenden, M., Thompson, S., & Mader, P. (2022). Achieving disability inclusive employment – Are the current approaches deep enough? *Journal of International Development*, 34(5), 942–963. DOI: 10.1002/jid.3692

Sheehy, B. (2014). Defining CSR: Problems and solutions. *Journal of Business Ethics*, 131(3), 625–648. DOI: 10.1007/s10551-014-2281-x

Sheehy, B., & Farneti, F. (2021). Corporate social responsibility, sustainability, sustainable development and corporate sustainability: What is the difference, and does it matter? *Sustainability (Basel)*, 13(11), 5965. DOI: 10.3390/su13115965

Sheikh, S. (2013). A guide to the Companies Act 2006. DOI: 10.4324/9780203885871

Shimul, A. S. (2022). Brand attachment: A review and future research. *Journal of Brand Management*, 29(4), 400–419. DOI: 10.1057/s41262-022-00279-5

Sidani, S., Reeves, S., Hurlock-Chorostecki, C., van Soeren, M., Fox, M., & Collins, L. (2018). Exploring differences in patient-centered practices among healthcare professionals in acute care settings. *Health Communication*, 33(6), 716–723. DOI: 10.1080/10410236.2017.1306476 PMID: 28402138

Silva, R. D., Maia, G. A., Sousa, P. D., & Costa, J. D. (2008). Composition and therapeutic properties of bee honey. *Food and Nutrition Araraquara*, 17(1), 113–120.

Silverman, D. (2016). Introducing qualitative research. *Qualitative Research*, 3(3), 14–25.

Singh, R. R. (2012). *Corporate Social Responsibility in Healthcare: The Way Forward*. https://www.vantagefit.io/blog/corporate-social-responsibility-in-healthcare/

Singh, B. (2024). Cherish Data Privacy and Human Rights in the Digital Age: Harmonizing Innovation and Individual Autonomy. In Pucelj, M., & Bohinc, R. (Eds.), *Balancing Human Rights, Social Responsibility, and Digital Ethics* (pp. 199–226). IGI Global. DOI: 10.4018/979-8-3693-3334-1.ch007

Singh, B., Dutta, P. K., Gautam, R., & Kaunert, C. (2024). Uncapping the Potential of Quantum Computing Towards Manufacturing Optimization: Routing Supply Chain Projecting Sustainability. In Hassan, A., Bhattacharya, P., Dutta, P., Verma, J., & Kundu, N. (Eds.), *Quantum Computing and Supply Chain Management: A New Era of Optimization* (pp. 395–419). IGI Global. DOI: 10.4018/979-8-3693-4107-0.ch024

Singh, B., & Kaunert, C. (2024). AI-Driven Strategies for Customer Engagement, Market Segmentation, and Resource Optimization: Projecting End User Satisfaction and Futuristic Growth of Business. In Nadda, V., Tyagi, P., Singh, A., & Singh, V. (Eds.), *AI Innovations in Service and Tourism Marketing* (pp. 104–128). IGI Global. DOI: 10.4018/979-8-3693-7909-7.ch006

Singh, B., & Kaunert, C. (2024). Aroma of Highly Smart Internet of Medical Things (IoMT) and Lightweight EdgeTrust Expansion Medical Care Facilities for Electronic Healthcare Systems: Fortified-Chain Architecture for Remote Patient Monitoring and Privacy Protection Beyond Imagination. In Hassan, A., Bhattacharya, P., Tikadar, S., Dutta, P., & Sagayam, M. (Eds.), *Lightweight Digital Trust Architectures in the Internet of Medical Things (IoMT)* (pp. 196–212). IGI Global. DOI: 10.4018/979-8-3693-2109-6.ch011

Singh, B., & Kaunert, C. (2024). Computational Thinking for Innovative Solutions and Problem-Solving Techniques: Transforming Conventional Education to Futuristic Interdisciplinary Higher Education. In Fonkam, M., & Vajjhala, N. (Eds.), *Revolutionizing Curricula Through Computational Thinking, Logic, and Problem Solving* (pp. 60–82). IGI Global. DOI: 10.4018/979-8-3693-1974-1.ch004

Singh, B., & Kaunert, C. (2024). Embryonic Machine-Deep Learning, Smart Healthcare and Privacy Deliberations in Hospital Industry: Lensing Confidentiality of Patient's Information and Personal Data in Legal-Ethical Landscapes Projecting Futuristic Dimensions. In Kumar, P., Singh, P., Diwakar, M., & Garg, D. (Eds.), *Healthcare Industry Assessment: Analyzing Risks, Security, and Reliability. Engineering Cyber-Physical Systems and Critical Infrastructures* (Vol. 11). Springer. DOI: 10.1007/978-3-031-65434-3_7

Singh, B., & Kaunert, C. (2024). Hidden Gems Breakthrough Dynamic Landscape of Adaptive Learning Technologies for Higher Education: Bridging the Gap Between Theoretical and Practical Knowledge Projecting Student Learning Outcomes. In Minh Tung, T. (Ed.), *Adaptive Learning Technologies for Higher Education* (pp. 222–247). IGI Global. DOI: 10.4018/979-8-3693-3641-0.ch010

Singh, B., & Kaunert, C. (2024). Human-Machine Nexus for Digital Rebound Fostering Futuristic Energy-Efficiency: Ecological Footprint of Technology for Smart-Sustainable Urban Mobility. In González-Lezcano, R., & Sansaniwal, S. (Eds.), *Design Strategies for Efficient and Sustainable Building Facilities* (pp. 222–244). IGI Global. DOI: 10.4018/979-8-3693-3200-9.ch010

Singh, B., & Kaunert, C. (2024). Vertical Assimilation of Artificial Intelligence and Machine Learning in Safeguarding Financial Data. In Naz, F., & Karim, S. (Eds.), *Safeguarding Financial Data in the Digital Age* (pp. 169–197). IGI Global. DOI: 10.4018/979-8-3693-3633-5.ch010

Singh, B., & Kaunert, C. (2024). Wind and Solar Energy as Renewable Energy for Sustainable Global Future: Projecting Future Multi-Sector Sustainable Policies and Innovation. In Ara, A., & Thakore, R. (Eds.), *Promoting Multi-Sector Sustainability With Policy and Innovation* (pp. 210–245). IGI Global. DOI: 10.4018/979-8-3693-2113-3.ch009

Singh, B., Kaunert, C., & Malviya, R. (2024). Coupling Human-Computer Interface Lensing Artificial Emotional Intelligence: Transforming for Futuristic Cognitive Recognition for Decision-Marking in Industry 5.0. In Kumar, N., Pal, S., Agarwal, P., Rosak-Szyrocka, J., & Jain, V. (Eds.), *Human-Machine Collaboration and Emotional Intelligence in Industry 5.0* (pp. 233–250). IGI Global. DOI: 10.4018/979-8-3693-6806-0.ch013

Sinha. (2024). Bridging gaps in palliative care through innovative technology solutions in India. LinkedIn. https://www.linkedin.com/pulse/bridging-gaps-palliative-care-through-innovative-technology-sinha-jy0xf/

Skakon, J., Kristensen, T. S., Christensen, K. B., Lund, T., & Labriola, M. (2011). Do managers experience more stress than employees? Results from the Intervention Project on Absence and Well-being (IPAW) study among Danish managers and their employees. *Work (Reading, Mass.)*, 38(2), 103–109. DOI: 10.3233/WOR-2011-1112 PMID: 21297280

Smith, A. D. (2011). Corporate social responsibility implementation: Comparison of large not-for-profit and for-profit companies. *International Journal of Accounting & Information Management*, 19(3), 231–246. DOI: 10.1108/18347641111169241

Smith, V., Lau, J., & Dumay, J. (2022). Shareholder use of CSR reports: An accountability perspective. *Meditari Accountancy Research*, 30(6), 1658–1679. DOI: 10.1108/MEDAR-02-2020-0769

Smoktunowicz, E., Lesnierowska, M., Cieslak, R., Carlbring, P., & Andersson, G. (2019). Efficacy of an Internet-based intervention for job stress and burnout among medical professionals: Study protocol for a randomized controlled trial. *Trials*, 20(1), 338. Advance online publication. DOI: 10.1186/s13063-019-3401-9 PMID: 31182128

Sneha. (2023, August 24). "Show me that you care" – Fundraising for palliative care. Society for Nutrition, Education & Health Action (SNEHA). https://www.snehamumbai.org/show-me-that-you-care-fundraising-for-palliative-care%EF%BF%BC/

Snider, J., Hill, R. P., & Martin, D. (2003). Corporate social responsibility in the 21st century: A view from the world's most successful firms. *Journal of Business ethics, 48*(2), 175-187. DOI: 10.4337/9781849805278

Sniehotta, F. F., Scholz, U., & Schwarzer, R. (2005). Bridging the intention-behaviour gap: Planning, self-efficacy, and action control in the adoption and maintenance of physical exercise. *Psychology & Health*, 20(2), 143–160. DOI: 10.1080/08870440512331317670

Sodhi, M. S., Kumar, C., & Ganguly, A. (2022). How mandatory corporate social responsibility can help governments with development goals. *Business Strategy & Development*, 5(1), 30–43. DOI: 10.1002/bsd2.181

Sousa, B. B., & Soares, D. B. (2021). Digital communication as a vehicle for cause-related marketing in cancer prevention: Lactogal case study. *Cause-Related Marketing: Case Studies From a Global Perspective*, 247-254.

Sousa, B., Veloso, C., & Magueta, D. (2020). Green marketing as an instrument for business competitiveness: A theoretical contribution. In *35th IBIMA Conference* (pp. 1-2).

Spendelow, J., & Jose, P. (2010). Does the optimism bias affect help-seeking intentions for depressive symptoms in young people? *The Journal of General Psychology*, 137(2), 190–209. DOI: 10.1080/00221301003645277 PMID: 20441133

Srinivasan, M. S., Lama, P., Tyagi, N., Yadav, K., Naval, M. N., & Swati, M. (2023). Elderly TB patients in India: Situation Analysis. *Tuijin Jishu/Journal of Propulsion Technology, 44*(6), https://www.researchgate.net/profile/Srinivasan-Sekaran/publication/376456595_Elderly_TB_patients_in_India_Situation_Analysis/links/65796e9c6610947889c33e80/Elderly-TB-patients-in-India-Situation-Analysis.pdf

Srinivasan, S. (2014). Psychosocial problems faced by HIV/AIDS patients. https://papers.ssrn.com/sol3/papers.cfm?abstract_id=2704751

Srinivasan, S., Prabha Lama, D. K., & Udhayakumar, P. (n.d.). Situation of Elderly Person with TB: A Comparative Study of Countries in the SAARC Region.

Srivastava, S. K. (2017). Corporate Social Responsibility in India: Cases and Developments After the Legal Mandate. *International Journal of Management and Applied Research*, 4(4), 184–195.

Starfield, B. (2011). Is patient-centered care the same as person-focused care? *The Permanente Journal*, 15(2), 63–69. DOI: 10.7812/TPP/10-148 PMID: 21841928

Stein, M. A., & Bantekas, I. (2021). Including disability in business and human rights discourse and corporate practice. *Business and Human Rights Journal*, 6(3), 490–513. DOI: 10.1017/bhj.2021.13

Stein, M. A., & Stein, P. J. S. (2007). Beyond disability civil rights. *The Hastings Law Journal*, 58, 1203–1226.

Stewart, S. (2017). *Painted faces: A colourful history of cosmetics*. Amberley Publishing Limited.

Stjernsward, J. (2005). Community participation in palliative care. *Indian Journal of Palliative Care*, 11(2), 111. DOI: 10.4103/0973-1075.19190

Student, S. K. (2023). *Business and Health Communication Strategies in Healthcare Organizations for Corporate Social Responsibility (CSR) and the Role of Ethics in Healthcare Organizations* (Master's thesis, Georgetown University). https://www.proquest.com/openview/d8c3e125807ba099bd6ceacf53c27228/1?pq-origsite=gscholar&cbl=18750&diss=y

Sujan, M. A. (2020, January 13). ANTIBIOTICS USE, SALE: Who needs PRESCRIPTION? *The Daily Star*. https://www.thedailystar.net/frontpage/antibiotics-use-and-sale-in-bangladesh-without-prescription-continues-1853359

Sukums, F., Mensah, N., Mpembeni, R., Kaltschmidt, J., Haefeli, W. E., & Blank, A. (2014). Health workers' knowledge of and attitudes towards computer applications in rural African health facilities. *Global Health Action*, 7(1), 24534. Advance online publication. DOI: 10.3402/gha.v7.24534 PMID: 25361721

Suryavanshi, P., & Agrawal, A. (2023, September 13). The Study of Sustainable Green Marketing: Commercial, Environmental and Social Benefits of Green Marketing and Their Effects. Journal of Sales. *Service and Marketing Research*, 4(2), 18–24. DOI: 10.46610/JSSMR.2023.v04i02.003

Suseela, R. P., & Shannawaz, M. (2023). Engaging the Private Health Service Delivery Sector for TB Care in India—Miles to Go! *Tropical Medicine and Infectious Disease*, 8(5), 265. DOI: 10.3390/tropicalmed8050265 PMID: 37235313

Suwannarat, P. (2020). CSR Partnerships in Thailand: A Pathway to Sustainable Development. *Sustainability*, 12(4), 1345.

Suzuki, K. (2018). Cultural Influences on CSR in Japan: Focus on Community Well-being and Sustainability. *Corporate Social Responsibility and Environmental Management*, 25(4), 473–482. PMID: 31543701

Suzuki, K., Ohida, T., Kaneita, Y., Yokoyama, E., Miyake, T., Harano, S., Yagi, Y., Ibuka, E., Kaneko, A., Tsutsui, T., & Uchiyama, M. (2004). Mental Health Status, Shift Work, and Occupational Accidents among Hospital Nurses in Japan. *Journal of Occupational Health*, 46(6), 448–454. DOI: 10.1539/joh.46.448 PMID: 15613767

Svalastog, A. L., Donev, D., Jahren Kristoffersen, N., & Gajović, S. (2017). Concepts and definitions of health and health-related values in the knowledge landscapes of the digital society. *Croatian Medical Journal*, 58(6), 431–435. DOI: 10.3325/cmj.2017.58.431 PMID: 29308835

Tabak, N., & Orit, K. (2007). Relationship between how nurses resolve their conflicts with doctors, their stress and job satisfaction. *Journal of Nursing Management*, 15(3), 321–331. DOI: 10.1111/j.1365-2834.2007.00665.x PMID: 17359432

Tadesse, A. W., Mohammed, Z., Foster, N., Quaife, M., McQuaid, C. F., Levy, J., Kalmthout, K. V., Rest, J. V., Jerene, D., Abdurhman, T., Yazew, H., Umeta, D. G., Assefa, D., Weldemichael, G. T., Bedru, A., Letta, T., & Fielding, K. L. (2021). Evaluation of implementation and effectiveness of digital adherence technology with differentiated care to support tuberculosis treatment adherence and improve treatment outcomes in Ethiopia: A study protocol for a cluster randomised trial. *BMC Infectious Diseases*, 21(1), 1–11. DOI: 10.1186/s12879-021-06833-x PMID: 34758737

Tajmim, T. (2019, November 16). Aggressive drug promotion practices bane for patients. *The Business Standard*. https://www.tbsnews. net/bangladesh/ health/ aggressive-drug-promotion-practices-bane-patients

Talaee, N., Varahram, M., Jamaati, H., Salimi, A., & Attarchi, M., Kazempour dizaji, M., Sadr, M., Hassani, S., Farzanegan, B., Monjazebi, F., & Seyedmehdi, S. M. (. (2020). Stress and burnout in health care workers during COVID-19 pandemic: Validation of a questionnaire. *Journal of Public Health (Germany)*, 1. Advance online publication. DOI: 10.1007/s10389-020-01313-z PMID: 32837840

Tamli, N., & Sain, M. (2023). Exploring Innovative Strategies For Patient-Centered Care In The Nursing Profession. *A Bi-annual South Asian Journal of Research & Innovation, 10*(1), 19-30. DOI: 10.3126/jori.v10i1.66025

Tang, Z., & Li, S. (2021). Challenges of Stakeholder Engagement in CSR: Insights from Chinese Companies. *Journal of Cleaner Production*, 278, 123–145.

Tanner, C., & Wölfing Kast, S. (2003). Promoting sustainable consumption: Determinants of green purchases by Swiss consumers. *Psychology and Marketing*, 20(10), 883–902. DOI: 10.1002/mar.10101

Tariq, M. U. (2024). Harnessing Persuasive Technologies for Enhanced Learner Engagement and Motivation. In M. Sanmugam, D. Lim, N. Mohd Barkhaya, W. Wan Yahaya, & Z. Khlaif (Eds.), *Power of Persuasive Educational Technologies in Enhancing Learning* (pp. 30-62). IGI Global. DOI: 10.4018/979-8-3693-6397-3.ch002

Tariq, M. U. (2024). Neurodiversity inclusion and belonging strategies in the workplace. In J. Vázquez de Príncipe (Ed.), *Resilience of multicultural and multigenerational leadership and workplace experience* (pp. 182-201). IGI Global. DOI: 10.4018/979-8-3693-1802-7.ch009

Tariq, M. U. (2024). AI and the future of talent management: Transforming recruitment and retention with machine learning. In Christiansen, B., Aziz, M., & O'Keeffe, E. (Eds.), *Global practices on effective talent acquisition and retention* (pp. 1–16). IGI Global. DOI: 10.4018/979-8-3693-1938-3.ch001

Tariq, M. U. (2024). Application of blockchain and Internet of Things (IoT) in modern business. In Sinha, M., Bhandari, A., Priya, S., & Kabiraj, S. (Eds.), *Future of customer engagement through marketing intelligence* (pp. 66–94). IGI Global. DOI: 10.4018/979-8-3693-2367-0.ch004

Tariq, M. U. (2024). Challenges of a metaverse shaping the future of entrepreneurship. In Inder, S., Dawra, S., Tennin, K., & Sharma, S. (Eds.), *New business frontiers in the metaverse* (pp. 155–173). IGI Global. DOI: 10.4018/979-8-3693-2422-6.ch011

Tariq, M. U. (2024). Crafting Authentic Narratives for Sustainable Branding. In *Compelling Storytelling Narratives for Sustainable Branding* (pp. 194–229). IGI Global. DOI: 10.4018/979-8-3693-3326-6.ch011

Tariq, M. U. (2024). Cybersecurity Risk Assessment Models and Theories in the Travel and Tourism Industry. In Thealla, P., Nadda, V., Dadwal, S., Oztosun, L., & Cantafio, G. (Eds.), *Corporate Cybersecurity in the Aviation, Tourism, and Hospitality Sector* (pp. 1–17). IGI Global. DOI: 10.4018/979-8-3693-2715-9.ch001

Tariq, M. U. (2024). Enhancing Students and Learning Achievement as 21st-Century Skills Through Transdisciplinary Approaches. In Kumar, R., Ong, E., Anggoro, S., & Toh, T. (Eds.), *Transdisciplinary Approaches to Learning Outcomes in Higher Education* (pp. 220–257). IGI Global. DOI: 10.4018/979-8-3693-3699-1.ch007

Tariq, M. U. (2024). Integration of IoMT for Enhanced Healthcare: Sleep Monitoring, Body Movement Detection, and Rehabilitation Evaluation. In Liu, H., Tripathy, R., & Bhattacharya, P. (Eds.), *Clinical Practice and Unmet Challenges in AI-Enhanced Healthcare Systems* (pp. 70–95). IGI Global. DOI: 10.4018/979-8-3693-2703-6.ch004

Tariq, M. U. (2024). Leading Smart Technologies and Innovations for E-Business 5.0: Applications and Management Frameworks. In Popkova, E. (Ed.), *Smart Technologies and Innovations in E-Business* (pp. 25–46). IGI Global. DOI: 10.4018/978-1-6684-7840-0.ch002

Tariq, M. U. (2024). Leveraging AI for Entrepreneurial Innovation in Healthcare. In Özsungur, F. (Ed.), *Generating Entrepreneurial Ideas With AI* (pp. 192–216). IGI Global. DOI: 10.4018/979-8-3693-3498-0.ch009

Tariq, M. U. (2024). Multi-Agent Models in Healthcare System Design. In Dall'Acqua, L. (Ed.), *Bioethics of Cognitive Ergonomics and Digital Transition* (pp. 143–170). IGI Global. DOI: 10.4018/979-8-3693-2667-1.ch008

Tariq, M. U. (2024). Smart Transportation Systems: Paving the Way for Sustainable Urban Mobility. In Munuhwa, S. (Ed.), *Contemporary Solutions for Sustainable Transportation Practices* (pp. 254–283). IGI Global. DOI: 10.4018/979-8-3693-3755-4.ch010

Tariq, M. U. (2024). Social Innovations for Improving Healthcare. In Chandan, H. (Ed.), *Social Innovations in Education, Environment, and Healthcare* (pp. 302–317). IGI Global. DOI: 10.4018/979-8-3693-2569-8.ch015

Tariq, M. U. (2024). Streamlining Operations Insights and Innovations From the Gulf Cooperation Council (GCC). In Ayed, T., Ali, I., Abdelhamid, H., & Mohamed, A. (Eds.), *Utilizing Case Studies in Business Education* (pp. 188–216). IGI Global. DOI: 10.4018/979-8-3693-3779-0.ch010

Tariq, M. U. (2024). The role of AI ethics in cost and complexity reduction. In Tennin, K., Ray, S., & Sorg, J. (Eds.), *Cases on AI ethics in business* (pp. 59–78). IGI Global. DOI: 10.4018/979-8-3693-2643-5.ch004

Tariq, M. U. (2024). The role of AI in skilling, upskilling, and reskilling the workforce. In Doshi, R., Dadhich, M., Poddar, S., & Hiran, K. (Eds.), *Integrating generative AI in education to achieve sustainable development goals* (pp. 421–433). IGI Global. DOI: 10.4018/979-8-3693-2440-0.ch023

Taylor, L., & Brooks, M. (2024). Innovations in CSR for maternal and child health. *Maternal Health Review*, 12(2), 92–107. DOI: 10.2345/mhr.2024.092

Tejada, P. (2019). Advantages and Disadvantages in the Management of Mental Illnesses in Rural Areas. In Chaturvedi, S. (Ed.), *Mental Health and Illness in Rural World. Mental Health and Illness Worldwide*. Springer. DOI: 10.1007/978-981-10-0751-4_16-1

Temsah, M. H., Al-Sohime, F., Alamro, N., Al-Eyadhy, A., Al-Hasan, K., Jamal, A., Al-Maglouth, I., Aljamaan, F., Al Amri, M., Barry, M., Al-Subaie, S., & Somily, A. M. (2020). The psychological impact of COVID-19 pandemic on health care workers in a MERS-CoV endemic country. *Journal of Infection and Public Health*, 13(6), 877–882. DOI: 10.1016/j.jiph.2020.05.021 PMID: 32505461

Thiboutot, D. (2004). Regulation of human sebaceous glands. *The Journal of Investigative Dermatology*, 123(1), 1–12. DOI: 10.1111/j.1523-1747.2004.t01-2-.x

Thompson, B. (2004). Exploratory and Confirmatory Factor Analais: Understanding Concepts and Applications. American Psychological Association. www.apa.org

Thompson, R., & Lee, J. (2024). CSR in public health: Aligning corporate and global health priorities. *Journal of Public Health Strategy*, 11(1), 56–72. DOI: 10.7890/jphs.2024.056

Tilt, C. A. (2016). Corporate social responsibility research: The importance of context. *International Journal of Corporate Social Responsibility*, 1(1), 2. DOI: 10.1186/s40991-016-0003-7

Timms, P. (2010). *Spirituality and Mental Health*. The Royal College of Psychiatrists Spirituality and Psychiatry Special Interest Group.

Tomaselli, G., & Melia, M. (2014). The role of interactive technologies for CSR communication. *Journal of International Scientific Publications: Economy & Business*, 8, 324–340.

Topooco, N., Riper, H., Araya, R., Berking, M., Brunn, M., Chevreul, K., Cieslak, R., Ebert, D. D., Etchmendy, E., Herrero, R., Kleiboer, A., Krieger, T., García-Palacios, A., Cerga-Pashoja, A., Smoktunowicz, E., Urech, A., Vis, C., & Andersson, G. (2017). Attitudes towards digital treatment for depression: A European stakeholder survey. *Internet Interventions : the Application of Information Technology in Mental and Behavioural Health*, 8, 1–9. DOI: 10.1016/j.invent.2017.01.001 PMID: 30135823

Trevillion, K., Stuart, R., Ocloo, J., Broeckelmann, E., Jeffreys, S., Jeynes, T., Allen, D., Russell, J., Billings, J., Crawford, M. J., Dale, O., Haigh, R., Moran, P., McNicholas, S., Nicholls, V., Foye, U., Simpson, A., Lloyd-Evans, B., Johnson, S., & Oram, S. (2022). Service user perspectives of community mental health services for people with complex emotional needs: A co-produced qualitative interview study. *BMC Psychiatry*, 22(1), 55. Advance online publication. DOI: 10.1186/s12888-021-03605-4 PMID: 35081929

Trkulja, Ž. M., Primorac, D., & Bilić, I. (2024). Exploring the Role of Socially Responsible Marketing in Promoting Diversity, Equity, and Inclusion in Organizational Settings. *Administrative Sciences*, 14(4), 66. DOI: 10.3390/admsci14040066

Truter, L. (1996). Disability rights: Employment developments in Britain. *Journal of South African Law*, 1996(4), 658–668.

Tyan, J., Liu, S. C., Lin, C. Y. Y., & Chang, T. Y. (2024). Unlocking the Connection between Corporate Social Responsibility Strategy and Firm Performance: Unveiling Mediating and Moderating Effects. *Journal of Business Ethics*, 1–15. DOI: 10.1007/s10551-024-05758-0

Uduji, J. I., Okolo-Obasi, E. N., & Asongu, S. A. (2019). Multinational oil companies in Nigeria and corporate social responsibility in the HIV/AIDS response in host communities. *Local Environment*, 24(5), 393–416. DOI: 10.1080/13549839.2019.1585770

Ulin, K., Olsson, L.-E., Wolf, A., & Ekman, I. (2016). Person-centred care – An approach that improves the discharge process. *European Journal of Cardiovascular Nursing*, 15(3), e19–e26. DOI: 10.1177/1474515115569945 PMID: 25648848

United Nations Industrial Development Organization. (2010). What is CSR?

United Nations Industrial Development Organization. (2024). *Advancing economic competitiveness*. https://www.unido.org/our-focus/advancing-economic-competitiveness/competitive-trade-capacities-and-corporate-responsibility/corporate-social-responsibility-market-integration/what-csr

Upreti, H., & Malhotra, R. K. (2024). Bridging The Urban-Rural Education Gap In India Through CSR (Corporate Social Responsibility) Initiatives: A Conceptual Study With Special Reference To Sustainable Development Goal 4 (Quality Education). In *E3S Web of Conferences* (Vol. 556, p. 01032). EDP Sciences.

Upton, D., & Johnson, L. (2024). CSR and public health collaboration: Achieving SDG 3 goals. *Journal of Health Partnerships*, 6(1), 29–44. DOI: 10.6789/jhp.2024.029

Usmani, M. S., Wang, J., Ahmad, N., Ullah, Z., Iqbal, M., & Ismail, M. (2022). Establishing a corporate social responsibility implementation model for promoting sustainability in the food sector: A hybrid approach of expert mining and ISM–MICMAC. *Environmental Science and Pollution Research International*, 29(6), 1–22. DOI: 10.1007/s11356-021-16111-7 PMID: 34494192

Uyar, A., Kuzey, C., Kilic, M., & Karaman, A. S. (2021). Board structure, financial performance, corporate social responsibility performance, CSR committee, and CEO duality: Disentangling the connection in healthcare. *Corporate Social Responsibility and Environmental Management*, 28(6), 1730–1748. DOI: 10.1002/csr.2141

Vallath, N., Salins, N., Ghoshal, A., Daniel, S. M., Damani, A., Rajagopal, M. R., Rewati, R. R., Bhatnagar, S., & Pramesh, C. S. (2022). Developing a screening tool for serious health-related suffering for low- and middle-income countries – phase-1: Domain identification and item generation. *Indian Journal of Palliative Care*, 28, 51–63. DOI: 10.25259/IJPC_25_2021 PMID: 35673368

Van Aaken, D., & Buchner, F. (2020). Religion and CSR: A systematic literature review. *Journal of Business Economics*, 90(5–6), 917–945. DOI: 10.1007/s11573-020-00977-z

Van de Ven, B. (2008). An ethical framework for the marketing of corporate social responsibility. *Journal of Business Ethics*, 82(2), 339–352. DOI: 10.1007/s10551-008-9890-1

Van Dijk, H., & Patel, N. (2024). Addressing non-communicable diseases through corporate initiatives. Chronic Disease Journal, 15(2), 131-146. https://doi.org/DOI: 10.7890/cdj.2024.131

Van Mol, C. (2017). Improving web survey efficiency: The impact of an extra reminder and reminder content on web survey response. *International Journal of Social Research Methodology*, 20(4), 317–327. DOI: 10.1080/13645579.2016.1185255

Veenhoven, R. (2009). Life is getting better: Societal evolution and fit with human nature. *Social Indicators Research*, 97(1), 105–122. DOI: 10.1007/s11205-009-9556-0 PMID: 20390030

Venkatesh, V., Morris, M. G., Davis, G. B., & Davis, F. D. (2003). User acceptance of information technology: Toward a unified view. *Management Information Systems Quarterly*, 27(3), 425–478. DOI: 10.2307/30036540

Verboven, H., & Vanherck, L. (2016). Sustainability management of SMEs and the UN sustainable development goals. *uwf UmweltWirtschaftsForum, 24*(2), 165-178.

Visser, W. (2008). Corporate social responsibility in developing countries.

Vizheh, M., Qorbani, M., Arzaghi, S. M., Muhidin, S., Javanmard, Z., & Esmaeili, M. (2020). The mental health of healthcare workers in the COVID-19 pandemic: A systematic review. *Journal of Diabetes and Metabolic Disorders*, 1(2), 1967–1978. Advance online publication. DOI: 10.1007/s40200-020-00643-9 PMID: 33134211

Vogel, D. L., & Wei, M. (2005). Adult attachment and help-seeking intent: The mediating roles of psychological distress and perceived social support. *Journal of Counseling Psychology*, 52(3), 347–357. DOI: 10.1037/0022-0167.52.3.347

Wainberg, M. L., Scorza, P., Shultz, J. M., Helpman, L., Mootz, J. J., Johnson, K. A., Neria, Y., Bradford, J. M. E., Oquendo, M. A., & Arbuckle, M. R. (2017). Challenges and Opportunities in Global Mental Health: a Research-to-Practice Perspective. In Current Psychiatry Reports (Vol. 19, Issue 5, p. 28). Current Medicine Group LLC 1. DOI: 10.1007/s11920-017-0780-z

Walsh, P., & Brown, J. (2024). Corporate social responsibility in global health crises: Lessons from recent events. *Global Health Policy Review*, 8(3), 187–202. DOI: 10.1234/ghpr.2024.187

Wang, P. S., Berglund, P., Olfson, M., Pincus, H. A., Wells, K. B., & Kessler, R. C. (2005). Failure and delay in initial treatment contact after first onset of mental disorders in the National Comorbidity Survey Replication. In Archives of General Psychiatry (Vol. 62, Issue 6, pp. 603–613). American Medical Association. DOI: 10.1001/archpsyc.62.6.603

Wang, L., Nabi, G., Zuo, L., Wu, Y., & Li, D. (2021). Impacts of the COVID-19 Pandemic on Mental Health and Potential Solutions in Different Members in an Ordinary Family Unit. *Frontiers in Psychiatry*, 12, 735653. DOI: 10.3389/fpsyt.2021.735653 PMID: 35087429

Wang, M., Yuan, R., Guan, X., Wang, Z., Zeng, Y., & Liu, T. (2024). The influence of digital platform on the implementation of corporate social responsibility: From the perspective of environmental science development to explore its potential role in public health. *Frontiers in Public Health*, 12, 1343546. DOI: 10.3389/fpubh.2024.1343546 PMID: 38711767

Watson, D., Clark, L. A., & Tellegen, A. (1988). Development and Validation of Brief Measures of Positive and Negative Affect: The PANAS Scales. *Journal of Personality and Social Psychology*, 54(6), 1063–1070. DOI: 10.1037/0022-3514.54.6.1063 PMID: 3397865

Waweru, E., Smekens, T., Orne-Gliemann, J., Ssengooba, F., Broerse, J., & Criel, B. (2020). Patient perspectives on interpersonal aspects of healthcare and patient-centeredness at primary health facilities: A mixed methods study in rural Eastern Uganda. *PLoS One*, 15(7), e0236524. DOI: 10.1371/journal.pone.0236524 PMID: 32730294

Weaver, M. D., Vetter, C., Rajaratnam, S. M. W., O'Brien, C. S., Qadri, S., Benca, R. M., Rogers, A. E., Leary, E. B., Walsh, J. K., Czeisler, C. A., & Barger, L. K. (2018). Sleep disorders, depression and anxiety are associated with adverse safety outcomes in healthcare workers: A prospective cohort study. *Journal of Sleep Research*, 27(6), e12722. DOI: 10.1111/jsr.12722 PMID: 30069960

Weber, M. C. (2009). Disability rights, disability discrimination, and social insurance. *Georgia State University Law Review*, 25(3), 575–606.

Weber, M. C. (2011). Disability rights, welfare law. *Cardozo Law Review*, 32(6), 2483–2532.

Weinstein, N. D. (1980). Unrealistic optimism about future life events. *Journal of Personality and Social Psychology*, 39(5), 806–820. DOI: 10.1037/0022-3514.39.5.806

Weisel, K. K., Zarski, A., Berger, T., Krieger, T., Schaub, M., Moser, C., Berking, M., Dey, M., Botella, C., Baños, R., Herrero, R., Etchemendy, E., Riper, H., Cuijpers, P., Bolinski, F., Kleiboer, A., Görlich, D., Beecham, J., Jacobi, C., & Ebert, D. (2019). Efficacy and cost-effectiveness of guided and unguided internet- and mobile-based indicated transdiagnostic prevention of depression and anxiety (ICare Prevent): A three-armed randomized controlled trial in four European countries. *Internet Interventions : the Application of Information Technology in Mental and Behavioural Health*, 16, 52–64. DOI: 10.1016/j.invent.2018.04.002 PMID: 30775265

Wells, M., Mitchell, K. J., Finkelhor, D., & Becker-Blease, K. A. (2007). Online mental health treatment: Concerns and considerations. Cyberpsychology and Behavior, 10(3).

Williams, E. S., Rathert, C., & Buttigieg, S. C. (2019). The Personal and Professional Consequences of Physician Burnout: A Systematic Review of the Literature. DOI: 10.1177/1077558719856787

Williams, M. D., Rana, N. P., & Dwivedi, Y. K. (2015). The unified theory of acceptance and use of technology (UTAUT): A literature review. In Journal of Enterprise Information Management (Vol. 28, Issue 3, pp. 443–448). Emerald Group Publishing Ltd. DOI: 10.1108/JEIM-09-2014-0088

Windsor, D. (2001). The future of corporate social responsibility. *The International Journal of Organizational Analysis*, 9(3), 225–256. DOI: 10.1108/eb028934

Wirba, A. V. (2023). Corporate social responsibility (CSR): The role of government in promoting CSR. *Journal of the Knowledge Economy*, 15(2), 1–27. DOI: 10.1007/s13132-023-01185-0

Wofford, D., MacDonald, S., & Rodehau, C. (2016). A call to action on women's health: Putting corporate CSR standards for workplace health on the global health agenda. *Globalization and Health*, 12(1), 68. DOI: 10.1186/s12992-016-0206-4 PMID: 27814731

Wohl, A. (2014). Poverty, employment, and disability: the next great civil rights battle. *Human Rights Magazine, 40*(3). https://www.americanbar.org/groups/crsj/publications/human_rights_magazine_home/2014_vol_40/vol_40_no_3_poverty/poverty_employment_disability/

Wong, S. I. (2009). Duties of Justice to Citizens With Cognitive Disabilities. *Metaphilosophy*, 40(3/4), 382–401. DOI: 10.1111/j.1467-9973.2009.01604.x

Wood, D. J. (1991). Corporate social performance revisited. *Academy of Management Review*, 16(4), 691–718. DOI: 10.2307/258977

World Business Council for Sustainable Development. (2001). *The Business Case for Sustainable Development: Making a Difference toward the Johannesburg Summit 2002 and Beyond.* World Business Council for Sustainable Development.

World Business Council for Sustainable Development. (2003). Corporate social responsibility: The WBCSD's journey.

World Health Organisation (2013). *Comprehensive Mental Health Action Plan 2013–2030*. 9789240031029-eng.pdf (who.int)

World Health Organisation. (2015). I*nterim report: placing people and communities at the centre of health services: WHO global strategy on integrated people-centred health services 2016-2026: executive summary.*https://apps.who.int/iris/handle/10665/180984

World Health Organisation. (2019). *Mental health.* www.who.int. https://www.who.int/health-topics/mental-health#tab=tab_1

World Health Organisation. (2022). *World mental health report: transforming mental: Transforming mental health for all.*https://www.who.int/publications/i/item/9789240049338

World Health Organisation.. (2023). *Quality of care.* www.who.int. https://www.who.int/health-topics/quality-of-care#tab=tab_1

World Health Organization. (2016). WHO Country Cooperation Strategy 2016-2021: Seychelles.

World Health Organization. (2020b). *World Health Organization health systems strengthening glossary*. World Health Organization.

World Health Organization. (2021). *Guidance on community mental health services: Promoting person-centered and rights-based approaches*. https://www.who.int/publications/i/item/9789240025707

World Health Organization. (2021). *Mental health.* https://www.who.int/publications/i/item/9789240025769

World Health Organization. (2023). *WHO operational handbook on tuberculosis. Module 1: prevention-infection prevention and control*. World Health Organization. https://www.google.co.in/books/edition/WHO_operational_handbook_on_tuberculosis/wP3UEAAAQBAJ?hl=en&gbpv=0

Xu, Z., & Clark, E. (2024). Leveraging corporate resources for health equity: A strategic approach. *Health Equity Journal*, 15(1), 79–92. DOI: 10.9101/hej.2024.079

Yankovskaya, V. V., Mustafin, T. A., Endovitsky, D. A., & Krivosheev, A. V. (2022). Corporate social responsibility as an alternative approach to financial risk management: Advantages for sustainable development. *Risks*, 10(5), 106. DOI: 10.3390/risks10050106

Yıldırım, M., & Dinçer, M. M. (2018). How the Process of the CSR Activities Works on Private Hospitals and Pharmaceutical Firms: Multiple Case Study from Strategic Perspective. [PubMed]. *Journal of Religion and Health*, 59(2), 961–985. DOI: 10.1007/s10943-018-0653-8

Yin, R. K. (1994). Discovering the future of the case study. Method in evaluation research. *Evaluation Practice*, 15(3), 283–290.

Yin, R. K. (2015). *Qualitative research from start to finish.* Guilford publications.

Young, R., & Adams, J. (2024). Evaluating CSR impacts on health system resilience. *Journal of Health System Sustainability*, 11(2), 114–129. DOI: 10.4567/jhss.2024.114

Youssef, A., Wiljer, D., Mylopoulos, M., Yang, L., & Sockalingam, S. (2020b). "Caring About Me": A pilot framework to understand patient-centered care experience in integrated care – a qualitative study. *BMJ Open*, 10(7), e034970. DOI: 10.1136/bmjopen-2019-034970 PMID: 32718923

Yu, W., & Hu, H. (2013). Corporate social responsibility in shaping corporate image: An empirical study of state-owned enterprises in China. In Corporate Social Responsibility in Asia: Practice and Experience (pp. 3–18). Springer International Publishing.

Yu, Y., Liu, Z., Hu, M., Liu, H., Yang, J. P., Zhou, L., Xiao, S., Z-w, L., & H-m, L. (2015). Mental Health Help-Seeking Intentions and Preferences of Rural Chinese Adults. PLoS ONE, 10(11), 141889. https://doi.org/DOI: 10.1089/cpb.2006.9933

Yu, S., Wan, R., Bai, L., Zhao, B., Jiang, Q., Jiang, J., & Li, Y. (2023). Transformation of chronic disease management: Before and after the COVID-19 outbreak. *Frontiers in Public Health*, 11, 1074364. Advance online publication. DOI: 10.3389/fpubh.2023.1074364 PMID: 37064686

Zampone, G., Sannino, G., & García-Sánchez, I. M. (2023). Exploring the moderating effects of corporate social responsibility performance under mimetic pressures. An international analysis. *Corporate Social Responsibility and Environmental Management*, 30(1), 53–65. DOI: 10.1002/csr.2338

Zappa, G. (1962). *L'economia delle aziende di consumo*. Giuffrè.

Zeller, C., & Thomas, H. (2024). Corporate engagement in disease prevention and health promotion. Public Health Management Review, 14(1), 56-72. https://doi.org/DOI: 10.7890/phmr.2024.056

Zhang, Q., Oo, B. L., & Lim, B. T. H. (2019). Drivers, motivations, and barriers to the implementation of corporate social responsibility practices by construction enterprises: A review. *Journal of Cleaner Production*, 210, 563–584. DOI: 10.1016/j.jclepro.2018.11.050

Zhao, J. (2021). Reimagining corporate social responsibility in the era of COVID-19: Embedding resilience and promoting corporate social competence. *Sustainability (Basel)*, 13(12), 6548. DOI: 10.3390/su13126548

Zinkin, J., & Williams, G. (2006). Islam and CSR: A study of the compatibility between the tenets of Islam and the UN Global Compact. *Available atSSRN* 905201. doi:DOI: 10.2139/ssrn.905201

About the Contributors

Gianpaolo Tomaselli is currently a Senior Manager within the Maltese Public Health Sector and he also lectures at the University of Malta's Department of Health Systems Management & Leadership (Faculty of Health Sciences). He obtained a Ph.D. in Healthcare Economics and Management from the University Magna Graecia of Catanzaro (Italy) with a dissertation on Corporate Social Responsibility (CSR) Communication. He has published several peer-reviewed works (journal articles, book chapters, edited books, conference papers, policy briefs, etc.) in the field of CSR, CSR in healthcare, and other healthcare management related topics.

* * *

Asif All Mahmud Akash holds a Bachelor's and a Master's (Thesis) degree in Public Administration from University of Rajshahi. His research has been published in reputable academic journals and featured in prominent daily newspapers. Asif's research interests encompass a range of critical areas, including regulatory governance, public health policy, governance of antimicrobial resistance (AMR), environmental governance, and gender mainstreaming.

S. M. Aamir Ali is an Assistant Professor of Law at Symbiosis Law School, Pune, Symbiosis International (Deemed University) Pune, Maharashtra, India. He is pursuing his Ph.D from West Bengal National University of Juridical Science (WBNUJS), Kolkata. He has completed his LL.M from National Law School of India University (NLSIU), Bengaluru, specialising in Human Right Laws and B.A. LL.B (Hons.) from Aligarh Muslim University, Murshidabad Campus. Along with his education and academic roles, he has also published over 27 academic research papers in National and International Peer Reviewed Journals, including 10 Scopus Indexed journals such as Novum Jus, Journal of Intellectual Property Rights (JIPR), Brazilian Journal of International Law, Manchester Journal of Transnational Islamic

Law and Practice, Brazilian Journal of Alternative Dispute Resolution, Economic Political Weekly (EPW) etc. Furthermore, he has contributed to Book Chapters with Internationally reputed publishers such as IGI Global, Springer Nature, Thompson Reuter, etc. He has also presented papers and participated in National and International Seminars, Workshops, and Online Faculty Development Programmes.

Mohamed Boulesnam holds a Bachelor's degree in Money, Banking, and Finance from Yahia Fares University (2007), and a Magister degree in Accounting from Al Al-Bayt University in Jordan (2010). He earned his Doctorate from Algiers University in 2015. He has been a conference professor at Yahia Fares University of Medea since 2010. His research interests include Corporate Social Responsibility and Social Accounting.

Sandra C. Buttigieg is Head of Department of Health Services Management, Faculty of Health Sciences, University of Malta, and Honorary Senior Research Fellow, Health Services Management Centre, University of Birmingham, UK. She is Consultant Public Health Medicine at Mater Dei Hospital, Malta. She is currently Global Representative-at-Large of the Health Care Management Division of the American Academy of Management. Sandra Buttigieg strongly advocates inter-/trans-disciplinarity within HSM in practice/research. She is on the Editorial Boards of PLOS ONE, International Journal of Human Resources Management, Health Services Management Research, Journal of Health Organization and Management, and Frontiers in Public Health. She is currently also Guest Associate Editor for Frontiers Veterinary Science. Professor Buttigieg participates in the EU-funded programmes: Horizon2020 - To REACH; COST Actions: CA 15222 – cost containment and quality of care (leader-WG 1); TD 1404 – NEOH (co-leader-WG 3); IS 1402 – Ageism (co-leader-WG 1); and IS 1103 – Adapting European Health Systems to Diversity (country-coordinator).

Concetta Lucia Cristofaro is associate professor in Human Resource Management at e-Campus University (Italy). Currently, she is adjunct Professor of in Organization theory, Conflict Management and Human Resource Management, Public and Private Organization at the Magna Graecia University. Her research is focused of intellectual capital, ITC, digitalization, family business, performance, gender diversity and knowledge management.

Akanksha Fouzdar holds a PhD in Public Finance from Dayalbagh Educational Institute, Agra. She qualified UGC NET JRF in 2018. She is currently working as an Assistant Professor at GLA University, Mathura. Dr. Singh specializes in macroeconomics, finance, and financial systems. Her research explores complex economic frameworks and financial mechanisms, contributing to the academic community with her extensive expertise and scholarly publications.

Frankline Zammit Galea works as Head of Gozo 6th Form School for Higher Studies.

Michael Galea is an academic at the Mental Health Department, University of Malta. He has worked extensively abroad, including in London, UK; in Nairobi, Kenya; and in Baltimore, MD, USA. He is a clinical psychologist by profession and has published a number of books on mental health, together with a long list of peer-reviewed publications.

Anuttama Ghose is an Assistant Professor of Law and Program Co-ordinator of BA LLB (Hons.) Program at the School of Law, Dr. Vishwanath Karad MIT World Peace University, Pune, India. She is also presently Heading the Centre for Innovation Incubation and Intellectual Property Laws (CIIIPL) at MIT WPU School of Law. She has completed her B.A LL.B (IPR Hons.) from the School of Law, KIIT University, Bhubaneshwar and LL.M with specialisation in the field of Intellectual Property Laws from Symbiosis Law School, Pune, India. She has completed her PhD in the field of Protection of Non-Conventional Trademarks from School of Law and Justice, Adamas University, Kolkata. She has previously worked as Vice-Principal and Assistant Professor of Law at Indian Institute of Legal Studies, Darjeeling, West Bengal. Apart from being an IPR enthusiast, she is a very keen researcher and has over 25 academic publications in National and International Journals to her credit. Her scholarly contributions extend to well-regarded Scopus Indexed Journals and Book Chapters with Internationally reputed publishers such as IGI Global, Springer Nature, Thompson Reuter, etc.

Priya Joseph holds a masters degree and an MPhil degree in Sociology. Passionate in the area of palliative care, her research area revolves around the emerging landscape of palliative care in India. Currently pursuing doctoral research at CHRIST University, Bangalore, India. ORCID id: 0009-0003-9484-1459.

Christian Kaunert is Professor of International Security at Dublin City University, Ireland. He is also Professor of Policing and Security, as well as Director of the International Centre for Policing and Security at the University of South Wales. In addition, he is Jean Monnet Chair, Director of the Jean Monnet Centre of Excellence and Director of the Jean Monnet Network on EU Counter-Terrorism (www.eucter.net).

Hartej Singh Kochher is a distinguished contemporary Indian author, esteemed legal scholar, and a dynamic force in academia. Holding a B.A. LL.B. (Hons.) from the University School of Law and Legal Studies, GGSIP University, New Delhi, and an LL.M. in Corporate Laws from the renowned National Law University, Jodhpur, Hartej combines a robust academic foundation with a passion for the intricacies of law. His professional journey is marked by impactful roles as an Assistant Professor of Law at institutions such as ICFAI Law School, Hyderabad; SRM University, Sonepat; University of Petroleum and Energy Studies, Dehradun; Dr. Vishwanath Karad MIT-World Peace University, Pune and currently at Vinayaka Mission's Law School, Chennai, India. Simultaneously pursuing a Ph.D. at GD Goenka University, Gurgaon, Hartej's research focuses on Competition Law in India, showcasing his commitment to legal scholarship. Hartej actively participates in national and international conferences, presenting papers on various legal subjects, further establishing his reputation as a thought leader in the legal community. His journey is characterized by a passion for knowledge, a commitment to excellence, and a continuous quest for intellectual growth.

Prabha Lama joined the Department of Humanities and Social Sciences, Graphic Era (Deemed to be University) as an Associate Professor in 2019. Currently Dr. Prabha Lama is the head of the Department of Humanities and Social Sciences, Graphic Era (Deemed to be University) since 2021. She possesses substantial and extensive experience of teaching in various faculty and has rich experience in teaching legal language, English literature and English communication. Dr. Prabha has published research papers and book chapters in UGC CARE, referred Journals including Scopus and. has also contributed as reviewer in various reputed journals. Furthermore, Dr. Prabha has been invited as a resource person in various reputed institutions in addition to chairing sessions in various events and occasions. She has been actively involved as a member of BOS and DRC as well as guiding and supervising PhD Students.

Maya M. is a sociologist with over a decade of teaching experience at the university level. She has worked extensively in the field of Sociology of Health and in the emerging landscape of Corporate Social Responsibility (CSR) in India.

Anna Maria Melina is Senior Researcher in Organization theory and Human Resource Management at University of Messina (Italy). Her research is focused of ITC, digitalization, healthcare, family business, small and medium business and knowledge management.

Himani Oberai holds a PhD in Human Resource Management and currently serves as an Assistant Professor and Area Chair of Communication at GLA

University, Mathura. Her research expertise encompasses various aspects of human resource management, sustainability, innovation, and organizational development. Dr. Oberai is recognized for her contributions to advancing HR practices and fostering sustainable organizational growth. At GLA University, she combines her academic knowledge with practical insights to educate and mentor students, shaping the future leaders in the field.

Nalini R. is an Assistant Professor in School of Management, SASTRA Deemed To Be University, Thanjavur, Tamilnadu, India. She has obtained her doctoral degree from Bharathidasan University, Trichy and has around 28 years of teaching experience. Her area of research is Marketing and Finance and has published 45 research papers in international and national level peer-reviewed (Scopus indexed) journals and 10 articles in other international and national level journals. She has also participated and presented papers in national international conferences and published case studies and book chapters. Her area of expertise is financial, cost and management accounting and currently handling accounting courses.

Md. Golam Rabbani is an Associate Professor in the Department of Public Administration at the University of Rajshahi, Bangladesh. He has been engaged in the field of health systems research for the past 17 years. Throughout his extensive professional career, he has contributed to over 50 research projects related to health and social policy. His research findings have been published in two books, seven book chapters, fifteen journal articles, and many conference papers. Most of his works have been published by prestigious publishers such as Springer, Sage, Routledge, IGI Global, and CRC Press.

Anjali Raghav is a Research Scholar at the School of Law, Sharda University, Greater Noida. She is a graduate in Law and has completed her Master's in Law from Sharda School of Law, Sharda University. She has over 3 years of experience as a criminal practising lawyer. Anjali has attended 21+ national and international conferences, webinars, seminars, and symposiums, along with paper presentations, and has participated in 4+ faculty development programs. She has over 25+ publications in various esteemed journals and books. Anjali is an active member at the Family Dispute Resolution Clinic, Meditation Centre, Greater Noida. She has a keen interest in the areas of Criminal Law, Intellectual Property Rights, Artificial Intelligence, Machine Learning, and Blockchain Technology.

S. Dinesh earned his Ph.D. in Business Administration from Madurai Kamaraj University and currently serves as an Associate Professor in the Sri Ramachandra Faculty of Management Sciences at the Sri Ramachandra Institute of Higher Education and Research. In his role, he oversees the Entrepreneurship Development

Cell and Online Programmes. With a rich background of 3 years in the financial services industry and over 14 years in academia, he brings a wealth of experience to his current position. Dr. Dinesh has successfully secured grants totaling 26.31 lakhs from various funding agencies. He is actively involved in organizing diverse training programs aimed at fostering entrepreneurial traits among students and the broader public. Recognition for his work, he received best paper awards from esteemed institutions such as IIM Nagpur, NGI GIs, Universiti Putra , NIED, and RVS IM. His commitment to online education is evident in the development of five comprehensive online courses.

Ankit Saxena is currently working as Associate Professor and Area Chair (Finance) at GLA University, Mathura. He is a Director Medalist from Dayalbagh Educational Institute, Dayalbagh, Agra. He qualified NET JRF in December, 2005. His academic interests are paradigms of Financial Inclusion, Indian Financial System, Behavioural Finance. He has been resource person to 20+ FDPs / Workshops on research methods and teaching pedagogy organized by various University, Educational Bodies viz. AICTE Training and Learning (ATAL) Academy and ICSSR.

Bhupinder Singh is working as Professor at Sharda University, India. Also, Honorary Professor in University of South Wales UK and Santo Tomas University Tunja, Colombia. His areas of publications as Smart Healthcare, Medicines, fuzzy logics, artificial intelligence, robotics, machine learning, deep learning, federated learning, IoT, PV Glasses, metaverse and many more. He has 3 books, 139 paper publications, 163 paper presentations in international/national conferences and seminars, participated in more than 40 workshops/FDP's/QIP's, 25 courses from international universities of repute, organized more than 59 events with international and national academicians and industry people's, editor-in-chief and co-editor in journals, developed new courses. He has given talks at international universities, resource person in international conferences such as in Nanyang Technological University Singapore, Tashkent State University of Law Uzbekistan; KIMEP University Kazakhstan, All'ah meh Tabatabi University Iran, the Iranian Association of International Criminal law, Iran and Hague Center for International Law and Investment, The Netherlands, Northumbria University Newcastle UK,

Bruno Barbosa Sousa is Adjunct Professor of Marketing at Polytechnic Institute of Cávado and Ave (IPCA), Portugal and PhD in Marketing and Strategy in Universidade do Minho, Portugal. Head of Masters Program - Tourism Management and Marketing Tourism (IPCA); CiTUR – Center for Tourism Research, Development and Innovation and UNIAG research member. He has published in the

Journal of Enterprising Communities, Tourism Management Perspectives, Current Issues in Tourism, Journal of Organizational Change Management, World Review of Entrepreneurship, Management and Sust. Development, among others.

Muhammad Usman Tariq has more than 16+ year's experience in industry and academia. He has authored more than 200+ research articles, 110+ case studies, 70+ book chapters and several books other than 4 patents. He is founder and CEO of The Case HQ, a unique repository for courses, narrative and video case studies. He has been working as a consultant and trainer for industries representing six sigma, quality, health and safety, environmental systems, project management, and information security standards. His work has encompassed sectors in aviation, manufacturing, food, hospitality, education, finance, research, software and transportation. He has diverse and significant experience working with accreditation agencies of ABET, ACBSP, AACSB, WASC, CAA, EFQM and NCEAC. Additionally, Dr. Tariq has operational experience in incubators, research labs, government research projects, private sector startups, program creation and management at various industrial and academic levels. He is Certified Higher Education Teacher from Harvard University, USA, Certified Online Educator from HMBSU, Certified Six Sigma Master Black Belt and has been awarded PFHEA, SMIEEE, and CMBE.

Srinivasan Vasan is an accomplished Assistant Professor (Research) in the Department of Humanities and Social Science at Graphic Era (Deemed to be University), Dehradun. He has previously contributed as Guest Faculty (Social Work) at Bharathidasan University, Tiruchirappalli, Tamil Nadu, where he served for two years. Mr. Srinivasan holds a Master of Philosophy degree from the Central University of Pondicherry, Pondicherry, India. His academic journey is marked by the publication of numerous research papers that cover a broad spectrum of subjects. His expertise spans across various areas including migration, ageing, women's and children's issues, public health issues, Tuberculosis, correctional administration, public policy, gender issues, artificial intelligence, and machine learning. Mr. Srinivasan's diverse research interests reflect his commitment to addressing complex social issues through an interdisciplinary lens, making significant contributions to both the academic and practical realms of social science.

Marzia Ventura is PhD in Economics and Management in Health and Post doctor in Social Capital at the University of Catanzaro "Magna Graecia"- Department of Law History Economics and Social Science. His activities are oriented towards the field of Intellectual and Social capital, Small and Medium Business and Knowledge Management. His publications appeared in academic journals and presented her research at several international conferences.

Index

www.ingramcontent.com/pod-product-compliance
Lightning Source LLC
LaVergne TN
LVHW080348011026
849161LV00009B/2224